School Discipline and School Violence

School Discipline and School Violence

The Teacher Variance Approach

Irwin A. Hyman
Temple University

with

Avivah Dahbany
Franklin Township Public Schools

Michael Blum
Riverton Public Schools

Erica Weiler
Temple University

Valerie Brooks-Klein

Mariann Pokalo
Atlantic Mental Health Center

Allyn and Bacon
Boston • London • Toronto • Sydney • Tokyo • Singapore

Vice President, Education: Nancy Forsyth
Editorial Assistant: Kate Wagstaffe
Marketing Manager: Kris Farnsworth
Sr. Editorial Production Administrator: Susan McIntyre
Editorial Production Service: Ruttle, Shaw & Wetherill, Inc.
Composition Buyer: Linda Cox
Manufacturing Buyer: Megan Cochran
Cover Administrator: Suzanne Harbison

Library of Congress Cataloging-in-Publication Data

Hyman, Irwin A.
  School discipline and school violence: the teacher variance
approach / Irwin A. Hyman with Avivah Dahbany . . . [et al.].
    p.   cm.
  Includes bibliographical references and index.
  ISBN 0-205-15812-9
  1. School discipline—United States.   2. School violence—United
States—Prevention.   3. Behavior modification—United States.
I. Title.
LB3012.2.H97 1997
371.5—dc20   96-10506
                                              CIP

Printed in the United States of America

10 9 8 7 6 5 4 3 2 1   01 00 99 98 97 96

To Rachael
What More Could a Father Ask?

Contents

Preface

In the fall of 1957, for my first teaching assignment, I entered a third-grade classroom of thirty-four unruly children in a small, rural, New Jersey school. Between kindergarten and my appearance, my charges had had seven teachers. This class of eight-year-olds, which in the minds of many were considered incorrigible, exuded a message that they were not about to be easily disciplined. Rumors circulating about the previous failed professionals included allegations that one had died of the stress of trying to manage her unruly charges. Another teacher was reported to have broken a leg when she was pushed down the stairs while attempting to slow her starved students from their rush to the lunchroom. Others had suffered various unidentified indignities that resulted in their speedy departures.

Like my unsuccessful predecessors, I had received no formal courses in administering school discipline. But there was one distinct difference between them and me. I had absolutely no formal training in education. When I entered that classroom, with a so-called emergency certificate from the New Jersey State Department of Education, the closest I had come to training in teaching was an undergraduate course in educational psychology.

What I did have going for me were three things: First, my undergraduate training in anthropology, sociology, and psychology had enabled me to develop a conceptual framework for understanding and analyzing behavior. Second, I had a high level of interest in working with young people. Third, I had extensive experience coaching and teaching children and youth in a variety of settings. I had been a leader in the Boy Scouts, a Red Cross Swimming and Water Safety Instructor, and a gymnastics instructor for the YMCA. In terms of school discipline and all other aspects of instruction, however, I entered a teaching career with little more to go on than the practical examples of my own childhood teachers and the advice and examples offered by my peers.

When consulting my colleagues in the school about discipline, the conventional wisdom was reduced to a few simple maxims, which included the following: "Don't be too friendly; you're not here to win a popularity contest," "Don't smile 'til Christmas," and "If you have to get rough, don't leave any marks on the children." The latter bit of advice was rather confusing, because I knew that corporal punishment had been illegal in New Jersey schools since 1867. But none of these maxims really helped me to translate the theories and research about human learning, behavior, and motivation that I knew from my undergraduate training to the classroom. I did know that effective discipline could not be reduced to a few simple beliefs, because the children in my class were so varied in personality, socioeconomic background, academic level, and intelligence.

What to do with Bobby, who was constantly moving; with Jane, who still did not recognize preprimer words; with Rachael, who wanted to read fifth-grade books, and was already bored and tuned out to instruction that endlessly repeated what she already knew? What about Jimmy and Joe, of the "ready fists," and Larry, the follower who could not avoid getting into trouble?

I decided that my fellow teachers were as ignorant as I was about the complexity of discipline problems. They had some inventive ideas for ways to punish children, but not for preventing misbehavior with challenging children. I returned to my academic roots to find answers in theories and research. As I searched the literature, I found it to be heavy on theory and light on application. I often found that one question generated another. Most important, I learned that the causes of misbehavior are myriad and that discipline techniques are more easily discussed than applied. There are no easy answers. This is especially true as I write this book, considering the problems and stresses of contemporary American life.

The prevention and amelioration of misbehavior intrigued me so much that within two years of teaching, I had entered the school psychology program at Rutgers University. While teaching fifth and sixth grades, I conducted research in my school and classroom on various styles of teaching as they related to discipline. These studies led to a dissertation that demonstrated that democratic, nonpunitive techniques of motivation and encouragement are far superior to other approaches to preventing misbehavior (Hyman, 1964).

This book is a culmination of over thirty-five years of experience in education and a testament to my continuing belief in the power of prevention and positive approaches to discipline. Its research supports these beliefs. This book demonstrates that all misbehavior may be understood within a theoretical construct that leads to applied and practical solutions to prevention and management. Quick fixes such as putting children's names on the board, criticism, sarcasm, put-downs, detention, corporal punishment, or suspension may be effective in the short run. But experience and research tell us that they do not teach or model new behaviors. These and other types of punishments all have counterproductive features that result in feelings of fear, humiliation, or anger.

Although this book was designed as a comprehensive text on school discipline, it differs from almost all other texts on the subject. We do not present the subject matter from a purported "value-free" point of view. Approaches to discipline, as defined in any society, are flavored and directed by the political, social, and moral ideology of the adherents of any particular point of view. We affirm that students are entitled to the same constitutional freedoms and respect as are adults.

We document throughout this book that the worst, and least effective, type of discipline is based on the use of power, fear, and punishment. We offer a scientifically supportable thesis about the nature and prevention of and "cure" for misbehavior in schools. Our writing reflects an "advocacy" view for positive, student-enhancing, esteem-building, preventive approaches to discipline. Because discipline is such an emotional issue, we ask only that dubious readers weigh the evidence we present and base their disagreements on counterevidence, rather than on "gut" feelings, individual anecdotes, or popular assumptions.

Teacher variance, the topic of this book, is the grandchild of child variance (Morse & Smith, 1980; Rhodes, Tracy & Head, 1977). Our current conceptualization is based on five orientations that have flowed from the original studies. Simply put, we believe that by taking the Teacher Variance Inventory—III (TVI), you can determine your underlying philosophy and beliefs about school discipline. This book will help you understand each orientation and how to use the theory in everyday classroom management. We hope that this book offers you insights into your own best approach to discipline and helps you to develop a consistent and effective plan to enhance learning in your classroom.

This book was made possible by the contributions of many of my graduate students, who are credited throughout. However, Avivah Dahbany and Mike Blum have made major, original contributions. Valerie Brooks-Klein developed the TVI-R. Mariann Pokalo and Erica Weiler contributed to editing, typing, and conceptualizing. Although much of the book is written in the first person, and frequently presents examples from my personal experiences, I also talk about "our" views and what "we" think. So when I use plural pronouns, I am referring to Drs. Pokalo, Blum, Dahbany, and Klein, and Ms. Weiler.

We all have school, clinical, and research experiences with school discipline. Although we offer a comprehensive overview of the literature and research, we also rely on techniques developed from our own extensive, daily experiences with alienated, disruptive, and disturbed students and their frustrated teachers.

Avivah Dahbany has worked as a school psychologist in New York City and New Jersey for more than fifteen years. As a result, she has developed extensive experience with adjudicated youth and their families. She has been an adjunct instructor for more than five years, teaching undergraduate courses in introduction to psychology and educational psychology, as well as graduate courses in tests and measurements, psychological testing, and psychological counseling. She has also been a consultant to a hospital pediatric evaluation unit and to the New Jersey Department of Corrections. After completing a clinical internship, she obtained her doctorate in school psychology from Temple University in 1996.

Mike Blum has more than ten years of experience as a clinical and school psychologist. He has worked as a school counselor in an inner-city school. He has five years of experience as a staff psychologist in a special school and partial hospital setting for children with severe behavior problems. He is currently a working school psychologist.

Erica Weiler, while this book was being written, was a doctoral student in school psychology. She worked as a mental health technician in a psychiatric hospital and worked with me as a cotherapist with adolescent groups. She made major contributions in researching selected topics such as emotional abuse as well as editing, organizing, and typing the text.

Valerie Brooks-Klein has had extensive experience as a high school teacher and school guidance counselor. Besides her involvement in research in a psychiatric hospital, she has worked with adolescents in psychotherapy and conducted rehabilitation therapy with people with traumatic brain injuries. She is a consulting school psychologist.

Mariann Pokalo is a supervising psychologist in a community mental health center. She has worked in a variety of school and institutional settings during the past twenty years. She is a consultant to Head Start and schools for disruptive youth. She is an expert on children and youth who are fire setters and on child abuse and its aftereffects. During the past fifteen years, she and I have collaborated on numerous studies and clinical casework involving school discipline, abused students, conduct disorders, and school violence.

This is a book written by and for educators who are devoted to the development of non-punitive, effective school discipline.

Acknowledgments

Many people over the years contributed to this book and the underlying concepts. We owe a debt to the Rhodes, Tracy and Head who developed the framework of child variance and especially to Bill Morse, who helped us in the early development of the teacher variance model.

Many former students contributed to the development of various versions of the Teacher Variance Inventory. Special acknowledgments are due to Dolores Lally and Naomi Lennox who helped develop the original version and contributed to the validation of later editions. Sue Sirica and Dolores Webster conducted extensive research in developing the fourth version, which is included in this book.

Dolores Switaj supervised an important segment of the process studies of various discipline training programs. Thanks are due to the many school psychology graduate students at Temple University who also contributed to this research. Long gone from Temple University, but not forgotten, is Dr. Dolores Lally, who conducted much of the research on the first process study in the 1980s.

Andrew Shanock conducted the research on school violence. Gretchen Britton contributed much of the material on sexual harassment and Donna Perone and Lori Romano contributed material on undercover agents in schools. Jessie White contributed to the section on strip searches.

Andy Osborn and Laureen Milano contributed information on smoking and Shawn Weston, Nurit Lahav, and Michael Selbst contributed material on substance abuse.

Special thanks go to Kenneth Cassie, a true gentleman and scholar, who voluntarily and unstintingly edited two complete versions of this book. His timely and helpful editing were invaluable in meeting deadlines. Thanks to reviewers Roger Cunningham, The Ohio State University; Judy Witkov, Moraine Community College; Dale Knapp, California State University, Los Angeles; Barbara Meyers, State University of New York, Oneonta; and Marlene Anthony, North Georgia College. Also, we owe a great debt to our editor, Nancy Forsyth, whose patient and ongoing suggestions made this book possible.

Introduction

We believe this book fills a long-missing gap in teacher training. However, to benefit from this book and the Teacher Variance approach, it is necessary to identify your own beliefs about punishment and discipline. **Before reading further, you should respond to the *Survey of Attitudes Toward Children* (SATC) and the *Teacher Variance Inventory—III* (TVI), which are presented in the next pages. There are no right or wrong answers on this scale; pick the responses that reflect your own beliefs. After taking the scales, be sure to score yourself by using the scoring keys, which are in the appendices.**

After completing the scales, continue in this introduction, which includes a summary of the meaning and use of the scales.

Survey of Attitudes toward Children

Directions

The following statements represent commonly held attitudes. You will probably agree with some and disagree with others. Please read each statement carefully. Then indicate your agreement or disagreement by circling the appropriate number according to the following code:

1—Strongly Agree	2—Mildly Agree	3—Neither Agree Nor Disagree	4—Mildly Disagree	5—Strongly Disagree

When you are done, use the score sheet in Appendix 1 to score yourself.

1. Physical punishment should not be allowed in the schools.	1	2	3	3	5
2. A child should never tell an adult that he or she is wrong.	1	2	3	4	5
3. Corporal punishment is just and necessary.	1	2	3	4	5
4. Children are not being allowed enough freedom today.	1	2	3	4	5
5. Corporal punishment is an effective deterrent to school discipline problems.	1	2	3	4	5

6. Corporal punishment is absolutely never justified.	1	2	3	4	5
7. Children have no moral obligation to remain loyal to their parents no matter what the circumstances.	1	2	3	4	5
8. Someone in the schools should be given the opportunity to punish children by paddling.	1	2	3	4	5
9. Training in adherence to the authority of teachers hinders the development of self-reliance in children.	1	2	3	4	5
10. You can't change human nature.	1	2	3	4	5
11. Scaring a student, now and then, by promise of a whipping is likely to have negative emotional consequences.	1	2	3	4	5
12. Loyalty on the part of children to their parents is something that parents should earn.	1	2	3	4	5
13. Physical punishment is an effective way to control student behavior.	1	2	3	4	5
14. Corporal punishment should be used frequently as a method of discipline.	1	2	3	4	5
15. Children "owe" their parents a great deal.	1	2	3	4	5
16. Children are the constitutional equivalents of adults, and thus should be accorded the same rights.	1	2	3	4	5
17. If you spare the rod you will spoil the child.	1	2	3	4	5
18. Children in school have to earn their rights.	1	2	3	4	5
19. Because paddling and spanking students may have negative consequences, we should discontinue the practice.	1	2	3	4	5
20. If a child acts mean, he or she needs punishment rather than understanding.	1	2	3	4	5
21. A young child's thoughts and ideas are his or her own business.	1	2	3	4	5
22. Corporal punishment is not necessary in modern education.	1	2	3	4	5
23. Children should have the opportunity to evaluate the educational materials they will be using in school.	1	2	3	4	5
24. Because corporal punishment has not eliminated school disciplinary problems, society should abolish it.	1	2	3	4	5
25. Because teachers act *in loco parentis* (in place of parents), they should be permitted to physically punish a student.	1	2	3	4	5
26. Children should be grateful to their parents.	1	2	3	4	5
27. When teachers hit students as punishment, they teach them that "might makes right."	1	2	3	4	5

Now that you have completed the scale, turn to Appendix 1 for the scoring instructions and to Appendix 2 for the norms.

Interpreting the Survey of Attitudes toward Children

Appendix 2 offers percentiles for the SATC from a national sample of 608 professionals, including teachers, psychologists, social workers, and administrators. A score between 48 and 81 falls approximately within the average 68 percent of people tested. The lowest possible (least punitive) score is 31, and the highest possible (most punitive) is 112.

Our sample includes very different types of professionals, and therefore there is a very wide spread of scores. A score above 81 suggests that your attitudes are shaped by beliefs that children (1) naturally owe respect, allegiance, reflexive obedience, and loyalty to authorities; (2) need to be physically punished in both home and school when they misbehave; (3) are best motivated by fear; (4) have too much freedom; and (5) are not entitled to the rights accorded adults. You are likely considered by peers and students to be very strict and perhaps rigid. If you scored below 48, you are probably considered very liberal by your peers. Your attitudes reflect beliefs that children (1) are entitled to the same rights as adults, modified only by developmental limitations such as judgment, cognitive ability, and factors that would adversely affect health and safety; (2) should never be hit; (3) have the right to plan relevant parts of their lives without undue adult intrusion; (3) have the potential for goodness and achievement, which is best brought out through rewards, encouragement, and freedom to make choices; and (4) should never be coerced by authoritarian, punitive techniques.

Teacher Variance Inventory III (TVI)

The TVI was designed to allow you to determine your basic orientation or philosophical assumptions regarding discipline. The scale's brief scenarios describe common classroom misbehaviors and are followed by items describing five ways to either diagnose or solve each discipline problem. Before you begin, decide if you want to respond in the book, duplicate the scale and score sheets for your own use and respond on the copies, or make up your own score sheet by hand copying Appendix 3.

The five-point scale allows you to indicate both your first choice and the strength of your beliefs in regard to the five approaches. When you have completed the scale, turn to Appendix 3 for scoring instructions.

Teacher Variance Inventory III

This questionnaire lists reasons why student behaviors occur in school and what to do about them. There are ten scenarios divided into two sections. Five scenarios offer choices about the cause of a particular behavior; the remaining five offer choices regarding recommendations for the behaviors.

Please respond to all ten of the scenarios, otherwise the results will not be valid. This is not a test; there are no right or wrong answers.

DIRECTIONS: 1. For each scenario rate **how important** each available response is in order to determine the cause of the behavior.
2. After you have indicated the **level of importance** for each of the five responses select one response you feel is the single best response by circling the letter before that statement. **Should you find it difficult to select one statement as being the best, just pick the one that you agree with the most, as indicated in the sample below.**

(Continued)

Section 1

SAMPLE: Tom is an eight-year-old who has severe tantrums when he doesn't get his way in class. To understand the cause of this behavior, how important is it for the teacher to determine if:

		Not Important		Important		Very Important
(A) He has poor inner controls.	(A)	1	2	3	4	(5)
B. His behavior is encouraged by the attention he receives from his parents and teachers.	B	1	(2)	3	4	5
C. There may be a nutritional deficiency which causes these tantrums.	C	(1)	2	3	4	5
D. His individual needs are not being met in school.	D	1	(2)	3	4	5
E. The assignments in class are too difficult for him.	E	1	2	3	4	(5)

Note that in the above sample, the respondent considered both A and E as "very important," and then decided on A as the "single best response."

1. Jane is not achieving as well as her teacher expected. To understand the cause of this behavior, how important is it for the teacher to determine if:

		Not Important		Important		Very Important
A. Unresolved interpersonal conflicts with the teacher are interfering with her work.	A	1	2	3	4	5
B. Jane is being consistently reinforced for good working habits.	B	1	2	3	4	5
C. The classroom noise level and structure are conducive to good work habits.	C	1	2	3	4	5
D. She has had her eyes checked recently.	D	1	2	3	4	5
E. She could benefit from a cooperative learning experience.	E	1	2	3	4	5

2. As soon as Gwen completes a small part of her assignment or activity, she places her head on her arms for a few minutes. To understand the cause of the behavior, how important is it for the teacher to determine if:

		Not Important		Important		Very Important
A. She is suffering from lack of sleep.	A	1	2	3	4	5
B. There is sufficient reinforcement to maintain on-task behavior.	B	1	2	3	4	5
C. She needs more help than the class size will allow.	C	1	2	3	4	5
D. She is daydreaming as a defense against anxiety.	D	1	2	3	4	5
E. She is fulfilling her need to function at her own pace.	E	1	2	3	4	5

3. Mike often becomes inattentive in class. To understand the cause of the behavior, how important is it for the teacher to determine if:

		Not Important		Important		Very Important
A. Mike has had his vision and hearing checked recently.	A	1	2	3	4	5
B. The classroom environment, i.e., seating arrangement, lighting and noise level contribute to his inattentiveness.	B	1	2	3	4	5
C. Underlying emotional conflict is preventing him from paying attention.	C	1	2	3	4	5
D. The classroom work is fulfilling his individual academic needs.	D	1	2	3	4	5
E. Reinforcement would increase Mike's time on task.	E	1	2	3	4	5

4. Karen continually taps her fingers on her desk, fidgets, or shuffles her feet when seated for an activity. To understand the cause of the behavior, how important is it for the teacher to determine if this is:

		Not Important		Important		Very Important
A. A reaction to being seated with disruptive students.	A	1	2	3	4	5
B. An indication of frustration to which the teacher should attend.	B	1	2	3	4	5
C. An indication of Attention Deficit Disorder.	C	1	2	3	4	5
D. A behavior she has learned to use to relieve her anxiety about being asked questions by the teacher.	D	1	2	3	4	5
E. A subtle, perhaps unconscious, attempt to disrupt the class.	E	1	2	3	4	5

5. Tommy stands in front of the class calling out obscene words. The teacher tells him to sit down and he just curses more. To understand the cause of the behavior, how important is it for the teacher to determine if:

		Not Important		Important		Very Important
A. Tommy is showing off to impress his peers who are hostile to school authority figures.	A	1	2	3	4	5
B. His language is a genuine expression of his frustration with the rules and expectations of the class which don't address his unique needs.	B	1	2	3	4	5
C. Tommy is displaying hostile feelings toward the teacher.	C	1	2	3	4	5
D. Tommy has a neurological disorder such as Tourette's Syndrome, and cannot control himself.	D	1	2	3	4	5
E. His obscene language results from copying other people's behavior and he has not learned to express anger in a more appropriate way.	E	1	2	3	4	5

(Continued)

Section 2

DIRECTIONS: 1. For each scenario rate the **level of effectiveness** of each available response in changing the problematic behavior.
2. After you have indicated the **level of effectiveness** for each of the five responses select one response you feel is the single best response by circling the letter before the statement. **Should you find it difficult to select one statement as being the best, just pick the one that you agree with the most.**

SAMPLE: As the children line up to go to lunch, Dean cuts in front of John. The two boys begin shoving each other. Rate the effectiveness of each intervention:

		Not Effective		Effective		Very Effective
A. Establish better instructions and routines for transition periods.	A	①	2	3	4	5
Ⓑ Find ways to help Dean's feelings of inferiority which are driving him to be first in line.	Ⓑ	1	2	3	4	⑤
C. Recommend a physical exam to understand the cause of Dean's irritability.	C	1	2	③	4	5
D. Find other ways to fulfill Dean's need for love and belonging.	D	1	2	3	④	5
E. Establish a reward system for Dean when he is able to line up appropriately.	E	①	2	3	4	5

Note that in the above sample, the respondent rated each response and then selected B as the "single best response."

6. When Ken asks for assistance, he is demanding and insists on getting an immediate response. Rate the effectiveness of each intervention:

		Not Effective		Effective		Very Effective
A. Respond to him only when he asks for help appropriately.	A	1	2	3	4	5
B. Convince his parents and doctor to try Ken on Ritalin to see if this will increase his impulse control.	B	1	2	3	4	5
C. Find ways to relate to Ken to help him accept authority figures.	C	1	2	3	4	5
D. Adjust the curriculum to match Ken's instructional level.	D	1	2	3	4	5
E. Recognize this is a genuine expression of need for recognition and respond with acceptance.	E	1	2	3	4	5

7. Pat has become involved in many fights with other girls. Her classmates complain that she has become a bully. Rate the effectiveness of each intervention:

		Not Effective		Effective		Very Effective
A. Recognize when Pat is becoming frustrated and allow her to express her feelings of frustration and anger in a safe atmosphere.	A	1	2	3	4	5
B. Suggest that the school initiate a program in peer mediation or conflict resolution.	B	1	2	3	4	5
C. Accept that Pat has an intense, reactive temperament and do not get upset when she does.	C	1	2	3	4	5
D. Teach Pat to recongnize what thoughts trigger her angry responses.	D	1	2	3	4	5
E. Make a referral for family therapy since angry outbursts are probably part of the family's history.	E	1	2	3	4	5

8. Dan's desk area and locker are a mess. Rate the effectiveness of each intervention:

		Not Effective		Effective		Very Effective
A. Speak with his parents to determine if he does this at home as a way to defy authority figures.	A	1	2	3	4	5
B. Reward him for maintaining a neat desk and locker.	B	1	2	3	4	5
C. Teach organizational strategies to the whole class.	C	1	2	3	4	5
D. Treat him as if the disorganization is caused by a learning disability and help him organize each day.	D	1	2	3	4	5
E. Allow Dan to determine his own style for keeping materials and schoolwork.	E	1	2	3	4	5

9. Kelly stamps her feet and screams whenever she does not get her way. Rate the effectiveness of each intervention:

		Not Effective		Effective		Very Effective
A. Ask Kelly's parents to be sure Kelly is getting enough sleep and a daily breakfast.	A	1	2	3	4	5
B. Encourage Kelly to work out her anger in appropriate ways through playground games.	B	1	2	3	4	5
C. Ignore the temper tantrums in order to promote extinction of such behavior.	C	1	2	3	4	5
D. Prevent further tantrums by creating a warm and accepting atmosphere in the classroom.	D	1	2	3	4	5
E. Remind her of the rules of the classroom and warn her of the consequences of her outbursts.	E	1	2	3	4	5

(Continued)

10. Stacy's work is of high quality yet she has poor interpersonal skills. Rate the effectiveness of each intervention:

		Not Effective		Effective		Very Effective
A. Tell Stacy you accept her preference to be alone and let her interact in her own way.	A	1	2	3	4	5
B. Find ways to increase Stacy's trust in others so she can develop relationships.	B	1	2	3	4	5
C. Provide opportunities for social interaction with other children, with the support of social skills training.	C	1	2	3	4	5
D. Recognize that Stacy has a shy temperament that can be accommodated but not changed.	D	1	2	3	4	5
E. Modify, through discussion, Stacy's irrational beliefs that she is better off alone.	E	1	2	3	4	5

Teacher Variance and School Discipline

Interpreting the TVI

This book presents a strong, data-based case to convince the reader that (1) there are at least five distinct approaches to prevent, diagnose, and remediate problems of misbehavior; (2) the best approach to discipline is the one with which each teacher is most comfortable; (3) the causes of misbehavior are complex, and therefore so are the solutions; and (4) as a nation, we are too punitive, and our excesses of punishment in general and its overuse in schools cause many more discipline problems than they cure.

Teacher variance, the topic of this book, reflects the belief that each educator has a unique set of beliefs, experiences, and attitudes that determine his or her approach to discipline. To be used most effectively, these attributes should be grounded in theory. The goal of this book is to familiarize the reader with five major orientations to discipline that flow from the child variance constructs of Rhodes, Tracy, and Head (1975) and Morse and Smith (1977). Teacher variance includes cognitive/behavioral, psychodynamic/interpersonal, humanistic, ecological/systems, and biophysical approaches to discipline. Each of these is grounded in a separate body of assumptions about how children's personalities and behaviors develop. Therefore, within a particular system, one derives an understanding of how personality disorders and misbehaviors develop and how to design and implement programs of prevention and remediation.

Readers, by taking the Teacher Variance Inventory—III, will identify the approach with which they are most in tune. They then can focus on the use of that approach to diagnose and treat misbehaviors.

Your primary orientation on the TVI was established by adding the number of times you chose each category as the "single best response." These are the responses you made when requested to circle only one letter. Although choosing your major orientation using this approach is useful, we have found that many teachers' disciplinary responses are based on the context of a situation. That is, they may use several types of disciplinary techniques in a single situation. This may work in the short run, but long-term success is often dependent on an understanding of the theoretical, diagnostic, and applied principles each orientation entails. Therefore, it is important to know the relative strength of each of your beliefs in the various orientations.

Using the total weighted scores, you may have discovered high scores in more than one orientation. These determine the relative strengths of your belief in each orientation. Multiple high scores suggest that you (1) have a good understanding of each approach and therefore view several equally efficacious responses as equally efficacious, (2) are willing to try anything, (3) responded in a shotgun manner by approving many alternative ways of handling the problem, or (4) believe that each problem requires a situation-specific response, regardless of theory. Whatever the case, the purpose of the scale is to help you to first determine your *major preference* and become an expert in that approach.

When you really understand one theory, if what you try does not work, you should go back to the theory to determine why it did not work. For instance, using behavioral theory, if giving a first-grader stickers as a reward for good effort does not work, you do not give up on rewards. You assume that the stickers were not strongly desired by the child, and you find a better reward. If you assume, using psychodynamic theory, that a student's aggressiveness with classmates is caused by sibling rivalry at home, and the aggression continues after the rivalry is reduced, you must reexamine your original diagnosis. An alternative hypothesis could be that the acting out at school may be the result of frequent spanking by an aggressive father with whom the child identifies.

When you complete this book, you will have identified your own primary orientation to discipline. You will understand its roots and how to consistently apply the theory to solve discipline problems. When a particular technique based on this theory does not work, you will be able to return to the theory to understand why it did not work, rather than willy-nilly trying something else.

When you have mastered one approach, your goal may be to become the "complete disciplinarian." By mastering this book, you will be able to understand all the approaches and to use those that are most effective in specific situations. For instance, let us assume that Ms. Jones has successfully used a token economy to ensure on-task behavior with most of her third-graders. However, Johnny hates Ms. Jones and is in a power struggle to prove he is in control. His behavior says, "There is no way you can bribe me to behave." In this case, Ms. Jones might find that psychodynamic/interpersonal theory offers her the tools to help her communicate effectively with Johnny to find out why he hates her and why he needs to be in control. If she can broaden her belief system regarding control, she will be able to communicate in an effective manner to reduce Johnny's anger and his need to control her.

Although the purpose of teacher variance is to identify your own theoretical base for discipline practices, all disciplinary techniques used in the classroom may not be completely tied to one single theory. For instance, an ecological/systems approach may be used in organizing classroom seating while a behavioral approach might be helpful for rewarding a child for not getting out of his seat. But, underlying each of these techniques is a separate belief system about what causes children to misbehave. From that belief flow the techniques that individual teachers, in their own particular context, find successful.

Some people hate theory or are unable to connect theory and practice. For these we have developed a process approach, which we include in Chapter 9 as part of the ecological/systems approach. In two studies, the latest based on an examination of eighty-four programs, we have found nine sets of techniques or processes that are common to many discipline training models (Dahbany & Hyman, 1995; Hyman & Lally, 1982).

The Background of Teacher Variance

In the late 1970s, the National Institute of Education (NIE), a government center established to conduct educational research, began to publish the results of a series of studies on the causes and effects of school violence. Policy makers were very interested in disciplinary techniques that helped prevent and control school violence. These methodologically sound studies offered a national database on school safety, crime, and disruption (National Institute of Education [NIE], 1977, 1978). The focus on violence in and around schools provided a springboard for a decade of efforts to develop methods of prevention and to examine what schools do and do not do about disruptive youth.

Although NIE was interested in violence and disruption by students against schools and peers, they were also interested in violence by educators against students. In 1977, the NIE presented a conference on corporal punishment in schools that brought together noted scholars and practitioners to examine the widespread practice of hitting schoolchildren. Staff from the newly organized National Center for the Study of Corporal Punishment and Alternatives in the Schools (NCSCPAS) participated in that conference. The results of the conference were issued in a report and an academic text (Hyman & Wise, 1979).

After the conference, NIE expressed interest in reviewing effective alternatives to corporal punishment. Under contract to the NIE, the NCSCPAS reviewed literature on the effectiveness of all preservice and inservice training programs that could be identified at the time (Hyman, Bogacki et al., 1979). We examined most of the texts and program outlines used in the most widely used college courses and inservice training programs (Hyman & Lally, 1982; Dahbany, 1996). After identifying hundreds of books and training programs, we realized the need to organize them into some conceptual framework. We used the child variance model developed at the University of Michigan (Morse & Smith, 1980; Rhodes et al., 1975). The child variance model was later developed into the teacher variance approach, which stresses that it is teachers' views about children that vary. The basis of teacher variance is the belief that effective discipline occurs best when teachers use theory-driven approaches that match their own value systems; this is the focus of this book.

This book helps people learning to be teachers to make choices compatible with their beliefs and to prevent misbehavior. It is full of practical suggestions that flow from theory. These will help you diagnose childrens' needs and develop constructive and effective interventions for today's classrooms.

Summary

Until the late 1970s, training in school discipline was sparse. There were no comprehensive texts on the topic. Most primary texts currently used for school discipline courses present overviews that describe all of the currently popular programs (Blum, 1994). Teacher training institutions considered good classroom discipline to be predicated on good teaching. If teachers were masters of instruction, they would not need to learn a body of information involving the history, theory, research, and practice of discipline.

Misbehavior, student alienation, school violence, and other forms of deviance from school norms cannot be solved by only using fair, consistent punishments. The answer is more likely to consist of a whole array of techniques of primary and secondary prevention (Hyman, 1990b). Organized approaches that focus on punishment, no matter how well intentioned, will not succeed in the long run as well as approaches that concentrate on prevention and remediation.

There are no simple answers to the problems of misbehavior. Solutions work only if they have goodness of fit among teachers, students, parents, and the school. Teachers vary in the ways in which they approach the problem. We believe that any individual teacher's understanding of discipline may be matched to at least one of five theoretical orientations to behavior and misbehavior. The task of the teacher variance approach is to help teachers identify and apply the techniques with which they feel most comfortable, competent, and successful.

Chapters 1 and 2 will help you to understand the underlying reasons for using these scales and how best to use this text for personal growth as an effective disciplinarian. The scales will help to point you toward the theories with which you are most consonant. You will learn to assiduously apply them to real-life situations. When this is accomplished, you will master the difficult science and art of school discipline.

$$C \ h \ a \ p \ t \ e \ r \quad 1$$

Misbehavior and Schools' Responses

Chapter Objectives

This chapter provides a history of how misbehavior has been defined and five models or approaches to help you organize and understand the concepts of school discipline.

After reading this chapter, you should be able to:

1. Understand how misbehavior has been defined historically in schools
2. Understand the causes of misbehavior
3. Cite and explain a uniform method of reporting school discipline infractions
4. Understand five models or approaches used to conceptualize school discipline

What Is Misbehavior?

Misbehavior has always been a concern for those who deal with children and youth. Misbehavior, violence, and disruption have been recurrent themes in schools for centuries (Newman, 1980; Travers, 1980). Historically, students have rarely met the expectations of school officials (Garinger, 1936; Henson, 1977). Since the earliest days of recorded history, few generations have failed to complain about the misbehavior of their youth. Clay tablets from Sumer written in 2000 BC discuss concerns about the misbehavior of youth (Hyman & Wise, 1979). The Ten Commandments admonish children to honor their fathers and mothers. The Puritans, who established education in America, emphasized original sin and the potential for the devil controlling children's behavior. Although especially concerned about evil and punishment, the Puritans came from a Europe that also was noted for widespread beatings of children. The Puritan preoccupation with sin and punishment in child-rearing is still maintained by some contemporary groups (Hyman & Pokalo, 1993).

The centrality of beliefs about sin, misunderstandings about child development, and stresses of modern life all contribute to modern-day confusion about disciplining children. Religious beliefs and social traditions of the Judeo-Christian world have contributed heavily to our conceptions about the nature and extent of misbehavior. Until relatively recently, educators and parents considered a swat on the behind the best remedy for misbehavior. Concepts such as prevention, reinforcement, and individual differences of both students and teachers have only recently begun to affect education.

Until the late nineteenth century, only about 50 percent of potential students were enrolled in schools (Travers, 1980). At the turn of the century, the severity, frequency, and duration of misbehavior and delinquency in the schools was much less than in modern times. Disruptive youth in schools were expelled or discouraged from attending school and conducted their misbehavior in the streets. In the middle of the twentieth century, schools established mandatory attendance, and educators sought to understand the causes and prevention of misbehavior.

The advent of educational psychology, the child study movement, research in child development, studies of individual differences, evolving concepts of freedom and individual rights, sociological studies of crime, and other factors converged in the 1920s and 1930s, resulting in a major shift in our understanding of misbehavior. Schools became institutionalized, and teaching became an organized profession. Educators used social and educational science to understand causes of misbehavior and to create effective discipline techniques.

Because various behaviors reflect community values and standards, each school decides its own definitions of misbehavior. Purvis (1976), working in the context of southern states such as Louisiana and Mississippi, conducted one of the early studies to objectify misbehavior. His list of punishable misbehaviors included:

1. Excessive talking in the classroom, hallway, lunchroom, etc.
2. Indecent language or gestures
3. Insolence toward school staff
4. Stealing
5. Smoking
6. Drug use
7. Fighting or attacking school personnel
8. Defacing and vandalizing school property
9. Gambling
10. Throwing objects in class or around school grounds
11. Loitering in unauthorized places
12. Dishonesty
13. Petting
14. Tardiness
15. Rudeness
16. Not bringing required instructional materials to class
17. Absenteeism from class or school
18. Leaving class or school without permission
19. Disobeying requests of school staff

20. Not completing assignments
21. Inattention to classroom activities
22. Possession of weapons
23. Habitually breaking the dress code
24. Body odor
25. Cheating
26. Extortion of other students
27. Organized protests

In 1979, using the work of Purvis (1976) as a base, we developed a comprehensive approach for reporting misbehavior (Berkowitz, Hyman, & Lally, 1984; Dougherty, 1991; Farley, 1983; Kreutter, 1982; Pokalo, 1986; Strauss-Fremuth, 1991). With the help of an entire school staff, we developed the *Uniform Discipline Reporting System,* which may be modified for individual school record keeping (Berkowitz, Hyman, & Lally, 1984). The categories for this system are summarized in Figure 1.1.

Using a computer program, the *Uniform Discipline Reporting System* tracks misbehavior and the methods used to prevent, correct, or punish it. After identifying the specific offenses, teachers record information about such factors as against whom the offense was committed, offense location, relation to gang activity, actions taken for victims, immediate action by teacher, recommended further action, and final outcome. Teachers enter data on scanning sheets, and computer-generated summaries help to analyze specifics about overall school trends, misbehavior profiles on individual students, responses by teachers, and effectiveness of remedies.

Focusing on specific definitions of misbehavior and consistent punishments may well contribute to the overall success of any school discipline program. However, what educators actually do and say about misbehavior is ultimately dependent on deeply held beliefs. These stem from a variety of religious, family, demographic, and idiosyncratic factors. Effective discipline occurs best when the individual teacher uses a theory-driven approach that matches most closely his or her own value system. That is the teacher variance model and is the focus of this book.

Causes of Misbehavior
Research has shown many causes for misbehavior. Although the reasons for some incidents may be easily understood, it is more likely that a variety of variables contribute to most misbehaviors. For instance, school misbehavior can be caused by:

1. Dysfunctional families
2. Inadequate teaching
3. Punitive school climates
4. Economic stress on families and schools
5. Inadequate principals
6. Ineffective school district policies
7. Students' biological and emotional disabilities
8. The way society is organized to deliver child and youth services
9. Peer pressure

FIGURE 1.1 **National Center for the Study of Corporal Punishment and Alternatives' Uniform Discipline Reporting System (Offense Details)**

Defiance

01–Failure to follow specific instructions by a person in authority
02–Arguing beyond acceptable limits
03–Raising of voice beyond acceptable limits
04–Use of profane language
05–Display of an obscene gesture
06–Refusal to follow a school rule
07–Dishonesty in dealing with another person
08–Creating a disturbance
09–Leaving the classroom without permission
10–Other

Defacing School Property

01–Littering
02–Creating graffiti
03–Throwing books
04–Purposely destroying school property
05–Accidentally destroying school property
06–Throwing other objects (specify in written note)
07–Pulling fire alarm
08–Setting a fire
09–Other

Illegal Activities

01–Stealing
02–Trespassing
03–Possession of weapon
04–Extortion
05–Gambling
06–Possession or use of drugs
07–Selling drugs
08–Other

Assault or Abuse

01–Hitting, punching, or kicking
02–Making verbal or gestural threats
03–Reckless endangerment (e.g. shooting gun in public, speeding on school grounds, setting off firecrackers)

04–Unnecessary use of force
05–Verbal sexual harassment
06–Physical sexual harassment, molestation
07–Sexual assault, including attempted and completed rape
08–Assault with a gun
09–Assault with knife
10–Assault with weapon other than gun or knife
11–Other

Fighting between Students

01–Hitting, punching, kicking, choking, etc.
02–Making verbal or gestural threats
03–Verbal taunting
04–Slapping, poking, pushing
05–Other

Activities Interfering with School Performance

01–Not completing assignment, homework, etc.
02–Excessive talking in class
03–Inattentiveness in class
04–Not prepared for activity
05–Failure to return to/from parent
06–Creation of disturbance
07–Leaving classroom without permission
08–Carrying a beeper
09–Other

Breaking Miscellaneous School Rules

01–Smoking
02–Leaving school grounds without permission
03–Making excessive noise
04–Tardiness
05–Truancy
06–Cutting class
07–Loitering
08–Use of profane language
09–Display of obscene gesture
10–Dishonesty in dealing with another person
11–Other

10. The size of the students' birth cohort
11. Individual students' failures to accept responsibility for their own behavior (Duke, 1982; Hyman, Flanagan, & Smith, 1982)

Because the reasons for misbehavior are complex, what actually constitutes misbehavior may be a matter of dispute, and many tend to gravitate toward simple, punishment-oriented, short-term solutions. Attempts to clearly define misbehaviors are challenged by changing attitudes, shifts in values, and emerging social problems. Behaviors defined as unacceptable change over time and vary between cultures, subcultures, societies, ethnic groups, regions, states, neighborhoods, and school districts. For instance, when data on school misbehaviors suddenly shot up from one year to the next in the Philadelphia schools, some panicked. However, examination of the data showed that the increase in numbers of offenses was mostly attributable to the banning of student-carried phone beepers.

Stereotypically, in inner cities, minority students who carry beepers are often assumed to be involved in drug trafficking. Yet, like their peers in the suburbs, some unknown percentage of these students carry beepers to keep in touch with working parents, their part-time employers, and their friends. The banning of beepers in Philadelphia suddenly increased the total number of students apprehended for breaking school rules.

Issues and Models for Understanding School Discipline

Six conceptual frameworks for discipline appear to meet reasonable standards of clarity and widespread use. They include:

1. Legalistic, discipline code models based on enforcement of rules
2. Moral education, which has emerged as part of the political agenda of the 1980s but was the original basis for discipline and character development in colonial schools
3. The framework of Charles Wolfgang and Carl Glickman (1980, 1986)
4. Donald Willower's Pupil Control Ideology (Willower, Eidell, & Hoy, 1967)
5. The total school model developed by Daniel Duke and Vernon Jones (1984)
6. Teacher variance, the major topic of this book

Discipline Codes as a Legalistic Model

Traditionally, punishment has been the major model for dealing with discipline problems. However, punishment has often been ineffective, counterproductive (suspending students for truancy), inconsistent, and overused with certain groups such as minorities and the poor.

Educators in different regions, states, school districts, and school buildings vary widely in the way they define misbehavior, relative severity of misbehaviors, and punishment for different misbehaviors. In the 1970s, policy makers recognized the need to bring some consistency and order to schools' reactions to misbehavior. Many thought that the schools, like the judicial system, should be governed by a reasonably uniform set of rules and penalties. This concept, rooted in the idealization of consistency, led to the movement for schools to develop discipline codes (National School Resource Network, 1980).

Leaders of the discipline code movement of the 1980s encouraged state departments of education to develop model discipline codes (National School Resource Network, 1980). Although this was a step in the right direction, there is little valid evidence that codes resulted in a marked decrease in misbehavior (Lally, 1982). Despite the proliferation of discipline codes, witness the panic over school violence, a decade later, in the 1990s. School disruptions and violence did not decrease when emphasis on rules and punishment increased (Hyman & D'Allesandro, 1984a, 1984b). Although discipline codes may have helped to make punishments more consistent in some cases, they have never been shown to effectively deal with the root causes of misbehavior. A rigid adherence to discipline codes, and other simplistic answers, can result in inappropriate punishment if the codes objectify legality and consistency and ignore justice. For instance, the following is a real-life example of how a well-written discipline code was abused by a punitive administrator who was dedicated to consistency of rule enforcement.

In the mid-1980s, I was consulting in an inner-city high school regarding discipline problems. The district Director of Discipline and I were investigating a complaint from a parent about the disciplinary actions meted out by an assistant high school principal, Mr. James. The parent's sixteen-year-old daughter, Kisha, had been suspended from school for defacing property.

Mr. James, who had suspended Kisha, was indignant that the parent had complained about this punishment to the central administration of the school. He remonstrated that the school discipline code clearly stated that three days of suspension was the penalty for defacing property, an act she had committed. However, the story was not so simple.

In the girls' lavatory, Kisha saw that someone had written on the wall, "Kisha is a slut." Kisha obliterated this offensive statement with a marker. As she was finishing the job, a teacher entered the lavatory and sent Kisha to the office. After hearing her story, Mr. James took out the discipline code and showed her the penalty for defacing school property. He then gave her the standard lecture about needing to have pride in the school and how defaced property was a blot on everybody. Despite her protestations that she did not mean to deface property and that she had never been in trouble before, he stated, "Rules are rules and they are not made to be broken. You broke the rules, and you are suspended for three days."

According to Mr. James, Kisha became quite indignant and told him that he was not fair. She claimed that he did not understand. She added a few more colorful phrases, which riled Mr. James. He informed her that if she said another word he would add two days to the suspension. She countered with, "Go ahead and suspend me for the whole year. I have had enough of you and your stupid rules." He added two days of suspension, as indicated in the discipline code, for disrespect.

The Director of Discipline pointed out that the discipline code contained a statement indicating that penalties should always be considered in terms of extenuating circumstances. He and I tried to explore, with Mr. James, alternative approaches to suspension, as were allowed within the guidelines. Because Kisha's initial motivation was not to deface the wall, but to cover the slur to her name, he could have made the punishment fit the "crime." Kisha could have been required to clean the wall, thereby removing the offensive statement and her efforts to hide it.

Mr. James could have used the behavioral technique of overcorrection, by having Kisha clean the whole wall. He could have used psychodynamic or cognitive/behavioral techniques in discussing other ways in which she could have handled her emotions when she saw the inscription. Unfortunately, mitigating circumstances were a concept foreign to Mr. James. Rather, taking the easy way out, he administered punishments "by the book." Like too many disciplinarians, he was unable to appreciate the subtleties of causality and the relation between justice and legality. He did not consider Kisha's past lack of disciplinary problems, her chagrin at being called a slut, her mother's incredulity that Kisha had been suspended for a whole week for a simple, nonmalicious act, or the possible effects of this punishment on Kisha's future behavior and attitude toward school, school rules, and school administrators.

The example of Kisha illustrates how discipline codes can be misused when applied simplistically. As this case suggests, they represent a step in the right direction, but they too frequently represent an attempt to codify rigidity and homogenize punishment rather than develop more complex, lasting solutions. They are too often punishment oriented, as Mr. James illustrated, and do not lay out the conditions under which students will be positively motivated to behave.

We support discipline codes as a rational method of outlining approved and disapproved behaviors. However, we are wary of their use as a mainstay of discipline policy independent of well-conceived programs of prevention and remediation. Let us now turn to a more conceptual model for understanding discipline.

Moral Education and Character Development

During the late 1980s, a small but highly visible group of educators and scholars began to promote the concept that misbehavior was a direct result of parents' and schools' inability to train children in traditional, universal truths and values that are necessary for the development of proper behavior (Bennett, 1994; Bloom, 1988). It is assumed that the development of good character leads to respect for others and values necessary for a civilized attitude. Advocates of this position have promoted curricula that fall under the rubric of moral or character education.

The call for moral education is based on the assumption that an entire generation has grown up in a moral vacuum (Rosenblatt, 1995). Centers such as the Center for the Fourth and Fifth R's (Respect and Responsibility), started by Professor Thomas Lickona of the State University of New York in Cortland, and others sprang up in the early 1990s. This movement is dedicated to teaching moral behavior to young schoolchildren and represents diverse approaches and opinions. However, much of the activity in this area is associated with a conservative political agenda based on the belief that some very specific, universal truths must be taught.

Concepts of morality, whether stated overtly or implied, are at the base of all discipline training programs. All promote specific assumptions about what is right, good, proper, and just. For instance, all discipline training programs emphasize respect for others, nonviolent solutions to conflict, and self-control (Blum, 1994).

Character education is a preventive approach to discipline. If children learn proper values at an early age, the theory goes, they will respect adults, obey authorities, be considerate and kind with peers, and obey the rules. In sum, they will not misbehave because they have developed a conscience, which results in self-discipline. If conscience acts as a brake on the slippery slope to misbehavior, then one must assume that the stronger the conscience, the more well behaved a student will be. The problem occurs when we attempt to define the exact rules that govern a child's conscience. Consider the following as a self-test of your orientation to morality.

You are observing a group of students in the schoolyard. Jimmy, a somewhat passive, easily victimized, overweight boy is being teased. He is teased about his weight, his family, his poor grades, and his lack of athletic ability. Although most of the teasing is done by Joe, a boy with his own problems, five other students are standing around observing. They are not actively teasing Jimmy, but some are smiling, and two are encouraging Joe. You should:

1. Immediately stop what is happening by telling the students to disperse.
2. Punish Joe for being mean.
3. Punish all the students for their participation and make them apologize.
4. Ignore the situation and let the students solve their own problems.
5. Tell Jimmy's parents to take him for self-defense classes.
6. Teach the children to be empathetic and caring and to come to the defense of underdogs.
7. All of the above.
8. None of the above.

Responses 1 and 4 would suggest that you do not believe that it is your responsibility to teach students to be decent to each other. If they do not learn that in the home and church, how can you do the job? Responses 2 and 3 indicate that you may believe that the best way to teach proper behavior is through punishment. That goes along with the "spare the rod, spoil the child" philosophy of discipline. Response 5 implies that you believe that "might makes right" and that victims must learn to protect themselves. Because you obviously can not always depend on authorities to protect you, you must take justice into your own hands. Response 6 suggests that you may have "wimpy" ideas that people should learn to be cooperative and caring rather than competitive and aggressive. After all, the latter traits are responsible for United States' greatness in the marketplace and in the sports arena.

Now if you are mad because you feel that we ridiculed any or all of your answers, you are beginning to get the message about moral education. The problem with approaching discipline from the perspective of morality and the inculcation of moral values is that values are highly subjective. Most of us agree that children should have high values, good character, well-developed morality, and the ability to care about others. But whose values, what kind of character, what view of morality, and about whom should children care? These questions transform a seemingly simple concept into a morass from which any rational educator may find no escape. This may be an overstatement if you grew up or teach in a small, relatively homogeneous community where "traditional moral values" have predominated. You may identify with communities where there is a moral consensus among politicians, parents, church leaders, educators, and so forth. The flip side is that in such a place traditional values may conflict with constitutional values such as dissent, individual rights, due process, and the freedom to refuse to conform to majority thinking. So which are the real "traditional" values? The polarity between the political right and the political left as they conceptualize the teaching of morality crosses all models.

The Conservative View

Conservative theorists consider that certain moral imperatives are inviolable. Universal truths exist that transcend cultures and must be passed on, basically unchanged, from generation to generation. These values are often rooted in religion and must be taught through the home, schools, the judicial system, and other agencies. In the United States, the Judeo-Christian values promoted by conservative curricula include:

1. Promotion of two-parent families with the father working and the mother at home
2. Sexual abstinence before marriage
3. Abstinence from smoking, drinking and drugs
4. The immorality of gay and lesbian lifestyles
5. Forbidding abortion
6. Patriotism
7. Obedience to and respect for authority
8. Politeness
9. Courtesy
10. Honesty
11. Prayer
12. Humility
13. Reverence for God

These values, many of which were taught in colonial schools, are still included in the curricula of contemporary private religious schools, where they are often integrated into the regular curricula. They are taught in specific religious classes and intertwined with other subjects. Parents send their children to these schools because of the values taught, so there is generally no real conflict with teachers and school officials. However, many public schools must cater to diversified communities that reflect varied values, some of which may be in direct conflict with those proposed.

The Liberal View

Liberal theorists generally have no problem with absolute values being taught in private schools where parents choose to send their children. However, with regard to teaching morality in public schools, liberals view values and morality through a prism of relativity. In a multicultural, multiracial, and multiethnic society, who is to say which specific values are correct? In a break with the past, this relativistic view was promoted in the 1970s through various curricula that prompted students to think through the meaning of values within specific cultural contexts. The flagship of the movement and the target of conservatives was "Values Clarification," a program developed by Raths, Harmin, and Simon (1966; 1978). Also, curricula in social studies were developed to encourage students to understand the relevance of values different from their own by taking a relativistic approach to the practices of each culture. Rather than being locked into their own values, students were encouraged to understand and appreciate the values, religious beliefs, and practices of other cultures.

Among the important values stressed in the liberal approach are critical inquiry; empathy; due process; freedom of thought and action; the concept of a just society; objectivity; tolerance; personal responsibility in all areas, including sexual behavior, family planning, reasoned argument and dissent; cooperation as opposed to competition; truth; and equality of opportunity. Obviously there are overlaps between conservatives and liberals in agreed upon values, but what about the differences?

Who Is Correct?

The problem is that both sides make good points. Both sides want students to learn to care about others, to respect others' rights, and to be responsible citizens. The public seems to agree with the teaching of those sorts of values. A poll taken in Maryland's Baltimore County Schools, where a broad-based values program is taught, reflects strong public support for the teaching of values. In answer to the question, "Is it necessary and appropriate for public schools to teach values?" the percentages of respondents answering "yes" included 98 percent of the school administrators, 85 percent of the parents and guardians, 84 percent of Baltimore businessmen, 68 percent of the school staff, and 75 percent of the students.

Assuming this survey is somewhat generalizable, and considering the numbers of children who attend private religious schools, it seems clear that Americans value values. From a policy point of view, it is impossible to determine who is correct about what values to teach. So what should public schools do?

To answer this question, one could begin with data from social science. Then one must match those findings with political necessity.

The assumptions underlying any public school morality curricula should reflect widely held values, beliefs, and yearnings. But they must also be consonant with the reality of people's lives. For instance, throughout history there have always been those who called for a return to "traditional" values, especially those promoted within the nuclear family. The underlying assumption is that good discipline is dependent on "good" homes, which some translate to mean intact homes. But Census Bureau data tell us that in 1990 only 26 percent of households with children were intact. The Bureau also says that between 1985 and 1989 almost half the nation's households moved. Furthermore, by 1994, approximately 20 percent of our children were growing up in poverty. So, for the foreseeable future, we cannot return to values based on a family structure, geographic stability, and economic security that does not exist.

American schools have always been concerned about premarital sex. To prevent any show of interest about sex, many schools have had long-standing rules against couples publicly holding hands, hugging, kissing, or any other open displays of affection. Contemporary schools are sometimes wracked by debates concerning student use of contraceptives, abortion, and teenage pregnancy. Both sides have legitimate arguments as to whether to treat these problems within either medical or moral frameworks. Although both liberals and conservatives agree that sexual intercourse among teenagers is not a good idea, they disagree about what and how to teach about the issue. However, historical and contemporary facts suggest that no culture has ever overcome adolescent hormones. Even in good old colonial times, data on prenuptial pregnancies run as high as 40 percent in some areas (Fischer, 1989).

As for contraceptives and abortion, few educators who teach about or mention these controversial topics feel completely safe. Almost always some parents or community groups feel strongly about these issues and sex education in general. The best approach may be to teach all sides of the issue as part of the curriculum. If parents do not want their children to hear others' views, the students should have the right not to attend. However, even this solution is not acceptable to all, because we are dealing with varied views of morality.

In the final analysis, moral education has gained such political significance that its curriculum manifestations will most likely be shaped at district and regional levels. The outcome will be influenced more by ideological rhetoric than by rational examination of social science data.

Turning to less controversial approaches to discipline, we now consider some of the other major approaches. These were identified by examining more than eighty discipline training programs (Blum, 1994; Dahbany, 1996).

Wolfgang and Glickman's Approach

Wolfgang and Glickman's work is important, not because it pioneered an original approach to discipline, but because their texts summarize many popular discipline programs. In their first edition, Wolfgang and Glickman (1980) conceptualized classroom discipline along a linear continuum based on techniques teachers use to control classrooms. This approach has historical precedents dating to the 1930s, when educational researchers began to examine the differences between authoritarian and democratic teachers. Although laissez-faire teachers were also studied in the early days, this model is rarely considered legitimate among contemporary experts in school discipline.

Since the early studies of H. H. Anderson (Anderson & Brewer, 1946) researchers have used various labels to identify the two opposite ends of the continuum of teacher control of students. At one end are teachers who have been labeled authoritarian, dominative, teacher-centered, custodial, and direct. At the other end are teachers who are labeled democratic, integrative, student-centered, humanistic, and indirect. Essentially, the continuum separates teachers in terms of their approach to motivation of children. At one end are those who believe that punishment and force are necessary to control children. At the other end are those who believe that reinforcement, praise, and persuasion will encourage children to learn and not misbehave.

Along the continuum, Wolfgang and Glickman conceptualized three constructs based on teachers' beliefs about discipline and control: relationship/listening, confronting/contracting, and rules/rewards/punishment rubric.

Relationship/listening includes both humanistic and psychoanalytic thought. Advocates of this approach agree that students are the masters of their destiny. They also believe that the focus is on the inner child, as opposed to outward behavior. Here, the role of the teacher is to create the type of environment where children are comfortable enough to freely express their feelings. While students battle with their inner emotions, the teacher needs to be an empathic listener. This viewpoint is apparent in the works of Carl Rogers (1969), Thomas Gordon's Teacher Effectiveness Training (Gordon, 1974), and Raths et al.'s Values Clarification (1966).

The confronting/contracting school of thought includes theorists from gestalt, developmental, and social psychology. The whole child must be viewed by the interrelationship of internal and external forces affecting him or her. The teacher constantly interacts with the child, being a clarifier, establishing and enforcing boundaries. However, mutually acceptable solutions to conflicts are formulated. This theoretical view includes such writers as Rudolph Dreikurs (1968, 1977; Dreikurs & Cassel, 1972) and William Glasser (1969, 1978, 1985, 1986), whose approaches are discussed later.

Rules/rewards/punishment theorists share the idea that childrens' development is directly affected by the environment. That is, external forces change human behavior. No consideration is given to inner emotions. Therefore, in school, the teacher becomes the controller of the environment, responsible for selecting appropriate reinforcements and punishments. This theoretical view includes such writers as Skinner (1953, 1968, 1971), Dobson (1970), Engelman (1969), and Canter and Canter (1976).

Pupil Control Ideology

In the 1960s and 1970s the works of Willower, Eidell, and Hoy (1967) and Flanders (Amidon, Flanders & Casper, 1985) had a major impact on teacher discipline training. Their concepts of pupil control are rooted in the early works of social psychologists such as Adorno (1950) and Lewin (Lewin, Lippitt, & White, 1939), who studied the effects of authoritarian, ethnocentric versus democratic personality and leadership styles. Although some may consider their work dated, their constructs still offer a valid conceptual understanding of classroom discipline.

Willower et al. (1967) developed the Pupil Control Ideology (PCI) instrument to study disciplinary attitudes of school personnel. With the help of a twenty-item questionnaire, these researchers conceptualized PCI along a continuum, ranging from "humanism" to "custodialism." Educators with a custodial pupil control ideology stress the maintenance of order by use of punitive sanctions. Students are viewed as irresponsible and undisciplined, and therefore they must be strictly controlled. In contrast, those individuals with a humanistic pupil control ideology stress an accepting, understanding, trustful view of students. Students are viewed as responsible and capable of self-discipline.

A series of studies of pupil control ideology revealed some interesting findings. They indicated that custodial teachers were lecture oriented, whereas humanistic teachers were more oriented toward accepting and developing students' ideas. The classroom climate of humanistic teachers tends to be characterized by high levels of cognitive activity and a stress on divergent rather than convergent thinking. As a result, students tend to be more enthusiastic than in custodial classes, where there tends to be more passive listening.

Elementary school teachers tend to be more humanistic than are junior high or high school teachers. Also, teachers tend to become more custodial during the initial period of socialization to schools (Hardesty, 1978; Hoy, 1983; Willower et al., 1967). This has been explained by assimilation into the culture of the school where the "don't smile until Christmas" ideology seems to permeate (Jones, 1982). Women tend to be less custodial than men, but the grade level that is taught influences this relationship (Multhauf, Willower, & Licata, 1978). Studies using other methodologies suggest that men tend to favor more punitive discipline techniques (Benedict, 1974).

Pupil control ideology studies focus mainly on the first years of teacher socialization to the culture of the school. Extrapolating from the data presented, one might expect that, as teachers become more experienced, they would increasingly become more punitive. However, some evidence suggests that this may not be true in all situations, especially when teachers rely on objective observations, have some knowledge of the discipline literature, and resist peer pressure to be punitive (Tully-Marchon, 1987). For instance, studies of the use of corporal punishment indicate that less experienced teachers are more likely as a group to use corporal punishment (Rust & Kinnard, 1983).

Most teachers know that immediate punishments of appropriate intensity, duration, and frequency, which allow no escape and no rewards, are usually effective in causing immediate cessation of certain behaviors (Bongiovanni, 1979; Hyman, 1990). In truth, with many students, a quick reprimand, a harsh look, or removal from class may immediately solve the problem. Through experience, however, many teachers learn that these techniques do not work with most of the students who are behavior problems.

For instance, when Johnny, who loves to socialize in class, is scolded to stop talking, he does. The teacher's belief that scolding works is thereby reinforced. But ten minutes later, Johnny talks out of turn, and the teacher scolds him again. This time he stops talking for twenty minutes, again reinforcing the teacher's belief in scolding. Then, forty-five minutes later, he curses at the teacher when she loudly and severely scolds him for again talking out of turn.

The teacher then sends Johnny to the principal, who keeps him for half an hour. Johnny comes back to class and is good the rest of the day, which again reinforces the teacher's belief in punishment. However, the following school day, the routine is usually repeated with students like Johnny. The teacher has not really taught him why he should behave or rewarded him for not talking. If the scolding were a real punishment, by definition, Johnny would not talk out of turn again.

These kinds of experiences with punishment are repeated daily by hundreds of thousands of teachers who fail to critically examine the long-term effectiveness of their control techniques. Punishment does not teach new behaviors; it generally does not get at why the student misbehaves; and it tends to lower self-esteem, thereby increasing the student's likelihood to act out (Kolko, 1992; Litovsky & Dusic, 1985).

Duke and Jones's Organizational Approach

Duke and Jones (1984) believe that discipline cannot be comprehensively studied along one continuum. They view discipline within a larger organizational context and consider misbehavior from a systemic framework. That is, true improvement in school behavior will follow an analysis of the system and organizational changes to deal effectively with individual and group problems. They define discipline approaches as fitting into one of three distinct categories: models, paradigms, and systems.

Models are defined as plans of action typically grounded in theory or conventional wisdom. However, they often lack empirical support. Examples of models include William Glasser's reality therapy (Glasser, 1969, 1978), Rudolf Dreikurs's work on logical consequences and motive attribution (Dreikers, 1968), Thomas Gordon's Teacher Effectiveness Training (Gordon, 1974), and Lee Canter's Assertive Discipline (Canter & Canter, 1976).

Paradigms are conceptual frameworks used to guide systematic or programmatic research on student behavior. Programs that fit into this category come from empirical investigations of specific teacher behaviors, classroom organization, and school climate. They use acceptable research methodologies and analytical tools and are supported, at least to some extent, by theory.

Examples of programs within this category include the Teacher Effectiveness literature (e.g., Brophy & Evertson, 1976; Evertson & Emmer, 1982a, 1982b) and the School Effectiveness literature (e.g., Goodlad, 1984; Rutter, Maughan, Mortimore, & Ouston, 1979).

Systems approaches are comprehensive and often eclectic sets of recommendations based on research and practice. The goal is to help educators create schoolwide or classroom plans for minimizing student misbehavior. According to Duke and Jones (1984), systems do not necessarily originate from a specific body of research, nor do they focus solely on prevention. The assumption underlying most systems is that behavior problems are endemic to schools. Therefore, educators must be prepared for any circumstance. Examples of systems include Madeline Hunter's (1990) Instructional Theory into Practice (ITIP) and Duke's (1980) Systematic Management Plan for School Discipline (SMPSD).

Summary

The five general approaches presented so far offer a brief overview of ways in which school discipline may be understood. The legalistic approach of using discipline codes offers a written, clear policy guide for dealing with misbehavior. However, these codes are rarely updated, tend to be punishment driven, and do not focus sufficiently on prevention, positive motivation, or corrective remediation and treatment. Supporters of moral education believe that misbehavior results from inadequate attention to development of good moral character and lack of adequate conscience. Wolfgang and Glickman (1986) and Willower, Eidel, and Hoy (1967) consider teaching along a linear continuum that focuses on the behaviors teachers exhibit in their attempts to control their classrooms. A continuum from authoritarian to democratic teaching styles does appear to predict student misbehaviors (Hyman, 1964), but there is less evidence that teacher personality or behavior can be made to move significantly in any one direction on that continuum. Duke and Jones (1984) organized the discipline literature by the level of proof for the validity of the various approaches.

Although Wolfgang and Glickman (1986) recognize the importance of the different theories of child development, they loosely interpret the various theories on a continuum. However, teachers' disciplinary behaviors are more likely formed from clusters of beliefs, emotions, and experiences that may be related, but probably do not exist on a linear continuum. In addition, although attitudes may remain consistent, behaviors may change as a function of school and community demands. For example, a teacher who believes that misbehavior should be ignored and good behavior rewarded might be severely reprimanded by the principal who observes students "getting away" with talking in class. If the norms of the school are to insist on absolute obedience to rules, the teacher will be pressed to enforce school standards. To do otherwise would result in "misbehavior" by the teacher. This type of blocking of an individual teacher's desire to follow his or her own dictates, which often are based on successful experiences, can result in less effective classroom management.

The work of Willower et al. (1967) still has validity in identifying teacher control ideology. But like Wolfgang and Glickman, defining teachers unidimensionally is too simple to help explain the nuances of discipline and to change teacher behavior to improve discipline. Duke and Jones (1984) recognize the multifaceted nature of school discipline but, unfortunately, do not offer an adequate conceptual/theoretical base for classifying teachers.

The intent here is to present overviews of multiple approaches within the overriding, theory-driven approach of teacher variance. This approach, which harnesses individual teacher belief systems, offers a unique and practical way to approach school discipline.

Key Terms

abuse

assault

confronting/contracting

defacing

defiance

discipline code

linear continuum

misbehavior

moral education

organizational approach

pupil control ideology

relationship/listening

rules/rewards/punishment

self-discipline

Application Activities

1. One way to develop a discipline code for a school district is to form a committee of administrators, teachers, parents, and students so they can all have input. Assign two students to play each of these roles and to develop definitions of misbehavior for activities interfering with school performance and consequences for misbehavior.

2. Ask the students to collect a few discipline codes from the local area's school districts. Have the students take either a conservative or liberal point of view and discuss the issues in the discipline code.

3. Have students attend a local school board meeting. Have the students report to the class

the issues discussed and identify the conservative and liberal points of view presented at the meeting.

4. Using Wolfgang and Glickman's linear continuum, develop approaches for a teacher to handle Michael's classroom issues (see case studies in Chapter 2).

5. Using the pupil control ideology, develop a humanistic and a custodial method for a teacher to handle Chris's classroom issues (see case studies in Chapter 2).

6. Discuss and classify the four other discipline approaches according to Duke and Jones's organizational approach.

Suggested Readings

Duke, D. L. (Ed.). (1982). *Helping teachers manage classrooms*. Alexandria, VA: Association for Supervision and Curriculum Development.

Duke, D. L., & Jones, V. F. (1984). Two decades of discipline: Assessing the development of an educational specialization. *Journal of Research and Development in Education, 17,* 25–35.

Glasser, W. (1984). *Control Theory: A new explanation of how we control our lives.* New York: Harper & Row.

Hunter, M. C. (1990). *Discipline that develops self discipline.* El Segundo, CA: TIPS Publications.

Hyman, I. A., Weiler, E., Dahbany, A., Shanock, A., & Britton, G. (1994, October 29). Policy and practice in school discipline: Past, present, and future. Invited presentation to the National Education Goals Panel, Washington, DC. [This paper as well as a list of other publications, workshops, and services are available through the National Center for the Study of Corporal Punishment and Alternatives, Temple University, Ritter Annex, Philadelphia, PA 19122 (215-204-6091)].

Jones, V. F., & Jones, L. S. (1990). *Comprehensive classroom discipline: Motivating and managing students* (3rd ed.). Boston: Allyn & Bacon.

Rogers. C. (1969). *Freedom to learn.* Columbus, OH: Charles E. Merrill.

Wolfgang, C. H., & Glickman, C. D. (1986). *Solving discipline problems* (2nd ed.) Needham Heights, MA: Allyn & Bacon.

$Chapter$ 2

Punitiveness and Teacher Variance

Chapter Objectives

After reading the chapter, you should be able to:

1. Know your orientation regarding your attitudes toward children and best discipline fit as measured by the Survey of Attitudes toward Children and the Teacher Variance Inventory
2. Know which grade level teachers, school personnel, and geographical regions tend to be more punitive than others
3. Be aware of the history and evidence of punitiveness in American society toward children
4. Understand the rationale behind the development of the teacher variance theory

Please do not begin this chapter until you have filled out and scored the two scales at the end of the Introduction. The first part of this chapter discusses the concept of punitiveness, which is measured by the Survey of Attitudes toward Children.

Punitiveness

When we first started offering discipline workshops to professionals, an interesting phenomenon occurred in the early stages of almost every presentation. Discussions of the meaning and usefulness of punishment in changing behavior almost always resulted in heated exchanges among the participants. Views about the rights of children often split the participants along a conservative-to-liberal continuum. This inevitably led to polarization of the audience, with neither side prevailing. These heated, sometimes vehement debates uncovered deeply held convictions that were invulnerable to reason and data during these confrontations. It was clear that arguments over these "gut" issues took up too much time and deterred us from expeditiously moving on to the rest of the full-day workshop on alternatives to punishment.

Rather than depending on research and expert opinion, teachers, parents, and policy makers tend to rely on "gut" beliefs regarding misbehavior and delinquency. As described above, significant minorities of professionals rely on their own "gut" feelings about some aspects of discipline instead of turning to the research on what really works (Kaplan, 1995; Sofer, 1983). The ways in which we were treated and punished as children and students never escape us. One of the best predictors of how parents or teachers will discipline children is how they were disciplined themselves (Eron, Walder & Lefkowitz, 1971; Graziano & Nemaste, 1990; Hyman, 1990a; Kaplan, 1995; Lennox, 1982; Mishkin, 1987; Patterson, 1982; Pokalo, 1986; Sofer, 1983; Straus, 1994).

Punitiveness as Measured on the SATC

There are clear differences in levels of punitiveness between professions and regions as measured by the Survey of Attitudes toward Children in the Introduction (Kotzen, 1994). Yet, using norms based on these comparisons is like comparing apples and oranges because training, work tasks, and professional values vary by groups and regions. Also, the meaning of the scores can not be taken literally. High scorers do not necessarily carry out their punitive philosophies, nor are low scorers necessarily permissive. In fact, effective disciplinarians with low scores believe in rules and manners, but try to persuade and convince children to abide by rules. They may even involve students in rule making. High scorers tend to believe in universal truths and rules that they state and enforce, but their actions might be modified by the discipline norms of their particular school. Most teachers fall within the middle range. No matter where you work, however, scores above ninety-one are considered quite punitive, whereas scores below forty-one place you well below the usual punitive range for most professionals who work with children.

The percentiles given in Table 2.1 on page 30 are for a mixed group of professionals and specialties. As might be expected, principals, whose jobs are often associated with discipline, control, determining and carrying out punishments, and staff supervision, tend to have the highest, most punitive scores. Psychologists and counselors, who are most focused on mental health and prevention of and understanding the causes of misbehavior have the lowest, least punitive scores.

One surprising finding in these data is that high school teachers appear to be less punitive than middle school and elementary school teachers. This does not fit the findings when we have run workshops with all types of teachers. These particular data, however, represent a large number of high school special education teachers who attended two workshops. Special education teachers as a group tend to be less punitive than other teachers, because of training and experience. So when the data were pooled, their numbers outweighed the relatively small number of regular high school teachers.

As might be expected, there are significant regional differences in levels of punitiveness, as demonstrated in Table 2.2 on page 30. For example, the South and Southwest of

TABLE 2.1   Comparison of Mean Scores on the SATC between Different Educator Groups

Group	Number of Respondents	Mean* Scores	Standard Deviation
Principals	48	79.13	14.20
Elementary teachers	48	77.63	14.91
Middle school teachers	17	76.88	13.25
High school teachers	30	69.93	15.41
Special ed. teachers	22	64.64	18.77
Counselors	17	61.88	16.83
School psychologists	211	58.62	13.97

* Higher scores are more punitive.

the United States, where almost all states still allow the use of corporal punishment on students, is statistically significantly more punitive than most other regions.

If possible, you should enlist a group of peers to take the test. You can then compare your score with others in your area. This will provide a basis for understanding yourself in relation to where you live and what you do. If you find that your scores indicate more punitive attitudes than appears to be warranted in your school district, you may want to think about their meaning in terms of your success in school discipline. Of course, attitude scales do not always correlate with actual behavior. Your classroom behavior may be shaped by the demands of the students, the requirements of the principal, peer pressure, and the standards and values in the community.

The most important variable is how your level of punitiveness affects your interpretation of your theoretical orientation as indicated on the TVI. For instance, if you are very punitive and behaviorally oriented, you may tend to focus on aversive punishment techniques, rather than reinforcement. You would support your reliance on punishment by selectively referring to behavioral research supporting your point of view. You would tend to ignore or discount the majority of research in behaviorism that indicates that reward is the most effective method of changing behavior (Alberto & Troutman, 1990; Bongiovanni, 1979; Skinner, 1953, 1982).

If you are very high in humanism, your total devotion to permissiveness might be counterproductive in certain situations. You might ignore the research and experience of peers who have tried to develop open, humanistic classrooms in schools that were not prepared for this approach. For instance, students who are used to authoritarian methods of control cannot be expected to immediately develop internal controls when they encounter a permis-

TABLE 2.2   Regional Differences in Levels of Punitiveness

Region	Number	Mean	Standard Deviation
South	204	68.88	18.89
Northeast	296	63.58	14.29
Midwest	80	62.95	16.81
West	28	58.25	14.94

sive teacher. As a result, if you unendingly depend on a permissive classroom climate in this situation, you are bound to have chaos. This will generally result in censure from parents, peers, and administrators.

Your belief in punitiveness is a generally static trait that reflects all of your experiences, attitudes, and beliefs. It guides the unifying theory that determines how you discipline children. Yet attitude scales are not always the best predictors of how you will behave in a particular situation. Contextual factors such as administrative demands, peer pressure, student differences, curricular requirements, employment conditions, and community values may change how you teach and how you discipline without really changing your belief system.

In addition to the above, Americans' faith in the efficacy of punishment shapes school discipline at many individual and institutional levels. Because of this, punitiveness in the United States deserves further discussion before moving on to the five teacher variance approaches.

America the Punitive

Through the nineteenth century, U.S. teachers relied heavily on corporal punishment and humiliation to foster achievement and maintain order. Teachers were often neither educators, instructors, nor trainers. They were valued as disciplinarians who specialized in the use of the rod and cowskin, the ruler, and switch (Finkelstein, 1989). Discipline, based on fear, resulted in the prominent display of paddles, switches, leather straps, and even whipping posts (Hyman & Wise, 1979). In the words of an Oregon teacher, these instruments of discipline "were silent but forceful admonitions to potentially disruptive students" (Finkelstein, 1989). The crucible for violence against authority may well have existed in the punitive atmosphere of Puritan society.

Many acts of child abuse begin with the precept that verbal and physical assaults on children are necessary to change behavior. Many people believe that the more intense the pain, the less likely that misbehavior will be repeated (Axelrod, 1983a, 1983b; Bongiovanni, 1979). In the campaign against corporal punishment in schools, it has become clear that too many in the United States are obsessively punitive. Punitiveness includes overt acts in which physical or psychological pain is inflicted, and acts of omission that result in painful, psychologically destructive conditions in homes, schools, and society.

The United States' punitive public policy toward misbehavior, deviance, and nonconformity suggests that we are a nation that prefers solutions based on punishment rather than prevention and rehabilitation. This attitude mitigates against any meaningful prevention of problems such as child abuse, delinquency, or school violence (McCord, 1988a, 1988b, 1991; Patterson, 1982; Patterson, Capaldi, & Bank, 1990; Straus, 1991, 1992). Covert punishment by legislative neglect is a type of punitiveness that affects the lives of millions of American children in inadequately funded schools. For instance, in schools serving poor children, meager resources are often used to provide services after misbehavior and violence have occurred rather than to offer comprehensive prevention programs.

When relative wealth and potential resources are taken into account, we are probably the most punitive country among all of the Western democracies (Children's Defense Fund, 1991; Hodgkinson, 1991; Hyman & Pokalo, 1993; The National Commission on Children 1991; National Committee for the Prevention of Child Abuse, 1991a, 1991b). The source of our punitiveness is a cluster of beliefs nurtured by the authoritarian right (Altemeyer, 1988; Barnhart, 1972; Hyman, 1990; Jones, Gasiewski, & Hyman, 1990a; Miller, 1980). The justification for our punitiveness toward children lies deeply embedded in religion and tradition (Greven, 1980, 1991; Jones et al., 1990; Pokalo, 1986; Wiehe, 1989).

The results of our punitiveness are evidenced by comparison with other Western democracies (Hyman, 1995). We have:

1. High infant mortality rates
2. A low percentage of gross national product spent on education (Hedges, Laine, & Greenwald, 1994)
3. A relatively poor record of providing programs and services for schooling and employing the disabled
4. The highest rate of incarceration and execution of people who committed crimes as juveniles
5. Very poor legislative support for families in terms of provisions of programs such as day care, family leave, sick leave, and vacations (National Commission on Children, 1991)
6. Great resources expended to punish unauthorized talk, pictures, objects, and thoughts of sex, although we still have the highest teenage pregnancy rates (our rates are twice as high as those of England, Wales, France, and Canada; three times as high as Sweden; and seven times as high as the Netherlands)
7. A continued fruitless "war on drugs" that emphasizes levels of punishment, as opposed to treatment and prevention, which have resulted in jammed courts and overflowing jails

Despite the evidence about our levels of punitiveness, we are changing as a society. Many policy makers, including judges, legislators, criminologists, police, and educators, over the years, have recognized the causes of misbehavior and violence rather than promoting and extolling "get tough" policies. Child abuse laws, protection from spousal abuse, drug treatment programs, juvenile justice, and the schools have gradually moved away from our punitive roots.

Polls reflect a slow but discernible erosion of support for hitting children. Studies in the 1980s indicate that 90 percent to 95 percent of Americans approved of parental spankings (Straus, 1989). A Harris poll in the late 1980s demonstrated that approximately 86 percent of the respondents then supported this practice (Hyman, 1989a), whereas data in 1994 suggest that currently approximately 60 percent to 70 percent of Americans support parental spanking (Straus, 1994). Most states do not allow spanking of foster children. As of 1995, only 23 states still allowed paddling in schools. Although a Gallup Poll of teachers in 1989 showed that only 38 percent disapproved of school paddlings, the National Education Association, the largest group representing teachers, has a policy against it (Elam, 1989a). In comparison, a Harris poll in which we were involved showed that 54 percent of parents were against hitting schoolchildren (Hyman, 1989a). As of 1996, all but a few of the national organizations representing children in any setting had taken a stand against corporal punishment in the schools.

Teacher Variance

To understand teacher variance and determine your own "best discipline fit," you should have taken the scales provided at the end of the Introduction. If you have not, you should now turn back and take the Survey of Attitudes toward Children and the Teacher Variance Inventory (TVI). After you have scored yourself, turn back to this chapter.

Teacher variance enables you to apply your own theoretical orientation in everyday situations. You will also learn what to do, within you own system, if a specific disciplinary technique does not work with an individual student. If you concentrate on the approach with which you are most comfortable, you will improve your skills in a way that does not ask you to change your beliefs. Once you master one approach, you may become curious about the approach that is next closest to your belief system. This may occur when you begin to realize that some approaches appear to be more effective in some situations than in others. You may choose to learn a second theory-driven orientation. Finally, you might want to master all of the material in this book to gain a better understanding of the many theories and techniques of discipline. In so doing, you will be able to match, based on strengths and weaknesses of each theory, disciplinary techniques to specific situations and misbehaviors.

The Teacher Variance Inventory (TVI), which was developed to measure teacher orientation, went through several revisions as a result of what we learned in workshops with teachers (Marchon-Tully, 1987). The TVI-III, included in this book, is a vastly improved version of the original scale. This latest version integrates contemporary theory and approaches. In addition, we have collapsed it to five approaches that are theoretically clearer than the original six approaches.

If you choose to become an expert in more than one approach, you may then decide which techniques might best be used in specific situations and how to combine approaches with individual students. At this point, however, we suggest that after you finish reading this chapter, you turn to the chapter based on the orientation reflected by your highest score on the TVI.

To get the most out of this book, we advise that you study one approach intensively. Examples of programs that fit into the various approaches are given. At first, try specific techniques in simple situations where the model should work easily. Then begin to apply your approach to more complex problems. If a particular technique does not work, go back to the system and analyze it. Try to determine within the system what you did wrong.

Although the purpose of teacher variance is to help you identify the theoretical base for your discipline practices, we recognize that all disciplinary techniques that you use in the classroom may not be completely tied to one single theory. For instance, you may use an ecological/systems approach in organizing your classroom seating, and you might use a behavioral approach for rewarding a child for not getting out of his or her seat. But underlying each of these techniques is your own belief system about what causes children to misbehave. From that belief flows the techniques that you, in your particular context, find successful.

With teacher variance, when a technique does not work, you will return to the theory to understand why it did not work. For example, in the cognitive/behavioral model, if you reinforce a student to improve his behavior and the technique does not work, you would not assume that reinforcement does not work. Rather, you would assume that you used the wrong reinforcement and attempt to find one that would be more successful.

The eventual goal for any professional who wants to be the "complete disciplinarian" is to understand all the approaches and to be able to use those that are most effective in specific situations. For instance, let us assume that Ms. Jones has successfully used a token economy to ensure on-task behavior with most of her third-graders. However, Johnny hates Ms. Jones and is in a power struggle to prove he is in control. His behavior says, "there is no way you can bribe me to behave." In this case, Ms. Jones might find that psychodynamic/interpersonal theory offers her the tools to help her communicate effectively with Johnny to find out why he hates her and why he needs to be in control. If she can broaden her belief system regarding control, she will be able to communicate in an effective manner to reduce Johnny's anger and his need to control her.

The case examples presented throughout this book illustrate examples of problems that may be diagnosed and remediated from any of the five teacher variance frameworks. The case of Chris, presented at the end of this chapter, is used throughout the text to demonstrate the basic concept of teacher variance; namely, that there are at least five ways of preventing, diagnosing, and remediating any discipline problem. In addition, we have included several other cases that may be approached from each orientation and can be used for exercises at the end of each chapter.

Some people hate theory or are unable to connect theory and practice. By examining all of the programs, we have found seven sets of techniques that are common to many discipline training models. From these we have developed a process approach that offers strategies for those who find teacher variance uncomfortable or unworkable. However, we urge that you attempt to master the theory and practice most closely tied to your belief system and be open to other possibilities.

The Basis for Selecting the Five Models

We used four specific criteria for selecting each of the five models or orientations. For example, to be considered humanistic, a program must:

1. Use similar methodologies for determining the underlying concepts and for studying behavior and misbehavior
2. Share a common view for explaining behavior and misbehavior
3. Share a common theory of the origin of behavior
4. Propose solutions to misbehavior that are consistent with the theory

The success or failure of a model depends on how teachers buy into it. Individual teacher beliefs, preferences, and attitudes can make or break any schoolwide discipline plan. Success of any plan depends on whether it is philosophically consistent with participants' belief systems and levels of punitiveness. For instance, most teachers are somewhat familiar with behavioral techniques and claim that they use them regularly in their classrooms. However, we have found that many so-called adherents to this approach really do not believe in the efficacy of rewards, the heart of behavioral theory. They are reluctant to follow basic tenets of the approach, such as ignoring bad behavior and systematically reinforcing good behavior.

Despite the existence of individual, underlying beliefs about the nature of behavior and misbehavior, there is evidence that teachers rarely tap them in a consistent and coherent manner. In a recent study of teacher variance theory, findings suggested that teachers tend to respond to contexts rather than consistently applying theory to diagnose or remediate problems across settings (Brooks-Klein, 1995). For instance, psychodynamic theory suggests that oppositional behaviors may indicate poor self-esteem. Acting out (misbehaving) may reflect an attempt to compensate for feelings of inadequacy. Therefore, when a student acts out, the solution is to focus on building the student's self-confidence rather than emphasizing punishment for minor misbehavior. Ms. White might diagnose Tom's cursing in class after receipt of a low grade as a sign of disrespect, worthy of severe punishment. Yet when Tom curses at a peer on the playground for failing to catch a ball, which he said was thrown too hard, she may interpret this as frustration exacerbated by feelings of inadequacy. In both cases, however, his behavior could be interpreted consistently as manifestations of feelings of inadequacy.

An interesting finding from the study by Brooks-Klein (1995) was that teachers who took the most training programs in school discipline tended to be the most punitive. The explanation of this finding could be that:

1. Teachers who were most punitive and least effective kept shopping for courses to match their approach
2. These teachers never really learned any one approach in depth and therefore tended to revert to punishment when any particular approach failed
3. When they superficially tried an approach that was inconsistent with their own orientation, it failed, thereby reinforcing their belief that punishment works best

Table 2.3, on page 36, will allow you to obtain an overview of teacher variance and to contrast and compare the different approaches.

Conclusion and Case Studies

In conclusion, in this chapter we have stated that we believe punishment may sometimes be necessary as one technique of discipline, but discipline should never be **based** on punishment. We personally, scientifically, morally, and emotionally oppose punitive techniques as the mainstay of school disciplinary policy. It is now time to turn to the teacher variance approach, in which we deal directly with the theory and the nuts-and-bolts issues of school discipline.

Throughout this book, we offer real case studies to illustrate various points. One purpose of the book and the teacher variance approach is to demonstrate that there are at least five distinct ways to diagnose and treat misbehavior. To accomplish this, we use a single case throughout the book, and we give examples of how each theory may be applied to diagnose and remediate the problem behavior. The case of Chris is presented below. Chris is a composite of problems that are faced by elementary school teachers. After the case of Chris, we offer three other cases that we believe are representative of typical discipline problems at various grade levels. Although the case of Chris is analyzed through the book from each of the five teacher variance approaches, we offer the other cases for similar analyses by the readers.

TABLE 2.3 Comparison of the Teacher Variance Approaches

Model	Theory	Diagnosis	Goals of Interventions	Intervention Techniques	Key Terms	Notable Names
Behavioral/ Cognitive–Behavioral	Behavior, thoughts, feelings, and emotions are learned according to principles of reinforcement and punishment.	Problem identification Identify target behavior Identify antecedents & consequences Identify new behaviors Gather baseline data Identify self-dialogue Identify reinforcements	Decrease undesirable behavior Decrease dysfunctional thinking Replace targeted undesirable behaviors with acceptable behaviors	Use reinforcement Group contingencies Self-control interventions Contingency contracting Reinforcement schedules Graph baseline and treatment schedules Use punishments sparingly Use relaxation techniques	Reinforcement Punishment Modeling Shaping Ignoring Time out Overcorrection Isolation Token economy Irrational thoughts	Bandura Elias & Clabby Ellis O'Leary Pavlow Premack Shure Skinner Watson
Psychodynamic/ Interpersonal	Behavior and personality are a function of internal, inherent drives and motivations in interaction with significant others, developmental stages, & individual life experiences.	Analyze student record Obtain history of child & child-rearing practices Interview parents & previous teachers Develop anecdotal record Determine crucial stages Obtain psychoeducational assessment	Help student gain insight Strengthen ego functions Enhance self-image Help student develop socially appropriate impulse expression Help staff understand student's dynamics	Psychotherapy (play, family, individual, group, biblio-therapy) Self-analysis Peer projects Self-esteem activities Psychodrama Counseling (teacher, peer) Staff changes	Psychosexual stages (id, ego, supergo) Defense mechanisms Unconscious Oedipal complex Electra complex Psychosocial stages	Adler Albert Berne Dreikurs Erikson Freud Ginott Piaget
Humanistic	All people are born with a 'tabula rasa' with an inherent capacity for empathy, goodness, & strivings for competence & self-actualization.	Determine unmet needs Determine demands for conformity Determine factors that diminish worth Identify punitive, non-democratic practices	Provide for realization of student's strivings Organize for creativity, individuality, & curiosity Provide prosocial models Provide moral education	Open education Participatory democracy Empowerment Alternative schools Roleplaying/Rap sessions Cooperation vs. competition	Self-actualization Self-sufficiency Individual rights Alienation Cooperation Democratic	Allport Goodman Herdon Hoit Maslow Rogers Rosseau
Biophysical	Behavior is greatly influenced by brain structure and chemistry, genetic programming, and health status.	Gather information on health status and health history Observe affect, energy, & appearance Obtain eating, sleeping, medication history Engage family physician Refer for evaluation	Maintain optimum health state for each student Provide appropriate medical, nutritional, educational, physical, & psychological interventions	Medication and drug therapy Specific remediation Biofeedback, hypnosis etc. to reduce stress Change nutrition Therapy (psychological, speech, physical)	Brain damage Attention deficit disorder PKU Cerebral palsy Diabetes Asthma Autism Temperament	Bender Chess Cruickshank Delacato Fernald Frostig Kephart
Ecological/ Systems	Personality & behavior are a function of the interaction of all ecological and interpersonal forces that impact on individuals.	Identify consistency of behavior in system Identify student's norms Identify self-fulfilling prophecies Identify class ecology (physical, climate) Identify teacher behavior & style	Restructure classroom ecology Restructure school ecology Restructure school system policy Change community attitudes Influence legislature to make new laws Provide positive climate	Climate assessment Sensitivity groups Prioritizing change Develop task forces Empowerment from top Data-based decisions Model building theory Conflict resolution Class control techniques Appropriate curriculum	Learning styles (teacher & student) Class & school climate Classroom management Organize settings (temporal, spatial, interpersonal) Birth order Family systems theory	Barker Canter Curwin & Mendler Duke Glasser Gump Jones Kounin Lewin Redl

Chris

Chris, an eleven-year-old sixth-grader, is the oldest of three children in a blended family. He lives with his mother and stepfather. The youngest sibling, who is one year old, is the biological daughter of Chris's mother and stepfather. The parents work at blue-collar jobs, and their combined income places them at the middle-class level.

Around the time that his biological parents were in the process of divorce, Chris had problems in kindergarten. On completion of kindergarten, he was placed in a transitional first grade for one year. He was then promoted to a regular first grade. Reports from kindergarten and first grade indicate that he was restless, had problems with fine motor skills, and was sometimes oppositional. He was periodically clinging and dependent, but this behavior disappeared by the end of second grade. In second grade, the teacher reported that he was able to do the work, and actually did very well in some areas "when he wanted to." He periodically misbehaved, and the teacher did have trouble getting him to attend to his work at those times. Also, he sometimes seemed to daydream. Teacher reports through the current grade are consistent, except that as he has become older he has become more disruptive in class.

In the current sixth grade, Chris is reported by his teacher, Ms. Jones, to be inconsistent in following directions. She indicates that he is often out of his seat, frequently talks out of turn, and has made aggressive statements and gestures toward other students when they have told him to sit down or to stop bothering them. He has never physically attacked his peers.

In the afternoon, Chris spends relatively little time at seat work compared with his peers. His teacher, Ms. Jones, believes that he is not learning in class, although he is able to pass tests when she makes him study in class. As a result of his erratic performance, she referred him to the school psychologist for testing.

Mike

Mike, a sixteen-year-old high school student, has been in trouble since approximately age thirteen. He comes from a middle-class family and lives in a comfortable suburb. His teachers report him to be defiant in class, a shirker of responsibility, and probably a heavy user of marijuana. He often sleeps in class and rarely completes his homework. Although it is clear that he could get good grades, which he sometimes earns, he generally views school as a great place to socialize.

Until about age twelve, Mike's achievement test scores and grades were average to above average. Elementary school teacher reports indicate that he was often restless and sometimes suspended for openly defying authorities. However, after suspension, he was usually good for a few months.

At approximately age twelve, Mike began to smoke and hang out with some of the students considered to be troublemakers, and his grades began to go down. He sometimes appeared to be depressed, and at other times he seemed to be very excitable and out of control.

In high school, Mike is frequently tardy to class, sometimes cuts school, and clearly is not much interested in learning. He wears black clothes, two earrings in one ear and one in another, and has long hair. He talks about quitting school, but his parents will not sign for him. His main interest seems to be a rock band he has formed with some friends.

Mike's parents, who originally wanted him to go to college, will be happy if he finishes high school. They say they have a hard time controlling him. They do not know what to do with him, because they have tried every punishment they know. Mike's older brother, who never gave them such a hard time, is in college. His ten-year-old sister is obedient, cheerful, active in sports, and a straight A student.

Jameel

Jameel is a twelve-year-old, fifth-grade, inner city, African American boy who has academic and behavioral problems. He lives with his maternal grandmother, who has been the primary guardian since his early years. Three younger siblings reside nearby with Jameel's natural mother, whom he visits regularly. However, by choice, he remains with his grandmother and transient maternal relatives. Jameel's father, who has a history of drug-related incarcerations, lives nearby but has infrequent contact with him.

Jameel, who was underweight at birth, currently enjoys good health. His low birthweight and associated complications may have been caused by his mother's use of illegal drugs during the pregnancy. The limited hospital records she has shared with the school nurse are inconclusive regarding any developmental problems. Jameel's mother has refused to give the school any information that she believes is private.

Generally, Jameel's life at home is disorganized and disrupted. The grandmother tries to provide him with adequate supervision, but she is often tired and unable to monitor his whereabouts. The discipline is not always consistent and is dependent on which adult in the home chooses to deal with Jameel's behavior problems. Jameel seems to resent the authority of the grandmother, yet he clearly loves her. The natural mother is overwhelmed with her own stresses and does not provide much supervision or parenting to Jameel.

Jameel's neighborhood is a difficult one for children. There is not much room to play, and there is little opportunity for safe activities. Children witness shootings, fights, and drug sales in their neighborhood on a daily basis. Jameel expects violence, and although he fears being hurt, he is resigned to the possibility. The housing project in which he resides is notorious for gang-related violence.

Jameel had difficulty mastering reading readiness skills and was retained in first grade. Current teachers believe that part of Jameel's academic problem is his lack of interest in schoolwork, laziness, and a "bad attitude." He seems to resent authority, but he has developed a fairly good relationship with a female guidance counselor who has a gentle approach with the students. Otherwise, he is disrespectful and has told teachers that he does not have to listen to anybody. Jameel is frequently truant and leaves class without permission. He says that grades mean nothing to him, and he does not care if he completes high school. He denies gang membership but admits that he has many friends who are in gangs.

Attempts to work with Jameel's family have generally been futile. As a result, teachers believe that his family does not care much about him.

Juanita

Juanita, a 7½-year-old second-grader, was referred to the school psychologist because of behavioral problems including temper tantrums, crying, and academic difficulties. She is the youngest of eight children being raised primarily by their paternal grandparents, who live in the home. Their mother works as a live-in housekeeper and is home only on Sundays. Their father works long hours at two menial jobs and is rarely available to the children. Only Spanish is spoken in the home, and therefore interpreters are required for school–home communication with the grandparents.

Juanita was a full-term baby with no difficulties during birth. She reportedly achieved normal developmental milestones, according to the grandmother. Juanita attended a regular kindergarten and first grade but is reported to be immature and unable to learn basic reading skills. She had frequent temper tantrums and other displays of anger.

Juanita's current teacher, who taught sixth grade in a mostly white, blue-collar neighborhood school, was assigned to this school and to second grade against her will. She admits to having little patience for younger children and says she is overwhelmed by the language problems in this school with 30 percent Hispanic children. She believes that Juanita's immature behavior, inability to progress in reading, and constant crying are too disruptive to the class. In addition, she reports that Juanita never stays in her seat and is always walking around the room.

When Juanita is especially difficult, she is frequently sent to sit in an upper-grade class, where she remains quiet and complacent. When she cries, she is sometimes sent to the counselor's office, where she is allowed to play with the toys and hang out with the counselor and other "difficult kids." Some teachers and the counselor claim that Juanita can be cooperative and is able to learn, but others believe she has a severe emotional problem.

Despite the teachers' reports, when the psychologist observed Juanita in class on a random basis, she discovered that the girl was on task 80 percent of the time. She gets out of her seat only during transition times or during reading seat work, and she often goes to the teacher for help. Her temper tantrums and crying, especially those observed during free play periods, occur mostly when she is teased by classmates. It was noted that she appears to have a significant problem understanding English.

Key Terms

child abuse
corporal punishment
disciplinarian
humiliation
misbehavior

physical abuse
punishment
punitiveness
verbal abuse

Application Activities

1. Tabulate the results of the Teacher Variance Inventory and Survey of Attitudes toward Children in your class by sex, age, and future profession. Are there trends in your class? Are there differences between the scores and the students' attitudes and behavior?

2. How were you disciplined at home as a child? In school as a child? How do you think it has affected your attitude toward children and discipline?

3. Research the National Education Association, American Psychological Association, National Association of School Psychologists, and other professional organizations' resolutions regarding corporal punishment and discipline.

4. Obtain a copy of the United Nations Convention on the Rights of the Child. What countries have ratified them to date?

5. Get the latest copy of the Phi Delta Kappa/Gallup Poll's *Public Attitudes Towards the Public Schools* and their *Teachers' Attitudes Towards the Public Schools.* What are the national trends regarding discipline in the schools?

Suggested Readings

Elam, S. M. (Ed.). (1989). *The Gallup/Phi Delta Kappa Polls of attitudes towards the public schools: A twenty year compilation of educational history.* Bloomington, IN: Phi Delta Kappan. [The September issue of the Phi Delta Kappan publishes the Annual Gallup Poll each year.]

Elam, S. M. (1989). The second Gallup/Phi Delta Kappa poll of teachers' attitudes towards the public schools. *Phi Delta Kappan, 70*(10), 785–798.

United Nations Convention on the Rights of the Child: Unofficial summary of articles. (1991). *American Psychologist, 46*(1), 50–52.

Relevant Journals

American Psychologist
School Psychology Review

Phi Delta Kappan
Journal of School Psychology

Addresses for National Organizations

American Psychological Association, 750 First Street, NW, Washington, DC 20002-4242
National Association of School Psychologists, 4340 East West Highway, Suite 402, Bethesda, MD 20814

National Education Association, 1201 16th Street, NW, Washington, DC 20036-3290
American Federation of Teachers, AFL-CIO, 555 New Jersey Avenue, NW, Washington, DC 20001-2079

Chapter 3

Behavioral/Cognitive–Behavioral Approach (BCBA)

Chapter Objectives

After reading this chapter, you should know:

1. The underlying assumptions, theory, and goals of the behavioral approach
2. The strategy for problem diagnosis using the behavioral approach
3. Developing intervention and treatment using behavioral techniques
4. The underlying assumptions, theory, and goals of the cognitive–behavioral approach
5. The strategy for problem diagnosis using the cognitive–behavioral approach
6. About developing intervention and treatment using cognitive–behavioral techniques
7. Reward, reinforcement, and punishment techniques
8. The considerations needed to use techniques
9. Programs using the behavioral and cognitive–behavioral approaches
10. The various techniques used to teach social skills
11. Four behavioral-oriented programs
12. Three cognitive–behavioral programs
13. Research and critique of the behavioral and cognitive–behavioral approach

The behavioral/cognitive–behavioral approach within the teacher variance rubric is actually an amalgamation of two separate, but related, traditions. These are behaviorism and cognitive–behavioral theory. If you are strong in the behavioral/cognitive–behavioral orientation, you believe that

1. Behavior, feelings, thoughts, and beliefs are learned.
2. All learning occurs as a function of principles of reinforcement and punishment.

3. Reinforcement is the most powerful shaper of behavior.
4. Behavior, thoughts, and feelings can be reported, measured, predicted, and controlled.
5. Behavior can be modified through systematic reinforcement, withdrawal of reinforcement, punishment, or rational persuasion.
6. New behaviors, thoughts, feelings, and beliefs can be learned to replace those that are irrational, self-destructive, and self-defeating. This may be done by use of reinforcement, self-talk, rehearsal, and practice.

You can, by following basic principles of behaviorism or cognitive–behavioral theory, eliminate misbehaviors and cause appropriate behaviors to appear (Alberto & Troutman, 1990; Axelrod, 1983a; Bandura, 1977; O'Leary, 1977; Skinner, 1968, 1982).

Many underlying assumptions, especially with regard to the belief that all behavior is learned and can be unlearned, are shared by "pure" behaviorists and cognitive–behaviorists. However, behaviorists attempt to analyze and change only *observable behaviors* by using methods of reinforcement and extinction. The term *behaviorism* evolved to behavioral analysis and more recently *functional analysis*. This latter term highlights the roles of reinforcement or escape-motivated behaviors and places increased emphasis on understanding all events or contingencies related to the behavior. Behaviorists focus on the use of extrinsic motivators and generally do not deal with thoughts, feelings, and emotions. These terms are only useful with behaviors that can be observed, measured, and changed.

If you lean more toward the cognitive–behavioral approach, you may base your practice on the belief that children can learn to: (1) identify irrational destructive thoughts, feelings, and beliefs; (2) learn to develop *internal dialogues* to defeat those thoughts; and (3) begin to act on new thoughts they have learned through both verbal and actual rehearsal of new behaviors (Elias & Clabby, 1984, 1988; Ellis, 1979; Goldstein, Sprafkin, Gershaw, & Klein, 1980; Kendall & Braswell, 1982; Spivack, Platt, & Shure, 1976).

We assume that you, as a preservice or in-service teacher, have taken a basic course in psychology. In that course, you covered the principles of behaviorism and read about the research of prominent behaviorists such as Pavlov and Skinner (Hilgard & Bauer, 1981; Morse & Smith, 1980). It is not our purpose here to offer a complete discussion of the underlying theories and research. Nor can reading this chapter teach you to expertly apply behavioral and cognitive–behavioral techniques. We assume that if you have a behavioral preference, based on the TVI, a brief overview will refresh your memory and update your knowledge in terms of the basics. References at the end of the chapter will help you to find other resources so that you can study the field extensively enough to become an expert. We strongly recommend that you attend some hands-on advanced workshops and visit programs that are devoted exclusively to behavioral approaches. The following is a brief review of basic concepts, especially as they apply to education.

Underlying Theory

Behaviorism

Behavior is lawful and can be understood by breaking it down to strings of simple, linked events that are then understood through a functional analysis of the events that contribute to it. The research of B. F. Skinner (1968), which has had the most direct influence on education, demonstrates that the future rate of any behavior, including misbehavior, increases if it is followed by reinforcement.

Many "neo-Skinnerians" have translated his theories for use in the classroom (Axelrod, 1983b, 1983; Homme, 1970; Madsen & Madsen, 1991; Walker & Shea, 1976). These writers share a common belief that a student's misbehavior can be altered and reshaped into a more socially acceptable behavior by directly manipulating the student's environment through the systematic use of *rewards*.

Behaviorists are not concerned with the early origins of a people's problems, unless it helps them to understand the mechanisms by which behaviors were shaped through reinforcement. Similarly, behaviorists assign little importance to feelings or emotions, which can not be observed. Nor do behaviorists expect misbehaving pupils to insightfully discover the reasons they break the rules. Specifically, behaviorists believe that teachers must ascertain what is happening in the classroom environment that reinforces the student's misbehavior.

For instance, Billy may be rewarded by peer laughter or praise as a result of his making fun of the teacher. Or his ridicule of the teacher could be escape-motivated behavior. When the teacher, as punishment, orders Billy to leave the classroom, Billy is rewarded if he dislikes the teacher and the subject being taught. In either case, until the teacher analyzes the results of his or her behavior, the student is controlling the contingencies, all of the events surrounding the misbehavior.

Operant reinforcement theory states that you can change or strengthen any behavior by reinforcement. In other words, you can increase the probability of desired behaviors by certain operations. These include giving students things that are rewarding to them, such as stickers, social praise by important adults, or free time.

Most behaviorally based strategies for improving children's academic and social functioning in the classroom focus on the manipulation of consequences or contingencies through the use of reinforcement. That is, students are rewarded *after* they exhibit appropriate behavior. Reinforcement procedures have been applied effectively to achieve diverse goals, such as developing social skills (Odom, Hoyson, Jameison, & Strain, 1985), eliminating autistic behaviors (Foxx, 1982), eliminating anxiety, increasing assertiveness, toilet training, increasing self-control (Bellack & Hersen, 1985), and eliminating a wide variety of classroom disruptions (Fowler, 1982).

Despite the general success of reinforcement procedures, behaviorists are always investigating methods to improve the use of applied behavior analysis (Carr, Newsom, & Binkoff, 1980). These efforts led to the development of functional analysis, which assumes that all behaviors, especially misbehaviors that are repetitive, are perpetuated by established patterns involving either reward or escape. Functional analysis includes the assessment of *antecedents* and *consequences* or *subsequent events* to determine their functional relationships. In other words, what environmental stimuli or events result in which specific behaviors or misbehaviors?

For instance, if Stan fights frequently in class, it is assumed that aggression serves a specific function for Stan. He may find that it serves as a mechanism for avoiding or escaping from something (e.g., getting sent out of the classroom). Or it may help him to get attention from peers, teacher, or parents.

An appropriate analysis provides sufficient information to describe, in objective, behavioral terms, the events surrounding the misbehavior. The first step is to identify the specific *target behavior* we want to eliminate. In the case of Stan, fighting is the target behavior. The next step is to develop a description of events antecedent to the target behavior. This requires collecting observations of the immediate classroom setting and perhaps data about other settings that include environmental stimuli that result in Stan's aggressive behavior.

It is important to collect all necessary data about the setting, such as class size, seating, class activities when fighting occurs, time of day, whom he fights with most, the verbal and physical behaviors of the students before the fighting, and the nature of his aggressions. You should also gather related data about fighting and aggression in the home, on the playground, and in other settings, and parental response to the target behavior.

The *discriminative stimulus* is the specific stimulus, person, or event that triggers the misbehavior. It is called discriminative because the person must be able to discriminate between it and other similar stimuli that do not lead to reinforcement. For instance, Stan may discriminate clearly between boys who are stronger than he and those who are not. Therefore, he will only become aggressive with those who are clearly weaker. This is because he learned from previous experiences that the punishment of being beaten outweighed any positive consequences he might derive from the attention he received for his aggressive behavior.

Special attention is paid to those events or interactions that appear to either reinforce or punish the misbehavior. The specific targeted behavior, in this case Stan's aggression, is then carefully described in behavioral terms. In Stan's case, cursing by the classmate whom he attacks may appear to be the antecedent event. However, closer evaluation of the data shows that cursing, in general, does not trigger the aggression. Stan finds certain words particularly demeaning. For instance, he may have a learning problem, and any statement that implies that he is dumb, lazy, a "jerk," or a "retard" could infuriate him, especially if it is spoken when he is trying to do his work and if it is spoken by one of the better students in the class.

The last step in a functional analysis is to describe the *consequent* or *subsequent events*. These are the events that occur after the misbehavior. In the case of Stan, who was left back and is therefore bigger and stronger than most of his classmates, the consequence that serves as reinforcement to Stan may be the attention in the form of crying that his behavior elicits from the offender. Or the fighting might be escape motivated, because whatever punishment is meted out prevents him from having to struggle with his schoolwork for a while after fighting. Finally, it could be praise he receives from his parents, who resent other kids making fun of him. They may congratulate him when he comes home and tells them that he "punched out one of those snotty, stuck-up kids" who make fun of him.

At the simplest level of treatment, if functional analysis enables the teacher to anticipate a misbehavior and to avoid or redirect the potential offender's attention, the misbehavior may be averted. In the case of Stan, possible solutions could include seating him away from students who make fun of him, rewarding students who do not provoke him, giving him constant praise for work that is geared to his level, setting up rewards for his not fighting, or convincing his parents to stop praising him for any type of aggression. Ample research evidence suggests that relatively simple techniques, based on behavioral principles, can solve difficult classroom problems (Hamlet, Axelrod, and Kuerschner, 1984).

Cognitive–Behavioral Theory

While holding to the basic concept that behavior is learned, cognitive–behavioral practitioners conceptualize misbehavior as the result of inadequate, inappropriate thinking or lack of learned thoughts and feelings that lead to socially acceptable behavior (Ellis, 1979; Meichenbaum, 1977). At the core of the cognitive–behavioral approach is the cause-and-effect relationship between thoughts, emotions, and behaviors. These are learned, and therefore people contribute to their problems by the way they interpret events in their lives. We can help students to "unlearn" irrational, self-destructive thoughts, feelings, and emotions by teaching them to attack them through rational thinking.

If Sally flunks many tests in the fourth and fifth grades, she may begin to believe that she is stupid, in spite of the facts that her IQ is high and her parents were having grave financial problems that stressed her family during that period. She also had a punitive, denigrating teacher who was very sarcastic about Sally's poor grades.

As a result of a combination of bad experiences affecting her grades, Sally may learn to think, "I am a dumb girl. All teachers must know I am a dumb girl and that I will not be able to pass many tests. No matter what I do, teachers will think I am stupid. Why bother to study, since I will fail anyway? Anyway, if I don't study, I can always blame that on my poor grades. I did well in some tests, but it was because they were easy and I was lucky."

The goal of cognitive–behavioral approaches is to help students to reorganize or restructure their thinking and feeling in a manner that is consistent with reality and that is adaptive to the school setting. New feelings and actual social skills can be learned through effective instruction by therapists or teachers. As a result, appropriate behaviors will replace misbehaviors.

Remember that behavior analysis focuses only on *overt* and observable behavior. But cognitive–behavioral practitioners believe that feelings and thoughts can be measured objectively through quantification on scales. For instance, a scale of 1 to 10 is a familiar concept to most educators. Students can rate any feelings or beliefs easily on such a scale. We often ask students to rate their level of happiness or anger, with 1 being very unhappy or very angry and 10 being very happy or having no anger. Measures on these scales can be used as before-and-after treatment indicators of success of interventions.

Cognitive–behavioral theory focuses on helping children to unlearn faulty, irrational patterns of thinking and feeling. Cognition, feelings, and behaviors are all learned and interactive. We feel what we think and behave as we feel. Because we have learned certain dialogues about ourselves and how we should act, we can learn new ways of thinking if we become convinced that the old ways are harmful. Rather than focusing on changing overt behaviors through reinforcement, cognitive–behaviorists attempt to identify the self-destructive, irrational thoughts, beliefs, or feelings of the person. For instance, a very common belief among students who misbehave is, "The teacher hates me and picks on me no matter what I do. So I might as well be bad and at least give her as much grief as possible. That will really fix the teacher."

The most irrational aspect of the above statement is that "it will really fix the teacher." In reality, the student will end up with the most grief. Therefore, the cognitively oriented therapist/teacher/counselor working with the student would attack the belief system by helping the student to understand that he or she is the one receiving the most grief. Because dealing with misbehavior calls for "teaching" new thinking patterns, cognitive–behavioral techniques are a natural for educators.

Assumptions of BCBA

Behavior and Misbehavior Are Learned through Reinforcement

If you scored high in BCBA on the TVI, you believe that even the worst-behaved student in your class learned his or her obnoxious behavior, thoughts, and feelings and was not born as a "bad seed." This is not a generally accepted notion. Many ignore the role of reward in learning acceptable behavior and tend to believe that children should be good just because they should be good. They often resent the idea that you should reward someone for good behavior and consider it bribery when it occurs.

By definition, bribery is a reward for doing something illegal. Yet we all receive rewards in every sphere of life. The best analogy is that adults are "bribed" in the form of salaries to get them to work. Yet, few complain if workers are "bribed" through merit pay or bonuses for good work. We all perform for some type of reinforcement. You also believe that through reason, rational persuasion, and practice of new behaviors, thoughts, and feelings, students can unlearn irrational beliefs about themselves and others and learn new ways of acting. You know that your "worst" students have learned to think and feel in ways that are self-destructive, but they can learn appropriate ways of thinking and behaving.

In applying the principles of reinforcement to the classroom, you understand that when Johnny curses in class and you yell at him, your attention reinforces his behavior if it fails to stop the cursing. If your yelling was effective punishment, it would cause the cursing to cease. You also understand that reinforcers may vary as a function of the student, the situation, and the person administering them.

Your beliefs are supported by research on behavioral interventions that have demonstrated a clear preference for positive, rather than negative, corrective techniques by both teachers and children (Reimers, Wacker, & Koeppl, 1987). You believe that denigrating verbal reprimands, lecturing, and nagging are ineffective in eliminating misbehavior (Hyman, 1990a). You know that correction is necessary at times, but you also know that praise plus soft reprimands are more effective at decreasing disruptive misbehavior than praise plus loud reprimands (O'Leary, Kaufman, Kass, & Drabman, 1970; Van Houten, Mackenzie- Keating, Sameoto, and Coleavecchia, 1982).

Behavior and Misbehavior Can Be Observed, Measured, Predicted, and Controlled

If Jane refuses to do her homework, the behaviorist will attempt to find rewards that will induce compliance. Six-year-old Jane may do her homework to earn stickers, toys, or extra time to play. These would be laughable to fifteen-year-old Joe. However, if he can earn points that can be cashed in for enough money to buy a new skateboard, which he has wanted for more than a year, he will zip through the assignments as if he had invented homework.

In the case of Jane, the cognitive behaviorist would explore her irrational beliefs about the reasons for not doing her homework and the consequences. With this approach, we might discover that she thinks she is stupid and that doing homework will only expose her stupidity on a daily basis. We could have her rate her feeling of stupidity on a scale. For instance, we might have her rank all of the students in class for brightness and see where she puts herself. Or we could construct a scale from one to ten, with one being very stupid and ten very smart, and have her assign her place on the scale.

After obtaining a rating of how stupid Jane believes she is, we could then offer arguments to show she is not stupid and then give examples of homework she can do. After working with her, we would then have her re-rank herself on the scale to see if her thinking has changed. If it changes, and she reports not feeling stupid anymore, we assume that she has rejected old ways of thinking about herself and learned new feelings.

Consider the case of inappropriate out-of-seat behavior. A typical behavioral response is to assume that Jimmy has been rewarded for getting out of his seat by such reinforcers as teacher attention or peer approval. If this is true, eliminating the attention and approval should result in elimination of the behavior.

A cognitive–behavioral analysis of Jimmy would not exclude the behavioral explanation, but it also would include an analysis of Jimmy's thinking and feeling about getting out of his seat. For instance, Jimmy might say that he really feels in control when he gets out of his seat and the teacher yells at him. He might say, "Yeah, I know I shouldn't get out of my seat, but the teacher yells at me anyway. She is always picking on me. I like getting her upset because I hate her."

The goal would be to try to help Jimmy understand that his thinking is irrational and self-defeating. Why does he dislike the teacher? Could it be that his own behavior is causing her to be angry at him? Is he really getting back at her, or is he ultimately the one who will suffer? How else could he handle his anger at her? These questions should prompt new thinking about the situation and consideration of alternative behaviors. In other words, he needs to "unlearn" his faulty beliefs and to learn new beliefs that are adaptive. The important points in understanding both behavioral and cognitive–behavioral strategies are observability, measurability, and predictability of behavior.

Reinforcement Is the Most Powerful Shaper of Behavior, and Punishment Is the Least Effective Deterrent

Overwhelming research indicates that reward is the most powerful shaper of behavior and that competent use of *contingency management* can change most behaviors (Axelrod, 1983a; Bongiovanni, 1979; Wolery, Baily & Sugai, 1988). This involves arranging reward to fit each contingency, and sometimes using punishment (Axelrod, 1983b). It is important to understand the technical definitions of reward and punishment. These form the basis for the behavioral management of various contingencies.

Table 3.1, on page 48, presents a matrix that summarizes various approaches to understanding the basic principles of contingency management. In the matrix, three types of negative approaches are contrasted with positive reinforcement. When considering techniques to complement reinforcement, it is important to consider all three possibilities rather than positive punishment alone.

TABLE 3.1   **Contingency Management Techniques**

	Response Outcome	
	Increase Good Behaviors by Using	**Decrease Bad Behaviors by Using**
Give	Positive reinforcement, such as praise, tokens, merit points, etc.	Positive punishment, such as verbal reprimands, unpleasant consequences
Remove	Negative reinforcement, such as stopping or removing unpleasant consequences	Negative punishment, such as time out from a rewarding or pleasant class situation

In the matrix, *positive reinforcement* is synonymous with reward. Reward is an event or stimulus that increases the likelihood of behavior occurring. For instance, if you praise a child every time he or she correctly spells a word and the child increases spelling accuracy, you may assume that your praise was reinforcing. In other words, the child was motivated to increase spelling ability to receive your praise.

The type of reinforcement and the rate at which it is delivered determine the procedure's success. Most teachers do not actually predetermine and monitor their rate of reinforcement. However, when working with severely disturbed or developmentally delayed students, it is important to identify the most successful reinforcement schedules.

If a procedure or reinforcement does not work, it must be assumed that whatever was given to the student was not truly reinforcing or was not being administered at the most appropriate rate. Immediacy of reinforcement is an important consideration.

Positive punishment is an event or stimulus that decreases the behavior preceding it. For instance, if admonishing a child once or twice for yelling across the room stops that behavior, you may assume that the admonishment was a punishment. However, if your admonishment did not decrease the yelling, it was not a punishment.

Suspension is a popular punishment technique used for misbehavior that is frequently not a punishment. If a child receives frequent in-school or out-of-school suspensions for particular misbehaviors, and those misbehaviors do not decrease, it is obvious that suspension is not a punishment. In fact, we have found that some students enjoy suspension because it gets them out of classes that they find to be more punishing than the conditions of suspension. The most patently absurd use of suspension is as a punishment for truancy or class cutting!

Controversy surrounds the use of punishment procedures, their effectiveness, and the ability to generalize to various settings. Overall, they may be effective when alternative techniques are not helping. They can produce very quick, short-term results. However, we absolutely oppose the infliction of physical pain, euphemistically called corporal punishment, in any school. Some make a case for the use of carefully controlled *aversive procedures,* which include the use of mild electric shock, slapping, water sprayed in the face, or other noxious stimuli, to reduce extremely self-injurious and aggressive behaviors. These procedures should only be used under supervision, in certain very restricted settings, and only after all reinforcement procedures have failed. Even then, we question the long-term usefulness of aversive techniques. Careful functional analysis will usually negate the need for aversive techniques.

Overcorrection is a type of punishment that includes two stages: a restitution phase, in which the child must correct any negative effects of his or her behavior, and a positive practice phase, during which the offender practices more appropriate behaviors, usually in an exaggerated fashion. For instance, if Johnny calls Jane a bad name, he will be required to apologize and then to practice frequently addressing her in an appropriate manner.

Time-out, which is widely misunderstood and too often abused, is a negative punishment; it removes the student from a positive experience and results in a decrease in the undesirable behavior. There are three types of time-out:

Exclusionary time-out occurs when the child is removed to the back of the room and must sit facing away from the class. Exclusionary time-out has been demonstrated to alter the behavior of target as well as nontarget children (Wilson, Robertson, Herlong & Haynes, 1979).

Nonexclusionary time-out is accomplished by sitting the child away from the class but allowing him or her to watch the class without participating. *Seclusionary* time-out occurs when the student is temporarily removed from the classroom.

Response cost refers to the removal of a positive reinforcer each time a misbehavior occurs. An effective method of using response cost is to take back tokens, stars, or stickers that have been given as rewards. For instance, in a *token economy,* children are given tokens as rewards for good behavior. Tokens are like salaries for piecework, except that in this example workers earn actual money based purely on productivity. The harder the students work to obey the rules and achieve academically, the more tokens they receive. At a designated time, students exchange tokens for various rewards, just as a piece worker can buy more with the additional money earned for being more productive.

Response cost has been found to be a time-efficient and effective classroom intervention procedure (Witt & Elliot, 1982). This technique is one of the most successful with students with severe conduct problems.

When parents cooperate in a behavioral plan, we sometimes use a variation of response cost that involves actual money. A student may start the week with a fixed amount of tokens at school and money at home. Tokens and money are taken away for specific misbehaviors. We frequently include bonus tokens and money that can be earned for outstanding acts, such as when the child offers to help or do something nice for a peer, sibling, or parent. At the end of the week, tokens or checks on a paper are exchanged at home for money or are added to the pool of money saved to purchase something.

The reward system must be in writing and fully understood by adults and children. Students at home and school can earn or lose a predetermined number of tokens for each behavior. The system fails if the child can manipulate it or the adult is arbitrary or inconsistent in following the rules.

Negative reinforcement, or removal of something the student finds aversive is rarely used. A good example is when students are placed in in-school suspension with the opportunity to rejoin the class when they agree to change their behavior. For instance, Johnny is sent to in-school suspension for two days. However, he may return to class after he recognizes his misbehavior and agrees not to do it again. It is negative reinforcement if Johnny feels the suspension is aversive compared to his regular classroom.

If asked to choose which techniques to use, research would support positive reinforcement as the most efficacious. The other three techniques involve some type of negative approach. Although some students seem to respond only to these approaches, there is always the danger that they will be overused. We suggest that a reinforcer be used to develop an appropriate behavior at the same time that a punishment is used to eliminate a misbehavior.

Irrational Thoughts and Feelings Can Be Unlearned

Cognitive–behaviorists believe that misbehavior may result from a student's irrational feelings and thoughts about the rules and regulations at school. Some students may expect teachers to recognize them whenever they raise their hands. Other students may think that the teacher should always punish guilty parties and never make a mistake. Some students may believe that a teacher always picks on boys or girls, even when the evidence suggests otherwise. Another common belief is that teachers must always grade fairly.

Personal beliefs that may result in misbehavior are often based on expectations established in the home. For instance, some children believe that they must always earn an A or that they should never get in trouble. There are also students who believe, contrary to reality, that they are bad, stupid, or lazy and therefore behave consistently according to that belief. Both views are irrational and result in tremendous pressure, anxiety, and self-destructive behavior.

Behavioral/Cognitive–Behavioral Diagnosis

Before adopting a treatment or remediation strategy, diagnosis must take place. In the behavioral/cognitive–behavioral approach, it is crucial to target the behavior that must be extinguished or the basic irrational thoughts, beliefs, or feelings that need to be deconstructed. Behaviorists measure observable misbehaviors or target behaviors in terms of frequency, intensity, and duration. They also record the contingencies surrounding the target behavior. In the cognitive approach, objectivity is important, but data are provided by the subjects through their descriptions of their thoughts, reasoning, and feelings that explain and perpetuate the misbehavior. These data also can be used to compare with observable behavioral changes.

In our workshops, to fully understand the power of teacher variance, participants view videotaped scenarios of common classroom misbehaviors. Each scenario is diagnosed and remediated within the five orientations. For purposes of this book, we use the written scenario of Chris (see page 37) , which will be analyzed from each of the five teacher variance perspectives.

Because behavioral and cognitive–behavioral techniques differ somewhat, we will demonstrate how a behaviorist would approach the problem, then we will examine how a cognitive–behaviorist would diagnose and treat the problem. Finally, we will examine a classroom situation in which a combined approach might be used.

Behavioral Diagnosis

Problem Identification

After examining the cumulative folder, the school psychologist decides to determine if the teacher is willing to try a behavioral approach with Chris. The major purpose of the initial interview by the school psychologist, in terms of behavioral diagnosis, is to identify the specific problem. The following is a brief summary of the interview:

Psych: Well, Ms. Jones, I understand you are having a problem with Chris.

Teacher: Yes, he is really hyper and aggressive. He is very difficult to manage. He can't seem to sit still, and he constantly argues with me when I make simple requests. I have tried everything to get him to behave. Maybe he belongs in a special class.

Psych: Can you describe exactly what he does that bothers you?

Teacher: He can't sit still and doesn't seem to want to conform. He just won't obey the rules.

Psych: Yes, but what specific behaviors bother you most?

Teacher: He is so hyper.

Psych: Yes, give me examples of how he is hyper.

Teacher: He always gets out of his seat.

Psych: Does he do it all day, at about the same rate?

Teacher: No, I guess most of it is in the afternoon.

Psych: What does he do when he gets out of his seat?

Teacher: Well, he usually just wanders around.

Psych: What other things bother you?

Teacher: When he wanders around class, he isn't doing his schoolwork, and he bothers other children. Maybe he has an attention disorder and needs Ritalin.

Psych: So the main thing that bothers you is that he doesn't stay in his seat. The other things happen when he is not in his seat.

Teacher: I guess so, but maybe he really doesn't belong in this class.

Later, in the initial consultation, Ms. Jones revealed that she is constantly correcting Chris when he gets out of his seat. He sometimes sits down, but then he repeats the behavior until she gets upset and sends him to the principal. The corrections are usually lectures about why he should be good, how he is being bad, and threats of the dire consequence of being sent to the principal. However, the corrections do not seem to be effective because he repeats his oppositional and defiant behaviors.

During the interview, the psychologist attempted to do the first thing needed to diagnose the problem from a behavioral perspective. Ms. Jones needed to spell out the specific behavior or behaviors that she wanted to eliminate.

The Target Behavior
In identifying the target behavior, it is necessary to first decide what behavior is undesirable. When asked what bothered her most, Ms. Jones indicated three things: (1) getting out of the seat without permission, (2) refusal to accept her directions when she told him to sit down, and (3) talking out of turn.

It is important to describe the behavior as observable responses. Ms. Jones indicated that getting out of the seat did not include standing up or moving around the desk, which did not bother her much. What really bothered her was when he got out of the seat and bothered other children or did things that were against class rules. It would be okay for him to get out of the seat to sharpen a pencil or get books out of the class library at appropriate times. Therefore, she was able to spell out the specific out-of-seat behavior that she wanted to eliminate.

When Ms. Jones reprimanded Chris, he would often mumble to himself, make faces at her, mimic her, or ignore her. Except for "making a face," these are all specific and observable. When asked to spell out more about "face making," she indicated that he would scowl. This was still rather vague, and she agreed that his facial expressions are different at different times, and that the other reactions to her reprimands were more important to be eliminated.

It is necessary to determine if the misbehavior is excessive. According to the teacher, Chris was out of his seat at least two or three times every day, whereas most other children never got out of their seats without permission. Therefore, his behavior was determined to be excessive and unacceptable. The next step is to count how often it happens during sample periods and to determine what events (antecedents) seem to precede each out-of-seat event that is tallied. This involves collecting *baseline data.*

Antecedents and Consequences or Subsequent Events

Antecedent factors that need to be examined include when and where the behavior occurs. What is the class doing at the time? In this case, most of the out-of-seat behavior occurred in the afternoon. In the morning, the classes were more structured with reading and math groups and lots of worksheets for desk work. Further discussion indicated that in the afternoon there was less structure, the curriculum varied, and there was more transitional time during breaks between activities. So it appeared that an antecedent to much of the out-of-seat activity was lack of formal structure and instruction. Interpersonal factors of importance include issues such as, who is associated with the behavior, how are they associated with it, is there any history between those others and the target student, and what disabilities might contribute to the problem? What typically occurs after the target behavior? Typically, according to the teacher, she yelled, threatened, or sent Chris to the office in response to his defiance.

Desired Behavior

It is important to define what behaviors you want to substitute for the undesirable behavior. Ms. Jones at first stated that she wanted Chris to be in his seat all afternoon unless he was told he could get up. She also wanted him engaged in work, especially in the afternoon when he was supposed to be in his seat. However, on further questioning, it became clear that other children were allowed to get up without permission to sharpen pencils, to throw things away, or to obtain materials such as books, paper, etc.

Finally, what Ms. Jones defined as desirable behavior was that Chris should only get up to do what is allowed and that when she asks him to sit down, he should promptly comply. She believed that if she could accomplish that she could then go on to encourage him to do more work at his desk in the afternoon.

Talking out of turn was defined as talking without raising his hand and also doing that in conjunction with verbally abusing her. She was asked if she objected to students excitedly calling out her name during a lesson when they thought they knew the answer. Although this bothered her somewhat, she did not mind that type of enthusiasm. What angered her was Chris's sarcastic, inappropriate, and sometimes mean comments about what someone in the class said or did and his cursing.

Gathering Baseline Data

Assume you are Ms. Jones, Chris has been a constant irritation, and you would just as soon see him removed from your class. But the school psychologist does not seem to think the child is a special education candidate and suggests that you work together to diagnose the problem and develop a treatment or corrective plan. Even if you subscribe to the behavioral approach and agree that you can change behavior through the principles of reinforcement, you are very busy.

So what does the psychologist suggest? You should add to your burden by gathering baseline data. You think, " This is just what I need. More work! I don't have to count how often Chris gets out of his seat every day. It is too much, and that's all I have to know. How can I take the time out to check off each time he gets out of his seat?"

But, if you are a real behaviorist, you say to yourself, "I know that this is going to be more work in the short term. But by counting when he gets out of his seat each day, over a week or two, I will see a pattern that will help me to diagnose the problem. It will also help me to know if my treatment program is working, and how well it's working."

Collecting baseline behavior data is simply a method of counting how often the student performs the target behavior. In the case of Chris, you would count how many times he gets out of his seat during a period each day. Because you notice that it is most often in the afternoon, you can tally all afternoon or do it during specific periods.

You will be developing an observational record by counting frequencies of behavior. This is easy to suggest but not so easy to do if you are very busy teaching. Once you determine when you are going to do it, you need to figure out who will do it. Here are some suggestions with the obvious advantages and disadvantages of each:

The teacher can collect the data. You can use a prepared paper that is kept on your desk, a clipboard you carry with you, a counter of the type you click each time, or a piece of masking tape on your wrist. The advantage of doing it yourself is that you do not have to train anyone, you know exactly what you are looking for, and you can make adjustments in timing if you want. The disadvantage is that you have to take the time to be alert during the tallying period.

An aide is ideal, if you have one in class. The students are familiar with the aide's presence in class, he or she can easily be trained and monitored, and you can just continue to teach without thinking about anything else.

College students are accessible in most areas where there are schools. This is a largely untapped resource for gathering observational data. Many schools host practicum students and student teachers from college and university teacher training programs. But another resource that is rarely used are students from a local community college who are taking courses in human development, child psychology, or a similar course. Very often college instructors are happy to allow them to fulfill course requirements by conducting observations of children in class. Of course, you could allow them to conduct other types of observations and studies, as long as they collect data for you. Also, high school students, especially those in future teachers clubs, can help.

The major advantage of using college or even high school students is that they do not cost money and they are usually eager to cooperate. However, they may not be available every day. Also, if they are not doing this as part of their own schoolwork, where completion of the project is mandated to obtain a grade, they may not complete the task. The problem with high school students is one of confidentiality. You must be sure they are not connected in any way to the observee and that they will not talk about their observations to anyone else.

Other possible observers are parents, volunteer grandparents, volunteers from community groups, and peers. Although any of these may be reliable and helpful, the issues of confidentiality must be addressed.

Rates of Recording

Frequency recordings require that the observer keep a tally of the number of times a particular behavior occurs over a certain period (per hour, per morning, and so forth). This procedure is most appropriate for short-duration behaviors such as hitting, talking out, or even academic behaviors such as reading errors.

Duration recordings yield information regarding the length of time that a child engages in a certain behavior. This method is best used for extended behaviors such as being out of seat, daydreaming, and so forth. In the case of Chris, you might want to obtain both frequency and duration data.

Interval recordings give some indication of both the frequency and the duration of the behavior. This method is especially suited for extended behaviors. A data sheet divided into certain intervals is prepared. During each consecutive interval, the observer (or teacher) records whether the target behavior occurs.

Time sampling recording is more convenient than duration and interval recordings, yet still provides an accurate record of performance. The observer notes only what a child is doing at the end of the interval. Behaviors before or during the interval are not recorded.

The *measurement of lasting products* is the closest to a teacher's everyday experience. You simply measure the tangible output of a student's work. Resulting products may be measured immediately on completion or at a later point. This is used mainly for recording academic performance. Behavior analysts have in recent years developed extensive literature on curriculum-based measurements that allow for short-term probes of daily or weekly achievement (Rosenfield, 1987). This technique allows you to assess whether improved behavior results in improved learning.

The choice of recording technique depends on the nature of the behavior being studied, as well as whether the observations are to be done by the classroom teacher or by an outside observer. If you are not sure which to use, just try the one that makes the most sense to you. It will soon be clear if your method is working and if the data are helpful.

It is best if the behavior is measured throughout modification procedures. Frequent feedback on the effectiveness of treatment techniques is helpful, and larger numbers of recordings enhance accuracy. Also, the use of several different observers is preferred, but not necessary.

Determine the Goals of Intervention

This is the last stage of the diagnosis procedure. In the case of Chris, a possible set of initial goals would be to eliminate at least 50 percent of his out-of-seat behavior during the first two weeks of treatment and 80 percent by the end of the second two weeks. In addition, you might decide that he should be engaged in learning at his seat by the end of the first two weeks at least 40 percent of the time and 60 percent of the time at the end of four weeks of treatment. It is important to make the goals reasonable and obtainable, so that the student feels successful in obtaining reinforcement or rewards. Remember that the two major goals of the behavioral approach are: (1) to reduce the occurrence of negative behaviors in a setting and (2) to increase the frequency of positive behaviors in a setting.

Behavioral interventions are designed to impact directly on the target behavior, by either decreasing or increasing it. Some interventions are directed toward the child's environment. School psychologists can generally consult with you in deciding which strategies are most appropriate. Perhaps the most fundamental concept is to start with the easiest, most obvious strategy and gradually increase it until results are obtained.

Behavioral Treatment/Intervention Techniques

The core of treatment in this approach is reinforcement in the classroom. In general, reinforcement is delivered by the teacher. However, far too many educators fail to enlist the help of parents in providing reinforcers (Budd, Leibowitz, Riner, Mindell, & Goldfarb, 1981). Other effective methods include self-monitoring/self-reinforcement (Christie, Hiss, & Lozanoff, 1984) and peer reinforcement (Greenwood, Carta, & Hall, 1988). Approaches such as these three have been found to be very effective in maintaining productive school behavior.

Whatever your plan, it must be convenient for you, and you must feel comfortable and confident that it will work. That is the whole reason for teacher variance. When teachers offer a host of reasons why the various behavioral techniques did not work or could not possibly work, it is time to give up on this solution and explore techniques with which the teachers are more comfortable.

The first step in changing Chris's behavior is to determine the most effective reinforcers. Once you have examined antecedents and consequences, you can hypothesize about what reinforces the undesirable behavior. Therefore, the first step, after baseline is achieved, assuming teacher attention is the reinforcer, is for Ms. Jones to try planned *ignoring* for a week or two (Alberto & Troutman, 1990; Axelrod, 1983b; Hall, Lund & Jackson, 1968; Kazdin, 1984; O'Leary, 1977; Pfifner & O'Leary, 1987). In other words, she will ignore Chris's out-of-seat behavior, except if he is attacking or actively bothering a classmate.

During the period of ignoring, Ms. Jones must continue to collect data on the number of times Chris gets out of his seat. If planned ignoring works, Chris will gradually stay in his seat for longer periods. Eventually, his out-of-seat behavior should be eliminated. However, if planned ignoring does not work, Ms. Jones must determine appropriate reinforcer or reinforcers.

In the case of Chris, as in most cases, the student is the best person to determine reinforcers. So here is how his teacher might go about deciding how to reward him:

Teacher: Chris, you know I have been watching you for the last few weeks. Do you know about how many times you get out of your seat every afternoon?

Chris: Why were you watching me? You don't watch the other kids like that.

Teacher: Well, you know that you are the only one who is out of his seat so many times.

Chris: But I can't help it. I just can't sit still sometimes.

Teacher: I understand that, and I don't mind your getting up to stretch or sharpen your pencil. But many of the times you are doing things that bother others. Then I end up yelling at you. Do you know that every afternoon you are out of your seat about five times each hour? Wouldn't you like to help yourself stay in your seat? That would stop me from yelling at you all the time.

Chris: You don't yell at any of the other kids. You are always picking on me.

Teacher: Well, maybe I am picking on you. I am sorry about that, but I am tired of yelling at you, and you must be tired of hearing me. So let's see if we can make a bargain to stop all this stuff. How would you like to earn some rewards for not getting out of your seat?

Chris: What kinds of rewards?

Teacher: What would you like to earn, that I can give you? Or maybe there is something that your parents can get you.

Chris: You mean like a new Nintendo game?

Teacher: Yes, you could earn points for not getting out of your seat. Then you could cash in those points with your parents. I know that they would be willing to let you earn things. They told me they would be happy to do something like this because they don't like what has been happening. Also, we can arrange for you to earn privileges in school.

Chris: Like what?

Teacher: I know you like artwork and gym. I can arrange for you to take an extra gym class at the end of each week, if you earn it. I can also give you extra art time each day.

Chris: You mean I can get all that for just staying in my seat? But I don't know if I can do it all afternoon.

Teacher: Don't worry. I don't expect you to do it all right away. Here is how we will do it: Each day you start out with five points. If you stay in your seat, except when you ask permission, all afternoon, you get all five points. You lose a point each time you get out of your seat. So even if you are not perfect, you can get points. We will set up a chart to show how many points you earn each week. We will also make a chart showing how many points each thing is worth. If you want to change your rewards and add new ones, we can do that. How does that sound?

In this example, the teacher used response cost. Rather then giving him points for each good behavior (positive reinforcement), or using a token economy, she allowed Chris to begin the week with "money in the bank." That is, she gave the reinforcers ahead of time and Chris lost them for misbehavior. She could just as well have given him a token for each designated period during which he stayed in his seat. Of course, the reinforcers suggested represented only a few of a wide range available to teachers, especially when they work with parents. Reinforcers will vary in desirability from student to student.

One reason reinforcers are effective in modifying behavior is that they provide students with ongoing feedback about how well they are doing. There is nothing vague about a clearly structured reinforcement program with well-defined target behaviors.

Types of Reinforcers

There are two general categories of reinforcers (Blackham & Silberman, 1975). *Primary* or *unconditioned reinforcers* are those that offer immediate gratification and are associated with satisfying basic, primary biological needs. The most frequently used primary reinforcers are various foods that taste good. Of course, these are rarely used above the preschool level.

A *conditioned reinforcer* is one whose ability to reinforce behavior results from an association with other reinforcers. Tokens and money are examples that allow the "purchase" of rewards from a menu from which the child can choose. The menu can include age-appropriate items such as stickers, prizes, free time, or special trips, and so forth.

Praise is a conditioned reinforcer because it reinforces a variety of behaviors. Praise is also referred to as a *social reinforcer.* It includes teacher attention, approval, and positive statements after desirable student behavior. The eventual goal is to always move from material reinforcers to social reinforcers so that the student "internalizes" the reinforcement.

Any reinforcement program should take into account the disabilities and assets of the student. For instance, if Chris is a very good artist, giving him extra time for art is an excellent reinforcer. If he is diagnosed with attention deficit hyperactivity disorder, demands for staying in his seat might be modified by reinforcement for shorter periods of in-seat behavior than might be expected if he did not have that disability.

Identify Appropriate Reinforcers.   *Self-determined reinforcement* allows the student to take part in the process of setting goals and determining reinforcement levels. Teachers and parents should let the child determine rewards within predetermined guidelines. Although reinforcers such as stickers, games, and attention from adults work well for most young children, it becomes more difficult with adolescents. In school they might want more free periods, freedom from homework, or other privileges. At home they may want expensive items or things such as more access to the car, freedom to attend dubious concerts or parties, or extended curfews. It is crucial that school and home work together to provide reinforcers that are powerful enough to shape behavior.

Individual children may have needs that are different from what might be suggested by the literature. Most of the research suggests that rewards should occur as soon as possible after correct behavior, but I have worked with exceptions in which children were willing to delay gratification for bigger rewards. Ask the student what he or she wants. What rewards will be more reinforcing than the misbehavior? You also should consider what reinforcers have been used effectively in the past. Parents and former teachers can help with this.

If you think this is bribery, you should stop here. You either are not behaviorally oriented or you need to reread what we have said about this approach.

Group contingencies occur when the whole class gets reinforced for certain behaviors. This is a very important concept for classroom teachers, because some children may resent that one child gets rewarded for behavior that most of them exhibit anyway. So, in the case of Chris, why not reward the whole class with tokens for staying in their seats? That way everybody benefits.

Some teachers may find group contingencies to be very practical, because individual records and reinforcement schedules may interfere with the flow of the class. But if they are integrated into the regular schedule, they become part of the daily routine. Each student receives reinforcements that depend on his or her own behavior, as well as that of the group.

Be careful that children do not threaten or bully those who interfere with group rewards. Do not let individual students be in a position to prevent group reinforcement.

Classroom "games" in which children compete as parts of teams are particular types of group contingencies. These procedures take advantage of the reinforcing value of winning a game to motivate students to perform appropriate behaviors. For instance, the team at a table in the lunchroom that is the quietest could get an extra bonus above a predetermined reward for any team that meets a basic standard. This could include extra time on the playground, in the library, or at free period.

Self-control interventions follow from the belief that students can modify their own behavior. Self-control takes several forms. Self-recording requires that students record their own behavior, and many times this alone reduces disruptiveness. It increases awareness of behavior, provides feed back, and so promotes modification of that behavior. This approach may be useful with adolescents who do not agree with the teacher's estimate of how often they misbehave.

Contingency contracting between a teacher or parent is very helpful (Homme, 1970). It clearly spells out the exact behavior and goals to be reached before the agreed-on reinforcement is dispensed. The process involves negotiation and a written contract. This is the most effective type of approach for children and youth above fourth- or fifth-grade level.

Contingency contracts generally should: (1) offer immediate rewards for short periods of correct behavior, (2) allow for frequent reinforcement, and (3) be constructed so that initially there is always a reasonable chance for reinforcement.

The key to contingency contracting is that the child gains a sense of accomplishment and satisfaction for correct behavior. Sometimes, despite the general recommendation that reinforcers occur frequently, some children or adolescents will delay gratification to obtain big-ticket rewards.

Ian was a ten-year-old who had a history of temper tantrums, fighting in school, opposition to teacher requests, and hitting his mother. He was afraid of his father, who was very big. His father always tried to reason with Ian, but when that did not work, spanking, time-out, and grounding were used. However, by the time I saw the family for therapy, no punishment worked.

After the parents agreed to minimize punishment and try a behavioral approach, in cooperation with the school, they argued about reinforcers. While his parents suggested small items, trips with his father, and money, Ian wanted big-ticket items. He demanded an expensive skateboard and a new bike that cost $250.00. Ian's demands outraged his parents, but after several sessions I convinced them to try it, especially because Ian's behavior in school could not get much worse.

We agreed on a monetary system using both response cost (starting a reward system with money "in the bank") and positive reinforcers (money earned for each good behavior). For instance, if Ian did not lose his temper in school for a whole day, he kept the 75 cents which was in his "bank." If he lost his temper once, he lost 50 cents of the money in the "bank" (response cost) and was only entitled to 25 cents. If he took out the trash at home he earned 50 cents. He lost it all for losing his temper twice. Table 3.2 is a sample response cost and reinforcement schedule.

It was possible for Ian to earn almost $6.00 a day for being good. With bonuses, he was able to increase that amount. Fortunately, his affluent and grateful parents were able and willing to provide the money for the greatly improved behavior at home and school. This

TABLE 3.2   Daily Reinforcement Schedule for Ian Based on Response Cost, Using Money as Reinforcer

Behavior	Frequency	Reward*	Frequency	Reward	Frequency	Reward	Frequency	Reward
School								
Fighting	0 times	1.00	1 time	.25	2 times	0	3 or more	0
Cursing	0 times	.50	1 time	.25	2 times	.10	3 or more	0
Losing temper	0 times	.75	1 time	.25	2 times	0	3 or more	0
Breaking class-room rules	0 times	.50	1 time	.25	2 times	.10	3 or more	0
Refusing teacher request	0 times	.50	1 time	.25	2 times	.10	3 or more	0

*Bonus Reinforcers***

Homework completed—.50 for each day

Desk clean at checkup—.25 for each day

Home								
Cursing	0 times	.50	1 time	.25	2 times	.10	3 or more	0
Losing temper	0 times	.75	1 time	.25	2 times	0	3 or more	0
Refusing parent request	0 times	.50	1 time	.25	2 times	.10	3 or more	0
Hitting mother	0 times	1.00	1 time	.0	2 times	.00	3 or more	0

*Bonus Reinforcers***

Taking out trash—.50

Setting table—.25

Completing homework without nagging—.75

Doing something nice for mom—1.00 for each day

Eaning A on test— 1.00 for each test

Earning B on test—.50 for each test

Earning C on test—.25 for each test

Perfect report for the day from teacher—1.00 for each day

---

* The first column represents how much money he keeps from the pool of money he starts with each day. Second and third columns indicate the amount left from the pool for indicated number of transgressions.
**Bonus reinforcers: These are straight reinforcers that are added to the pool of money when he performs indicated positive tasks.

program was instituted in March, and Ian earned his skateboard and bike by the beginning of the summer.

Differential reinforcement of other behaviors (DRO) is an easily applied technique and should be used before attempting any type of punishment procedure. The teacher simply reinforces the child for any behaviors during a period when the target misbehavior does not appear. In the case of Ian, cursing and fighting are examples of misbehavior to be avoided.

Differential reinforcement of alternative behavior (DRA) occurs when the teacher reinforces the behavior that is incompatible with the disruptive behavior. If a student is reading a book he or she cannot, at the same time, start a fight with a classmate. The two can not occur at the same time. In the example, Ian was rewarded for doing something nice for his mother, which is incompatible with not being nice.

Extinction requires withholding all reinforcement from a previously reinforced behavior to decrease that behavior. Ignoring a behavior each time it occurs is an example of extinction.

Modeling is a simple, nonintrusive technique that can often help to shape students' behavior. The use of modeling is an important concept in the behavioral model. This strategy can be especially helpful for providing disruptive children with an example to imitate. Models can be: (1) peers, (2) fictitious or idealized characters, or (3) an important adult. Modeling with peers is accomplished when you praise a student for appropriate behaviors during a time when the target child is misbehaving. When Chris is out of his seat, Ms. Jones might say, "I am really happy with the way John has been working hard at his seat." She should also praise Chris when he is in his seat and praise others during the day for in-seat behavior.

If, in the case of Chris, ignoring and modeling do not work to decrease misbehavior, it must be assumed that other things are sustaining and reinforcing his out-of-seat behavior. These could include escape from boring seatwork or work that is too difficult to accomplish without help. Reinforcement might come from being near another student whose seat is across the room. It is possible that you may never discover the exact reinforcer, but you can discover more powerful reinforcers to get him to stay in his seat.

Determine Appropriate Reinforcement Schedules. A *continuous reinforcement schedule* is an arrangement in which reinforcement follows every appropriate behavior. An *intermittent* or *partial reinforcement schedule* is when reinforcement follows only a portion of the desired behaviors.

You must recognize that reinforcers may change over time. The student may become satiated or bored with a reinforcer that worked previously. Therefore, if contingency management seems to be losing steam, check the efficacy of the reinforcers by asking the students about their desirability.

Varying the amount of reinforcement as well as the type and the time at which reinforcement is presented will alter the results. It is best to initially offer a certain amount of reinforcement and increase the quantity only when that amount proves ineffective.

Graph Baseline and Ongoing Targeted Behaviors during Reinforcement Treatment Schedule. Graphing is helpful because it allows you to obtain a clear visual picture of the targeted behaviors over time. There are many ways to graph data. We recommend, if you want to become an expert, that you refer to the appropriate texts in the references, consult with an expert, or read copies of behavioral journals such as *The Journal of Applied Behavior Analysis*. Typically, the bottom, horizontal axis is used to show time, and the vertical axis shows numbers or percentages of behaviors. Figure 3.1 is a graph that might show the story of Chris. Note that the vertical axis indicates number of out-of-seat behaviors. The horizontal axis shows days (it is often a good idea to show actual dates) of baseline and treatment. Assume that during the treatment phase Chris is reinforced for periods during which he remains in his seat.

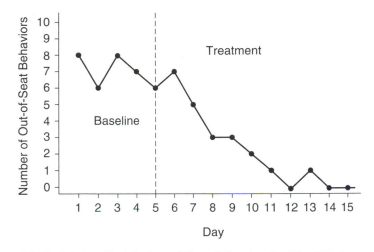

FIGURE 3.1   Chris's Out-of-Seat Behavior for Two Weeks

Classroom researchers often use an ABA design to determine if the reinforcement is really working. In this design, you obtain baseline recordings, before the student knows anything about the program. Then you have a trial of reinforcement during which the behavior should begin to extinguish. Finally, you stop the reinforcement schedule to see if the behavior increases as a function of no reinforcement.

In the case of Chris, Figure 3.1 clearly shows that there was a drop over the two weeks as Chris was reinforced for staying in his seat. In most cases, if the correct reinforcers are used, improvement will be noted quickly. If not, another reward or combination of reinforcers may be tried. In this way, effort will not be expended on ineffective approaches. This low cost in time when treatments are ineffective is a distinct advantage of the approach.

As with the case of Chris, most teachers do not take the time to set up an ABA or "reversal design," which means that the teacher returns the child to baseline conditions. If the behavior deteriorates to baseline levels, then the intervention was a factor in producing the desired results. Reinstating the intervention to again acquire the preferred behavior is necessary.

A "multiple baseline" procedure involves the focus of the intervention on a completely different target behavior. Repeated acquisition of appropriate behavior demonstrates an intervention's efficacy.

Use Punishments (i.e., Seclusionary & Nonseclusionary Time-Out, Soft Reprimands, Negative Reinforcement) Sparingly.   Time-out is a punishment that is frequently used in lower grades and in preschool. Time-out is a type of negative punishment, which we described previously. Because it is so widely used, and too often abused, a thorough discussion is warranted.

The rule of thumb is that the removal time in minutes should not exceed the child's age. However, the research on effectiveness shows that the correct duration is best determined by what works. In school settings, short periods of time-out can be very effective when used in conjunction with positive reinforcement programs. Long periods of time-out (over 30 minutes) begin to involve ethical problems that may come back to haunt you.

Some classes use a cardboard box or a special booth for isolation time-out. Unfortunately, the presence of these enclosures all too often leads to their overuse. When you are tired and frustrated, it is very tempting to just remove behavior problems. Out of sight and out of mind may make life easier in the short run, but it is a formula for long-term problems.

Time-out should be reserved for extreme behaviors such as hitting, cursing, or lying. These are actions that are not only inappropriate but also unacceptable. Minor misbehaviors such as talking out of turn, pushing in line, and the million other daily irritants should not be punished with time-out. If time-out becomes routine, it probably will lose its effectiveness.

Time-out is effective if the student enjoys class. But the process of sending a student to time-out should not be reinforcing. For instance, if a student enjoys irritating you, and you respond by yelling and screaming as you send him or her off to time-out, you have been defeated.

Below is a summary list of do's and don'ts for the effective use of time-out:

- Do establish clear procedures and time limits for going to and remaining in time-out. Post a description of the offenses deserving time-out in a prominent place.
- Do tell students what rules they have broken and calmly request that they go to time-out.
- Do prepare options for students who refuse time-out.

Calmly repeat those options if a student refuses and give him or her time to consider what to do.

- Do not send an errant student to the friendly counselor for time-out, where he or she will be counseled instead of punished.
- Do not send students to the principal, where they may sit in the outer office to be entertained by the comings and goings of secretaries, other students, and school staff.
- Do not yell, scream, or threaten students when you send them to time-out.
- Do not forget that the student is in time-out.

In conclusion, time-out, when used as part of a total system of contingency management, can be an effective method for reducing misbehavior. It should not be the equivalent of a sentence in the Gulag or solitary confinement in a federal penitentiary. Finally, it should not be confused with in-school suspensions, detentions, or other exclusionary procedures, which are rarely used as part of a systematic approach to improving behavior.

Summary of the Behavioral Approach

Behavior modification, and its minor variants in practice, contingency management, applied behavioral analysis, and functional analysis, all offer advantages. It is a systematic approach that can be learned effectively in a relatively short period. Its principles can be incorporated into teaching and become natural aspects of teaching behavior. Also, desirable results can be achieved rather quickly. The basic theory is parsimonious and easy to understand. It can be applied in any setting and can work with all children. It may capitalize on nonverbal communication such as pats on the back, smiles, hugs, and nods of approval; it eliminates constant contact with the child; it encourages success; and its orientation is positive, reinforcing good feelings and self-concept.

Cognitive–Behavioral Diagnosis

As discussed previously, the cognitive–behavioral approach is rooted in behavioral theory. But rather than focusing on rewards and punishments administered by the teacher for various behaviors and misbehaviors, the emphasis is on teaching misbehaving students new ways of thinking, feeling, and acting. Let us now turn to the case of Chris and examine the diagnosis and treatment plan using a cognitive–behavioral approach.

Problem Identification

The major purpose of the initial diagnosis is to identify the specific misbehaviors that need to be eliminated. Unlike the behavioral approach, the focus turns to the thoughts and feelings that cause the misbehavior. Different theorists use different language to describe the thought processes, but essentially we attempt to uncover the internal dialogue or *self-talk* that is assumed to be behind all behavior. Therefore, the core of diagnoses in the cognitive–behavioral approach is the identification of irrational, self-destructive thinking. If the antecedent thinking can be changed, then the consequent behavior can be changed by processes we will discuss in the treatment section. To illustrate the similarities and differences between the two approaches, we again interview Ms. Jones about Chris. In this case, the school psychologist wishes to help her understand the problem from a cognitive–behavioral perspective:

Psych: Well, Ms. Jones, I understand you are having problems with Chris.

Teacher: Yes, he is really hyper and aggressive. He is very difficult to manage. He can't seem to sit still, and he constantly gets into fights. I have tried everything to get him to behave. Maybe he belongs in a special class.

Psych: Can you describe exactly what he does that bothers you?

Teacher: He can't sit still and doesn't seem to want to conform. He just won't obey the rules.

Psych: What bothers you most?

Teacher: He is so hyper.

Psych: Yes, give me examples of how he is hyper.

Teacher: He always gets out of his seat.

Psych: And what do you do when he gets out of his seat?

Teacher: I tell him to return. Sometimes he talks back to me.

Psych: What does he do when he gets out of his seat?

Teacher: Well, he usually just wanders around until I catch him.

Psych: What feelings or ideas does he express when you confront him? What does he say?

Teacher: Well, he can really get nasty. He seems to want to defy me. Especially when he wanders around class and he isn't doing his schoolwork. He bothers other children. Maybe he has an attention disorder.

Psych: Exactly what does he say? Give me an example of a recent time when he was out of his seat. What did you say; what did he say?

Teacher: Well, yesterday afternoon I told him to sit down, and he refused.

Psych: Tell me exactly what happened. Make believe you are narrating a scene from a film and you are reading from the script. What was the time, the setting, and so on?

Teacher: It was around two in the afternoon. I was helping Jane with her homework. It was study time. Chris had wandered around several times, and each time I told him to sit down he did. This time he started to complain. He claimed he was only going to sharpen his pencil. I said he always seems to be sharpening his pencil.

Psych: How did you say it? Was it in a joking way, or was it in an angry or calm voice?

Teacher: I guess it was a little sarcastic. Anyway, he flipped out. He started yelling that other kids are allowed to get out of their seats all the time, which isn't true. He claimed he is the only one I yell at. He claims I pick on him just like all the other teachers, that no one likes him anyway, and why don't I just suspend him? Then he said something to the effect of, "There is nothing you can do to hurt me. I don't care if you kick me out of school."

Psych: What did you do?

Teacher: I told him to be quiet and sit down. His response to that was that I could go f_ _ _ myself. At that point, I sent him to the principal, which was what he wanted. He is now cooling his heels at home. Maybe he really doesn't belong in this class.

Later in the initial consultation, when she was finished venting her anger, Ms. Jones revealed that she is constantly correcting Chris when he gets out of his seat. He sits down, but then he repeats the behavior until she sends him to the principal. The corrections are usually lectures about why he should be good, how he is being bad, and threats of the dire consequences of being sent to the principal. However, the corrections do not seem to be effective, because he repeats his misbehaviors.

Identify Antecedents and Consequences.   An analysis of the antecedents is possible from accurate behavioral descriptions by teachers and the students' reports of their behavior and feelings. In the case of Chris, it is clear that the out-of-seat and defiant behavior occurs mostly in the afternoon. It also appears that it generally happens at times other than actual classroom lecture. That information helps us to decide that it is important to consider how to analyze what is happening in reality, as opposed to the student's perception of that reality.

The traditional behaviorist would generally not put much emphasis on antecedents, other than those in the classroom. However, a functional analysis does require, as was discussed previously, a more comprehensive description of all possible, relevant antecedents. The cognitive–behavioral practitioner wants to know what caused the irrational thinking that resulted in the misbehaviors in the classroom.

We will now reexamine the case of Chris, using the cognitive–behavioral approach.

Preliminary Analysis

It is clear that some of Chris's attitudes about himself and school were developed around the time of his parents' divorce. This was a time when he was beginning formal instruction in readiness skills and beginning reading and arithmetic. The history suggests that he may not have been sufficiently mature for formal instruction at the end of kindergarten or that he may have had a mild learning disability. The history indicates that his image of himself as a student is not good.

A common reaction by young children to divorce is to blame themselves for the parental split. This happened around the time of Chris's problems in school. Perhaps he thought he should have been home more with his mother during her most difficult times.

All of the above data help us to understand where, when and why Chris developed an angry attitude toward teachers. Yet, we will not focus on those factors, as would a psychodynamic theorist, but rather on how to change Chris's feelings that no matter what he does, the teachers are out to get him. It is important to know about these factors in developing strategies to attack his distorted thinking.

Identify Specific Misbehaviors and Dysfunctional Thoughts, Feelings, and Emotions to Be Eliminated.   The psychologist not only attempted to discover the specific misbehaviors but also to discover what the child was thinking, feeling, and saying in response to the teacher's statements and demands. Although one would assume that Chris knows that he should not get out of his seat without permission, we must also assume that he knew that when he curses at the teacher, he is going to get suspended.

When Chris returns to school, the school psychologist or the teacher with cognitive–behavioral skills needs to talk in a nonthreatening way about what happened. The goal is to reveal what Chris was thinking and feeling as the scenario that led to his suspension was unfolding.

We have had hundreds of such conversations, and Chris represents a composite of them. It is likely that the talk will reveal that Chris feels that, no matter what he does, his teacher does not like him. His self-talk might be something like, "All I did was get up to sharpen my pencil. You should listen to Ms. Jones nagging me. Boy, does she hate me. She is just like the rest of the teachers. That really tees me off. Well f_ _ _ her, she's not going to tell me what to do. Let her suspend me. I don't care. I'll fix her."

Now the elements of *irrational thinking* are reflected in his self-talk. "All I did was get up to sharpen my pencil." Chris needs to recognize that that is just not true. He was up a lot of other times. But this rationalization helps sustain the next belief that may or may not be true.

"You should listen to Ms. Jones nagging me. Boy, does she hate me." She is obviously very angry at him, but there are some good reasons, based on objective behavior, for her to be angry. Although she is angry, she may not hate him. However, assume the worst-case scenario, which is that she detests him. Again, does she hate him because he is a detestable person or because he does detestable things? Does he believe he is a detestable person?

"She is just like the rest of the teachers." How is she like the other teachers? Was there never a teacher who liked him, was nice to him, or did not act like Ms. Jones?

"That really tees me off." From a cognitive–behavioral perspective, this is a very important point in making the diagnosis. What events trigger the feelings that result in maladaptive, self-defeating behavior? Chris really gets angry and starts to lose it when: (1) a teacher gives him orders he does not like and (2) the teacher's reprimands remind him of other teachers, who he thinks are all unfair. That thought results in the next thought, which then results in the expression of the anger.

"Well f_ _ _ her, she's not going to tell me what to do." Now, this is the most serious and irrational part of this self-dialogue. Chris says to himself that the teachers can not tell him what to do. Although he may reject what she tells him, she can tell him what to do. He may not do it, but if she can not make him do it, she has access to others who can make him do it.

"Let her suspend me. I don't care. I'll fix her." This is a very common belief among oppositional, defiant students. Many believe that they are really getting back at the teacher by their defiance. It may be true that the teacher is annoyed, angry, and frustrated. In the end, the teacher always "wins" by using the authority of the school to punish the student. Furthermore, although the student may say he or she does not care, it is usually very easy to point out that the student ends up with more grief than the teacher. This may come from a combination of school authorities, parents, and sometimes peers.

Irrational Thoughts and Feelings Can Be Unlearned.   The first step in "unlearning" dysfunctional thoughts is to recognize them. The next step is to acknowledge the behaviors that are related to them and then to consider alternative ways of thinking and acting.

The cognitive–behavioral practitioner would sit down with Chris and discuss the thinking described in the section on identification of specific irrational thoughts. If Ms. Jones is the person to do this, she must do it in a nonjudgmental manner. She must be able to help Chris measure his perceptions against reality. She might even try a classroom discussion of the rules and how often they are broken. This must not be done in a manner that publicly sanctions Chris. It might be done better in a small group with other students who have similar problems. Perhaps some of them are even his buddies. She also might ask the psychologist to take this initial step or to guide her in how to do it. Once she learns the approach, she will be able to do it on her own.

After Chris recognizes or admits to his thinking, it is important to consider the usual sequence of events around the time of his misbehavior.

The usual sequence begins with Chris getting out of his seat at the wrong time. This is followed by: (1) initial demands to conform to the rules, (2) reprimands for not following the rules, (3) threats of punishment, (4) oppositional responses from Chris, and (5) punishment. Because this chain of events is repeated, one must assume that the punishments are not effective. If they were, after a few trips to the office or a few suspensions, Chris would change his behavior. Does Chris recognize this? If he does, then the next question is, "Chris, if it is not a punishment to be suspended, you must think it is a reward. But is it really a reward?"

Thorough discussion will usually show that he really gets a lot of grief from his parents, school authorities, and misses much classwork when he is suspended. This may be ignored by him in the short run, but the problem of missed work can spiral into later issues around grounding at home, grades, and promotion. Once he admits this, Ms. Jones is on her way.

Next, two things need to be done. Identify the "triggers" that get Chris angry and help him discover alternative ways of thinking, feeling and responding to each trigger.

It seems clear that as soon as Chris is given what he considers an "order," which the teacher considers a request, he begins to feel that she is picking on him. The consequent reaction is anger, followed by oppositional behavior.

The trigger, then, is any request by the teacher that makes him believe that she is picking on him. Because as soon as he thinks that, he gets angry, he must learn to not be angry when he thinks that the teacher is picking on him. It may well be that she is picking on him. Or the teacher may be able to prove that she is not picking on him. Whatever the case may be, he must recognize that the trigger leads to behavior that really does not cause much distress to the teacher, because she can just get rid of him. However, he ends up the loser in the long run.

Identify New Thoughts, Feelings, or Emotions to Replace Targeted Misbehaviors.   If Chris will acknowledge that his thoughts that: (1) teachers always pick on him, (2) his feelings of anger are okay, and (3) he is getting revenge on the teacher by his misbehavior are all either wrong, or at least lead to bad consequences, then he can go to the next step. This is accomplished by listing alternative thoughts, feelings, and responses to the teacher's requests. Assuming this level is achieved, let us consider the following dialogue:

Teacher: Well, Chris, you do admit that I yell at other kids when they don't obey, but you still think I am picking on you.

Chris: Yeah, I guess I am not the only kid you pick on.

Teacher: Yes, but the others don't seem to feel I am picking on them.

Chris: Maybe you don't pick on me all the time, but you do pick on me.

Teacher: Just for the sake of argument, let's assume that I do pick on you sometimes when I am upset. You admitted that what happens when you get angry, especially when you curse at me, gives you more grief than it gives me.

Chris: I guess that is true, but I can't help it. I always get angry when people are mean to me. It's just the way I am.

Teacher: No, it's the way you think you have to be. You just learned to be angry.

Chris: I can't help it. My father is the same way. He used to always lose his temper. I used to cause it a lot because I was so bad.

Teacher: No, you are not bad; you have just learned to act bad. Everybody gets angry, but we can learn to think before we act on our anger. For instance, the other day when I asked you to sit down, there were several ways you could have handled it.

One, you could get angry and curse. The consequence is that you get sent to the office. Two, you could tell me you think I am picking on you, and I could say we will discuss it later, after you sit down. Three, as soon as you felt that I was picking on you, which really gets you angry, you could take ten nice slow, steady, deep breaths to calm down, and then sit down. When you were calm, you could ask to talk to me later about how you felt. Four, you and I could set up a plan so that as soon as you start to really get angry, and before you begin to curse and defy me, you could go to the principal's office and calm down and then return when you are ready. Five, you could decide that you are not a bad boy, which I don't think anyway, and begin to try being good, so that I don't yell so much at you. What do you think? Would any work?

All of the above are steps in the right direction. There are a variety of solutions to any problem, and Chris must learn that he can learn new ways of dealing with problems. It would be better for the teacher to help Chris to come up with some of these answers himself. But initially, most children his age need some help in learning to think about alternatives.

Identify Proper Self-Dialogue Based on ABC (Antecedents-Behavior-Consequences).   Once Chris decides on ways to deal with his anger about being picked on, he needs to develop a self-dialogue to use when the triggers for his anger appear. This is done by recognizing the chain of events, which include *antecedents, behavior, and consequences (ABC)*. Here is one such self-dialogue that he might use when the teacher makes a request: "I know that I get mad when she starts giving me orders. I know that she thinks I am bad. I am not bad, and if I lose my temper I will look bad. I better take some deep breaths and calm down before I blow it."

Another might be, "I am starting to get mad. She is out to get me again. If I stay in the class, I am going to blow up. I better leave and go to the principal's office like we planned. After I come back, I will calmly tell her how I feel."

Of course, there are whole curricula that help teach children alternative ways of dealing with social problems (Goldstein, 1989; Shure, 1992). Sometimes it is worthwhile to teach these skills to a whole class for the benefit of a few children. This way they get the message from peers. Also, in class they can practice and role play.

Gather Baseline Data of Observable and Measurable Targeted Thoughts, Feelings, or Emotions.   We recognize that most teachers will be busy enough teaching new thinking to misbehaving students without worrying about measurement issues. However, cognitive–behavioral therapists often use scales to measure rates of success. In the case of Chris, at the beginning of the training, the teacher could make up an anger scale for Chris to indicate how angry he gets when he believes he is being picked on. Ratings are usually on a scale of one to ten. His scale could be as follows:

1	2	3	4	5	6	7	8	9	10
Not Angry		Little		Somewhat		Fairly			Very Angry

It is not really necessary to put in the words under the numbers between 2 and 9, but in some cases it helps, especially with younger children.

Use Behavioral Rehearsal.   You might think of the cognitive–behavioral approach as a method of training students to learn new scripts for their appearances on the stage of life: a *behavioral rehearsal.* Yes, that sounds trite, but it is apt. If actors must learn to act in a new play, they must first learn their new lines and then rehearse them, before going on stage. But even if they do not learn the lines and believe them in terms of the part they are to play, they may still learn the part through actual practice. So what if they ad lib a little!

Use Relaxation Procedures for Anger Control.   Teaching *relaxation skills* can be very helpful for dealing with anger. Methods such as deep muscle relaxation, imagery, deep breathing, yoga, self-hypnosis, and meditation can be easily learned by any college student or teacher. If you learn these skills as an undergraduate, they will help you learn to relax under stress, and you will be able to use acceptable techniques in class to help students who are stressed and angry. Students usually enjoy relaxation sessions.

Next, we turn to one more overview of the use of the BCBA in teacher variance before considering a few model programs.

Combining Behavioral and Cognitive–Behavioral Approaches

In the case of Chris, we examined traditional behavioral and cognitive–behavioral approaches separately. In both models, we considered the theory and basic techniques. In the following case, we present an integrated approach in which we apply the common underlying assumptions of both approaches and pick and choose techniques that best fit the situation.

Ms. Smith, a sixth-grade teacher, had two students with completely different personalities but similar problems. Shy, withdrawn Jane and aggressive, demanding Rob both lacked peer acceptance. Neither had any close friends, yet both expressed desires to have friends. I asked Ms. Smith to describe some specific situations in which these children had difficulties with classmates.

Ms. Smith told her class that they were to choose social studies projects. She listed some possible topics on the board, and at the students' request, agreed that they could work on projects in groups. She informed them that they had three days to pick their topics and workmates.

After the announcement of this assignment, Ms. Smith observed the students at lunch as they busily formed alliances. As might be expected, friendship patterns were more important than the particular topics in determining who worked together.

As usual, Jane was quietly eating lunch at the fringe of a group of the more popular girls in the class. As the children got up to return their lunch trays, Jane approached Sue, one of the class social leaders, and asked to work with her on the project. Sue politely informed Jane that she already had a project group, dropped off her lunch tray, and ran to the playground. Jane appeared sad and dejected, shrugged her shoulders, and slowly wandered out of the lunchroom.

During the same lunch period, Rob joined a group of boys who were talking about a possible topic for their project. Rob insisted that he be a part of the group. However, Joe, one of the more assertive boys in the class, informed Rob that the group had already been formed on the way to the lunchroom. An argument ensued, and Rob, feeling rejected and angered, responded in his usual manner: He began to curse at Joe and call names.

Joe tried to ignore the verbal assault, until Rob threatened to overturn Joe's food tray. Joe dared Rob to try, but before an actual physical struggle ensued, Ms. Smith intervened.

Most teachers are familiar with the above scenario and often understand many of the reasons children are rejected by others. For instance, Ms. Smith knew that Jane, a rather shy girl, had recently moved to this school district. Most of the children had attended school together for many years, and social groups were well established. This made it extremely difficult, even for an outgoing, active sixth-grader, to break into the groups.

Rob was frequently bullied by an older brother and a father who belittled and demeaned him. His father, somewhat of a social outcast in the community, constantly warned Rob that his classmates should never be allowed to push him around.

Because of her understanding of the problem, Ms. Smith was sympathetic to the plights of both children. She tried to get the class to be more understanding. Yet both children were unable to sustain relationships. We decided that both Jane and Rob needed to act differently. They both were unable to deal with rejection by peers. Jane gave up too easily, and Rob was too persistent. The result was that they had developed bad feelings about themselves and their classmates. They needed to learn social skills to make friends and to handle rejection.

Learning Social Skills

Behaviorists, observing the interactions in the lunchroom, would objectively describe the specific actions of Jane, Rob, and their classmates. It is assumed that both children learned the traits they exhibited in those interactions. Once the specific behaviors are "targeted," they must be unlearned. This can be done by teaching new behaviors that are more likely to result in positive outcomes.

Research shows that children can be taught a variety of positive *social skills*. These include initiating conversations, sustaining conversations, playing cooperatively, reacting to rejection appropriately, dealing with peer ridicule, and controlling their own aggressive impulses. Children who learn these skills begin to feel better about themselves. Let us apply social skills techniques to the problems of Jane and Rob.

It is obvious that Jane, who is rather shy, has not developed the skills to make friends. When she is rejected, she quickly withdraws and gives up. Ms. Smith can use the following techniques:

Feedback: The teacher can be helpful by describing for Jane, in an unemotional manner, what she observed. She must help Jane to objectively understand what happened. Ms. Smith and Jane need to agree about the important behaviors that occurred before they talk about how Jane felt. After that, they should discuss Jane's feelings and the possible feelings of Sue.

Instruction: The teacher can help Jane to "target" the specific behaviors such as initiating and sustaining conversations, offering to help others, asking for help, and observing actions and interests of popular students. Also included would be instruction in dealing with rejection. Ms. Smith should explain to Jane that she was not rejected because there is something wrong with her, but because she has not properly identified all of the specifics in the situation. For instance, she has not used techniques to make new friends before asking to join an already existing clique. It may have been better to identify other children who are not part of existing cliques and make friends with them.

Modeling: Ms. Smith could model appropriate behaviors for making new friends. Or she could have Jane read or watch videotapes in which "new kids" make friends. She can thereby observe the appropriate behaviors in action.

Role Playing: The teacher would take the part of another child, and Jane would play her normal role. Then they would switch, and Jane would play the part of the other child. This will help her to understand the nature of the interactions. Also, the teacher could introduce the topic of meeting friends as a lesson for the class. In this situation, children role play specific interactions.

Behavioral Rehearsal: Once Jane understands the specific skills she needs, she can practice them. She can do this with the teacher during role playing sessions in the class or in her mind. The teacher and Jane should identify several new situations, in which, after sufficient practice, she attempts to make friends.

In Vivo Implementation: Jane must, on her own, begin to use her new skills in various situations. She should report to Ms. Smith what happened after each incident. They can analyze the situation together and share in her success.

Dealing with Anger

Social problem solving is a preventive approach. The teacher must target the specific skills needed and present the class with scenarios in which the skills can be used. This avoids pointing the finger at any particular child and thereby makes it more "digestible" to those who need it most. Children enjoy discussing common social problems that are relevant to their everyday lives. They can demonstrate expertise during role playing and discuss various solutions and the consequences of each. It is important for the teacher to do this as an academic exercise and to let children discuss viable solutions and not voice her own judgments about the worth of any particular resolution of a problem.

Social problem solving is simple enough for any teacher to use. In the case of Rob being denied membership with the project group, Ms. Smith might prepare a number of lessons for the class on how to deal with feelings of rejection and anger. She can describe a situation, have the children role play, base discussions on television shows, or make video-tapes. Because there is so much violence on TV, children can discuss solutions to scenes many of them have viewed. In fact, this offers a good technique to undermine TV's message that violence is an easy solution to problems.

Ms. Smith should list on the board each solution the students generate. Beside each solution, she should list possible consequences. The class can then vote on the best ways to deal with anger and rejection. Then, students can use behavioral rehearsal to practice dealing with a variety of potentially troubling situations.

Rob needs to learn new ways of thinking to resolve his problems. First, he must engage in the process of social problem solving. Ms. Smith can present a variety of situations similar to the one in the lunchroom, in which aggression is one of the possible responses to rejection. Rob needs to think ahead about what to do if Joe turns him down. What are the consequences of calling Joe names? Joe could: (1) give in and let Rob join the project group, (2) ignore him, (3) call Rob names, (4) tell the teacher, or even (5) punch him. What are the consequences of each of those events?

Most likely, if Rob persists, he will get into trouble. Because this situation is typical for Rob, it can be used as a model for learning the skills needed to handle his feelings of rejection and anger. He needs to develop, as a result of learning social problem-solving skills, an internal dialogue for thinking ahead.

Ms. Smith can discuss the situation privately with Rob when he is calm and ready to talk. She can individually go through the process described above. Instead of saying how bad it is to hit another student, she should unemotionally facilitate Rob's thinking about the various consequences of hitting another child. However deplorable it might be, one viable consequence of Rob beating up Joe is that Joe might have let him join the group. However, the teacher can help Rob to understand other negative consequences, such as Joe's ongoing resentment of Rob.

Reinforcement is a most important part of a problem-solving approach. Both teacher and classmates should reinforce children who use appropriate problem-solving strategies. This can be done by verbal praise, by giving rewards, and by having the student reenact how he or she successfully dealt with the situation.

Although this may sound too sophisticated for sixth graders, try to present a similar problem to your class. If you are a doubter, you will be pleasantly surprised to discover the range of consequences and possible solutions that emerge.

Examples of Behavioral Programs

Hundreds of behavioral programs could be presented here, as could many example of cognitive programs in the next section. We have selected some model programs to discuss, even though the citations for some suggest that the programs are dated. But we have selected some older programs because they have been successful. We present a summary of a sample of both types of programs in Table 3.3. As part of becoming an expert in this area, it would be useful to pick one or two programs and read the primary sources.

TABLE 3.3 Examples of Behavioral Programs

Program	Underlying Theory	Assumptions	Diagnosis	Intervention/ Remediation	Research
Behavior Analysis Program of Follow-Through	This is a follow-up to the Head Start Program. It is based on the behavioral technique of reinforcement.	Behavior can be controlled through provision of rewards (e.g., tokens, praise).	Teacher and student target misbehavior by developing a list of effective, available rewards. Children receive tokens when displaying positive behaviors. Tokens are then exchanged for rewards.	Contingencies are consistently reexamined for their reinforcing value to each student. An important feature of this program is also the training of parents in behavior modification techniques.	There is a growing body of research applying behavioral principles to the classroom (e.g., Martens & Meller, 1990). Maccoby & Zellner (1970) found this approach to be superior in terms of the student's acquisition of basic skills.
The Rose School Program	Based on a token economy model, this program illustrates an approach to applied behavioral analysis that is useful in enhancing group cohesion and positive group behavior.	Individual and group behavior can be positively affected by reinforcement of clearly defined appropriate behaviors.	This type of program is widely used with adolescents who are oppositional, defiant, and delinquent. Inconsistency of rule enforcement and lack of rewards for good behavior are almost always the major antecedents in the lives of students with conduct problems.	On an individual basis, students receive privileges and positive reinforcement for achieving higher levels of appropriate behavior on daily and weekly bases. On a group level, the teacher determines the suitability of reinforcers and provides acceptable ones as the class reaches specific levels associated with points that are earned.	Parese (1989) has found this approach to positively affect group behavior and enhance group cohesion.
Red Light Green Light/ GOALS	A behavior modification program that provides immediate feedback and reinforcement of positive behaviors.	Immediate feedback is a more effective change agent for certain people (e.g., young children, seriously emotionally disturbed individuals, etc.). It also assumes that verbal praise or advice given by peers provides an effective means of producing and maintaining positive behaviors in the classroom.	Individual charts are used for monitoring students' behaviors. Time blocks of half-hour intervals are indicated on each chart. For each interval, a certain number of points can be earned based on the student's behavior.	Throughout the school day, teachers and students provide "positive" and "helpful hints," which are directed toward specific appropriate behaviors. Students then earn points corresponding to a specific zone (e.g., green/yellow/red). In addition, a response cost method is used, whereby individuals can lose points for infractions of rules. Furthermore, bonus points can be given to help reinforce positive behaviors. Students earn privileges based on the zone they achieve (green being the best).	Barbetta (1990) has found this program to be effective in meeting the needs of students who require immediate reinforcement.
Special Education Learning Center Program	Uses a behavioral approach to handle the more behaviorally disordered students.	A therapeutic classroom management program is needed to provide education to the most disruptive and violent students.	Behaviors to be extinguished must be targeted, and contingencies surrounding the misbehavior must be understood.	This program employs a system of reinforcements, physical interventions, and team support to carry out the behavioral curriculum.	The staff at the Special Education Learning Center in Hartford, CT has used this program for over 10 years with demonstrated success. However, no empirical evidence has been found.

The Behavior Analysis Program of Follow-Through

Many people are familiar with the Head Start Program, which has been in existence since 1965. Head Start attempts to provide preschool children with academic, social, nutritional, medical, and other services similar to those of more privileged children. Project Follow-Through was instituted in the fall of 1968 as an experimental program to follow up on the gains of Head Start (Maccoby & Zellner, 1970). Because Follow-Through was an experimental program, prominent theorists had an opportunity to submit primary school programs (grades K–3) that would enhance children's learning. The Behavior Analysis Program was sponsored by Dr. Donald Bushell, Jr., from the University of Kansas. Bushell's program, with modifications, still exists in some school districts. The original version was based on systematic reinforcement procedures as the major motivator for children's learning.

A core element of the program is the method of teacher/student determination of effective, available rewards. Subsequently, a "menu" of rewards is developed. The menu lists all the reinforcers and is prominently displayed in the classroom. The teachers carry tokens with them that they use for immediate reinforcement of positive behaviors. Children collect the tokens and exchange them for rewards. Each item on the menu has its own value in tokens. If items on the menu lose their reinforcing value, the "price" is lowered or new reinforcers are added to the menu.

Tokens alone are not used as motivators. Teachers also use social praise when giving tokens. The goal is that the praise, which is paired with the token, will eventually become the reinforcer. Finally, the intrinsic, self-praise will motivate students to learn.

Teachers were trained extensively in behavioral techniques and considered themselves to be in control of the class in their roles as behavior modifiers. If students were not functioning well, it meant that they were not trying to earn tokens at an effective rate. Rather than blaming the child, the teachers examined the contingencies that would lead the child to want to desire more tokens. These could include such factors as the teachers giving more attention to the child, simplifying the tasks, or providing adequate reinforcers.

An important feature of the program was the training of parents in behavior modification. In the original program, parents were hired to function as behavior modifiers for five to seven weeks. The reasoning was that behavioral principles work as well at home as in school and that the best results could be obtained through parental cooperation. Both money and the opportunity to become part of the educational system were powerful reinforcers to encourage parents to learn the system. Selection and training procedures assured some parent involvement in the classroom throughout the year. Unfortunately, funding cuts eventually reduced this very important component of the program.

Because of the strong behavioral orientation, teacher, parent, and student behaviors and progress were closely monitored. Adults were constantly encouraged to continually assess the effectiveness of reinforcers and to add new rewards as needed.

Misbehavior was assumed to be the result of reinforcement. The teacher's job was to discover what reinforcers were maintaining the misbehavior. Ignoring minor misbehaviors was a major strategy for eliminating reinforcers such as teacher attention. Time-out was generally used for unacceptable behavior such as hitting. Misbehavior, however, was not a major concern in evaluating this program. Compared with many other programs in the

Follow-Through experiment, this approach was superior in terms of students' acquisition of basic skills (Maccoby & Zellner, 1970).

Red Light–Green Light/GOALS (Immediate Reinforcement)

Levels systems are commonly used in behavior modification programs. However, in schools the reinforcements associated with the attainment of specific levels often are not received by the students until the following school day, when points have been tallied. The delayed privileges may not be effective for young students or seriously emotionally disturbed students. Barbetta (1990a) presents a behavior modification program called "Red Light–Green Light," which was developed to meet the needs of those groups of students. Students receive different levels of privileges or restrictions throughout the day. This provides almost immediate feedback and reinforcement of behaviors.

At the beginning of the schoolyear, the class meets to develop classroom rules. The rules are then translated into different types of activities that normally take place during the school day. For example, "Have Good School Behavior" may be translated to mean no talking in line, using a quiet voice during lunch, or putting materials away when done. The results are then read by a student before the class's engagement in an activity. Throughout the school-day, teachers and peers give "positives" and "helpful hints." Positives are statements of praise directed toward specific appropriate behaviors (e.g., "Johnny, you did a good job of keeping your hands to yourself during the lesson"). Helpful hints are statements of advice or suggestions related to a problem situation. They also can be used as a preventive measure (e.g., "Let's be careful to throw away all of your trash today. Yesterday, there was paper left on the floor."). Other individual reinforcements are also determined by the students.

Individual charts are used for monitoring students' behaviors. Time blocks of half-hour intervals are indicated on the chart. For each half-hour interval, students have the opportunity to earn one to three points (Red Light Zone), four to six points (Yellow Zone), seven to nine points (Green Line Zone), or any number of bonus points. Using response cost, students lose one point for each infraction of a rule during the period. For more serious offenses, more points may be deducted. Bonus points may be given by the teacher to individuals or to the class to help reinforce positive behavior. At the end of each half hour, the teacher totals the points earned during that timeframe. The total will indicate which zone the student is in. Attached to each student' desk is a laminated "traffic light" in which the student places the correct color disk. Students earn privileges according to the category of their behavior. The privileges should be easily administered and transferable to mainstream activities. For example, Green Light students may be allowed to be errand runners, have access to a special "Green Light Box," and eat lunch in the cafeteria. Yellow Light students may be allowed to spend free time at their desk with a peer, be called to line after Green Light students, and be permitted to cue peers. Students in the Red Light Zone may be restricted to their seats, called to line last, and have to eat lunch in the classroom. Barbetta gives several variations to this program and suggests that it be individualized to the management concerns of each classroom in which it is employed.

A major focus of this program is encouragement of peer praise and good advice. It is believed that this ingredient provides an effective means of producing and maintaining positive behaviors in the classroom.

Examples of Cognitive–Behavioral Programs

Table 3.4 presents an overview of sample cognitive–behavioral programs. We have selected several widely used programs to discuss in more detail.

Myrna Shure's Interpersonal Cognitive Problem-Solving Program

In the late 1970s, Shure and colleagues (Spivack et al., 1976) postulated that parents needed to teach their children to think for themselves in terms of problem solving. As cognitive behaviorists, they assumed that misbehavior resulted when children were unable to think of the possible consequences of their actions. The failure to consider consequences is the result of lack of learning rather than some inborn tendency toward misbehavior or genetically programmed impulsivity. They developed a set of skills and steps needed to learn problem solving.

Spivack et al., (1976) identified three skills considered important for problem solving: (1) the ability to generate alternative solutions; (2) the ability to anticipate consequences and, for children ages nine and older, (3) the ability to develop a step-by-step plan of action that will result in achieving the desired goals and the resolution of interpersonal problems. Based on extensive research, Myrna Shure (1992) developed a series of curricula entitled *I Can Problem Solve* (ICPS).

Shure's curricula teaches problem solving to children. She does not teach children what to think or do, but how to think so they can successfully resolve problems with peers and authority figures. The program also teaches children about how they and other children feel and offers options for reaching their goals.

Shure believes that, as early as age four, children who can think about their own and others' feelings, consequences of actions, and alternative ways to solve problems show fewer behavior problems than youngsters who merely react impulsively. Two decades of research indicate that the ICPS program can help some children, of various ages and IQ levels, become: (1) less easily frustrated, (2) less likely to fly off the handle when things do not go their way, (3) less impatient, (4) less socially withdrawn, (5) more caring about others, (6) more likely to share and take turns, and (7) better able to make friends than other children.

For preschoolers, lesson-games teach early language concepts that can set the stage for later problem solving. The words *same* and *different* can help children recognize that hitting and kicking are kind of the same because they both can hurt someone. They then learn to think of something different to do. Children learn that different people feel different ways about the same thing, that feelings change, and that we learn about feelings by watching, listening, and asking.

TABLE 3.4   Examples of Cognitive Behavioral Programs

Program	Underlying Theory	Assumptions	Diagnosis	Intervention/ Remediation	Research
Albert Ellis's Rational Emotive Education	This is an outgrowth of Ellis's rational emotive therapy, which is based on the premise that it is not life events that cause a person to experience severe distress. Instead, it is the way a person views the events that causes the emotional reaction.	Intense negative emotions are the result of irrational thinking. However, these learned irrational beliefs can be changed to a more rational way of looking at life's events.	One must analyze an individual's perception of a situation, which includes the activating event (A), that person's beliefs (B), and the consequences (C), or emotions and behavior. Ellis calls this the ABC model of rational thinking.	Several techniques are used to help individuals think more rationally. These include arguing against assumptions that are not fact, and helping people use a more realistic vocabulary (e.g., "I would prefer that . . ." versus "I should . . ." or "I must . . .").	A recent review of outcome studies (Hajzler & Bernard, 1991) on various school-aged populations revealed positive effects on rational thinking, internal locus of control, anxiety, self-esteem, and behavioral problems. However, the authors caution readers that their conclusions are based solely on studies that were available for examination.
Myrna Shure's Interpersonal Cognitive Problem-Solving Program	A cognitive behavioral approach, this program suggests that if children can learn to think straight (e.g., problem solve), they can relieve their emotional tension.	Misbehavior results when children are unable to think of the possible consequences of their actions. The inability to do this is the result of a lack of learning.	This program has been found to be effective with those students who have difficulty getting along with peers and authority figures. According to Shure, this approach can be taught as early as age four.	Shure & Spivak (1982) have developed a set of skills and steps needed to learn how to problem solve. This includes (1) the ability to generate alternative solutions, (2) the ability to anticipate consequences, and (3) for children nine years of age and older, the ability to develop a step-by-step plan of action that will result in achieving the desired goals and the resolution of interpersonal problems.	Two decades of research had indicated that this program has helped children become (1) less easily frustrated, (2) less likely to become angry when things do not go their way, (3) less impatient, (4) less socially withdrawn, (5) more caring about others, (6) more likely to share and take turns, (7) better able to make friends than other children.
Elias and Clabby's Social-Cognitive Decision-Making & Problem-Solving Skills	This program flows directly from the work of Shure & Spivak (1976), which stresses a core set of skills that incorporates affective and behavioral components.	Misbehaving students lack decision-making skills or the ability to understand feelings and problem situations.	Similar to interpersonal cognitive problem solving program (Shure & Spivak, 1976), this program appears to be most effective with those individuals who have difficulty making decisions, solving problems, identifying feelings, and getting along with others.	Elias and Clabby have identified six components that need to be learned: behavioral self-control, developing constructive relationships with peers and adults, understanding feelings and problems situations, decision making, planning and anticipating obstacles, and applying their learnings to everyday situations.	Extensive research with Elias & Clabby materials has shown a positive impact on children as they negotiate the transitions to middle and high school.

After learning other problem-solving concepts, children are ready for games and dialogues that teach solution and consequential thinking skills, using their own and others' feelings. They learn that if one solution does not work, or is not a good idea, it is possible to try a different way. Most important, teachers and parents are taught ICPS *dialoguing,* a problem-solving communication style. For example, Cheryl's teacher talked to her this way:

T: What happened? What's the matter?

C: It's mine!

T: What happened when you grabbed the clay?

C: She hit me.

T: How do you think Vicki feels when you grab from her?

C: Mad, but I don't care. It's mine!

T: How did you feel when Vicki hit you?

C: Mad.

T: Grabbing is one thing you can do. Can you think of something different you can do so she won't hit you, and you both won't be mad?

C (to V):   Can I have the clay?

V: NO!

T: Oh, you'll have to think of a DIFFERENT, new idea.

C (to V):   If you let me have the clay, I'll build you a castle. Do you like that?

Happy with their own solution, Cheryl felt proud, and the teacher did not have to explain why children should share. This should not be taken to mean that children should always end up with what they want. Good problem solvers can better cope with disappointment, too. One ICPS teacher told Johnny why he could not have play dough at an inconvenient time and asked, "Can you think of something different to do now while you wait?" This child thought for a moment, then gleefully shouted, "I'll go paint." If the teacher had simply said "I can't help you now; why don't you go paint?" the child probably would have whined, "I don't want to paint, I want the play dough."

Initial ICPS and behavioral gains appear to last when measured one and two years later. Impulsive children become less impatient and less likely to explode in the face of frustration. One child, who shied away when the teacher tried to help her into the group, made a dramatic move during the 11th week of the program. She told a group in the doll corner, "If you need a fireman, I'm right here." One of the children who previously ignored her then noticed a pretend fire.

Shure claims that ICPS thinking can prevent serious problems from occurring. The ICPS approach suggests that if children can think straight, they can relieve their emotional tension. Cheryl, who had options, and Johnny, who could not wait, offer good examples of how ICPS can work as a preventive curriculum and as a provider of language to use in solving conflicts.

Elias and Clabby's Social-Cognitive Decision-Making and Problem-Solving Skills

The work of Elias and Clabby (1988, 1989) flows directly from the work of Shure et al. There is a great similarity between the programs, which stress a core set of skills that incorporate affective and behavioral components. The Elias and Clabby materials focus on the elementary and middle school grades and are supported by extensive research, showing positive impact on children as they negotiate the transitions to middle and high school. The skills include six components, which Elias and Clabby call Critical Social-Cognitive Problem-Solving Skills:

Behavioral self-control is an important component in helping all impulsive children. This requires teaching children to: (1) listen carefully and remember accurately, (2) remember and follow directions, (3) converse appropriately with peers, (4) converse appropriately with adults, (5) keep control of self when frustrated and angry, and (6) resist provocation by others.

Constructive relationships with peers and adults are important in establishing an ability to handle conflict. The necessary skills include the ability to: (1) trust and be comfortable with peers, (2) trust and be comfortable with adults, (3) share feelings with classmates, (4) select praiseworthy friends, (5) appropriately ask others for help, and (6) appropriately give help to others.

Many students who misbehave, especially those who are aggressive, lack the skills to *understand feelings and problem situations.* Therefore, they must learn to: (1) recognize other's feelings, (2) recognize their own feelings, (3) put problems into words, and (4) clearly state their goals in problem situations.

Decision making is an important skill for everyone. However, students who frequently misbehave generally lack the skills to systematically think out problems. Therefore, they must learn to: (1) consider more than one way to solve an interpersonal and intrapersonal problem, (2) consider positive and negative consequences of their actions, (3) accurately link various consequences to each alternative solution to a problem, and (4) decide which solution is to their advantage.

Planning and anticipating obstacles are skills used by many successful people. However, misbehavior suggests an inability to anticipate obstacles. Therefore, it is important for students to learn to: (1) consider how a solution should be carried out, (2) anticipate possible obstacles to the solution, (3) recall past experiences with the options selected, and (4) be able to discuss personal examples of past experiences and their failures and successes.

The final step in Elias and Clabby's approach is to teach students to *apply their learning to everyday situations.* This requires practice in group settings and one-on-one sessions. Students must be able to: (1) discuss possible compromises with others, (2) demonstrate personal initiative in resolving problems, (3) demonstrate that they believe that problems can be resolved positively, and (4) apply problem-solving thinking to academic and interpersonal situations.

Summary of Sample Programs

We have considered a variety of behavioral and cognitive–behavioral approaches to prevention and amelioration of discipline problems. The developers and publishers of many of these and similar programs offer workshops and in-service training. Or, by understanding the underlying theory and using these examples, and perhaps with some help from your school psychologists or other similarly trained consultant, you may wish to develop your own curriculum program. We will now present a critique of this model of teacher variance.

Summary, Research and Critique of Behavioral/Cognitive– Behavioral Theory and Techniques

Despite their reliance on the scientific method and simplicity, the behavioral approaches are criticized by those who believe that behavioral control of others is unethical. In the school setting, some think that institutions and bureaucracies have no right to control and manipulate an individual's behavior.

Behavior modification is attacked on philosophical and practical grounds, which suggest that this model does not help children resolve underlying "inner" problems. It is believed that, in many cases, behavior modification may change the symptoms but does little to alleviate the actual problem. Another limitation is that this approach may have harmful effects if not used correctly. It can be abused by insensitive and unethical practitioners. In addition, behavior modification, as opposed to cognitive–behavioral approaches, does not consider emotions important, it does not let children use their rational abilities, and precise record keeping is needed to determine its success.

Yet, behavioral techniques have been demonstrated to be very powerful in shaping and changing people's behavior. They are the only successful alternatives to drugs for a variety of problems such as anxiety and depression. Applied behavioral analysis (ABA) and functional analysis work well with children with severe disabilities, depression, anxiety, and obesity, and in ever-increasing numbers of problems. Yet, many, including teachers, are deeply suspicious of techniques that control and modify others. In a democratic society, in which free will is extolled, we do not want others to manipulate us. The movie *Clockwork Orange* presents the classical dilemma. Should we rob, even the most vicious psychopaths, of their free will in order to condition them not to commit crimes?

Some educators find ABA practices unacceptable, unethical, and immoral because of the attempt to "bribe" students to do what they should do anyway. Some suggest that this model does not help children resolve underlying "inner" problems. Extrinsic rewards are no substitute for intrinsic motivations. Therefore, ABA may change the symptoms, but it may do little to alleviate underlying problems. Also, because the approach is so powerful, especially in the use of aversive procedures, there is always the risk of abuse when applied by insensitive and unethical practitioners.

ABA requires precise record keeping to determine its success. Many teachers complain that with 25 to 35 students in their class, they do not have the time to keep specific data on even one student throughout the day. Similarly, Doyle (1990) adds that ABA's complex systems of token economies, contingency management, and ignoring undesirable behavior while reinforcing desired behavior may not be practical for individual classroom teachers. This is because most educators lack the assistance of independent observers and support personnel.

Despite the documented effectiveness of the strategies and techniques of ABA, educators have been slow to adopt them for everyday use in the classrooms (Skinner & Hales, 1992). Some researchers (e.g., Axelrod, 1993) have suggested reasons that educational personnel reject ABA principles and procedures:

1. The tendency of educators to use the same procedures, even though evidence supports more effective approaches
2. The historical image of ABA as a procedure appropriate only for institutionalized people and animals
3. The resistance by many to the perceived "control" produced by ABA procedures as opposed to behavior change from "within"
4. The lack of positive exposure from the media
5. The perception of many educators that classroom behavior is caused by a variety of factors outside of a behavioral explanation, such as a developmental or psychodynamic orientation

Most behaviorally based strategies for improving children's academic and social functioning in the classroom has focused on the manipulation of consequences. These reinforcement procedures have been applied effectively to a diverse group of social goals, such as social skills development (Odom et al., 1985) and classroom disruption (Fowler, 1982). However, the manipulation of consequences has not always proven successful as a means of altering children's behavior (Carr et al., 1980). As a result, researchers are beginning to look at the effects of manipulating behavioral antecedents. For example, as described earlier, Hamlet et al. (1984) used a stimulus-control paradigm to investigate the effects of demanded eye contact between teachers and students as a setting event for compliance.

Studies have also assessed the effectiveness of decreasing undesirable behavior. Research on behavioral interventions has demonstrated a clear preference for positive over reductive techniques by both teachers and children (Reimers et al., 1987). In addition, with regard to verbal reprimands, Van Houten et al. (1982) discovered praise plus soft reprimands to be more effective at decreasing disruptive behavior than praise plus loud reprimands delivered from across the room.

Response cost, in contrast, has been found to be a time-efficient and effective classroom intervention (Witt & Elliot, 1982). Similarly, exclusion time-out, one type of time-out procedure, alters the behavior of target as well as nontarget children (Roberts, 1988; Wilson et al., 1979).

Recent methods of delivering reinforcement have been employed that decrease teacher involvement while maintaining program effectiveness. These include self-monitoring/self-reinforcement (Christie et al., 1984; Merrett & Houghton, 1989), peer reinforcement (Greenwood et al., 1988), and home-based interventions (Martens & Meller, 1989; Turco & Elliot, 1986). These three have been found to be effective in maintaining productive school behavior.

The cognitive–behavioral approach offers a technique that is much like teaching. It can be used with individuals and the whole class. Curricula in social problem solving and self-talk can be proactive and used for prevention. The limitation is that the practitioner must be trusted by the student(s) and must be able to talk rationally and calmly when discussing issues. Also, the practitioner/teacher must be able to discuss his or her own possible contributions to the misbehavior without becoming defensive.

Cognitive–behavioral approaches seem rational. However, a review of outcome studies suggests that their effectiveness is not yet convincing, especially with older students, in terms of skills and new thinking generalizing to real-life situations (Blum, 1994). Also, although it may be easy to teach them in class, there is relatively little evidence that children's actual behavior changes dramatically from this curriculum approach. Furthermore, many oppositional students, especially adolescents, openly resist the training if they can. Even when they are forced to learn the techniques, there is little evidence they carry through in real-life situations.

We have now examined behavioral theory, practice, and programs. This should provide you with sufficient information to begin to become expert in this area. Next we turn to a completely different approach.

Key Terms

ABC (antecedent, behavior, consequence)
antecedent
aversive procedures and techniques
baseline data
behavior modification
behavioral rehearsal
behavioral self-control
conditioned reinforcement
consequences
consequent events
contingency contracting
contingency management
continuous reinforcement schedule
decision making
dialoging
differential reinforcement of alternative behavior
differential reinforcement of other behavior
discriminative stimulus
duration recordings
exclusionary time-out
extinction
feedback
frequency recording

functional analysis
group contingencies
ignoring
in vivo implementation
instruction
intermittent reinforcement schedule
internal dialogue
interval recordings
irrational thinking
measurement of lasting products
modeling
negative reinforcement
nonexclusionary time-out
observable behavior reinforcement
operant reinforcement
overcorrection
overt behavior
partial reinforcement schedule
positive reinforcement
primary reinforcement
relaxation skills
response cost
reward

role playing
seclusionary time-out
self-control interventions
self-determined reinforcer
self-talk
social problem solving
social reinforcement

social skills
subsequent events
target behavior
time sampling recordings
time-out
token economy
unconditioned reinforcement

Application Activities

1. Diagnose Juanita from a behavioral approach. Develop intervention and treatment using reinforcement and reward techniques.

2. Diagnose Michael from a behavioral approach. Develop intervention and treatment using punishment techniques.

3. Diagnose Jamal using a cognitive behavioral approach. Develop intervention and treatment using reinforcement and reward techniques.

4. Diagnose Chris using a cognitive behavioral approach. Develop intervention and treatment using punishment techniques.

5. Develop a social skills training program for Juanita using Shure's I Can Problem Solve program.

6. Develop a social problem-solving program for Jamal using Elias & Clabby's Social Decision-Making Skills.

7. Develop a social skills training program for Michael using Elliott and Gresham's Social Skills Intervention Guide.

8. Develop a whole-class lesson plan for social skills development using Ellis's Rational Emotive Education.

Suggested Readings

Alberto, P. A., & Troutman, A. C. (1990). *Applied behavioral analysis for teachers* (3rd ed.). Columbus, OH: Merrill Publishing.

Beck, A. T. (1976). *Cognitive therapy and emotional disorders.* New York: New American Library.

Elias, M. J., & Clabby, J. F. (1989). *Social decision-making skills: A curriculum guide for the elementary grades.* Rockville, MD: Aspen Press.

Elliott, S. N., & Gresham, F. (1991). *Social skills intervention guide.* Circle Pines, MN: American Guidance Service.

Ellis, A., & Bernard, M. (1983). *Rational-emotive approaches to the problems of childhood.* New York: Plenum.

Ellis, A., & Dryden, W. (1987). *The practice of rational emotive therapy.* Secaucus, NJ: Stuart Lyle.

Morris, R. J., & Kratochwill T. (1983). *Treating children's fears and phobias: A behavioral approach.* New York: Pergamon Press.

Shure, M. (1992). *I can problem solve (ICPS).* Champaign, IL: Research Press.

Skinner, B. F. (1953). *Science and human behavior.* New York: Macmillan.

Stephens, T. M. (1992). *Social skills in the classroom.* Odessa, FL: PAR.

Waksman, S., Messmer, C. L., & Waksman, D. D. (1988). *The Waksman social skills curriculum* (3rd ed.). Austin, TX: PRO-ED.

Wolery, M., Bailey, D. B., & Sugai, G. M. (1988). *Effective teaching: Principles and procedures of applied behavioral analysis with exceptional students.* Needham Heights, MA: Allyn & Bacon.

Walker, H. M., McConnell, S., Holmes, D., Todis, B., Walker, J., & Golden, N. (1988). *The Walker social skills curriculum: The ACCEPTS program.* Austin, TX: PRO-ED.

Walker, H. M., Todis, B., Holmes, B., & Horton, G. (1988). *The Walker social skills curriculum: The ACCESS program.* Austin, TX: PRO-ED.

Chapter 4

Psychodynamic/ Interpersonal Approach

Chapter Objectives

After reading this chapter, you should know:

1. The assumptions, interventions, treatment, and techniques of the psychodynamic/ interpersonal model
2. Freud's three components of the mind and defense mechanisms
3. Adlerian theory
4. Erikson's psychosocial stages of development
5. Berne's transactional analysis
6. Piaget's theory of moral development
7. Kohlberg's theory of moral development
8. Examples of psychodynamic/interpersonal models, including Dreikurs, Dinkmeyer, Albert, Berne, Redl and Wattenberg, and Ginott

The Psychodynamic/Interpersonal Approach (P/IA) within the teacher variance model is based on the assumption that all personality and behavior develop as a result of interactions with significant others during crucial developmental stages. If you are strong in this approach, you believe that:

1. Personality and behavior are strongly influenced by inherent, genetically programmed drives and needs.
2. Various drives and needs emerge at specific developmental stages.
3. Personality is shaped by the nature of the interaction with parents and significant others during each stage.
4. Misbehavior may occur if children and youth do not make adequate adjustments during each developmental stage.

5. The nature and quality of parenting during the stages of development up to about five or six years of life are crucial in determining later adjustment.
6. Misbehavior is often the result of patterns of inadequate or deviant parenting passed from one generation to another.
7. Misbehavior is almost always associated with poor self-image and low self-esteem.
8. Misbehavior is often a function of behavior that has not matured during a particular developmental period or of inadequate ability to handle anxiety.

Underlying Theory

Psychoanalytic Foundations

The psychodynamic/interpersonal approach is rooted in the works of Sigmund Freud (1933) and later his daughter Anna Freud's (1965) work with schoolchildren (Hall, 1979). Freud began his career in the late 1800s and published his first book on psychoanalysis in 1900, at a time when behavior was attributed to the chemistry of the mind and consciousness. Freud postulated that behavior was driven by unconscious impulses and drives. You will recall from earlier course work that he theorized that the mind is made up of three components: the *id* or libido, the *ego,* and the *superego.* His structure of personality is reviewed in Table 4.1.

Psychoanalysis is based on the assumption that we are driven by inherited, instinctual impulses. These impulses are controlled by the appropriate development of the ego and superego during critical developmental stages. Because these developmental stages occur most often within the context of the family, misbehavior is best understood by studying a child's history within the family. Freud believed that to develop a full and healthy personality, people must master various stages. These stages are the oral, anal, phallic, latency, and genital.

During these stages, both parents have important roles. However, Freud, who focused more on the development and problems of males, conceptualized the father as being pivotal in the development of the personality characteristics that most directly affect discipline. He considered the father the primary force underlying the development of the superego or conscience. This occurs during the "Oedipal stage" for boys and the "Electra stage" for girls, around three to five years of age, when children establish their sexual identity. The major love object for children is the opposite-sex parent. But the family and society do not allow this relationship. To avoid sanctions by the opposite-sex parent, the child learns to identify with the same-sex parent.

Defense Mechanisms
Defense mechanisms are procedures that the ego uses to defend against anxieties aroused under extreme pressures. In the struggle for balance between id, ego, and superego, children may become anxious when one system predominates. They attempt to control anxiety by unconscious "defense mechanisms." Lack of appropriate defense mechanisms or overuse of them leads to self-defeating, "neurotic behavior," which may manifest as misbehavior.

TABLE 4.1   Freud's Organization of Personality

	System		
	Id	**Ego**	**Superego**
Function	Reduces or eliminates tension The pleasure principle avoids pain and finds pleasure	Executive of the personality Controlling and governing the id and superego Balances the needs of the person with the external world The reality principle postpones the discharge of energy until the actual object that will satisfy the need is present	Moral representation of the personality that consists of the values and traditions of the society handed down from parents to children Strives for perfection
Processes	Reduces tension by either impulsive motor activity or image formation Primary process, or wish fulfullment, is a mental image of an object needed to reduce tension	The secondary process uses thoughts and reason to develop a plan of action to obtain the actual object that will satisfy one's needs Reality testing is putting a plan of action into effect to determine if it will work and satisfy one's needs	Consists of two subsystems The ego ideal is what the child's parents consider to be morally acceptable The conscience is what the child thinks the parents consider to be morally bad
Purpose	Subjective reality of an inner world of the mind with no regard to the external world	Separates the subjective world of the mind from the objective world of the environment	Subjective reality of an inner world of the mind with no regard to the external world
Product	Product of evolution consisting of impulses and reflexes	Product of interaction with the environment	Product of socialization and culture

In psychodynamic thinking, neurotic, self-destructive behavior leads to a negative self-concept, which in turn can lead to misbehavior.

For instance, every teacher has had a class clown like Joe. Joe never misses an opportunity to make a wisecrack, to mimic others, and to make himself the center of attention just to get a laugh. Joe is also very bright, but his grades are poor because of his misbehavior. A psychodynamic explanation of Joe would suggest that he sees himself as a clown rather than a serious student. Here is what Joe subconsciously says: "When I was in the first grade, I tried very hard and failed at a few tests. Everybody told me that I was smart and could do it if I try. But when I really try, I fail; therefore, I must be stupid. But even if I'm stupid, people seem to like me when I act silly. In fact, I'm better at being silly than I am at being a good student. Besides, I get very nervous when I try to do well in school. Even when I do well, it's probably because the test is too easy, the teacher likes me, or it's just a fluke. I know that they say I have a high IQ, but I don't believe it."

It is clear that Joe gets quite anxious when he tries to do well in school. It is also clear that he gets a lot of attention for being a clown. He defends himself from the anxiety that he feels about schoolwork by using several defense mechanisms. He uses *denial* of the reality that he really is bright because, in his mind, brightness is associated with good grades. He thinks he cannot obtain good grades, because a few times he failed and was made to feel stupid. Even when faced with good test scores, he distorts the reality that he really earned the good grade.

In addition to denial, Joe uses the defense mechanism of *rationalization*. Rationalization is the process by which he makes excuses for his clownish behavior, which clearly gets him in trouble. He convinces himself that his sense of humor is much more valued in the long run than good test grades.

Projection is another defense mechanism that is widely used by misbehaving children. Brian is always getting into fights. Although he does not physically start all of the fights, he constantly needles other children. As a result of his behavior, teachers are vigilant when he is around. Sometimes, he may even be an innocent bystander, but he still gets blamed for starting the fight.

Brian's self-concept is that he is a courageous and valiant defender of himself and his family honor. His behavior is only a reaction to a hostile environment. Therefore, his aggression and anger are appropriate because he projects all blame on others. When confronted with solid evidence of his misbehavior, rather than deal with the anxiety that would be aroused if he were not the valiant person that he perceives, he blames others for what happened.

Displacement is often related to family dysfunction. Sara's father is abusive toward her and her mother. Although she is very angry with him for beating her and her mother, Sara is unable to effectively retaliate. In addition, her brother has begun to act toward females the way that her father has. As a result, Sara has developed an intense dislike of males. Sara is afraid to express her anger at her father, who will in turn beat her up. However, she can relatively safely take it out on her male teachers, because they are unlikely to physically retaliate. This type of displacement is very difficult to work with because, if Sara realizes that some males are decent, she might become quite anxious at having to form a relationship that might end up in a beating.

Regression is a defense often seen in young children with new siblings in the family. Frankie, a first-grader, begins to wet his pants, suck his thumb, and become clinging and whiney. This behavior can be easily explained from a psychodynamic point of view. Although Frankie received a lot of attention for being a "big boy" like his father, he now finds that his parents' attention is focused on the dependent behavior of the new daughter. Frankie is unconsciously fearful that he will lose the love of his parents. His anxiety is allayed by regressing. This newly developed immature behavior results in more attention from his parents.

Sublimation is the process by which unacceptable drives and needs are rechanneled into socially accepted activities. This is ultimately the most civilized method of dealing with unacceptable needs and drives. High achievers in academics, sports, and cultural and vocational activities have successfully sublimated strong primary drives. However, unconscious sexual drives may break through the defensive sublimation. For instance, teachers may be shocked when they hear that Jane, usually described as a wholesome, straight A, top athlete, all-American-type 17-year-old, was caught experimenting with marijuana or having sex with her boyfriend. Because all people are driven by the pleasure principle, even Jane, a "goody-goody" student and a highly successful sublimator, could not completely control her curiosity and libidinal drives.

Repression and *suppression* are processes by which the ego attempts to forget about unpleasant memories. In repression, a dangerous memory, idea, or perception is forced out of the conscious mind. In this process, a barrier is erected between the memory and the conscious mind. Teachers must understand repression, especially because it may help to explain abnormal-appearing student sexual behavior caused by sexual abuse. Because this type of abuse interferes so severely with normal development, the child may try to completely repress the experience. But it is so overwhelming that it may lead to a breakdown of the defense mechanism. The child may even develop another personality, which is one that was not abused and has nothing to do with sex.

For instance, one of the results of early abuse is sexual acting out (Walker, 1988). Therefore, any sign of excessive interest in a child's own genitalia, frequent talking about sex, continual flirting, and promiscuity would lead to a hypothesis of early sexual abuse.

For example, frequent masturbation in primary grades is very disturbing to teachers and other children. However, this should not be treated as a disciplinary problem but should suggest to the teacher, after medically ruling out urinary infection or other disease, the possibility of either actual sexual abuse, molestation, or exposure to adult sexuality. This could include witnessing older children or adults or watching inappropriate television. The hypothesis of early sexual abuse should always be considered, no matter what the age, when students appear to be excessively interested in sex. This determination should be made by a trained professional, because uncovering early memories can be extremely disturbing and possibly cause psychosis. Furthermore, there is great controversy regarding some therapists who, through either unconscious suggestion or as a result of ideology, discover lost memories of sexual abuse (Ceci & Bruck, 1995).

Suppression is a process by which a person consciously pushes memories out of the conscious mind. Unlike repression, in which the memories are not available, in suppression the memories are available to the conscious mind. For instance, Sean, a fifth-grader, was caught cheating on a social studies test. He had written crib notes, which were up his sleeve during the test. He was so anxious that when he got up to leave, the notes dropped out of his shirt sleeve and were seen by the teacher. The teacher was infuriated and loudly berated Sean in front of the other children. The following year, Sean developed a great deal of anxiety about taking tests. As a result, his grades began to suffer. His parents were puzzled because Sean had generally been a good student despite the incident during the past year. His parents knew that he had been studying diligently and that he really wanted to do well.

During the initial interview in therapy, Sean admitted to me that he had cheated during the previous year. He had been able to keep the information a secret and had struggled through fifth grade. However, he did not make a big deal of the cheating incident, because it was only one part of his history. In his responses on projective tests, for which he was asked to make up stories about children in various ambiguous situations, there were under-lying themes of cheating and getting caught. He often described children in the pictures dis-gracing themselves. Sean made no connection between the cheating incident and his current problem with tests. However, it was apparent that, although Sean had suppressed many of the memories about being disgraced in class, the anxiety aroused by the uncon-scious memories made him extremely fearful that he would do something during a test that would suggest that he was cheating. He used an inordinate amount of energy to control these fears and was not able to concentrate on the test. In therapy, Sean was able to discuss all of this and gain insight into what was happening. As a result, he realized that, although he should not have cheated, many other kids do cheat, and it does not necessarily mean that he is unworthy and never capable of love and respect from teachers. He accepted that he had been punished by the situation and had punished himself for almost a year. His super-ego was satisfied, and his ego allowed him to remember that he had cheated but that he had repented, and he was now an OK person.

Adlerian Theory

One of Freud's disciples, Alfred Adler, departed from his mentor's belief in the primacy of inborn instincts. Adler's theory of individual psychology is based on the belief that all behavior is purposive, that is, *goal directed.* All of our actions are performed to serve a pur-pose or obtain a payoff. Adler did not deny the existence of inborn drives, but he believed that the primary drives are related to the need for social interaction. He believed that chil-dren are inherently social beings and are governed by certain social determinants such as the drive for acceptance and approval.

Adler observed that when children did not feel accepted, competent, or to belong to desired groups, they developed bad feelings about themselves. To account for this, he devel-oped the concept of the *inferiority complex,* which may result in misbehavior when children are frustrated in the drive towards competence. He and his disciples translated the theory for use in the school situation. The focus is on helping teachers to understand the underlying causes of behavior rather than giving them specific techniques to use. That is, individual children must be understood in terms of their uniquely determined goals. Rather than focus on unconscious drives and motivations, he focused on people's conscious perceptions of their perceived inferiorities.

Adler's theories are important for educators because Rudolf Dreikers and Donald Din-kmeyer applied them to the development of major discipline training programs. These actual programs are discussed near the end of this chapter.

Erik Erikson's Psychosocial Theory

Erik Erikson's (1964, 1968, 1982) eight stages of man represents an important psychosocial construct that builds on traditional psychoanalytic theory. Erikson posited that (1) there are psychosocial stages of ego development that exist side-by-side with the psychosexual stages described by Freud; (2) personality development takes place throughout the life cycle; and (3) each stage has a positive as well as a negative component. His major contri-bution is the concept that individuals have to reorient themselves and decide their identities at each stage. Because Erikson's stages are taught in basic psychology and development courses to most undergraduates, we review them briefly in Table 4.2 and present examples of how they are relevant to school discipline.

TABLE 4.2   Erikson's Stages of Psychosocial Development

Stage	Ages	Developmental Tasks	Significant Relationships
Trust vs. mistrust	Infancy Birth to 18 Months	The infant needs to trust that the basic needs of feeding, caring, and safety are met.	The relationship with the initial caretaker, usually the mother
Autonomy vs. self-doubt	Toddler 18 months to 3 years	The toddler needs to develop control of body functions such as feeding, elimination, and dressing.	Relationships with both parents or primary caretakers
Initiative vs. guilt	Early childhood 3 to 6 years	The young child needs to explore the environment for the sake of activity and curiosity.	Relationships with the nuclear family and close family friends
Industry vs. inferiority	Later childhood 6 to 12 years	The older child needs to develop confidence in his or her ability to do things successfully, such as schoolwork.	Relationship with the extended family, neighbors, teachers, and peers
Identity vs. role confusion	Adolescence 12 to 18 years	The adolescent needs to develop an identity not based on the desires of others, but based on one's own interests and desires.	Relationships with peer groups

Adapted from *Childhood and Society* by Erik H. Erikson. Copyright © 1950, 1963 by W. W. Norton & Company, Inc., renewed Copyright © 1978, 1991 by Erik H. Erikson. Reprinted by permission of W. W. Norton & Company, Inc.

In the first stage, trust versus mistrust, when care is inadequate, inconsistent, and rejecting, the child learns fear, suspicion, and mistrust of caregivers, including teachers. If this mistrust is not resolved, the child may be doomed, to protect the ego, to a life of fear, mistrust, and self-defeating behaviors. Students who turn to self-destructive, delinquent behavior never learn to compensate for the lack of appropriate nurturance during this first, crucial stage of development.

In the second stage, autonomy versus self-doubt, either overprotective or overdemanding parents can cause the child difficulties in later life. At this crucial stage, if the parents are overly critical or excessively punitive, the feelings of doubt, worthlessness, and shame will predominate over a healthy sense of autonomy. The result may be students who are chronic underachievers. They have frequent rationalizations for low grades, inadequate or missing homework assignments, and lack of interest in extracurricular activities.

Too much autonomy, especially in the absence of realistic limits, also can be harmful. The result can be overbearing, demanding, selfish children who demand of everyone and give to nobody.

Children who leave this stage with serious feelings of shame and doubt will have great difficulty at other stages of life when they need to establish autonomy, especially during adolescence. Correcting the problem at this stage is a lot easier than dealing with it in adolescence.

During initiative and guilt, if children are made to feel stupid, silly, or ridiculous when they initiate play, express ideas, or act out fantasies, they may develop into guilt-ridden adolescents and adults. As students, they may be easily manipulated by peers. They may be concrete in their thinking and unable to act creatively in solving social problems.

During the stage of industry versus inferiority, if children's efforts and enthusiasm are thwarted, ridiculed, or denied, they will develop a sense of inferiority. Feelings of inferiority result in giving up easily in school, rarely completing assignments, and misbehaving to divert attention from school failures. These students may later identify with counterculture groups at either end of the political spectrum. They are equally vulnerable to becoming either Dead Heads or Skinheads.

During identity versus role confusion, inconsistent enforcement of school rules cause immature students great difficulty. A person with a mature world view recognizes that consistency and fairness are not always forthcoming and that it cannot be achieved by self-defeating rebellion against authority. Immature adolescents, however, often refuse to follow any school rules because some of them are not properly enforced.

The adolescent who is unable to achieve a positive identity develops role confusion. Approximately 20 percent of adolescents have great difficulty in the struggle to find themselves (Diamenti, 1992). This is especially true when they arrive at this stage with feelings of mistrust, shame, doubt, inferiority, guilt, and confusion about who they are. Students with healthy role identities harness their youthful energy by becoming active in socially approved work, clubs, organizations, and causes. Those with role confusion may identify with antisocial behaviors, be easily recruited into cults or gangs, develop addictions, and be lead to self-destructive lifestyles. For girls, this may mean promiscuity and its inherent stigmatization by peers and school staff. Take the case of Marybeth, who was referred to me because of frequent rule breaking, suspected promiscuity, and depression.

The Case of Marybeth

I saw Marybeth when she was a 16-year-old boarding student in a private, independent school. Her parents put her there because she had reported them twice to the child abuse authorities. All of the children in her family were physically and psychologically abused by both parents when the parents were drunk or high. The mother frequently checked herself into drug rehabilitation centers for weeks at a time. The father, who denied his addictions, was of little help in caring for the children when the mother was away. Most of the charges were for neglect, rather than life-threatening physical abuse, and the parents were sent back to their therapists and drug rehabilitation.

Marybeth was very attractive and had been a model since she was young. She was the oldest of four children and was frequently left to care for her siblings. She talked about her siblings as "my kids," and she took on major child-rearing responsibilities when the parents were physically or psychologically unavailable. Fortunately, a live-in housekeeper and grandparents were available to provide transportation and basic needs.

The school staff saw Marybeth as an angry, rebellious, flirtatious rebel. She was referred to me by her roommate because of increasing depression, suicidal ideation, promiscuous behavior that seemed to her friends to be self-destructive, and refusal to obey dorm rules. She often managed to attract staff attention to herself and her friends and as a result they all were disciplined, primarily because of her misbehavior.

In school, despite her tardiness, truancy, and oppositional behavior, and because of her high IQ, Marybeth always managed to obtain passing grades and sometimes made the honor role. Some teachers were surprised at her flashes of brilliance and insight. She had few female friends and generally had trouble relating to her classmates. She disdained the staff who taught in the private Catholic schools she attended and enjoyed subverting school staff when they tried to enforce rules, especially those rules that she considered unreasonable. This behavior ended in expulsions from several of the schools.

Unfortunately, because of failure to completely resolve any of the first five critical psychosocial stages, especially because of abuse from her parents and because of her need to identify herself as a healer rather than an abuser, Marybeth tended to date boys she could nurture and "save." Or she selected boys who would completely indulge her in return for sex, which she confused with love. She was able to attract rich, egocentric, selfish young men who sometimes demeaned her in public and convinced her to do their homework and minister to them when they did not feel well.

I consulted with Ms. Reston, Marybeth's English teacher, who was also her dorm parent. She had tried to get close to Marybeth but felt quite rejected. Her statements, demeanor, and voice inflections all suggested that unconsciously she was jealous of Marybeth, who seemed to flaunt her beauty, brains, and affluence to manipulate peers and school staff and to subvert dormitory rules. Marybeth "played the game" with Ms. Reston by feigning remorse, agreeing with the logic of the almost weekly lectures, and then again breaking the rules.

This case is presented to exemplify the complexity of understanding and diagnosing problems that result from faulty opportunities to develop appropriately through Erickson's stages. From the beginning, trust was not established. Marybeth's parents did not provide opportunities for autonomy, initiation of adequate exploratory behavior and related self-esteem, or praise for her sense of industry. Finally, neither parent provided appropriate role models to establish identity.

In therapy, Marybeth responded very well to empathetic listening. Some of her issues were resolved by psychodynamic, insight-oriented therapy. She made the connection between her own upbringing and the reasons she allowed herself to be abused by boys. She also recognized that she was not completely responsible for her siblings and began to garner a larger network of adult support. She began to identify the healthy as well as the neurotic aspects of her need to "save" people and began to consider the helping professions as a possible career.

With consultation, Ms. Reston also began to understand her own internal conflicts about Marybeth. She began to understand that, rather than lectures, Marybeth needed someone to listen to her. Furthermore, Ms. Reston expected that the attention she gave Marybeth should be returned by loyalty and obedience. She had difficulty accepting that Marybeth saw her as an authority figure but was also looking for female role models who could accept and respect her.

The example of Marybeth demonstrates how poor parenting and the stresses of contemporary society can make adolescence a most difficult period of life. It is especially challenging, even for young people who are basically well adjusted, when they must deal with adult bodies and responsibilities and yet be financially dependent on parents during the stage of identity versus role-confusion. ■

Eric Berne's Transactional Analysis

Eric Berne, originally trained in psychoanalysis, was a psychiatrist in California, who, in the 1950s, developed an approach to therapy called Transactional Analysis (TA). He envisioned TA as a rational approach to understanding behavior. It is framed within the belief that all individuals can learn to "trust themselves, think for themselves, and make their own decisions" (Berne, 1969). Berne believed that TA could be used anywhere people had to deal with others, such as home, work, and school.

Operating from the basic premise that every person is born to be a "winner," TA offers a positive way of looking at ourselves and others (Harris, 1969). Even though a "loser" image may occasionally appear, the potential exists for people to exercise a great deal of control over their lives. According to this model, people have the ability to identify behaviors they want to change and the ability to implement the change. To change, people must identify their own ego states. Berne hypothesized that these ego states consist of permanently recorded scripts in the brain. There are three ego states that form the basis for Berne's concept of personality: the *Parent,* the *Child,* and the *Adult.* These are reviewed in Table 4.3.

If the parent ego state reflects parents who are constantly negative, derogatory, and punitive, the student and later the adult might be dominated by a negative, punitive parent ego state without knowing why. Students with this problem may seem utterly self-destructive by constantly repeating misbehaviors for which they are frequently caught and punished. When asked for the cause of these repetitive misbehaviors, they often respond by stating, "I don't know why I did it." The truth may well be that they really do not know why.

If the child ego state develops beliefs that "I'm not OK" rather than "I'm OK," the student may be constantly oppositional, yet continue to get caught and punished.

The adult in a student can also cause problems when it is not appropriate. Consistent experiences of unreasonable demands of parents can result in resistance in children. Increases in resistance and oppositional behavior may engender increasing cycles of punishment and perceived rejection from parents. Conversely, when reasonable demands are made, when parents constantly praise children, their child ego state says "I'm OK." As the parent state and the child state interact within the child and between the child and parents, multiple scripts are recorded. These unconscious scripts then determine the behavior that children will carry with them to school.

For instance, when Tina, who grew up in an overly critical and punitive home, entered first grade, her modus operandi was determined by her ego states, as it is with all children. The parent state tells her, "You must be good, you must behave, etc." Therefore, she listens to the teacher and appears overly submissive. However, because she is dominated by the parent state, she is demanding, critical, and harsh with playmates.

TABLE 4.3   Berne's Structural Analysis of Ego States in Social Activities

	Ego State		
	Parent	**Adult**	**Child**
Functions	Enables individuals to act effectively as parents of children	Needed for survival as it deals with the outside world	Contains intuition, creativity, spontaneous drive, and enjoyment
	Learns responses automatically, which saves time and energy	Regulates activities of parent and child	
		Mediates between parent and child	
Forms	*Direct,* or *active ego state,* in which people respond as their parents would have responded		The *adapted child* modifies responses to parental wishes, or withdraws
	Indirect, or *influence,* in which people respond as they think their parents would have wanted them to respond		The *natural child* is spontaneous

Adapted from: Berne, E. (1964). *Games people play.* New York: Grove Press. Copyright © 1964 by Eric Berne. Reprinted by permission of Random House, Inc.

Transactional Analysis stresses the importance of touch and recognition in the development and maintenance of personality adjustment. TA proposes that each person has an innate need for strokes (recognition) and will design a life script (plan) during childhood that is based on early beliefs about him/herself and others. Strokes may be (1) positive or negative, (2) contact or noncontact, or (3) conditional or unconditional. Strokes shape early beliefs about oneself. Inappropriate stroking can result in repetitive, stereotyped games with others. For example, because of repeated negative strokes, some children may develop a life script of "I am not OK." As a result, they resort to "acting out" to receive attention. This reinforces their "not OK" scripts and serves as an excuse for not improving behavior.

Transactions are units of human communication that can occur on the social level, which is overt or manifest, and on the psychological level, which is covert or latent. Transactions occur every time a person interacts with another. Three types of transactions originate from the ego states and may occur in any combination: complimentary, crossed, and ulterior. These are reviewed in Table 4.4 on page 96.

Complementary transactions are important for effective discipline because it is extremely important for teachers to remain in the adult ego state when managing student behavior.

Crossed transactions are often the source of misunderstanding between teachers and students. For instance, when Ms. Grant, a 12th-grade teacher, says, "Tim, you are a spoiled brat; you don't deserve to be in my class and I am going to send you to the principal to pun-

TABLE 4.4 Berne's Types of Social Transactions

	Type of Transactions		
	Complementary Transactions	**Crossed Transactions**	**Ulterior Transactions**
Definition	Communication proceeds smoothly and can proceed indefinitely	Communication is broken off	Involves more than two ego states simultaneously
	Simple complementary transactions occur in superficial working and social relationships		Angular ulterior transactions involve three ego states
			Duplex ulterior transactions involve four ego states
Interactions	Parent to parent	When an adult/adult transaction is attempted but the response is a parent/child or child/parent	If a salesman tells a customer that "This one is better but you can't afford it," it is an Adult/Adult transaction on the social level. The customer responding as an Adult would agree with the salesman. However, the ulterior psychological level is talking to the customer's Child, who responds with "I'll take it" regardless of the financial burden it entails.
	Adult to adult		
	Child to child		
	Parent to child		
	Child to parent		
	Parent to adult		
	Adult to parent		
	Adult to child		
	Child to adult		

Adapted from: Berne, E. (1964). *Games people play.* New York: Grove Press. Copyright © 1964 by Eric Berne. Reprinted by permission of Random House, Inc.

ish you," she is using her parent ego to address Tim as if he were a child. He will therefore respond like a child rather than as an 18-year-old high school senior.

Ulterior transactions initiated by teachers cause many ongoing discipline problems. A typical example occurs when Mr. Bowers says, "I've done everything I can for you, Steve, and you still get into fights almost every day in the class." The ulterior communication is, "I've had it with you. I can't stand you." (Curwin & Mendler, 1988).

With its easily understood theory and emphasis on communication, TA was readily adapted as a classroom discipline approach (Ernst, 1973). When applied to the classroom, TA's major components are (Overman, 1979): (1) understanding transactions, which are based on a person's state of mind when communicating with others; (2) analysis of the three ego states; and (3) the teacher's role in avoiding passivity and stressing the need for students to think and care for their own needs.

Passivity refers to behavior that discounts a situation, the significance of the situation, or a solution to a situation. Teachers need to avoid or minimize passive behavior in the classroom. For example, Mr. Bond says, "I can't do much to stop Reggie's aggressive behavior except report him to the principal. After all, his father and mother are both aggressive, obnoxious people, and he is just following in their footsteps."

Problem solving is used as a means of reducing passivity in the classroom. The key to problem solving is the belief that something can be done to improve a situation without controlling other people. In the above example, Mr. Bond could call Reggie's parents and say, "You know, I know that Reggie is not happy underneath and you can't enjoy the constant calls about his fighting in school or his suspensions. We have a problem that we can solve only if we work together. I know that you have problems with Reggie at home, and they are not so different from my problems with him at school. Let's try to work on this together."

Contracting is the procedure for translating problem solving into action. Generated from the adult ego state, contracts state explicitly what behavior will occur. Contracting will work if the teacher recognizes a crossed transaction and negotiates a written contact with the student. It should recognize each person's role in solving the problem and what each must do to solve the problem. For example, Mr. Gates agrees not to talk to Jim as if he were a baby, and Jim agrees to stop whining if he is asked to do something he does not like. Instead, he will ask to discuss it when Mr. Gates has time, he will tell Mr. Gates exactly why he cannot do it, and if it is unreasonable, Mr. Gates will negotiate a change in the requirement.

Berne proposed that people have various scripts that they use in particular situations. These scripts are used to play "games." Classroom "games" that students play must be understood in order to stop them (Ernst, 1973).

For instance, students may play "uproar" by engaging in such activities as knuckle cracking, finger tapping, or pen clicking. When admonished by the teacher, such students say they are being picked on and shortly resume the game with another form of distraction.

Playing "clown" is often a popular game. The "clown" is generally well liked by the teacher and students, and can be found mimicking the actions of teachers or others to the delight of his or her peers. This is usually done when the teacher's back is turned.

Students playing "make me" simply refuse to do assignments or to perform necessary requirements. When questioned, these students will directly challenge the teacher, placing the teacher in the position of a persecutor.

TA recommends that teacher strategies for dealing with games of misbehavior should include (1) analyzing the game that the student is playing, (2) refusing to play the game, (3) allowing the child to find his or her own solution, and (4) giving strokes or attention that affirm the child's worth.

Research-Generated Developmental/ Interpersonal Theories

We have discussed theorists who have developed their approach from purely psychodynamic considerations. All have some roots in psychoanalytical theory, although some presented moved from theories of instinctual, sexual, pleasure-driven needs toward more socially oriented needs. However, all posit the importance of stages and the crucial nature of caregivers who interact with children as they pass through each stage.

Piaget and Kohlberg are not usually thought of in terms of misbehavior, school discipline, and the development of appropriate curricula to improve school behavior. They fit the psychodynamic/interpersonal model because their theories are based on stages; each stage relates to appropriate and inappropriate behavior, and in each stage childrens' perceptions and behaviors are shaped by interactions with caregivers. Misbehavior, especially when it transgresses against others, can usually be considered within a framework of morality. Our major understanding of the developmental aspects of childrens' concepts of morality has emerged from the prolific research of these two psychologists and their disciples.

Piaget's Stage Theory of Moral Development

Piaget (1932) defined respect for rules as the essence of morality. He believed that commitment to rules depends on our attachment to others. Piaget's research helps us to understand discipline in terms of the developmental limits of children's understanding of "good" behavior and the appropriate consequences of "bad" behavior. His stages of moral development are reviewed in Table 4.5.

At every stage of development, children are required to obey both stated and implied rules. Studies by Piaget indicate that young children's moral judgments about rules are restricted by their own egocentricity (Riley, 1992).

Younger children tend to favor heteronomous or *expiatory* (Piaget, 1932) morality, as shown on Table 4.5. In expiation, the circumstances of the misdeed or the intent of the individual are not relevant to the punishment, which, in their minds, should be fixed, consistent, and as severe as possible.

An example of expiatory thinking occurs when five-year-old Tommy breaks several small crayons as he tries to learn to copy letters. He knows that it is "bad" to break things and that he may be punished. He may even think that he is bad for breaking the school pen-

TABLE 4.5   Piaget's Stages of Moral Development

Stage	Heteronomous Morality	Autonomous Morality
Definition	Children think that rules are rigid and cannot be changed. They learn that breaking rules leads to punishment.	Adults learn that rules are made by a consensus of people. Punishment is not automatic, but based on why the rule was broken.
Relationships	Relationships are based on inequality and constraint. For instance, the inequality between a parent and child requires the child to adhere to adult rules.	Relationships are based on equality and cooperation between individuals.
Attitudes	The *morality of constraint* or *moral realism* attitude is that rules are rigid, made up by others, are not open to negotiation, and have to be obeyed.	The *rational* moral attitude is that rules are made by agreement and can be negotiated, are accepted with consent, and are based on cooperation and respect.
Judging Right and Wrong	Adult decisions are considered to be fair. Learning right and wrong is based on one's observable behavior and consequences of actions.	Fairness is based on equal treatment of individuals, or based on the need of the individual. The intention of the behavior is the most important consideration.
Punishment	Punishment is automatic and based on observed behaviors that are considered wrong by adults.	Punishment is based on the intentions of the individual and equal to the degree of the offense.

Adapted from: Hogan, R., & Emler, N. P. (1978). Moral development. In M. E. Lamb (Ed.). *Social and personality development* (pp. 200–233). New York: Holt, Rinehart, & Winston.

cils. If his teacher yells, blames, or punishes and threatens Tommy, if he continues to break crayons, this reinforces the stage of development in which laws that govern conduct are fixed, unchangeable, and ruled by punishment. The understanding teacher explains that it was an accident, and that Tommy did not intend to break the crayons. This helps the child, when he is developmentally ready, to learn that it is the intention (trying to do something positive) that overrules the outcome.

From fifth grade on, children's verbal abilities expand, and they begin to understand that rules can be negotiated and disputes settled. At this stage, children begin to understand that rules and punishments can be modified or suspended as a result of intention or extenuating circumstances. For instance, during playground activity, a group of children are playing baseball. Billy, who is playing second base, looks up to catch a fly ball. As Doug is running as fast as possible to second base, he does not see Billy, who is backing up to catch the ball, and slides into Billy. Billy is furious and thinks that Doug should be thrown out of the game. The children negotiate and agree that Doug did not intend to run into Billy and, therefore, it was an accident. The children agree to start the play over again.

Sixth- and seventh-graders, in the stage of cooperation and reciprocity, begin to understand that rules are not always rigidly enforced. Reciprocity implies that the transgressor has some degree of self-punishment or guilt because of the recognition that the trust involved in the social bond has been broken. For instance, when Stan punches Frank in the face for saying something negative about Stan's mother, he may begin to feel guilty about breaking Frank's glasses. Although Frank should not have said anything about Stan's mother, Stan recognizes that Frank did not deserve to have his glasses broken. At this level, although Frank is still angry with Stan, he would say he was sorry for breaking the glasses. At an even higher level of moral development, he might offer restitution by offering to pay for the glasses.

In summary, Piaget's theories fit into the psychodynamic/interpersonal framework because he emphasizes the synergy between fixed stages of moral development and social interaction. In early stages, parents and other significant adults begin to shape the way that children will understand rules and consequences. As the child moves out into the world, peers and other caregivers influence the child's emerging sense of morality. The highest stage of morality exists when a person internalizes morality as a social contract that is observed as a matter of mutual cooperation and care rather than because of fear of punishment.

Kohlberg's Stage Theory of Moral Development

Lawrence Kohlberg (1980) is perhaps the most well-known developmental psychologist in the area of moral development. His view of moral development is based on the concept, similar to Piaget's theory, that stages of moral development are predetermined by cognitive structure. That is, the biological development of the brain and thinking form universal boundaries that constrain levels of moral reasoning. Within that context, the content of moral reasoning is determined by situational circumstances, parental inculcations, school discipline, religious training, and other external variables.

Kohlberg conceptualized three levels of moral development or judgment that ultimately influence students' behavior in school. Each of these levels is divided into two stages. The evolution of moral development proceeds through the preconventional level (up

TABLE 4.6   Kohlberg's Stages of Moral Development

	Levels		
	I. Preconventional Level	**II. Conventional Level**	**III. Postconventional Level**
Definition	Moral judgment is based on individual needs and the understanding that others make the rules.	Moral judgment is based on the individual accepting the rules of one's family, culture, society, and country. Individuals may ignore their own needs to satisfy the needs of their group.	Moral judgment is based on ethical principles an individual adopts, which develop into the values and mores to live by.
Stages	*1. Punishment– Obedience Orientation* An individual learns what is right and wrong based on the physical consequences of actions.	*3. Good Boy–Nice Girl Orientation* An individual learns what is right by having action approved by others.	*5. Social Contract Orientation* An individual understands that what is right is determined by the society, such as laws made in a democracy.
	2. Instrumental Relativist Orientation An individual learns what is right based on needs. An individual will do things for others if it will fulfill personal needs.	*4. Law and Order Orientation* An individual learns that laws are rigid and have to be followed to maintain society. Authority must be respected, and doing one's duty is a necessity.	*6. Universal Ethical Principle Orientation* An individual decides what is right based on conscious choices based on abstract and ethical principles.

Adapted from: Kohlberg, L. (1969). Stage and sequence: The cognitive–developmental approach to socialization. In D. A. Goslin (Ed.), *Handbook of socialization theory and research* (pp. 347–380). Chicago, IL: Rand McNally.

to age seven), the conventional level (up to age ten), and the postconventional level (up to age thirteen), as outlined in Table 4.6.

Up to stage 1, children will attempt to avoid pain, restrictions of freedom, or the anxiety associated with fear of getting caught. At stage 2, children begin to understand concepts of sharing and fairness but interpret them pragmatically. At stage 3, children have learned to enjoy the goodwill of others and seek to gain their approval and please them. Children begin to develop empathy and affection and appreciate those feelings from others. At this stage, children begin to understand the importance of intention and motivation.

At stage 4, children realize that authority and rules maintain the social order. In the fifth stage, toward the end of high school, many students' respect for law and order is replaced by understandings of the social contract between individuals and society. Correct actions tend to be defined in terms of the standards, requirements, and rights that are commonly accepted in society. Although recognizing legal restrictions, children begin to understand the rights of the individual. At stage 6, the highest level of moral development, individuals decide on a set of self-chosen ethical principles. Those who reach this stage develop sophisticated concepts of justice, equality of human rights, and respect for individuality and dignity. Unfortunately, few people are considered to reach this stage.

Most school discipline policies tend to reflect the first four stages and therefore do not provide a model for actions based on the last two stages. Schools that model participatory democracy and universal ethical concerns are more likely to encourage students to develop a higher sense of morality and sophisticated rationales for good behavior, based in part on empathy.

Summary

In summary, we have now reviewed the major theoretical approaches that fall within the psychodynamic/interpersonal rubric. Each of the theorists discussed has been written about extensively and has been interpreted and reinterpreted by many. We hope that you understand how Freud contributed to this area by conceptualizing the concepts of drive, intrapersonal and interpersonal dynamics, and the importance of stages. If you wish to become an expert in the individual approach, you will find references in this text. However, from this point, we attempt to integrate the various theories in a way in which they can be translated into the classroom. Therefore, the following sections draw on the various theories and use terms that may overlap or seem to go together.

For instance, when we talk about Freud's concept of the superego, we might also refer to Berne's concept of the parent ego state or Kohlberg's preconventional level.

Assumptions of the Psychodynamic/Interpersonal Approach

Behavior Is Strongly Influenced by Inherent, Genetically Programmed Drives and Needs

All of the psychodynamic/interpersonal theorists recognize, with differing emphasis, the existence of inherited, biological structures that are capable of programming behavior. What is of most interest, as we approach the twenty-first century, is that the acceptance of instinctual drives significantly waned after the 1950s. This occurred as behaviorism began to dominate theory and research in psychology and education. However, recent brain research, studies of other primates, and theories of linguistics support the argument for underlying, genetically determined brain mechanisms that drive behavior. Although the concept of instinct is still generally reserved for use in descriptions of other species, modern psychobiological researchers are describing what Freud first called instinctual drives.

The psychodynamically oriented teacher must have a thorough understanding of normal behaviors at the various developmental stages. Because these behaviors are biologically and psychodynamically driven, neurosis may result from thwarting of the acquisition of appropriate skills, thinking, and personality attributes. For instance, a very common problem arises with girls who become pubescent earlier than their peers. Take the case of Molly.

Molly is a well-nourished, healthy fifth-grader. Both of Molly's parents were early maturers. Most of Molly's classmates are prepubescent, but she has started to develop secondary sexual characteristics. Her genetic history was not programmed by the arbitrary grade assignments of the public school. When her body was ready, pubescence began, and with it, the accompanying feelings and drives.

Molly is beginning to act in a manner consistent with biology and evolution. But her teachers are disturbed by her flirtatious behavior. As she begins to have mutual interest in older boys on the playground and out of school, some of her girlfriends become jealous and angry. They begin to gossip about her and call her a "slut," even though she has had no sexual encounters. The immature boys in her class also spread stories, and some brag that they have "felt her up" or "groped her." Most disturbing, some of the male teachers, who may be unconsciously attracted to this taboo woman–child, overreact and make snide comments about her dress and her manner.

As a result, Molly begins to believe that there is something wrong with her and her body. However, her parents, understanding the problems of early pubescence, tell her to be proud of herself and that what is happening is perfectly natural. In this case, educators have the potential to help Molly to accept herself and her behavior and develop a healthy ego. Or, they can, through demeaning, sarcastic, and punitive behavior, encourage her to accept the ego identity that they give her as "oversexed," and therefore she may act out these beliefs.

Misbehavior Is a Function of Inadequate Defenses Needed to Control Drives

The classic psychoanalytical theorists focus on the more primitive needs for sex, power, and revenge, whereas the more psychosocially oriented theorists focus more on needs to be accepted and to be competent. Fulfillment of these needs is dependent on the strength of the drive and opportunities offered by caregiver-dominated environments. At the earliest ages, children seek instant gratification, and most learn that they must delay gratification and accept that some needs may not be gratified.

Healthy children learn to defend themselves from the frustration and anger associated with not getting what they want through anxiety and defense mechanisms. For instance, seven-year-old Greg sees a box of delicious chocolate candies in Sara's desk. He is sitting close enough that he could reach over and grab some without being discovered. However, as he is about to secure a delicious morsel, he becomes anxious. He still wants the candy, but his superego begins to act as a censor, telling him that it is not right to steal. His reality-testing ego says that he has a good chance of getting away with the theft, but he becomes more anxious as his superego more stridently reminds him of the immorality of stealing. It also reminds him that Sara is his friend, and that it would be wrong to steal from anyone, let alone a friend.

Greg defends against the anxiety aroused by the competition between the desire to satisfy his needs for chocolate and the realization that it would be wrong to steal by rationalizing that he really does not need the candy in the middle of the day. He suppresses all thoughts of candy and sublimates by returning to his schoolwork.

Jimmy, who sits on the other side of Sara, also sees the candy. He has a very poorly developed superego. Therefore, he is not anxious about doing something wrong, nor does he feel much anxiety about getting caught. He defends against low levels of anxiety regarding the possibility of getting caught by the rationalization, "I deserve that candy because I don't get hardly any at home. I know I can eat it before I get caught. If I get caught, I don't care, because I hate this class; besides, Sara thinks that she is better than me. She's a dork." He uses the defense of denial, in thinking that it does not really matter if he gets caught. He also uses projection by blaming the stealing on Sara, based on his perception that she deserves to have her chocolate stolen.

Depending on the child's age, various defense mechanisms, described previously, are used to ward off the anxiety aroused by libidinal needs. As children develop, each stage provides for progressive lessons in delayed gratification and the development of more sophisticated defenses. For instance, all teachers are familiar with chronic misbehavers who frequently use projection and denial as defenses when caught. They claim, "I didn't do it," or, "It wasn't my fault; it was Sara's fault."

The failure to control instincts results in "acting out." Sexual acting out involves undue interest in sexually related activities, including promiscuity. Typical problems include student notes filled with sexual words and ideas, frequently drawn pictures of naked people, and constant insertion of sex and sexual innuendoes in conversations. Student masturbation in class is a problem in this area that is encountered at one time by most teachers. Consider the case of Jenny.

Jenny was a kindergartner from a very restrictive, critical home, where there was a lot of conflict between her parents. Frequently, when Jenny was seated at her desk or in a circle with her peers, it was noted that she seemed to daydream. She would invariably begin to masturbate and sometimes rock back and forth. Psychological evaluation showed that Jenny was very unhappy at home and at school. Her main source of gratification was her fantasy world. Masturbation was a pleasurable activity that enhanced her fantasies, although they were not sexual in an adult sense. Of course, sexual abuse must always be considered when this activity is frequent.

Evaluation indicated that Jenny had not been abused, but her drawings and diagnostic interview with her parents showed that the family sleeping arrangements would have made it possible for her to hear or even see her parents having sex. This was never established; however, the important issue is not the masturbation, but Jenny's use of it to escape a world that gave her little gratification. Jenny was not able to develop adequate defenses against the anxiety she felt about her need to masturbate in class or the anxiety she felt about the world. Therefore, she escaped the anxiety by entering her own fantasy world.

It is natural for young children to touch and play with their genitalia during the preschool stages. Knowledgeable preschool teachers simply distract children from this activity by involving them in other, more interesting, pleasurable, but socially acceptable endeavors. The child learns that this type of self-gratification must be delayed until he or she is alone. By the end of first or second grade, healthy children will significantly decrease or stop this activity.

If teachers respond to masturbation with disgust, ridicule, or severe punishment, the child may begin to see himself or herself as disgusting, ridiculous, and unworthy. The drive for pleasure through sexually related behavior will normally resurface in adolescence, after going through a stage of latency. The healthy child will then be driven toward sexual activity as part of shared venture with another person.

The psychodynamics of the situation involve both a sense of morality (the superego, the parent ego state, or the conscience) and an understanding of reality (governed by the ego or adult ego state). The child's ego aids in reality testing, which results in cessation of masturbation in school. When the primitive need to masturbate is felt in school, the child becomes anxious. The anxiety causes the child to use various defense mechanisms such as sublimation (finding socially acceptable activities that are gratifying), suppression (pushing the need back in the conscious mind), or repression (pushing the need into the unconscious, so that it is not felt).

Nonaggressive or passive–aggressive acting out is typified by students who are noted for underachieving, clowning, wisecracking, losing assignments, cutting class, truancy, procrastination, and being an "itch." Consider the case of Ryan, a fifteen-year-old underachiever. He has an IQ of 135, which suggests that he is very bright and could easily earn As and Bs. However, his grade point average is about C minus.

Ryan hates his teacher and almost never brings in his homework assignments. His consequent failure in the class contributes to his low self-esteem, anger, and the impulse to get revenge when his teacher publicly criticizes him. He thinks, "I'll fix her, when she turns her back. I'll give her the finger, so the other kids see it. She'll look like an ass. I hate her, and the more she criticizes me, the less I'll do my homework." This attempt to assert power and get revenge reflects a regressed and unrealistic type of thinking. His aggression takes the form of not doing his schoolwork as a way of getting revenge. He is unable to recognize the self-defeating nature of this act. Also, although he may or may not get caught and punished, he served the needs of his ego–child state, his id, or his striving for autonomy.

Aggressive/antisocial acting out refers to actual fighting, extortion of other students, bullying, stealing, and vandalism. Chronic acting out against all the rules is a sign of a poorly developed or missing superego. The extent to which acting out violates the school or community standards varies. For instance, fist fights may be part of the macho culture in a particular community. Therefore, fighting in school may not be severely punished. In another community, where any outward expression of emotion is frowned on, fighting might be severely punished. But the psychodynamic/interpersonal approach suggests that, although the "punishment should match the crime" philosophy might work well in the criminal justice system, educators should first understand why the "crime" was committed. The case of Jane illustrates how defenses against anger can break down.

Jane was a fourth-grade girl who was referred for excessive fighting in school. Her parents were religiously conservative middle-class people who had recently moved from the Midwest to a new school district in the East. Previously, Jane had been a compliant, obedient, and conforming child. Raised in a small midwestern town, behavior in her elementary school was governed by dictates of politeness, trust, and respect for each other's rights.

Jane was very angry about the move to the hectic suburban world of the East Coast. However, she was raised not to express anger openly, especially against her parents or other adults. Her parents were shocked when Jane's new teacher reported that she was constantly in fights with both boys and girls in her class. These fights were not always provoked by her, but she was quick to respond to any slight. Her fighting was characterized by pushing, shoving, and hair-pulling. On one occasion, she punched a boy sitting next to her.

Jane's parents were referred to me to determine why this formerly compliant, agreeable child had changed so dramatically. Psychodynamic evaluation techniques, including drawings, sentence completion, and a play session, showed that Jane was extremely angry but was not allowed to express these feelings at home. She had never been taught to deal with her feelings appropriately, and when she went to the new school, her anger finally broke through her defenses. Despite this, she initially denied being angry and would only admit to her sadness at being at a new school.

As part of the therapy, Jane was encouraged to shift her physical expressions of anger to verbal expressions. In school, she began to curse at the other children instead of hitting them. This upset her teacher and parents greatly; however, she eventually learned to express her anger in a more acceptable way after going through this transition. She learned to say something like, "What you are doing really gets me angry, but I am just going to ignore you."

All Behavior Is Purposeful

The psychodynamic/interpersonal approach is based on the assumption that all behavior and misbehavior is driven by conscious and unconscious needs. Whether it is goal directed, toward psychosocial accomplishments, or driven merely by the pleasure principle, behavior can be understood by analysis of a person's social/emotional history. In comparison with the other teacher variance views, this theory depends most heavily on techniques involving detailed, historical information to determine the purpose of misbehavior. These techniques, which are spelled out in the section on diagnosis, include (1) family, medical, social, educational, and emotional history; (2) projective tests to discover unconscious needs, fears, and fantasies; (3) analysis of drawings, stories, dreams; and (4) observations during structured and unstructured activities. Let us consider a typical problem for teachers that can be understood from a psychodynamic perspective.

An inordinate need for attention causes many discipline problems. We must always ask, "Where did that need originate?" There are multiple explanations, some indicating that the exact opposite types of parenting may yield the same results. For instance, consider the case of Derek.

Derek, an energetic, nonstop, six-year-old, was referred to me for his outrageous behavior. His clowning repertoire in class included a constant stream of funny facial expressions, inappropriate statements, and physical activity. The latter included dancing on and crawling under desks. He particularly enjoyed imitating animals such as bears, snakes, and wolves.

Family history showed that Derek was accustomed to an overabundance of attention for anything that he did. His parents considered his misbehaviors to be amusing. As an only child and grandchild, he was constantly indulged and rewarded for his imitations of other adults and TV characters. Whenever Derek failed at a task, or refused to comply with a parental request, he would act in a regressed, immature manner. Derek was given too much autonomy for his age. He thought that he was equal to adults, that he was in charge in most situations, and that anything that he did to get attention was legitimate. There were never any logical consequences for his behavior, so he just acted on impulse. However, it was no mystery that the purpose of the clowning behavior filled his unrealistic need for autonomy. He failed to understand that true freedom must be tempered by self-restraint.

Classroom interventions were aimed at providing him with ample opportunities for legitimate recognition, with support from his parents. For instance, each day he was invited to imitate a different animal. But he also had to tell something about the animal and include drawings and tapes of the animal, which his parents helped him to prepare. When he found that he could not do a different animal each day, he asked to do one a week, and his inappropriate sounds stopped.

Although clowning can be relatively innocuous and easy to understand, the purpose of stealing may be more difficult to understand. Stealing by children and youth may not necessarily be for the acquisition of the stolen object. Stealing may be rooted in feelings of low self-worth and self-esteem. Often, the things that children steal are of little real value. We have seen many cases in which children have stolen candy or money to give the stolen property to other children to gain approval.

The purpose of stealing by children may be to gain esteem, worth, or power. However, these motivations may be unconscious. For instance, children may be quite truthful when they claim that they did not know why they stole something. That is, the actual motive for stealing is buried deep in the unconscious, but the act of stealing serves the purpose of enhancing the ego. Diagnostic information can help to reveal the purpose for stealing and set the stage for evolving a plan to help the child. If stealing is related to low self-esteem, classroom and home activities to help the child to gain self-esteem will eliminate the stealing.

The Preschool Years Are Crucial in Determining School Adjustment

Freud's belief that basic personality traits are determined by the time a child is six or seven years of age is partially supported by temperament research, which is discussed in Chapter 6. The psychodynamic/interpersonal approach emphasizes the importance of the interaction between inherited drives and environment in the early stages of life. A healthy personality is rooted in the successful accomplishment of early sequential developmental tasks.

At the early stages, children are dependent on appropriate parenting. They have limited coping mechanisms to deal with deviant parenting. Their defenses are often confined to a repertoire of compliance, withdrawal, or oppositional behavior. For instance, a four-year-old girl who is sexually abused by her father often has little recourse but to comply. However, the stages of later personality disorder and school discipline problems, especially with male teachers, may result from that compliance.

Professionals who work with children who have conduct disorders, and who are repeatedly apprehended and punished, understand the dynamics of their repetitive misbehavior. Although much delinquent behavior is caused by the lack of superego, or poorly developed superegos, some may be explained by superegos interacting with self-images riddled by feelings of unworthiness. In early childhood, these repeat offenders may have developed superegos at times when they were also severely rejected, criticized, and punished. As a result, they come to view themselves as bad, unworthy people. In school, these students may be caught in an unending cycle of repeated misbehavior. It is likely that their frequent punishments result from their superegos' unconscious maneuvers, which cause them to get caught. Yet when asked why they repeated an offense when they knew it was likely that they would be caught, they cannot explain why they did it.

The roots of delinquency may be grounded in punitive parental behavior regarding feeding, toilet training, and resolution of Oedipal issues. By first grade, frequently punished, predelinquent students already feel unloved, unlovable, and unworthy. As victims of rejection during the oral–sensory, trust–mistrust stages, they may become career criminals, labeled as sociopaths and psychopaths. These victims of early rejection will never be able to trust anyone completely, and they will never know why. This is why successful dynamic therapy is dependent on their gaining insight into and recognition of their early rejection.

In addition to early rejection, other deviant parent behaviors during the preschool years can negatively impact school adjustment. For instance, harsh toilet training can cause problems of self-esteem.

George, a third-grader, frequently loses his temper. His teacher, Ms. Jones, has noticed his perfectionistic propensities. Often his homework papers and seatwork assignments are so full of repetitive erasures that they are wrinkled and difficult to read. At least once a day he breaks out in tears or curses and balls up his seatwork and throws it on the floor. When others comment on his behavior, he lashes out at them with statements such as, "I can't stand to hand in sloppy work," or "I want to make sure everything is correct."

An interview with George's parents showed their perfectionistic traits. Developmental history indicated that George was very oppositional during toilet training, and his mother "had to be" extremely strict. He was frequently punished or ridiculed for soiling himself; yet his parents rarely praised him for going a day without an accident.

George developed a sense of shame, doubt, and anger at his parents during early toilet training. To defend against the consequent anxiety, he identified with his father's traits of perfectionism, fastidiousness, and fear of failure to resolve his needs to defy his parents.

Educational strategies included stories, videotapes, and constant personal assurance from the teacher that it is OK to not be perfect. The parents had several sessions with the school psychologist, during which the dynamics of the problems were explained, and plans for treatment were developed. George learned that you can be loved, even when you make mistakes.

Misbehavior Is Often the Result of Transgenerational Patterns of Inadequate or Deviant Parenting

Without appropriate intervention, deviant parenting patterns may be repeated through many generations. Neurotic parents are likely to raise neurotic children. Psychotherapeutic intervention is often necessary because (1) the neurotic, self-destructive behavior of the school-child has often been fixed at earlier stages; (2) the forces driving the misbehavior are buried in the unconscious; (3) the child's self-destructive behavior at home and in school often results in rejection, which leads to poor self-esteem; and (4) the parents' inappropriate, neurotic parenting style results from their own unconscious conflicts. Take the case of Jessie, whose academic difficulties and aggression illustrate these four points.

When I first saw Jessie, he was a very large fourteen-year-old who was referred for frequent fighting, running away from school, and inconsistent classwork. From kindergarten on, he was frequently referred to the school psychologist. His hyperactive behavior and poor socialization skills included refusing to follow directions or share with his classmates and hitting his peers.

Both the mother and her father had trouble learning to read, suggesting a genetically based learning disability. Both of Jessie's grandfathers were known for their short tempers and readiness to smack their children. In addition, Jessie's father related that when he was beaten up by other kids, his father beat him for losing the fight. Jessie's maternal grandmother was a "screamer," who was always critical of her daughter.

Both parents admitted that they have "short fuses." They also reported that Jessie, who is the oldest of four boys, terrorizes his siblings. Although he has been in that role in the family, ever since he was about five or six years old, neighborhood children and classmates have picked on him and made fun of him. It has only been since he entered early adolescence and had a growth spurt, accompanied by an extra thirty pounds, that the teasing diminished.

Jessie reported that he was born with a temper, and "there is nothing I can do about it. That's the way I am." From as early as he could remember, the cycle of violence in the home was characterized by a specific pattern. First he would bully and terrorize his siblings. Next he failed to comply with his parents repeated requests to stop. This was followed by beatings, slappings, kickings, and screaming by whichever parent was involved. Finally, the cycle began over again as he took out his anger and frustration for the beatings on his siblings.

Older children with periodic temper tantrums usually have at least one parent and one grandparent who had the same problem. In these families, parents perpetuate the belief that there is little that can be done about one's temper. The parents of these children often have harsh superegos and rarely develop past Piaget's expiatory level or Kohlberg's punishment–obedience level in terms of their own moral development.

The teacher could not help Jessie much until the parents got help. The major initial goal of therapy with Jessie's family was to stop the cycle of misbehavior, threat, counterthreat, violence, and calm before the next cycle. Although both parents admitted that hitting and screaming did little good, they had great difficulty giving up these patterns of transgenerational, intrafamilial violence. I worked on building Jessie's self-esteem in group therapy. This was enhanced by a girl in the group who recognized Jessie's need for nurturance. She sometimes treated him as a little child who did not feel loved. After nurturing behavior, he always calmed down.

In this case, the dynamics of the family were so complex, and crises so frequent, that progress was very slow. I was able to help Jessie's teachers understand that his anger and aggressive behavior was often displaced on them and his peers as a result of incidents that occurred in his home. After extensive therapy, his parents became more nurturing, and they encouraged him to verbalize his angers and frustrations, rather than to act aggressively. This improvement at home significantly reduced the acting out in school.

We often hear frustrated educators say that what bullies and aggressive kids need is a good swift kick in the behind. Yet, as this example shows, that type of punishment is more often the cause than the cure for aggression.

Misbehavior Is Almost Always Associated with Low Self-Esteem

Most frequently misbehaving students have low self-esteem (Brassard, Hart & Germain, 1987; Garbarino, Guttman, & Seeley, 1986; Straus, 1994). Family and educational histories invariably illuminate how parents, early caregivers, and teachers cause this problem. Both physical and verbal assaults on children, in addition to constant criticism, denigration, and sarcasm, are surefire methods of destroying self-esteem.

Through the most perilous stages, when libidinal needs overcome rational thinking, parents and teachers must help set limits in a manner that enhances rather than destroys the child's sense of accomplishment and understanding of the rules, expectations, and taboos of life. Children and youth must be nurtured through each stage so they are able to deal effectively with unconscious needs and drives that shape the self-concept.

The real world constantly demands performance of all of us. But, in general, the daily academic demands of schooling and the performance demands of organized sports can be unrelenting in assaulting children's sense of competence. Take for example a D grade that twelve-year-old Sammy brings home from school. Sammy is capable of at least C or B grades, but is in a slump. Let us look at two extremes in terms of how a parent might react.

Mother Destroyer would say something like, "Oh, I see you have failed again. This is the third D in a row. Are you going to make a habit of being a loser? Lately you just don't care about anything but your TV and videogames. You don't care that I am so embarrassed about you, that I hate to admit that you are my son. Now I have to face your teacher about these ridiculous grades you have been getting lately."

Mother Supporter would say something like, "That's OK. I know that you aren't pleased with your grades, but grades aren't the most important thing in the world. You don't seem to be too happy lately. Let's try to find out why you are having problems. You know I still love you. Anyway, we all have slumps, and your grades do not mean that you are stupid or anything like that. Besides, you got a great hit in the baseball game last week."

Teachers can either reinforce or help change parental practices that lower students' self-confidence. But, to help change them, the teacher must diagnose the problem.

Psychodynamic/Interpersonal Diagnosis

Within the psychodynamic/interpersonal framework, most misbehaviors are viewed as the result of neurosis. Because misbehavior is self-defeating, it is neurotic and the result of faulty reality testing. Poor reality testing is the lack of the ability to objectively evaluate the demands and requirements of the external world and adequately separate them from internal, egocentric thinking. The purpose of diagnosis is to map the source and nature of neurotic thinking and determine its roots in the web of interactions within the unconscious, subconscious, and conscious mind. Once this is done, teachers can develop strategies to defeat neurotic thinking and enhance self-esteem.

Diagnosis provides information to assess the child's perception of the situation and the extent to which misbehavior might be caused by internal or external factors. Because behaviors appropriate in one stage of life may be inappropriate in other stages, knowledge of development is needed for accurate assessment. It is important to note that the absence of deviant behavior does not necessarily indicate that the child is emotionally healthy. For instance, a student with a weak or distorted superego could be fearful, compliant, and respectful when a feared teacher is present. However, in the absence of authority figures, that same student could be a sadistic bully. The goal of diagnosis in this model is to determine the core problem.

Desirable diagnostic information includes:

1. The history of the individual's early interpersonal relationships
2. Past and present family dynamics
3. Transgenerational methods of discipline
4. Descriptions of how parents helped children deal with drives and needs at developmentally critical periods (i.e., Freud, Adler, Dreikurs)
5. Determination of the adequacy of the child's defense mechanisms
6. An understanding of the student's perception of the situation
7. An assessment of the type, level, and sources of the student's anxiety
8. An assessment of the extent to which internal and external factors influence the student's perception of the problem
9. An assessment of the nature and extent of the child's self-esteem

To develop the skills to use all this information, you will need to study extensively and obtain help from someone such as your school psychologist.

Often, misbehavior reflects a *fixation* or regression to behavior that was developmentally appropriate at an earlier stage. For instance, consider the case of Stan.

Stan, a thirteen-year-old, is always whining about rules, is frequently out of his seat, often makes silly noises in class, and repeatedly calls out of turn. In other words, he is a pain in the neck to have in class. His behaviors might be developmentally appropriate in primary grades, but not in middle or high school.

Almost every teacher has had a Stan. Stan's behavior often results in ridicule and teasing by peers and frustration and repeated punishments by teachers. These reactions cause a cycle of loss of esteem and more frequent attempts to gain attention, control, and power by his behaviors. Despite frequent reprimands and attempts at reasoning and explanations of the natural consequences of his behavior, nothing seems to change. Understanding of this type of behavior lies in a careful analysis of Stan's social/emotional history.

Understanding may be based on many sources of information. In the case of Stan, diagnosis can come from talking with him, other students, parents, the school nurse, previous teachers, and others. Even though teachers are not trained in clinical interviewing and projective testing, you may want to learn some of these skills from your school psychologist.

Mental health consultation with your school psychologist will help you develop psychodynamic diagnostic skills, including insight about yourself and how you perceive your problem students. This approach assumes that your problem with Stan may be based on unconscious beliefs about him. For instance, extreme anger at some of Stan's behavior could suggest that, rather than being objective about the problem, your deep-rooted feelings, experiences with someone like Stan, and other subjective beliefs are being transferred to the situation. For instance, you could unconsciously associate him with your older brother, who always got you into trouble. The repeated themes or scenarios that took place between you and your brother could unconsciously prevent you from being objective about how to understand and deal with Stan, who, after all, may differ in many important ways from your brother.

Psychodynamic practitioners recognize the power of the unconscious or subconscious in making decisions. Therefore, psychodynamically oriented therapists are usually required to go through a course of therapy themselves. As a teacher oriented to this approach, it may not be necessary to have therapy, but you must be willing to examine your own background, behaviors, and hidden motives when working with children. This may be accomplished through mental health consultation with a psychologist.

It is now time to apply the psychodynamic/interpersonal approach to the diagnosis of Chris (see page 37).

Analyze Student's Cumulative Folder and Other Available Records

When I first began to teach, I was warned that I should always give each child a fresh start in my class. I should ignore previous school records, comments by past teachers about my students, and other information, lest I develop a self-fulfilling prophesy about each student. This may be appropriate if negative information is used to predict a bleak future. However, the psychodynamic/interpersonal approach mandates that we examine the past, not only to determine potential problems, but to search for strengths. This approach, based on a medical, diagnostic model, depends on previous records and history to develop diagnostic hypotheses and then to test them and rule out those that do not apply. For instance, if a student like Chris is doing poorly in academic areas, there are a number of possible hypotheses to test.

Some hypotheses to test to account for Chris's poor schoolwork are that he (1) lacks the intellectual ability to work at the grade level required; (2) has adequate intelligence, but has a learning disability or attention deficit disorder; (3) has a new or preexisting illness (i.e., anemia, brain tumor, diabetes) or physical disability (i.e., vision or hearing deficit); (4) has emotional problems, including low self-esteem, which are rooted in home or school and result in lack of achievement.

Assume that the preliminary description of Chris is accurate. The first impression suggests that we can rule out a strong possibility of numbers 1 and 3 above. Because the records, teachers' reports, and statements by his current teacher provide evidence that he can do the work when he is motivated, he has adequate intelligence. An examination of the record will show if he frequently misses school, which might suggest a chronic illness. The nurse's records would show further information. Chris's attendance is regular, and there have been no sudden changes in his pattern of behavior related to illness. It is always possible that the nurse and his parents missed something, but let us assume that is not the case.

It is possible that Chris has a learning disability. If this were the case, his achievement test scores would most likely show weaknesses in specific areas. His weaknesses would also show as consistent low grades in specific areas. For instance, if he had a reading disability, his cumulative record would show slow reading development and gaps in learning. Also, this would show up in instruction. Further, if the disability was associated with an attention deficit disorder, teacher comments would help in the diagnosis.

The information provided indicates that the most likely hypothesis is that Chris's academic problems stem from emotional factors.

Obtain a Social, Developmental, and Educational History and Determine Transgenerational Patterns of Childrearing

Too many teachers seem to believe that when they meet with parents, they must tell the parents something. Yet parents know much more about their children than do teachers. Parents are a gold mine for understanding children, but you must know how to gather the information.

Most parents come to school expecting to be told about their child. Often they get the message that this is a chore for the teacher and a pain for the school. Too often, conferences are arranged during daytime, parental working hours and scheduled for limited time. Teachers may become defensive if they are questioned about appropriate educational techniques for the child and when they do not seem to know important things about the child. Furthermore, parents of children with chronic behavior problems may have been in trouble themselves when they were in school. Even if they were not, they soon become wary of repeated conferences during which they continue to learn how bad they and their children are. Finally, chronic misbehavior in school is often a reflection of the same misbehavior at home. We have heard parents express their frustration by saying to teachers, "If I knew how to make Johnny behave, do you think he would be a problem in school? You are the expert. Tell me what to do."

If Chris's parents feel defensive, they may deny or minimize his problems at home and blame the school. If you were to meet with his parents you might start the conference by asking them to tell you about Chris. What was he like when he was younger? Did he have any particular problems at various stages? Did either of them have similar or related problems as children? How did he handle the divorce? How well does he get along with siblings? What are his interests, hobbies, and strengths? How does he feel about school and his teachers? What have they tried with him that works and does not work?

A complete list of questions for gathering social, developmental, and educational data may be obtained from your school psychologist, social worker, or counselor.

Interview Previous Teachers, School Nurse, and Others Who Know the Student

To obtain information from colleagues, try to schedule a quiet time when they are not in the middle of lesson plans, not in the teacher's room with other staff, and have not just completed a very rough day. Be prepared to ask some very specific questions that will help you to determine what is happening with the child. Try not to ask questions that require a "yes" or "no" answer. For instance, rather than asking, "Was Chris a good student?" you might ask, "What kind of student was Chris when he was in your class?"

Attempt to obtain a clear picture of the student from the teacher's response. The response should be clear enough for you to picture it as a movie scene being played in your mind. For instance, if you are interviewing a teacher about Chris, and the teacher says, "Well, Chris was an inconsistent student," you need to elicit examples of specific scenarios that illustrate his inconsistencies.

One trick in interviewing for hypothesis testing is to make believe you are a detective. From previous information, make hypotheses that you then test by asking appropriate questions. For instance, let us assume you make the hypothesis that Chris's problems are related to a poor relationship with his stepfather. The first question you might ask of Chris's previous teacher might be a general one, such as, "What do you know about Chris's relationship with his stepfather?" or "Can you tell me what you know about Chris's family life?" Then you might follow up with more specific questions to determine the exact nature of the problems between Chris and his stepfather.

When interviewing previous teachers, it is always a good idea to have first reviewed the child's cumulative folder. Some students do well in one grade or with one teacher and then do very poorly, in the same subject, with another teacher. Therefore, it is important to try to determine how objective the teacher's reporting might be.

Be careful in interpreting the meaning of grades. Be sure to ask specific questions about the quantity and quality of work. Consider grades in comparison with objective achievement scores. These tests may not always be reliable for every individual administration. A student could be sick, upset, or not motivated on the day he or she took the school-wide achievement tests. However, over several years, these test results can be very helpful for comparison with teacher grades in determining a student's level of motivation, interest, and achievement.

When examining the cumulative folder, note days absent each year. Frequent absences may suggest medical, motivational, or teacher–student interaction problems.

Some cumulative folders include teacher comments and anecdotal reports, either on the cumulative records or on copies of report cards, which are included in the folder. I have found that teacher comments, even though brief, can provide valuable information about a child. When examining these, look for patterns that are reported consistently by teachers. Be cautious, because these comments sometimes say more about the teacher than the child. Look for teacher comments that appear inconsistent with those of other teachers. If these are especially negative or positive compared with other comments, investigate why.

School nurses, especially in elementary school, are often valuable sources of information. When they are nurturing caregivers, parents and students confide in them. Other sources of information include guidance counselors, administrators, and coaches. Although this sounds very tedious, if you are oriented toward the psychodynamic/interpersonal approach, you will realize the value of obtaining as much information as possible.

Interview Parents

Unfortunately, in too many cases, teachers view parents as the enemy who caused the student's problem in the first place. Rather, it is better to conceptualize the parents as part of the solution. The psychodynamic/interpersonal model suggests that misbehavior and deviance develop within the family. But blaming is a nonproductive and destructive approach to dealing with parents whose children are behavior problems in school. Because there is ample evidence that parents can successfully participate in the education of their children, the most potent way to improve discipline is for parents and teachers to share information and plan strategies together. Some schools, as a way of recognizing the importance of collaborative efforts, require that teachers visit parents at home on a regular basis.

It is important to make a distinction between understanding and blaming. The reason for gathering information is to diagnose the source of the student's problem. Your attitude must be strictly neutral and objective when meeting with parents. If your goal is to validate feelings that the parents are to blame, parents will eventually get the message and become defensive and uncooperative.

If you approach parent interviews in terms of mutual respect and collaboration, you will find that most parents will become quickly cooperative. If you are frustrated with a student's behavior, it is very likely that the parents have similar frustrations. It is important to create an atmosphere in which both parties share their frustrations and begin to plan together. The following are good and bad ways to begin a parent interview about school discipline. Let us consider the case of Chris Smith, Ms. Jones's misbehaving student.

Wrong

Teacher: Mr. and Mrs. Smith, Chris has been quite a problem to me. He doesn't seem to want to obey the rules. Sometimes he is moody and other times he seems okay. Sometimes he is lazy and just refuses to do the work.

Parent: Well, Ms. Jones, Chris doesn't seem to be very happy in your class. He tells us that you don't like him.

Correct

Teacher: Mr. and Mrs. Smith, I asked you to come here so we can talk about how we can help Chris. I wonder if you could tell me about how he is at home.

Parent: Has he been a problem in school again?

Teacher: Well, let's not talk about that right now. I am trying to understand Chris, and you are the experts because you live with him. You know him better than anyone.

Parent: Well, what do you want to know?

Teacher: How does Chris react when you ask him to do his homework?

In the first dialogue, the teacher's first statement immediately put the parents on the defensive. Of course, Mr. and Mrs. Smith know that Chris is a problem. They've been hearing it for years. The last thing they need is a meeting with the teacher telling them how bad Chris is. The opening statement by Ms. Jones caused them to think something like, "Here we go again. Another teacher telling me how rotten my kid is. I know she is blaming me for the problem, and I am not going to take it. I am going to let her solve the problem herself. I am not going to let her off the hook."

In the second dialogue, even when given a prompt, Ms. Jones refused to repeat the often-heard litany about how bad Chris is. As a result, the parents might be thinking, "Gee, this teacher really wants to listen to us. She seems to understand that we're just as frustrated and unhappy as the teachers." In this scenario, the teacher has established rapport and the potential for mutual sharing of information.

You may feel uncomfortable delving into information about such topics as divorce, parenting styles, possible alcohol or drug use in the family, etc. Therefore, if you feel extremely uncomfortable in terms of the type of information that you feel is necessary, you could ask your school psychologist, social worker, or counselor to conduct a more in-depth interview.

When you are interviewing parents, be sure to obtain specific information. When a parent describes an event, you should be able to develop a complete mental picture of what happened. For instance, let us assume that you ask Ms. Smith how Chris gets along with his siblings and she responds, "Well, just like any other typical brothers and sisters. They fight once in a while." Some follow-up questions would be: (1) How often do they fight? (2) When do they fight? (3) What types of things do they fight about? and (4) How intense are the fights? Then ask for a description of a typical fight situation, detailing the setting, what preceded the fight, what happened during the fight, and how the parent handled the fight.

When talking to parents, make a list of the areas that you think will produce important information. The areas that are generally of interest will include:

1. The child's and parent's reactions to important developmental tasks such as feeding, toilet training, sharing, complying with requests, temper tantrums, etc.
2. The child's early and continuing relationships with siblings
3. The child's early and continuing reaction to authority figures
4. The child's history of academic difficulties and how they are handled by the parents
5. The parent's typical methods of disciplining the child
6. The ways in which the child's parents were disciplined by their parents
7. The child's reactions to stressful situations such as death, divorce, or disability of a parent, relative, or close friend
8. History of any traumatic event such as chronic illness, abuse in home, school or other setting
9. The child's friendship patterns

If the misbehaving student is an adolescent, several areas that can affect behavior include:

1. Rejection and acceptance by peers
2. Reactions to pubescence
3. Identification with model adults
4. Reaction of parents to child's attempts at autonomy
5. Reaction of parents to dating
6. Attempts by parents to control various aspects of the child's life
7. Reaction to child's use of leisure time

An important issue in contemporary times involves the impact of media on children's lives. Television viewing should always be questioned in terms of time and content. For instance, does a student who is aggressive in class watch much TV violence? Does he or she have trouble separating the fantasy of Ninja movies from real life? Does the student believe that real-life karate experts like Bruce Lee or Chuck Norris can really vanquish ten or fifteen foes at a time?

Develop a Systematic Anecdotal Record of Student's Behavior and Misbehavior in Various Situations and Examine Your Own Objectivity

Valuable information for diagnosing student misbehavior may be obtained from teachers' anecdotal records (Prescott, 1957). To begin, use a notebook with a vertical line dividing each page. On the left side, keep anecdotal records of events in the classroom. The anecdotes should be a random mixture of "normal events" in the everyday classroom life of the child you are observing. In addition, keep an ongoing record of events that involve the child's misbehavior. Each recording should include the day, the time, the setting, and an accurate description of who did and said what. This should include what you said and did before, during, and after the event.

The use of classroom observations is discussed fully in the ecological/systems approach. The basic technique for the objective recording of behavior is the same in any approach. However, from a psychodynamic/interpersonal approach, it is assumed that there will be some bias in the way in which you pick events to record. For instance, if your hypothesis about Chris is that his hostility to other students in school is related to possible sibling rivalry at home, you would look for events that test your hypothesis. You would record events such as bickering with other students. These events might include loud protestations when someone "butts in line," complaints that other students are given more opportunity to answer questions in class, or snide remarks when a classmate performs well.

It is important to recognize your psychodynamic bias so that it does not interfere with the observation and recording of data that do not support your hypotheses. As long as you objectively record incidents in the left-hand column of your record sheet, you can make any interpretation you wish in the right-hand column. The accuracy of your hypothesis will be demonstrated when it is repeatedly noted in the right-hand column with supporting, objective reporting of incidents in the left-hand column.

After a week or two of recording of anecdotal events, review the record sheet for recurring patterns of behavior. Do they support your original hypotheses or help you develop new ones? Use the right side of the page to jot down your hypotheses, comments, interpretations, and intuitive feelings about the reasons for the events and how they may be related to the child's self-image, parental expectations, and other psychodynamic constructs.

To make hypotheses, you should review crucial developmental stages. Can the behavior observed be explained by Freud's oral, anal, phallic, or genital stages; Erikson's stages of trust versus mistrust, autonomy versus shame and doubt, initiative versus guilt, industry versus inferiority, identity versus role confusion, or intimacy versus isolation; Piaget's stages of expiatory punishment (outcome) versus reciprocity (intention); Kohlberg's stages of obedience and punishment, instrumental–relativistic orientation, nice girl/good boy, law and order, social contract, and universal ethical principles?

Consider which of the dynamic constructs appear to contribute to the child's behavior. Which drives and needs are not being met in the life of the child you have been evaluating? If you can determine which needs are not being met, you can then understand why the child is feeling anger, frustration, and defeat. This will explain the child's neurotic, self-defeating, and destructive behavior.

Remember to consider your own dynamics. For instance, in the case of Chris, does he remind you of an older sibling whom you disliked, a classroom bully who bothered you when you were a student, or traits in yourself that you do not like? Now let us construct an anecdotal record for Chris.

Anecdotal Record   *Impressions*

Friday, Oct. 3, 1:30 P.M.
social studies lesson
The class has just taken out their books and are quietly reviewing the chapter they read for homework. I was walking around the classroom. Chris kept asking Bob questions about the assignment. Bob gave him an answer and then Chris wanted to talk about other things.

Chris: Hey Bob, were we supposed to read the whole chapter?

Bob: Yeah, don't you remember the teacher told us just before the end of the lesson yesterday?

Chris: Did you read the whole chapter?

Bob: Yeah, I did.

Chris: What was it about?

Bob: Come on, Chris; leave me alone.

Chris did not do homework again.

Chris: Come on, you creep, why won't you help me?

Bob: Chris, you are always doing this. Why don't you just do your homework yourself like you are suppose to?

Chris makes unreasonable demands and if no compliance he gets hostile.

Chris: (loudly) F___ you, Bob.

Teacher: Chris, what did I hear you say?

Chris: Nothing.

Teacher: I heard you cursing at Bob. I also heard you asking him to help you with your assignment that you were supposed to do last night.

Chris: I needed help, and my father wouldn't give it to me, and my mom was too busy with my new sister. How can I do my homework when it is too hard for me? Nobody wants to help me.

Teacher: Chris, I've told you a million times, if you want help, ask me. Besides, I will call your parents and find out if we can't arrange for them to give you more help with your homework.

Chris: Don't do that. They will just yell at me. Nobody seems to care anyway.

Teacher: OK class, let's get on with the lesson.

In the above anecdotal record, you will notice that the time, the date, and the lesson are included. Also, a short narrative is followed by an actual recording of who said what and how they said it. Obviously, you can't remember every word, but the idea is to approximate it as closely as possible. The way you write your impressions will be determined by your specific psychodynamic orientation. Let us consider a few possibilities here. A theme that predominates this anecdote is that Chris has not done his homework and is asking for help. In examining multiple anecdotes, if this theme appears, it is one of the recurring patterns that you need to note under impressions. A second theme is one that indicates that Chris annoys other students with unreasonable requests, and when he is rejected, he curses. Again, if this is a recurring pattern, it should be noted.

Using Erikson's stage theory, it would appear that Chris is not playing by the rules. The rules are that you should do your homework and not depend on others. At this stage, competence and good self-esteem are based on completion of projects with little or no help. A pattern of failures to complete assignments followed by lack of help suggests that Chris will go through this stage feeling inadequate and inferior.

Chris's anxiety about feeling inferior is defended by rationalization and projection. He rationalizes that he did not do the work because it was too hard. Yet, we know that Chris is capable of completing the assignment. He also projects blame on his parents and others, whom he claims never want to help him. This is a projection, because he has been offered help many times by his teacher and his parents. Furthermore, if he were not so annoying to his classmates, many would be happy to help him.

The above impressions could be written into the right-hand column as statements, suggestions for further investigation, or proof for specific hypotheses.

Obtain Psychoeducational Assessment through Objective and Projective Procedures and Interview

Neurotic misbehavior is related to unconscious needs, drives, and motivations. If students do not understand the reasons for their misbehavior, it is nearly impossible for them to gain insight into solving their problems. Furthermore, they can hardly be expected to tell a teacher or psychologist what is occurring in their unconscious or subconscious minds. To tap information from these inner recesses, psychologists and psychiatrists have developed projective tests.

Projective tests, such as the Rorschach (inkblot test), sentence completion tests, thematic apperception tests, and open-ended clinical interview questions all provide vague or neutral stimuli to which a person can respond in any way. These responses reflect the unconscious. Although as a teacher you were not trained to administer and interpret projective tests, if you understand the basic theory, you can interpret information from the unconscious from a variety of sources within the context of the classroom.

In the process of making tentative diagnoses, you may or may not have anecdotal records. It is preferable to gather that information, but it is understandable, especially if you are a secondary teacher, that you may not have time to record the necessary information. However, revealing information can come from student reports and student discussions.

Assignments such as student reports about their summer vacations can provide valuable insights. It is up to you to provide formats for gathering information. For instance, you might request that the students write about (1) how they spent their past summer, (2) their best and worst summers, and (3) the ideal summer. The contrast between all of these will provide fascinating information about their inner lives.

After grading of the papers, ask further questions about what the student felt or meant about specific passages. Ask the student to expand on those themes.

Ask yourself, "What is the child trying to do in life?" and "What is the child up against in the struggle to accomplish his or her goals?" There are a host of assignments you can give students to answer these questions. For instance, ask students to draw a map of their neighborhood and other places that are important to them and then describe their activities on a normal day after school. The map can be used to outline where they go and what is important to them. The pictures, especially by younger children, may reflect important feelings and events in their out-of-school lives. For instance, do the pictures depict happy, sad, or neutral expressions on people's faces?

Movies and TV shows are important sources of projective information. Although the stimuli in these cases may not be ambiguous, the interpretations of events can aid in understanding the child's motivations, needs, and desires. Discussions and reports about movies can focus on questions such as:

1. What was the hero of the movie trying to do?
2. How did various characters in the movie feel about what was happening?
3. What would be the most desirable outcome to the events that took place in the movie?
4. Were certain actions moral, immoral, or amoral?
5. How did you feel about certain characters, and what would you do if you were in their places?

All of this information will help you to understand and diagnose the student.

In examining student responses, if they seem bizarre or much different than might be expected, consult your school psychologist. Also, consider that the process of trying to understand students through their writings, comments, and interpretations of media will help you to become a more sensitive, insightful, and introspective professional.

If Stuck, Obtain Mental Health Consultation from Your School Psychologist

Every school has some access to school psychologists, but not all are trained to do mental health consultation (Brown, Pryswansky & Schulte, 1991; Caplan & Caplan, 1993; Conoley & Conoley, 1992; Meyers, Parsons, & Martin, 1979). Many classroom problems can be solved if teachers are willing to examine their roles in determining the solution rather than blaming the child. This is most often done collaboratively. The psychologist will try to help the teacher to determine if the problem is based on the teacher's (1) lack of skill, (2) lack of knowledge, (3) lack of objectivity, or (4) lack of self-confidence in dealing with the student, or some combination of these. If the teacher is open, cooperative, and trusts the confidentiality assured by the consultant, this is a very successful approach for helping students. The importance of trust and the nature of the interaction between the consultant and consultee is somewhat like psychotherapy. However, it is not meant to be psychotherapy but mutual problem solving. In the case of Sam and Ms. Brown, which is described below, I used this technique to help her understand that she was not being objective, because she was angry at Sam. She really knew what to try, at least as a first step, but could not.

Sam was an overweight thirteen-year-old who seemed bent on making life miserable for some of his teachers. He had a history of overly severe discipline at home, constant ridicule by peers, and refusal to cooperate in school. In kindergarten and first grade, he could not share, was sometimes aggressive, and had trouble sitting still. He had difficulties in learning to read, although he apparently had normal intelligence. In third grade, he was classified as having a learning disability (LD) and placed in special education.

Sam's parents sought psychotherapy, and for two years he was with a therapist who taught him to express his anger verbally rather than physically. This was a great improvement over his past disruptive behavior. Sam believed that when he was frustrated in class it was better to curse and make noises than to be aggressive or destructive. He considered this to be great progress, but unfortunately, Ms. Brown, his language arts teacher, did not agree with either solution to his anger.

Sam knew that he could control his anger if he tried. He also knew that he could really upset some teachers if he made noises or cursed in class. He could always say that this was better than striking out at others. He knew that Ms. Brown was a perfect victim. Ms. Brown was an attractive, articulate young woman with five years of experience teaching in the LD program of Sam's middle school. When she called me, she was obviously frustrated, angry, and ready to kill. The following is a condensation of our conversation:

T: I know that Sam has problems, but I can't allow him to curse and make noises when he is frustrated. We have rules in this school about cursing. He must be suspended if he can't control himself.

Me: But isn't this one of the reasons he was placed in your class?

T: Yes, but he is emotionally disturbed. He should be in a class for kids with emotional problems, not in an LD class.

Me: Can you recommend that he be placed in such a class in your district?

T: There are none, and he is apparently not sick enough to be placed out of our school district. But I can't allow this.

Me: So you are saying that you are stuck with him.

T: Yes, but not with his cursing. It disrupts the whole class. He should be suspended each time he curses or makes weird sounds.

Me: But isn't that what they tried? Did it work?

T: No, but we do have school rules.

Me: Why do you think he keeps doing it?

T: I guess he loves to irritate me. I know he doesn't do it with some of his other teachers.

Me: If he is doing it to irritate you, I guess he is doing a good job.

T: I know! I know! I should ignore it. But that goes against my grain. Besides, if I ignore it, all the other kids will think it is OK to curse and make noises whenever they feel like it.

Me: Well then, what are you going to do?

T: Do you think I should ignore the cursing? It goes against my grain to let him get away with it. I will listen to your advice, but I don't like the idea.

Me: I didn't say you should do it. If you feel uncomfortable, don't. Besides, if I tell you to do that and it doesn't work, you will blame me.

T: (Laughs) No, I won't blame you. But I guess I could try it for a little while to see if it works. Besides, after talking to you, I don't feel so angry.

Me: Well, call me in a week or two and let me know what happened.

What Ms. Brown really wanted was to have Sam removed from her class because she was so angry at him. But she knew this was not possible unless he was provoked to really bad behavior. Intellectually, she knew what to do, but at a feeling level she could not do it. She thought that if she gave in, Sam would get the best of her. She was caught in a dilemma between a possible rational solution and her anger at Sam.

If I told Ms. Brown what to do (that is if I really knew), and what I told her worked, she would call me more frequently and attribute all wisdom about Sam to me. Why should she try to solve problems herself, when she could go to the great oracle?

If I told her what to do and it did not work, then her belief in the hopelessness of the situation would be confirmed. It would also confirm her belief that I did not know what I was talking about.

She needed to be free to try a variety of techniques without any assurances that they would work. We needed to work together to find the best approach. I could offer an objective, outsider's view of the situation, and she was free to try what she wanted. Therefore, we collaborated to try to solve the problem.

Of course, this is a small sample of what might take place in collaborative consultation between a school psychologist and a teacher. The teacher has specific classroom expertise in the areas of curriculum, learning and behavior for the average student, and knowledge of what has and has not worked for him or her in the classroom. The psychologist has generic problem-solving skills, objectivity, and comprehensive training in the diagnosis of human behavior. Their combined expertise can yield solutions that each of them separately could not find.

Goals, Objectives, and Techniques of Intervention

Psychodynamic interventions focus on the child's accepting that there is a problem, trying to understand the nature of the problem (insight), eliminating neurotic, self-defeating defenses, and developing a healthy set of dynamics, including a good self-image. In the best of all possible worlds, every child and family that needed it would receive psychotherapy aimed at meeting these goals. However, this is not always possible, and there are many effective interventions, based on psychodynamic theory, that can be used in schools and homes.

When direct psychotherapeutic intervention is warranted, the teacher's role is actually limited to the observation of students for the purpose of screening or monitoring treatment. Although teachers are never ethically or legally permitted to perform psychotherapy, they can and often do act therapeutically and are able to create therapeutic classroom climates. When therapeutic strategies are employed, the teacher is entitled to consultation with the therapist to receive guidance in helping the child.

There are many possible interventions with the psychodynamic/interpersonal approach. The school psychologist and other professionals will consult with you in deciding which strategies are most appropriate. Perhaps the most fundamental concept is to start with the easiest, most obvious strategy and gradually increase complexity if warranted. Do not be afraid to probe for deeper understandings; you and your students can only benefit from your own increased insights, because the focus on increased individual growth and development makes psychodynamically oriented activities appropriate for all children.

In the behavioral approach, the goal is to change a child's behavior. However, the psychodynamic/interpersonal approach mandates that a major objective is to *help the student gain insight into the reasons for his or her neurotic self-defeating behavior.* It is only through self-understanding and self-analysis that one can make appropriate changes. In other words, we do not control what the child does; we provide the climate in which he or she can feel free and safe to discover the reasons for misbehavior. We can then help the child to use the insight to plan appropriate changes.

In the case of Chris, it is important to discover the true effects of the divorce, remarriage, and birth of a half-sister. Also, it is important to help him to discover that he really is bright enough to do the work. He needs to understand that his use of projection, denial, and rationalization are only cover-ups for his fears that he is really an inadequate, inferior person.

I have never worked with a child who was referred for misbehavior who felt good about himself or herself. Therefore, another objective is to *strengthen ego functioning by improving self-esteem and reality testing.* Many students who misbehave have no understanding of cause and effect. Often they will deny that they did what they did, or they will deny that what they did was worthy of punishment. Statements such as, "I lost my homework," "It wasn't my fault," "You're always picking on me," "It's not fair" are common reactions to reprimands. Projection is the most troubling of all the reactions to disciplinary procedures, because it suggests that the child's reality testing is extremely limited. Therefore, a major goal from a psychodynamic/interpersonal approach is to help children understand how they can face reality without being made to feel worse.

Schooling includes a prescribed series of tasks such as listening to lectures, reading assignments, answering questions in class, homework, complying with rules, and test taking. Students who misbehave invariably feel incompetent, inadequate, inferior, and unable to adequately perform in some or all of these areas. However, these feelings are often repressed or suppressed in an attempt to function with some sense of ego strength.

In conducting school psychology evaluations of students who misbehave, I wish I had a nickel for every time I recommended that the student be placed with a warm, empathetic teacher who can provide structure and direction with a minimum of punishment. These are the conditions necessary for a child to feel safe enough to deal with inner feelings. Poor reality testing indicates that the student is afraid to face subconscious or unconscious feelings of inadequacy, unworthiness, and inferiority. In a safe environment, with an understanding teacher, a student will be able to express these feelings and be able to discover that others also have them. The teacher can help this type of student to understand that worthiness is not dependent only on the ability to produce academically at the level desired by parents or others. The student can learn that the important thing is to function within one's own ability and to accept one's limitations and to build on strengths.

A major issue that divides the psychodynamic/interpersonal approach from most of the others is the deterministic view for the existence of primary drives for pleasure and self-enchancement. Most theorists posit that anger is a natural reaction when drives and needs are not satisfied. If anger is natural, then aggression must also be an inherited part of our nature. An objective of this approach is to help the student to *develop socially acceptable expressions of impulses such as anger, which result in misbehavior.* Therefore, it is important to learn to rechannel anger and aggression. These feelings cannot be eliminated if they are instinctual.

Techniques of Intervention

From the earliest ages, children learn at different stages and in different levels of cognition that there are acceptable ways of expressing their anger. At the most primitive level, children bite. Because this is an instinctual reaction, it is not appropriate to bite the child back or to hit the child. It is more appropriate to restrain the child from biting while the child screams and yells as an expression of their anger. It is also appropriate to help children to rechannel their energies into other activities after discovering what is frustrating them.

After biting, children learn to hit. Again, this is a primitive instinctual method of expressing anger. Hitting children back does not teach them anything except that the one who wins is the one with the most strength. It is more appropriate to teach the child to verbally express his or her anger. By school age, most children have learned not to bite and hit and are struggling with verbal methods of expressing their anger. Again, if children curse in class, a teacher would not curse back at them or call them names. It is better to recognize that anger is an expression of frustration and to discover the causes. Attempts to stamp out anger through punishment and exclusion will invariably fail.

Fighting, vandalism, cursing, and sexual molestation of fellow students are the most serious expressions of anger in school. Each of these suggests unmet needs and neurotic behavior. These students have not learned to sublimate their drives, which have emerged in a very primitive form.

Sublimation involves acceptable expressions of unmet needs. For instance, aggressive boys have typically been channeled into sports, where their anger can be expressed in socially appropriate ways. Contact sports, such as football, lacrosse, soccer, and wrestling, are outlets for anger. But more important, these and other sports stress the need for discipline and self-restraint to succeed.

Besides providing for sublimation activities, schools may to a limited extent, provide for *abreaction*. Abreaction is a process by which unconscious and subconscious thoughts, feelings, and ideas are brought to the surface. For instance, a boy who is constantly inappropriately touching girls may be unconsciously working out unresolved issues with his mother or sister. In psychotherapy, the abreaction of an emotion occurs as the patient gains awareness of the relationship between his or her inappropriate behavior and unconscious feelings of anger and frustration.

Teachers, of course, are not psychotherapists, but they can understand the therapeutic process and apply it in the classroom. This can be done through discussion of movies, books, and plays. For instance, a teenage girl who hates her male teachers may not be able to connect this behavior with her anger at her father. Discussions around these themes can occur to help the student to let out her anger about fathers in general without actually going into personal issues.

The following is a list of techniques that might be explored in the case of Chris. They are listed here for you to consider. We have not spelled each one out, because at this point you need to explore what you think might work. But before considering these, you should make up a complete case history for Chris and then plan interventions based on your diagnosis.

Specific techniques you might wish to consider for Chris include:

1. Individual psychotherapy
2. Group psychotherapy
3. Family psychotherapy
4. Play therapy
5. Bibliotherapy–videotherapy (Dreyer, 1992)
6. Self-analysis through writing and discussing an autobiography
7. Peer projects
8. Big brother/sister
9. Esteem building activities within the classroom and school
10. Environmental/staff changes
11. Psychodrama and role playing
12. Peer counseling

Environmental interventions are the simplest. These are aimed specifically at the setting or people with whom the child interacts. Specific strategies include:

1. Modifying the environment to fulfill students' individual needs (i.e., flexible seating arrangement for an insecure child)
2. Encouraging others to help students to enhance their self-images
3. Providing the opportunity for the students to identify with appropriate adult models such as supportive, nurturing authority figures
4. Encouraging the development of prosocial behaviors, especially the expression/control of impulses in appropriate ways
5. Using special curriculum materials to help students improve their self-images and to learn more about their own problems

6. Improving students' academic skills through appropriate instruction so they feel good about school
7. Helping to change students' distorted perceptions by using relevant books as therapeutic material through such techniques as bibliotherapy (Dreyer, 1992)
8. In crisis situations using life space interviewing (Wood & Long, 1991) for on-the-spot problem resolution by first eliciting and accepting the student's view and exploring possible solutions

   Preventive strategies include:

1. Developing a positive relationship with the child, perhaps using TA models
2. Providing the opportunity for identification with appropriate persons in the environment
3. Encouraging the healthy expression of emotions through art, music, writing, dance, drama, and play
4. Working through normal developmental issues in groups with other children
5. Providing parents with education, guidelines, and remedial strategies with an understanding of current behavior in terms of early development and family dynamics

When you discuss which approaches you might use, be sure to spell them out and determine that they can really be instituted. Will the teacher, parents, and school authorities allow you to do them? This approach requires an especially high level of insight, patience, and determination for school staff. But it also offers promise of long-term gains for pupils and staff.

Examples of Psychodynamic/Interpersonal Programs

Table 4.7 on pages 126–127 offers a summary analysis of sample programs from the psychodynamic/interpersonal approach.

Dreikurs and Dinkmeyer

The bond between Adler, Dreikurs, and Dinkmeyer (Dinkmeyer, McKay & Dinkmeyer, 1980) is the agreement that all behavior, including misbehavior, is orderly, purposeful, and directed toward achieving social recognition (Dreikurs, 1968). When students are unsuccessful in obtaining the recognition they desire, a pattern of misbehavior begins. An attempt is made to fulfill inner needs by annoying, destructive, hostile, or helpless behavior (Wolfgang & Glickman, 1986). The role of the teacher is to help students understand their "mistaken goals" and provide them with other options for group acceptance. As a result of this intervention, it is suggested that students will rationally change their own behavior. Using an Adlerian framework, they define four major goals or "mistaken goals" that subconsciously motivate misbehavior: (1) Attention getting occurs when an individual who is constantly looking to belong and be recognized in the class resorts to acting in ways that demand incessant praise or criticism; (2) Power and control may be the goal of the below-average student who feels

TABLE 4.7   Examples of Psychodynamic/Interpersonal Models

Program	Underlying Theory	Assumptions	Diagnosis	Intervention/Remediation	Research
Driekurs & Dinkmeyer	Based on the work of Alfred Adler, which indicates that all human beings are motivated to belong and be accepted by others.	All behavior, including misbehavior, is orderly, purposeful, and directed toward achieving social recognition.	The four mistaken goals that subconsciously motivate misbehavior include attention getting; power and control; revenge; and helplessness or inadequacy.	Involves the use of natural or logical consequences and the process of encouragement. Natural consequences are naturally occurring events to specific situations. Logical consequences are results that follow certain behaviors and are arranged by the teacher.	Equivocal results have been found because of the complexity of this approach and the difficulty in determining what procedures results in which outcomes. However, some studies have shown an increased teacher knowledge and application of Adlerian concepts after training.
Albert's Cooperative Discipline	This approach is based on the theories of Adler and Driekurs.	Both internal and external forces shape student's behavior and misbehavior.	Albert outlines a five-step School Action Plan, which includes: (1) pinpoint and describe the student's behavior, (2) identify the goal of misbehavior (from the four noted in Driekurs & Dinkmeyer), (3) choose the intervention techniques for the moment of misbehavior, (4) select encouragement techniques to build self-esteem, and (5) involve parents as partners.	Six basic guidelines include (1) focus on the behavior, not the student, (2) take charge of negative emotions, (3) avoid escalating the situation, (4) discuss misbehavior later, (5) allow students to "save face," and (6) model nonaggressive behavior.	Empirical data for Albert's model have not been found in the literature.
Transactional Analysis	Based on the work of Eric Berne, which indicates that every person has an innate need for recognition (strokes) and will design a plan (life script) during childhood that is based on early beliefs about self and others. These early beliefs are then reinforced by each person engaging in repetitive, stereotyped "games" with others.	Every person is born to be a winner, and therefore, people have the ability to identify behaviors they want to change and the ability to implement the change.	The goal is to identify in which "ego state" an individual is functioning, which includes the child, adult, or parent (similar to Freud's id, ego, and superego). Then one must identify the "game" that is being played (e.g., attention getting, oppositional behavior, etc.).	Although there are various treatments for each diagnosis, the following general strategies have been described: (1) analyze the game that the student is playing, (2) don't play the game!, (3) give strokes or attention that affirm the child's worth, and (4) allow the child to find his/her own solution.	Most of the research on TA was conducted in the 1960s and 1970s. A computerized search of the literature revealed no current studies analyzing TA and classroom discipline. Most of the research focused on the impact of TA on psychotherapy.

Redl and Wattenberg's Mental Hygiene	Redl & Wattenberg have translated psychodynamic concepts into classroom procedures. The model provides insight into both psychological and social forces that affect student behavior in classroom groups.	The group is distinctly different from the individual, and the teacher must understand group processes, as well as individual differences, to effectively teach and maintain order. It is also assumed that group behavior in the classroom is influenced by how the students perceive the teacher.	Diagnostic strategies include: forming a hunch, gathering facts, applying hidden factors, taking action, and being flexible. Teachers need to identify the various roles a student may play, such as leader, clown, fall guy, and instigator. Each of these roles provides a person with a sense of belonging to the group.	Teachers maintain group control by: (1) addressing the problem before it becomes serious, (2) helping students to regain control, (3) teaching students the underlying causes of misbehavior and helping them to foresee probable consequences, and (4) rewarding good behavior and punishing negative behavior.	Because this program is theoretical in nature, there is no empirical support for the Redl & Wattenberg model in the literature. One of Redl's interventions methods, Life Space Intervention, is being field validated (Wood & Long, 1991).
Hiam Ginott's Approach	The theory originated from Ginott's work on the relationship between adults and children. It is a communication model that espouses the use of congruent communication between adults and children.	Adults significantly impact on children's self-esteem through the messages they send. Ginott sees the adults (e.g., teachers) and their behaviors as the most important element in maintaining discipline.	By addressing the situation rather than the individual's character, adults communicate that they know what is going on, they know what they want changed, and they are aware of the person's feelings. Helpfulness and acceptance are continually being conveyed.	Adults at their best send sane messages, express anger appropriately, avoid labeling students, avoid the perils of praise, and are brief when correcting students. Also, "I" and "You" messages are used to convey how adults feel about the situation.	There are no empirical data in the literature to support Ginott's model of discipline.

unable to live up to the expectations of self or others. The result is an attempt to compensate for the perception of inferiority by bragging, clowning, being the boss, or forcing oneself on others; (3) The drive for revenge results from an inability to gain attention or power. Revenge seekers see themselves as having unequal status because of what others have done to them. Blaming others, these students may resort to achieving status by bullying, putting down, and humiliating others. They may also resort to malicious gossip.

A mistaken self-perception of helplessness or inadequacy occurs when students believe that they cannot do anything right or when they see themselves as total failures. They have given up on the possibility of belonging to or gaining status in a peer group. According to Dreikurs and Cassel (1972), they see themselves as nothing more than "blobs." This unfortunate situation may occur as the final stage in a series that begins with (1) attention getting, which often leads to (2) power struggles, which when thwarted, lead to the desire for (3) revenge, which may be unsuccessful or result in "apprehension," leading to (4) using disability as an excuse. This mistaken thinking is very serious and difficult for students and teachers to overcome.

Disciplinary problems must be approached by using consequences that are impersonal and not the result of arbitrary personal authority. Adlerian theory, as explained by Dreikurs, relies on the use of logical consequences and encouragement to elicit positive behavior, rather than punishment of discipline problems or excessive praise for compliance.

Dreikurs fully recognizes the impact that a good teacher has on a child. He views the democratic educator as the ideal. According to Dreikurs, a democratic teacher provides guidance, encouragement, and recognizes achievement. In addition, a democratic instructor works at cooperating with others and sharing responsibility in team efforts (Dreikurs & Cassel, 1972, p. 19).

Once teachers understand the issue of mistaken goals and the impact these have on classroom climate and learning, they are prepared to move to the important issue of discipline. Dreikurs does not believe in the use of punishment, negative reinforcement, or excessive praise. Instead, he substitutes "natural/logical consequences" and the process of encouragement. These are results that follow certain behaviors and are arranged by the teacher. It should be noted that these consequences are not weapons used by the teacher. Logical consequences must be explained, understood, and agreed to by students. They should also relate as closely as possible to the misbehavior, so students can see the connection between them.

According to Dreikurs, consequences must be applied each and every time misbehavior occurs. This helps students to make their own choices about how they will behave. Children learn to rely on their own inner discipline to control their actions. Additionally, they learn that poor choices will result in unpleasant consequences (Charles, 1989). Dreikurs explains that classroom group discussions are an ideal place in which to set the limits of behavior in the class and to devise logical consequences for any misbehavior (Chance, 1985).

Natural consequences are those that follow as a direct result of action. For instance, a burnt finger is the natural consequence of touching a hot stove (Hyman et al., 1982). There is no outside intervention to either make this happen or to stop it. Most children learn that the natural consequence of putting their hands on a hot stove is pain. Children learn to cope with the world as a result of experiences with natural consequences. However, parents should not always allow all natural or dangerous consequences to occur.

A natural consequence of running out into the street without looking could be serious injury or death. Therefore, an alternative set of consequences is desirable. The child could be restricted to a fenced yard, or the parent could teach the child that pain may accompany dashing into the street. This is done by associating the street with something that causes the child pain. The parent could teach the child to look both ways and tell the parent when he or she is ready to cross the street. These alternatives follow logically from the illogical behavior of dashing into the street without looking. In each of these, the child is being offered a choice to avoid bad consequences.

Logical consequences are those that do not follow directly from the act, yet are reasonably related consequences. A distinction is made between consequences and punishment. For instance, logical consequences express the reality of the social order, that is, rules of living. Punishment, in contrast, teaches the power of personal authority.

A logical consequence is sensibly related to a misbehavior, whereas punishment generally is arbitrarily imposed, with no connection to the behavior. A logical consequence involves no element of moral judgment, whereas punishment inevitably is concomitant with moral censure. Logical consequences are concerned only with what will happen in the present, whereas punishment is concerned with the past. Finally, logical consequences occur without the anger (open or concealed) that frequently accompanies punishment.

The logical consequence procedure is to be used in tandem with students' accepting the consequences for their misbehavior or correcting the behavior. Logical consequences follow immediately after the misbehavior. They should also relate as closely as possible to the misbehavior, so students can see the connection between the two.

In schools, consequences should not be used as weapons by teachers. They should be explained, understood, and agreed on by the student before intervention is begun. This technique may be very effective if the goal of the student is attention getting, because this behavior can be relatively easily pointed out to students.

Adlerian theory places a great deal of emphasis on the use of *encouragement.* Children must be encouraged to do the correct thing, because they are capable of self-determination. Because we choose to behave properly, we can also choose to misbehave.

Encouragement is a crucial aspect to the approach. Through encouragement, children develop attitudes that help them to correct and avoid future mistakes, in contrast to *praise,* which implies a value judgment. Encouragement:

1. Places value on children as they are
2. Shows faith in children and helps them develop faith in themselves
3. Demonstrates belief in the child's ability, wins the child's confidence, and builds self-respect
4. Recognizes a job "well done"
5. Uses the classroom as a group to facilitate development of the child
6. Integrates the group, because it does not pit one child against another
7. Assists in the successful development of various skills without stressing competition
8. Recognizes strengths and focuses on assets
9. Uses the child's interest to facilitate learning
10. Deemphasizes emotional problems while emphasizing self-determination

Driekurs and Dinkmeyer's adaptations of Adlerian psychology have the strengths of using democratic principles in a democratic society. The approach develops a system of mutual respect, it allows children time to solve their own problems during class discussion, it involves the entire class in decision making, it helps to aid in the socialization of the student, it includes in the Systematic Training for Effective Teaching (STET) training materials a step-by-step procedure to obtain goals, and it includes natural and logical consequences (Wolfgang and Glickman, 1986). Charles (1989, p. 86) adds that this model helps students to ultimately build an inner sense of responsibility and respect for others.

In contrast, Chance (1985, p. 102) points out that Dreikurs's approach is not as well defined or structured as other discipline models. In addition, Charles (1989, p. 86) presents the same criticism here as he did with Ginott's model: How does one handle the hard-to-manage classrooms, especially when students defy the teacher? Dreikurs does not address how this is to be done. Further criticisms suggest that teachers may not always be able to determine a child's true goal, that a passive child would be very difficult to help with this approach, and, at times, it can be hard to determine natural or logical consequences.

The research on Dreikurs' model is equivocal because the model is somewhat complicated, and it is therefore difficult to determine which procedures result in which outcomes. A review of ten efficacy studies completed before 1979 indicated more about the inadequacy of the methodologies than how effective the programs were. However, three studies that included pretest and posttest measures (two used control groups) suggested that the approach might reduce vandalism, improve attitudes of trained staff, and improve some behaviors of disturbed students (Hyman, Bogacki et al., 1979).

The few more recent studies identified are not much more convincing than the pre-1979 studies. Consider, for example, a case study by Gamble & Watkins (1983), which incorporated the approaches of Alfred Adler and William Glasser. A treatment plan was presented addressing the therapeutic relationship, classroom interventions, and family interventions. Although these researchers found both models to be highly useful in effecting change in misbehaving children, the use of both approaches together makes it extremely difficult to assess the Adlerian approach on its own merit. In addition, concepts such as logical consequences were used in the family intervention phase as opposed to the classroom intervention plan. Finally, with a sample size of one, it is hard to generalize these findings, regardless of the number of discipline models used.

Another study attempted to correlate an eleven-week collegiate course in Adlerian skills with teacher attitude change (Kibler, Rush, & Sweeney, 1985). The Minnesota Teacher Attitude Inventory (MTAI) was used to measure attitude change. Results indicated the development of positive attitudes toward the Adlerian democratic principles of child discipline, as well as significantly higher MTAI scores in the treatment group. Increased MTAI scores continued up to twelve weeks after treatment. However, limitations again included a small sample size and an inability to generalize findings to other populations. In addition, subjects were not randomly assigned to groups. Similarly, Cady (1983) found that teachers participating in an eight-day summer workshop made significant gains on the MTAI, in the direction of a student-focused, nonauthoritarian perspective. Gains were also seen on tests of knowledge and application of Adlerian concepts, and these gains only diminished slightly after three months. It should be noted that one threat to internal validity was the self-selection of the teachers into the instructional groups.

In general, it is known that global attitudes do not necessarily predict behavior in specific situations. The research cited suggests that Adlerian types of training do result in participants' changes of attitudes as measured by scales after training. Whether these attitudes toward more democratic teaching survive over time or actually translate into effective disciplinary procedures is not really known.

Albert's Cooperative Discipline

Linda Albert's (1989) Cooperative Discipline is a kindergarten through twelfth-grade in-service training program based on the theories of Adler and Dreikurs. Both internal and external forces shape students' behavior and misbehavior. Albert views cooperative discipline as a "hands-joined," two-pronged approach to classroom management. In the spirit of democratic principles, teachers are cooperative leaders who guide students by offering choices, setting limits, and involving them in the process. The focus is on corrective and preventive approaches. According to Albert (1989), the goal of cooperative discipline is to build positive relationships, as well as self-esteem to enable students to freely choose appropriate, positive behavior.

A five-step action plan gives teachers a practical framework for dealing with misbehavior. Students needs are addressed through the completion of five action steps (School Action Plan): (1) pinpoint and describe the student's behavior, (2) identify the goal of the misbehavior, (3) choose the intervention techniques for the moment of misbehavior, (4) select encouragement techniques to build self-esteem, and (5) involve students, parents, and others as partners.

Cooperative discipline is identical to Dreikurs's theory in terms of defining the drives for misbehavior as the need for attention, power, revenge, or the avoidance of failure. The ultimate goal of student behavior is to fulfill the need to belong. Albert goes further than Dreikurs by providing many specific strategies and techniques to deal with students' drives. Consequently, much of Albert's discussion in her book focuses on how to appropriately minimize these four needs. She outlines six basic guidelines for intervention: (1) focus on the behavior, not the student; (2) take charge of negative emotions; (3) avoid escalating the situation; (4) discuss misbehavior later; (5) allow students to "save face"; and (6) model nonaggressive behavior.

In an attempt to build self-esteem, Albert emphasizes encouragement strategies. She states that teachers need to allow mistakes, build confidence, focus on past success, make learning tangible, and recognize achievement. The ideal classroom climate to encourage the development of self-esteem provides for the "five As," which include acceptance, attention, appreciation, affirmation, and affection (1989, p. 117).

Albert's approach differs from Dreikurs's in terms of emphasis on parental involvement. According to Albert (1989), parents play a vital role in the cooperative discipline process. For example, before discipline problems occur, parents are to be notified about cooperative discipline (e.g., written policy statement). Also, to inspire parental cooperation, educators must establish an atmosphere of mutual support (e.g., talk about misbehavior in objective terms, anticipate success). Furthermore, parents should be initially notified about a School Action Plan by telephone. As a result of this contact, a conference may be planned to discuss the School Action Plan or develop a Home Action Plan. During this process, both parents and teachers are encouraged to provide input.

Linda Albert's cooperative discipline approach, as with other Adlerian models, attempts to develop a system of mutual respect, involves a step-by-step procedure according to goals, may not be the best method for the more hard-to-manage students, and may not be useful to help determine a child's true goal in a specific situation. However, Albert (Personal Communication, 1995) claims that her strategies for dealing with students' needs for power and revenge (to appear in her second edition) demonstrate how her approach can be successfully used with difficult students in many school districts. However, anecdotal evidence and testimonials, as are available for STET and for Dreikurs's approach to discipline, do not offer scientific support. Few empirical data specifically focusing on the efficacy of cooperative discipline were found in the literature. Newlon and Arciniega's (1983) study suggests student gains in knowledge, understanding, and application of Adlerian principles and teacher improvement toward greater positive perceptions of selected students' behavior.

Transactional Analysis for Teachers

Teachers tend to like TA because it offers a tool for productive verbal confrontation (Ford, 1984). Verbal game-stopping is seen as a powerful step to terminate manipulative behaviors of problem students. In addition, by helping students through the stages of this approach, teachers help develop their own maturity. Another strength is that TA provides a construct that enables teachers to critically evaluate their verbal/nonverbal interchange with students. This model helps students to learn to communicate with their adult ego state and helps them to differentiate feelings into parent, adult, and child ego states.

Transactional analysis is a psychodynamic approach that deals with the cognitive level. Teachers are encouraged to determine the games they play in relation to their feelings about themselves and their interaction with others. The intention is to develop the teacher into an OK person who deals with others typically at an adult level.

Transactional Analysis saw its heyday in the 1960s and 1970s, when most of the research in this approach was conducted. A dissertation done by Niblett (1979) reported several studies suggesting significant results in the use of TA with teachers and students: For example, Peek (1975) found short-term positive changes in self-concept for 48 delinquents. In addition, deSantis (1975) discovered positive effects on truancy and suspension rates for a high school class. Further, Harbin (1975) noted positive changes in teacher talk behavior. Finally, Cooper (1977) showed a significant positive relationship between knowledge of TA and positive teacher attitude toward students. However, no significant difference existed between the experimental and control groups for teacher attitudes toward students.

An underlying problem with TA theory is that much current developmental research indicates that children remember little about their experiences before the age of five. Despite Berne's assertions that all early experiences are absorbed as part of the parent ego, the data suggest that these early experiences are not processed and stored properly until the brain matures around the age of five. As with other psychodynamic/interpersonal models, limitations of TA fall into two categories: time consumption and complexity (Ford, 1984, p. 20). Many teachers have reported feeling limited by the amount of time needed to stop verbal game-playing in the classroom. Others found difficulty in the amount of complexity and confidence required for an effective use of TA. For example, it may be hard for people to distinguish which of the three ego states is speaking. In addition, it is believed that the adult as a rational ego state in the early years of life is weak and can easily be replaced by the child's or parent's demands (Wolfgang & Glickman, 1986). Furthermore, there does not seem to be a clear plan for changing students' misbehaviors. Finally, as found with Teacher Effectiveness Training (TET), TA may not be an effective method with those children who are nonverbal or who demonstrate language difficulties.

A computerized search of the literature uncovered no current studies analyzing TA and classroom discipline. In fact, it appears that very little research has been done assessing the impact of TA in any area other than psychotherapy.

The few studies focusing on TA and students have shown mixed results. For example, Bechstrand (1973) attempted to change the locus of control of 90 students by analyzing the relationship between TA and written expression. Findings suggested that there was a significant difference in locus of control for the experimental group. In contrast, McCormick (1973) compared TA with behavior modification in the treatment of juvenile delinquents. However, he found little evidence that TA was superior to behavior modification in working with this population.

It is clear that more research is needed with TA and children before this can be considered an empirically supported model.

Fritz Redl and William Wattenberg's Mental Hygiene and Hiam Ginott's Approach

The works of Redl and Wattenberg (1951) and Ginott (1969, 1971) contributed greatly to the translation of psychodynamic theory to the problems of schoolchildren. Many of their concepts and techniques are still widely used.

Redl and Wattenberg stressed diagnostic thinking by the teacher and focus on group management. This involves forming a first hunch, gathering facts, understanding hidden factors, taking action, and being flexible. According to Redl and Wattenberg, teachers maintain group control through various influence techniques (Chance, 1985). These include:

1. Helping students develop self-control techniques that address the problem before it becomes serious
2. Teacher use of eye contact, physical proximity, encouragement, humor, and playful ignoring
3. Situational assistance techniques (when students cannot regain control without assistance from the teacher), such as helping students over a hurdle, restructuring the schedule, establishing routines, removing the student from a situation, removing seductive objects (causing one to be distractible), and, when necessary, physical restraint
4. Appraising reality techniques that help students to understand underlying causes of misbehavior and to foresee probable consequences that include offering encouragement, criticism, setting limits, and clarifying situations once the disciplinary difficulty has been stabilized

5. Pleasure/pain techniques that involve rewarding good behavior and punishing bad behavior. Punishment should be used only as a last resort because it can be extremely
   counterproductive. They are adamantly against corporal punishment and even add that
   overpraising can have detrimental effects.

Ginott (1965, 1969, 1971) believed that adults significantly impact children's self-
esteem through the messages they send. In an effort to keep this impact positive, he developed specific skills for dealing with parent–child and teacher–student conflicts.

Ginott introduced the differences between "I" and "you" messages, which were later
expanded by Thomas Gordon (1974), in his Teacher Effectiveness Training (TET), which is
discussed in the chapter on humanism. Ginott's model is somewhat unique in that it stresses
that teachers should exemplify good behavior in their own personal conduct, thereby offering ego-ideal models (Charles, 1989; Chance, 1985). Although many of the techniques are
widely used and seem to make sense, there are few empirical studies to support either model.

Summary, Research, and Critique

A major strength of the psychodynamic/interpersonal approach is that it emphasizes a thorough understanding of why a particular child misbehaves. Often, the mere process of studying a student causes teachers to change their behavior in positive ways. Furthermore, as
teachers begin to gain insights into psychodynamic principles, they are better able to understand misbehavior in a broader, diagnostic context. As a result, they begin to develop habits
of hypothesizing and testing the hypotheses by trying different strategies. The major weakness with the approach is that it requires a great deal of reading, studying, and consulting
with others to really become proficient. Furthermore, in regular classrooms, some of the
techniques, such as the use of abreaction to deal with anger, are not appropriate. Many
teachers want quick answers and techniques that are immediately effective. This approach
does not provide for quick fixes.

When you choose the psychodynamic/interpersonal approach to classroom management, you make a commitment to study the child and the personality structure. You agree
to become familiar with the basic philosophy of the psychodynamic viewpoint and to apply
that knowledge to your educational setting. You agree to employ a certain program consistently and completely. In addition, you realize that you must monitor the progress of the
child. This can be done by use of anecdotal records, talking to the child, and observing the
child's behavior by use of systematic techniques. Although this takes some initial planning,
you will find that it eliminates daily discipline alterations and, actually, saves time. Besides
that, you might be willing to invest some time and energy to gain the control and understanding of the class that you want to have.

Difficulty in analyzing some problem behaviors or situations can be brought to the
attention of the school psychologist. Every problem behavior deserves consideration for
psychodynamic intervention; however, you may notice that it is not appropriate in all situations. Also, it may be necessary to seek additional interventions outside of the school setting. This is especially true if therapy is needed and not available in the school.

Psychodynamic approaches are especially appropriate when the concern is with long-term personality change. Teachers must be aware that intervention may not result in the immediate cessation of problem behaviors.

This approach is applicable to situations in which a student's ability to establish relationships and test reality are not severely impaired, because insight is important for change to occur. Also, success is often dependent on good adult role models who have some insight into their own behavior when they interact with oppositional, defiant students. They must also be aware of appropriate developmental norms, so that they can set appropriate standards for classroom behavior and be able to help parents to set appropriate limits at home. Without many of these, prognosis may be poor.

Key Terms

abreaction
complementary transactions
crossed transactions
defense mechanism
denial
displacement
ego
encouragement
expiatory
fixation
goal directed
id
inferiority complex

logical consequences
natural consequences
parent/child/adult
praise
projection
rationalism
regression
repression
sublimation
superego
suppression
ulterior transactions

Application Activities

1. Diagnose Juanita from a psychodynamic/interpersonal approach. What defense mechanisms is she using? Develop intervention and treatment plans using Freudian theory.

2. Diagnose Michael from a psychodynamic/interpersonal approach. Where is he according to Erikson's psychosocial development stages? Develop intervention and treatment plans using Adlerian theory.

3. Diagnose Jamal using a psychodynamic/interpersonal approach. Where is he according to Kohlberg's moral development stages? Develop intervention and treatment plans using transactional analysis theory.

4. Diagnose Chris using a psychodynamic/interpersonal approach. Describe his ego functioning according to Freudian theory. Develop intervention and treatment plans.

5. Develop a whole class lesson plan using Albert's cooperative discipline model.

Suggested Readings

Adler, A. (1979). In H. L. Ansbacher & R. R. Ansbacher (Eds.), *Superiority and social interest: A collection of later writings* (3rd rev. ed.). New York: Norton.

Albert, L. (1989). *Cooperative discipline*. Circle Pines, MN: American Guidance Services.

Berne, E. (1964). *Games people play*. New York: Grove Press.

Dinkmeyer, D. C., McKay, D. C., & Dinkmeyer, D. Jr., (1980). *Systematic training for effective teaching (STET)*. Circle Pines, MN: American Guidance Service.

Dreikurs, R. (1968). *Psychology in the classroom* (2nd ed.). New York: Harper & Row.

Dreikurs, R., & Soltz, V. (1964). *Children: The challenge*. New York: Meridith Press.

Erikson, E. H. (1963). *Childhood and society* (2nd ed.). New York: Norton.

Erikson, E. H. (1968). *Identity: Youth and crisis*. New York: Norton.

Ernst, K. (1972). *Games students play*. Berkeley, CA: Celestial Arts.

Freud, S. (1949). *An outline of psychoanalysis*. New York: Norton.

Ginott, H. (1971). *Teacher and child*. New York: Macmillan.

Hall, C. S. (1954). *A primer of Freudian psychology*. New York: Penguin Group.

Kohlberg, L. (1981). *The philosophy of moral development*. New York: Harper & Row.

Piaget, J. (1970). *The science of education and the psychology of the child*. New York: Orion Press.

Piaget, J., & Inhelder, B. (1969). *The psychology of the child*. New York: Basic Books.

Redl, L. E., & Wattenberg, W. W. (1951). *Mental hygiene in teaching*. New York: Harcourt, Brace, & Jovanovich.

Chapter 5

The Humanistic Approach

Chapter Objectives

After reading this chapter, you should know:

1. The philosophical and historical roots of the humanistic approach, including Comte, Guarino, Rousseau
2. The assumptions, goals, interventions, treatment, and techniques of the humanistic approach
3. John Dewey's progressive education
4. Maslow's holistic–dynamic theory of personality
5. Carl Roger's client-centered therapy
6. Kohn's theory of teaching caring, noncompetitive, altruistic behavior
7. Neill's theory of open education
8. Kohl's theory of open education
9. Rath and Simon's Values Clarification
10. Gordon's Teacher Effectiveness Training
11. Research and critique of the humanistic approach

The humanistic approach within the teacher variance model comprises a constellation of beliefs that intertwine with philosophy, psychology, history, religion, politics, ethics, and psychobiological research. Of the five models that we consider, none is more capable of stirring heated, impassioned controversy and political action.

If you are strong in the humanistic approach on the Teacher Variance Inventory, you believe that:

1. All people are born with an inherent capacity for empathy, caring, curiosity, spontaneity, and goodness and strive toward being competent, loved, and self-actualized.
2. All children have an innate desire to learn.
3. Children's desires to learn are stifled when schools frustrate their unique needs, their individual learning styles, and their need to become competent in their own way.

4. Bureaucracies, such as schools, which are organized in hierarchical, authoritarian structures, suppress individuality, unique styles of self-expression, and self-actualization.
5. Misbehavior occurs when students are not allowed to learn in their own ways or to express and fulfill their unique needs without hurting others.
6. Misbehavior occurs when students rebel against the unjust authority and tyranny of meaningless rules, regulations, and curricula.
7. Participatory democracy should be taught as a process in schools.
8. The focus of education should be on the process and joy of learning, rather than on memorizing and regurgitating specific course contents and facts to pass tests.

If you scored high in humanism on the TVI and also had a low score on the Survey of Attitudes toward Children, indicating that you are less punitive than the norm, your peers may judge you as being too liberal. In the minds of many Americans, liberalism and humanism are synonymous, in that both terms apply to people who do not necessarily, automatically subscribe to "traditional values." When we present teacher variance workshops in schools, especially in rural areas, teachers who identify themselves in this category also state that they are different from most staff members. They are often viewed as being too liberal, idealistic, and naive and are sometimes perceived as covert or overt rebels. If they teach in conservative areas of the country, they inevitably run into severe conflicts with administrators.

If you scored high on humanism and sometimes feel you do not quite fit into the discipline approaches in your school, you are not alone. Resistance to rigidity, authoritarianism, and punitiveness has been a hallmark of humanist movements throughout Western history. Humanism is a philosophy that strives to free the mind and spirit from narrow, parochial thinking. This is an approach that helps students to broaden their thinking, to examine themselves, and to develop methods of critical inquiry. In other words, humanism, liberalism, and liberal arts are inexorably intertwined.

A Brief Historical Perspective

In education, the term *humanism* was first used during the Renaissance, when there was a surge of interest in individualism and rebellion against Church-dominated authority over all intellectual, spiritual, and social aspects of life (Cordacso, 1963). Batista Guarino, an early theorist and supporter of the humanities, helped define them in 1459. He stated, "Learning and training in virtue are peculiar to man: therefore our forefathers called them 'Humanities,' the pursuits, the activities proper to mankind" (Cordacso, 1963, p. 43).

Batista Guarino's concept of education anticipated the first humanist movement, which occurred in the early sixteenth century. It was represented by a revival of interest in Greek and Roman studies. After a long period in education dominated by ecclesiastic concerns of the Catholic Church, this early humanism opened the way for later interest in the concept of liberal education.

Unfortunately, as often happens in educational reform, by the end of the sixteenth century, humanistic education became associated with slavish adherence to drill, memorization of passages and facts, translation, and recitation in Latin and Greek. Grammar and linguistic meanings of the ancient Greek and Latin cultures were predominant in the schools. Students spent long hours in memorization, regurgitation of facts, translations of long passages, and drills. The biblical injunctions of complete obedience to authority led to a climate characterized by monotonous, sometimes cruel demands for compliance, resulting in many misbehaviors, which typically were "remedied" by beatings.

The revolt against the Catholic Church was an important aspect of the sixteenth century. This part of humanism resulted in the imposition of memorization of religious catechisms, creeds, and church services to the already overbearing rote requirements of the humanistic curricula. In fact, by the end of the sixteenth century, humanistic and religious education were one and the same. Eventually, the English Latin schools that represented this genre of education were transplanted to colonial America. Those schools perfected techniques of corporal punishment of schoolchildren (Greven, 1990, 1991; Manning, 1979). How interesting that the early meanings of humanism, associated with rote learning, religious indoctrination, and stress on obedience to authority, eventually became associated with a diametrically opposed educational philosophy.

In the seventeenth century, humanistic realism and sense realism represented the next steps toward eventual curriculum reform. This was reflected in a revolt against the formalism of earlier humanistic education and a greater concern with self-enhancement through the study of ancient literature. Efforts were made to teach practical skills, theoretical and applied science, mathematics, and morality. There was an attempt to individualize education, an important stepping stone to the evolution of contemporary humanism. Most schools, especially those in England, continued the practice of corporal punishment throughout this period.

It was not until the eighteenth century that major philosophers began to truly articulate approaches that led to our common understanding of contemporary humanism. Perhaps the most formidable and well-known humanist theorist was Jean-Jacques Rousseau. Rousseau extolled the values of nature as opposed to civilization, cities, and science. He rejected concepts of original sin and the need to discipline and train children according to the reigning views of morality and education. He proposed that education provide children with opportunities to develop their own natures, powers, and inclinations. This concept, tied to his view of the Utopian world of the "savage," was at extreme odds with most of education in his time and for many educators today.

Rousseau is remembered for his dethronement of reason, the exaltation of passion and his views of the value of nature and naturalness in moral and educational development (Manuel & Manuel, 1979). Rousseau stressed that education should come from within and in interaction with all of life. He strongly believed that children are basically positive and good. Therefore, if education is ever to have real meaning, it must be based solely on the child's life and experiences (Cordacso, 1963).

Although Rousseau never recommended the dissolution of curricula in education, in his most famous educational treatise, *Emile,* he stressed the need to allow for free expression of children's natural goodness, curiosity, and love of nature. Formal education should not begin until the age of twelve. Because the child's natural inclination toward morality is inherent, it is not until the age of fifteen that students should learn about morality and religion as they apply to life and society.

Much nineteenth century educational theory was based on the writings of Rousseau. His assumptions about individuality, instincts, tendencies, and natural development laid the groundwork for developmental psychology. "His insistence on the study of the phenomenon of nature . . . [led to] . . . the scientific movement in education; his advocacy of an education which prepared the individual to live in society led to sociological theories in education" (Cordacso, 1963, p. 34). Important features of his philosophy included:

1. His belief in the goodness of the child
2. His belief that human nature is essentially good, as opposed to prevailing religious concepts of his time of original sin
3. His opposition to religious and educational indoctrination and punitiveness designed to suppress or eradicate the purported inherent badness in children
4. The importance of letting children determine their early learning agendas and their own learning styles.

These are all aspects of the concept of naturalism that still survives among educational theorists. However, many of his related beliefs were and still are rejected as impractical by most educators, especially with regard to discipline.

In the nineteenth century, the tremendous growth in science and technology, the advent of industrialism, and the growth in democracy led to a continuation of educational interest in education as a means to improve social welfare. Humanitarian impulses in democratic societies focused on universalization of education and separation of schools from church influences. This period heralded the attempt to introduce scientific thinking into the schools with the development of educational psychology. Froebel and others carried forth the humanistic tradition by advocating that educators provide for free activity, creativity, and social participation. However, humanism as a philosophical force during this period was vastly overshadowed by new discoveries and growth in the social, biological, and physical sciences. Faith in technology, science, and industrialization became predominant. As larger numbers of children began to attend school, and as cities grew, the bureaucracies so despised by humanists grew and became inevitable in education.

Contemporary Humanism

In the twentieth century, humanism has frequently been identified with any educational movement that has tried to break away from traditional, restrictive, and punitive methods of teaching. These methods stress mastery of the so-called basics, drill, memorization of facts, and regurgitation of those facts, as the major means of the measurement of a child's worth.

In the 1960s, many educators, often associated with humanist/liberal philosophies, struggled to replace educational practices that reflected outdated beliefs about learning, change, and the nature of individuality in social and political structures of America. The struggle was based in part on the realization that scientific knowledge, and much of the factual information presented in school texts, was doubling every ten years. Adherents of change believed that schools were not attending to the increasingly rapid transformations in technology, communications, transportation, and cultural exchange. They realized that change had become the major reality of the postindustrial society. They proposed that it was pure folly for education to depend solely on teaching facts. They posited that the emphasis on drill, the dependence on rigid curricula and static texts, and the denial of the importance of feelings, subjectivity, and intuition were stifling to creativity. The inevitable result of using outdated methods to teach large numbers of youths was alienation, rebellion, and a citizenry unable to meet the challenges of work, society, or personal growth in a changing world.

Associated with this trend was a growing fear of expanding bureaucracies and the use of technology to control rather than to free people. The infant environmental movement was beginning to provide data that cast deep suspicions about the motivations of scientists, the reality of scientific objectivity, and the honesty of the industrial/military/scientific establishment. The public was learning about the effects of insecticides and the safety of atomic energy and its waste products. In short, many turned away from science and into themselves. Humanism, which expresses the importance of the individual, represented a counter-cultural movement that revived many of the beliefs of Rousseau.

The term *change agent* became popular in the 1960s, and many of those seeking structural change in education were to some degree associated with humanism. These included proponents of progressive education, open education, and education of the whole child, curricula that promote the importance of process over content, cultural relativity, values education, sensitivity training, and most recently cooperative learning and the whole-language approach. Traditionalists were bound to react as schools began to experiment with alternatives based on experiential, subjective, and individually oriented approaches to education. In the realm of school discipline, most of these approaches were associated in the minds of many with permissiveness and left-wing political ideology.

As part of an organized attack on these new concepts, which challenged the precepts of "basic education" and the teaching of "traditional values," the political and religious right coined the term *secular humanism.* Secular humanism is a redundancy that could just as well be called humanism. Although secular humanism is not recognized by most scholars as a distinct philosophy, it has great significance as a code word for conservatives to pejoratively portray individuals whom they consider to be too liberal. The implication is that these individuals are antireligious, antiestablishment, anti–law and order, and anti-American.

For some, secular humanism has become a term of derision and a rallying cry for the far right's most impassioned opposition to change. In the 1960s and 1970s, this opposition resulted in vigorous political action that has had a strong influence on public education policy during the 1980s, especially with regard to school discipline (Hyman, 1984; Hyman & D'Allesandro, 1984a). As a result, social policy toward misbehavior shifted from a preventive/rehabilitation model to a law-and-order, punishment model (Hyman, 1984; Hyman & D'Allesandro, 1984b; Stagliano & Hyman, 1983).

Psychological Roots of Contemporary Humanism

John Dewey was a philosopher/educator/psychologist who promoted *progressive education* as a major challenge to predominant educational philosophies, which had changed little since colonial times. Dewey preferred that his philosophy of education be called experimentalism (Dewey, 1958) or instrumentalism (Runes, 1955). He clearly falls under the rubric of naturalistic humanism (Davidson, 1953) and pragmatism. His approach in many ways reflects the humanistic ideas we have already discussed.

Dewey agreed with Rousseau and other humanists that both inner experiences and the experiences of living cannot be separated from education. Education should be experiential; that is, you must focus on teaching children and not subjects. Idiosyncratic principles govern how children learn and what they learn. Educators cannot act as if the curriculum is unrelated to children's life experiences and the reality of the world in which they live. Education and life are inseparable, and therefore schools should teach practical skills, inquiry, and the process of democracy (Dewey, 1958).

Dewey's rejection of the formalism of American schools is reminiscent of the humanists of the Renaissance. He went further in stressing the importance of self-discipline, freedom, and the relativity of values, truth, and morality. He stressed the need to help students to learn to think and act on their own. He emphasized, as did the positivists, the importance of the scientific method in all realms of thinking.

Abraham Maslow's holistic–dynamic theory of personality and his concepts of needs and self-actualization contributed greatly to contemporary humanism (Hall & Lindzey, 1970). Until the 1960s, psychoanalytic/psychodynamic psychology and behaviorism were the predominant forces that connected theory to practice. Both are based on their own forms of observation, description, and research. Each considered themselves as part of the body of scientific psychology. Both theories, as we discussed in previous chapters, had major impacts on education in terms of their descriptions of the development of personality, behavior, and misbehavior.

Maslow identified himself as a humanistic psychologist and so turned away from gloomy theories of determinism. He rejected the darkly lurking libidinal forces of psychoanalysis and the rigid, simplistic rewards and punishments of behaviorism. Whereas many theories of personality and behavior had been based on pathology, Maslow claimed, in the humanistic tradition, that we should study positive traits such as "gaiety, exuberance, love, well being," creativity, and the striving for competence and actualization (Hall & Lindzey, 1970). He claimed that at infancy we appear to be born with the will toward health, wellbeing, and the accomplishment of our fullest potentials. Misbehavior, rebellion, and pathological conditions occur when our *basic needs* are not met.

The basic needs exist in a hierarchy that begins with (1) physiological (hunger, warmth, etc.) needs. They then continue up the hierarchy with needs for (2) safety, (3) affection/affiliation/love, (4) cognitive/physical mastery, (5) esteem, and (6) *self-actualization*.

Self-actualization is achieved by relatively few people, although we can still strive toward it. It occurs when a person attains a perfect state of equilibrium in which all needs are fulfilled and functioning draws on the creative aspects of human nature. Maslow studied famous actualized historical contemporary individuals such as Lincoln, Thoreau, Eleanor Roosevelt and Albert Einstein. They all shared common characteristics such as highly developed senses of intimacy, realism, spontaneity, acceptance of self and others, and humor based on philosophical issues rather than hostility. They were all tremendously creative, resisted conformity to culture, and identified with the human condition (Hall & Lindzey, 1970).

In addition to the basic needs, we all have meta-needs such as the desire for "justice, goodness, beauty, order, and unity," which are just as instinctive as are the basic drives (Hall & Lindzey, 1970).

As with Gestalt psychology, Maslow's humanism held that the whole is more than the sum of the parts. We can still scientifically study people, but we must ask the correct questions. We must accept subjective reality and find ways to measure it. Maslow's work contributed to the beliefs of Carl Rogers, who carried humanism to a scientific and applied zenith in the 1970s and 1980s.

Carl Rogers's theory flows from his work as a psychotherapist, rather than directly from philosophical and academic endeavors. As with other humanists, he broke with traditional approaches in his field. In the 1940s and 1950s, psychotherapy was dominated by a medical model that placed emphasis on diagnosis and rigidly formulated approaches to treatment. Through practice and research, Rogers discovered that patients (he called them clients) got better if the therapist was viewed as an empathetic listener. He called his approach *client-centered therapy,* because the focus is to understand the client and to help the client to set the agenda for movement toward mental health. Client-centered therapists are trained to endeavor at all times to attempt to understand and enter into the subjective, emotional life of the client. The therapy is called nondirective, because the client determines the course of therapy.

According to Rogers, for client-centered therapy to be effective, therapists must have faith that, without specific direction, clients will be able to uncover and use their innate drives toward health and actualization. To create a safe, trusting atmosphere, the therapist must display genuine warmth, be completely nonjudgmental, and communicate unconditional positive regard for the client. This is done by accurate and empathetic reflection of the client's feelings and thoughts.

Rogers's alliance with traditional humanism is apparent in a statement made in a speech in 1985, after thirty years as a practitioner, researcher, and scholar. Looking back on his career, quoting from his writings, Rogers (1987) said:

> My views of man's most basic characteristics . . . [include] . . . such terms as positive, forward moving, constructive, realistic, trustworthy. . . . My belief in that statement has been confirmed in individual therapy, in small groups, in large groups, and in groups consisting of antagonistic factions . . . in the nurturing climate I endeavor to create the actualizing tendency . . . [that is] . . . a tendency to grow, to develop, to realize full potential. (Rogers, 1987, p. 180)

Rogers's humanism applies to discipline by offering children unconditional positive regard for them as human beings, despite their misbehaviors. Trust that they will improve is vital. He conveys this through empathy. Rogers says, "Empathy is itself a healing agent. . . . It releases, it confirms, it brings the most frightened client into the human race. If a person can be understood, he or she *belongs*" (Rogers, 1987, p. 180).

In the climate of change in the late 1960s and early 1970s, Rogers's (1969) book *Freedom to Learn* was among many humanist tracts that blasted American education. He stated that American education was, "as a whole, the most traditional, conservative, rigid, bureaucratic institution of our time . . . [it] can [cause] . . . [students to] . . . revolt against the whole social value system, revolt against the impersonality of our institutions of learning, revolt against imposed curricula" (Rogers, 1969, p. vii; Rogers & Skinner, 1976).

Empathy, Cooperation, and Social Responsibility

Everyone is familiar with the ubiquitous art form manifested in bumper stickers. For years, parents proudly displayed stickers extolling their high school sports teams. However, relatively recently some proud parents have displayed stickers indicating that their children were honor students in a particular school. This was too much for those who espouse competition and aggressiveness. I saw, to my dismay, a sticker that said "My kid beat up your honor student."

If you will remember, as opposed to other theories about the causes of behavior and misbehavior, humanism proposes that the major inborn traits of infants are positive. There is growing evidence to suggest that infants are instinctively prosocial, empathetic, and cooperative. In recent years these basic assumptions of humanism have received some surprising support from laboratory research with infants. Much of this has been integrated into educational theory by Alfie Kohn, a humanist theorist who first came to national prominence for his book, *No Contest: The Case Against Competition* (Kohn, 1986).

Kohn's first book makes the argument that our obsession with competition is a major flaw in our society. Emphasis on competition actually decreases, rather than enhances, productivity (Kohn, 1986). At the individual level, competition is destructive of self-esteem, because it can only come about by valuing one's self in relation to being better than another. Kohn went on to investigate how schools could teach children to care (Kohn, 1990, 1991). He contends, after reviewing several hundred research studies, that, "cynicism is not realism.... Human beings are not only selfish and self-centered, but also decent, able to feel—and prepared to try to relieve—the pain of others.... It is as natural to help as to hurt" (Kohn, 1991, p. 498). He goes on to review studies by developmental psychologists that demonstrate that newborns are more likely to cry and to cry longer when they hear another infant crying than when hearing loud noises. Ten- to fourteen-month-old toddlers will respond with agitation and distress when exposed to another's unhappiness. By the time of preschool, children frequently demonstrate prosocial behaviors, including caring. His essential message is that positive, prosocial genetic programming of children can easily be tapped by parents and educators who wish to focus discipline on promoting positive behaviors rather than squashing misbehavior.

In the process of establishing his thesis, Kohn attacks behaviorism and the concept that we must use external reinforcers to motivate children to be good. His stress on encouraging caring, noncompetitive, altruistic behavior in schools is reflected in the contemporary movement known as cooperative learning (Hike, 1990). Cooperative learning attempts to build self-esteem as a result of helping others rather than competing with them (Slavin, 1986). However, although there is an underlying egalitarian philosophy inherent in the theory and techniques of cooperative learning, there is often a pragmatic use of behavioral methods in the actual classroom application of the approach (Slavin, 1987).

Ironically, while cooperative learning was beginning its heyday in the 1980s, open education, the most humanistic of the current educational theories, was dying. Many of its premises are being revived, transformed, and newly admired in movements such as cooperative learning, whole language, and the magnate school movement as we approach the end of the century.

Assumptions of the Humanistic Approach

Unlike the psychodynamic/interpersonal approach, which is rooted in a complex series of assumptions, humanism has in common with behavioral/cognitive–behavioral approach a somewhat simple set of assumptions. These assumptions are all related to faith in the possibility for goodness in humankind.

All People Are Born with an Innate Capacity for Empathy, Goodness, and Caring

The basic assumption underlying all humanistic thought is that the potential for goodness is innate. Our inborn nature is essentially good and never evil. As a species, we have a natural desire to act in ways that fulfill our need to be good. Self-actualization is intimately associated with goodness and is achieved within an accepting and nurturing environment. Basically, to be good is to be normal. Maladaptive behavior occurs as a result of punitive parenting and of authoritarian technological and bureaucratic environments that cause feelings of insecurity as well as the diminution of individual worth. Any factors in the environment that frustrate the drive toward self-actualization can cause dysfunction.

Emphasis on efficiency and centralized control (as in schools) results in the alienation of the individual. Identity groups (religion, class, race, etc.) may lead to unhealthy competition and conflict and may, at times, inhibit individual growth. An underlying assumption is that bureaucracy, institutions, etc., cause diminution of worth.

All Students Have an Innate Desire to Learn

It is difficult to prevent children from learning and exploring their surroundings. In all other species in which parents care for their young, as soon as safely possible, exploration is allowed and encouraged to enhance learning. In all social animals, including humans, survival is dependent on learning, which occurs through cooperation and social interactions.

In contrast to tribal cultures, which are in tune with nature, we prescribe what and when a child will learn, based on concepts of learning that are driven by the bureaucratic entities that control our lives. As a result of this artificial channeling of innate desires to learn, we create inordinate discipline problems by overcontrolling learning at early ages and extending the period between the end of childhood and the beginning of adulthood. As a result, bureaucratic control suppresses natural desires to learn and turns too many children and youth against themselves and the system.

In contemporary, postindustrial societies, most educators and schools have lost touch with the child's innate desires to learn as part of an organic whole. The things that children are taught and the people who teach them may not always reflect the natural tendency toward cooperation and an organic balance. This balance can only occur when we facilitate the child's need to learn specific things, in specific ways, on the child's time schedule. Consider the cases of Sara and Jimmy as examples of suppression and facilitation of innate desires to learn.

Four-year-old Sara is a bright, inquisitive child. She has a six-year-old brother in the first grade. Because both of her parents work outside the home, Sara must wake up at 7:00 AM so that her parents can take her to day care. Her desire to learn and explore in the morning are circumscribed by her parents' needs to prepare themselves and their children for the day's activities. Her parents do not have time to play with her in the morning. Nor do they want her to play with her brother, because they do not want to pick up toys at the end of the day. Therefore, after Sara and her brother are dressed and while her parents attend to morning responsibilities, the children are encouraged to watch TV.

Sara, refreshed after a night's sleep, and driven by her natural desire to learn, would like to pull out her toys and become involved in active learning. However, instead she becomes a passive learner. Rather than picking her activities and being driven by the curiosity of the day, she is seduced into watching material, carefully designed to hold childrens' attention, that has been chosen by an executive in a far-away TV corporation.

If Sara chooses to watch cartoons, there is little likelihood that she will learn cooperation and empathy, which are natural instincts. Instead, she may view the 19 millionth rerun of the Road Runner being chased by Wiley Coyote or Bugs Bunny blowing up Yosemite Sam.

After being forced to sit in a car and being restrained by a seat belt for a half-hour, Sara begins day care. This particular day care, which caters to the yuppie crowd, is cognitively oriented and stresses formal learning to prepare future college students. Unlike day care based on the British infant school model or American models that stress learning through play, children are allowed relatively little free play time. Sara's teacher has very definite rules about when children should sit and learn and when they should rest. Sara has not taken an afternoon nap at home for more than a year; however, in day care, she is forced to "nap" during nap time.

Unlike her parents, however, Sara's teachers allow some flexibility for real individual expression. Sara loves to finger paint. In day care, she is allowed to get paint on her face, smock, and hands. When she is done with painting and is ready for another activity, she knows that she must clean up. There are no rules or sanctions for paint that remains on the smock or clothing. However, at home, her impulses to smear finger paints on paper are severely restricted. Sara's mother is extremely fastidious and abhors paint on any surface or in any form other than on a painting that has been framed and hung on a wall. She will allow Sara to use a paintbrush and watercolors to smear, but the use of fingers is verboten.

When Sara arrives home, her parents are both exhausted from the day's work, yet her mother insists on some quality time each day. Her concept of quality time is to work with the child on readiness skills that are stressed in day care. These include letter identification, directionality, and copying. Sara wants to play with her mother, but this activity is not part of the agenda.

Let us look at the case of another child whose home environment is very different from that of Sara. Four-year-old Joey has a two-year-old sister and comes from an intact family. One of the few rules in this family is that the children are not permitted to watch television, because the parents believe that television is "junk" and they do not want their children to "waste their minds." Joey's mother runs a small advertising agency from their home and spends as much time with her children as possible. She often lets the children initiate games that she plays with them. She reads to them every night before they go to sleep. So that she can operate her business, she takes Joey and his sister to day care in the morning and picks them up in the early afternoon. Joey's father is a pilot and is frequently away from home.

Joey's home environment may best be described as permissive. His parents grew up at the tail end of the 1960s, during the "hippy" generation. In their home, peace, love, and respect is paramount. Their children are encouraged to play together and are provided with many opportunities to explore and to learn from their environment. If Joey is happy, it does not matter whether he is dirty or making a mess of the house.

Obviously, Joey's adjustment to day care is quite different from that of Sara. Like in his family environment, Joey is not restricted at day care. Aside from snack and nap time, there is little structure at the day care, and the children are encouraged to do what they like to do. He is permitted and encouraged to be creative, play new games, and develop friendships. The only rule is that the children share and be kind to each other. At day care, the children are showered with affection.

In contemporary, technological cultures, every child who enters kindergarten wants to learn. However, by the time children end first grade, some have been crushed by inane insistence that everyone learn by sitting in seats, following prescribed curricula, adhering to rules of when, how much, and what should be taught. The result is often misbehavior or underachievement.

All Students Come to School with a Hierarchy of Needs and Drives toward Self-Actualization

Everyone wants to be loved by someone, to feel competent, and to be appreciated, valued, and respected by peers. Every student in school has these needs. At the secondary level, this includes the bikers, the druggies, the trouble makers, the jocks, the preppies, and the nerds. Each is trying to become actualized. Even the students who seem most incorrigible desire, in their own way, a sense of self-worth and are moving toward their own distorted view of actualization. But they can never become actualized because many of their most basic needs were never met. However, the humanist treats them with unconditional positive regard and gives them an environment that provides them with the most basic needs such as adequate food, shelter, and safety before moving to satisfy the more advanced needs.

Misbehavior results when children's needs are frustrated or when we make demands that they perform at levels that mistakenly assume that prerequisite needs have been met. Contemporary humanism relies heavily on Maslow's hierarchy in understanding needs. But more important, one must recognize that healthy children are striving toward their own goals. Schools that frustrate that striving create discipline problems.

The humanist does not see misbehavior as a sign of "badness," but rather as an expression of lack of opportunity to strive toward "goodness."

Some teachers exclusively stress cognitive/physical mastery. They pride themselves on being tough graders, no-nonsense lecturers, and exacting in their demands for high-quality work. They may well help students fulfill needs related to this area. However, these teachers may neglect students' needs for affection/affiliation/love and self-esteem. Despite high-quality, subject-oriented instruction, constant and demeaning criticism may "turn off" those students who do not have sufficient reservoirs of self-esteem.

Misbehavior May Occur When Curiosity and Spontaneity Are Repressed

Each child is unique and must be allowed to explore the environment freely and to be spontaneous and honest in expressing feelings and thoughts. Of course, when curiosity and spontaneity lead to actions that might impinge on the rights of others, caregivers must appeal to the child's innate understanding that one must not hurt another. Children whose own basic needs have been met for physiological satisfaction, safety, and affection/affiliation/love will easily respond to limiting their behavior if it hurts others.

Children's curiosity at home or in school is stifled when others tell them what they should know and when and how they should learn. For instance, Joe, a fifth-grader, suddenly becomes very interested in oceanography. He should be allowed to devote most of his school time and leisure activities to pursue his new-found interest. Because this topic covers, among other subjects, math, science, literature, and biology, he will gain new knowledge as part of satiating his curiosity. For instance, if he wants to know how the oceans contribute to weather patterns, he will have to learn something about physics, temperatures, probability, and geography. All of this will require reading and the acquisition of new vocabulary words. He does not need to learn these separately, at different assigned times of the day and with specific textbooks. He will learn about many subjects as part of the organic whole of the topic. The satisfaction of curiosity is dependent on the student learning how to learn. It is the process of learning that is more important than the facts. Once the process of learning, which is unique to each child, is established, the innate desire to explore will be continually regenerated.

Parental or teacher pressure to force learning in ways that are antagonistic to the child's own learning style and particular type of curiosity can easily backfire. This can lower achievement because the parents may not fulfill children's needs that are lower on the hierarchy than the need to achieve in school. That is, if the parental support, love, and affiliation is perceived by the child to be dependent on academic performance, the child may rebel. Take the case of Jake.

Jake was obviously a bright twelve-year-old. His achievement test scores were all about two or three years above his grade level. His IQ was 130. His parents, both highly educated, upwardly mobile, and hard working, seemed responsible and concerned about his education. There was only one problem. Jake was described by both his parents and his teachers as a pain in the neck. They expressed a complete sense of failure in their attempts to motivate Jake to do well in school. This bright, curious, active boy suddenly seemed to turn off at around fourth grade.

Not that Jake was a troublemaker, like some of his more aggressive friends who also did poorly in school. He never got into fights. His teachers more often described him as an "itch." Jake's excuses for not completing assignments ran the gamut from the banal to the bombastic. He was becoming a true con artist. In many ways, he was amusing and enjoyable. But the bottom line was always the same—Jake would not do his work.

Jake's father described homework sessions as more difficult than negotiating between representatives of labor and management. It seemed that Jake spent his life mastering every conceivable method of avoiding homework. He did not openly defy his parents; however, he had raised procrastination, prevarication, evasion, and the "disappearing act" to the level of art forms.

Children like Jake frequently have highly successful parents. These parents are usually well educated and have come to assume that their children will automatically be motivated to do well. Unfortunately, we have not yet found a gene that determines the desire to please parents or do well in school. Very often, this seems strange to parents, because as preschoolers these children are often so spontaneous and eager to learn. Frequently these students have older siblings who seem to breeze through school. So why are the Jakes of the world so different?

Underachievers can have low, average, or high IQs (Hyman, 1988, 1989c). In general, their achievement is uneven. They may get As in subjects they like and then fail the very same subject the following year if they do not like the teacher. If they do not like subjects, getting them to work is a gargantuan task by any standard. Although some underachievers function at a consistently low level, inconsistency is the hallmark of most. Because of their demonstrated ability in subjects that meet their needs, or with favored teachers, who are usually of the nurturing, accepting type, they are particularly frustrating to those who try to motivate them. It sometimes seems that their chief goal in life is to "get your goat" whenever you try to help them.

Children achieve when their basic needs are met and when they are allowed to seek self-actualization in their own manner. Some underachievers may blossom in small, private schools that promote humanistic values and stress the importance of the process of learning through self-motivation.

Bureaucracies Threaten Individuality, Privacy, and Our Sense of Freedom and the Right to Be Unique

Too many schools, especially large high schools, are hopelessly rigid institutions, riddled by overworked, bored, and demoralized staff. In many cases, it is clear that the school is organized for the convenience of educators rather than students.

Many large megaschools have embraced a multitude of sometimes conflicting and often inane rules and regulations that are counterproductive in allowing the development of free-spirited, creative students who learn to share and care for others. The movement away from the small, intimate schoolhouses of yesteryear into large regional factories has resulted in the shuffling and warehousing of our most precious resource, primary-grade children.

In the name of cost-effectiveness and efficiency, a typical large, contemporary elementary school may include 500 to 1,000 students. They learn early to negotiate the interpersonal distance involved in large institutions. The size of these schools results in the need to control the movements and activities of large groups of children who as a result become numbers on a logistics chart. Consider the following misbehavior of a principal and her recess aides in such a school.

Jill, a gifted, caring second-grader, was raised to believe in fairness and justice. Her concern for others and her astuteness regarding social inequity was a marvel to behold. She often came home to describe how children had been mean to each other and how teachers' actions were inappropriate. Teachers and peers often praised her ability to mediate conflict and defend children who were being teased or ridiculed. In almost all cases, her perceptions were right on target. Despite her indignation at senseless and unfair bureaucratic edicts and actions, she never acted out against authorities and always strove to be a perfectly behaved child. However, one day she came home with a story that really infuriated her parents.

Because of the large numbers of students at each lunch shift, the recess aides conceptualized their task in terms of crowd control rather than the movements of eager young children. They insisted that students must move in a quiet, orderly, and obedient manner from the lunchroom to the playground. Recess involved approximately one hundred active first- and second-graders, after sitting in their seats most of the morning and after being forced to eat in a quiet, controlled manner at lunch. By recess time, these children needed a break. Naturally, after conforming to classroom and school schedules and curricula over which they had no control, they were ready to break loose.

To conform to adult standards, these children were requested to control all of their impulses until they came to the playground. Once on the playground, they were also required by the aides to play "nicely." The injustice occurred when some children did not obey. As a result, the aides forced all of the children to practice standing in line and being quiet for more than half of their recess period. This action displayed their complete ignorance of the children's natural exuberance, spontaneity, and joy at being outside and free of the shackles tying them to their desks.

The possible thoughts of the children who were behaving might be: (1) "This is unfair, but heck, the world is unfair, so there is nothing I can do"; (2) "I am helpless against authority, and this means I better learn to comply with anything else they might do that is unfair"; (3) "This is unfair so I will figure a way to get back at them"; (4) "This is unfair but I will figure out a better way to misbehave without getting caught"; or (5) "Why should I behave? I'm just going to be punished anyway."

Jill's parents initially discussed the issue with her in terms of the child's indignation that she was being punished for the behavior of others. It was decided that she would talk to some of the other children to determine how they felt about the situation. Meanwhile, her parents contacted some other parents. Some were angry about the situation, some had not heard about it, but few were willing to take on the bureaucracy.

Jill, after talking to a group of children, organized a club made up of children who were angry about their unjust punishments. The purpose of the club was to try to figure out a solution to the problem. One of the children who was afraid to join the club told the lunchroom aides that the club had been formed as a "hate the lunchroom aides club." The aides reported this to a teacher. Without accurate information, the teacher accused the children of conspiring to get the aides fired.

By the time the whole incident was relayed to the principal, the facts had further changed. Without going into detail, he perceived the incident as a direct attack on his bureaucracy. However, after several phone calls from parents and a letter from Jill's parents suggesting other methods for dealing with the children, the principal finally agreed that practice punishment drills were not appropriate.

Unfortunately, this practice had been institutionalized. During the following two years, by late September, Jill again reported a repetition of the previous year's events. This was followed by another round of parental complaints and cessation of the punishment drills. The story of Jill reflects the inertia of institutionalized practices in schools. Clearly the punishment drills offered the school a simple and immediate way of controlling large groups of students. The messages the children learned were contrary to humanistic values.

This model discourages reliance on large bureaucratic structures in education. Misbehavior is seen as a symptom of negative reactions to these bureaucracies, authoritarian controls, and senseless rules. It promotes the use of alternative schools and more humane attitudes toward students' problems.

Misbehavior Is Minimized When Schools Become Just Communities

Just schools provide for fair and equal treatment of all individuals in similar situations. Justice, which is based on equity, is clearly rooted in the humanistic assumptions of the Declaration of Independence and the preamble to the Constitution of the United States (Bybee & Gee, 1992).

Just schools teach and model the democratic ideals that govern the laws of our country. This includes teaching students about the rights, duties, and obligations that are due society. In the classroom, this is exemplified by listening to others, respecting their rights to individual dignity, and fulfilling responsibilities. Teachers have a responsibility to allow free speech in the classroom, while providing for the safety, security, and privacy rights of each student. Although there may be a need to punish violations, in a just society, based on the highest ideals of the Constitution, there should be little need for retribution if justice is available to all people.

School policymakers and administrators can create just schools when they learn that students cannot flourish when bureaucracy functions in ways that are against the true nature of students. The leadership must use its knowledge and power to provide proper guidance and support for students. Correction of deviance must occur in a nurturing and natural milieu so that all children will model acceptable norms of civility and respect for others.

The humanistic concept of justice, when applied in schools, can result in safe, orderly, and happy institutions for learning. Lawrence Kohlberg's concept of the just community, based on his last two stages of moral development, provides a humanistic framework for establishing justice in the schools. Moral education, based on these stages, suggests guidelines for a curriculum that focuses on choices rather than imperatives. For instance, John steals some pencils from the desk of Jill. Because John is eight years old, he can hardly be considered a hardened criminal. His teacher, Ms. Hawn, could easily punish John. However, as a humanist, she is more interested in helping John to understand why he stole the pencils and what effect the theft had on Jill and the other class members. In a supportive and nurturing way, she stops the lesson and conducts a class meeting. Because the other children know about the theft, and will talk about it behind John's back, she believes that it is better to discuss the issue openly.

Ms. Hawn begins the discussion, not by accusing John or making him feel like a criminal, but by saying, "Class, we need to discuss why people sometimes take things from others. There are times when I would like to take things that do not belong to me, and I am sure that most of you have had that experience. We know that John took Jill's pencils, but we do not know why he did it. So let's all discuss experiences that each of us have had in which we had wanted to take things that didn't belong to us, but we didn't. If you want to admit the times that you did take something, that's OK too, but tell us how you felt about it afterwards, why you think that you did it, and how you think that the person you took it from felt."

The purpose of this approach is to elicit a sense of community and support within the classroom. John is not treated as an outcast or criminal, but rather as a person whose needs were fulfilled at the expense of another. It is understandable that we all have these needs, but the point of humanism is to appeal to the goodness in the "offender" rather than to seek retribution.

Humanistic Diagnosis

Turn now to the case of Chris (see page 37) to consider diagnosis based on this model.

Determine Unmet Needs from a Hierarchy

Using Maslow's theory, consider which needs are not being met. We know that Chris experienced the breakup of his family around the age of five. Surely Chris's needs for safety and stability were sorely tested. If one does not feel safe, it is important to be vigilant and protective. A child who does not feel safe may either withdraw into fantasy or actively and aggressively seek to control an unstable environment. Certainly if adults are the providers for the fulfillment of safety needs, they are not to be trusted when they violate the trust inherent in the relationship between the caregiver and the child.

It is apparent that Chris's needs for safety have been frustrated. The safety provided by a stable home was shattered by the divorce. Part of children's sense of safety is provided by their physical surroundings. They feel secure in their own homes around their toys and other familiar objects. The physical structure of the home provides safe places to explore, to hide, and to be nurtured. Chris lost all of this as a result of the divorce by trusted and loved adult caregivers. Chris learned that adults may not always be reliable providers of safety.

In addition to loss of safety, Chris's needs for affiliation and love were denied by the conflict between his parents and later between his mother and his stepfather and his biological father. He was unsure of his mother's love when she gave birth to his half-sister. Could he depend on a stepfather who now had his own biological child, Chris's half-sister?

The record shows that Chris had some problems with fine motor skills while in the primary grades. He had some trouble learning how to read and may have had a learning disability. Testing showed him to have adequate intelligence. Although it is clear that he had some early problems in learning to read, he was able to mobilize his strengths to compensate, and he did learn to read. A humanistic approach would have recognized these problems and allowed him to learn at his own rate. Instead, he was placed in a transitional class, which in essence kept him back for a year. It is clear that Chris's needs for cognitive and physical mastery were not met in the early years.

Diagnosis of Chris, using a humanistic framework, suggests that Chris may never progress adequately until the needs mentioned above are met. Self-esteem and self-actualization cannot be established when lower-level needs have been frustrated.

Diagnosis involves relating to the student. Using nondirective Rogerian techniques, the student may be encouraged to share feelings, perceptions, and beliefs about himself or herself. Gentle questioning that conveys true interest in the child will help to determine which needs have not been met. This approach may begin with (1) an exploration of physiological needs. It may be followed by the determination of unmet (2) safety, (3) affiliation/love, (4) cognitive/physical mastery, (5) self-esteem, and (6) self-actualization.

Although determining unmet needs from a predetermined hierarchy is extremely helpful, each child experiences the world in his or her own unique way. Therefore, it is the existential reality of the meaning of the unmet needs that is important. For instance, rejection by peers may be extremely disturbing for most adolescents. This can cause a frustration of the need for affiliation and love, which can result in lack of self-esteem, anger at specific peers, and actual aggression directed toward them. Conversely, some teenagers may be much more disturbed about rejection by an older, idolized sibling or a parent. In either situation, the reaction may be the same.

Tie Unmet Needs to Specific Misbehaviors

Unlike the psychodynamic or behavioral approaches, the humanistic theorists have not developed an elaborate system of diagnosis. This is not necessary, for two reasons: First, unmet needs underlie all misbehavior. Second, each person has unique ways of understanding and dealing with unmet needs. This existential aspect of individual diagnosis cannot always be used to sort students into predetermined categories. To diagnose the causes of the misbehavior, the teacher must establish an open and trusting relationship with the student and parents. This relationship will enhance the communication necessary to understand the child. The parents and student will be encouraged to willingly relate all of the background information necessary to understand the problem.

It is important to recognize that all misbehavior can be related to the frustration of children's needs. No matter how egregious a student's behavior may be, a humanist understands that the misbehavior masks an inner person striving toward goodness, competence, and self-actualization. Therefore, the school bully must not be viewed as an innately cruel person. Some place in the bully's background, the concerned teacher will find unmet needs.

Humanistic teachers must have a clear understanding of the various needs so that when talking with the students or parents, they are provided with opportunities to discuss whether the needs have been met. In diagnosing unmet safety needs, the teacher, Ms. Jones, could have the following conversation with Chris:

T: Chris, what did your old house look like?

C: Which house do you mean?

T: The house you used to live in before your parents got divorced.

C: Oh, that was a nice big house. We had a big lawn, and I had a nice bedroom all to myself.

T: Oh, do you share your bedroom now with your brother?

C: Yeah, and he is always taking my things out and not putting them back.

T: It sounds like you weren't too happy to leave that house.

C: Yeah, I really liked it there. I could keep all of my toys away from my brother. I was really angry when my parents got divorced.

T: So you were really angry.

C: Yeah, I didn't want to leave my house and my friends. Sometimes I still think that it was my fault that they got divorced.

T: Why did you think that it was your fault?

C: Because they were always arguing about how to make me behave.

T: How did you feel when they were arguing about you?

C: I felt sad, because I caused so much trouble. I made my parents angry at each other. I made the problems.

T: Do you think that you were the only reason why your parents argued?

C: Sure, they didn't talk that much to each other or spend much time together. But when I was bad, they'd start fighting about me and then about other things. It was my my fault that they started yelling in the first place.

T: You must feel terrible if you believe that you were the cause of your parents' problems.

C: I feel so bad sometimes. We had to move and lost our house, and we had to make new friends. It was hard. I promised myself that I would try to be good. I don't want my Mom to hate me more than she does already.

By using reflection of Chris's statements and feelings, Ms. Jones enabled him to express his feelings. In addition to reflection, Ms. Jones tries to convey unconditional positive regard. This term, coined by Carl Rogers, is a reflection of the attitude of a true humanist. In this case, despite his aggressive and uncooperative behavior, it is clear that Chris is hurting. His needs for safety and love have been thwarted. His low level of academic work causes low self-esteem, to further complicate the problem.

Identify Sources of Suppression of Needs Satisfaction

Determine if parents, teachers, or school organizational demands for conformity are sources of frustration. Are there organizational, personal, or curricular factors in the school that diminish the student's feelings of individual worth? Identify authoritarian, punitive practices and educators who reject democracy as a process.

In the case of Chris, it is clear that the demands placed on him by his parents, his stepfather, the learning environment, and his own needs are incongruent. Examination of the school record, talks with Chris and his parents, and observation of his behavior clearly demonstrate that stresses from the family and the school have kept him from moving toward self-actualization. As mentioned previously, the diagnosis is dependent on a thorough understanding of the humanistic perspective. Information is gathered from past records. But the major sources of suppression emerge from discussions that occur within a framework of mutual trust and support between the teacher, Chris, and his parents.

Goals, Objectives, and Techniques of Intervention

Provide for the Realization of Each Student's Needs

Use of the humanistic approach to misbehavior means that you, as both a teacher and a human being, believe that people are essentially good and are born with a basic goodness that is fulfilled throughout life. It means that you perceive normal behavior as being a result of growing up in a warm, accepting, and nurturing environment. Conversely, misbehavior occurs when children grow up in rejecting, demanding, and critical environments. All children need a wide latitude to feel free to express themselves. Overall, adoption of this approach means that you believe that a nurturing classroom and school climate allows the child's basic thrust toward goodness to emerge.

You need to provide the proper climate to help students to realize the possibilities to strive toward self-actualization. To do this, ask yourself the following: What are the forces in the environment that lead to feelings of individual worthlessness? Does the school/classroom provide for expression and acceptance of honest portrayal of feelings? Is the school/classroom placing too much emphasis on cognitive, rational learning rather than intuitive and alternative methods of problem solving? To what extent does the value of conformity inhibit individual differences in your class? Can you help the student accept others?

What Are the Forces in the Environment That Lead to Feelings of Individual Worthlessness?

It is obvious that Chris has had problems related to both his parents' divorce and his early academic difficulties. He does not feel good about himself and tends to feel that he is not very smart or competent. Also, his safety needs have never been secured. To help Chris, his parents and teachers must begin to give him unconditional positive regard. Unlike the behaviorist, the humanist will not selectively praise Chris. Although not accepting his misbehavior, Chris and his teachers will discuss the meaning of the misbehavior. For instance, let us assume that Chris is constantly out of his seat. The teacher will not correct or reprimand him each time that this happens. Rather, the teacher will wait until an opportune time to discuss this behavior with Chris. The following dialogue might occur:

T: Chris, I notice that you have been getting out of your seat a lot today. You seem to be restless. I wonder if something is bothering you. I understand that you sometimes get this way.

C: I didn't bother anybody, Ms. Jones.

T: Well, I'm not accusing you of anything; I realize that you didn't bother anybody.

C: How come you are talking to me about it, if I wasn't bad?

T: Do you think you're bad, Chris? Is that why you think that I am talking to you?

C: Yeah, all the other teachers always yelled at me for not staying at my desk.

T: No Chris, I realize that you have a hard time staying still, but I also know that you are still learning in class. As long as you don't bother anybody, I can allow you to get up and move around. But I noticed that some days you do it more than others, and I worry that something is bothering you. Did anything happen at home or school this morning that upset you?

C: Yeah, my little sister was sick and neither of my parents would help me with my homework last night. They said that they would check it in the morning, but they were too busy.

T: Oh, so that's why you didn't have your homework this morning.

C: Yeah. It was pretty hard to do.

T: Well, if you find the work too hard, I would be happy to help you. I guess it's my fault if I give you homework you can't do on your own. Maybe I should see if some other students are having the same problem.

C: I hate homework. I wish you wouldn't give us homework.

T: Why don't you bring that up in class? We could all talk about it. If it doesn't help, maybe we could all find out why and then figure out what to do about it.

In the above scenario, the topics shifted from out-of-seat behavior to homework. Chris was surprised that his teacher did not yell at him. She had accepted his not turning in his homework in the morning, and he brought up the topic as a possible reason for being upset. It could be that he is lying about the reason for not doing his homework, because in the past he has had many excuses.

Ms. Jones is not concerned about whether Chris did the homework. This is only a reflection of his feelings of academic inadequacy and perceived rejection by his parents. She refuses to focus on out-of-seat behavior and failure to hand in homework because she realizes that this would only contribute to Chris's feelings of incompetence and rejection. She sees these actions as expressions of his feelings of alienation. She is free to admit that she may be responsible for the problem with the homework. She is willing to discuss the issue with the whole class. If the class agrees with Chris, or expresses genuine feelings against homework, she is willing to consider alternatives. They might change the type of homework, do it in school, institute a homework helpline, or have a trial period during which they do not do any homework. It is important that she recognized the legitimacy of Chris's feelings and is willing to take action in his behalf.

When problems occur, Ms. Jones will consider them as symptoms of failure by those who prevent Chris from rediscovering the inner person who wants to move toward actualization. She will continue to help Chris explore his behavior without judging what is good and what is bad as long as he does not hurt others.

Does the School/Classroom Provide for Expression and Acceptance of Honest Portrayal of Feelings?

In the above scenario, Ms. Jones attempts to provide an accepting and nurturing atmosphere. However, she may place herself at risk in doing this. A humanist provides an open setting within a school that is quite often a closed setting. If Ms. Jones's principal is a traditional administrator, she will be very unhappy if she observes the class in which Chris is allowed to get out of his seat without reprimands. She also will insist that Chris be required to complete homework each day, as are the other children. She may suggest specific punishments for noncompliance. Ms. Jones realizes that punishment has been used continuously with Chris and has not had a salutary effect. In fact, she believes that punishment is ineffective and counterproductive because it further damages Chris's sense of competence and self-esteem. She anticipates that eventually, by fully accepting Chris and believing in him, within the classroom environment, she can help him begin to recognize his true potential.

Is the School/Classroom Placing Too Much Emphasis on Cognitive, Rational Learning Rather Than Intuitive and Alternative Methods of Discovery and Problem Solving?

Chris has been taught by traditional methods that have not worked well. He was introduced to formal instruction before he was ready. His lack of readiness skills and the emotional upheaval of the divorce should have signaled to the school that Chris needed more time before formal instruction was instituted. It is clear that his early misbehaviors were signs of unfulfilled needs. His daydreaming, his aggressive behavior, and his restlessness were all indications of his unhappiness. School should have been a haven for Chris, not a punishment. He needed a place where music, art, and physical activities could allow him to deal with his pain. Understanding and nurturing teachers, providing for creative expression, would have given him the opportunity to begin formal learning when he was ready.

To What Extent Does the Value of Conformity Inhibit Individual Differences in Your Class? Can You Help the Student Accept Others?

Most teachers insist that all students stay in their seats. They seem to believe that there is a direct connection between a seated behind and a learning mind. However, there is lots of evidence that even children with attention deficit disorder can learn while moving. A humanist would never insist that children sit just for the sake of an orderly classroom.

A host of meaningless, arbitrary rules exist in most classrooms and schools. Why do many teachers assume that every child's bladder fills at the same time and therefore must be relieved according to the teacher's schedule? Why is it that only in schools do we insist that mealtime cannot be an enjoyable situation in which all participants are allowed to talk? Who ever got the idea to blow police whistles in the lunchroom when an adult decides that the children are too noisy?

Conformity only serves to enforce diminution of individual worth. It stifles creativity and causes rebellion. Ms. Jones, in dealing with Chris and the other students in her class, recognizes that Chris has a need to move about, whereas most other students do not. She has discussed this with the class, and they recognize this also, so they do not resent Chris. Even if half the class was like Chris, Ms. Jones would find a way to enhance their learning while they were moving.

Organize the Class or School to Maximize Expressions of Individuality, Curiosity, and Creativity

In the 1970s, when *open education* was enjoying widespread support, I was a consultant to an emerging high school that would model the humanistic ideals of open education. The principal was an extremely bright, articulate, well-read, intellectual who was outgoing, energetic, and enthusiastic. He was given two years to recruit teachers from throughout the school district as the new high school was being built.

During the last year before the building was complete, the high school shared a building, using a split schedule, with a junior high school. The principal, whom we will call Ben Bader, was adored by students, staff, and parents. He was available, insightful, humorous, and responsive to the needs of others. He recruited a staff that believed in the humanistic approach to education. Part of my job was to help the students and staff conduct a needs and climate assessment. Everyone helped to develop a process-oriented school that would enhance creativity and individuality. This would be an open system that would be constantly able to change and renew itself.

There was only one problem. Although Ben was highly valued by those with whom he worked in developing the new school, he was strongly resented by some of the other administrators, including his boss, the superintendent. They disliked his disregard for bureaucracy, his flaunting of rules and regulations that were not consonant with humanistic concerns, and his ability to stimulate students to question authority. Ben was trying to create an open system within a closed system.

Ben's downfall occurred over the problem of smoking. The school board passed a rule that the new high school would not allow students to smoke in the school. They would be allowed a small area outside of the building. Although Ben was against adolescent smoking, when students complained to him, he suggested that they form a committee and investigate the issue. The students were learning to engage in participatory democracy. He empowered them to conduct research on their own, to poll other students, and to write a report and make their own recommendations to the school board.

The student committee knew all of the arguments against allowing them a smoking area. But they also knew that teachers had a smoking room, that there were no state rules against them smoking if their parents allowed it, that there was no insurance restriction against it, and that they had been told a lot of untruths and half-truths by the superintendent. Armed with a sheaf of evidence, they spoke at a public meeting of the school board and presented a blistering rebuttal of the board's reasons for not allowing a smoking area for students.

Although the students' exercise in participatory democracy and attempt to work within the system was exemplary of the humanistic ideal, it did not endear them to the superintendent or most members of the Board of Education. In fact, they were furious. Their response suggested that they believed that it is OK to teach democracy in classroom, but do not dare to practice it until you graduate.

This illustrates the difficulty of trying to develop an open system within a closed system without the full support and understanding of those in power. However, as Mr. Bader demonstrated, it can be done by people who are willing to take the heat when the philosophy is extended beyond the confines of the classroom or school.

In the case of Chris, Ms. Jones was willing to explore options within the classroom that might violate school policy or parental expectations. The possibilities of no homework, allowing students to roam the class at will, or spending class time discussing what the class should do might be disconcerting, fearsome, and downright subversive to others in authority. But, given these organizational changes, Chris will be able to grow.

The humanist must define and modify environmental pressures that may interfere with the individual's efforts toward self-actualization. Ms. Jones may choose to use sensitivity groups to help Chris and his peers understand the pressures each lives with. She may attempt to provide opportunities for Chris and others to become involved in determining school policy about issues that are important to them. This is possible through student representation at administrative meetings, student input into a discipline handbook, and so forth. She will modify her teaching to account for individual choice in curriculum, make curriculum relevant to minority group students, and allow for active student roles in the learning process. She might have students participate in community services projects that are integrated into the curricula they choose.

Provide a Humanistic Moral Education Curriculum to Enhance Innate Prosocial Beliefs and Behavior

Humanists believe that caring, altruism, empathy, and other humanistic values are genetically programmed behaviors; therefore, they should be supported and enhanced by schools (Kohn, 1986, 1990, 1991). For instance, the San Ramon Valley (California) Unified School District emphasizes the inherent goodness in children and their potential for caring, cooperativeness, and prosocial behavior. These values are nurtured by activities such as cooperative learning, literature-based reading programs that stimulate discussions about empathy and caring, discipline based on the value of being good for the sake of goodness (rather than fear of punishment), and community service projects.

Humanistic schools should help staff and students to respect each other. They should convince everyone that sarcasm, ridicule, "put downs," and other types of verbal assault are inherently destructive. They should foster the desire of students to want to "do good" because it is the right thing to do, rather than to avoid "doing bad" for fear of punishment.

Holistic humanistic interventions focus on the problem at the systems level. Although systems intercessions are difficult, especially when initiated by individual teachers, they are possible. Viable interventions that can begin the process of change include alternative classrooms or schools, work–study programs, open education, and schools without walls.

Techniques of Intervention

Unlike the behavioral or the psychodynamic approaches, the techniques used in the humanistic approach may vary, based on individual differences and needs. The overriding concern is to provide an atmosphere in which the student feels safe to express inner emotions. The techniques that have most often been used are briefly discussed here.

Process Groups

Various types of *process groups* provide opportunities for students to express themselves openly and honestly and to share their feelings with others. Sensitivity groups, T groups (leaderless groups used for training members in group processes), rap groups, Gestalt therapy groups, and others are associated with various humanistic movements. Most share the belief that the leader should play a minimal role and that the group members should share the responsibility for determining the procedures, processes, and goals of the group. This resonates with the philosophy of humanism, which is based on the assumption that each person, in a safe and supportive social situation, will move toward sharing, cooperation, empathy, and individual actualization.

Humanistic groups are not conducted in a didactic manner. The teacher/leader may institute a group at any time that seems appropriate and may suggest a topic. For instance, if Chris is having a bad day, and begins to have an altercation with Joe, Ms. Jones would stop the class and begin a group session by saying, "I think Chris and Joe are having a problem, class. Let's talk about what is happening."

In a nonjudgmental manner, Ms. Jones would encourage open discussion between Chris, Joe, and interested classmates. She would focus on feelings and reasons for what happened, rather than discussing punishment for the misbehavior. Once Chris and Joe calm down, and understand why each did what they did, she or other students might promote the opportunity for further discussion of methods to avoid this type of conflict in the future.

During the peak years of open education, sensitivity groups proliferated. They served both students and staff. A frequent goal of these groups was to sensitize participants to racial, ethnic, and sexual differences. Unfortunately, a sizable minority of group leaders were poorly trained, unethical, and used poor judgment regarding the nature and goals of groups that would be suitable for use in schools. As a result, sensitivity training was condemned by many policymakers and citizens. However, judicious use of these groups can be very helpful in allowing students to be aware of their own feelings and to learn to *empathize* with others.

Many group exercises have emerged from the process groups of the 1960s and 1970s. For instance, a trust exercise can involve two students, June and Jill. June stands about a foot or two behind Jill. Jill is instructed to fall backwards. She is told to trust that June will catch her before she hits the floor. June places her extended hands about six inches to a foot behind Jill's shoulder blades so that she may easily catch June as she falls backwards. If June has a great deal of trust in her own strength, she may stand further back and catch Jill after she has fallen a greater distance. However, usually the person is caught before falling more than a foot or two.

Another exercise helps students learn to listen to each other. Two students sit about two feet apart and concentrate on each other's faces. Each student focuses on a short dialogue spoken by the other. This is done by repeating as accurately as possible everything the other student says. Repetition occurs after every three or four sentences. It is interesting to see how long each participant can concentrate on the other.

There are a host of other exercises designed to establish trust and empathy with others (Simon, Howe & Kirschenbaum, 1972).

Role Playing

Role playing is a technique that may be included in any type of process group. However, it also can be used independently. This technique helps participants to "get into the shoes" of another person. A powerful exercise is called role reversal. For instance, when Ms. Jones becomes frustrated with Chris's refusals to do work, she could set up a role reversal situation. Chris plays her role and she plays the role of Chris. The teacher's accurate portrayal of Chris will help him to realize how difficult the teacher's role may be. Furthermore, if Chris accurately portrays the negative things the teacher does, Ms. Jones may understand how Chris feels. Student comments about the accuracy of the role playing will help Chris and Ms. Jones gain a better understanding of each other.

Psychodrama

The technique of *psychodrama* emerged from the psychodynamic approach, but is relevant to the humanistic classroom. In psychodrama, students are assigned roles and goals as part of a dramatization of a particular issue or event. Usually their roles are the opposite from their normal behavior. This is a little different from role playing, which is a technique within psychodrama, because a whole scenario is planned. After the psychodrama, the class and participants discuss the meaning of the events and the feelings that accrued.

Affective Curricula

Many *affective curricula* help students deal with their feelings. Besides the standard ones, published by major companies, many arrive periodically in the mail of educators and psychologists. Values Clarification (Simon, Howe & Kirschenbaum, 1972) is a prototypical approach to a humanistic affective curriculum. The range of topics and the variety of publishers are too extensive to discuss here. The common goal of most of these affective curricula is to promote recognition of one's own feelings, beliefs, and values and to appreciate those of others. Many of the programs help students learn to express their feelings without hurting others.

For instance, Ms. Jones might say to Chris, "I understand that you are angry at Joe. Your feelings are genuine and you can express them; however, acting out these feelings and hurting someone is inappropriate. So it's okay to tell Joe that you are angry and what he did to make you angry, but you are not allowed to hit him."

Humanistic Programs

Some examples of the humanistic approach are presented in Table 5.1 on pages 162–163. More detailed discussions follow.

Open Education

The humanist concern for individuality, freedom, and self-directed learning was expressed in a number of seminal books at a time when America was awakening from the postwar stupor of the 1950s (Gross & Gross, 1969). However, a great deal of credit for the growing humanist movement in American education is owed to the humanist revolt in England. There, in 1921, Summerhill, a boarding school associated with "ultrapermissiveness," was opened. It became famous throughout the world with the publication of *Summerhill* in 1960 (Neill, 1960, 1966).

TABLE 5.1   Examples of Humanistic Programs

Program	Underlying Theory	Assumptions	Diagnosis	Intervention/Remediation	Research
Open Education	Teachers and students should be treated as "moral equals" and the same rules apply for everyone.	Children's innate abilities and curiosity will develop in a natural manner at each child's own pace. Thus, teachers must be responsive to the ways students naturally grow and develop.	Teachers must determine each student's needs and relate these unmet needs to specific behavior.	The emphasis is on observing, listening, and understanding children so that a flexible and suitable environment can be created (Rich, 1985). For example, modifications of classroom arrangements (e.g., moving furniture) may be necessary. According to Kohl (1976), the best way to handle a discipline problem is by using a fable or story that can be discussed without embarrassing anyone.	Strong support for open education has not been found in the literature.
Raths & Simon's Values Clarification	Behavior change will occur if students are able to focus on issues in their lives and if they are stimulated to consider the following processes: (1) freely and thoughtfully select from alternatives, (2) be happy with their choice and affirm it publicly, (3) do something with that choice within one's own life pattern. The ultimate goal is to change one's behavior and not one's values.	Discipline problems are caused by two factors: (1) when students with unclear expectations experience considerable inner turmoil, and (2) when both the identified misbehaving student and the school (e.g., teacher, administrator, etc.) have clear but different values and when either or both are unable to accept each other's differences.	The key is to identify behaviors that signal value confusion. Raths et al. (1978) have noted eight behaviors that may signal this type of confusion: apathy, flightiness, uncertainty, inconsistency, drifting, overconforming, overdissenting, and role playing. It was suggested by the authors that clear values could help change some of these behaviors.	Unlike other discipline models, the values clarification approach does not provide immediate steps for the teacher to take when dealing with discipline issues. Instead, this is a model used over a long period. What teachers can do is avoid directive statements that judge, influence, or impose values. Also, teachers should avoid all control in the forms of reinforcement, physical intervention, and isolation. The following behaviors should be done overtly: (1) look and listen for value indicators from the student, (2) listen carefully, (3) ask questions that probe the elements of a true value, and (4) use formal group exercises.	In general, research on values clarification has lacked enough methodological rigor to support its effectiveness. Some studies have indicated student improvement in value-related behavior, but there have been few well-designed empirical studies to support an increase in self-concept, movement toward self-actualization or better thinking processes (e.g., Lemming, 1981).

Program	Underlying Theory	Assumptions	Diagnosis	Intervention/ Remediation	Research
Gordon's Teacher Effectiveness Training	The theory underlying TET was first conceptualized by Carl Rogers. He held that, given empathetic understanding, warmth, and openness, one will choose what is best for oneself and will become a fully functioning person.	TET assumes that "the quality of the teacher–learner relationship is crucial if teachers are to be effective in teaching anything" (Gordon, 1974).	The model acknowledges two kinds of student behavior: acceptable and unacceptable. Once this is understood, the idea of problem ownership is introduced. It is the "no problem" area where the most effective teaching and learning can take place (e.g., the problem is owned by both the teacher and the student).	Gordon has identified a six-step process, which includes: (1) defining the problem, (2) generating possible solutions, (3) evaluating the solutions, (4) deciding which solution to implement, (5) determining how to implement the decision, and (6) assessing how well the solution solved the problem. In addition, this model supports the use of "language of acceptance." This is shown by the use of empathetic acknowledgment responses, open-ended questions, active listening, and the use of "I" messages (placing responsibility for what is happening within the person experiencing the problem).	Despite widespread use of TET, the research has yielded mixed results. At this time, there are a limited number of adequately designed outcome studies. Recent studies do tend to support the conclusion that TET training can change teacher attitudes and behavior in a direction consistent with the assumptions of the TET model.

Despite ridicule, sarcasm, and fear expressed by many traditionally oriented educators, Summerhill not only survived, it thrived. In addition, it also passed an extensive review by British educational officials in 1949 (Gross & Gross, 1969). Later reports indicated that graduates, when matched with peers from traditional schools, were indistinguishable in terms of accomplishments in life.

Despite the fears of *traditionalists,* the example of Summerhill, reports of the British Infant School Movement (Featherstone, 1971; Plowden, 1967) and a series of publications resulted in the open education movement in America. Important concepts were explicated in such books as *Crisis in the Classroom* (Silberman, 1971), *The Open Classroom Reader* (Silberman, 1973), *The Open Classroom* (Kohl, 1969), *How Children Fail* (Holt, 1982), *How Children Learn* (Holt, 1967), and *Teacher* (Ashton-Warner, 1963).

Herbert Kohl (1969, 1979; Rich, 1979), a major American theorist of humanism and open education, believes that teachers and students should be treated as "moral equals" and that the same rules should apply to everyone (Rich, 1985). According to Kohl, the open teacher, when questioned or challenged, does not resort to bullying. He or she is open and responsive to criticism. In addition, the teacher should also have the strength to admit failure (Kohl, 1979).

In Kohl's model, equal importance is assigned to teacher–student relations and the classroom environment. Therefore, he believes, when necessary, teachers should not hesitate to modify classroom arrangements. This might include rearranging furniture, changing schedules, or stopping a lesson to consider an important emerging issue. Also, separate and private places may be needed both for small-group work and for solitary thought.

The teacher's objective is to create an environment in which trust and responsibility can evolve. Each teacher needs to determine the extent to which the school system will permit an open classroom. Compromises will need to be made with administrators and other teachers.

Kohl's approach provides a flexible, open-classroom setting, in which the teacher displays such positive traits as responsiveness, naturalness, openness, closeness, and toughness (Rich, 1985). An attempt is made to create an environment that will best nurture natural development. What is constructed is an environment with much freedom to learn, explore, and create. As a result, it is believed that students will likely find their classroom a happy place and will usually enjoy their school experiences.

As with other applications of humanistic principles, Kohl does not allow students to harm themselves, others, or property. The entire class needs to see that rules are enforced and that the teacher is the enforcer. This latter deviates somewhat from more democratic approaches to enforcing discipline that typify humanism in education. When limits are tested, it is the teacher's task to respect the student's strengths while consistently enforcing the limits. If a discipline problem should arise, affecting the entire class, Kohl states that the best way to handle it is by using a fable or story that can be discussed without anyone being embarrassed.

A contemporary American version of the humanism reflected in Summerhill is the Sudbury Valley School, founded in 1968 in Framingham, Massachusetts. This is a school where students, without restrictions, structure their own educational experiences (Mezzacappa, 1992). Traditionalists fear that children will not learn in such an environment. The founder and director, Dan Greenberg, states, "There is no question that children learn best when they're engaged in something on their own initiative" (Mezzacappa, 1992). For example, if students are interested in a single topic such as skiing, baseball, physics, or history, they are allowed to spend as much time as they wish in pursuit of their own, intrinsic interests. Faculty members act as guides and friends and function on an egalitarian footing with the students.

The school is a participatory democracy, where together students and staff vote on all curricular and administrative decisions. Discipline problems are handled by an all-student rotating judicial committee, which bases its decisions on the School Meeting Law Book, a document developed by students and faculty.

The Waldorf Schools, founded in 1919 by Rudolph Steiner in Stuttgart, Germany, are another example of humanism that has spread to the contemporary American educational landscape. The name *Waldorf* comes from the fact that the school was instituted for employees of the Waldorf-Astoria cigarette factories. Currently, there are more than 500 schools around the world, with about 120 of them located in the United States. These are private schools that focus on the humanistic belief that children's innate abilities and curiosity will unfold in a natural manner at each child's own pace. Experience in art, music, and movement will enhance and encourage the development of cognitive skills such as writing, reading, and math.

Reading is not stressed as an important and necessary skill in the child's early education. Rather, the Waldorf philosophy, in common with the contemporary whole-language approach, introduces reading gradually through storytelling and writing. Compared with most schools, the classes are small, with only eleven children to a class.

Although most contemporary schools stress that they teach the whole child, the Waldorf schools actually do this. They encourage curiosity and a desire to learn for learning's sake rather than focusing on the memorization and retelling of facts. The organic whole is emphasized. Classrooms are enhanced with soft, natural colors and objects from nature, such as flowers, woven baskets, and ceramic and wooden eating utensils. Plastics, TV, and other representations of the postindustrial, technological age are avoided as mediums for learning. The teacher as a person is more important than the teacher as a specialist in a particular curriculum. In some situations, the teachers stay with the students all the way through the eighth grade.

The Waldorf schools represent a quite contemporary and growing alternative to modern factory schools that focus on jamming bits and pieces of information into children's heads. These schools are not concerned with economic efficiency or standardized curricula; rather, they are concerned with individual development.

Opinions differ about the nature, meaning, and impact of open education in America. But all advocates of the movement consider education as a process, not just a means to prepare for later life. "Children need to be themselves, to live with other children and with grownups, to learn from their environment, to enjoy the present, to get ready for the future, to create and to love, to learn to face adversity, to behave responsibly, in a word, to be human beings" (Plowden, 1967). In the early 1970s, I was involved in several studies and consultations to open education programs. One effort resulted in a scale that measured eight major dimensions of Open Education (Keller & Hyman, 1973). These include:

1. A democratic teaching style
2. Individualization of instruction geared to students' interests
3. Informality in classroom structure and functioning
4. Diversity of student activities based on individual interests
5. Diagnosis of problems based on individual goals, interests, and abilities rather than on comparison with others
6. Stress on cooperation as opposed to competition
7. Productivity in terms of clearly purposeful activities by students that relate to and extend beyond the classroom
8. Classroom activities that are of interest to the students and provide them with personal and academic satisfaction.

Humanism in American education took a real drubbing in the 1970s and 1980s. In many cases, the humanistic roots of open education were lost in attempts to reorganize space, administration, and curricula. The political right vigorously attacked the curriculum, which in many cases was poorly conceived and taught by educators who were drafted into an approach that was alien to their beliefs about children and education. School boards and architects went into a frenzy of building "modern" schools without walls separating classrooms. The underlying concepts of freedom, individuality, and self-determination were rarely implemented. Among the movements that suffered was the values clarification approach.

Raths and Simon's Values Clarification Model

Raths, Harmin, and Simon (1966) defined a value as the outcome of a three-part process. First, after thoughtful consideration of consequences of various alternative choices, students must make their own decisions. Second, once a choice is made, they should be happy enough with their decision to affirm it publicly. Third, they should be able to take actions based on their decisions, and they should be able to incorporate those actions into their lives.

Students need to focus on major issues and moral decisions in their lives. If they are enabled, in a nonthreatening atmosphere, to consider their value, then students will change behavior, demonstrating more purposeful, proud, positive, and enthusiastic behavior patterns (Raths, Harmin, & Simon, 1978). Thus, the ultimate goal in value clarification is to change behavior.

Raths identified (1) apathy, (2) flightiness, (3) uncertainty, (4) inconsistency, (5) drifting, (6) overconforming, (7) overdissenting, and (8) role playing as behaviors that signal value confusion. He believed that clear values could help change some of these behaviors.

According to this model, discipline problems are caused by two factors. The first occurs when students with unclear values experience considerable inner turmoil, which leads them to engage in a variety of behaviors in an attempt to restore themselves to more fluid functioning (Curwin & Mendler, 1988). In this process of restoration, they may participate in behaviors that may conflict with the prevailing school system (e.g., refuse to do homework, skip classes). The second factor occurs when both the identified misbehaving student and the school (administrator, teacher) have clear but different values and when either or both are unable to accept each other's differences.

Unlike other discipline models, the values clarification approach does not provide immediate steps for the teacher to take when dealing with a student engaged in a disruptive act (Wolfgang & Glickman, 1986). Instead, this model is a technique to be used over a long period. People do not acquire or change values every few minutes. Time and exploration need to occur before change can come about.

In the humanistic tradition, the teacher should avoid directive statements that judge, influence, or impose values. In addition, the teacher should avoid all control in the forms of reinforcement, physical intervention, and isolation. The teacher should (1) look and listen for value indicators from the student; (2) listen carefully, paraphrasing or repeating the student's thoughts; (3) ask questions that probe the elements of a true value; and (4) use formal group exercises.

Formal lessons are presented that allow students to actively explore their individual attitudes and values, as well as alternatives to them. Here, the teacher functions primarily as a guide, asking questions without imposing his or her values. Students learn to understand and explore alternative values, ultimately choosing a course of action from a selection of alternatives (Marotz, 1983). Simon and deSherbinin (1975) claim that values clarification can help students be more purposeful, become more productive, sharpen critical thinking, and have better relations with each other.

There are many testimonials and positive anecdotal reports about values clarification. Proponents claim that it helps underachievers to (1) improve attitudes toward learning, (2) actively participate, (3) raise questions and alternatives, (4) persevere, and (5) become self-directed without the fear of being corrected (Wolfgang & Glickman, 1986). It enables students to communicate effectively in a nonjudgmental, accepting atmosphere, stimulates thinking, and can be used informally or formally anytime and anywhere during the school day (Curwin & Mendler, 1988).

In general, research on values clarification has lacked enough methodological rigor to support its effectiveness. Some studies indicate student improvement in value-related behaviors, but there has been little well-designed research demonstrating improvement in self-concept, movement toward self-actualization, better thinking processes, and reductions in dogmatism (Covault, 1973; Greco, 1977; Guziak, 1975; Leming, 1981).

Not until more reliable and valid measures are developed to better differentiate between those with "clear" and "unclear" values and not until the central components of values clarification are better defined will this model be fairly and accurately assessed.

Practical limitations of values clarification include that it does not tell teachers what to do when faced with disruptive behavior. Values clarification is basically an indirect, preventive method of dealing with misbehavior (Wolfgang & Glickman, 1986, p. 189). Therefore, this model must be used with other methods. Also, this approach advocates nonjudgmental teacher support toward any student value. However, this is extremely difficult to maintain when one student says he is going to "hurt" another individual. Even if a teacher were to be as nonjudgmental as possible, it would still be difficult to be completely accepting of all values. Furthermore, some critics (e.g., Stewart, 1975) contend that teachers and students find the values clarification activities boring and sometimes embarrassing. Others have said that the techniques of this model ignore the importance of normative values that make groups and cultures cohesive.

Gordon's Teacher Effectiveness Training

Teacher Effectiveness Training (TET) was developed by Thomas Gordon (1974), whose original ideas dated from his attempts to help parents deal effectively with their children. It is partially based on Carl Rogers's model of client-centered therapy, with emphasis on techniques that facilitate understanding, warmth, and openness.

TET offers communication skills and problem-solving methods that are claimed to improve the quality of the teacher–learner relationship. This is crucial if teachers are to be effective in teaching anything (Gordon, 1974). An effective teacher–student relationship includes:

1. Openness or transparency, so that each is able to risk directness and honesty with the other
2. Caring, when each knows that he or she is valued by the other
3. Interdependence of one on the other
4. Separateness, to allow each to grow and develop his or her own uniqueness, creativity, and individuality
5. Mutual needs meeting and no-lose conflict resolution, so that neither's needs are met at the expense of the other's needs

Gordon acknowledges two kinds of student behaviors: those that are acceptable and those that are unacceptable to the teacher. These behaviors are thought to vary depending on place, time, concern, incident, changes in the teacher, changes in the student, and changes in the environment (Gordon, 1974).

Once it is understood that there are these two kinds of behaviors, the idea of problem ownership is introduced (Chance, 1985). For example, a problem is owned by the teacher if a student's behaviors interfere "with the teacher's meeting his or her needs, or cause the teacher to be frustrated, upset, or irritated" (Gordon, 1974, p. 38). In contrast, a problem is owned by the student if it only affects the student and does not interfere with the teacher's right to teach. Conflicts may also be owned by both teacher and student. However, it is only in the "no problem" area that effective teaching and learning can take place. The goal of TET is to increase the amount of teaching–learning time by decreasing the amount of time it takes to deal with problems.

Gordon explains that teachers should avoid responding to students with roadblocks to communication. These roadblocks consist of twelve categories, which include:

1. Ordering, commanding, and directing
2. Warning and threatening
3. Moralizing, preaching, giving "shoulds" and "oughts"
4. Advising, offering solutions or suggestions
5. Teaching, lecturing, giving logical arguments
6. Judging, criticizing, disagreeing, blaming
7. Name calling, stereotyping, labeling
8. Interpreting, analyzing, diagnosing
9. Praising, agreeing, giving positive evaluations

10. Reassuring, sympathizing, consoling
11. Questioning, probing, interrogating
12. Withdrawing, distracting, being sarcastic (Gordon, 1974; pp. 48–49)

Students who hear these roadblocks frequently interpret them as comments about their abilities. According to Gordon, the danger in this is that "your messages of today becomes his self-concept tomorrow" (Gordon, 1974, p. 51). It should be noted here that Gordon, in the humanist tradition, sees the use of both rewards and punishments, or using the teacher's power to try to control the student's behavior, as a manipulation and misuse of power by the teacher. This eventually will lead to defensive behavior on the part of the student.

Instead of teachers sending roadblocks, Gordon says what is needed is the "language of acceptance," which will encourage students to do their own problem solving. This is shown by the use of passive listening, empathic acknowledgment responses, open-ended questions or statements, and active listening. Another effective means of communication is required when a student's behavior causes a problem for the teacher. Gordon recommends using "I" messages. Statements such as, "John, I can't continue this lecture while you are talking," place responsibility for what is happening within the person experiencing the problem. The teacher tells the student what is happening, the effect the student's behavior is having on the teacher, and that the behavior is unacceptable.

A third central component of TET, in addition to teaching listening skills and "I" messages, deals with changing the classroom environment in such a way as to prevent unacceptable behavior and increase the amount and degree of quality instructional time (Chance, 1985). There are many ways to improve the environment. Depending on the needs at the time, it can be enriched, impoverished, restricted, enlarged, rearranged, simplified, and systematized. Planning ahead is accomplished by informing students about what is expected of them in the future (Chance, 1985).

No matter how effective an environment a leader creates, conflicts with students are inevitable. Gordon has identified three methods for handling such conflicts. Method I involves the settlement of a conflict by the teacher using power to win. In contrast, Method II is when the teacher "gives in," resulting in the student winning. TET has rejected the first two Methods and favors Method III, the no-lose method, in which a solution is sought that is acceptable to all parties. It is actually a system for negotiating the settlement of a conflict, so that nobody loses.

Method III consists of a six-step process (Gordon, 1974) which includes (1) defining the problem; (2) generating possible solutions; (3) evaluating the solutions; (4) selecting the best solution; (5) determining how to implement the solution; and (6) assessing how well the solution solved the problem. These six steps help to provide a logical sequence to resolve classroom conflicts.

An additional benefit of Method III is that it can be used to facilitate classroom rule setting (Chance, 1985). These meetings allow students to participate with the teacher to develop classroom rules and guidelines for conduct.

Three options are provided for those individuals who fail to abide by an agreement through Method III. The first step is to confront the students and remind them of their commitment. If this fails, the second alternative is to repeat the six-step process of Method III in an effort to arrive at a better, more acceptable solution (Gordon, 1974).

A frequent observation about the strength of Gordon's model is its focus on the positive, accepting relationship it fosters between teacher and students. According to Wolfgang and Glickman (1986), the strength of TET is that it goes beyond the abstraction of being a "good" teacher. Instead, it prescribes specific teacher actions and methods to attain that end. Another strength of this model is the development of student responsibility, which results from children being encouraged to solve their own problems. Ford (1984) also likes TET's sensitivity to the student's feelings in difficult situations. Furthermore, this model requires democratic rule-setting practices and helps teachers decide problem ownership. Finally, Tauber (1990) explains that, by teaching communication skills, TET promotes the most effective discipline, namely, self-discipline.

As with many of the previous models of discipline, one of the limitations of Gordon's Teacher Effectiveness Training (TET) is that it does not totally address the problem of disruptive or violent students. For example, the use of "I" messages may not be strong enough when a student becomes violent or explodes with rage. Thus, it is not clear what can be done during an act of violence. Another limitation questions Gordon's underlying assumption of rationality. At what point are children cognitively capable to make rational decisions? What about young children or intellectually limited youngsters? For these students, the teacher may need to tell them what is in their best interest. Similarly, children with language difficulties or who are nonverbal will have a hard time expressing their emotions.

Another limitation suggests that TET may actually require some techniques that are better suited to therapy. Because teachers are neither trained as therapists nor authorized to engage in therapy, they may do more harm than good (Rich, 1985). Finally, the biggest complaint about Gordon's approach is that too much time is required to adequately listen and solve problems with one student while the rest of the students are waiting.

Despite the widespread use of TET, there are a limited number of adequately designed outcome studies. The research has yielded mixed results. The studies reviewed tend to support the conclusion that TET training can change teacher attitudes and behavior in a direction consistent with the assumptions of the TET model (Blume, 1977; Chanow, 1980; Dennehy, 1981; Dillard, 1974; Emmer & Aussiker, 1990; Percy, 1990; Thompson, 1975).

What is not as convincing is the effect of TET on students. Yet, there is some evidence that students in the classes of teachers trained in TET may improve in some areas such as attitude, interest in school, competence, achievement test scores, school attendance, and behavior (Aspy, 1977; Dennehy, 1981; Laseter, 1981; Nummela, 1978; Thompson, 1975). Again, the problem of poor methodology limits us from making definitive conclusions about this popular program.

Summary, Research, and Critique

When compared with other Western democracies, the United States is not very humanistic. In fact, the values of cooperation, sharing, and "doing one's thing" are considered by many to be actually anti-American. Furthermore, schools are not organized around these values. Schools are bureaucracies and focus on competition, achievement, and group management in the classroom. It is difficult for any teacher to set up an open classroom in a closed system. Although there are many humanistic teachers, there are few who are allowed to operate their classroom on a purely humanistic basis. This is true despite the fact that the research on this approach is as adequate as the research in the other areas.

For instance, Robinson and Hyman (1984) conducted a meta-analysis of fourteen studies that evaluated the effectiveness of human relations training programs that were all based on humanistic theories. All studies used experimental and control groups and sound statistical procedures. Positive effects were found for 79 percent of the programs. The major goal of the training programs was to change teachers' or preservice teachers' attitudes and learning climate. Better designs would have indicated whether these factors resulted in "better" students in humanistic terms.

In conclusion, humanism is an approach that requires a deep sense of the potential goodness in all people. It is apparent that humanism is not reflected in mainstream education. Furthermore, in more conservative areas, humanistic language, techniques, and philosophy may occasion outright hostility. It is clear that if you are a humanist, your beliefs may have a positive effect on your interaction with students; however, you may find it difficult to operate a completely humanistic classroom. If you are in a situation where it is not possible to completely carry out your philosophy, you can still selectively and judiciously use many of the techniques discussed.

Key Terms

affective education

basic needs

client-centered therapy

empathy

open education

process groups

progressive education

psychodrama

role playing

secular humanism

self-actualization

traditionalists

Application Activities

1. Diagnose Juanita from a humanistic approach. Where is she according to Maslow's theory of personality? Develop intervention and treatment plans using humanistic techniques.

2. Diagnose Michael from a humanistic approach. Develop intervention and treatment plans using Rogerian theory.

3. Diagnose Jamal using a humanistic approach. Develop intervention and treatment plans using Kohl's open education approach.

4. Diagnose Chris using a humanistic approach. Develop intervention and treatment plans using Rath & Simon's values clarification model.

5. Develop a whole class lesson plan using Gordon's Teacher Effectiveness Training model.

Suggested Readings

Dewey, J. (1944). *Democracy and education.* New York: Free Press.

Ellsworth, J. T., & Monahan, A. K. (1987). *A humanistic approach to teaching and learning through developmental discipline.* New York: Irvington.

Gordon, T. (1991). *Discipline that works: Promoting self discipline in children.* New York: Plume-Penguin Group.

Kohl, H. (1976). *The open classroom.* New York: Schocken Books.

Kohn, A. (1990). *The brighter side of human nature: Altruism and empathy in everyday life.* New York: Basic Books.

Kohn, A. (1991). Caring kids, the role of the schools. *Phi Delta Kappa, 72*(7), 496–506.

Maslow, A. H. (1968). *Toward a psychology of being* (2nd ed.). Princeton, NJ: Harper & Row.

Maslow, A. H. (1970). *Motivation and personality* (2nd ed.). New York: Harper & Row.

Neill, A. S. (1960). *Summerhill.* New York: Hart Publishing Co.

Neill, A. S. (1966). *Freedom not license.* New York: Hart Publishing Co.

Rath, L. E., Harmin, M., & Simon, S. B. (1978). *Values and teaching* (2nd ed.). Columbus, OH: Charles Merrill.

Rogers, C. (1961). *On becoming a person.* Boston, MA: Houghton Mifflin.

Rogers, C. (1983). *Freedom to learn.* Columbus, OH: Charles E. Merrill.

Silberman, C. (1971). *Crisis in the classroom.* New York: Vintage Books.

Silberman, C. (1973). *The open classroom reader.* New York: Vintage Books.

Slavin, R. (1983). *Cooperative learning.* New York: Longman.

Chapter *6*

The Biophysical Approach

Chapter Objectives

After reading this chapter, you should know:

1. The historical roots of the biophysical approach
2. The current research in the biophysical approach
3. Various conditions that affect the perceptual and organizational aspects of brain functioning
4. The various components of temperament
5. Medical diagnosis of neuropsychological functioning
6. Neuropsychological tests
7. The three components of attention deficit hyperactivity disorder
8. The various disorders caused by chemical imbalances in the brain
9. The techniques used for intervention in the biophysical approach
10. Critique of the biophysical approach

The biophysical approach within the teacher variance model emphasizes biological determinism. If you came out high in this area on the Teacher Variance Inventory, you believe that:

1. Everyone is born with genetically determined traits such as intelligence, athletic ability, and temperament
2. Behavior is adversely affected when individuals are not in an optimal state of health
3. Misbehavior may be caused by biologically based disorders of affect, attention, or learning or inherited vulnerabilities such as alcoholism
4. Misbehavior may be the result of unidentified physical disabilities such as visual impairment, auditory impairment, hormonal imbalance, or disorders of metabolism
5. Misbehavior may be the result of inadequate nutrition
6. Misbehavior may be the result of ingestion of inappropriate or illegal substances

Proponents of the biophysical approach emphasize the importance of *nature over nurture* in explaining behavior and misbehavior. However, although determinism is related to *heredity,* interventions are still possible. Proponents advocate that medical interventions are underused because of faulty screening, inadequate developmental and family histories, and improper diagnosis of a variety of misbehaviors.

Biological Determinism, Social Darwinism, and Issues of Race and Class

In Western culture, until relatively recent times, *biological determinism* predominated beliefs about people's fates. Biological determinism is the belief that genetic and biological inheritance determines one's personality, traits, limitations, abilities, and expectations for success. *Social Darwinism* is an extension of biological determinism that applies Darwin's principals of natural selection to class and race. It posits that individual biophysical characteristics such as intelligence, athletic ability, and height are inherited and are part of the larger gene pool of each social class and racial group. Those who inherit traits that facilitate dominance of others will emerge at the top. This is nature's way of ensuring survival of the fittest in every society. In an industrial or postindustrial society, most people who are in lower classes are there because they do not have the biological traits such as intelligence, perseverance, and enterprise needed to succeed. Their inferior abilities, biologically determined, doom them and their progeny to remain in the lower strata of society.

As with humanism, the biophysical model has major social and political implications. In contemporary times, there are periodic debates based on the relative importance of nature (biology) and nurture (environment) as determinants of people's success. These debates often result when the theories are applied to differences in racial groups in terms of their abilities to succeed in modern societies. These debates clearly cloud scientific considerations and even research based on biological determinants of abilities and behavior.

Beginning around 1994, there has been renewed interest in biological determinism. Proponents of heritability (the belief that traits such as intelligence are inherited) have presented data that could have profound effects on education and social policy into the next century.

Proponents of heritability of intelligence, using comparative studies of racial groups, have consistently claimed that 60 to 80 percent of intelligence is due to heredity (Herrnstein & Murray, 1994; Scarr-Salapatek, 1971). However, once comparisons are made between racial groups such as African Americans and whites, the predictions of intelligence are complicated by issues of socioeconomic status and prejudicial social, economic, and educational treatment of minorities. When issues of social equity become entangled in the nature–nurture controversy, political polarization is inevitable. For instance, Arthur Jensen (1980) and Herrnstein and Murray (1994) argue that the average genetic potential of African American populations is about ten to fifteen points lower than that of white populations. They claim that these differences account for lower socioeconomic status and higher rates of criminal behavior. However, most psychologists, including ourselves, reject racially based biological determinism as an explanation of intelligence and misbehavior (Scarr-Salapatek, 1971).

Adherents of social and racial equity fear public support for the concept of heritability as it is related to biological determinism. They oppose research that might demonstrate the innate superiority of certain racial, ethnic, or sexual groups, which would lead to social policy based on those limitations. A new debate on some aspect of these issues seems to emerge each decade as some adherent of biological determinism produces research to support racial or sexual differences.

No group wishes to be considered genetically inferior on any trait, and groups targeted as inferior will inevitably decry the claims of biological determinists. They claim that, taken to extremes, biological determinism is also used to explain the superiority of groups within a relatively homogeneous gene pool. For instance, darkness of skin may be used, as it is in India, to define a caste system. But even when skin color is not an issue, and the population is indistinguishable on any apparent physical characteristics, heredity based on family history, hair color, or height may be used to explain superiority.

Some data support the contention that poor people are more prone to use aggression and violence to solve problems, or at least they get caught and are more often convicted at higher rates than groups above them on the economic ladder (Hyman, 1995). It is possible that biophysical factors such as vulnerability to alcoholism, drug addiction, attention deficit disorders, and learning disabilities may go undetected or untreated more frequently in lower socioeconomic groups. Furthermore, because there is some evidence that poor people may more frequently resort to spanking and physically abusing their children (Hyman & Grossman, 1993), children from impoverished homes may be more subject to brain injuries, which may result in violent behavior. Also, lack of adequate prenatal care, poor nutrition and medical care, and overall stress in life also may contribute to brain deficits.

Biology and Mental Illness

In the 1800s, when psychology emerged as a science separate from medicine and philosophy, many believed that all mental disorders would eventually be related to identifiable structures or chemical imbalances of the brain and nervous system (Morse & Smith, 1980). However, the idea of social Darwinism was discounted by most researchers in this area, which focused on determining biological bases of various medical syndromes. There were important milestones in the nineteenth century. For instance, in 1846, Seguin identified Down's syndrome as a genetically transmitted abnormality, and in the early 1900s a series of twin studies provided evidence for hereditary factors in the transmission of schizophrenia. In the 1990s, exponential growth of neuroscience has demonstrated that many mental illnesses, including psychoses, anxiety disorders, and depression, are related to chemical imbalances in the brain and can be treated successfully by medications.

Temperament and the Resurgence of Biological Determinism

Despite the ascendance of *environmental determinism,* during the 1940s and 1950s, scientists conducting research on individual differences in infants and children found evidence of heritability in mobility, perceptual responses, sleeping and feeding patterns, drive endowment, quality and intensity of emotional tone, social responsiveness, autonomic response patterns, biochemical individuality, and electroencephalographic patterns (Thomas and Chess, 1977; Thomas, Chess, & Birch, 1968).

Contemporary with the studies of *temperament,* other research began to provide mounting evidence for evolutionary, biological, and neuropsychological bases for behavior. Hereditary traits may make a person more prone to depression, anxiety, and other mental health problems. For instance, recent studies have demonstrated that obesity has a strong biological determinant, making it tremendously difficult for some people to maintain low body weight. Yet, they are blamed for their obesity, and the discrimination against them is injurious. They are less likely to marry, more likely to be poor, and earn far less than those who are not obese (Kolata, 1993). Men who are short are 10 percent more likely than taller men to live in poverty, and many studies show that taller men do better in the business world (Kolata, 1993). Teachers are not immune to stereotyping students. A number of studies of students have demonstrated that teachers tend to favor students who are physically attractive.

Biology and Aggression

In recent years, molecular science has investigated the neurobiological basis of a number of personality traits. Of special interest to us is the possible relation between biology and aggression. Although it is unlikely that a single gene can predict violence, scientists have discovered that the genetic programming for *neurotransmitters* (chemicals that transmit signals between neurons) may offer a powerful clue to predicting violent behavior.

Studies comparing fraternal twins, who share half of their genes with one another, and identical twins, who have identical genes, suggest that impulsive, aggressive behavior may be inherited. Low levels of the neurotransmitter seratonin have been associated with high rates of aggression. Some neuroscientists indicate that the heritability of the types of traits that lead to low levels of seratonin may account for between 20 and 40 percent of explosive behavior (Angier, 1994). Other studies have shown that high levels of certain hormones such as testosterone, the male hormone, are associated with high levels of aggression. Another hormone, vasopressin, can cause violent, aggressive behavior in animals. However, the same hormone in animals helps males to bond with their mates and protect their young. Most interesting is the fact that people's thinking and habits may change the levels of various chemicals in the body. There is clear evidence, however, that various drugs that alter the levels of neurotransmitters and hormones can reduce aggressive and violent behavior.

With relatively few exceptions, studies of extremely violent people show that they tend to have some neurological deficits such as *learning disabilities,* low intelligence, and lack of brain mechanisms to control angry feelings. There is evidence that smart people have more efficient neural wiring to transmit information. For instance, people who have earned doctorate degrees have much more complicated neural webs than do high school dropouts (Begley, 1993).

In summary, it is clear that the late 1900s witnessed a resurgence of research for understanding behavior as a function of heredity and biology. New discoveries and significant applications of molecular biology and genetic engineering are advancing at warp speed compared with the growth of the knowledge base in the other teacher variance approaches. In this chapter, we barely touch the topic and limit ourselves to a discussion of biophysical factors that seem most relevant to school discipline.

The Medical Model and Special Education

In recent years, there have been pressures to eliminate diagnostic categories and classifications in educating children with disabilities. The attempts by policymakers to reform all categorical programs, especially those involving children with "mild" disabilities, have resulted in programs of accelerated mainstreaming and total inclusion in regular classrooms of all children with disabilities. This approach deemphasizes the diagnosis-driven thinking that predominates the biophysical approach, which is usually referred to as the *medical model* in education. The biophysical approach, although philosophically in agreement with all well-supported attempts to mainstream children with disabilities, rejects some basic concepts of this movement.

Proponents of the *regular education initiative* and the *inclusion* movements contend that problems lie within the classroom and that treatment programs for many problems are so similar that it is wasteful of resources to spend inordinate time in differential diagnoses. In practice, they tend to use classroom-based, very focused behavioral and educational techniques to diagnose and remediate problems. Many reject the biophysical notion of comprehensive diagnosis as being part of an outdated medical model in education.

The "medical model" emphasizes (1) identification of the presenting problem, (2) diagnosis, and (3) remediation or treatment of both the symptoms and the underlying causes. It is dependent on advances in the behavioral and medical sciences and on sufficient quality and quantity of well-trained diagnosticians. Educational classifications/categories such as emotionally disturbed, learning disabled, and communication disordered are not diagnoses. They cannot be considered consistent with the biophysical approach because they consist of merely generic terms devised by educational bureaucrats to simplify placement. These terms are far removed from current medical/psychological nosology and research in diagnosis and treatment/remediation.

The movement toward inclusion, with its rejection of the medical model, is reminiscent of the proclamations of Thomas Szasz, who, in the 1960s, claimed there was no such thing as mental illness. His thinking helped fuel the deinstitutionalization movement. This exacerbated problems of homelessness and mental illness.

Although programs based on the medical model certainly have problems, they offer a rich variety of services that help children with disabilities to function in the least restrictive environment. The success of this model is dependent on accurate, ongoing assessment, diagnosis (categorization of disabilities), and treatment/remediation strategies.

Surveys of school psychologists, whose role as diagnosticians is pivotal to the medical model in education, generally favor returning children with disabilities to regular education when possible (Hyman & Kaplinski, 1995). However, there is deep suspicion of any totally inclusive model that does not provide for (1) adequate diagnosis; (2) accurate, periodic assessment of all biophysical and emotional factors; and (3) sufficient funding for appropriate support services. Many believe that, when it is run properly, with adequate use of mainstreaming, resource room, and declassification of children ready to return to regular education, this system works pretty well. This system, based on the medical model, although not perfect, ensures that many of the individual needs of classified children are met by low student–teacher ratios and educators who want to work with exceptional children. Placing exceptional children, especially those with oppositional behavior, back in the regular classes that could not handle them in the first place puts more pressure on the total system.

Success of the biophysical/medical model depends on accurate diagnosis. This must be followed by adequate funding, good training of staff, knowledge of current biomedical and behavioral research, and ongoing teacher assessment on each child's Individual Education Plan. If the psychoeducational treatment or medical intervention does not improve the student's functioning, further diagnosis may be considered.

Assumptions of the Biophysical Approach

Behavior Is Adversely Affected When Individuals Are Not in an Optimal State of Health, Which Can Best Be Maintained by Prevention

The core assumption of the biophysical approach is that good health is a cornerstone for good behavior. Many preventable medical syndromes may result in misbehavior. These problems can result in misbehavior when they (1) impact on mood, affect, or the ability to control impulses; (2) cause cognitive deficiencies that result in inability to function adequately in school, which may lead to low self-esteem and consequent acting out; and (3) cause such physical stigmata that the student is ridiculed and alienated from staff and most peers.

Other approaches of teacher variance conceptualize all misbehavior flowing from dysfunctions that relate to the environment and internal psychological mechanisms. Although all emphasize prevention, the biophysical orientation, through public health research and prevention programs, has historically provided dramatic and convincing proof for the success of this model. Examples include well-established protocols for prenatal care, broadscale inoculations, public education about hygiene, early diagnosis and treatment of childhood diseases, public nutrition education to reduce heart disease, and screening for genetic problems. Schools have nutrition, dental, visual, hearing, and other types of medical screening in addition to immunization requirements and safety education. We are now able to prevent major infectious diseases that in the past resulted in brain damage from high fevers or secondary infections and created educational and behavioral problems in schoolchildren.

The biophysical model stresses the importance of early school diagnosis and intervention when there are sudden and drastic changes in students' functioning or when deviant behavior persists past a reasonable period of attempted correction. Evaluation of the problem must begin with a review of the child's medical history. With the help of the school nurse and the parents, all recent medical possibilities are explored.

There Are Major Categories of Physical Dysfunction That May Cause Misbehavior

Gross neurological dysfunction can cause a host of academic and behavioral problems, including inborn errors of metabolism, intrauterine damage of the fetus, hereditary syndromes, infectious diseases of the brain, seizure disorders, aneurysms, cancer, and head injuries. Any of these problems can cause learning disabilities, attentional problems, problems of impulse control, and retardation. Trauma to the brain may damage the impulse control systems. In addition, the ability to make moral judgments and to engage in normal social intercourse may be hindered. Beyond the more obvious damage to the neurological system, there are more subtle problems that affect learning and behavior. The most prevalent of these educationally related, medical syndromes are discussed in the following section.

Perceptual and *organizational deficits* include problems of encoding, associating, and decoding information. The most easily determined problems include damage to organs and areas of the brain involving sensory inputs that facilitate hearing, seeing, and touching or feeling. If students cannot see or hear properly, they become frustrated. Most schools include adequate screening by the school nurse. But this only rules out the most obvious problems. For instance, a child may have a subtle loss of high-frequency sounds that impairs the ability to benefit from phonetic instruction. Also, this loss might result in certain speech sounds dropping out so that the child does not always hear completely the instructions given by teachers. Both of these deficits elicit angry responses by the teacher, who believes the student is being recalcitrant.

Even if the brain receives messages, problems of visual, auditory, and kinesthetic perception and association can result in academic difficulties and poor social skills. Some of these may be so subtle that they must be inferred from results of neuropsychological and educational evaluations. Deficits in either auditory or visual memory and inability to make adequate associations between material learned by rote may impair academic functioning. For instance, students with deficiencies in auditory memory will have difficulty learning to read phonetically. They will require more dependence on whole-word memory of words than on beginning analytic ability based on word sounds. Failure to provide adaptive teaching will often cause frustration and misbehavior.

Finally, there are problems of output. For instance, some students may be able to read and remember what they have read or heard in class lectures. But they might have an expressive writing disorder, which impairs their ability to efficiently take notes, write reports, and respond fast enough on written tests. Many of the oppositional students I have had in therapy have this problem. Because of it, they procrastinate, or never hand in reports and homework, and they rarely complete written tests. Their frustration in writing causes emotional problems and feelings of failure. Yet, they are correctly perceived by teachers and parents as having average or better intelligence. Their feelings of failure then are reinforced by teachers and parents, who label them as lazy. If these problems are undiagnosed by adolescence, many students become serious behavior problems and are often substance abusers.

Chemical imbalances in the brain cause a wide variety of personality and behavioral disorders that can result in school misbehavior. Brain chemistry accounts for shyness, hypersensitivity, impulsiveness, obsessional thinking, anxiety, poor concentration, and inability to control anger and aggression.

Allergies can cause a number of seemingly unrelated problems in the classroom. They can cause headaches, agitation, short temper, and hyperactivity. Constant nasal/pharyngial irritation can result in coughing, labored breathing, sneezing, and other problems that distract the learner, classmates, and the teacher. Furthermore, some of the medications used for allergies may cause additional problems. Antihistamines can cause drowsiness, and decongestants can cause sleep loss, irritability, and lack of ability to concentrate. Fear of deadly asthma attacks can cause parents to be overprotective at home. The victim may suffer from hypochondriasis or a reluctance to take responsibility in school. Some students with this condition may rebel and refuse to take their medicine regularly, become oppositional in school, and overcompensate in their efforts to prove that they are not crippled.

Hormonal imbalances may cause dysfunctions in metabolism, menstrual cycle, size, and energy levels. Although rare, students who have overactive thyroids may be hyperactive, and those with underactive glands may be phlegmatic and seriously overweight. Adolescent girls, as a result of menstrual problems, may have emotional correlates to premenstrual reactions that cause irritability, depression, or inability to concentrate.

Hormonal problems that create difficulty with metabolism include diabetes and hypoglycemia. Both of these can cause periods of low energy and irritability that interfere with learning and social interactions.

Intake of *harmful substances* can fall within two categories: purposeful and harmful substance abuse, which includes the use of both legal and illegal stimulants and depressants; and unintentional intake of noxious chemicals and poisons, which can affect mood and learning. Uppers such as amphetamines can cause angry, paranoid behavior, and downers such as marijuana can result in silly, giggly behavior or sleeping in class. Diet pills, which often include amphetamines such as Dexedrene, which some students take to stay up while cramming for exams, and caffeine can all cause irritable behavior when ingested in amounts that are excessive for each individual. Addictive cigarette smoking, especially in an era of smoke-free schools, can cause chronic disciplinary problems, as any high school administrator knows.

Legitimate medications may have powerful side effects that result in disturbed and disturbing behavior. These can include cold remedies, especially those with strong decongestants, antibiotics, and other commonly used medicine.

Lead poisoning affects approximately 17 percent of American children from six months to six years of age who have dangerously high levels of lead in their blood. Approximately twelve million young children live in old houses where lead paint is potentially toxic (Behrman, 1992). Approximately 5.9 million children younger than six years of age live in the oldest housing with the highest lead content of paint. The 17 percent of our children with high lead levels (greater than 15 ug/dl) are at risk for future neurobehavioral and cognitive deficits, mental retardation, behavior problems, and attention deficit as the results of lead poisoning.

Lead poisoning may be an undetected cause of many discipline problems in schools. This possibility is increased in schools that serve large numbers of poor children who live in old, deteriorating homes. In a study of more than 2,000 children, a dose–response relationship was shown between the frequency of behavioral and attentional problems in school and the lead content of shed baby teeth. Follow-up on a smaller sample of these children at eighteen to twenty years of age has shown that those with the highest lead content in their teeth at six to eight years of age were six times more likely to have dropped out of school and seven times more likely to have a reading disability than those children with the lowest lead content (Behrman, 1992). Common toxic brain symptoms include disorientation, concentration difficulty, emotional lability, lowered intellectual ability, speech difficulty, gait difficulty, memory problems, delusions, and hallucinations (Templer, Spencer, and Hart-lage, 1993).

Malnutrition is a bigger problem than most people realize and is not always recognized as a contributor to disciplinary problems. Malnourishment can occur in every socioeconomic level; however, children living in poverty are at an increased risk. A study conducted by the Center on Hunger, Poverty, and Nutrition Policy at Tufts University showed that the rate of child poverty increased by 49 percent in the 1980s and 1990s (Cohen, 1994). The rate increased by 56 percent in inner-city areas, 36 percent in rural areas, and the largest rate of growth in the suburban areas, which rose by 76 percent in the past twenty years. Demographics of malnutrition are related to poverty groups, which make up 14 percent of suburban, 32 percent inner-city, and 22 percent of rural children, based on 1992 figures.

Malnutrition may begin in infancy or may occur sometime during the child's school years. Other causes of malnutrition include poor dietary habits associated with poor hygiene, chronic disease, finicky eating habits of the child or the food provider, or disturbed parent–child relations (Behrman, 1992).

Malnutrition does not invariably result in loss of weight. Fatigue, lassitude, restlessness, and irritability are frequent manifestations. Restlessness and overactivity are frequently misinterpreted by parents as evidences of lack of motivation. Malnurishment may be self-induced, as in cases of anorexia, bulimia, and other problems that occur in some adolescents.

Everyone Is Born with a Genetically Determined Temperament That, In Interaction with the Environment, Can Result in Misbehavior

Temperament is an inborn trait that determines a persons basic behavioral style. Although traits are genetically programmed and are apparent in infancy, children's futures are governed by how well their temperament "fits" their abilities, motivations, and opportunities. The early research by Thomas and Chess (1977) suggested that there are basically nine types of traits. Some that can eventually impact on school discipline problems include adaptability, which is the ability of the child to modify his or her behavior as a result of environmental changes or mediation by adults; mood, which is level and intensity of behavior in terms of pleasant or unpleasant affect; activity, which is the amount of physical motion during sleeping, eating and playing; and distractibility, which is the ability or lack of ability to remain focused on the activity.

Despite the importance of genetic determinants of temperament, most researchers recognize that temperament interacts and is intertwined with the environment. This interaction affects both the child and the parent. For instance, if a child has a high level of distractibility, matched by his parents' distractibility, the parent–child interactions can be disastrous. A highly distractible child needs a patient and supportive parent to learn to focus. If the parent becomes anxious and impatient about the child's lack of attention, it is likely that punitive interactions will occur. This match between parents and children or teachers and students is conceptualized in terms of "goodness of fit." A good fit occurs when a child's capacities, motivation and temperament are matched by the demands, expectations and opportunities of the environment.

A Major Role of Teachers Is to Recognize the Symptoms of Possible Medical Problems Related to Misbehavior and to Adapt Teaching to Identified Disabilities

The biophysical approach in education relies on teachers' ability to recognize possible indicators of pathology that may cause misbehavior. You are not expected to be a physician or a neuropsychologist. But teachers can make tremendous contributions to diagnosis and treatment by keeping careful records of students' behavior and working closely with the school nurse, who will help make referrals. In addition, when physicians and psychologists are trying different medications or interventions, ongoing behavioral observations in the classroom can be crucial in ensuring successful treatment.

Diagnosis in the Biophysical Model

Using the biophysical approach, teachers can be invaluable in identifying potentially undiagnosed medical problems. Teachers can contribute by (1) acting as screening and referral sources, (2) observing and identifying patterns or symptoms that may reflect physiological problems, and (3) monitoring behavioral patterns and symptoms after medical or specialized interventions (Marchon-Tully, 1987).

The biophysical approach requires a good understanding of developmental stages and expectations. Knowing what is normal behavior at each age helps to recognize real deviancy. However, as a teacher, you are not expected to make diagnoses. In fact, we caution you to never tell parents that their child has a particular syndrome, even if you feel very strongly about it. Since most teachers do not have ready access to school physicians, you can discuss your belief with the school nurse. Also, well-trained school psychologists should be knowledgeable about learning and behavioral problems that have a neuropsychological base. Speech pathologists or therapists, special education teachers, and reading specialists may also be helpful if the problem appears to fall within their area of expertise.

A cautionary example of a perversion of this model is provided by the overdiagnosis of attention-deficit disorder (ADD). Too many ill-advised teachers and administrators, without competent psychological and neurological assessment of their students, pressure parents and pediatricians to place hyperactive children on Ritalin. Hyperactivity can be caused by a variety of problems, and even when ADD or attention deficit hyperactivity disorder (ADHD) exists, some children respond quite well to environmental interventions.

If you support this model, your abilities will increase as you explore each malady that a student has and you become familiar with the behavioral effects of medications. You can purchase a *Physicians Desk Reference,* which is published each year by Medical Economics Data Publishing Company. This compendium, available in most book stores, provides information about the nature and side effects of all approved medications. However, this should always be used with caution and, in general, communication to parents or physicians about concerns about medications or their side effects should be through the school nurse.

It is helpful to be familiar with students' eating, sleeping, and activities that may be related to misbehavior. You should be quite knowledgeable about developmental patterns of behavior, such as the amount of sleep children require at various ages. We do not provide an overview of these topics here, because it is assumed that every teacher has taken some course work in development, especially related to the age-group with which they work.

In the following section, we provide information about the diagnosis of the common biophysical problems that may be related to misbehavior. We begin with an understanding of temperament, which is posited as a set of inherited traits that, in interaction with specific classroom environments, may be related to misbehavior.

Determining Temperament

Specific temperament factors have been related to children's success in school (Martin, 1988, 1989). For instance, children who persist tend to receive fewer orders and restrictions than those who appear unable to persist. Children who tend to withdraw receive more instructions, orders, and restrictions. Children who approach receive more feedback and reinforcement. Children who are low in task orientation (activity, persistence, and distractibility) are typically recipients of controlling and directing teacher behavior. These findings are substantiated in studies of children with learning and other disabilities (Goldberg & Markovitch, 1989; Keogh and Burstein; 1988).

The Temperament Assessment Battery for Children (Martin, 1988, 1989) is a teacher response scale that you can use to diagnose temperament factors related to classroom discipline. This will help you to determine to what extent the student really deviates from the norm.

Scale measures related to discipline include (1) activity related to the students' tendency to wiggle, move out of their seats, run rather than walk, and ability to sit quietly; (2) distractibility, which is the tendency to be easily distracted and interrupted by things such as noises, events outside of the classroom, outsiders entering the classroom, and so forth; and (3) persistence, which is related to patience and persistence on tasks, despite interruptions and level of difficulty.

Martin (1989) believes that too many professionals see high levels of activity and distractibility and low levels of persistence as associated with various pathological conditions. As a result, a disease model is used to create diagnoses such as ADD. This medical model leads inevitably to the search for medical cures involving the use of drugs. Martin suggests that these traits should be considered as normally distributed in the population, just as are height, intelligence, and athletic ability.

Martin's approach leads to biophysical interventions based on methods related to goodness of fit rather than to the use of drugs. For instance, if a child is too big for the assigned desk, a teacher would obtain a bigger desk. If a child is inept at sports involving eye–hand coordination, the child can be directed toward sports that do not require batting, catching, kicking, or throwing balls.

In reviewing studies of activity level, distractibility, and persistence, it is apparent that most teachers have a greater affinity for children who are less active and distractible and more persistent. They tend to be less warm and helpful to children who are less persistent, more active, and distractible. Teachers are more critical of children who display low attention and high distractibility (Martin, Nagle & Paget, 1983). Although children with these traits tend to have low achievement over the school years, it is not clear whether their lower grades are related to negative teacher reactions or to their inability to concentrate on schoolwork. Many children with behavior problems exhibit these traits. The goodness-of-fit hypothesis dictates that in dealing with these children, teachers should have temperament styles characterized by ability to provide structure, patience, and warmth. Although we have never seen this done, matching could be based on observations of teachers and their scores on an adult temperament scale.

In understanding misbehavior in active, distractible, and nonpersistent children, one should determine whether the misbehavior is related to temperament or caused by ADD with or without hyperactivity. In the former case, medication would not be indicated, whereas in the latter case the use of medications such as Ritalin might be helpful in reducing the activity level. Research by Martin (1988) and others indicates that, especially with children in the primary grades, misbehavior tends to increase with decreasing ability to conform to the classroom demands for order, control, and persistence. Lack of motivation, failure to complete assignments, and poor grades may escalate into belligerent and aggressive behavior.

Although Martin and others do not assume that high or low levels of activity, distractibility or persistence necessarily indicate a pathological condition, the medical model suggests that an organic dysfunction in the brain may cause hyperactivity. This may lead teachers who are knowledgeable about ADD to immediately pressure parents to obtain medication for the child before adequate diagnosis is completed.

Diagnosing Neuropsychological Dysfunction

There has been a dramatic increase in research that correlates childhood brain dysfunction with the incidence of emotional and behavioral problems (Brown, Dingle, & Landau, 1993; Gadow, 1992; Kruesi et al., 1990). Brain disorders are diagnosed by a variety of professionals, most often by neurologists.

Gross Neurological, Perceptual, and Organizational Dysfunction

Neurologists usually begin with patient history and a basic examination of coordination, reflexes, balance, muscle strength in each side of the body, and visualization of the retina. These are all noninvasive techniques to determine the presence of pathological conditions of the brain. Patient reports of such problems as memory loss, confusion, distorted perceptions, loss of vision, sudden changes in feelings, and sudden loss of control of emotions may lead to a series of more complicated tests. Neuropsychological techniques include a wide range of nonintrusive and mildly invasive techniques to assess the brain, which require the services of other specialists and equipment to monitor brain functions.

Neurologists often talk about hard signs, which are obvious indicators of neurological disorder. These include loss of memory, gross loss of coordination, and the speech problems of most victims of cerebral palsy. Soft signs, which are not usually detected with magnetic resonance imaging (MRI) or computed tomography (CT) scans, are more subtle, such as minor dysfunctions in coordination, discrepancies in cognitive abilities, and subtle speech and language disorders. After a basic neurological examination, the child may be referred for more specific procedures and evaluations, including speech and language testing, psychological assessment, and various electrical tests of the brain.

Many school problems, which show up as soft signs, are not recognized until teachers determine that something is wrong. But teachers must be sophisticated enough to recognize these indicators, which are most often discrepancies in an individual student's performance. For instance, if a child can read very well orally but writes on a level that is at least two years below expectation, a neurological dysfunction should be considered. Although you are probably an expert in this type of educational screening, we can discuss commonly used procedures that are implemented to assess neurological functioning.

Many educators mistakenly believe that specific abilities are exclusively located either in the left or right hemispheres of the brain. In general, it is true that the left hemisphere tends to govern verbal and analytical abilities and that the right hemisphere controls nonverbal and holistic abilities. But these basic facts were translated by some to mean that left-dominant people are more scientific and analytical and that right-dominant people are more creative. Curricula were developed to "train" specific hemispheres of the brain. However, most neuroscientists now believe that the brain functions as an integrated whole and that every area of the brain is to some extent involved in all activity.

In too many cases, practical and financial limitations make extensive neurological diagnosis the exception rather than the rule. As a result, it is probable that many behavioral problems have an undiagnosed neurological component (Short & Shapiro, 1993). Some studies show that up to 63 percent of children with identifiable brain dysfunction exhibit behavioral and personality problems (Quay & Werry, 1986).

Common syndromes that can lead to behavioral problems include closed head injury, seizure disorders, a host of genetically based neurological diseases that impair learning and attention, and *explosive disorders,* which generally result from impairment in the frontal lobes and other areas of the brain.

Teachers actually perform basic neuropsychological assessments when they test for readiness skills in preschool and primary grades. These include fine motor coordination used in copying and drawing and large motor skills used in skipping, running, and throwing. Teaching and testing all reflect childrens' ability to perceive, organize, and remember information. Seeming inability of children to follow directions in sequence, to attend for developmentally appropriate periods, to follow rules, to sit still, and to comply with social and moral conventions may all be indicators of neurological dysfunction.

Many school psychologists are trained to assess neuropsychological functioning. They especially look for discrepancies in abilities that can signify neuropsychological dysfunction. Neuropsychologists use more extensive tests and often can locate specific areas of damage in the brain. These areas are determined as a result of dysfunction in certain skills, cognitions, or behaviors.

Although the number of neuropsychological problems associated with misbehavior is immense, there are common syndromes that require some regularly used testing procedures. Attention deficit disorder (ADD), learning disabilities, explosive/impulsive behavioral disorders, and closed head injuries all have been researched and diagnosed through the use of these assessment techniques.

Advanced Neuropsychological Tests

Sophisticated technologies are available to diagnose observable brain dysfunction. Methods of investigating brain activities include the electroencephalograph (EEG) (Becker, Velasco, Harmony, Marosi, & Landazuri, 1987; Fuller, 1977; John et al., 1983; Satterfield,

Schell, Backs, & Hidaka, 1984; Quay & Werry, 1986), the brain electrical activity mapping technique (BEAM) (Selz & Wilson, 1989; Torello & Duffy, 1985), computer tomography (CT), magnetic resonance imaging (MRI) (Jernigan, Hesselink, & Tallal, 1987; Tallal & Curtis, 1990), positron emission tomography (PET) (Decker & Howe, 1981; Fuster, 1990; Rothenberger, 1990), brain stem evoked responses (BSER) (Obrzut, Morris, Wilson, Lord, & Caraveo, 1987).

Many depend on expensive procedures and some scans are considered invasive because they used injected radioactive substances (Selz & Wilson, 1989). All are used for research and diagnosis to determine the causes of ADHD, mental retardation, seizure disorders, brain injury, and learning disabilities. Newer, noninvasive technologies continue to be developed, and if you adhere to the biophysical model, you can keep abreast of the field by reading everything from the Tuesday Science section of the *New York Times* and other popular sources to professional journals.

Explosive/Impulsive Disorders and Head Injury

A difficult and puzzling problem for teachers are students who do not seem to learn from their mistakes. These students, who constantly get into trouble, are frequently explosive and often steal, cheat, lie, and fight. Although they sometimes cry and promise to never commit the same indiscretion again, they invariably repeat the offenses. They are particularly difficult when they are subject to rages when frustrated by seemingly inconsequential and reasonable demands or sanctions. Some of these students probably have some dysfunction in their frontal lobes, an area related to moral behavior, planning ability, facility to make rational/ethical decisions, and ability to process emotions.

Frontal lobe dysfunction can be of unknown origin and sometimes difficult to detect without the types of sophisticated evaluations just discussed. Others are obvious because they result from known head injuries, seizures, and comas. Accidents are the major cause of morbidity and mortality in children older than one year of age, and head trauma is the injury most responsible for death (Behrman, 1992). It is estimated that 100,000 children are hospitalized annually in the United States because of head injury, and 5 to 10 percent have long-term mental or physical handicaps as a result (Behrman, 1992).

Most head injuries somehow involve an automobile. These often include autos hitting bicycles or motorcycles. Falls and nonaccidental trauma (child abuse) also account for a significant number of head-injured children. Twice as many boys are injured than girls (Behrman, 1992). The degree of brain trauma depends on many variables, including age, velocity of the fall, whether the injury was a closed or open wound, and whether the victim used protective gear.

Memory difficulties are the most frequently occurring symptom after a head injury. This can greatly impact school performance. Students who return to school too soon after trauma and those who do not receive compensatory instruction can become easily frustrated and develop "catastrophic reactions" typical of recovering head trauma survivors. Other symptoms of brain injury include decreased arousal, slowness of information processing, apathy, impoverished behavior, vigilance deficits, impulsivity, and tangential thinking (Templer, Spencer, & Hartlage, 1993).

Some research indicates that about 11 percent of people with traumatic brain injury emerge from their comas with episodic outbursts of anger and aggression (Papas, 1993). A small group of students who have been in coma may develop personality changes.

Learning Disabilities (LD)

In preschool years, a tragic and often predictable scenario begins with unidentified learning disabilities. A happy, well-adjusted child, Bob, enters a preschool program. The teacher reports to the parents that Bob seems to lack certain readiness skills. These may include ability to recognize letters, numbers, or sounds. Or the teacher may note problems in fine motor coordination. However, because these skills are not necessary to complete preschool, and because Bob is a happy, extroverted child with good verbal skills, nothing is done.

In kindergarten, where readiness skills begin to become important, Bob's teacher becomes concerned because he cannot recognize the sounds of letters that she has gone over repeatedly. Furthermore, Bob has trouble copying as well as other children. During a visit to the pediatrician, Bob's parents are assured that he will catch up because he appears to be a bright child.

Because Bob is well adjusted in many ways, seems to be bright, and is never a behavior problem, he is passed to the first grade. Bob's teacher recognizes that he is quite capable and believes that his beginning reading problem can be remediated by extra drill at school and at home. Each night Bob's mother works with him on his homework as his siblings are allowed to watch television. Although Bob is about a year behind at the end of first grade, he is promoted.

By third grade, despite frequent tutoring and continual drill, Bob has fallen almost two years behind in reading. His third-grade teacher decides that because Bob is so obviously bright, he must be lazy. She puts continual pressure on his parents to ensure that he completes all homework. Meanwhile, Bob is beginning to recognize that he cannot read as well as his peers. They sometimes make fun of him because of his poor reading. In addition, his teacher and parents sometimes become frustrated and angry when he appears to have forgotten material that they were sure he had previously learned.

Bob begins to resent the extra tutoring that is pushed on him, and his mother and father have lost patience with his attempts to avoid doing his homework. Bob is convinced that he is stupid and begins to hate reading. He does everything possible to avoid homework. To divert attention away from his academic deficiencies, he begins to misbehave and associates with other students who are alienated from school.

By eighth grade, Bob is labeled a troublemaker. He and his friends begin to experiment with drugs and alcohol and enter the counterculture in the school.

Unfortunately, we still see many cases similar to Bob. Too often bright children are able to barely compensate for learning disabilities, and the result is that they never receive a complete evaluation. Even when they are identified early, many of these students do not receive adequate emotional support to deal with the feelings attendant to their deficiencies. In our experience, a large number of alienated, unhappy students fit into the above scenario. For this reason, early identification and treatment is important.

Most learning disabilities are associated with some types of minimal brain dysfunction (Adelman, 1994; Tallal, Sainburg, & Jernigan, 1991; Welsh, 1994). The dysfunction leads to some type of perceptual or processing problem in the brain, which may result in academic failure or misbehavior (Quay & Werry, 1986; Tramontana & Hooper, 1989). The causes of the dysfunction are varied and can include prenatal injury, infection, anoxia during birth, brain disease and trauma, various types of deprivation related to low socioeconomic status, family violence, environmental pathogens, and genetic factors (Hinshaw, 1992). Generally, it is difficult to determine the actual cause of the problem, but diagnosis should always begin with a thorough family history that traces academic/learning problems at least as far back as the student's grandparents on both sides of the family.

A comprehensive evaluation for learning disabilities may include testing by psychologists, reading specialists, neurologists, speech therapists, and others. However, normally psychological and academic evaluations can suffice. You can help the assessment process by using a common sense approach that I developed early in my career. This simple educationally based model conceptualizes the brain as a box that provides for input, processing, and output. Figure 6.1 illustrates this idea.

On the left side of the figure are the channels through which the brain receives information. The processes that occur in the brain to perceive, sort, remember, and comprehend are listed within the middle box, which represents the brain. Output occurs through processes such as saying, reading, and writing, as shown at the right. Note that the box indicating emotions is also part of the brain and affects how association and processing occur. If significant negative emotional factors interfere with the cognitive processes, misbehavior and less efficient learning occur. Learning disabilities can consist of a breakdown in any one or combination of abilities to perceive, process, and output information as a student attempts to deal with daily academic tasks.

You can informally diagnose LD by breaking down the student's ability to handle each of the tasks indicated in Figure 6.1. For instance, some students with LD have excellent

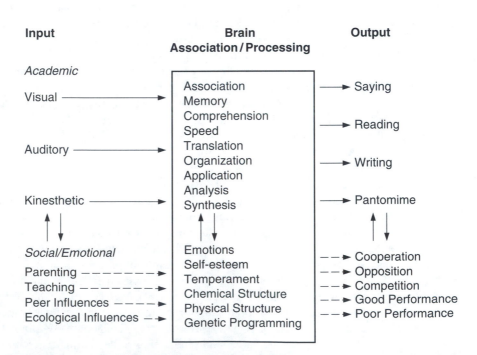

FIGURE 6.1   An Output/Input Model for Understanding Learning Disabilities

visual perception and memory. Therefore, they can learn to read whole words and remember their shape. However, they may have very poor auditory perception and association skills that render them incapable of using phonetic approaches to learn reading. Phonetics depends on good auditory memory and association. All teachers should have some familiarity with these processes, because many misbehaviors may result from physiological limitations in academics rather than laziness, rebellion, or lack of motivation. Failure to recognize appropriate instructional channels early in the first grade often results in later misbehavior.

Although there are many arguments about the exact definition of LD, experts agree that it is different from mental retardation (lately called developmental disability). It is generally identified as a significant discrepancy between intellectual ability and academic performance. A student whose academic functioning is significantly below what would be expected may have LD. For instance, a fifth-grade student with an IQ of 100, which is average, would be expected to read at the fifth-grade level. This student would be expected to earn at least C grades with a reasonable amount of effort. However, if the student's reading or math functioning is at the third-grade level, the discrepancy between expected functioning and actual functioning suggests, but does not in itself indicate, LD.

In opposition to the discrepancy model, recent research (Fletcher et al., 1994) suggests that both students with discrepancies and those without major differences between IQ and achievement may have the same types of problems that make it difficult for them to read. Nine problem areas include:

1. Deletion of phonemes
2. Inability to separate figure from ground
3. Poor short-term verbal memory
4. Poor nonverbal short-term memory
5. Difficulty with speech production
6. Limitations in vocabulary and the ability to find words
7. Deficiencies in rapid naming of things
8. Problems in visual/motor coordination (copying)
9. Deficiencies in visual attention.

This research strongly suggests that at the core of all learning disabilities are linguistic deficiencies in phonological awareness (Stanovich & Seigel, 1994).

Attention Deficit Hyperactivity Disorder (ADHD)

Steve, a bright fourth-grader, was having significant problems paying attention in class. He was constantly on the move, frequently fidgeting when seated, and continually made inappropriate comments to the teacher and classmates. He often lost his temper, but his inability to fight resulted in periodic beatings by his classmates. When Steve's parents came to me for consultation, it was apparent that they were seriously concerned because Steve was nothing like his two well-adjusted siblings.

Initially, Steve was very cooperative, although he at times made inappropriate comments such as, "If you don't let me do what I want, I'm gonna punch you in the stomach." It didn't take long to see how his lack of social skills caused him to be an outcast.

Psychological testing indicated that Steve had an IQ of 125, and although he initially had trouble reading in first grade, he suddenly caught on and began to read. Therefore, although he had some early indications of a learning disability, he was able to do the academic work. The problem was that he only wanted to complete assignments that he thought were relevant.

Family and developmental history showed that the father and grandfather had problems paying attention, although both were extremely bright. No other significant information showed specific biological reasons for Steve's problems with attention and inappropriate social behavior. Steve's mother was a professional counselor, whose parenting strategies seemed appropriate, but ineffective. After considering all of the information available, I decided to suggest family and group therapy and recommended an evaluation by the family pediatrician. After an evaluation and consultation with the pediatrician, we decided to try Steve on several doses of Ritalin. We asked the teacher and parents to track Steve's behavior by using the Actor Scale, which is one of many rating systems used to diagnose ADD. We also used a placebo design that allowed us to determine whether Steve's behavior improved simply by virtue of taking a pill or by the actual use of Ritalin.

The results of our experiment demonstrated a dramatic change in Steve's social and academic functioning. On ten milligrams of Ritalin in the morning and at lunch, Steve was able to attend in class and to act much more appropriately. In group therapy, he began to pay attention and to practice social skills. My experience with Steve was seminal in a series of individual placebo studies to develop an effective way to determine if psychostimulants are truly effective with each child. The use of this technique is discussed in the remediation sections. Let us next discuss the nature of attention deficit hyperactivity disorder (ADHD).

In the early 1990s, teachers, parents, pediatricians, and others discovered an epidemic of attention deficit disorder also known as attention deficit hyperactivity disorder (ADHD). Although reasonable estimates suggest that 3 to 5 percent of school-aged children may have ADHD (Barkley, 1990), it became fashionable to label children with a wide range of misbehaviors as having this syndrome and to blame it for the behavioral problems of large numbers of students.

Every teacher has had at least one student who just cannot sit still, cannot concentrate, and seems forever disorganized. These students may be angry, impulsive, and apparently unable to learn from experience. These symptoms may be caused by a variety of stressors, such as excessive academic pressure, physical or psychological abuse, parental conflict, or divorce. Also, young children who are slow to mature may exhibit these symptoms. At least 85 percent of these maturationally immature children, if provided with appropriate educational programs and psychological support, outgrow the problem by adolescence. However, the child who truly has ADHD may continue into adulthood to be inordinately hyperactive, inattentive, and impulsive.

The official diagnosis of ADHD is based on a description in the *Diagnostic and Statistical Manual,* Fourth Edition, usually called DSM-IV (American Psychiatric Association, 1994). There are three types of ADHD: (1) attention-deficit/hyperactivity, (2) attention-deficit/hyperactivity predominantly inattentive type, and (3) attention-deficit/hyperactivity disorder, predominantly hyperactive-impulsive type.

A child must have at least six of the symptoms listed in Figure 6.2 *before* the age of seven, and they must have been present for at least six months.

FIGURE 6.2   Diagnostic Indicators for ADHD From DSM-IV

Inattention

- Often fails to give close attention to details or makes careless mistakes in schoolwork, work, or other activities
- Often has difficulty sustaining attention in tasks or play activities
- Often does not seem to listen when spoken to directly
- Often does not follow through on instructions and fails to finish schoolwork, chores, or other duties in the workplace (not because of oppositional behavior or failure of comprehension)
- Often has difficulty organizing tasks and activities
- Often avoids, dislikes, or is reluctant to engage in tasks that require sustained mental effort (such as schoolwork or homework)
- Often loses things necessary for tasks and activities (e.g., toys, school assignments, pencil, books, or tools)
- Is often easily distracted by extraneous stimuli
- Is often forgetful in daily activities

Hyperactivity

- Often fidgets with hands or feet or squirms in seat
- Often leaves seat in classroom or in other situations in which remaining seated is expected
- Often runs about or climbs excessively in situations in which it is inappropriate (in adolescents, this may be limited to subjective feelings of restlessness)
- Often has difficulty playing or engaging in leisure activities quietly
- Is often "on the go" or often acts as if "driven by a motor"
- Often talks excessively

Impulsivity

- Often blurts out answers before questions have been completed
- Often has difficulty awaiting turn
- Often interrupts or intrudes on others

If a child is not hyperactive and impulsive, he or she may have a condition referred to as *undifferentiated attention deficit disorder.*

American Psychiatric Association: *Diagnostic and Statistical Manual of Mental Disorders, Fourth Edition.* Washington, DC, American Psychiatric Association, 1994. Reprinted with permission.

There is often an overlap between ADHD and learning disabilities. Studies vary and indicate that anywhere from 30 to 60 percent of children with attention deficit may also have learning disabilities (Barkley, 1990).

Approximately 60 percent of children with ADHD also are diagnosed as having oppositional defiant disorders or the more serious designation of conduct disorder. Many of these students, by adolescence, develop addictive disorders, frequently including dependence on cigarettes. Furthermore, there is ongoing debate over the existence of various subtypes of ADHD.

Diagnosis should be based on multimodal measures, including history, neurological evaluation, cognitive and academic functioning, rating scales, actual observed behavior in various settings, and personality testing. Continuous performance tests have recently gained attention for diagnosing ADHD. These are tests in which the child presses a computer key continuously as part of a purposely boring task that appears on the screen. Diagnosis is too often made primarily on the basis of rating scales, which identify such factors as levels of attention, hyperactivity, aggression, oppositional behavior, or social interaction. These are filled out by parents or teachers and are therefore subject to biases by the raters.

Chemical Imbalances of the Brain

Chemical imbalances of the brain can result in a variety of personality traits and behavior problems. However, many of these problems, such as anxiety, depression, and rage, can also be situational and not based on neurochemical problems. Therefore, it is important to refer suspected cases to your school psychologist.

There are many mental disorders listed in DSM-IV that are believed to have a chemical basis. We have selected some that are most commonly related to school discipline problems.

Anxiety disorders may cause a variety of acting out behaviors. Students are often anxious because of feelings of inadequacy and suspicion of others. Also, children who have been physically, psychologically, and sexually maltreated might have posttraumatic stress disorder, which falls within the general category of an anxiety disorder. In all of these disorders, students are generally afraid that something is going to happen to them. Those fears may lead them to take aggressive initiatives in preventing something from happening. For instance, if John has been beaten frequently by his father when his father appeared angry, John may perceive anger by his teacher or another student as a signal of an impending attack. His reaction may be to attack first to protect himself.

A disorder called substance-induced anxiety disorder can be the result of overdependence on drugs such as alcohol or marijuana to relieve anxiety. Absence of these drugs in the system may result in uncontrolled anxiety, which leads to agitation and explosiveness. Furthermore, heavy dependence on caffeine as a stimulant, when overused, can cause agitation.

Diagnostic indicators of anxiety are well known to most teachers. These include nail biting, fighting, nervous tics, and other repetitive habits. Also, children with high levels of anxiety have difficulty concentrating enough to study. As a result, low academic achievement may be an indicator of an anxiety disorder. Usually students with this problem report that when they sit down to study, they just cannot concentrate. Also, they may report trouble falling asleep. They often mention that they cannot fall asleep because their minds keep racing. In some cases, this disorder may be mistaken for ADHD. If you suspect an anxiety disorder related to a student's misbehavior, you should refer the student to the school psychologist.

Depression and manic depression or bipolar disorder may underlie the angry and aggressive behavior of students who are diagnosed with conduct disorder. It is difficult to ferret out the underlying depression because, on the surface, these students are so defiant and oppositional. They often act as if they do not care what happens to them. They often take life-threatening risks in the commission of crimes and in the use of drugs. They may drive at reckless speeds while drunk or attack someone who is obviously their physical superior.

Obvious signs of depression include overt expressions of sadness, statements about the hopelessness of life, helplessness to change events, talk about suicide or actual threats or attempts to kill oneself, talk about dead people being better off, disheveled appearance, lack of hygiene, and eating or sleep dysfunction. Very often, the circumstances of a child's life may be good indicators of possible depression. These include emotional, economic, and social impoverishment.

Depressed students who are not acting out may become behavior problems because of refusal to do schoolwork and resistance to normal school activities. Punishment is ineffective with children like this because they are already so discouraged that punishment only reinforces their sense of helplessness.

Obsessive–compulsive disorder can lead to misbehavior when the student's obsessions include antisocial acts. For instance, a fifteen-year-old foreign-born student, Parvis, was referred to me because he refused to participate in group activities and assigned projects in school. Although he was not overtly hostile, he refused to comply with teacher requests. I discovered that he also refused to eat lunch with any other students, and he frequently tapped five times on wood. Students who observed this strange behavior made fun of him and created more problems for the teacher.

Clinical interview showed that when he was six years old, his parents moved to the United States and he was enrolled in public school in a middle- to upper-middle-class suburb. Because of his dark skin and foreign accent, classmates frequently teased him, especially in places like the lunch room, where they were not observed by school staff. Initially he complained to his parents, who told him he must stick it out until his peers accepted him. As he got older, the teasing continued. He was afraid to express his anger at his peers, and he did not want to lose face with his family by admitting that he was frightened to fight back. He began to develop compulsive rituals, such as tapping wood, which he believed had power to protect him. However, his anger could not be completely bottled up. He began, at the age of thirteen, to hit his mother as part of another obsessive ritual.

Parvis developed a "word game" during which he demanded that his mother guess what word he was thinking. Each time she guessed a wrong word, he hit her. Over a two-year period, as Parvis's anger at schoolmates increased, the beating of his mother became more severe. His father rarely intervened, because he thought that the mother had done something to deserve the beatings.

Intervention involved short-term use of clomipramine, a medication that helped to decrease the compulsive behavior, psychotherapy to reduce the anxiety that triggered his ritualistic acts, and training in assertive techniques to deal with rude classmates. After much cajoling, I convinced the father to intervene. I further insisted that, if no other help was available, the mother must call the police. Although she never did this, the threat was a good deterrent. Finally, I alerted the school authorities, and they stopped the teasing.

Diagnosis of Other Biophysical Conditions Associated with Misbehavior

As mentioned previously, teachers can contribute to diagnosis by keeping careful records of students' behaviors. We discuss observational techniques in the chapter on the ecological/systems approach. It is important to be especially aware of any drastic changes in behavior or affect. These may occur suddenly and be of long duration and intensity, or they may appear as mood swings during the day. We will not even try to discuss medical testing for conditions such as allergies and hormonal imbalances and the many other conditions that may affect school behavior. However, you might want to investigate the myriad other conditions that may be considered when evaluating possible physiological correlates of misbehavior.

Testing for the intake of harmful substances or substance abuse is of major relevance to school discipline. Use of easily available substances such as cigarettes and alcohol may be easily diagnosed by any teacher who can smell. Addicted smokers usually carry the odor of tobacco on their clothes, in their breath, and on their hair. Unfortunately, nonsmoking students may smell because of heavy smoking in their homes. Students addicted to alcohol usually imbibe during the day. They often try to mask the smell of alcohol on their breath by using mints, chewing gum, and spray fresheners. If you are suspicious, you will probably eventually smell the child's breath.

A variety of chemical tests ascertain the use of illegal substances. After alcohol, the most commonly abused substance is marijuana. Testing for this substance is usually done from urine samples. Unfortunately, the most widely used screening tests are those that are least expensive and least sensitive. Therefore, most tests done through schools and local agencies should not be considered as definitive. Actually, the assessment of use can be made by a trained psychologist or drug counselor. Judgments can be made by interview, appearance, friendship patterns, objective paper and pencil tests, and teacher reports. In my work as a therapist, I have rarely encountered a youth who did not "confess" to pot use during confidential therapy. I frequently double the amount of use based on their reports of frequency, because heavy, daily users intuitively know that this level is of major concern to therapists.

Accurate urine screening depends on the student's size, weight, and time of last use. Also, the "quality" of the marijuana will affect test sensitivity. Many of the youth in my therapy groups have received negative test results within one to two days of use. When they know they are going to be tested, they drink massive amounts of water, and some take an herb called golden seal, which is a mild diuretic. Therefore, a successful testing program must be random so that the student cannot prepare to defeat it.

Observations of malnourished children often show limited attention span and poor academic achievement. They have increased susceptibility to infections. Muscular development is inadequate, and the flabby muscles result in a posture of rounded shoulders, flat chest, and protuberant abdomen. Such children often look tired; the face is pale, the complexion is muddy, and the eyes lack luster.

Hormonal imbalances and allergies both can result in headaches, hypermanic or hypomanic behavior, mood swings, and tiredness. These problems of course require appropriate medical referral for diagnosis.

Specific Diagnostic Considerations

Teachers may have limited input once a referral has been made to the school psychologist or outside medical or clinical specialists through the school nurse or child study team. In complicated cases, every effort should be made to obtain the help of competent specialists, especially those who are used to working with educators. Specialists such as board-certified child psychiatrists, clinical psychologists, neuropsychologists, and speech and language therapists are not always geographically convenient. If not, it may be wise to seek out specialists at a university teaching hospital or other premier facility.

The Case of Chris

A biophysical approach to Chris's problems (see page 37) would begin with a thorough developmental, social, and educational history. We would want to discover whether any other members of Chris's family exhibit problems of inattentiveness, restlessness, and early readiness or academic deficiencies. Chris's history, especially indications of restlessness and fine motor coordination problems, suggest the possibility of organic problems. His ability to concentrate at certain times could indicate either that he does not have ADD or that, in certain situations, when he is motivated, he is able to screen out extraneous stimuli and focus.

Furthermore, it is possible that Chris is one of those children who has a combination of ADD and a mild learning disability. Teacher diagnosis would include careful observations of Chris in various situations. Anecdotal reports over a several-week period can be provided to the school psychologist as part of a comprehensive evaluation. The psychologist will probably ask you to fill out a rating sheet that can be used in diagnosing ADD. We cannot overstress the importance of observations in diagnosing ADD.

The psychologist may use rating scales, psychological tests, or a computerized test that measures a student's attention. A good diagnosis of ADD always includes multiple assessment techniques. A medical assessment will be necessary for final diagnosis. This is usually done by the family physician or pediatrician. However, diagnosis by a pediatric neurologist is generally preferable. In the case of Chris, a trial on a psychostimulant such as Ritalin might show improved ability to attend and a decrease in oppositional behavior. We would prefer that no Ritalin trials are given in the school unless they include different doses; ongoing; objective assessment; and a triple-blind technique (Hyman, Wojtowicz, Lee, et al., 1996). This means that neither the teacher, parent, nor child will know whether the pills contained Ritalin or a placebo, or which dosage is being tried at any one time. It should also be noted that approximately one-third of people taking Ritalin have improved concentration even if they do not have ADHD. Therefore, prescribing Ritalin should be done with the best possible diagnostic considerations.

Intervention Techniques

Because most medical intervention techniques related to misbehavior in the biophysical model require physicians and allied health professionals, teachers' roles are usually to observe student behavior and inform the appropriate personnel of pertinent information. Teachers can become an important part of the treatment plan by being alert to the potential side effects of medications. For instance, antihistamines for allergies may make students drowsy. This behavior could be interpreted as laziness or low motivation. Decongestants can cause tenseness and irritability. Some of the psychotropic drugs for behavioral problems can cause tremors, restlessness, and sleeplessness.

Many medical intercessions must be complemented by classroom modifications or special teaching strategies. These changes may be indirect, such as avoiding confrontations with students whose medication makes them irritable. Direct interventions include modified instruction for students with learning disabilities or classroom seating that minimizes distractions for children with ADHD.

Interventions in the biophysical model include (1) medications and drug therapy, (2) specific cognitive/perceptual/academic remediation, (3) psychotherapy, (4) diet and nutritional therapy, (4) speech and physical therapy, and (5) biofeedback techniques. Because of the exhaustive literature on each of these, we only discuss a few of these areas that are of most direct relevance to disciplinary problems.

Medications and Drug Therapy for Behavioral Problems

The range of medications for problems indirectly related to misbehavior is vast. The biophysical approach does not mandate that you become a pharmacist or physician. However, you can become sufficiently informed when a student is placed on medication. You can determine the characteristics of all medication by referring to the *Physicians Desk Reference,* consulting your school nurse, or asking your druggist. You also may want to consult with the student's physician. We briefly discuss some of the psychotropic drugs directly used to ameliorate behavioral and academic problems.

Tricyclic antidepressant medications with brand names such as Norpramin, Tofranil, and Pamelor are prescribed for student populations for the treatment of depression, anxiety-related disorders including school phobia, attention deficit hyperactivity disorder, enuresis, sleep disorders, inattention, impulsivity, lack of motivation, separation anxiety, and obsessive–compulsive disorders (Schatzberg & Cole, 1986). Although the evidence regarding the efficacy of antidepressant medication for children has been inconclusive, they are widely used. Tricyclic antidepressants have also been used as a second-line treatment (after stimulant failure or contraindication in the presence of other problems such as tics) for children with ADHD.

Clomipramine has been used with some success with children exhibiting obsessive–compulsive behaviors such as rituals of cleaning, counting, and checking, as well as disturbing thoughts. Lithium has been endorsed in child psychiatry as an effective treatment of bipolar disorder, depression, and severe impulsive aggression (Schatzberg & Cole, 1986). Of course, none of these drugs is without side effects, and reactions must be closely monitored.

Clonidine (Catapres) and propanolol (Inderal) were originally used to treat high blood pressure. Clonidine has been effective in the treatment of Tourette's syndrome as well as ADHD. In ADHD, clonidine has been useful in regulating mood and activity level and is most beneficial when used in conjunction with a stimulant. Propanolol has been used to treat uncontrollable rage reactions, impulsive aggression, and self-injurious behavior. Recent evidence has shown benefit of propanolol in ameliorating anxious symptoms of posttraumatic stress disorder, hyperventilation, and test and performance anxiety.

Methylphenidate, the chemical name for Ritalin, was introduced in the 1950s to avoid the side effects and potential abuses of amphetamines, which seemed to help hyperactive children (Brown & Borden, 1989). Ritalin is the most popular treatment for ADD and probably the most widely used medication for children with behavior problems. The drug company that sells methylphenidate sometimes has trouble keeping up with the demand. During one period in the early 1990s, they had doubled their sales in two years, and the demand outstripped the available supply. For this reason, methylphenidate deserves special attention.

It is estimated that 1 to 2 percent of all elementary school children are prescribed some type of stimulant medication (Brown, Dingle, and Landau, 1993). Of those children diagnosed as ADHD, 80 to 90 percent have been treated with a central nervous system stimulant at some point. The three most widely prescribed stimulants for children with ADHD are methylphenidate, dextroamphetamine (Dexedrine), and pemoline (Cylert). Children receive methylphenidate more than dextroamphetamine and pemoline.

One theory of why stimulants work with on ADHD children is that the area of the brain that controls attention is not working efficiently. The stimulant will "speed up" the functioning in these parts of the brain and therefore enhance the child's ability to slow down and concentrate. Another way of thinking about it is that children with ADHD are underaroused in comparison with normally developing children and that psychostimulants act by normalizing the arousal level. A favorable drug response has often been viewed as confirmation of a diagnosis of ADHD (Brown & Borden, 1989). Contrary to this belief, "normal" children and adults experience enhancement of attention and concentration, so this cannot, in itself, be considered confirmation of diagnosis of ADHD.

Placebo Protocols to Determine Effectiveness of Ritalin

Because psychostimulants can have positive effects on concentration and short-term alertness in almost all people, it is important to determine if they are really helping students. Furthermore, although the short-term benefits of stimulant medication have been established, long-term learning benefits have not been adequately documented. It may be that the standardized achievement measures that have been used to measure treatment outcomes are not sensitive to the level of change expected during relatively brief treatment periods (Brown & Borden, 1989). Some research with curriculum-based measures has demonstrated positive short-term academic gains (Pehlam et al., in press).

There is evidence that different dose levels impact different areas of performance, with lower dosages of methylphenidate associated with optimal cognitive performances and higher dosages associated with enhanced social performance (Carlson & Brunner, 1993). Improvement in social behaviors include following rules, positive peer interactions, and increased percentage of time attending (Pehlam, 1993). There are large individual differences related to various doses, so it is crucial to determine which dose works best for each individual. Because of this, medication assessments should include a variety of measures to tap important areas of classroom functioning.

Ritalin is a "Schedule II" drug, which means that it has a high potential for abuse and dependence; yet many physicians ignore or deny this. Many claim that children can stop and start the use of Ritalin without any adverse reactions. This is just not true. Side effects tend to be similar for all stimulants and include insomnia, irritability, growth retardation, rebound effects, and decreased appetite (Brown et al., 1993). These effects can be managed by administering the medication early in the day, and after lunch or supper. If possible, administration should be avoided in the evening so as to not interfere with sleep. Physicians should also regularly monitor height and weight, because these can be adversely affected by overdose (Brown et al., 1993). It is often desirable to implement drug-free weekends and vacations (Pehlam, 1993).

It is important to consider that only a minority of children who do respond positively to medication show sufficient improvement for their behavior to fall entirely within the normal range; the rest are improved but their behavior is not normalized, and additional treatments are needed (Pehlam, citing Abikoff & Gittleman, 1985). It is the glue that will help the student to stay in a seat and to concentrate. But it alone will not increase motivation to want to learn. Many ADD students do learn on the run without drugs, but most teachers do not allow that kind of behavior in class. There is evidence that children who have been treated with psychostimulant medication for periods up to fifteen years have failed to provide any evidence that the drugs improve the long-term prognosis for children with ADHD. Consider the case of Judy, a fifteen-year-old, who was referred to me in the late 1980s.

The Case of Judy

I was consulted by Judy's parents because of a sudden decline in grades while she was attending a private preparatory school. Judy had been diagnosed with ADD at age six by a very prominent psychiatrist. He specialized in this disorder and prescribed Ritalin for most of his patients. Unlike most professionals, he did not insist on complementary psychotherapy, behavioral interventions, or academic modifications.

Judy's parents reported that she responded quite well to the Ritalin. Her grades began to steadily improve, and by fourth grade, she consistently earned As and Bs. She did not take Ritalin during the summers and often refused to take it on the weekends. Despite this, her parents often argued that she needed her medicine at all times.

Reports from the school indicate that Judy identified with a small group of students who spent a lot of time playing Dungeons and Dragons. Judy frequently dressed in all black clothes, sometimes wore black nail polish and lipstick, and appeared depressed. She was going through an identity crisis that had little to do with ADD. Actually, part of her problem was related to her anger at her parents for forcing her to take Ritalin and their avoidance of dealing with her need to have some control of her life.

Judy complained bitterly about being forced to take Ritalin, but she did not have the nerve to defy her parents. Also, she had been so dependent on the idea that she needed the Ritalin that she was afraid to stop for any length of time for fear that she would need it to pass tests. I suggested the use of a placebo protocol to determine if the Ritalin was really helping her.

By use of a placebo protocol, we were able to determine that Judy did not require Ritalin any more. However, she still used it when studying for and taking exams. This experience suggests the importance of the services of a school psychologist who is familiar with the behavioral pharmaceutical effects of Ritalin and any other drug used to facilitate learning.

Specific Cognitive/Perceptual/Academic Remediation

Students with learning disabilities, traumatic brain injury, and other disorders of the brain often require special academic remediation to minimize the frustration associated with these problems. Rarely can medication alone help to solve the academic and behavioral problems associated with brain dysfunction.

There have been many fads and outright frauds associated with the remediation of learning problems. Some of the more notable approaches that have not survived examination by independent researchers have included nutritional regimens, antihistamines, chiropractic manipulation of the jaw and palate, and eye exercises.

Successful remediation activities for learning disabilities have generally focused on direct teaching of reading skills by emphasizing each students' strengths rather than weaknesses. Strengths and weaknesses can be determined through competent psychological evaluation and informal instruction. There are a multitude of programs, including those promoted by the Orton Society, the Fernald Approach, and canned curricula promoted by numerous publishers. It would be advisable to consult with a school psychologist or special education teacher who has training in the field of learning disabilities if you desire specific techniques.

Students with behavioral problems who also have learning disabilities present a dilemma in terms of treatment focus. Some theorists claim that because many of their behaviors are related to academic failure, the major focus to improve their behavior should be the amelioration of their academic difficulties. They assume that once these students are able to function adequately, they will not have poor self-esteem and consequent misbehavior. Conversely, others suggest that children with learning disabilities generally have to work much harder than others to achieve the same academic goal. Their recognition of this fact and the perseverance required may be sufficient to cause low self-esteem as a result of being "different."

In my experience, heavy emphasis on academic intervention is necessary in the early years. At these stages, children with learning disabilities need to learn to "break the code" so that they can learn to read rather comfortably. However, as they get older, many of these children do require help in planning their time, structuring their activities, and they may need supportive psychotherapy to deal with the stress of maintaining good grades and having adequate social and recreational activities. In sum, although learning disabilities have a biophysical base, most of the interventions must be educational and behavioral.

Psychotherapy

Most psychotherapy involves talking and problem solving between the patient and therapist. Most of the research on psychotherapy has been conducted by psychologists, and most of the practice is conducted by therapists without medical degrees. However, psychotherapy is considered by many, especially insurance companies, as a medical specialty. Insurance reimbursement supports the practice of psychotherapy in private offices, hospitals, mental health agencies, Medicaid, and Medicare. Furthermore, the growth of school-based partial-hospitalization programs and "wrap-around" services are beginning to bring more psychotherapy into schools, where it has traditionally been conducted by school psychologists, counselors, and social workers.

As part of the medical model, medication is often a necessary adjunct to psychotherapy, especially to alleviate the symptoms of psychosis, depression, and anxiety. Because of all of these factors, we have included psychotherapy in the biophysical chapter.

If one of your students is in psychotherapy, you should obtain parental permission to consult with the therapist. With the exception of school-based personnel, most therapists have limited knowledge of schools and classrooms, and it is often crucial that you form a therapeutic alliance with the therapist. Besides helping to implement a classroom plan to complement the psychotherapy, you can be alert to changes in the student's behavior that may be relevant to the therapist's efforts.

Competent therapists normally develop specific therapy goals and outline procedures to accomplish those goals. For instance, a structured behavioral plan may include consistent rule-enforcement. This must be coordinated between the home and the school. It may require that you and the parents only threaten a punishment if you are sure you can enforce it. The therapist may request that the student be given lots of praise, reinforcement, and success experiences to enhance self-esteem.

There is good evidence that classroom teachers can provide a therapeutic atmosphere that will enhance student emotional and social growth. Without being a psychotherapist, you can implement classroom strategies that mirror good therapy. At least seven processes occur in successful psychotherapy that can also be used in the classroom (Burton, 1976).

Good *rapport* between the therapist and patient and the teacher and student are essential in forming a therapeutic alliance. This occurs as a result of mutual trust between all parties. The adult must be able to convey genuine feelings of interest, concern, and empathy. The successful therapeutic teacher is a consistent source of emotional support. Carl Rogers, who we discussed in the chapter on humanism, describes the quality of "unconditional positive regard" as necessary for effective therapy. This also applies to teacher–student relationships.

Tension reduction occurs when patients/students believe that it is safe to express their innermost feelings, fears, and anxieties. In general, because of the explicit agreement of confidentiality, it is more likely that the greatest amount of disclosure occurs between patients and therapists. However, it is not surprising that students will disclose histories of sexual and physical abuse, pregnancies, and problems with drugs to empathetic and understanding teachers.

Learning of new skills, cognitions, and feelings is an important part of the therapy relationship. Patients/students learn to correct inappropriate/incorrect thinking and behavior about themselves and toward others. Depending on the orientation, this may include such learning processes as cognitive and emotional insight, practice of new interpersonal skills, or repeating new internal dialogues. Teachers can help children to learn more about themselves and why they misbehave when many of the other conditions for successful change occur.

Approval and *disapproval* are constants in most relationships. However, therapists convey disapproval of the patient's/student's behaviors rather than of the patient. This can be done by outright statements, questions, body posture, or facial expressions. Therapeutic teachers have this unique skill.

Suggestion and *persuasion* are important elements in helping patients/students to change. In a therapeutic alliance, the patient/student should not feel obligated or morally sanctioned for not making immediate changes in their thoughts or actions. They know they are free to determine their own needs and time schedules and that they alone must make the final decision. They are free to debate, accept, or reject the suggestions of the therapist. Therapeutic teachers tend to be democratic and nonpunitive in their approach to suggestion and persuasion.

Modeling of the therapist/teacher is a common process in successful therapeutic situations. In my own experience, it is surprising how many of my adolescent patients envision themselves becoming psychologists.

Reality testing is the process by which patients/students learn whether their perceptions, understandings, and feelings match reality. For instance, I had a student who frequently did not meet her responsibilities. Rather than admit that she had made a mistake, she frequently stated that there was a misunderstanding. When "caught" repeating a misbehavior (defacing property in my office building), she incidentally apologized and acted as if her behavior should be immediately forgotten. No matter how perceptive a patient or student may appear, if their behavior does not match reality, they cannot successfully change.

Reality testing can occur in many ways. Billy, a sixteen-year-old patient, constantly projects blame on others. Even when he was caught stealing, he denied that it was his fault. Billy was unable to accept blame because he thought that the stealing was something that he had to do because he was a bad person. When he finally began to understand that he was not an inherently bad person and that his stealing was related to his anger at others who constantly ridiculed him, he was ready to change.

For Billy, reality testing consisted of trying new roles. As he began to deal directly with his anger, he could express it verbally to others, and the need to steal was diminished. As he tested his new role, he found that others began to treat him in a more positive way, and he began to realize that his old way of thinking was dysfunctional.

In summary, psychotherapy has been demonstrated to be an effective approach for children with emotional problems. In some cases, medication and therapy must be used in tandem. It is important for teachers and therapists to work together to help students achieve their goals. Although teachers are not psychotherapists, by understanding the important aspects of psychotherapy, they can create a therapeutic milieu within the classroom.

Biofeedback, Hypnosis, and Other Techniques to Reduce Stress

Relaxation techniques can be very helpful with children who are anxious, tense, and angry. Although the techniques themselves can be taught reasonably by a minimally trained professional, they should only be used by competent psychologists and psychiatrists and other professionals who have a broad understanding of behavioral problems. Relaxation techniques are based on the assumption that a person cannot be tense and relaxed at the same time. Also, when a person is tense or anxious, there is always accompanying muscle tension. Therefore, if a person can be trained to relax muscles on command, the physiologically accompanying tension or anxiety is reduced.

Deep muscle relaxation is a technique in which subjects learn to relax their muscles. Two techniques are generally employed. In the older, Jacobson technique, subjects generally lie down and are given instructions to breathe slowly and deeply. They are then told to focus on each muscle group of the body and to relax those muscles. Eventually, through practice, individuals can train themselves to relax on command. A newer, behaviorally oriented technique involves tensing and then relaxing each muscle group. As this is done, the subject will use words such as "tense" and "relax" as these procedures occur. Eventually, as result of the pairing of the words with the relaxation, subjects can master relaxation by using verbal signals.

Imagery occurs when the subject is taught to breathe deeply and slowly while imagining a scene that is completely relaxing. After training, the subjects can return to the scene quite easily to achieve a state of relaxation.

Self-hypnosis is a technique that involves several of the other procedures. Subjects begin by closing their eyes and concentrating on one hand. Initially, they are told to focus on all the sensations in one hand and to imagine that it is floating upward. They eventually follow this and other instructions on their own so that they can invoke a hypnotic trance without help from others. Establishment of the trance, which is merely a state of focused suggestibility, occurs through the use of deep breathing, imagery, and muscle relaxation.

Biofeedback can reduce the frequency of distressing symptoms such as anxiety or minimize physical symptoms such as pain (Hodes, 1989). Biofeedback apparati measure electroactivity in the skin and muscles. The equipment allows subjects to visually observe how well they are relaxing by watching a needle or computerized graph that displays electrical activity correlating with tenseness and relaxation.

Changes in Nutrition

Behavioral problems, based on the biophysical model, may be treatable with improvement in nutrition. Treatment programs fall within traditional and alternative forms of medicine. Most licensed physicians and nutritionists use standard blood tests and other medical procedures to determine deficiencies. In the traditional view, treatments for medical problems that may be related to misbehavior, such as obesity, hypoglycemia, malnutrition, eating disorders, and severe acne, must be prescribed by adequately trained personnel. School nurses may be involved in treatment procedures; however, teachers are rarely consulted on these issues.

Alternative medicine, often based on homeopathic or holistic approaches, often is based on natural ingredients in treating nutritional problems. Treatment recommendations can often be obtained in natural food stores and other organizations that promote these approaches.

From time to time, particular nutritional fads emerge. One such fad was the Feingold diet. This fad was promoted in the 1970s and was touted as a solution for children with behavior problems. This diet assumed that children were acting out because of an allergy to specific additives in foods. This approach removed all food additives from a child's diet. There has been little evidence to support this contention. One review of research concluded that there is no firm evidence of behavioral toxicity (such as hyperactivity or antisocial behavior) resulting from dietary substances, including sugar and caffeine, in normal children (Quay and Werry, 1986). The *New England Journal of Medicine* (1994) also reported that no association was found between children's sugar intake and behavioral or cognitive change.

Speech and Physical Therapy

Some students may become behavior problems because of physical disabilities that result in peer ridicule and low self-esteem. For instance, children may be ridiculed by peers because they have a lisp, stuttering, a variety of articulation problems, or orthopedic problems. These problems, coupled with ridicule, may cause some students to develop low self-esteem, anger at peers, and hostility toward adults who do not protect them. This combination may result in acting-out behavior.

Most schools provide some level of speech, physical, and occupational therapy to help children to overcome their problems. Your job as a teacher is to work with therapists to enhance their efforts. For instance, children who require glasses, hearing aids, or prosthetics may require constant support because of their reluctance to use devices that make them look different from others. Your efforts as a teacher may include techniques to convince the student's peers to accept and encourage the use of these mechanisms.

Summary and Critique

Unlike the others models in teacher variance, much of the diagnosis and treatment in the biophysical model depends on others. However, teachers play an important role as early screeners and identifiers of possible biophysical problems. They also can be keen observers, reporters, and implementors in assisting diagnosis and treatment. The strength of the model lies in the extensive resources of medical research, diagnosis, and treatment. Unfortunately, the comprehensive medical model is too expensive to implement in most school settings, and therefore, if parents do not have sufficient resources, the model is of little use.

Like education, even medical approaches are sometimes subject to fads and panaceas. Often teachers have neither the knowledge nor the clout to prevent ineffective and unproven medical treatments of students, nor to stem the overuse and misuse of powerful psychostimulants and psychotropic medications. However, when teachers are well informed, they have at least a chance of steering parents and other school personnel to authoritative sources for information.

Key Terms

allergies
anxiety disorder
attention deficit hyperactivity disorder
biofeedback
biological determinism
chemical imbalance
environmental determinism
explosive disorder
gross neurological dysfunction
harmful substances
heredity
hormonal imbalances
imagery
inclusion
lead poisoning
learning disabilities

malnutrition
medical model
modeling
nature versus nurture
neurotransmitter
organizational deficits
perceptual deficits
persuasion
rapport
reality testing
regular education initiative
relaxation techniques
self-hypnosis
social Darwinism
temperament
tension reduction

Application Activities

1. Diagnose Juanita using the biophysical approach. What kind of temperament does she have? Develop an intervention and treatment plan using the biophysical approach.

2. Diagnose Jamal using the biophysical approach. Do you think he has a chemical imbalance? Why or why not? Develop an intervention and treatment plan using the biophysical approach.

3. Diagnose Michael using the biophysical approach. Does he have a neuropsychological dysfunction? Why or why not? Develop an

intervention and treatment plan using the biophysical approach.

4. Diagnose Chris using the biophysical approach. Does he have a learning disability? Why or why not? Develop an intervention

and treatment plan using the biophysical approach.

5. Develop a hierarchy of teacher intervention procedures using the biophysical approach.

Suggested Readings

American Psychiatric Association. (1994). *Diagnostic and statistical manual of mental disorders* (4th ed.). Washington, DC: Author.

Chess, S., & Thomas, A. (1986). *Temperament in clinical practice.* New York: Guilford Publications.

Jordan, N., & Goldsmith, P. (Eds.). (1994). *Learning disabilities: New direction for assessment and intervention.* New York: Allyn & Bacon.

Maxmen, J. S. (1991). *Psychotropic drugs: Fast facts.* New York: W. W. Norton & Company.

Pinel, J. P. J. (1993). *Biopsychology* (2nd ed.). Boston, MA: Allyn & Bacon.

Reynolds, C. R., & Fletcher-Jansen, E. (Eds.). (1989a). *Clinical neuropsychology techniques of diagnosis and treatment.* New York: Plenum Press.

Reynolds, C. R., & Fletcher-Jansen, E. (Eds.). (1989b). *Handbook of clinical child neuropsychology.* New York: Plenum Press.

Thomas, A., Chess, S., & Birch, H. G. (1968). *Temperament and behavior disorders in children.* New York: New York University Press.

Thomas, A., & Chess, S. (1977). *Temperament and development.* New York: Brunner/Mazel, Inc.

Turecki, S., & Tonner, L. (1985). *The difficult child.* New York: Bantam Books.

Chapter 7

Ecological/Systems Approach (ESA)

Chapter Objectives

After reading this chapter, you should know:

1. The seven assumptions of the ecological/systems approach
2. The eight causes of misbehavior

Rooted in sociological theory, the ecological/system approach (ESA) is based on observational studies of individuals and groups in natural settings. The ESA assumes that personality, behavior, and misbehavior are a function of the interaction and interdependence between people and all factors in their environment. Because it is so all-inclusive, the ESA is covered in three chapters. Chapter 8 covers theory and assumptions of the model; Chapter 9 presents diagnosis and application; and Chapter 10 offers a process analysis of disciplinary techniques across many programs, sample programs, and a critique of the approach.

If you tested high in the ecological/systems approach (ESA) on the TVI, you believe that:

1. Misbehavior cannot be completely explained by one single theory of personality development
2. Misbehavior is the result of an ongoing, complex interaction of all ecological and interpersonal forces within the system, which include the student's total life experiences with every aspect of the environment
3. Misbehavior can be caused by dysfunction between the student and any particular system in the environment
4. The appropriateness or deviancy of most behaviors is a function of the setting and is not inherent in the behavior itself

5. Alienation, underachievement, and misbehavior can be successfully addressed through appropriate modifications in systems ecological factors, curriculum adjustments, and teaching styles

6. Individual misbehavior should be viewed as a symptom of malfunction of the system, rather than in terms of individual student actions

7. Misbehavior can be perpetuated by stereotyping, inaccurate assumptions about role identification, institutional rigidity, and suppression or denigration of cultural and personal diversity

8. The real solution to discipline problems is within the system rather than in the individual. Solutions at any systems (organizational) level require accurate diagnosis of problems within the system, empowerment of staff to correct problems, assessment procedures for evaluation of change, and mechanisms for self-correction and self-renewal

Underlying Theory

Previously presented models are based on very specific assumptions and theories about human nature and learning, and focus on the individual. Unlike these other approaches, the ESA emphasizes the importance of each teacher as an instructional leader. The ESA accounts for all behavior and misbehavior as a function of the interaction between individuals and the environments. It is rooted in astute methods of observation (Barker, 1968; Barker & Wright, 1954; Gump & Kounin, 1961; Kounin, 1970; Lewin, 1951; Plas, 1994; Proshansky, Ittelson & Rivlion, 1970), and it is closer to traditional educational thought than the other models because it emphasizes working with students as members of groups, whether at the class, school, or school system level.

Without being aware of ESA, many educators "naturally" apply its principles in the everyday administration of discipline. That is, their approaches reflect their own experiences, observations, and expectations with various children in different settings. It is a "common sense," pragmatic, experiential approach to discipline based on the belief that well-administered schools, adequate resources, and effective teaching are the primary antidotes to misbehavior. Proponents believe that schools and classrooms should be orderly settings in which educators determine and administer rules and regulations.

Rather than using theory, teachers rely on intuition, experience, the modeling of their own teachers or colleagues, and community norms to discipline students. Yet a thorough understanding of the underlying theory of ESA will help to avoid the mismanagement of students caused by inaccurate stereotypes, negative self-fulfilling prophesies about children, and counterproductive authoritarian control procedures. It is important to understand the sociological underpinnings of ESA.

The sociological aspect of ESA flows from research showing how cultural background and group identity affect individual behavior (Bennett, 1995). In a pluralistic society, schools can serve as "melting pots" in which children from all groups or subcultures are encouraged to accept the values, attitudes, and norms of the predominate white middle-class culture. Or they can encourage diversity in beliefs, languages, and customs, while fostering a common appreciation for democracy. In either case, the friction between the desires of the school and those of students and their families are always a potential source of resentment, alienation, and consequent misbehavior.

Anomie, Deviance, and Systems Theory

Misbehavior may occur as a result of what the French sociologist, Durkheim (1951, 1956), called anomie or social disruption (Morse & Smith, 1980). Anomie occurs when the norms and values of society change faster than do those of individuals. Rapid social changes result in confusion, disempowerment, and alienation of those individuals and groups that cannot adapt to sociological shifts. For instance, change from a manufacturing base into a service economy and the loss of manufacturing jobs to offshore workers has economically and socially stressed working class families, and therefore schools feel the impact.

Once a high school education was sufficient for economic security, but in the 1990s even an undergraduate degree does not guarantee employment. As the tax base erodes and as family dysfunction increases, great stress is placed on schools to discipline large numbers of students who are pessimistic about their futures. Skills, values, and attitudes that once served students and their families are outdated, and those who cannot adapt may be perceived as deviant.

In the ESA, deviancy is defined by the context, or the contrast between the person's behavior and the norms for the group. For example, a talkative, noisy, hyperactive student might be considered deviant in one classroom and not in another. Different reactions to misbehaviors can cause problems for the teachers and students, because deviancy is defined differently by each teacher (Eno, 1985; Kuriloff, 1973).

Student deviancy may reflect membership in groups that are demeaned by those in power. Students identified as jocks, greasers, druggies, deadheads, skaters, ravers, goatropers, rednecks, or bikers may be resented and disliked by some other groups in the school. The student is labeled or stereotyped as if he or she possessed all of the negative qualities ascribed to that group. Once a student is stereotyped, teachers may unconsciously establish self-fulfilling prophesies that guide their teaching strategies and approach to discipline (Biddle & Thomas, 1966; Rosenthal & Jacobson, 1968). Consider a typical scenario in which stereotyping can result in misbehavior as a function of *self-fulfilling prophesies*.

The Case of Jim

Ms. Bradon, a high school English teacher, is serving as a hall monitor. Just after the final bell rings, she sees Jim, a fifteen-year-old with long hair, a motorcycle jacket, and black boots walking casually down the hall. His appearance, which is different from the norm for the school, suggests deviancy. His appearance immediately causes Ms. Bradon to label Jim as a druggie, and she assumes that he is up to no good. Perhaps he is returning from smoking a joint or doing something else illegal. As a result of her labeling, she is very tense, angry, and out to prove that she can handle any druggie in her school.

In a harsh, demeaning manner, Ms. Bradon orders Jim to stop and explain where he has been. Her intent is to show Jim who is boss, to let him know what she thinks of his clothing and his long hair, and to show him that he is not fooling her. In other words, she has labeled Jim, decided that he is guilty, and is letting him know how she feels about people like him who cannot get to class on time. Because the guilt is established in her mind, she begins the punishment by yelling at him in a denigrating manner. This sets up the self-fulfilling prophesy.

Jim could be late for class and walking slowly for a number of reasons. This is not to say that he is not guilty, but it would be better to assume he is innocent until proven guilty. It is possible that he was not feeling well and vomited in the lavatory, that his class was on the other side of the building and was dismissed late, that he lost something and went back to his locker to see if it was there, that he has a heart condition and cannot move too fast, that he is preoccupied with the loss of a girlfriend, or that he is depressed and thinking of suicide because his life is so miserable.

Jim's response to the "guilty until innocent" verdict by Ms. Bradon is to let her think she is right, because he feels that he has already been tried and convicted. He thinks, "You can go to hell, teacher. You think that I'm breaking the rules; I'll show how I can really break the rules." In other words, as a result of labeling, setting up a prophesy of how he would act, Ms. Bradon got what she predicted.

The *ecological* aspects of ESA are well illustrated in the actions of Ms. Bradon as she confronts Jim. Her power in the hallway, her authority as a teacher, and her disdain for people who look like Jim escalate the situation. An ecological theorist, observing the interaction between Jim and Ms. Bradon, would be interested in how the system itself might be dysfunctional. For instance, using systems theory, an investigator might determine what factors in the school contribute to Ms. Bradon's belief that all students who look like Jim are always guilty of something. Is this idea supported by subtle statements from the principal when he meets with teachers, or is it sustained in unchallenged statements made frequently by school staff in the teachers' room? Have there been a series of school disruptions caused by students who look and dress like Jim? Do the parents of students identified as part of Jim's subculture cause problems for school staff? Did Ms. Bradon have some bad experiences with students or people outside of school who dress like Jim? These and a host of other factors would be investigated to diagnose what is going on in the system.

Using *general systems theory,* the problem of Ms. Bradon and Jim would be solved at a systems level. Answers to the questions posed above will help us to design intervention programs. For example, if frequent derogatory comments by school administrators fuel staff anger at students who look like Jim, the administrators would be given feedback and asked to develop positive approaches to dealing individually with students, whether or not they fit a label.

General Systems Theory (Plas, 1994) emphasizes a "big picture" approach, and says the world cannot be understood by reducing it into independent pieces of information and knowledge. Applied to school discipline, each incident of misbehavior is viewed as part of a unique system that has its own idiosyncratic reactions to deviancy. Diagnosis and remediation of the problems within the system depend on understanding the total system (Fisher, 1986). Expertise in ESA is complemented by familiarity with *family systems theory,* which considers a child's misbehavior as a symptom of family dysfunction (Fine, 1994). For instance, if children feel free to disrespect their parents, they are likely to exhibit the same behavior in school.   ■

Reasons for Misbehavior

The complex causes of school misbehavior involve many factors, including the size of birth cohorts, family factors, the political and economic structures of society, school-related factors, teachers, peer groups, the media, and students themselves.

How the Size of Birth Cohorts Contributes to Misbehavior

Most criminal behaviors occur during adolescence and young adulthood (Krauss, 1995). The size of the cohort of children born each year will generally predict the crime rate and the rate of school misbehavior 15 years later, as is illustrated in Figure 7.1 on page 210.

Schools feel the impact of large birth cohorts when larger than usual groups of children enter kindergarten. Schools must decide between increasing teaching staff or increasing class size. When funding is not available to employ more teachers and hire more counselors and school psychologists, the school's ability to respond to early signs of delinquency is limited. Teachers are more stressed when they must deal with larger numbers of disruptive students.

In 1994, the number of adolescents in the United States was approximately 60 million, and the anticipated number around the year 2000 will be 70 million. Although in 1994 the overall crime rate decreased, the rate of homicide and assaults credited by the FBI Uniform Crime Reports each year to impoverished, inner city youth is staggering. Based on current projections, schools and the justice system can expect an epidemic of crime and misbehavior by the year 2005. If the conditions that cause high crime rates do not change, we may be faced with a blood bath in impoverished neighborhoods and the schools that serve them.

Some Family Factors that Contribute to Misbehavior

Divorce can have both short- and long-term effects on school behavior. Divorce has a grave emotional impact on some children (Berna, 1993). Further, because divorce generally devastates family income, children of divorce tend to live within greatly restricted economic means. Reduced income for both parents creates further stress. Home and school misbehavior increases when single parents are not able to cope with their reduced income or the increased demand of primary care of the children. If both parents in divorce are involved in parenting, misbehavior is likely if parents are not consistent in discipline styles. For instance, a guilt-ridden parent who left the home may be overly permissive and indulgent with the children. As a consequence, the other parent must enforce limits. These problems may spill over into the school.

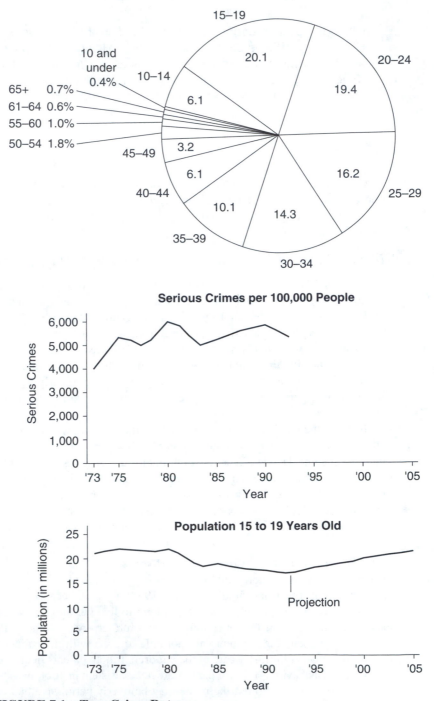

Percentages of Age Group Arrests in Cities in 1992

- 15–19: 20.1
- 20–24: 19.4
- 25–29: 16.2
- 30–34: 14.3
- 35–39: 10.1
- 40–44: 6.1
- 45–49: 3.2
- 10–14: 6.1
- 10 and under: 0.4%
- 50–54: 1.8%
- 55–60: 1.0%
- 61–64: 0.6%
- 65+: 0.7%

Serious Crimes per 100,000 People

Serious Crimes

Year

Population 15 to 19 Years Old

Population (in millions)

Projection

Year

FIGURE 7.1   Teen Crime Rates

Source: Federal Bureau of Investigation

Teachers' divorces may cause deterioration in their ability to manage student disruption. Although this problem might well fall within the purview of our discussion on teacher factors that may cause misbehavior, we present it here because it really has to do with families.

The most common classroom symptom of teacher divorce is loss of patience with students. Little things such as minor misbehaviors, unfinished assignments, or excessive exuberance, which a previously effective disciplinarian handled with ease, may become overwhelming. Teachers may strike back at misbehaving students and then feel guilty and depressed. Or they may rationalize their behavior and blame the students.

Economic stress on families may exacerbate existing disciplinary problems or create the conditions for misbehavior. Recurring periods of inflation and recession typify our economy. Since the 1980s, economic pressures have necessitated dual employment in most families. When both parents are fully employed, they frequently have few emotional resources left to deal with their children's school problems. Latchkey children, those who carry their house keys with them so they can enter their homes after school, find that their free time allows sufficient autonomy to engage in inappropriate or illegal activities. The plight of these children has been recognized by schools and other agencies. Some communities provide before- and after-school programs within students' school buildings, "phone a friend" programs that latchkey children can call if they feel anxious or lonely at home, and homework helplines.

When working reduces the time available for one's own children, parents are less likely to volunteer to lead community groups such as Scouts or Little League. Hard-pressed municipalities have fewer resources to support supervised recreational programs, and good day care often is available only to those who can afford it. What is lost to children are these programs that contribute to self-discipline, help children develop good coping skills and positive self-esteem, and provide productive uses of free time.

Child abuse, which often has a profound impact on students' behavior in school, is a major problem in our country. Children who are physically or emotionally abused at home may present either overtly aggressive or sometimes violent behavior in school or they may be withdrawn and fearful. Sexually abused children frequently display inappropriate sexual behavior in school. Therefore, as a teacher, you must recognize and report signs of abuse that are reflected in misbehavior. Most schools have training programs in this area.

How Political and Economic Structures of Society Contribute to Misbehavior

The Federal Individuals With Disabilities Education Act (formerly PL 94–142) mandates that local schools place every child with disabilities in the "least restrictive environment." If the least restrictive environment for a misbehaving student is deemed to be the regular classroom, the teacher must deal with a student that he or she might not want to have in the class.

Current inclusion legislation, which may result in children with severe behavior problems being placed back into regular classrooms, may have a tremendous impact on teachers' attitudes about misbehavior. If full inclusion of these students is mandated, without sufficient funding for support services, misbehavior in regular classes will increase and regular teachers will need to develop more expertise in dealing with the problem.

Youth unemployment of over 50 percent of minority, inner-city adolescents and large numbers of rural youth, many of whom are school dropouts, reflects our society's failure to prevent associated misbehavior and delinquency. This condition creates a soil rich with the nutrients from which misbehavior grows.

When lower- and middle-class youth cannot find summer jobs, the potential for misbehavior increases. When upper-class children are left on their own with money and no need to work, they are ripe for misbehaviors related to sex, drugs, and drinking. Problems generated by lack of constructive activity will not disappear if policymakers continue to struggle over the ideology of the solutions.

Addictive behaviors, including cigarettes, alcohol, and drug abuse cause many disciplinary problems for schools. Schools' usual response is punishment, including suspension and expulsion. However, there is growing evidence that prevention-oriented programs, especially those that teach students to resist peer pressure to use drugs, do reduce drug use among adolescents (Pellow & Jengelenski, 1991). Yet a historical analysis of drug abuse demonstrates that since the passage of the Harrison Act in 1914, punitive approaches to addictions have not only failed, but have created other severe problems for society. These are discussed in the last chapter. Punishment creates adolescent criminals, who increasingly present problems for schools and clog the courts, the jails, and our limited treatment facilities. In the long run, these approaches cost our schools and our society dearly.

How School-Related Factors Contribute to Misbehavior

Schools have frequently been criticized because, rather then serving as bastions for teaching the process of democracy, they too often serve as little islands of autocracy (Dewey, 1961). When schools violate individual rights (Kirp, 1973, 1982; Kirp & Yudoff, 1974), stress conformity and obedience (Rogers, 1969), and discourage creativity and dissent (Gross & Gross, 1969), they foster rebellion among some segments of the student population. Paradoxically, students are taught in class about principles of democracy such as freedom, responsibility to the community, justice, and fair play; yet, those values too often are not modeled in the way schools are run.

The Safe Schools Study (National Institute of Education, 1978) clearly demonstrated that large schools, located in distressed neighborhoods, governed by ineffective or authoritarian principals, are most likely to have high rates of misbehavior, disruption, and violence. Overly punitive and rigidly bureaucratic schools often promote rather than prevent misbehavior. They tend to implement ineffective and inane rules, emphasize competition over cooperation, and inappropriately violate students' rights.

How Inadequate Funding May Result in Increased Discipline Problems

Despite popular beliefs to the contrary, substantive evidence indicates that school productivity, grades, and scores improve as funding increases (Hedges, Laine, & Greenwald, 1994). Although good teachers may deal effectively with a large variety of misbehaviors, there are those students who require extensive special services of school psychologists, social workers, counselors and alternative schools. These services are expensive.

How Teachers Contribute to Misbehavior

Often teachers unwittingly create problems by not communicating adequately with parents. They may believe that parents either do not adequately discipline children or that they do not care enough. Blaming parents does not solve the problem. Furthermore, some teachers with considerable discipline problems are often their own worst enemies. Take the example of Ms. Rodgers.

Ms. Rodgers was an experienced teacher who had almost thirty years in the same large city school district. When she first began teaching, her school system was well funded and highly regarded for academic excellence. Many of her students were from working-class ethnic backgrounds, discipline problems were minimal, and there was a great deal of parental and student respect for teachers, many of whom had themselves grown up among the ethnic groups in the city. These families, and once-abundant employment opportunities, gradually disappeared.

Ms. Rodgers was an extremely bright person whose children all graduated from prestigious colleges and obtained professional degrees. Although she and her husband had come from working-class families, they had obtained a high level of economic security and social status. Her husband was a successful businessman, and both were dedicated to the arts. She had stayed in teaching because of her desire to remain active and contribute to society.

Every year Ms. Rodgers referred at least a third of her students to the school psychologist. She seemed to constantly have behavior problems. When I first met with her, we discussed two of her referrals. During my first visit to her fifth-grade class, it was obvious that the approach she used to teach poor children from a public housing project was no different from what she had probably used 25 years previously. The setting was formal, seats were all neatly arranged, and the bulletin boards were well provided with pictures and articles that had no relation to the lives of her students, who were required to maintain their seats and constantly be on task. Problems associated with poverty such as hunger, abuse, violence, and family dysfunction were acknowledged, but not considered in her instructional strategies. The children did not seem to want to conform to her rules. About 30 percent of teaching time was spent dealing with issues of control.

Ms. Rodgers used screaming, sarcasm, threats, and ridicule to control the children. The students resented her tone of voice, her implications that they would never learn, and her denigration of their values and beliefs. Ms. Rodgers claimed that in the "good old days," minimal amounts of these methods worked. She reasoned that when misbehavior increased, more of the same would work. She had become her own worst enemy. She was burned out by her inability to face a changing population of students, whose basic needs had to be met before they could learn in school. Her expectations were so low that she just did not expect much academic success from her students.

Although Ms. Rodgers is an extreme example, too may teachers think that increasing misbehaviors require increases in punitive techniques. Their failures to maintain discipline often contribute to *burnout,* which renders them even more incapable.

Poor instruction may account for more than 50 percent of classroom misbehavior (Rosenfeld, 1987). Teachers who are unable to accurately recognize appropriate instructional levels for each student cause major discipline problems. The frustrated student may become withdrawn or hostile. Difficult curricula can result in a wide range of misbehaviors from clowning to explosive refusals to do assignments. When classes are too easy, bored students may cause disruption. They may ignore homework that they consider beneath their ability level. Bright students can be quite inventive in avoiding homework and in fooling parents and teachers. When they are caught and confronted, they may become openly hostile or resort to passive aggression.

Emotional maltreatment by educators, a major cause of student anger, alienation, and rebellion, includes verbal assault, put downs, ridicule, isolation and rejection, punitive sanctions, peer humiliation, and sexual corruption (Brassard, Hart, & Germane, 1987; Hyman, 1990a; Leffler, 1988). This topic is discussed in detail in Chapter 10. Unfortunately, despite the prevalence of emotional maltreatment of students and its relation to misbehavior, there is little research on the topic (Code of Professional Responsibility for Teachers, 1992; Hyman, 1990; Hyman & Weiler, 1994).

How Peer Groups Contribute to Misbehavior

Contemporary Western society pays a price for extending childhood and adolescence. Adolescents' social and economic dependency on parents is often incongruent with their physical maturity as compared with all pretechnological societies. The biological, intellectual, and emotional status of the typical 17-year-old boy equips him to compete with much older adults in terms of many skills. The average 14-year-old girl is capable of bearing children and performing routine maintenance functions involved in rearing them.

Despite eons of evolutionary programming that bestows adolescents with attributes and aptitudes for survival, in our postindustrial society, they are generally judged as incompetent to function as adults. This extended period of adolescence, reinforced by youth-oriented media, advertising, and manufacturing, has created an adolescent peer culture that is driven by the need to be different from adults. Sometimes these needs extend to opposition and aggression against mainstream adult values.

Peer groups that are allowed to develop norms and values contrary to the decent treatment of others are a major contributor to misbehavior and delinquency. Drug-oriented gangs and loosely knit, antisocial peer groups are particularly difficult for parents, schools, and other agencies. For instance, once adolescents embrace the values of the drug culture, no matter where they attend school, they will always find compatible peers. My experience as a psychologist in a private "prep" school bears out this observation. Some parents, who have the economic resources, attempt to save their children from their hometown druggie friends by sending them to boarding school. This rarely works, because other parents, with similar problems, have the same idea. So the students just substitute druggie friends in public school with similar, easy-to-find friends in private school.

How the Media Contributes to Misbehavior

Educators know that there is nothing like TV to transform children and youth into zombies. Students with short attention spans in class will sit at home, staring for hours at the unending entertainment provided by TV. There is now a sufficient body of research to indicate that TV can cause a multitude of learning and behavior problems in school (American Psychological Association, 1993).

Frequent TV viewing:

1. Decreases social gatherings away from home, community activities, family conversations, and household care
2. Results in depressed reading ability and lowered scores on measures of creativity
3. Of violence results in aggressive and undesirable behavior, although the relationship is not direct and is mediated by other factors so that some children are affected more than others
4. Results in harmful stereotypes of white men as models of desirable behavior and promotes women and minorities as possessing a variety of undesirable traits
5. Of aggressive sexual acts against women can increase willingness to aggress against females
6. By adolescents of sexual scenes of highly attractive actors and actresses causes them to be less satisfied with their own sexual status and have distorted perceptions about sex and sexuality as compared with peers who watch relatively little programming with sexual content

Children from academically oriented homes will more often watch educational TV, and children from less advantaged backgrounds tend to pick TV with high action and low educational value (American Psychological Association, 1993; Liebert & Sprafkin, 1988).

Unrealistic fight scenes from "karate movies," ranging from Power Rangers to Bruce Lee sagas, may convince students that people who are punched in the face, hit over the head by baseball bats, or slammed head-first into walls do not sustain cuts, bruises, broken bones, and serious internal injuries. Defiance of school rules and norms are encouraged by media depictions of children and youth happily and successfully deceiving, ridiculing, and sometimes aggressing against peers, parents, teachers, and other adults. Inappropriate heroes and anti-heroes model violence to solve problems and offer anti-establishment roles to emulate.

On the positive side, TV can help children improve reading and math skills, learn academic subjects, and accept cooperation, nonaggressive problem solving, generosity, and friendliness from well-prepared educational television. Techniques that capture childrens' attention and shape their thinking have been used successfully on programs such as Sesame Street, Mr. Rogers, and Reading Rainbow.

How Students Themselves Contribute to Misbehavior

In general, a family's socioeconomic and educational level, family structure and values, birth order, number of siblings, and support systems have somewhat predictable influences on children and their behavior in school (Fine, 1994; Plas, 1994). The ESA, however, although allowing for these outside influences, also stresses that misbehaving students must assume some of the responsibility for changing their behavior and attitudes. Proponents of the ESA set limits on the amount of deviancy allowed before the system must change the setting in which the student is schooled.

Students who have untreated predispositions to violence, poor motivation to meet the demands of schools, and lack of responsibility and appropriate moral behavior toward others may need special help. The regular classroom teacher should not be expected to become a therapist. Schools and society must provide sufficient environmental alternatives such as special education classes, alternative schools, and hospitalization when necessary.

For a variety of reasons, some students become alienated from authority. This can range from passive resisters to outright aggressors. Take the case of Jay Jones, a twelve-year-old who was raised in a home of reasonable privilege.

The Jones family sat across from me in my office. Mrs. Jones tearfully related an incident during which her only child, Jay, had hit a teacher while on the playground. The teacher's "offense," according to Jay, was that she unfairly blamed him for starting a fight. According to Jay, she should have believed his account that the other kid started the fight by making fun of him. The teacher had no right to grab Jay to protect the other kid, who "deserved to be smashed." He reported that his anger escalated when he was taken to the principal. His verbal abuse of the teacher, the principal, and everyone else involved in the incident finally resulted in a call to his parents to take him home.

Jay, a small, wiry twelve-year-old, looked me in the eye. He sneered, curling half of his upper lip, and began his repertoire of well-practiced facial acrobatics. He then began his verbal assault: "I will beat that kid up when I go back to school. I'll smash him any time I want to. No teacher's gonna stop me, and you can't stop me either."

As we continued our verbal exchange, Jay became increasingly agitated. His mother, sitting next to him on the couch, placed her hand on his shoulder as he got up to come toward me. He wiggled, shoved, and raised his fist at her. His father, sitting on the other side, was growing visibly angry, but was obviously restraining his impulse to smack his son.

Mrs. Jones said, "Now you're really seeing how he gets when he loses his temper. He does this all the time at home, but this is the first time he has ever hit a teacher. He hits me sometimes, and I'm beginning to become afraid of him. This is no way to feel about your own child."

Her last statement appeared almost incomprehensible when one observed Mrs. Jones, who at 5'10" and 160 lbs was surely capable of handling her diminutive son. As we discussed this inconsistency, I discovered that Mr. Jones, who was even larger, had no compunctions about smacking his son, a fact that was not lost on Jay.

As Jay's rhetoric continued to escalate, he got up and began a macho display of shadow boxing. As he danced back and forth between me and his mother, he extolled his toughness and his power over his mother and his teachers. The following dialogue ensued:

Me: Jay, it's not good for you or your mother to believe that you can control her physically.

Jay: Yeah? What are you gonna do about it?

Me: I am going to teach your mother how to physically restrain you without hurting you.

Jay: You and what army?

While making this last statement, he gave me a light punch on the arm, whereupon I jumped out of my chair, took him to the floor and immobilized him with a basket hold. This is a method to be used only by those trained in this technique of physical restraint, to control violent behavior without hurting the aggressor.

Jay screamed, yelled, kicked, and struggled for at least fifteen minutes, as I calmly held him in passive restraint and talked with him. As this occurred, his parents were at first dumbfounded that a child psychologist should be laying on the floor on top of their child. They became amused as I talked calmly, joked about my actions, and explained to them that part of Jay's problem was that he felt invulnerable and free to lose his temper both at home and at school.

I let Jay get up when he agreed that he was calm. He went back to sit on the couch beside his mother. He admitted that I could control him, but stated that his mother could not. To demonstrate, he began punching his mother in the leg. I instructed his mother to do the same thing that I had just done. Much to Jay's surprise, he again found himself on the floor with his mother's legs wrapped over his, and his arms crisscrossed and held from behind by his mother. He resisted for another fifteen minutes, and when his mother began to get a little tired, she was relieved by her husband. By the end of the one-hour therapy session, Jay had spent almost forty minutes on the floor in physical restraint.

During the following two weeks, Jay tested his mother on several occasions. Without anger, his mother swiftly immobilized him. After that, Jay's physical assaults on his mother stopped. But we needed to know why Jay went to school angry.

His developmental, social, and educational history showed that Jay resented being small. Other children teased him. Also, he had a mild learning disability that made him feel inferior, although he had above average intelligence. His parents vacillated between excessive punishments, spankings, and not following through on threats. As he became immune to increasing levels of punishment, his school and home problems escalated. His mother became depressed, helpless, and rejecting. His father began to withdraw.

Jay's frustration with slow progress in school led to angry responses at teachers and parents, who seemed unfair in their demands. Children sometimes teased him about both his height and his poor schoolwork. His model for dealing with frustration came from home, where his parent's anger led to spankings. His life became a series of confrontations and punishments that were increasingly ineffective. Intervention was complex but successful.

The Joneses agreed to stop spanking. I taught them anger control methods to deal with their own feelings. They learned to prevent escalation of Jay's outbursts by calmly listening to his complaints and not reacting punitively to his profanities and verbal threats. The constant punishment cycle was eliminated by a use of a combined school/home reinforcement program in which Jay earned points for things he highly desired.

I helped Jay to identify the basis of his hostility and feelings that aroused his anger and led to his temper tantrums. His teachers agreed to let him go to the counselor if he thought he was going to "lose it." We worked on strategies such as relaxation training to calm down. He practiced, through role playing, how to respond to teasing so that he would not get into trouble. The reward system began to work, and he demonstrated to himself and his caretakers that he could control his temper. His self-confidence began to improve as he spent more time learning and less time in conflict.

The above situation illustrates the complexities when a student's coping style conflicts with the norms of the school. Although we provided a variety of adjustments to the environment, Jay had to accept some of the responsibility. He had to decide that rules were not made to be broken.

Jay's case was relatively easy to ameliorate. However, complex ecological factors may not be so easily managed when the student is old enough to be relatively independent. The following case illustrates the difficulties faced by teachers and parents when an adolescent has learned to cope independently. It shows how problems may occur when single parents must work full-time, when latchkey children gain too much independence, and when there are no after-school resources or supervision available.

A Case of Sex in the Afternoon

Mrs. Harris was a relatively young mother who came to therapy with a big problem. This attractive woman, in her early thirties, had married quite young. Her husband was a carpenter who married her after she became pregnant. Even though the family income was adequate when they married, she decided to work through most of her pregnancy. However, after the birth of her daughter, she wanted to stay home.

Several years after they were married, her husband found good employment in another state, and the family moved. But, despite a rise in income, they found it difficult to maintain their standard of living. She obtained an excellent position as a secretary and was quite happy. She placed her child in day care, and she loved her work. Everything went well until the child was about ten, and the parents began to quarrel continually. They finally decided to divorce.

At the time of the divorce, Mrs. Harris had advanced in her job. After the divorce, she was faced with the problem of supervision of her daughter. She did not want to move, even though she had no relatives and few friends in the area.

Mrs. Harris explained to the therapist that her daughter Jean was a bright, well-adjusted fourteen-year-old whose boyfriend was a nice fifteen-year-old schoolmate named Paul. One day Mrs. Harris came home early from work to discover her daughter and boyfriend in the kitchen. Paul was sitting at the kitchen table having a beer while Jean was ironing a shirt. It was the shirt she had worn to school.

When Jean and Paul arrived at the Harris home after school, Jean decided to wash the blouse and panties she had worn during the day, along with the other laundry. However, she had not bothered to put anything on to replace them.

Shocked and chagrined, Mrs. Harris concluded something sexual had occurred between removal of Jean's clothes and their entry into the washing machine. She was angry, sad, and confused. Jean was embarrassed, defensive, and hysterical. Paul "headed for the hills" at the first opportunity.

After this incident, Mrs. Harris and Jean fought for several months, during which time Jean's schoolwork began to deteriorate. She began, for the first time, to talk back to teachers and rebel. Previously obeyed school rules became a big issue.

As things became worse, Mrs. Harris came to see me. She returned with her daughter. After listening to them argue, I decided to have Jean and her boyfriend come in together.

Without going through the whole story, it was obvious that there was no real pathology in the situation. Although Jean was very bright and mildly rebellious, she had been on her own after school most of her life. She watched a great deal of TV, especially the "soaps," during her preteens and early teens. Mother and daughter had a generally good relationship.

Paul, although probably not as bright as Jean, came from a home where everybody, including the kids, worked in the family business. At a relatively early age the children had their own money, which they had earned, and a lot of freedom from supervision when they were not working.

Once Jean and Paul admitted to me that they were having sex, they told me in confidence that they had no plans to give it up. They really enjoyed it, and although Mrs. Harris was very unhappy, they felt she was resigned to it. During the family sessions that ensued, it was obvious that the essential issue was one of control.

Television, a hefty allowance, and early independence had resulted in Jean's establishing her own set of values. As a latchkey kid, she had learned to be responsible and independent. Because her mother came home late from work, Jean faithfully carried out her chores, including preparing supper, washing clothes, etc. Her mother, a single working woman, provided for the family, but Jean had, at an early age, become the homemaker. Adult responsibility led Jean to think that it was appropriate to control all aspects of her behavior. This created conflict in school, where authorities insisted on maintaining control of her behavior.

Paul, believed that, because he worked and contributed to his family, he should be allowed to do what he wished. In terms of mental health criteria, neither he nor Jean had emotional problems. Although the school might consider their behavior reflective of conduct disorders, the diagnostic criteria were not met. Because they were physically mature and functioning independently, they just wanted to be treated like adults; they had proved that they could function like adults.

Mrs. Harris thought that her daughter was just too young to be in an ongoing sexual relationship. But what could she do to stop it? She could forbid Paul from being in her home when she was not there, but she knew that the kids would find another place to make love. Paul's parents both worked, and therefore his house was empty frequently. As a condition for coming to therapy, all three had agreed not to tell Paul's parents about the intimate relationship.

Mrs. Harris could not afford to come home early or to hire an adequate person to monitor her daughter between 3:00 PM and 6:00 PM. There were no after-school activities except for major sports. There was no YWCA close enough, and the church they attended had no weekly activities for young people. One might argue that Mrs. Harris already set the pattern, and it was too late to do anything. However, because Jean and Paul did not want to upset Mrs. Harris, they agreed to try to refrain from having sex in Jean's home.

For some, the solution might be considered a wimp out. After all, since when should a fourteen-year-old do what she wants? What right does a fifteen-year-old boy have to a mature sexual relationship? This age-old problem is illustrated by Romeo and Juliet. Even in that structured society, parents were unable to control the lives of their teenagers.

Essentially, Mrs. Harris was not able to control certain aspects of her child's time. She lived in a community where there were few adolescent-oriented after-school activities. She had no nearby relatives and few close friends. Her situation is not unlike that of many other single parents. ■

The above true case illustrates how the economic and social realities of contemporary American society militate against parental control of many children. Support services and volunteer activities that provide for after-school supervision of children of working parents are minimal. Social policy in America is not focused on the types of supports that families really need to recreate the "good old days" when small towns, extended families, and non-working mothers watched over children and youth.

In summary, we have considered some of the most prominent systemic causes for misbehavior. Birth cohorts, families, society, schools, teachers, peer groups, the media, and students themselves are intertwined in causing the conditions that result in misbehavior. Solutions require a multifaceted approach, as promoted in the ESA.

The ESA recognizes current realities and is based on assumptions related to those realities. We now turn to these assumptions.

Assumptions of the Ecological Systems Approach

Individual Misbehavior Must Be Understood as a Function of Ecological/Systems Factors

As we have discussed, the ESA is concerned with the relationship of individuals to settings. This orientation considers important internal forces such as needs, drives, innate patterns, biological urges, physiological conditions, and external forces such as organizations, families, politics, stimuli, reinforcers, punishers, social rules, mores, taboos, cultural patterns, and social conditions. The individual reflects all of the above forces, and misbehavior in the classroom must be understood within that context.

At the classroom level, good group management skills depend on effective instruction. It is not expected, as in other models, that the teacher have a good grounding in a particular personality theory. Rather, in the ESA, the teacher must understand the dynamics of the classroom and be able to apply the techniques of effective instruction. Interesting, enthusiastic and appropriate levels of instruction help minimize misbehavior.

Individual Misbehavior Should be Viewed within the Context of Roles and as a Symptom of a Systemic Problem

In all of the other approaches in the teacher variance model, individual diagnosis is paramount. However, in the ESA, we attempt to discern how individual misbehavior reveals the student's identity with a particular group. In the section on deviance, we discussed the case of Ms. Bradon and Jim as an illustration of how stereotypical views, shaped by physical appearance, dress, race, ethnic group, or socioeconomic class, can influence a teacher's behavior.

Individual discipline problems are always viewed as one part of a system. The ESA focuses on how the system creates similar problems. The solution lies in an understanding and amelioration of the misperceptions and stereotypes that create problems.

Behavior and Misbehavior Are Seen as Normal or Deviant According to the Setting

The setting designates what is "normal" and "abnormal." For instance, yelling and cheering may be appropriate in a physical education class, but these behaviors would be completely inappropriate in a typical English class. In the ESA, the teacher sets the standards for appropriate behavior. In this sense, the ESA flows directly from traditional beliefs and practices in education. Because teachers vary in discipline styles, students must learn to adjust to the standards of each class.

In the classroom, the teacher is the instructional leader. The basis for guiding teaching is the extensive research on teacher efficacy. Although each teacher's individual style and standards are important, they must be reasonably congruent with research findings about good classroom management.

Teacher expectations and disciplinary techniques are limited by community standards. The "permissiveness" that would pervade a humanistic classroom would probably be unacceptable in a conservative, rural community. Conversely, a very strict, punitive teacher may not be acceptable in a liberal, suburban New England community.

Misbehavior Is Caused by Dysfunction in the Match between the Environment and the Individual

Most contemporary societies are characterized by various stereotypical groups. Each group has its own norms. In America, these stereotypes are strongly reinforced through the media. For instance, in the 1970s a popular TV sitcom about education was entitled "Welcome Back Kotter." Even though the dress and some of the language of this show is dated, the series is periodically replayed (most currently on Nickelodeon) because of the enduring message about the fallacies of stereotyping.

Mr. Kotter is portrayed as a somewhat "hip" teacher who was able to relate to the subculture of city students who were mostly from working-class families. In general, these students were not oriented to learning or to the value system of the school. However, Mr. Kotter, by using humor and creativity, was portrayed as reaching these alienated youth. Although he maintained an adequate level of decorum and classroom control, he was able to allow the students the freedom to express themselves in the way that they knew best. In this case, the teacher was able to match his style with that of the students.

In contrast to Mr. Kotter, the principal, who had a fund of pejorative labels for the students, viewed them as a "bunch of sweat hogs." The principal expected the students to match with the environment he considered appropriate for education. But his concept of adequate and proper education was at odds with the norms of the students. Therefore, a mismatch occurred, and misbehavior followed.

The ESA could consider that either Mr. Kotter or the principal could deal appropriately with the students. In general, Mr. Kotter used classroom ecological techniques to make learning interesting and stimulating. The principal, despite his negative attitudes, could use a wide range of school, community, and home resources to attempt to motivate the students. However, he could also, as was portrayed in the sitcom, function at such a punitive level that a self-fulfilling prophesy would occur.

Misbehavior Can Be Perpetuated by Self-Fulfilling Prophecies

Educators can actually encourage students to misbehave in accordance with the adult's expectations. These self-fulfilling prophesies are particularly troublesome when they are associated with racial and economic labeling. In impoverished city school districts, there are teachers who are "burned out" by years of struggle against schools plagued by lack of resources and students faced with overwhelming odds against success. Some teachers just give up. In an unpublished study I conducted in preparation for Congressional testimony, I asked a random sample of inner-city African American and Hispanic students why they behaved in some classes and not in others (Hyman & D'Alessandro, 1984b). The most frequent single response was that they misbehaved mostly in classes where they believed that the teachers "don't care about us or give us any respect." The students' main response to "uncaring" teachers was to make the teachers' lives miserable. The cycle of teacher anger and apathy and student alienation and disruption reinforces the self-fulfilling prophesy that "these students" do not care about education.

Appropriate evaluation and remediation based on the ESA requires an accurate assessment of all the self-fulfilling prophesies about various groups. It is useless to treat individual behavior while ignoring how that misbehavior is embedded in the social constructs of the school and the community.

Suppression of Diversity Causes Misbehavior

Although the ESA stresses matches between various environments and the individual, it also focuses on understanding the nature, quality, and interrelations of various groups in the school and community. Economic struggles over limited employment and resources can result in ethnically or racially based derogatory stereotypes and escalating angry dialogue between politicians, parents, students, and educators from different groups. This type of community conflict may lead to aggression between adolescents, which spreads to the schools.

The contemporary mix of ethnic, racial, language, and religious groups is enormous. School staff and students need to learn about different cultural and ethnic values. Behavior that might be benign in one culture might be interpreted as threatening or disrespectful by someone from another culture. For instance, Ms. Saxon, an Anglo teacher, expects Julio, a Puerto Rican student, to look her in the eye when she is reprimanding him. However, in his home, he is expected to show respect by looking down when he is being scolded. Ms. Saxon reads his behavior as disrespectful and becomes increasingly angry at his refusal to look at her.

African American street language is full of expletives. In many cases, this has become such a staple part of adolescent, macho language that male students may inadvertently use it as part of everyday speech in school. Although constant obscenities are not acceptable to parents or school authorities, this type of language should not become a major reason for repeated suspensions. Rather, the school can implement remediation programs using role playing, videotapes, and other techniques to help students to differentiate where that language may or may not be appropriate.

Our legal, moral, and ethical standards demand that educators understand diversity in terms of values and behavior. Good discipline within the ESA perspective requires appropriate staff and student training and sensitization to the traits of each students culture. The form and content of disciplinary policies and practices must be sensitive to each group's needs to minimize disruption.

Organizational Change Can Be Accomplished through Systems Approaches

Organizational change can be forced by a variety of crises, including economic loss or gains, drastic changes in leadership, or political mandates. However, long-lasting, positive change is usually dependent on systematic use of theory-based approaches such as field theory, systems theory, or chaos theory. All of these fall within the rubric of organizational development, a topic which is discussed in Chapter Eight.

Organizational change in schools can only occur when policymakers allow for accurate diagnosis of the problem, empowerment of staff, assessment procedures for evaluation of change, and mechanisms for self-correction. Analysis for change assumes that all elements of the system are interdependent and that the whole may be greater than the sum of its parts. Before change is implemented, program evaluation research methods must be planned. This may include the use of climate assessment, field analysis, focus groups, and participatory decision making. Actual techniques of change are discussed in the next chapter.

Summary

In this chapter, we have explained the theory behind the ESA. In the ESA, diagnosis and remediation intertwine and are dependent on an understanding of all factors that affect misbehaving students. Yet misbehavior must be understood as a symptom of the system. Remediation requires a thorough understanding of all of the factors in society that contribute to the development of children and youth.

At the school and classroom levels, the underlying assumption about misbehavior is that effective schools and teachers will minimize misbehavior. Effective administrators provide for a safe, secure, and comfortable atmosphere in which teachers use disciplinary techniques based on positive motivational techniques and effective methods of punishment. Teachers conduct a well-managed, appropriately paced, businesslike classroom.

In the next chapter, we focus mostly on diagnosis and treatment at the classroom level, with an overview and example of diagnosis and remediation at the community and school levels. Consistent with this model, we are most concerned to interdict against those systems factors that allow or encourage deviance.

Key Terms

addictive behavior

anomie

burnout

child abuse

deviant

divorce

ecological

economic stress

emotional maltreatment

family systems theory

general systems theory

media influences

poor instruction

self-fulfilling prophesy

sociological

youth unemployment

Application Activities

1. What systems factors are possible causes for Juanita's misbehaviors?

2. What systems factors are possible causes for Jamal's misbehaviors?

3. What systems factors are possible causes for Michael's misbehaviors?

4. What systems factors are possible causes for Chris's misbehaviors?

Suggested Readings

American Psychological Association. (1994). *Violence and youth: Psychology's response* (Vol. I). *Summary report of the American Psychological Association Commission on Violence and Youth.* Washington, DC: Author.

Durkheim, E. (1968). *Education and sociology.* New York: Free Press.

Durkheim, E. (1973). *Moral education: A study in the theory and application of the sociology of education.* New York: Free Press of Glencoe.

Fine, M. (1994). A systems-ecological perspective on home-school invention. In M. Fine and C. Carlson (Eds.), *The handbook of family-school intervention: A systems perspective.* Boston: Allyn & Bacon.

Guttman, H. A. (1991). Systems theory, cybernetics, and epistemology. In A. S. Gurman & D. P. Kniskern (Eds.), *Handbook of family therapy* (Vol. II, pp. 41–64). New York: Brunner/Mazel, Inc.

Plas, J. M. (1994). The development of systems thinking: A historical perspective. In M. Fine & C. Carlson (Eds.), *The handbook of family-school intervention: A systems perspective.* Boston: Allyn & Bacon.

Chapter 8

Diagnosis and Remediation Using the Ecological/Systems Approach (ESA)

Chapter Objectives

After reading this chapter, you will know:

1. How to use the ecological problem solving matrix to develop primary, secondary, and tertiary interventions in the home, school, and community
2. How to diagnose the ecology of the classroom
3. Characteristics of teacher effectiveness
4. Diagnosis of school climate
5. Intervention for and history, diagnosis, and treatment of anger in the classroom
6. Primary, secondary, and tertiary prevention strategies when dealing with angry, aggressive students
7. The five stages of aggression
8. The development of aggression in students
9. Skinner's eight-step peer mediation program

Diagnosis Using the Ecological Problem-Solving Matrix

From an ESA perspective, misbehaviors should be considered in terms of the larger system within which the student functions. Of course, in reality, most problems are handled at the classroom level. However, organizational development, a systemic approach to school dis-

TABLE 8.1   Problem-Solving Matrix for School Discipline

Diagnosis Category	Levels of Intervention				
	Primary Prevention	Secondary Prevention	Tertiary Prevention	Punishment	Restitution
Home					
Family structure	HA1	HA2	HA3	HA4	HA5
Family power	HB1	HB2	HB3	HB4	HB5
Family values	HC1	HC2	HC3	HC4	HC5
Other					
Schools					
Organization	SA1	SA2	SA3	SA4	SA5
Students and peer groups	SB1	SB2	SB3	SB4	SB5
Teachers and teaching	SC1	SC2	SC3	SC4	SC5
Other					
Community					
Values	CA1	CA2	CA3	CA4	CA5
Control	CB1	CB2	CB3	CB4	CB5
Opportunities	CC1	CC2	CC3	CC4	CC5
Other					

cipline and violence offers the best long-term framework for understanding and solving problems. The ESA framework we present here emerged from a four-year discipline and violence prevention project in Trenton, New Jersey, schools and resulted in the development of an ecological problem-solving matrix, presented in Table 8.1 (Hyman, 1990b). The matrix is designed to consider five levels of intervention within each system that impacts on a particular misbehavior. In each cell are codes that refer to solutions, which are described after we discuss the levels of intervention.

Primary Prevention

Primary prevention consists of activities meant to intervene before misbehaviors occur. Public health policy, especially in the universal use of vaccinations, offers a good example of primary prevention. Although vaccinations have eradicated many diseases, the initial costs for developing vaccines is quite high. Yet those costs are minuscule compared with the expense of medicines, hospitalizations, physician care, and loss of productivity associated with the diseases they prevent. The most effective inoculation against misbehavior, alienation, and violence is the provision of an environment that promotes and sustains adequate economic, social, emotional, and educational support for every child. This not only includes food, clothing, and shelter, but also adequate social, emotional, and educational support for families.

Secondary Prevention

Secondary prevention is used after misbehavior occurs. At this level, students have begun to misbehave, but it is relatively easy to intervene. This level works best when all parties hold the same values. For instance, John copies test answers from the student sitting next to him. If John and his parents value honesty, a simple reminder of the implications of cheating should be sufficient to deter further cheating. This approach will work because John will feel embarrassed about being caught, he will feel shame about his parents learning of his behavior, and he will understand the moral ramifications of the act.

Successful programs of secondary prevention require knowledgeable teachers who understand the causes of misbehavior and who feel free to consult with mental health professionals if they need help. Secondary prevention also may be thought of as correction.

Tertiary Prevention

Tertiary prevention is required when misbehavior becomes chronic or serious. This level of intervention mandates the services of trained professionals. The ESA model includes multilevel interventions that necessitate coordination between the home, school, and community agencies. School psychologists, specially trained teachers, school counselors, school social workers, and drug and alcohol counselors may collaborate at the school level. By the year 2000, it is predicted that many schools will adopt the model of wrap-around or school-based services that include all agencies and professionals to implement comprehensive treatment (National Education Goals Panel, 1994).

Punishment

Punishment is a procedure that reduces the probability of the misbehavior recurring. The ESA approach does not avoid the use of punishment when it is considered necessary. However, punishment must be reasonable and effective. This is too often not the case with chronic school misbehaviors such as class cutting, fighting, and disrespect of authority. Students who exhibit these and other misbehaviors are often repeatedly given in- or out-of-school suspensions or detentions. When this pattern occurs, it is obvious that these techniques are not punishing.

Research and experience indicate that punishment is the least effective way to change behavior (Alberto & Troutman, 1990; Axelrod, 1983b; Skinner, 1979). Its advantage is that it is usually relatively inexpensive, it can be administered easily by untrained staff, and students sometimes prefer it to wipe away the misdeed. It is only effective when it taps the student's sense of guilt. Chronic truants have often been frequently punished without any appreciable effect.

Restitution

Restitution is a technique in which the offender acts in a manner to compensate for what he or she did. For instance, a student who spraypaints a wall in the school might be given a choice of erasing the graffiti or repainting a portion of the building. The major advantage of restitution is that it is related to the misdeed and allows the student to "do something good."

Using the Matrix to Generate Solutions

We can use the ecological problem-solving matrix to examine a typical discipline problem, such as class cutting (Hyman, 1984, 1990b). Class cutting, for want of a better title, is a generic term that describes student misbehaviors including tardiness, failure to attend class, or absence from school. The most typical and palpably inane response of most schools is to suspend students who cut class. This response is particularly ineffective because students cut school because they do not want to attend or because they find other activities more interesting. Therefore, we must assume that the school is a co-conspirator in helping the student to avoid classes.

The matrix presented is meant to provide a systematic method of approaching problems such as class cutting. The first step in using this or your own matrix is to gather data concerning the cause of the problem. This can be done by individual and small-group interviews (focus groups) or by developing questionnaires. Sources of information should include students, parents, staff, etc. The development of surveys to collect data can be accomplished by staff committees, the school psychologist, or outside consultants. Although comprehensive data gathering is strongly advised, it is recognized that it may be resisted because of various limitations of staff and resources. However, without appropriate data, significant changes and ongoing renewal are not likely.

It is important to identify all of the demographic factors that contribute to a problem. In the problem-solving matrix, we have identified families, communities, and schools. Under each, we have listed specific aspects of those entities, such as family power and school organization. These subheadings are not meant to be definitive. Therefore, others can be added or some may be deleted, based on unique characteristics of each problem.

Determining causes and solutions is actually relatively easy. Implementing your plans is much more difficult, because many interventions involve coordination with parents, school, authorities, and various community agencies. Also, it is important to collect data to monitor the progress, success, and failures of each approach. The *Uniform Discipline Reporting System,* a computerized reporting system for tracking misbehavior, was developed for this purpose (Berkowitz, Hyman & Lally, 1984). One could use this system, which appears on page 15, to monitor the success of remediation across different school buildings or the system.

Table 8.1 provides an example of some interventions for class cutting at each level and in each setting using the ecological problem-solving matrix (Hyman, 1984, 1990b). The codes within each cell match the codes in the following list of interventions. You are encouraged to add remediations to each cell.

Solutions for the Problem-Solving Matrix for Class Cutting*

Home Interventions

Family Structure

HA1: Primary Prevention. Facilitate provisions for low-cost day care so that high school students are not responsible for caring for younger siblings during the school day.

---

*Hyman, I. (1990). Class cutting: An ecological approach. In R. Gupta & P. Coxhead (Eds.), *Intervention with children* (pp. 107–129). London & New York: Routlage.

HA2: Secondary Prevention. Offer small-group parenting seminars for parents of students who are beginning to cut class.

HA3: Tertiary Prevention. Set up behavior modification system with parents.

HA4: Punishment. Have school psychologist or guidance counsel check that the family understands the role of punishment.

HA5: Restitution. Help parents determine what types of restitution are applicable.

Family Power

HB1: Primary Prevention. Help parents to understand whether they are being manipulated by student.

HB2: Secondary Prevention. Keep parents informed of all cutting, and help them use corrective techniques.

HB3: Tertiary Prevention. Provide family therapy.

HB4: Punishment. Determine if punishment is too severe and nonproductive or too weak.

HB5: Restitution. Support parent in charge of discipline with suggestions and encouragement to develop restitution plans for student.

Family Values

HC1: Primary Prevention. Send newsletter home to parents containing the events of the month and include items on improved attendance.

HC2: Secondary Prevention. Permit special outings (special vacations, camping trips, etc.) with parents for students with perfect attendance. Arrange for completion of missed schoolwork.

HC3: Tertiary Prevention. Help parents to implement a behavioral program to increase motivation to attend school. If family is overly permissive, help them to understand the results.

HC4: Punishment. Assure parents that punishment may have to be used, and that they should not feel guilty. Conversely, if punishment is excessively used and is too harsh, help parents to understand that it becomes counterproductive.

HC5: Restitution. Convince parents of the value of restitution.

School Interventions

School Organization

SA1: Primary Prevention. Take all possible steps to assure that school is a safe, rewarding, and pleasant place to be.

SA2: Secondary Prevention. Reward improved or perfect attendance with tangible and social means, such as stickers, publicity, luncheons for parents and students, tickets to sporting or social events, etc.

SA3: Tertiary Prevention. Set up alternative school for chronic truants.

SA4: Punishment. Use after-school detention.

SA5: Restitution. Provide chores as an alternative to punishment.

School Students and Peer Groups—Prevention

SB1: Primary Prevention. Involve all students in ongoing projects to promote healthy school climate.

SB2: Secondary Prevention. Set up study buddy systems for students beginning to cut class.

SB3: Tertiary Prevention. Have peers counsel truants and class cutters.

SB4: Punishment. Have student disciplinary board determine punishments (this should be used with caution and close monitoring).

SB5: Restitution. Have students who cut help other students, for example, tutoring a less able student.

School Teachers and Teaching

SC1: Primary Prevention. Educate students that future employers will check their high school record for job reliability.

SC2: Secondary Prevention. Call parents of students who cut class, try to determine causes and develop an in-school plan to improve attendance.

SC4: Punishment. Restrict students' free time or desired school activities.

SC5: Restitution. Have student do classroom chores to make up for cutting.

Community Interventions

CA1: Primary Prevention. Community leaders, businesses, and others offer incentives such as certificates, award ceremonies, and credit coupons for purchase of meals at fast-food restaurants for students with good attendance.

CA2: Secondary Prevention. Businesses provide after-school work experiences dependent on acceptable student attendance.

CA3: Tertiary Prevention. Community leaders, athletes, police, and other adults with whom students identify become big brothers and sisters to chronic truants.

CA4: Punishment. Businesses may receive fines if they harbor or sell to truant students during school hours.

CA5: Restitution. Truant students are allowed to substitute detentions for truancy by completing specified hours of community service.

CB1: Primary Prevention. Students are informed of coordinated community effort to spot and report truant students.

CB2: Secondary Prevention. Truants are picked up by police and returned to school.

CB3: Tertiary Prevention. Chronic truants are required to attend therapy sessions.

CB4: Punishment. Chronic truants are required to spend time in youth correctional facilities.

CB5: Restitution. Chronic truants are offered opportunities such as cleaning up the town.

CC1: Primary Prevention. Local radio spots advertise after-school work opportunities for students with good attendance records.

CC2: Secondary Prevention. Community offers free counseling service and help line for parents of children who are beginning patterns of truancy.

CC3: Tertiary Prevention. Coordinated efforts by social services, community guidance centers, and other agencies offering low-cost psychotherapy for families of chronic truants.

CC4: Punishment. The community requires truants to work in services such as soup kitchens until their attendance improves.

CC5: Restitution. Truants help indigent people who never finished high school.

Additional categories such as recreation, sports, health, and nutrition may supplement the matrix. As an exercise, you might wish to take another problem area, such as student weapons possession, and fill in the cells. For example, a primary prevention approach at the family and school levels might be curricula informing children of the dangers of handguns. At the secondary prevention level, in the schools, metal detectors might be considered. At the punishment level, within the schools, staff must consider the efficacy of complete expulsion, suspension, or offering the possibility of restitution by a student who brought a gun to school.

When finished with that activity, turn to the case of Chris (see page 37), and let us begin approaching his problem from the diagnostic aspects of the matrix.

Identify the Misbehavior in Relation to Ecological/Systems Levels within the Macro and Microsystems

Because we have not given you a comprehensive history of Chris, and we have not described the school or classroom in detail, it will be helpful for you to make up possible scenarios about these factors. For our purposes here, we offer sufficient information to begin the process.

Community-Related Factors for Diagnosis

Every family has a community-based group role identity related to such factors as religious affiliations, socioeconomic status, political ideology, and recreational activities. From the information available, Chris's family would be considered blue collar or working class. Using the matrix as a guide, we would first want to determine the values and socioeconomic structure of the community. For instance, if the community is predominantly working class, it is likely that Chris and his family would feel comfortable in terms of their aspirations, family values, and interactions with neighbors and community institutions. Their schools would reflect their belief system.

Teachers in any socioeconomically homogeneous community may develop either negative or positive stereotypes about the students they serve. For example, in the case of Chris, if the teacher is unable to identify with or is unsympathetic to working-class values, she may be unable to objectively assess the true nature of his problem. However, she may realize that both parents must be employed to survive economically, that work is as highly valued as education, and that some parents may have two jobs to maintain their desired lifestyle.

Diagnostic considerations should include understanding of the community control mechanisms, with regard to aggressive behavior as they impact on Chris's interpersonal problems and disruptive behavior. For instance, has Chris's behavior caused problems with neighbors, and have his aggressive behaviors resulted in appeals to the police? Although this is unlikely, considering that Chris has never physically attacked peers, the way that communities control youth aggression tells us about institutional perceptions of the reasons for aggression.

It is important to identify whether the values of the community encourage and support the development of preventive or punitive attitudes toward children like Chris. For instance, do people generally believe that it is OK to have problems in school and that "the children will grow out of it"? Or, would Chris's problems be viewed as serious and in need of diagnosis and treatment or punishment?

Does the community provide adequate recreational activities, after-school programs, church youth groups, and other endeavors to help build the self-esteem of children like Chris? Does the community recognize the needs for these types of support services for families in which both parents work?

Within the matrix, it is possible to add as many categories as is desired. Under the community category, it would be helpful to identify whether Chris's misbehaviors are consistent across different settings. How is his behavior treated by neighbors and other authorities in the community?

Home-Related Factors for Diagnosis

Some questions concerning diagnosis of the family structure include:

1. Is the family intact?
2. Who is responsible for discipline?
3. Does the student have family responsibilities that help him or her develop self-discipline?
4. Does the parents' work schedule interfere with discipline and completion of homework?
5. Are one or both parents weak and unable to support the school's discipline policies?
6. Is the student's misbehavior related to a power struggle with his or her parents?
7. Do parents need support to help discipline the child at home?
8. Do the parents value conformity in school?
9. Are parents able to effectively communicate their values to the school and the child?
10. Are the parents supporting or undermining school authority?

In the case of Chris, using the above as a checklist, a number of questions are relevant. We have not presented all of the details, but they can be easily generated in terms of hypotheses. For instance, although his current blended family is intact, there is good reason to assume that the divorce impacted his life. It appears that, with both parents working, it is important to determine who does the disciplining and how much help he gets from each parent.

School-Related Factors for Diagnosis

School organizational diagnosis includes questions such as:

1. Is there a clear set of guidelines concerning school rules?
2. Are students and parents aware of consequences for specific misbehaviors?
3. Are guidelines mailed home once a year, sent home with students, and/or discussed in class?
4. Are guidelines followed in an overly legalistic manner that prevents fairness by ignoring individual circumstances?
5. Are guidelines inconsistently followed or ignored by individuals or groups of staff?
6. Do schools have appropriate staff to deal with the consequences of misbehavior (this may include detention personnel)?
7. Does the school have a motivational system to encourage appropriate behavior (this may include incentives such as awards or additional free time)?
8. Does the administration motivate teachers to encourage appropriate behavior among the students?
9. Do students have the opportunity for restitution of the misbehavior rather than punishment?
10. Do teachers understand individual reasons for misbehavior, or do they have an attitude of "The kid is bad and it's the parents' fault"?
11. Does the principal attempt to make school an interesting and rewarding place for students to be?

School and peer group diagnosis includes questions such as (1) What subgroup cultures exist and how does each encourage or discourage misbehavior? (2) Do students perceive teachers as favoring particular subgroups in terms of rule enforcement? (3) Have teachers attempted to use differential motivational techniques to reach various peer groups? (4) Have novel approaches such as peer counseling or peer tutoring been used? and (5) Have students been involved in planning discipline codes or monitoring fairness of administration of rules?

Teacher diagnosis includes questions such as:

1. Are significant numbers of teachers "burned out" and therefore apathetic or overly punitive about misbehavior?
2. Are there systems of rewards or recognition for teachers who motivate students to behave?
3. Are teachers involved in problem solving and planning regarding misbehavior?
4. Do teachers receive adequate information and consultation concerning students who misbehave?
5. Do teachers feel that they are supported by the administration in difficult cases?
6. Are teachers provided with time and encouraged to work with parents on discipline problems?
7. Is parent–teacher communication facilitated or discouraged by other staff such as pupil service workers?
8. Do teachers have adequate supplies of interesting texts and supplementary materials?
9. Are students taught at appropriate grade levels?

Many of these issues are relevant to Chris's problems. For instance, considering Chris's history, has Ms. Jones received adequate information and interpretation of his past problems? Is she using the most effective teaching strategies at the appropriate reading and interest level for Chris? We discuss some of these issues in more detail in the section on treatment and intervention.

Identify Self-Fulfilling Prophecies

School policies and teachers' perceptions may be based on negative stereotypes that feed into self-fulfilling prophesies. Federal laws regarding children with disabilities represent an attempt to counter stereotypes by integrating students into the least restrictive environments and carefully regulating the use of punishments, especially suspensions and expulsions. The regulations requiring least restrictive environment, mainstreaming, and inclusion represent attempts to stop segregating children in easily identifiable special education classes (Kirp, 1973). Desegregation is another attempt to bring people together to combat negative stereotyping and self-fulfilling prophesies.

In the case of Chris, it would be easy to stereotype him as a child with a learning disability or attention deficit disorder. This labeling could influence teachers to lower their academic expectations of Chris. He also could be stereotyped as the child of a blue-collar family that may not value education. Finally, as a child of divorce, he could be labeled as troubled and not easy to help. To avoid self-fulfilling prophesies, Ms. Jones, Chris's teacher, must examine her own attitudes about what these labels mean and how they may affect her instruction. This is not an easy task, but many effective teachers are able to accomplish it.

As a preservice teacher, you could begin by listing all of the labels you use to identify people. Then list common assumptions about those labels, such as "overweight people are jolly" or "jocks are dumb." Then challenge these beliefs by listing the names of people who support them and those who do not, and by doing some research on the topic at the library.

Diagnose the Ecology of the Classroom

Important ecological factors in the classroom include the (1) physical environment, (2) overall climate as determined by student feelings and perceptions, and (3) specific teacher behaviors that encourage student achievement and cooperation.

The Physical Environment.   Given the daily level of activity in a typical classroom, few teachers focus on the specific ecological factors within their surroundings that affect learning and discipline. These factors in the physical environment include all material elements that impact on learning. The following discussion should not be considered definitive, because there are always ecological factors unique to specific locations (Proshansky, Ittelson, & Rivlin, 1970).

The outside weather may initially predispose students' behavior in the classroom. For instance, young children eagerly awaiting the first snow may be quite restless in classrooms when snowflakes begin to appear outside the window. This distraction and the anticipation of playing in the snow may result in restlessness, inattention, and disruption. Hot, muggy weather may make it difficult for students of any age level to concentrate. Furthermore, heat and humidity are known to decrease tolerance for frustration, which may result in aggressive behavior (Baron & Ramsberger, 1978). The temperature in the classroom, especially when it varies significantly from normal levels of comfort, can further exacerbate restlessness, discomfort, and aggression in students.

The day of the week and the time of day are variables that influence students' attention and patience. Although we have identified no research on these variables, teacher experiences, student comments, and observations show differences in student misbehavior when comparing Monday morning with Friday afternoon. In terms of readiness to learn and paying attention, most educators would opt for Monday mornings. However, for some students, the usual pattern may be reversed. For instance, students of divorce who are in difficult custody situations may come to school on Monday agitated and angry after being forced against their will to spend the weekend with a noncustodial parent.

Periods before and after recess, lunch, and special activities may be problematic. For instance, fights on the playground may spill over into the classroom.

Seating arrangement and *available space* per student are important variables affecting student behavior (Perlmutter, 1994). There is ample evidence that overcrowding can cause aggression. Several studies have shown that students with clear visual access to the teacher are more likely to be attentive. Individual characteristics may modify student attentiveness and compliance as a result of seating and available space. For instance, studies of open space indicate that students have differential abilities to block out distractions. An excellent study of seating arrangement by Perlmutter (1994) indicated that a combination of specific seating arrangements and teaching strategies designed to limit distractible stimuli and provide quick accessibility to disruptive students can be effective in reducing misbehavior. He found that favored strategies such as seating distractible students in front of the room or in the back of the room are not very effective. His research indicated that the teacher's goals should be to restrict the student's accessibility to distractible stimuli such as windows, doorways, and other disruptive students, and to increase the teacher's accessibility to distractible students. This may best be achieved by seating the students in the second seats from the front of the end rows of traditional seating arrangements. Other studies have shown that accessibility to distractible students can be facilitated by semicircular seating arrangements with distractible students seated near the front end of the semicircle. Perlmutter (1994) suggests that, when students are seated in clusters or at tables, distractible students should be seated at the front end tables facing toward the middle. He cautions not to pair distractible and disruptive students in any seating arrangements and that serious misbehavior cannot be controlled by seating alone.

The architecture of the classroom, including such factors as dispersion of light and sound and location in the building can affect behavior. Some students find fluorescent lights to be distracting. Furthermore, inadequate lighting in some corners of the room may cause fatigue, which leads to irritability. Unfiltered noise entering the classroom may increase the distractibility of some students. The location of the classroom can impact on a number of factors regarding misbehavior and safety. Some examples include rooms located near (1) extremely busy corridors, (2) gymnasiums, (3) music practice rooms, or (4) exits through which intruders can easily enter.

Classroom Climate. *Classroom climate,* within this context, is the pervasive feeling arising from interpersonal interactions. The climate is determined by teachers' and students' personalities, behaviors, and styles. Classroom climate may be more than the sum of the

TABLE 8.2 Descriptions of Leadership Style

Autocratic	Democratic
Boss	Leader
Command	Invitation
Power	Influence
Pressure	Stimulation
Demanding cooperation	Winning cooperation
Imposing ideas	Selling ideas
Domination	Guidance
Criticism	Encouragement
Faultfinding	Acknowledge achieving
Punishing	Helping
I tell you	Discussion
I decide, you obey	I suggest, you decide

individual parts of the classroom. Table 8.2 indicates a number of dimensions that Dreikurs and Cassel (1972) identified with teachers as a function of democratic versus autocratic teacher leadership, which is a climate dimension we consider highly important in relation to discipline.

These dimensions of democratic versus autocratic classroom climate have been extensively studied and lend support to the concept that good discipline should be based on a classroom climate in which the teacher and students respect each other (Driekers & Cassel, 1972; Kindsvatter & McLaughlin, 1985; Kotzen, 1994; Lunenberg, 1984; McCrosky & Richmond, 1983; O'Hagan & Edmunds, 1983). This dimension of climate can be measured by either student responses, as illustrated by the Hyman A–D Scale presented in Figure 8.1 or by systematic observations of the classroom by using a scale such as Interaction Analysis (Amidon et al., 1985).

To take the Hyman A–D Scale, students respond to each item by indicating whether it occurs always to never by filling in the appropriate number. The score is determined by adding all the response numbers. However, before scoring, note that a number of the items on the questionnaire have asterisks before them. The score for these items must be reversed. To reverse the score, a 1 becomes 5 and 5 becomes 1, 2 becomes 4 and 4 becomes 2. Because 3 is in the middle, it cannot be reversed. These items are reversed to control for student's tendency to answer everything in the same direction.

After administering the scale to the class, the scores for each student are added, and a mean is obtained for the class. The scores can range from a low of 24 to a high of 120. Based on our samples, a mean of about 60 indicates neither a strong authoritarian or democratic classroom. Scores above 68 are authoritarian and scores below 54 are more democratic. Scores above 75 and below 47 are indicators of high authoritarian and high democratic styles. However, norms differ for each school district.

In several studies, we asked teachers to fill out the scale based on (1) how they think they are, (2) how they think the average student in the class will respond, and (3) how they would

FIGURE 8.1   Hyman A–D Scale

Below are twenty-four items that tell how you feel about your class. You also have a scoring sheet with five possible scores for each answer. Answer each item, using the scale below, to show if you believe that the item is true Always (1), Frequently, (2), Occasionally (3), Seldom (4), or Never (5). Please answer all questions using this scale.

1	2	3	4	5
Always	Frequently (almost always)	Occasionally (half and half)	Seldom (almost never)	Never

  1. The teacher is concerned with discipline. _____

  2. The teacher has confidence in the class. _____

*3. The class "picks" on certain kids. _____

  4. Different class members get chances to take some sort of responsibility. _____

  5. In class discussion, a kid's opinion is respected. _____

*6. The teacher's tone of voice is bossy. _____

  7. Everyone gets a chance to talk. _____

  8. Most members are interested in class activities and problems. _____

*9. The teacher makes the decisions for the group. _____

*10. One or two members of the class take over in discussions. _____

*11. The teacher picks on certain individuals more than others. _____

12. Most members feel bad if they let the class down. _____

*13. The teacher does things against the will of the class. _____

*14. Do you have the feeling that you would like to get out of the class? _____

15. The teacher permits us to cooperate with our friends. _____

16. The teacher tries to control rather than guide our activities. _____

17. The teacher tries to get everyone to take part in class activities. _____

18. Most kids are interested in class discussions and seem to enjoy them. _____

*19. The teacher treats certain kids better than the rest. _____

20. The teacher's feelings about many problems are the same as ours. _____

*21. The class is expected to agree with the teacher. _____

22. We express our opinions. _____

23. The teacher seems to enjoy new ideas. _____

24. Sometimes people become "so" involved in a class that they rarely think of themselves at all. The class is all that matters. How often does this happen to you? _____

*Note. Items preceded by an asterisk (*) must be reversed when scoring.

like the average student to think of the class. The scale actually measures four factors: (1) democracy in the classroom; (2) favoritism toward individual students; (3) teacher's bossy, controlling behavior; and (4) students' sense of loyalty and responsibility to class members (Kotzen, 1994).

Diagnosing the overall classroom climate can be very helpful for teachers who are willing to examine their own behavior. It may be especially useful to consider each of the A–D scale items to determine possible areas of change. For instance, a teacher may consider himself or herself treating all students equitably, yet students' responses on the A–D Scale may indicate a high degree of favoritism toward particular students. The teacher must be open to student perceptions and be willing to make changes. This may be accomplished by asking the students directly about what changes need to be made.

More detailed studies of specific climate factors have been conducted. These suggest that teacher leadership can affect climate dimensions, such as:

1. The cohesiveness of the class as a group
2. Students' satisfaction with the class and the teacher
3. The perceived difficulty of the curriculum and class lectures
4. The formality of procedures and norms in the group
5. The sense of goal direction by members of the class
6. The speed and pace of instruction
7. The diversity of curriculum materials and lecture style
8. The levels of cooperation versus competition
9. The friction between students and the teacher
10. The encouragement and acceptance of cliques
11. The level of student apathy
12. The sense of disorganization
13. The feeling of favoritism (Walberg, 1986)

All of these can influence individual and group misbehavior at some level. For example, students can develop a strong sense of group identity and cohesiveness against an arbitrary, demeaning teacher. In this case, cohesiveness can result in class actions to thwart the teacher and to get revenge. Conversely, a supportive, group-oriented teacher can harness group cohesiveness to mutually set and accomplish goals.

Diagnose Teacher Behaviors and Teacher Style

Studies that examine the relation between various teacher behaviors and classroom variables constitute the effective teaching literature. Much of the teacher efficacy literature reports studies of the correlation between specific teacher behaviors and class achievement. Achievement is generally determined by scores on standardized tests. These studies reflect the traditional belief that good teaching and high levels of achievement prevent or minimize misbehavior. This is consistent with the ESA regarding discipline.

There is an extensive literature relating to teacher efficacy (Walberg, 1986). It is assumed that most preservice training programs use texts that cover this material in one or more of their methods courses (Good & Brophy, 1994; Kindsvatter, Wilen, & Ishler, 1992).

We briefly cover those behaviors we think are most directly related to the prevention of misbehavior.

- *Businesslike* and *task-oriented* teachers are well prepared, offer well-organized lessons, make smooth transitions between tasks, and run the class smoothly and efficiently to minimize student free time for disruption.
- Organized, businesslike teachers should (1) be pleasant and polite to students; (2) show respect and genuineness in teacher–student interactions; (3) not be authoritarian, but be vigilant, fair, and consistent disciplinarians.
- High levels of *time on learning* or *engaged time* reflect well-organized lessons in which little time is spent nagging, talking about extraneous subjects, or disciplining (Kounin, 1970).
- *Clarity* in instruction minimizes time spent on discipline as opposed to teacher behaviors such as vagueness, uncertainty, bluffing, and disciplinary threats that generally are not carried out. Vagueness, as a general trait, can establish a disciplinary climate in which students constantly test the limits. Vagueness and inability to admit when you are wrong or do not know the answer will only undermine student trust and respect. If you do not know the answer to a factual question, it is best to initiate a plan to find the facts.

  Teachers whom students rank high on clarity (1) give individual help, (2) provide good explanations, (3) allow students time to think, (4) teach at appropriate speed, and (5) are enthusiastic. They also may have a good sense of humor, which is a very effective tool in diverting misbehavior.

- *Teacher enthusiasm* is rated high by students when teachers consistently (1) express enthusiasm during teaching and in regard to assignments, (2) display a cheerful attitude in the face of adversity, (3) take great pride in their students' achievements, (4) express high regard for their students, (5) have high expectations for students, and (6) are concerned and upset when their students underachieve or misbehave.

  Although enthusiasm is generally desirable to prevent misbehavior, it may not be effective in maintaining discipline with some types of students. One study showed that students of highly enthusiastic teachers were somewhat hyperactive and overstimulated (Brophy & Good, 1986). Although pupils with dull teachers are obviously bored and understimulated, not everyone has the energy or temperament to consistently maintain high levels of enthusiasm. Optimal results require at least a medium level of enthusiasm.

  Research on mentoring of students who achieve despite abysmal home and community conditions tells us about the importance of teachers who both care and enthusiastically show how they care. Students who survive poverty, abuse, and neglect and later achieve in life all say that one person who cared made a difference. Sometimes that one person was a teacher.

  Enthusiasm includes dimensions such as energy, vitality, stimulating presentation, clarity, relaxation, mobility, frequent use of inflection, gestures, eye contact, and expressiveness. One study indicated that students observing an enthusiastic teacher would see frequent (1) rapid, uplifting, varied vocal delivery; (2) dancing, wide-open eyes; (3) demonstrative gestures; (4) varied, dramatic body movements; (5) varied emotive facial expressions; (6) varied vocabulary with lots of adjectives; (7) ready, animated acceptance of ideas and feelings; and (8) high overall energy level. Of course, all of these behaviors require a reasonable energy level, which is often related to health and temperament.

- *Praise* and *positive encouragement* should always be used in teaching, but the amount and quality may vary according to the students (Good & Brophy, 1994). If praise and encouragement are not perceived as being sincere and honest, and if they are offered in a mechanical and repetitive manner, they will not be effective. Also, teacher praise of student behavior may correlate more positively to student attitudes than does student achievement, thereby being very important in preventing misbehavior (Brophy, 1986).

  Teacher criticism of students has received a great deal of attention in the literature (Brophy & Good, 1986; Rosenshine and Furst, 1973). Effective teachers use criticism sparingly, in the form of corrective feedback rather than personally demeaning statements about students. However, low levels of criticism probably do not do a great deal of harm, although they are certainly not necessary (Brophy & Good, 1986).

  Criticism should be delivered in the manner that separates the misbehavior from the student. For instance, it is acceptable for the teacher to say, "Your answer was wrong because you forgot to carry your ones," rather than, "How could you be so stupid as to not carry your ones?"

- *Direct* versus *Indirect teaching style* as it affects student achievement, attitudes, and behavior has been the topic of a great deal of research. These styles may be determined from an objective, systematic, observational instrument, the *Interactional Analysis Observational System* (Amidon, Flanders & Casper, 1985; Flanders, 1960).

  The indirect teacher behavior classifications include (1) accepts student feelings, (2) praises or encourages students, (3) accepts or uses student ideas, and (4) asks students questions. The direct teacher style categories include (5) lectures, (6) gives students direction, and (7) criticizes or justifies authority. In addition to these seven categories of teacher talk, there are two for student talk. These include (8) responds to teacher's solicitation and (9) initiates interaction. The final classification is (10) silence or confusion. We strongly recommend that all teachers periodically study their own classroom behavior, using this scale, by taping sample lessons. The results will indicate their typical methods used to control, direct, motivate and discipline students. The authors provide a manual and training tape (Amidon, Flanders, & Casper, 1985).

  When this scale is paired with the Hyman A–D Scale, teachers have two useful tools to examine their style. Self-examination can be helpful in determining what the teacher is doing to encourage or discourage misbehavior. For instance, whereas in certain classes, high levels of direct teaching and structure may be appropriate, commensurate high levels of criticism and punitiveness are not justified.

- *Questioning* and *probing* are important aspects of classroom discourse that can cause or prevent misbehavior. Overuse of higher-level questions with students who do not have a factual basis for answering can cause embarrassment, resentment, anger, and oppositional behavior. Overuse of low-level questions with bright students can cause boredom, rebellion, and underachievement.

  Preferential teacher characteristics are traits that help to minimize disciplinary problems and are important motivators for resilient (Anthony & Kohler, 1987), at-risk children who seem to rise above debilitating home and community environments and display good behavior and high achievement. Preferred teachers, who are liked by students and whom students tend to respect and obey, are considered by adolescents to be (1) trustworthy, (2) fair, (3) understanding, and (4) showing special interest in students (Galbo, 1984, 1987, 1989). Middle schoolers prefer teachers who convey qualities of caring, empathy, patience, good humor, nonthreatening demeanor, understanding of students' needs, and willingness to become involved with students both in and out of school, and who demonstrate the ability to make learning fun and interesting (Veaco & Brandon, 1986; Veaco & Smith, 1982). Other important qualities are (1) nurturance, (2) sensitivity, (3) respect for students, and (4) ability to treat misbehavior and their own mistakes as learning experiences (Geoghin, 1986; Goffin, 1989).

The classroom is only one part of the system that impacts on school discipline. We now consider school climate as it affects student discipline.

Diagnose the School Climate

Diagnosing the classroom climate is relatively easy within the ESA. Most teachers and administrators are familiar with the dimensions of classrooms that affect misbehavior. However, although most educators have heard of school climate, our experience suggests that few have conducted their own climate studies to improve school discipline. This approach requires a major staff commitment.

School climate includes all the aspects of the environment of a school that may affect learning and discipline. Communities, parents, students, teachers, and even the school building contribute to the climate. Effective discipline is dependent on a healthy school climate. Almost invariably, the principal is the chief determinant of the climate in any school building.

Ask any psychologist, counselor, or itinerant teacher who works in more than one school building about the differences between schools. Sitting in the teacher's room, watching the students at lunch, observing the secretaries, watching students and teachers in the halls, and attending staff meetings all offer valuable clues about the climate of a school as determined by the principal's leadership style.

The best method to diagnose school climate is to develop a questionnaire that is answered anonymously by students, staff, administrators, and even parents. It sounds impossible, but it is not. The process takes time, energy, and commitment. Also, effective change usually takes from three to four years of effort.

Climate assessment is used as the starting point for change and comprehensive improvement of discipline. As questions about discipline surface, they inevitably become embedded in larger issues concerning such dimensions as teacher morale, resources, and communication between teachers, administors, and parents. Successful change occurs only when administrators are committed to using climate assessment to develop a database about how members of the school community feel. When administrators waffle, change projects die.

Staff and consumers must be empowered to develop climate assessment instruments and to cooperatively create new programs. Although climate assessment instruments are available commercially, I believe that the process of self-development of the instrument is crucial. When staff toil over their own climate assessment, they achieve ownership of the problems and the solutions. Therefore, the process is as important as the product.

The following is an outline of the steps needed to complete a diagnostic assessment within the ESA. This method entails the belief that frequent discipline problems can best be understood within the total context of the school.

Problem identification is the first step in developing a climate assessment instrument. This is best done by setting up a steering committee. This may be representative of teachers, administrators, students, and parents, depending on the extensiveness of the project.

Technical assistance is important in terms of learning to write items for a climate assessment questionnaire. Help may be available from a teacher with some background in marketing or questionnaire development a school psychologist, university professor, or another outside consultant to help with the technical aspects. The goal is for several members of the school staff to become proficient in item development so that consultants will not be required for this task if another instrument is needed.

Problem clarification may take several sessions of brainstorming by the steering committee. After possible areas of concern are discussed, members of the steering committee meet with their constituents to confirm that all problem domains have been identified.

Items are then developed to measure the extent of problems in each area. This is where technical help may be necessary to develop a questionnaire that can easily be administered, scored, and interpreted. The questionnaire usually consists of statements to which the respondents can indicate their level of agreement. They are given a range of choice from "strongly agree" to "strongly disagree." Or, they may be asked how important something is by indicating a range from "not very important" to "very important."

The following is a sample of problem areas usually identified by steering committees working initially on school discipline projects. Following each is a sample item to which respondents would indicate some level of agreement.

Discipline.   Teachers begin climate assessment with the concept that they will only be dealing with items related directly to school discipline. However, although discipline items predominate initially, they become proportionate to other concerns as the teachers realize the interconnection between discipline and other aspects of the school climate. Discipline concerns usually regard issues such as consistency of enforcement, administrative support, and adequate punishments other than suspension. In schools that handle children with emotional or learning problems, there is usually less concern with punishment and more with trying to provide for more adequate incentives or rewards to motivate the students to behave better. A sample item is, "Discipline is administered consistently by the principal."

Physical Plant.   At the most basic level, teachers need a safe, clean building that facilitates the teaching process. For instance, I have worked with teachers of very disturbed children in buildings where the intercom system was either nonexistent or did not work most of the time. They had to leave the class or send another pupil when one of their students became highly aggressive. Furthermore, schools need space for in-school suspension rooms, assigned areas for after-school and Saturday detentions, and places for tutoring and counseling students who are having problems. A sample item is, "There is adequate room for student traffic in the hallways."

Physical Resources.   Teachers know that there are limits to resources. But they are concerned that at least minimal levels of resources are available. These include teaching materials, library books, extra staff to help with discipline problems, and availability of texts, pencils, chalk, and paper. Some students and school staff are inevitably concerned about the quality of food in the cafeteria, the adequacy of training of bus drivers to handle disruptions, and the cleanliness of the lavatories. A sample item is, "There are adequate supplies of paper during the school year."

Personnel Resources.   Teachers are very concerned about the availability of nonteaching personnel to help in monitoring halls, playgrounds, lunchrooms, and security. A sample item is, "We need more lunchroom aides."

Financial Resources.   Among important issues involving climate is the problem of teachers' salaries and distribution of monies. This is not unique to teachers; most employees would like higher salaries. However, this factor is related to teacher morale. Low teacher morale may result in apathy and lack of motivation to appropriately discipline children. A sample item is, "Teacher compensation for Saturday detentions is adequate."

Communication.   A major issue affecting school discipline is poor communication among staff. This includes intercommunication and intracommunication patterns involving teachers, administrators, and parents. It is especially problematic when communication between various groups is only in one direction. For instance, difficulty arises when administrators make all important decisions and communicate them downward to teachers while ignoring teacher suggestions. A sample item is, "The principal implements suggestions made by teachers."

Professional Support Services.   Professional support services include school psychologists, counselors, nurses, speech therapists, art teachers, music teachers, etc. Their availability and the nature of their service delivery is very important to teachers. A sample item is, "The school psychologist should spend more time directly helping teachers rather than just testing the children."

Morale.   When teachers construct climate scales, they are always interested in measuring the morale of their peers. In inner city schools, I have found that "burnout" is a big issue. This is most frequently related to feelings of helplessness, hopelessness, and anger at the system. In low income areas, the teachers often construct scales to give to parents to try to determine why the parents aren't more involved in their children's schoolwork. Not surprisingly, parental response most frequently indicates that parents with misbehaving children often feel helpless themselves. They often express the desire that the schools, rather than blaming parents, enter into a cooperative relationship to solve the child's problems.

Under the general category of morale, climate measures usually attempt to assess the type and extent of stress that typical teachers experience.

A sample item is, "I feel that I get no support from the school administration."

Other issues such as grading practices, student assignments, homework policy, and so forth, are measured by individual climate assessment instruments. Each school has its unique issues along with the general ones mentioned.

The construction, administration, scoring, and feedback of results takes about a year. The approach recommended here is intended as the first stage in a three- to four-year project to improve school discipline through the improvement of total school climate. Once the results of the assessment are obtained, the steering committee presents them to school staff and other constituencies. By using an assessment instrument, it is possible to quantify the results in a way that they can be prioritized. Details of this procedure may be provided by a technical expert or any basic book on measurement. Using the results of the survey, staff can determine which areas need the most effort. Among these may be the development of effective discipline policies, which are discussed in the next section. It is important to establish priorities, however, because most schools do not have the personnel and resources to solve every problem immediately.

ESA Treatment/Intervention Techniques

Develop Effective School System Discipline Policies

After the statistical results of the climate assessment instrument are summarized, a report must be developed. This report will be presented to all teaching staff and other targeted groups. These groups might include parents, administrators, or students who completed their own versions of this survey. The report should be in narrative form and easily readable but should also provide statistical data. These data result from finding the average level of agreement or disagreement with the items on the scale.

For example, on the item, "Most students generally respect teachers in our school," respondents are asked how strongly they agree or disagree. Scoring is based on a 5 for strongly agree; 4 for agree; 3, neither agree nor disagree; 2, disagree; and 1, strongly disagree. If the average score on this item is 1.5, it must be assumed that there is either a major problem of lack of respect for teachers or that it is only the teachers' perceptions. If a similar average score emerges from student responses to that item, there is definitely a problem.

In addition to ranking the items from those reflecting the highest indication of problems to the lowest, items can be grouped by area, and the average score for that area can be used to determine priorities. The results of the survey should be given to staff and others at an open meeting in which the steering committee discusses the results. Then staff are asked to prioritize the areas from those needing the most effort to those reflecting the least amount of concern. These discussions are always interesting because some strong-minded staff members always disagree with the results by attacking such factors as the credibility of the steering committee, the instrument, or the consultants who may have helped develop it. However, in the end, we have found that staff always agree with their own quantitative data.

After the prioritization, committees are formed to work in specific areas. These may include such areas as parent–school communication, teacher–administrator communication regarding specific issues, school rules and enforcement, discipline training for aides, and policy and resources for detention and in-school suspension.

Committees are generally formed by the end of the school year and may even begin to meet during the summer. With proper professional consultation and further data collection, they frame the specific nature of the problems they must address and how they will measure them and evaluate results of remediation efforts. The search for solutions includes reviews of the literature, visits to schools with model programs, and brainstorming over a wide range of possible solutions. This may take from three to six months, and sometimes plans do not emerge until the end of the school year. Furthermore, failure is assured if, during this process, the principal or other key administrators do not remain enthusiastic, flexible, and supportive of the processes of problem identification, ongoing program evaluation, staff empowerment, and released time for planning.

Programs to improve school discipline based on the ESA may be drawn from the many models presented in this book. In some cases the models may be accepted in total, and in others it is best to tailor them to the needs of each school. However, true climate assessment is ongoing, and it is assumed that as the climate changes, programs requiring reassessment that will involve organizational renewal.

Students such as Chris may have special needs with regard to discipline. The school discipline policy should focus on providing opportunities for restitution rather than punishment. For instance, it does little good to understand the basis for Chris's agitation and threats to other students, if he is continually suspended for this behavior, which breaks the school rules. It is known that both parents work and his sister is in day care. Therefore, if he is suspended, his parents will be punished also. It might be better to develop a program that allows Chris to "make up" for his angry behavior toward others. For instance, when he calms down, he could apologize or offer to do a good deed for the subject of his aggression.

Improve Classroom Management by Using Techniques Validated in the Effectiveness Literature

We have already briefly reviewed effective teacher behaviors that we believe are most related to good discipline. Here we provide strategies for modifying the classroom environment to prevent problems. Each of the effective teacher behaviors described in the literature must be used in ways that improve discipline within the ecology of the classroom. Techniques such as clarity, enthusiasm, engaged time, and seating arrangements can discourage misbehavior by (1) enriching, (2) impoverishing, (3) restricting, (4) enlarging, (5) rearranging, (6) simplifying, or (7) systematizing the environment. These techniques of intervention are discussed in the next chapter, in which we report on a study of more than 80 programs developed to improve classroom discipline.

In the case of Chris, it is important for the teacher to consider her contribution to his difficulties. It is too easy to blame his background for all of his problems. However, his daydreaming, aggressiveness, motivational problems, and erratic performance could be caused by lack of: teacher enthusiasm or humor, adequate curriculum planning, appropriate instructional level, interesting material, and adequate break times. She might overdo the amount of engaged time and direct instruction, and she might need to determine if she offers the class enough praise and encouragement. A host of other possibilities may be considered from the ESA perspective.

Deal Appropriately with Anger in the Classroom

Ecologists recognize that expressions of anger are inevitable in most group situations and are not necessarily destructive to the ongoing group process. Yet, student or teacher anger and expressions of aggression are probably the most disruptive phenomena in classrooms. Every teacher must learn to recognize and deal with this troubling emotion, which is expressed in many ways.

Anger is a feeling that may lead to actions such as verbal aggression, including sarcasm, name-calling, and putdowns, or to actual physical assault. Anger is not inherently bad. For instance, anger that another student received a higher grade could spur a competitor to study harder for the next test. Although some might not approve of this as a motivator for learning, from the ESA perspective it may be effective as long as the anger is focused on studying harder rather than on some overt act against the competitor.

Any discussion of anger should include definitions of hostility, aggression, and assertion. Hostility is a general response set to specifics in the environment. It can best be described as an attitude that can lead to angry verbal expressions or aggressive outbursts. Hostility easily generalizes, and hostile students are often those who are constantly oppositional, defiant, and ready to explode at the least slight.

Actual aggression consists of an overt attack, which normally involves an attempt to physically assault a person or property. Although aggression involves an attempt to hurt another, assertion is different. Although aggression is usually undesirable, assertiveness can be a valuable personality trait. Assertiveness involves protecting one's own integrity and self-worth and standing up for one's interests.

Discipline problems can actually be created because of teachers' confusion about the nature and appropriateness of aggression versus assertion. Some teachers encourage passive, dependent, and unquestioning behavior rather than assertive behavior on the part of students. This can lead to unnecessary confrontations over classroom power when an assertive student challenges the factual basis of a teacher statement, especially during teacher presentation or interpretation of curricular material. This does not automatically mean that the student is disrespectful. The worst-case scenario is when the teacher confuses the challenge concerning the correctness of the information with a challenge to personal authority. This may lead to confrontations, teacher–student expressions of anger, and resulting disciplinary action by the teacher, which are viewed as unfair and inappropriate by the class. The teacher's response should be to resort to authoritative sources. If the student is correct, he or she should be rewarded for appropriate assertiveness, rather than punished, as if vigorous questioning of the teacher were an aggressive act.

Teachers' anger can create disciplinary problems when it triggers or escalates student anger. Some teachers have difficulty appropriately expressing their anger at students or even admitting that they are angry. Many of my unsuccessful consultations with teachers were related to anger. These failures occurred because the teachers were unable to admit that they were angry at the student or with me. The culture of education suggests that teachers are not supposed to be angry at students and colleagues. They must act "professionally" at all times.

Teachers should avoid expressing their anger at students by such behaviors as yelling, nagging, being sarcastic, scapegoating, using unfair disciplinary practices, or lowering grades for reasons other than academic performance. Unfortunately, some teachers deny their anger to both themselves and others, even though the anger may be quite obvious to their students. Rather than examine their reasons for anger, their denial results in the development of more anger, which leads to a hostile classroom climate.

Teacher anger can be appropriately handled by using such techniques as "I" messages. Rather than angrily yelling at a student who disrupts a class, the teacher can say, "Your talking in class is interrupting my lesson, and if you continue, I am likely to become upset and will then have to take stronger action than just talking!"

Students' transitory expressions of anger do not normally require complicated diagnoses or extensive intervention strategies. Ignoring, using appropriate desist methods, inquiring in a nonthreatening way about the causes of the anger, and using nonsarcastic humor can often defuse it. Interesting lessons and appropriate pace are good methods of preventing frustration, which may cause student anger. However, if the student anger is chronic, more extensive techniques may be needed.

De-Escalate Potentially Explosive Situations

The treatment of violence in psychiatric settings led to the development of de-escalation procedures and therapeutic physical restraint, sometimes called safety mechanics. These techniques are widely used in public school settings that serve children with conduct disorders and severe emotional problems. Full understanding of the history, use, and abuse of these techniques is relevant if you plan to teach highly disturbed students (Crespi, 1990; Kinitzer, 1984; Miller, Walker & Friedman, 1989; Philips & Nasr, 1983; Rosen & DiGiacoma, 1976; Swett, Michaels & Cole, 1989; West, 1994). Yet, proper knowledge and appropriate skills concerning when and how to use therapeutic physical restraint are important elements in the armamentarium of crisis intervention. This is especially true in school buildings and special education facilities that house highly aggressive students.

Two common scenarios are likely to precipitate students' explosive behaviors in the classroom. The first scenario consists of the, "I am the boss and you better do what I say or else" routine. In this scenario, the teacher often makes a reasonable request such as, "sit down . . . get in line . . . hand in your paper . . . stop talking." Because of the student's predisposition at the time, this is all that is needed for an explosion. However, too often, teachers contribute to the escalation of the explosion when the student does not immediately comply. In this variant, the teacher's repeated requests for compliance begin to display increasing annoyance, impatience, and anger as the decibels increase. This then escalates to a threat such as, "If you don't sit down, I will make you sit down," or "get out of my classroom."

The second scenario occurs when the teacher emotionally maltreats a student. This usually involves such disciplinary or "motivational" techniques as sarcasm, name calling, ridicule, and putdowns that humiliate students. If the student already feels humiliated, alienated, defeated, and angry, the stage is set for the blowup. Whatever the cause, once a student explodes, de-escalation techniques should be employed.

Students' violent eruptions do not occur within a vacuum. Students who become violent almost always have histories of emotional deprivation or trauma. These events are related to:

1. Intense feelings of inadequacy
2. Feelings of rejection from significant others
3. Distrust, fear, and anger toward family, school staff, or peers associated with incidents such as teasing, scapegoating, or perceived unfair discipline

4. Agitated depression and suicidal thoughts such as the desire to kill others before killing themselves
5. Alienation from the culture of the school
6. Severe discipline by parents, teachers, or other caregivers that results in anger at all authority figures
7. Physical, psychological, or sexual abuse by caregivers or teachers
8. Lack of limit setting by primary caregivers
9. Frequent disputes with other students
10. Victimization by other students
11. Isolation from peers
12. The triad of fire-setting, cruelty to animals, and bed-wetting
13. Obsession with violent TV
14. Obsession with weapons
15. School failure
16. Violence in the community
17. Fear of loss of face in front of peers
18. Restriction of freedom
19. Failure to accept developmentally appropriate responsibilities such as completing chores or homework
20. Refusal to accept punishment

Some of these could be considered in the case of Chris, because there is adequate evidence that underlying anger is a major issue. An examination of background information may show that his anger has multiple sources. These may include anger at his parents for divorcing, his half-sister who has replaced him as the youngest child, the school for retaining him, the teacher for not allowing him to daydream, and his peers who seem able to attend to school. He also may be angry at himself because of his poor fine-motor skills and his restlessness in class. Each of these issues can be understood within the ESA. We will consider a few treatment suggestions and ask that the reader devise additional strategies.

Chris's anger at his parents' divorce may be somewhat ameliorated through discussion groups for children of divorce. These may be run by the school psychologist or counselor. Curriculum materials related to divorce can be helpful in discussion of common problems. In addition, these materials may be shared with the teacher and parents.

Chris's anger at his sister should be evaluated in terms of the ecology of the household. The teacher can begin this process by having Chris draw a map of his house and showing where he is and what he does during a typical day. It may be that part of Chris's problem is related to his living space. Perhaps the birth of his sister caused him to lose his own room. Maybe he is angry that she is allowed to take his toys or that she wakes him at night.

Perhaps the school should reevaluate their retention policy. Although it is too late for Chris, other children like him could benefit from promotion and additional help. There is convincing evidence that retention is generally not an efficacious technique to improve academic functioning. If Chris is much bigger and stronger than his classmates who are a year younger, perhaps an accelerated summer program and additional tutoring may allow him to catch up with his age-mates.

Daydreaming may be a sign of a generally boring classroom or that the instructional level is inappropriate. If instruction is wrong for Chris, it is probably inadequate for other students like him. Therefore, the teacher should conduct some curriculum-based measures to determine each child's functional level with the various curricula. Although Chris might find the reading quite easy, he might have great difficulty with math. It is possible that the teacher is required to instruct at one level, using cooperative learning and a whole-language approach. If this does not work for children like Chris, the curriculum should be changed.

Chris might benefit from having a study buddy who sits next to him and helps him to concentrate. The teacher would have to allow them to talk when necessary. The teacher might allow Chris to help devise a plan to channel his restlessness. For instance, every half-hour or when needed, Chris could go to the back of the room and stretch. If others complained about his freedom to do this, the teacher could arrange a group activity for all of the "restless" students.

If Chris's fine-motor skills interfere with written assignments and tests, instructional modifications are necessary. Chris could take oral tests, tape-record lectures, and use a computer for written assignments.

All of these are preventive methods for dealing with Chris's anger. When Ms. Jones witnesses Chris's aggressive statements and gestures toward other students, she should deal with the problem immediately. This will include staying calm, moving within close proximity of the situation without invading his space, and nonjudgmentally determining the cause of the situation. This is preferable to emotional reactions on the part of the teacher, who should model rational control of her own emotions. Shouting, threatening, or ordering immediate compliance may only escalate Chris's tendency toward aggression.

Behavioral Cues and Teacher Responses to Prevent Violence

Certain behaviors forewarn the informed about a student's potential for violence. These include:

1. Frequent challenges to authority
2. Sudden emotional withdrawal or psychological numbing
3. Frequent inappropriate facial expressions such as grimaces, smiles, and frowns
4. Excessive daydreaming
5. Restlessness/agitation
6. Overly obedient/constricted affect
7. Bringing weapons to school
8. Sudden lack of interest in or failure to complete schoolwork

Specific cues of an imminent outburst include:

1. Facial expressions of anger
2. Facial flushing
3. Widening or squinting of the eyes

4. Changes in vocal pitch and loudness
5. Clenched fists
6. Pacing, stomping, or other random movements
7. Body posture that appears rigid and/or coiled in readiness for action

Indirect aggression is often a harbinger of later interpersonal attacks. Indirect aggressive acts include:

1. Slamming, smashing, kicking, or throwing inanimate objects
2. Outbursts of crying, screaming, or insulting others
3. Verbal/physical tantrums
4. Excessive demanding, arguing, or complaining
5. Excessive cursing, expressions of anger, criticism
6. Excessive self-deprecation
7. Attempts to provoke others or to control them
8. Frequent challenges to authority

Direct aggression in school includes:

1. Destruction of property
2. Punching, hitting, smacking, shoving of peers or school staff
3. Cruelty to animals such as class pets
4. Throwing objects at peers or school staff
5. Extorting, terrorizing, or holding hostages with use of weapons

Although carrying weapons to school is a serious offense, the motivation should be established. Most weapon carrying is related to fear of assault rather than to intent to victimize someone.

Defusing aggression begins with attention to behavioral cues. For instance, if a student refuses to comply with a teacher request, before escalating the demand, the teacher should carefully assess the student's facial expression, body posture, tone of voice, and other factors that suggest an impending eruption. These data will determine the teacher's course of action.

Remain objective by avoiding the feeling that you must immediately challenge this unacceptable threat to your authority. Do not become preoccupied with losing face in front of the other students. This type of preoccupation is especially true of physical education teachers, who believe that they must not show any weakness in front of their class. To stay objective, force yourself to focus on the student's behavior rather then on how you feel about him or her.

Where is help from other staff if the situation gets out of control? As you begin to deal with the student's screaming, threatening gestures, throwing things, knocking over furniture, and other scary behavior, you must begin to make a plan about the ecology of the situation. Determine whether (1) you will need to immediately call for help; (2) you should send a student to get help; (3) you should tell the rest of the class to leave, and where they should go, and how long they should stay where you send them (you cannot send them to an unsupervised place for very long); and (4) you are strong enough to ward off a direct attack. Note what furniture you can keep between you and the attacker until help arrives.

Keep a safe distance between you and the student. If you are strong enough, stay between the student and the door so that he or she does not run out of the class or out of the school. If the student is too strong, don't get backed into the wall. Very often, after a blowup, the student wants to get out of the situation and, when calmed, will be glad to go to a counselor, psychologist, or other helping person.

Do not threaten punishments until the student calms down. Certainly do not make threats that you cannot enforce on your own such as, "If you try to knock over one more desk, I am going to stop you."

Keep your hands off the student unless he or she attacks you or others. It is better to move away than to try to grab a student unless you are trained in physical restraint techniques. Even then, the last thing you ever want to do is to physically engage an enraged student who may be out of control.

Anger is self-limiting, and therefore your strategy should be to wait it out if possible. To help students calm down, you can:

1. Use silence
2. Offer acceptance and recognition of their anger, frustration, and pain
3. Assure your availability to listen and stay with them
4. Encourage them to tell their side of the story
5. Allow them to relate facts and feelings in their own way, even if it involves profanity
6. Use empathetic/reflective listening
7. Allow and encourage expression of feelings
8. Restate facts and feelings
9. Attempt to clarify statements about the student's perceptions of events
10. Encourage the continued verbiage by giving leads and prompts such as, "Go on, tell me more about it . . . so how did you feel when I said that . . . what upset you most?"
11. Give information

When students are calm enough, you can:

12. Discuss with them the possible consequences of their aggression
13. Talk about alternative actions and consequences
14. Conduct them to a private, quiet, and calming setting

When students erupt, do not:

1. Lose your temper
2. Unrealistically reassure them
3. Make moral judgments of who is right or wrong
4. Disagree with or argue about their perceptions of the event
5. Try to stop, reshape, or control the tone or content of their verbalizations
6. Advise them about what they must do
7. Defend someone else's actions or statements
8. Lecture
9. Disagree with them in any way until they are calm

10. Belittle, denigrate, or ridicule their perceptions or ideas
11. Deny that a problem exists
12. Try to change the topic
13. Require that they justify their actions or feelings
14. Raise your voice
15. Move into their space
16. Menace them by such behaviors as clenched fists, posturing, or glaring
17. Become incensed because of their obscene language

Follow-up is necessary once a student has calmed down and can rationally describe what happened. This is a very important phase and if done properly it can reduce the likelihood of later aggression. The key to success in follow-up is to treat the blowup as an expression of the real problem. It reveals alienation, frustration, and a host of other emotions and life situations with which the student could not cope. At this stage, minimize discussion of the behavior and focus on what triggered the aggression and what can be done to avoid it in the future.

When the student has calmed down, allow him or her to save face. If school rules require a punishment, discuss possible punishments and need for punishment in such situations. Recognize with the student that the punishment probably will not change the conditions that caused the problem, but that society demands that people accept responsibility for their misbehavior. Try to respond to his or her anxieties appropriately, especially with regard to parental responses to the aggression. As soon as possible, talk the situation over with the student's family in a calm way and again focus on the conditions that caused the situation rather than on the immorality of aggression. Finally, remember that "to err is human; to forgive is divine"—anger and aggression are expressions of frustration and pain.

Use Physical Restraint Only When Necessary to Protect from Harm

All teachers have the right to use force when necessary to protect themselves, others, property, or to prevent student self-injury. Even states that do not permit corporal punishment do allow the proper use of reasonable force to control students. Its use is generally confined to special classes, often housed in schools for severely disturbed and violent students. However, it is a good idea for all teachers to have some training in restraint techniques, to minimize the chance of harm to students and themselves if physical force should be necessary.

Teachers who are well trained in de-escalation of violence avoid the use of force because they realize the temptations of overuse. The use of force offers a quick, short-term solution for dealing with aggressive students. This is especially true when injuries can be minimized by use of teams of experienced, well-trained staff.

Competent physical restraint training will include de-escalation techniques and practice in methods such as the baskethold (grasping students from behind in a manner that prevents them from hurting themselves or you), physical takedowns, and releases when students grab you. Training should emphasize:

1. Never try restraint unless you are strong enough
2. Do everything possible before using force
3. Do not use force if you cannot stay calm and think out what you plan to do

4. Be careful in a confined space or on a hard floor if you plan a takedown, because you or the student is more likely to get hurt
5. Calmly warn the child of the consequences if he or she attacks you
6. When possible, attempt blocks and other avoidance techniques, such as keeping furniture between you and the student, before engaging in a baskethold
7. Stay calm and talk to the student as you are holding him and assure him that as soon as he calms down you can release him

If you use physical restraint, you must be well trained because of the possibility of injury to yourself or the student. Rather than describing specific techniques here, we recommend that you seek training from experienced instructors.

Prevent and Interdict Aggression through Specific Programs

Every school should have a plan to deal with aggression. The plan should include all ecological, architectural, and personnel factors that can be used to prevent escalation and control the situation. A typical building contingency plan provides an outline for actions at any point in the building. Every classroom must have an intercom system so that the teacher can call for help. Furthermore, each teacher must have a plan to quickly summon other teachers who are physically capable of controlling a violent student. Acceptable practices must be clearly defined with regard to instructions to class members if a student begins to lose control and appears to be dangerous.

When a student begins to lose control, it may be necessary to request that the class leave the room. How this request is made, where the students go, and who should be notified are all details that should be spelled out in the building plan.

Primary prevention of school aggression includes the development of a supportive but firm climate. This may be accomplished by (1) catching a problematic student being good as often as possible, (2) providing appropriate chores and rules, (3) using humor, (4) being fair, (5) considering mitigating circumstances before reflexively punishing, and (6) imposing relatively consistent consequences while avoiding rigidity.

An essential aspect of primary prevention is discouragement of psychological maltreatment of students by peers and school staff. An informal monitoring of media reports of killings by students suggests that a high but unknown percentage of assailants are students who were frequently derided, scorned, and ridiculed by peers and sometimes by school staff.

Students who are extorted, bullied, and threatened by gangs may bring weapons to school to protect themselves. Vigorous prevention of harassment will reduce the likelihood of fearful students bringing weapons to protect themselves. Unfortunately, in some neighborhoods and on some school buses, the students' trip to school is the most fearful time of the day. Prevention of harassment may require involvement of other community agencies such as law enforcement. Metal detectors, although of questionable value in stopping students who are determined to smuggle weapons into school, may have a general deterrent effect.

Smaller schools are a primary deterrent to violence. When most school staff are familiar with students and their families, they will be able to foresee impending problems. They will recognize immediately when a student is distraught. This will enable them to intervene early by asking the appropriate questions of students, parents, and others to determine the potential for violence. At any early stage in this scenario, they may contact the school psychologist, counselor, or other appropriate resource. This may result in early clinical intervention.

Teachers and curricula that promote nonviolent problem solving will be helpful to prevent later violence. This includes programs such as Myrna Shure's (1992) "I Can Problem Solve" and training in peer counseling and mediation.

Secondary prevention of aggression occurs when an aggressive act appears to be in the making. Historically, at least two movements are related to school-based programs for the amelioration and treatment of both secondary and tertiary prevention of violent episodes. These include the conflict resolution/peer mediation approach applied in group settings and the development of crisis management, control, and restraint techniques discussed in the previous section. The former is based on philosophical beliefs about the nature of human interaction, and the latter is rooted in assumptions about mental illness, but the techniques they use are often identical. These approaches have elements of primary, secondary, and tertiary prevention, because the level of intervention is determined by the skill of the intervener in recognizing predisposers to violence and the severity of the event when the intervener arrives on the scene. We now turn to peer mediation, which became widely popular in the early 1990s.

Peer Mediation

Peer mediation represents a relatively new approach for both primary and secondary prevention of aggression. Contemporary peer mediation and conflict resolution techniques have roots in both hospital-based de-escalation procedures and the "peace and justice" era of the 1960s (Van Slyck & Stern, 1991). During the late 1970s, when the nation focused on the problem of school violence, crisis intervention and de-escalation procedures were introduced in schools. These intervention techniques were widely disseminated among educators who needed to handle disruptive or aggressive students. In the early 1980s the peer mediation movement was aligned with the cooperative education movement and was used in major U.S. cities such as San Francisco and New York (Van Slyck & Stern, 1991).

The peer mediation movement is a logical extension of de-escalation theory and practice. It is based on the concept that students can be taught de-escalation procedures to be used in school settings with peers. It differs from hospital-based programs in that it assumes that conflict is a normal part of life and a potentially positive force to promote personal growth and social change (Benson & Benson, 1993; Schrumpf, Crawford, & Usadel, 1991). Although numerous programs abound, we have chosen to present the techniques developed by Skinner (1995), who frames her approach within the context of cultural diversity.

Skinner selects student mediators by a variety of measures. They may be class leaders who are respected by others, or they may be alienated but influential students who themselves have problems of low self-esteem or impulse control. As part of their training in mediation, they are sensitized to cultural difference. For instance, there may be sex-based differences in interpreting the meaning of argument and debate (Tannen, 1990). Boys may enjoy arguments because they see them as a way of increasing their skills and achieving mastery over another. Girls may feel victimized by debate and verbal conflict. They may feel verbally assaulted and denigrated and therefore avoid such arguments and debates. Inner-city, African American males may see argument and debate as a sign of disrespect and deserving of retaliation. White males from families that stress rational thought and the suppression and avoidance of emotions such as anger may also wish to avoid debates. They may perceive any debate involving personal expression of emotion or emotional issues as superfluous to the resolution of problems.

African American, Italian, and Eastern European cultures encourage spontaneous expressions of emotion, which frequently includes dramatic use of hands and body language (Kochman, 1981). English and Scandinavian cultures tend to value control of the open expression of emotions. These legitimate cultural differences should be recognized and understood by mediators. Therefore, when an argument between two students of opposite backgrounds begins to escalate, cues might be misread, thereby increasing the anger by both parties. Consider an argument between Salim, who comes from Lebanon, and Jim, whose family heritage is British and German:

Salim: Jim, why did you laugh in class when I was reading that part from Romeo and Juliet out loud?

Jim: I don't know. Something was funny.

Salim: What was funny? (Salim wonders if Jim was laughing at him. His voice becomes louder as he uses his hands to help express himself.)

Jim: Listen, I have to get to my next class. I will talk to you later. (Jim begins to get uncomfortable about Salim's raised voice and hand waving.)

Salim: Just tell me what was funny. (Salim now feels he is being ignored. He steps in front of Jim, who has turned to walk away.)

Jim: Why are you waving your fist at me? I told you I don't have time now. Now get out of my way. You better not try anything! (Salim's hand waving and attempt to get Jim's attention was misinterpreted.)

Salim: I am not waving my fist. I just want to know why you laughed.

Jim: I wasn't laughing at you. I was laughing about what those words meant. This is ridiculous. I am not going to stand here and argue about such a silly thing.

Salim: What words were so funny? (Salim will forget the matter if he believes he wasn't insulted.)

Jim: I don't have time for this. (Jim turns to walk away—this action is a direct insult to Salim. It means he is being treated with contempt, when all he asked for were the words that were funny. He would actually like to know what he missed.)

In this situation, Jim's immediate response might have been adequate for someone he knew well or who was not part of a culture in which any possible insult is not treated lightly. Salim, who does not believe in violence, had no intention of becoming aggressive, but he was worried that he did not understand if there was something funny in the text he was reading. However, Jim's initial response made him wonder if Jim were laughing at him. Salim's hand waving and animated body language are typical in his culture, but to Jim they suggest real danger.

Skinner's program sensitizes student mediators to cultural differences such as those just described. She teaches students to be sensitive to the fact that a more spontaneous person might view the other party's lack of expression as an indication of contempt and ridicule. How each group expresses emotions should not be judged as good or bad, just different.

Because peer mediation removes disruption and potential violence from the teacher–administrator–punishment loop, it has great potential for reducing misbehavior in nonclassroom school settings. Furthermore, it may (1) transform alienated leaders into positive role models, (2) promote a win–win approach to dealing with conflict, (3) increase students' and teachers' perceptions of safety in the school, and (4) empower students to feel that they have a stake in how school functions.

Student mediators are trained to use an eight-step model when they see a dispute beginning or in progress.

Step 1 involves informing the disputants that they are welcome to the process of mediation. Although mediators must report crimes, serious threats, or actual abuse, they guarantee confidentiality otherwise. In this stage, they assure that they will listen to both sides, that they are not there to judge who is right or wrong, and that they will help the disputants come to their own solution.

Step 2 is devoted to an explanation, by one mediator or two working as a team, of the process of mediation. Mediators explain that:

1. Each disputant will have the opportunity to express their perceptions of the event.
2. The person first making a complaint will talk first, explaining his or her side.
3. Disputants must wait their turn to talk.
4. Mediators will not judge but merely ask questions to clarify and summarize their third-party, hopefully objective, perception of the situation.
5. When the mediator understands the situation, disputants will be encouraged to question and talk with each other.
6. Disputants will be encouraged, through their new insight into causes of the problem, to come to a compromise solution.
7. Disputants will draw up a contract of agreement regarding the causes and solution to the problem.
8. All three will sign the agreement, and the mediator(s) will contact both parties in a few days to determine if the agreement has been honored.

Step 3 is devoted to an explanation of the ground rules. These include (1) mutual display of respect for each other's right to talk; (2) no interrupting, name-calling, putdowns, threats, or fighting; (3) honesty as to each person's perceptions; (4) an agreed-on dedication to resolving the dispute; and (5) clear statement by each disputant to agreement with the ground rules.

Steps 4 and 5 focus on problem definition. In this phase, the mediators must work as traffic directors to be sure that each disputant feels fairly treated. The skills required are somewhat like those described in the indirect teaching style of the Interaction Analysis Scale. Good mediators help decide which issue will be discussed first. They ask questions, reflect feelings and ideas, restate and summarize information, and direct the parties to work on one issue at a time. If there are discrepancies in information presented, the good mediator skillfully teases out the truth. This is probably the most difficult task at this stage.

Step 6 is the time to begin problem solving. Disputants are encouraged to brainstorm possible solutions. Mediators ask questions such as, "How can this conflict be resolved?" or "What are you each willing to do to resolve this problem?" Mediators do not judge the value of various solutions; however, they can question the disputants when the resolutions do not seem realistic.

Step 7 is devoted to an evaluation of the solutions. Once disputants agree about what to do, they must discuss how realistic the solutions are, and they must agree that the solutions are evenly balanced so no one feels cheated. They must agree to the specifics of who will do what, when, where, and how. They must agree to tell their friends that they have resolved the conflict, and that if this resolution does not work, they will come back for more mediation.

Step 8 involves writing an agreement. The agreement should include a brief description of the conflict, the important issues involved, and the solutions. The disputants should be congratulated for their ability to solve conflicts by discussion, and if possible, they should shake hands, hug, or otherwise acknowledge that they are both to be praised.

Skinner's approach, which is similar in format to most other peer mediation training programs, requires that students use many of the skills employed in de-escalation procedures as described in the previous section.

Support and Encourage Parental Solutions

Few parents, especially when both work, are able to completely control their childrens' social relationships and activities. However, when families work to support each other, especially with help from schools, there is hope. Consider the case of the Lucas family.

Mr. and Mrs. Lucas came to see me about their daughter Lucy, a bright underachiever. Lucy, an attractive, slim fourteen-year-old, had an IQ of 135. Before adolescence, she was an excellent student who was well liked by her teachers. She was always described as being a shy, obedient, and pleasant child. Her parents were working, upper-middle-class professionals. A seventeen-year-old brother was an honor student.

Although both parents recognized the need for control, they tended to avoid the use of punishment. They stressed honesty and open discussion when discipline problems arose. However, as Lucy entered adolescence, she began to "hang out" with a new group of friends who lived in the new neighborhood to which they had moved. It was obvious that they were spending too much time together away from any adult supervision.

The Lucases became worried when Lucy began to lie about completion of her homework, and her grades declined. She began to angrily resist questioning by her teachers and parents. As compared with her former complacent, easygoing, good-natured self, she became edgy, secretive, and resentful. She indicated that she did not want to spend time with school activities or with her family, because she always had plans that involved her friends.

Mrs. Lucas become increasingly suspicious about her daughter's activities and on investigation discovered marijuana paraphernalia and liquor bottles hidden in Lucy's bedroom. On questioning, Lucy admitted smoking and drinking occasionally and stated, "All the cool kids in school smoke and drink. If you don't, kids think you are a nerd."

Not wanting to force an open confrontation, the Lucases began to exercise increasing control over Lucy's time. The struggle for control became more acrimonious as time went by. Lucy constantly complained that "all the other kids' parents let them go out weeknights, and let them go to unsupervised parties at each other's homes."

I suggested that Mr. or Mrs. Lucas call the school counselor. She admitted that smoking and drinking are problems at school, even among some of the "good" students. She had no idea exactly how extensive the problem was, because the school authorities refused to do a survey. They feared that the results might give the school unfavorable publicity, which they did not need. The counselor, of course, could not divulge what she knew about Lucy's friends.

Finally, at my suggestion, and against Lucy's wishes, Mr. Lucas decided to check with her friends' parents. He called them and asked if they would be willing to have a group meeting of the parents of the "gang." All the parents agreed to a meeting. Although all the teenagers were angry at Mr. Lucas and called him a dictator, they attended the meeting for fear that their parents would plot against them. At the meeting it became obvious that all the parents had similar concerns and fears. Yet they wanted their offspring to perceive them as reasonable and not out of step when compared with the other parents. Each adolescent, by claiming that all the other parents were fair, manipulated their parents into believing that they were "old fashioned" and dictatorial if they did not give their kids more freedom.

An additional meeting of the parents and adolescents resulted in more reasonable control over what their children did and when they did it. Although these two meetings did not solve all of the problems, they set the stage for further cooperative efforts between the parents to mediate the effects of the peer pressure.

Influence Legislatures to Change Laws That Perpetuate Misbehavior and Hostility between Role Groups

A comprehensive understanding of the ESA includes a recognition of the "big picture." Laws, regulations, and bureaucracies control the extent and shape of resources that affect misbehavior. We discussed this theme in detail previously. From an ecological perspective, without adequate social policy, it is difficult to imagine a true solution to problems such as violence in the inner cities, sexual harassment in schools, and addiction among adolescents. For instance, there is little question that school violence among adolescents in the inner cities is related to conditions of poverty, racism, and the availability of guns. Sexual harassment among students will continue until adequate education is provided. The maze of sometimes contradictory laws and regulations makes it extremely difficult to help students addicted to drugs or alcohol if they do not enter the legal system and become adjudicated delinquents. In all of these cases, because of limitations of health insurance, unless a student comes from a welfare family, or a reasonably affluent working family, it is unlikely that high-quality psychotherapy and medical treatment will be available for sufficient duration.

In contemporary times, minority and immigrant groups are at risk in a variety of social, political, economic, and educational arenas. The gang wars that accrue from intergroup tensions as a result of struggles between the various ethnic or minority groups reflect our nation's inability to convince the majority of the public that we as a nation will sink or swim together.

Laws requiring least restrictive environment for children with disabilities exemplify an ecological approach. Misbehavior and alienation are minimized by integrating groups of students who were formally subject to rejection, isolation, and teacher self-fulfilling prophesies. This approach has been successful when adequate resources, well-trained personnel, and supportive citizens have worked together.

Educators who have the vision to understand the relationship between individual misbehavior and the system within which it occurs must be willing to approach the problem from a public policy perspective. Although this may be unrealistic for most teachers, it reflects the most effective solution to discipline problems. However, true adherents of the ESA should make it their mission to inform the public about salient issues and must attempt to create viable solutions through political action.

Change Community Attitudes

Community attitudes, customs, and traditions have a great impact on school discipline. For instance, in areas in which high school sports are highly valued, prized athletes may be more indulged than their peers. There is evidence that the climate that values the macho, womanizer image of the athlete actually offers covert acceptance of indiscretions such as sexual harassment and date rapes.

Acceptance of violence between and toward students reflects community values. For instance, data we have presented previously suggest that the use of corporal punishment is more acceptable in southern and rural areas than in other parts of the country (Hyman, 1990a). Stereotypes of significant minority or ethnic groups within communities may lead to acceptance of violence between students who belong to those groups. It is not uncommon for police and school officials to be more lenient toward interpersonal violence among African American students than toward that between students from other groups. This is based on the belief that violence is a "more natural" method of problem solving among some minority groups.

In some communities, fervent and sometimes violent support of professional sports is seen by students as an acceptance of group fighting and brawling at competitive events. When communities tolerate this type of behavior, it is likely that schools will reflect public acceptance of aggressive misbehavior.

Many citizens recognize the need for community values that reflect cooperation, sharing, and nonviolent solutions to problems. Action is often spurred by both religious and nonreligious groups. The Quakers are an example of a group that willingly educates the public in nonviolent methods of rearing and teaching children. No matter what the source, most nonviolent training programs are rooted in beliefs that stress cooperation rather than competition, prevention rather than punishment, encouragement instead of criticism, and acceptance of diversity and individuality rather than conformity. When these values are stressed in the community, schools are given the resources and the moral imperative to develop prevention programs at the school level. Therefore, the ESA includes the use of school/community committees to solve discipline problems that are reflected by negative community values.

Community values may play a role in the case of Chris. For example, because Chris comes from a blue-collar family, community values may suggest that he will be less successful than students coming from higher socioeconomic groups. This prejudice may have contributed to the decision to retain Chris and may have an influence on the quality of his education.

Limit or Shape Perceptions of TV Programs That Promote Aggression as the Solution to Problems

We now have enough research on TV violence to indicate that it does promote and validate aggression and misbehavior (Liebert & Sprafkin, 1988). Yet, despite clear evidence about negative effects of TV, attempts to control portrayals of violence raise constitutional and regulatory issues that generate heated conflicts. As a teacher, you have limited ability to shape children's TV viewing habits. However, you can counteract the negative effects of TV, especially in relation to the encouragement of rule breaking and the promotion of misbehavior, aggression, and violence. Some classroom activities are indicated below. These can be used at all levels of prevention and intervention.

- Teach critical thinking and viewing skills about TV. Because many students now have VCRs, they can easily make copies of material on television. Help students to separate fantasy from reality and to understand that popular TV shows often appeal to our need for excitement, escape, and adventure. The repeated glorification of guns, exotic weapons, inappropriate sex, and impossible karate fights tends to numb students' ability to think critically about these subjects. For instance, they uncritically watch and accept the perception promoted on TV that frequent blows to the face result in little damage. Classroom viewing and critical discussion of these scenes can be effective in showing how ridiculous they really are.
- Creative writing can be developed through an understanding of story plots. Have students analyze the main characters, the themes, and the messages of movies that display violence as the main solution to conflict. After a year of watching kung fu movies and writing about them, some students will begin to ridicule the gratuitous violence. You may not be able to control students' viewing habits, but writing reports on the shows they see will help some to understand about the "vast wasteland."
- *Videotherapy* can be used in the same way that books are used in bibliotherapy. For instance, students whose misbehavior is related to factors such as parental divorce, having a learning problem, or being overweight can benefit from viewing movies that sympathetically depict their problems. Problems such as bullying in class can be dealt with by having the whole class view and discuss movies on that theme. Of course, you will have to preview the movies first to make sure that they are appropriate.
- Comparing movies and books also can be useful. Have some students read the book and then view the movie version of a story. Have class discussions about the quality of each, especially where graphic displays of gratuitous violence are featured.
- Use TV plots and outcomes to teach students social problem solving. Discuss how often they develop unrealistic expectations of life from TV depictions of family life, love, sex, crime, and the problems of young people. For example, TV is loaded with teenybopper movies and sitcoms that often depict adults as morons who are easily deceived, tricked, and manipulated. Some of these actually capture the angst of youth, but most of them have little socially redeeming value. Still, because students are watching them, use them to discuss real-life social problems.

This may be especially helpful in the case of Chris, who is verbally aggressive and tends to daydream. It would certainly be appropriate and helpful to analyze his TV viewing. It is likely that a child like Chris spends too much time watching TV. The content and quantity of TV viewing should be modified if it is determined that this activity contributes to his anger and tendency to withdraw.

Develop a School Safety Plan

Every school should have a *school safety plan.* This plan will be different depending on the community. The purpose of a safety plan is to provide for the protection of both staff and students in the case of a variety of problems. Safety plans should include methods of dealing with problems such as (1) a student's refusal to leave the room at the request of the teacher, (2) student attacks on a teacher, (3) fighting between students, (4) rumors that could ignite fighting, (5) vandalism, (6) stealing, (7) intrusion by strangers, (8) unauthorized presence of suspended students, (9) weapons possession, and (10) alcohol and drug use and distribution. This list is not meant to be inclusive, because local conditions many contribute to unique disciplinary problems.

A full discussion of school safety plans is beyond the scope of this book. Information on the development of such plans may be obtained by the National School Safety Center at Pepperdine College and other special interest groups.

Provide for Diversity

The ESA recognizes the importance of reduction of intergroup tensions as a major way of preventing disciplinary problems. However, we believe that in the foreseeable future, racism, ageism, and economic conflicts between various groups will sorely tax schools' ability to develop harmonious relations between various groups. The core struggle within education is currently over the development of appropriate curricula that value pluralism, recognize the contributions of all racial and ethnic groups, and teach the history, literature, and cultural values of groups other than those from Europe.

Psychological approaches to diversity include the use of sensitivity training, role playing, and the facilitation of communication between groups. Experts in these areas are widely available. Educational approaches include mainstreaming, inclusion, and work–study, which help to integrate children and adolescents with disabilities into a culture predominated by people without emotional, intellectual, physical, or learning disabilities.

Chris might be categorized by some teachers and peers as either a slow learner or a student with a learning disability. Others might consider that he has attention deficit disorder or that he is emotionally disturbed. Students with all of these problems are part of the diverse fabric of public schools. Chris's problem certainly is not severe enough to be considered for a special class placement. However, to minimize behavior problems from children like him, the school should provide adequate counseling for both Chris and his parents. A homework help line might assist children of working parents to do their homework if their parents are not available. The community could support an after-school program in each school building so that children like Chris could get extra help and recreation rather than returning home to watch TV.

Summary

In this second of three chapters on the ESA, we have discussed the diagnosis and remediation of misbehavior from a broad ecological perspective. We have addressed the problem most intensely at the classroom and school levels and touched on aspects of intervention at the community and legislative levels. Next we will examine discipline training models that are rooted in the ESA and consider a final integration and synthesis of the processes taught in 80 widely used texts and programs that propose solutions to the discipline dilemma.

Key Terms

available space
businesslike
clarity
classroom climate
direct teaching style
engaged time
financial resources
indirect teaching style
morale
peer mediation
personnel resources
physical plant
physical resources
physical restraint
positive encouragement
praise
primary prevention

probing
problem identification
professional support services
punishment
questioning
restitution
school safety plan
seating arrangement
secondary prevention
task-oriented
teacher criticism of students
teacher enthusiasm
technical assistance
tertiary prevention
time on learning
videotherapy

Application Activities

1. Using the school climate diagnosis strategies, diagnose your school.

2. Using the classroom climate strategies, diagnose your classroom.

3. Using the ecological problem solving matrix develop primary, secondary, and tertiary interventions for the home, school and community for students who do not do their homework.

4. Develop a lesson plan using Schrumpf et al. (1991) Peer Mediation program.

5. Develop primary, secondary, and tertiary prevention techniques for dealing with aggressive, angry students in the home, school, and community.

Suggested Readings

Baron, R. A., & Richardson, D. R. (1994). *Human aggression* (2nd ed.). New York: Plenum Press.

Dreikurs, R., & Cassel, P. (1972). *Discipline without tears.* New York: Hawthorn.

Goldstein, A. P., & Glick, B., with Reiner, S., Zimmerman, D., & Coultry, T. M. (1987). *Aggression replacement training.* Champaign, IL: Research Press.

Schrumpf, F., Crawford, D., & Usadel, H. C. (1991). *Peer mediation: Conflict resolution in the schools program guide.* Champaign, IL: Research Press.

Schrumpf, F., Crawford, D., & Usadel, H. C. (1991). *Peer mediation: Conflict resolution in the schools student manual.* Champaign, IL: Research Press.

Shapiro, E. S. (Ed.). (1994). School violence miniseries [Special issue]. *School Psychology Review, 23*(2).

Chapter *9*

Ecological/Systems Models and Processes

Chapter Objectives

After reading this chapter, you should know:

1. Kounin's five characteristics of successful classroom management
2. Canter's three characteristics of assertive discipline, three steps of limit setting, and three characteristics of verbal limit setting
3. Hyman's characteristics of authoritarian and democratic classrooms
4. Hunter's eight steps of effective instruction
5. Jones's three cluster skills to develop self-control
6. Duke's six control procedures for systematic management
7. Curwin & Mendler's three dimensions of discipline
8. Glasser's four inborn needs, and three kinds of class meetings
9. The eight categories of the ecological/systems process approach to discipline

Many of the discipline training programs that we have studied are eclectic. Some are actually rooted in ecological/systems theory and are described in the first section of this chapter. Table 9.1, on pages 265–268, offers a summary of programs that fit into this framework.

The second section offers a synthesis of common disciplinary techniques or processes that are advocated across programs, regardless of orientation. This process approach considers all of the ecological and systems factors that may be used to make a good "fit" between schools, teachers, and parents.

TABLE 9.1 Examples of Ecological/Systems Models

Program	Underlying Theory	Assumptions	Diagnosis	Intervention/Remediation	Research
Jacob Kounin's Study of Desists	Kounin's model is based on his many years of research in the area of group management. He emphasized how the handling of the misbehavior of one student affected others.	Mastery of group management techniques (e.g., with-it-ness, overlapping, smoothness) enables a teacher to be free from concern about classroom management problems (Kounin, 1970).	Kounin's approach focuses on the prevention of misbehavior. Thus, teachers need to look at their ability to manage groups, lessons, and the classroom environment.	Kounin outlines specific teacher techniques related to successful classroom management. These include with-it-ness (constantly alert to sights and sounds of the classroom), overlapping (attending to two events at the same time), smoothness (preplanning lessons), and group alerting (calling on students at random).	Kounin's work has been supported and expanded by the research on effective instruction (Brophy, 1983; Evertson, 1989). These findings have been translated into various training materials for teachers (Emmer, Evertson, Sanford, Clements, & Worsham, 1989; Evertson & Harris, 1995).
Lee & Marlene Canter's Assertive Discipline	Assertive discipline is based on the principles of assertiveness training, which evolved from social learning theory research. This behaviorally oriented approach explains how nonassertive personality styles are established, maintained, and treated.	Classroom teachers need to have clear expectations, must insist on correct behavior, and provide consistent follow-through regarding demands. In this model, both teachers and students have specific "rights."	In this model, teachers need to attend to their own needs, identifying those factors (e.g., negative expectations) that may be hindering their confidence and competence necessary to assert their influence and deal more effectively with discipline problems.	Five steps have been delineated: (1) recognizing and removing roadblocks (e.g., negative expectations); (2) practicing assertive response styles; (3) making a discipline plan that contains good rules and clear, effective consequences; (4) teaching the discipline plan to students; and (5) teaching students how to behave responsibly. Canter also notes that praise is the most effective technique that teachers have for encouraging responsible behavior.	The effectiveness of assertive discipline has been hotly debated in the literature (Canter, 1989; Render, Padilla, & Krank, 1989). Advocates feel that it provides for a more efficient use of class time as well as improves the teacher's ability to manage the class more effectively (Mandlebaum et al., 1983; McCormack, 1985). However, critics claim that assertive discipline is too harsh, overpowering for young children, undemocratic, and authoritarian (Charles, 1989; Render Padilla, & Krank, 1989a, 1989b). While the debate continues, assertive discipline has become one of the most popular programs in the country.

Continued

TABLE 9.1 *Continued*

Program	Underlying Theory	Assumptions	Diagnosis	Intervention/Remediation	Research
Hyman's Authoritarian–Democratic Classroom Climate Approach	This approach is based on theory and research on the authoritarian personality and on authoritarian/democratic teaching styles.	Democratic environments foster the development of internal controls. In contrast, external controls are developed in authoritarian settings.	This scale is administered to students anonymously. It offers teachers an objective measure of classroom climate. It allows teachers an opportunity to examine their classroom style on the continuum from democratic to authoritarian. Teachers can also use the scale to indicate: (1) how the teachers perceive their own classroom climate; (2) how teachers think their students will assess their classroom climate; and (3) how teachers would like students to perceive the classroom climate.	Although this scale does not offer any specific program for remediation, teachers can use scale items to assess student perceptions of their teaching style. Teachers can use the data obtained to change to a more democratic approach. They can readminister the test to assess their progress toward a more democratic approach.	Research by Hyman (1964) demonstrated that when teachers left the classroom for 45 minutes, students from authoritarian classes became out of control, whereas students from democratic classes maintained order as if the teacher were present. This supports the concept of internal or external controls in the classroom. In addition, Hyman & Lambert (1987) discovered that teachers' expectations of their classroom climate were generally consistent with their students' evaluations. It further showed that teachers who viewed themselves as authoritarian did not think they were as authoritarian as they would like to be.
Hunter's Instructional Theory into Practice	This theory is based on two decades of analyzing educational research and specifying the instructional skills characteristic of effective teachers.	Hunter's work led to the finding that effective educators need skills in seven basic areas: (1) content, (2) materials, (3) planning, (4) classroom management (5) human relations, (6) human growth, and development, and (7) instructional methods. As a result, effective instruction automatically reduces misbehavior.	Teachers' abilities to use these skills are noted through observations by a trained "coach" (e.g., school principal, supervisor, etc.). Meetings are held between teacher and coach to discuss what happened during the lesson and examine the teacher's reasoning in decisions related to instruction.	Intervention involves modification and monitoring of lessons, lesson plans, and student progress.	Even though there is agreement that the strategies described by Hunter are important ingredients in effective instruction (Goodlad, 1984; Jones & Jones, 1990), there are few studies evaluating the effects of the Hunter Model on student achievement (Donovan, Sousa, & Walberg, 1987; Mandeville & Rivers, 1991). Those that do exist have yielded mixed results.

TABLE 9.1 *Continued*

Program	Underlying Theory	Assumptions	Diagnosis	Intervention/Remediation	Research
Fredric Jones's Approach to Discipline	The main focus of this model is helping students develop self-control. It is based on thousands of hours of controlled classroom observations during the 1970s.	Classroom discipline problems are not as negative as they are depicted in the media and perceived by the public. Also, Jones found that teachers are frustrated in their efforts to manage classrooms. Furthermore, many teachers are unhappy because they have been inadequately trained in effective classroom management techniques.	Diagnosis involves identifying those teacher behaviors ineffective in dealing with classroom behavior. Jones notes that through training, most of the more effective approaches are teachable. However, they must be practiced, perfected, and added incrementally.	Jones identifies three clusters of skills that help to prevent misbehavior and help to deal with misbehavior when it occurs: (1) using body language to set and enforce limits, (2) using formal and informal incentives, and (3) providing efficient help to students.	Although there is no disagreement as to the importance of Jones's skills clusters in creating an effective classroom environment, no empirical data were found assessing the effectiveness of teachers' implementation of this model.
Duke's Systematic Management Plan for School Discipline	This theory is based on organizational development, encompassing the entire school system.	Discipline is a school-wide issue as opposed to just an individual classroom concern.	This approach involves the use of a questionnaire to ascertain the needs of the schools. Duke also advocated for the observation of the school, students, and teachers, along with interviews and evaluation of existing discipline data.	Duke outlines six control procedures useful for behavior problems: (1) problem avoidance; (2) problem acceptance; (3) problem compensation; (4) problem prevention, including rules, sanctions, and rewards; (5) problem intervention, including directive communication, behavior modification, and parent involvement; and (6) problem management.	Empirical validation for Duke's model is extremely difficult to obtain because it borrows from so many other discipline programs (e.g., Reality Therapy, Teacher Effectiveness Training, etc.).

Continued

TABLE 9.1   *Continued*

Program	Underlying Theory	Assumptions	Diagnosis	Intervention/ Remediation	Research
Curwin & Mendler's 3-D Discipline	This model is based on an integration of many discipline approaches. It helps teachers take charge of interpersonal conflicts within the classroom.	Educators can prevent behavioral problems by acknowledging that they will occur and by providing behavioral, interpersonal, and anxiety management skills.	This involves the identification and acceptance of behavioral problems, as well as acknowledgment that they will occur.	Curwin & Mendler (1988) describe three dimensions to discipline: (1) prevention (including the provisions of structure, direction, and flexibility), (2) action (implementing consequences, and monitoring and modifying the class's social contract), and (3) resolution (establishing individual contracts when the social contract fails to work).	No independent studies on 3-D discipline were found in the literature. However, a study by Curwin & Mendler in 1980–1981 found 3-D discipline to significantly reduce teacher stress and anxiety in the classroom.
William Glasser's Reality Therapy	Glasser was first recognized for his theory of reality therapy. Currently, he has applied control theory to the classroom. This approach rejects the traditional stimulus–response theory and contends that schools can and should be restructured to meet students' needs.	Discipline problems will be minimal, and quality schoolwork will occur when schools restructure to meet students' inborn needs (e.g., survival, belonging, power, freedom, and fun).	This involves identifying students' unmet needs and restructuring the environment in an effort to meet these needs.	Glasser advocates the use of class meetings, which should focus on problem identification and solutions. He also recommends that schools move from the traditional classroom structure toward small learning teams.	Extensive research has yielded mixed results. For example, some studies have demonstrated more positive attitudes toward schools, improved grades, and reduced anxiety (Cady, 1983; Houton & Slowik, 1982). In contrast, a number of studies found no gains in general student achievement or attitudes (Lynch, 1975; Welch & Dolly, 1980). Glasser claims that, in general, much of the research is invalid because it is not based on schools where teachers have been properly trained in his method (personal communication, 1995).

Jacob Kounin's Studies of Desists

Jacob Kounin is best known for his seminal work *Discipline and Group Management in Classrooms* (1970), which reflects extensive analysis of classroom videotapes. Kounin was interested in group management. He emphasized how handling the misbehavior of one student affected others. This effect on the group was known as the ripple effect.

From studies of the ripple effect came research on disciplinary and group management techniques (Anderson, Evertson, & Brophy, 1979; Borg & Ascione, 1982; Brophy, 1983; Brophy & Evertson, 1976; Brophy & Good, 1986; Good & Grouws, 1977; Walberg, 1986). From an analysis of the videotapes made in eighty different classrooms, Kounin discovered several dimensions of group management that promoted student involvement and reduced misbehavior (Chance, 1985).

After recognizing the universality of ripple effects, Kounin addressed the subject of desists and the manner in which they are issued. A desist is a teacher's attempt to stop a misbehavior. Effective desists include (1) clarity, which occurs when the teacher names the perpetrator, specifies the misbehavior, and lists the reasons for the desist; (2) firmness ("I mean it"), which is conveyed through voice projection and follow-through until the child stops the misbehavior; and (3) toughness, which is communicated when the teacher uses anger, threats, physical handling, and punishment. Although the latter offer short-term effectiveness, overdependence on them, especially if mean spirited, has long-term negative consequences.

Effective discipline may require a balance between teacher type, the teacher–class relationship, and the quality and potency of the desists (Chance, 1985). Effective classroom managers manifest high levels of "with-it-ness" and skills such as overlapping, smoothness, momentum, and group alerting.

A teacher possessing *with-it-ness* is constantly alert to the sights and sounds in the classroom. Student seating is arranged for maximum visibility. Whether attending to an individual or to a small group of students, the teacher always can scan the classroom. On detection, the teacher immediately acknowledges misbehavior.

Overlapping is the skill of attending to two events simultaneously. This enables the teacher to continue one activity while dealing with something else at the same time.

Teachers who handle extraneous matters and prepare the lesson ahead of time display *smoothness*. Once students are absorbed in their work, these teachers do not distract them. They leave the children alone and assist them individually, when needed.

Good *momentum* occurs when the teacher keeps the lesson moving, does not dwell on minor or understood portions of the lesson, and corrects students without nagging or interrupting the lesson. Students move from one activity to the next without having to wait for each other on each subpart of a transition. For instance, saying, "Everybody put your pencils away" is better than, "Row one, put your books away; now row two, put them away," and so forth. Overdwelling, or nagging students rapidly becomes useless as a desist technique.

Group alerting occurs when the teacher randomly calls on students and raises interest levels by making comments such as, "Now this is a difficult one." This includes evoking group choral recitation rather than individual responses, physically moving around the room, and requiring students to demonstrate their work products.

The strength of Kounin's approach is its focus on the prevention of spread of misbehavior. Many of today's discipline approaches incorporate and extend Kounin's suggestions for maintaining a good learning environment (Emmer & Evertson, 1981). Some teachers believe that Kounin's suggestions focus too much on control and do not emphasize prevention and correction. Behaviorists would criticize him in terms of his belief that you must immediately attend to all misbehaviors rather than ignore them. He offers no specific suggestions for corrective discipline or how misbehavior should be suppressed and redirected in more positive ways (Charles, 1989, p. 37).

Kounin's work has been supported and expanded by the research on effective instruction in both elementary (Emmer, Evertson, & Anderson, 1980) and secondary schools (Evertson & Emmer, 1982; Sanford & Evertson, 1981) and translated into training materials for teachers (Emmer, Evertson, Sanford et al., 1989; Evertson, Emmer, Clements, Sanford, & Worsham, 1989). These materials focus on establishing rules and procedures at the beginning of the school year. Teachers, whose students consistently gained in achievement, organized classrooms in a businesslike manner. Their characteristics include (1) rules and procedures that are carefully planned, (2) rules and procedures that are systematically inculcated in class, (3) both active and passive monitoring of student work and behavior, (4) instruction organized to maximize student task engagement and success, and (5) directions and expectations that are clearly communicated, reducing complex tasks to essential steps (Harris, 1991). Experimental studies of this approach indicate that teachers with these skills have more students who are on-task, who complete assignments, who are successful in class lessons, and who achieve academically (Evertson, 1985, 1989).

Lee and Marlene Canter's Assertive Discipline

One of the most popular discipline programs in the 1980s and early 1990s was developed by Lee and Marlene Canter (1976), who spent seven years observing master teachers. Assertive Discipline is based on the concepts developed in assertiveness training. This behaviorally oriented approach explains how nonassertive personality styles are established, maintained, and can be treated. Lack of assertiveness is primarily attributable to anxiety and lack of appropriate interpersonal skills (Kearney, 1988).

Assertive discipline posits that effective teachers need to have clear expectations, must insist on correct behavior, and provide consistent follow-through regarding demands. They also must provide warmth and support. Backing their requests with appropriate action, teachers are able to exhibit the confidence and competence necessary to assert their influence and deal more effectively with discipline problems.

Teachers have the right to (1) establish a classroom structure and routine that, within the confines of their own strengths and weaknesses, provides an optimal learning environment; (2) request appropriate behavior that meets the teacher's needs and encourages the positive social and educational development of students; and (3) ask help from parents and administrators.

Assertive discipline involves (1) recognizing and removing roadblocks to assertive teacher behavior and replacing of their own negative expectations of students with positive expectations; and (2) practicing assertive response styles. Teachers must make their expectations known to students by backing their words with actions. Students should receive positive benefits from compliance. Noncompliance should result in consequences that are related to the misbehavior.

Nonassertive or hostile response styles need to be eliminated. Teachers must learn to set limits. Canter states, "No matter what the activity, in order to be assertive, you need to be aware of what behaviors you want and need from students" (1976, p. 65). Steps in limit setting include (1) identifying specific behaviors that are expected from students, (2) making these behaviors explicit, and (3) following through for both compliance and noncompliance.

Verbal limit setting involves (1) requesting appropriate behavior by use of hints (reminders), such as *"I" messages* (telling students how behavior is affecting the teacher), questions, and demands; (2) delivering the verbal limit through the use of eye contact, tone of voice, gestures (e.g., facial expressions), use of students' name, and physical touch (light hand placement on the shoulder); (3) using the *broken record* technique, repeating the original message (this is especially effective when students seek to divert teachers from their intended message); and (4) following through on limit setting.

Appropriate follow-through for limit setting includes (1) making promises rather than threats; (2) selecting appropriate consequences in advance; (3) setting up a system of consequences that can easily be enforced, such as putting a student's name on the blackboard with the threat that an accumulation of a specific number of check marks for each misbehavior will result in suspension; (4) practicing verbal confrontations that call for follow-through; and (5) implementing a system of positive consequences. Positive consequences include attention from the teacher, complimentary notes about students to their parents, special awards such as certificates for achievement, special privileges such as taking care of the classroom pet, material rewards such as stickers and posters, rewards given by parents such as extra TV time, and rewards for the entire class for good behavior.

Advocates of Canter's assertive discipline believe that it more efficiently uses class time by effectively stopping misbehavior while instruction continues. In addition, assertive discipline promotes a single system of rules, rewards, and punishments that can be used for all age levels and all kinds of students. Teachers like its overall ease of implementation, its insistence on respecting teachers' and students' rights in the classroom, its emphasis on caring enough about students to limit their self-defeating behavior, and its insistence on support from administrators and parents (Ford, 1984). Further, Wolfgang and Glickman (1986) add that teachers can be confident and efficient with discipline, because assertive discipline offers a set program to follow.

Canter and Canter (1992) recently updated their widely used text to incorporate many principles that may be considered anathema to their many former adherents. In an about-face from previous thinking, and in concordance with more democratic approaches such as Adlerian-based programs (Albert, 1989) and approaches that use classroom problem solving (Glasser, 1985), the Canters now recommend greater student input for establishing rules.

Despite its widespread use, critics claim that Canter's assertive discipline is too harsh, militant, and overpowering for young children, and too demeaning to older students (Charles, 1985). It is accused of being undemocratic and authoritarian and suppressing negative behavior to the exclusion of building values for positive, responsible behavior. Thereby, it releases the student from personal responsibility and rational decision making, and it is really a version of behavior modification and take-charge teacher firmness with rules and consequences (McDaniel, 1989; Rich, 1985; Wolfgang & Glickman, 1980).

Because assertive discipline is so widely used and aggressively marketed, there have been heated debates about its effectiveness. The evidence supporting assertive discipline is not very convincing, although the number of studies exceed those on most other approaches in the ESA (Mandlebaum et al., 1983; McCormack, 1985; Render, Padilla & Krank, 1989a, 1989b; Rich, 1985; Smith, 1983). As with other efficacy research, most of the claims are based on outcome measures of teachers' perceptions rather than their actual classroom behavior or student behavior.

The debate will probably continue, and the Canters will probably periodically update their program as they incorporate many aspects of other contemporary approaches. Assertive discipline will persevere to enjoy widespread use because more than 600,000 people have already been trained in the technique, according to its authors (Canter, 1989). In our opinion, assertive discipline includes such a variety of ecological approaches that some elements of the program will always work in some situations. We are not convinced by the current research that this approach is necessarily superior to others in the ESA.

Hyman's Authoritarian–Democratic Classroom Climate Approach

In 1964, I arranged an experiment with a large number of fifth-grade classes for which I developed the Hyman A–D Scale, discussed in Chapter 8. This scale measures classroom climate along an authoritarian/democratic continuum. External controls, which are developed in *authoritarian* classrooms, depend on fear of punishment as the major deterrent to misbehavior. Authoritarian teachers emphasize competition, the assertion of power, and obedience. *Democratic* classrooms are those in which students have developed internal controls. Teachers in these classrooms emphasize cooperation, mutual goal setting, and shared responsibility. Students behave because they do not want to infringe on the rights of others.

Through the use of the Hyman A–D Scale, we identified authoritarian and democratic fifth-grade teachers. After measuring authoritarian and democratic climate through the student-administered scale, teachers were told by their administrators, without prior knowledge of this request, to leave their classrooms. They remained absent for forty-five minutes. The climate of the authoritarian classrooms deteriorated into complete chaos after the first thirty minutes. The students went crazy. Their model for control was punishment by an external authority—the teacher. It was interesting to note the progression, in the authoritarian classes, as time passed. As students became more confident of the teacher's absence, they became more unruly. In the democratic classes, you would not have known the teacher was missing. These children had internalized the values of their classroom. The students of the democratic classes functioned as though the teachers were present.

This experiment clearly demonstrates the difference between internal and external controls. Both types of classrooms provide structure and rules. Yet the democratic class gives the students a feeling that they have a "stake" in how the class functions. An ethos of fairness is clearly evident. Structure may be maintained without the use of punitive methods. Firm, consistent, and fair teachers do not have to be "mean." Providing structure and an orderly learning environment is consistent with democratic principles.

In another study, the scale was offered as part of an article in a magazine for teachers (Hyman & Lamberth, 1987). In this study, teachers were asked to fill out the scale as they thought their classes would, so that we could compare the teachers' perceptions of their style with those of their students. In total, this scale was administered to sixty separate classes with 1,834 students. Ninety-two percent of the teachers taught fifth to eighth grade, and represented twenty-one states and Canada. Forty-seven percent were from California, Illinois, Maryland, Texas, and Wisconsin.

For the most part, the teachers' expectations were consistent with their students' evaluations of their classroom climate. In general, these scores were in the high end of the authoritarian range. The teachers perceived an ideal classroom climate as being even more authoritarian than it already was. This is interesting because the respondents, who were quite authoritarian, apparently believed that they were not adequately in control. However, most respondents did indicate that their effectiveness as disciplinarians was above average.

This project was interesting for a number of reasons. It provided teachers with an opportunity to examine their classroom style without having to worry about administrative judgments. Most of the teachers who responded viewed themselves as authoritarian, but they did not think they were as authoritarian as they would like to be. Because a hallmark of authoritarianism is punitiveness, it may be that they thought they were not tough enough. These results suggest that, like many people, the respondents equate punishment with discipline. However, punishment is only one technique used to maintain discipline, and most research indicates that it is ultimately the least effective approach.

The Authoritarian–Democratic classroom climate scale can be used for initial diagnosis of the classroom climate. However, because there is no standard remediation program, teachers can examine test results and determine exactly which items on the scale suggest changes in classroom leadership style. Then the scale can be administered at a later time to determine if students perceived actual teacher changes. Unfortunately, there is little reason to believe that most authoritarian teachers might want to change their style so that students will behave when they leave the room or are away from authority figures.

Hunter's Instructional Theory into Practice (ITIP)

Madeline Hunter and her associates spent about twenty years analyzing educational research and specifying the instructional skills characteristic of effective teachers. They maintain that effective educators need skills in content, materials, planning classroom management, human relations, human growth and development, and instructional methods. Although Hunter acknowledges the importance of all of these areas, her theory focuses primarily on the elements of effective instruction.

Effective instruction, which automatically reduces misbehavior, includes teaching to an objective, selecting an objective at the correct level of difficulty, monitoring and adjusting instruction, and employing principles of learning. They may be incorporated into almost any lesson by:

1. Establishing an anticipatory set (e.g., focus the students' attention, develop readiness for instruction)
2. Stating the objective and its purpose

3. Maintaining the appropriate active, direct instructional input
4. Modeling correct responses
5. Monitoring students to check for understanding
6. Guiding practice around the facts, learning, and thinking involved in the lesson
7. Having students summarize by stating or writing what they have learned from the lesson
8. Planning for independent practice such as seatwork, homework, or project work

Students respond to this format by high rates of on-task behavior (Jones & Jones, 1990). However, there is a lack of convincing evidence for improvement in academic performance of classrooms which adhere to the model.

The strengths of Hunter's program lie in its clarity, utility, systematic approach to lesson preparation, and monitoring of student progress (Freer & Dawson, 1987; Jones & Jones, 1990). Problems lie in implementation, because it may be too rigidly applied, and coaching of teachers may not be consistent enough over time (Mandeville & Rivers, 1991). Furthermore, the approach is overly mechanistic and leaves little room for creativity (Gibboney, 1987a, 1987b). Slavin (1987), a proponent of cooperative education, claims that Hunter's model is nothing more than traditional instruction, which most teachers use anyway. Research on effectiveness is inconclusive (Mandeville & Rivers, 1991; Donovan, Sousa & Walberg, 1987)

Frederic Jones's Approach to Discipline

Frederic Jones emphasizes helping students to develop self-control (Jones, 1987). Jones's approach is based on extensive classroom observations during the 1970s.

Jones claims that classroom discipline problems differ from their depictions in the media and as perceived in the minds of the public. He did not find the kind of hostility and negative behaviors that many people believe exist in the schools. He found a great deal of "massive time wasting," which included students talking, goofing off, and walking around the classroom without permission. Fifty percent of available teaching time is spent disciplining students.

Many teachers are unhappy because they were inadequately trained in effective classroom management techniques. As a result, they use hostile and punitive control techniques. Jones identified three clusters of skills that helped to prevent and deal with misbehavior. These involve the use of body language, incentive systems, and efficient instructional and management techniques.

Jones maintains that approximately 90 percent of good discipline depends on effective body language. Therefore, his training program concentrates on helping teachers learn to use physical mannerisms to set and enforce limits. This involves eye contact, physical proximity, body carriage (e.g., good posture), facial expressions, and gestures. Effective body language communicates that the teacher is calmly in control, knows what is going on, and means business (Charles, 1989).

"An incentive system is a coherent program for generating work based on the systematic delivery of reinforcers" (Jones, 1987, p. 145). Jones describes formal and informal incentives.

Formal contractual incentives/rewards, such as paychecks, are explicit, negotiated, and mutually acceptable. Informal incentives govern almost all of our responsible, appropriate, adult behavior. These are based on implied agreements that we follow simply because they involve doing the right thing.

The third cluster of skills involves the providing of efficient help. Teachers who organize the class so that students are within easy reach, use graphic reminders, such as models or charts, that provide clear examples and instructions, minimize individual help and give students straightforward instructions and answers.

Through his approach, Jones has been able to isolate those behaviors seen in teachers who have established an effective system of discipline. He also has found that, through training, most of these behaviors are teachable. However, it is unrealistic to think that someone could read Jones's work, walk into the classroom, and immediately transform it into a highly efficient environment. The skills he describes must be practiced, perfected, and added incrementally.

Similar to Hunter's approach, there is no disagreement as to the importance of Jones's skill clusters for an effective classroom environment. However, no empirical data have been found assessing the effectiveness of teachers' implementing this approach.

Duke's Systematic Management Plan for School Discipline

Daniel Duke's Systematic Management Plan for School Discipline (SMPSD) is based on organizational development (Duke, 1980). It uses a questionnaire to ascertain the discipline needs of the school. Problems areas include (1) attendance, (2) truancy and class cutting involving criminal and noncriminal behavior, and (3) classroom misbehavior.

Six control procedures include (1) problem avoidance; (2) problem acceptance, relating to the school's ability to enforce certain rules and coping with the problems that may arise; (3) problem compensation, providing assistance to victimized students or teachers; (4) problem prevention, including rules, sanctions, rewards, and curriculum adaptation; (5) problem intervention, including control procedures such as directive and nondirective communication, behavior modification, problem referral, and parental involvement; and (6) problem management, which Duke claims is most effective.

Problem management and control strategies include special personnel, team troubleshooting, data collection, conflict resolution mechanisms, decentralized authority, smaller organizational units, and environmental redesign.

Implementation of SMPSD begins with the use of a needs survey developed by Duke. He also advocates observation of the school, students, and teachers, along with interviews and evaluation of existing discipline data. The second phase involves development and implementation of the plan, based on school needs and the goals of SMPSD. The final phase requires a periodic review and revision of the SMPSD program once it is implemented.

In discussing his Systematic Management Plan for School Discipline, Duke acknowledges that no one method, including his own, is best. Certain schools may need to borrow from several discipline programs. One strength of his program is that it incorporates some of the best attributes of existing programs, such as Reality Therapy, Teacher Effectiveness Training, Ginott's model, and Dreikurs's Logical Consequences Model. In addition, the program calls for reorganization or restructuring of schools to promote effective discipline. Furthermore, this approach opens communication lines and increases human relations activities (e.g., involvement of parents and the community) throughout the school system (Chance, 1985, p. 127).

A limitation of the Systematic Management Plan for School Discipline is that, as a schoolwide program, it is very difficult to get all staff and faculty members to do anything in the same manner. In addition, borrowing techniques and strategies from so many different models of discipline makes it extremely difficult to obtain any type of empirical validation for the program.

Curwin and Mendler's 3-D Discipline

Curwin and Mendler's approach, an amalgamation of many discipline techniques, emphasizes teachers taking charge of interpersonal conflicts in classrooms. Teachers must recognize that problems will occur. They must develop skills in behavioral, interpersonal, and anxiety management (Curwin & Mendler, 1988). The three dimensions (3-D) include prevention, action, and resolution.

The first dimension of 3-D discipline establishes an environment in which discipline problems are *prevented*. Important components of this dimension include providing structure and direction, as well as demonstrating flexibility. Cognitive, behavioral, and affective elements are blended in an effort to facilitate awareness. The seven stages of prevention comprise (1) increasing teacher self-awareness, (2) increasing student awareness, (3) expressing genuine feelings, (4) discovering and recognizing alternatives or other models of discipline, (5) motivating students to learn, (6) establishing social contracts with the class, and (7) implementing social contracts.

Curwin and Mendler emphasize that teachers must learn to deal with the stress associated with disruptive students. They believe that by practicing stress reduction activities before problems are encountered, teachers will be more effective in dealing with future conflicts.

Action, the second dimension, implements consequences for violating the social contract and active monitoring and modifying of the class's social contract. When discipline problems occur, the teacher should (1) choose the most appropriate consequence for violation of each rule, (2) implement the consequence, (3) collect data on effective and noneffective alternatives, and (4) avoid power struggles.

Resolution is used to reach out-of-control students. These students, who cannot comply with the social contract, require individual contracts. Individual contracts are needed when students (1) do not accept consequences established in the social contract, (2) chronically violate rules and disrupt the class, and (3) repeatedly refuse to follow specific rules of the social contract.

In these situations, teachers should (1) discuss preventive procedures with the student, (2) develop a mutually agreeable plan, (3) monitor the plan and revise it if necessary, and (4) use creative approaches. Teachers who have taken preventive measures and have consistently applied consequences to rule-breaking have little need for individual contracts.

Similar to the other discipline "systems," Richard Curwin and Allen Mendler's 3-D discipline offers a strong preventive element. In addition, it is structured, yet flexible, and it takes into account feelings and ideas of both teachers and students. Furthermore, 3-D discipline provides strategies and techniques from many different discipline models. However, encompassing a variety of theories and approaches can make 3-D discipline a difficult "system" to implement. Teachers need to understand many discipline models. Also, the eclectic approach makes Curwin and Mendler's discipline dimensions more difficult to evaluate. It is not clear how effective this approach may be with the more severely oppositional and defiant students who may refuse both social and individual contracts.

A literature search of Curwin and Mendler's approach yielded only one effectiveness study. This was a teacher outcome study conducted by Curwin and Mendler in 1980 to 1981 and cited in their book, *Discipline With Dignity* (1988). Inner-city elementary school teachers in upstate New York were provided with a five session, ten-hour 3-D discipline program. Results suggested that it significantly reduced anxiety felt by teachers at the end of the school day. Stress was reduced in managing disruptive behavior, supervising behavior outside of the classroom, being the target of verbal abuse, maintaining self-control when angry, being threatened with personal injury, and having personal property stolen or destroyed. This was not an outcome study of actual improvement in student behavior, and because it was conducted by the authors and was not replicated by others, the results must be interpreted with caution.

William Glasser's Reality Therapy

Psychiatrist William Glasser was first recognized for his theory of *reality therapy* (RT). This approach to psychotherapy consists of a combination of Glasser's humanism and his emphasis on patients accepting responsibility for the "here and now" rather than focusing on the past. In his books, *Schools Without Failure* (1969), *Control Theory in the Classroom* (1986), and *The Quality School (1992),* he extended his ideas to the schools. Because of Glasser's different emphasis in his earlier versus his later works, his model of discipline will be discussed in terms of pre- and post-1985 (Charles, 1989).

Before 1985, Glasser viewed behavior as a matter of choice. Teachers' roles are to learn reality therapy techniques so they can help students make good choices. Because the past cannot be changed, emphasis should be on the present and the future. Although it is obvious that the past may influence behavior, humans, with their rational minds, are able to make choices despite their pasts. Students can understand acceptable school behavior and can choose to behave appropriately (Glasser, 1985).

Students must desire to make good choices. Conversely, if misbehavior is perceived as desirable, students will make bad choices. Teachers must develop the skill to persuade misbehaving students to acknowledge and judge their own behavior. Rather than accepting excuses for misbehavior, teachers should focus on what is acceptable.

Before 1985, Glasser believed that schools offered students a good chance to be successful and to be recognized (Glasser, 1978). He thought that for many individuals, schools may have been the only place where these needs could be met. Success produced a sense of self-worth and a success identity, which ameliorated deviant behavior. However, students could not make more responsible choices until they became emotionally involved with people, such as teachers, who could model such choices.

Glasser believed that teachers hold the key to good discipline (Glasser, 1969). He continues to believe that it is the teacher's task to stress student responsibility. Classroom meetings are especially effective, because they help students to solve the problems of living in their school world (Glasser, 1969). These meetings should be a regular part of the curriculum. Students sit in a tight circle with the teacher and discuss matters that concern the class. The three types of class meetings are *open-ended, educational/diagnostic,* and *problem-solving.* Open-ended meetings are used to encourage students to imagine a variety of problem situations and develop solutions. These may be based on reality or fantasy. Educational/ diagnostic meetings are used to explore proposed curricula. The purpose is to determine students' knowledge and interests in the topic. In a problem-solving meeting, students deal with real life problems which affect the classroom. They follow specific problem-solving strategies and conclude with their commitment to a mutually agreeable plan of action.

During class meetings, participants should mutually establish rules that lead to success. Meetings should facilitate personal and group achievement. Group members should not accept excuses related to students' conditions outside of school or student commitment. When students exhibit inappropriate behavior, teachers should learn how to persuade them to make value judgments about the appropriateness of their behavior. Teachers should suggest suitable alternatives to misbehavior, including two or three options, when students are unable to generate their own. Students learn it is more satisfying if they abide by the options they chose. Noncompliance should be followed by conferences to work out the problem. This is part of the counseling methods of reality therapy that teachers need to learn. In extreme cases, it may be necessary to place students in a time-out room or in-school suspension to reconsider their behavior.

Persistent, caring teachers never lose the commitment to helping their students toward self-discipline. Through classroom meetings, teachers carry out continual review by focusing on problem identification and solutions.

Before 1985, Glasser claimed it was the students' responsibility to make successful choices. After 1985, he emphasized the schools' role in making discipline meet the needs of the students. He concluded that "no more than half of our secondary students are willing to make an effort to learn" and that "we have gone as far as we can go with the traditional structure of our secondary schools" (Glasser, 1986). This is the result of the schools' inability to meet students' needs and to keep them involved with learning.

Glasser posits five inborn needs, which are the needs for survival, belonging, power, freedom, and fun. Learning will not take place unless these five needs are met. This concept, central to control theory, explains that people are intrinsically motivated and are not responsible for external events (Glasser, 1986).

Glasser rejects the traditional stimulus–response theory and contends that schools, rather than expecting extrinsic motivators to work, can and should be restructured to meet students' needs. Use of his control theory will result in "quality" and "quality teachers" (Glasser, 1992). His insistence on the importance of inborn needs and his rejection of external reinforcement anchor his theory in the humanist camp; however, he rejects this suggestion (Glasser, personal communication, 1995).

Glasser's more recent works stress that schools must abandon their "boss management" approach, which creates adversarial relationships. The alternative is "lead management," in which teachers establish warm, noncoercive relationships with students. The crux of his current approach is that discipline problems will be minimal and quality school work will occur when schools restructure to meet students' inborn needs.

Glasser recommends that schools move from the traditional classroom structure toward small learning teams. Small learning groups of approximately four students provide for (1) a sense of belonging, (2) motivation for students to work on behalf of the group, (3) the opportunity for stronger students to meet their needs for power and build friendships by helping weaker students, (4) weaker students meeting their own needs by contributing to the group, and (5) freedom from overdependence on the teacher as they help each other (Charles, 1989, p. 129).

Glasser claims that learning teams increase work output and reduce discipline problems. His interest in these teams may stem from the growing literature supporting the efficacy of cooperative learning approaches (Johnson & Johnson, 1987; Slavin, 1987).

Glasser's model has a number of strengths and weaknesses. On the positive side, he offers an easily understood, structured, well-organized practical program that stresses discipline without resorting to punishment. One of the most appealing aspects of reality therapy is "the extent to which a student feels he has control over his own destiny" (Glasser, 1969, p. 123).

It is difficult understanding how Glasser's pre- and post-1985 theories fit together. Charles (1989, p. 130) speculates that one could view Glasser's model of discipline in an expanded form, in which the teacher first organizes the class to meet students' inborn needs and then continues to use the earlier intervention strategies for controlling and improving behavior. Other limitations of Glasser's approach are that it does not work well with students who do not care, class meetings are hard to schedule in secondary school, school changes may be difficult to accomplish within the school structure (e.g., changing the curriculum or the environment), and it is very hard to start fresh each day (Wolfgang & Glickman, 1986).

Glasser's reality therapy has been extensively researched and, as with most other programs, the results are mixed and methodology has generally been poor. Our review of the literature showed only research related to Glasser's original theory. Glasser (personal communication, 1995) claims that the research we have cited is not based on schools in which teachers have been properly trained in his method.

A number of studies found no gains in general student achievement, math achievement, student attitudes, scores on the Metropolitan Achievement Test, or changes on subscales of the California Test of Personality (Lynch, 1975; Masters & Laverty, 1977; Matthews, 1972; Welch & Dolly, 1980).

Some studies have shown students to have developed more positive attitudes toward school, increased knowledge, and better attitudes regarding the discipline concepts of reality therapy, generally better attitudes, improved grades over a six-week period, and a moderate reduction in anxiety (Browning, 1978; Cady, 1983; Houton & Slowick, 1982).

Some studies indicate that the use of some components of reality therapy may be helpful. For example, studies have shown reduced student arguing after a series of class meetings on the issue (Marandola & Imber, 1979), decreased problem behavior of highly disruptive students for several weeks after treatment (Gang, 1974), and significantly improved on-task behavior in the classroom after reality therapy counseling for four highly disruptive students (Atwell, 1982).

Overall, as with similar programs, research on the effectiveness of Glasser's model in the schools is not convincing. However, his basic ideas are consonant with well-supported concepts of prevention and positive remediation.

An Ecological/Systems Process Approach

The ESA is rooted in the assumption that all environmental factors may impact on student misbehavior. These factors include the range of disciplinary responses used by schools and teachers. Therefore, to master this approach, it is helpful to determine the nature and extent of disciplinary techniques available through widely used training programs.

To identify common elements or frequently taught strategies for effective discipline, we conducted two research studies (Dahbany & Hyman, 1995; Hyman & Lally, 1982). We identified the discipline techniques or processes advocated by each program. The results of our studies represent a synthesis of actual processes taught from an analysis of 80 programs, regardless of their purported underlying theoretical orientations. The programs examined were chosen because they were widely used to help teachers to deal with misbehavior. Table 9.2 compares the number of programs evaluated in the two studies.

The programs reviewed include techniques discussed throughout this book. Therefore, we present our findings with limited examples, where appropriate. The processes are organized into eight clusters and reported in tables that indicate the number of programs that teach each process. The tables offer data from the two studies, and the text includes definitions of the processes.

Teaching Teachers to Give Feedback

Table 9.3 presents the variables identified in the area of teaching teachers to give feedback.

Accepting students' feelings is a means of improving communication between teachers and students. To show that you accept your students' feelings, you can tell your students that you understand how they feel, that they have a right to feel as they do, and that they will not be embarrassed, humiliated, or punished for showing or expressing their feelings. However, you also must indicate that, although you accept your students' feelings, this does not mean that you will approve or accept inappropriate expressions of these feelings.

An example of how to deal with feedback is the empathetic responder mode (Goldstein, 1989). You must relate to students that you really believe that "nobody can help seeing things the way they see them, and nobody can help feeling the way they feel" (p. 431).

TABLE 9.2   Process Analysis Summary

	1995 Data	1982 Data
Number of programs analyzed	80	27
Number of programs validated by author	40	15
Percent rate of programs validated by author	50	56

**TABLE 9.3   Features of Programs That Instruct Teachers on
Feedback Techniques**

Variable	1995 Data (N = 80)		1982 Data (N = 27)		% Change	
	f	*%*	*f*	*%*		
Accept student's feelings	51	64	18	66	–	2
Accept student's ideas	46	58	17	63	–	5
Reflect/restate student's feelings	46	58	14	52	+	6
Reflect/restate student's ideas	37	46	12	44	+	2
Provide verbal feedback on student's behavior*	65	81				
State student's desirable/undesirable behaviors	54	68	13	48	+	20
Discuss student's negative behaviors	47	59	10	37	+	22

Note. *This is a new process that was not used in the 1982 study.

Although you may think that the students' ways of seeing things are wrong and should be changed, the students are genuinely expressing their feelings and perceptions. You must set aside your own feelings and put yourself in the students' shoes to understand them. This will enable you to develop a relationship with the students that is based on acceptance, respect, and understanding. Some authors (Dupont, Gardner & Brody, 1974) indicate that the teacher needs to realize that many students do not have experience recognizing or talking about their feelings because their families may have rejected, ignored, or denied the discussion and expression of feelings in their homes. So the students may be initially very uncomfortable dealing with their feelings in the classroom.

To enhance the development of feelings expression, you must foster an atmosphere of acceptance and respect for feelings. One way to promote an appropriate climate is to tell students that feelings such as sadness, anger, and excitement are genuine and that it is OK to express them verbally. You may relate anecdotes about your own experiences with expressing feelings.

When a student is having a hard time expressing feelings, teacher feedback can include acceptance and the encouragement of other students to express similar feelings. This helps suggest the universality of feelings and the concept that it is good to share them with others. It is important to stress that appropriate feedback when one expresses feelings, even when you do not understand them, should not include negative statements. You can relate that it is important to (1) state that teasing is unacceptable in the classroom, (2) discuss the uncomfortable feelings that students get when they are teased, and (3) model acceptance and respect for the expression of student feelings. The goal of appropriate feedback is to help students to accept, respect, and express their own feelings, as well as learn to accept and respect the feelings of others. For instance, "I understand why you feel angry at Johnny for calling you a name; you can tell him how angry you are and that you feel like punching him, but you cannot hit him."

Accepting students' ideas is another means of improving communication with students. Like the acceptance of feelings, the goal is to demonstrate understanding of the students' ideas, and acceptance that, even though they may be incorrect, students have a right to express them. They should never be embarrassed, humiliated, or punished for expressing ideas. You can show acceptance of the students' ideas by summarizing, clarifying, restating, and extending them. You can make it clear that accepting the students' ideas does not indicate that you approve or accept student misbehavior based on those ideas. For instance, "I understand that you think the rules are unfair, and some may be in particular situations, but you still should not break the rules."

When teachers give students an opportunity to voice their own opinions, the teachers are fostering a sense of ownership, independence, and power in the students, as well as a positive attitude for classroom participation. The teacher also fosters the students' feeling of belonging, self-esteem, and critical thinking skills, which leads to a circular process for further classroom participation (Albert, 1989). "Brainstorming" (Elias & Clabby, 1989) is a method to encourage multiple and sometimes creative solutions to a problem. It also improves problem-solving skills.

Reflecting or restating students' feelings indicates to students that you have heard and understood their feelings. Here you can paraphrase what the students have said to echo, or reflect, the students feelings back to them.

Teachers can use three ways to demonstrate that they accept students' feelings and behavior (Gordon, 1974, 1991). The first is not to intervene in interpersonal disputes between students, unless they become physical. The object is to convey trust in the students' ability to appropriately express feelings and to solve problems on their own. This should enhance the students' self-esteem.

Teachers sometimes are attentive but passive to student discourse about feelings. Therefore, the students may feel that their feelings have been accepted, but not necessarily understood. Gordon (1991) advocates the use of active listening because it indicates to the students that their feelings have been both accepted and understood. To do this, you must first focus on the meaning of what the students are saying. Then demonstrate this understanding by stating students' feelings in your own words. This allows them to either correct you if you misunderstood or to agree with you. Gordon (1991) believes that "Without feeling understood, people will seldom feel accepted" (p. 182).

Other programs (Ellsworth & Monahan, 1987) indicate that in any verbal interaction, the teacher needs to (1) give the person full attention; (2) not jump to conclusions; and (3) ask for clarification when not understanding. When you want to explore a point a student has made, you can say, "Tell me more about that," "How did that make you feel?" or "Would you carry that a little further?" When you do not understand what a student has said, you might say "I'm not sure that I follow... What do you think is the main point in what you have said?" When you are restating a students' feelings, you could start by saying, "Have I got this straight, that..." or, "During our discussion, we agreed..."

Reflecting or restating students' ideas is another way for you to show you understand what students are expressing. This is similar to reflecting or restating student feelings. It can be accomplished by paraphrasing the students' ideas and using them during the lesson.

Active student participation and involvement is important for a lesson to succeed (Savage, 1991). Encouraging students' agreements or disagreements to the teacher's statements is a way for students to express their ideas. You can indicate understanding by restating the students' response in a question form, saying, "Are you saying that...?" Reflection indicates that the teacher is noticing the students, but that no judgments, demands, or interpretations are assumed (Wood, Combs, Gunn & Weller, 1986). Reflection helps students to appraise their ideas and prepares them for increased verbal and cognitive monitoring of their own thinking. "When in doubt, reflect," is considered a basic guideline for teachers.

Providing verbal feedback on student behavior is a way of providing an objective, non-demeaning communication. It allows the students to understand and change their inappropriate behaviors without the need to be defensive. Verbal feedback includes letting your students know what you expect of them and letting them know what you will and will not accept in your classroom. It includes praising and encouraging good behaviors as well as discussing inappropriate behaviors.

Derogatory, demanding, and generally negative responses to inappropriate behaviors put the student on the spot, draw attention to the misbehavior, and set the stage for a power struggle. Verbal abuse of the student, including sarcasm, shouting, and displays of anger, only cause resentment and student loss of face. These counterproductive acts may result in the student's perceived need to retaliate.

Verbal feedback should be clear and firm (Savage, 1991) and may include hints such as, "Everyone should be working"; questions such as, "Would you please get to work?"; and I-messages such as, "I want you open your books and get to work" to initially request appropriate behavior from the students (Canter & Canter, 1992). Eye contact, hand gestures, using the student's name, moving toward the student (proximity control), and gently touching the student on the shoulder increase the effectiveness of the verbal communication. If students refuse to comply, refuse to take responsibility for their own behavior, or respond inappropriately to your demands, you can use the broken record technique.

The broken record technique helps to avoid verbal battles while insisting on the appropriate behavior. You state what you want from the student with a preface such as, "This is what I want you to do." Avoid getting diverted from your goal by firmly repeating your request a maximum of three times. If the student does not comply, be prepared to follow through with a consequence. For example:

Teacher: I want you to stop poking and shoving the people who are sitting next to you.

Carol: But I didn't mean to.

Teacher: That's not the point; I want you to stop poking and shoving the people who sit next to you!

Carol: But I didn't mean to.

Teacher: I understand, but I don't want you to poke and shove people who sit next to you.

Carol: All right, I'll keep my hands to myself, but if anyone calls me a name, there is going to be trouble.

Teacher: If you touch anyone again, you will lose free time for a week!

Stating students' desirable or undesirable behaviors is another way a teacher gives students feedback about their misbehavior. The teacher describes students' appropriate and inappropriate behaviors in precise, nonjudgmental terms. This may include how many times they misbehaved during a lesson. The goal is to help the students see their misbehavior as others see it, understand their own behaviors, and see how their actions affect others. This may motivate students to continue to behave appropriately as well as to develop a desire to change their inappropriate behaviors.

The sit and watch technique (Jackson, Jackson, & Monroe, 1983) requires the teacher to initially remove the misbehaving student from the group. The student then has to sit quietly, maintain a good attitude, and watch the other students for two minutes. Then the teacher asks the student to state why the student is sitting and watching. If the student cannot verbalize the misbehavior, the teacher states it, and asks the student to repeat it, and the teacher reinforces the repetition. Then the student is asked to state the correct behavior that has to be demonstrated to return to the group.

If the student cannot state the correct behavior, the teacher repeats it and asks the student to say it. The teacher reinforces the repetition. The student is then allowed back into the group, the teacher watches for the student to demonstrate the appropriate behavior, and then reinforces the student for positive behaviors.

Discussing students' negative behaviors helps teachers to communicate with their students and provide them with specific feedback about their inappropriate behaviors. The teacher can be trained to talk to the student in a one-to-one situation to try to find out the reasons for the student's inappropriate behaviors. In these discussions, the teacher helps the student understand the reasons why the student does not behave appropriately and jointly work on what can be done to change the inappropriate behaviors.

The I-message (Gordon, 1991) is a three-part verbal technique to deal with misbehavior. It is a nonblameful, nonevaluative message that tells students how the teacher is experiencing their inappropriate behavior. By giving an I-message, the teacher helps the students understand how their behavior is having a negative impact on the teacher or the class. The parts of an I-message include (1) describing the inappropriate behavior, (2) describing the effect it has on the teacher or the class, and (3) describing the teacher's feelings about the misbehavior. Instead of making a denigrating statement such as, "This class is full of motor mouths," you would say, "When there is so much noise in the classroom, I can't hear what anyone is saying."

Another method for discussing the student's negative behavior is included in control theory (Glasser, 1992), which offers a solution-oriented approach to misbehavior, thereby decreasing time spent on blaming or fault finding. For instance, rather than nagging, reprimanding, or blaming Jim, who says, "I don't want to do this seatwork; I hate it and I hate this class," you must approach the situation as a problem to be solved. You can reply to his refusal by using statements such as, "It looks like you have a problem. How could I help you to solve it? If you'll just calm down, as soon as I have the time, I'll talk it over with you. I think that we can work something out, but as long as you're doing what you're doing now, we can't work anything out." After the student calms down, you tell the student, "I want to help you work this out. I am not looking to punish you for what you have done. If there is a problem, let's solve it."

When Jim is ready to talk, you can help him examine the reasons for his refusals and develop a plan with him to help him refrain from this behavior in the future. Some questions you can use to discuss misbehavior include, "What were you doing when the problem started? Was this against the rules? Can we work it out so that it doesn't happen again? If this situation comes up in the future, let's work out what you can do and what I could do so we don't have this problem again."

Teaching Teachers to Use Diagnostic Strategies for Understanding Students and Student-Teacher Interactions

Table 9.4 presents the variables related to measuring behaviors and attitudes and diagnosing the reasons for misbehavior.

Systematic observations involve use of instruments generally developed for research on classroom behavior of students or teachers. The better instruments, such as the Interaction Analysis (IA) Scale (Amidon, Flanders, & Casper, 1985), provide categories of behavior that are clearly described in behavioral terms. A teacher or observer tallies the incidence or nature of the student behavior, teacher behavior, or student–teacher interaction across regular time intervals.

Teachers can systematically tally the incidence of specific misbehaviors. The teacher must define the behavior and determine when and how often to tally observations. An example of an observable behavior would be, "the student enters the room two minutes after the final bell rings," rather than, "the student is late to class" (Buckley & Walker, 1978).

Evaluation of the tallies enables the teacher to diagnose the nature and extent of misbehavior and to determine an intervention. This procedure was described in the chapter on behavioral approaches.

Some programs provide rating scales to assess social behavior in the classroom. Elliot and Gresham's (1991) diagnostic rating scale is linked to lesson plans to teach skills such as cooperation, assertion, responsibility, empathy, and self-control. A Social Skills Inter-

TABLE 9.4   Features of Programs That Instruct Teachers on Diagnostic Strategies

Variable	1995 Data (N = 80)		1982 Data (N = 27)		% Change	
	f	*%*	*f*	*%*		
Use of systematic observations*						
For students	49	61	12	44**	+	17
For teachers	17	21	9	33**	–	12
For student–teacher interaction	9	11	8	30**	–	19
Use of anecdotal information*						
For students	36	45	12	44**	+	1
For teachers	24	30	9	33**	–	3
For student–teacher interaction	15	19	8	30**	–	11
Identification of students' feelings by using observational techniques	20	25	12	44	–	19
Identification of students' feelings by dialogue	49	61	11	41	+	20
Identification of students' feelings through facial expressions, body language, etc.	28	35	10	37	–	2
Use of measures for teacher attitudes	9	11	8	30	–	19
Use of measures for students' attitudes	17	21	6	22	–	1

Note. *These two processes were listed as one process in the 1982 study, but were separated into two processes for the 1995 study. **Data from the 1982 study are repeated for both processes in this table in order to make a comparison.

vention Progress Monitoring record also is provided to assess the progress the students are making in the program.

Observation of teachers may focus on how a teacher spends instructional time, organizes the instructional environment, tries to improve student performance or self-concept, or uses varied verbal behaviors such as praise, lecture, or directions.

The Observer Checklist (Jackson, Jackson, & Monroe, 1983) requires listing each student and their goals on the length of the page. Space at the top of the page lists teacher behaviors such as praise and prompts to obtain appropriate behavior. The observer records the number of times the teacher demonstrates these behaviors.

The Teacher–Student Interaction Seating Chart (Evertson & Harris, 1993) helps the teacher obtain a record of the teacher–student interactions. It provides information about (1) how often teacher–student interactions occur; (2) where the attention is distributed; (3) which students receive teacher attention; (4) which students demand teacher attention by calling out, misbehaving, etc.; and (5) what types of teacher attention individual students receive. The teacher makes a seating chart for the class and labels each seat with the student's name. The observer uses notations to tally behaviors. Examples include academic questions (?), academic feedback (+), correction (c), prompt (p), reprimand (x), and student-initiated comment or question (*). Analysis of interactions involves making a chart and asking questions such as How many students are in the class? How many students were spoken to by the teacher? and What was the location of the students most spoken to and least spoken to? If each symbol on the chart weighed a pound, which way would the room tilt? Is there a pattern as to who received teacher attention? How would you describe it? How many of each type of interaction were noted? Was there a difference in response to boys and girls? How would you describe it? These questions can help the teacher to diagnose problem areas that cause misbehavior.

Anecdotal information involves completing informal, unstructured anecdotal reports of misbehavior. Teachers or observers typically make notes, write descriptions, or list reminders after an event occurs. Such reports usually concern incidents, reactions to discipline plans, or interactions and can be used to implement discipline strategies.

In some cases, you can check the accuracy of observations by checking with the student. For instance, "Bill, did you say that 'all teachers are old and dumb' or 'dumb and old'?" (Hunter, 1990). The student may ask, "What are you going to do with that?" and the teacher should respond with, "I haven't decided yet," because most students fear the unknown more than the known. The teacher can stop making the notes when the student behaves appropriately.

If the misbehavior continues, you can give the student a private notice, such as, "Susan, I don't think you realize how many times you call out the answers. This keeps others from having time to think. I'm going to record it each time on this pad so at the end of the period you can see what a habit it is. Remember, if you raise your hand, I will call on you."

Observations of teacher behavior, using tape recordings, colleagues, supervisors, or other outside observers, include informal descriptions of predetermined teacher behaviors in specific situations. These could include observations of discipline-related behaviors such as threatening punishments you cannot implement, the reasons you send students to the principal for punishment, or the reasons you use time out.

A positive reminder plan (Canter & Canter, 1992) uses a handy piece of paper and a pencil to keep track of events we might forget. If you are working on having Sylvia become more attentive in class, you can make a note of this and record how many times you praised her for staying on task. If she has an especially good day, it will remind you to send a positive note home.

Problem logs enable observation of student–teacher interaction. This consist of notes on specific situations or student–teacher interactions that help create or solve a classroom problem. These are often based on teachers' long-held beliefs that interfere with their relationships with students (Dinkmeyer et al., 1980). These beliefs can negatively affect your relationships with students. They include the beliefs that (1) Teachers need to be in control—this fosters student dependency or rebellion; (2) Teachers need to be superior, dominant, or overprotective—these behaviors limit students' ability to develop independence, responsibility, and self-discipline; (3) Teachers are automatically entitled to obedience and respect and do not have to show respect for students—students may then be distrustful and not demonstrate respect for the teacher; and (4) Teachers must always stand up for their rights, because if they ever give in they are perceived as weak—this belief erodes mutual teacher–student respect.

Perfectionism is an observable teacher quality that causes disciplinary problems. It is apparent when teachers show low tolerance for student mistakes, thereby causing some students to be become overly fearful and anxious about failure. The presence of these teacher traits can be observed by audiotaping or videotaping lessons or by colleague observation.

Identification of students' feelings, especially those that can be easily inferred by observable behavior, may be facilitated by using either a systematic or an anecdotal observation technique in the classroom. For instance, students who are instigators may lack confidence. They prefer to have others act out their feelings. Class clowns may feel inferior, so they entertain the class to gain acceptance. Scapegoats may continually endure this role or even appear to relish it because they have negative self-concepts. Blame and ridicule are forms of attention that assure the recipient an ongoing role in the group (Savage, 1991).

Observational data enable you to recognize these roles and the underlying feelings. You can develop strategies to help these students cope with their feelings. The instigator can be praised and recognized for good ideas; the class clown can be reinforced for humor in appropriate times and situations; and you can spread the responsibility for blame and solutions to the entire class.

The positive interactions checklist (Ellsworth, 1993) allows the teacher to observe and record nonverbal communication, which is as important as verbal communication. To assess students' attitudes and feelings, watch for the students to make eye contact or hand gestures, nod in agreement, and smile. Another way to assess the students' feelings is by noticing their level of physical closeness to their peers and to you.

Identification of students' feelings by dialogue is used when teachers are trained to identify students' feelings by using either systematic or anecdotal observation techniques using classroom dialogue. Class meetings facilitate diagnosis of feelings. These meetings often stimulate student–teacher dialogue and problem solving on issues that are of real and practical concern (Nelsen, Lott, & Glenn, 1993). During these meetings, you should help the group focus on solutions instead of consequences. You should (1) be patient and take time to learn the class meeting procedures, (2) allow the students to put problems on the class meeting agenda, and (3) allow the student who put the problem on the agenda to choose the solution rather than allowing the students to vote on the solution.

Teacher listening skills enhance students' desires to express their real concerns, needs, or wants. Students often disguise their real concerns by making general angry comments, such as, "I hate this class." This statement may mask frustration over difficulty understanding the class material (Jones & Jones, 1990). Empathetic, nonevaluative listening is commonly called paraphrasing, active listening, or reflecting. Listening skills are improved if you (Johnson & Johnson, 1991): (1) restate students' ideas and feelings in your own words; (2) start your remarks with "You think . . .", "Your position is . . .; (3) avoid any indication of approval or disapproval; (4) make your nonverbal messages match your verbal message, such as saying these things and looking attentive; (5) are as accurate as possible when you reflect the students' feelings; (6) do not add or subtract anything from the original student statement in the paraphrase; and (7) are able to put yourself in the students' shoes to try to understand them and what they are saying.

Identification of students' feelings through facial expressions, *body language,* and so forth, occurs when teachers are trained to identify student feelings by the students' nonverbal language in the classroom.

Feelings are generally accompanied by a physical reaction that is nonverbal. For instance, when people are embarrassed, their face turns red. Although nonverbal behaviors can be ambiguous and open to several interpretations, a teacher should become sensitive to the facial expressions and body language of their students to determine how they are feeling and what the goal of the misbehavior is, such as attention, power, revenge, or display of inadequacy (Froyen, 1993). This is labeled the recognition reflex, which is demonstrated in young students through smiling, grinning, an embarrassed laugh, or a twinkle in the eye. In older students, the recognition reflex is demonstrated through a change in their seating position, swinging a leg, or tapping their fingers.

Many programs provide lesson plans to help teachers train students in recognizing nonverbal behavior of their peers. For instance, in the lesson *How Can You Tell?* (Shure, 1992), students are taught how someone feels by watching them and listening to them. In subsequent lessons, the students are taught to watch, listen, and then ask others how they are feeling. In the lesson entitled *Recognizing Another's Feelings* (McGinnis & Goldstein, 1990), students are taught to watch people, paying close attention to such features as posture and facial expression. They notice most what and how the person does and says things. Students make a list of what they think the person is feeling and then decide whether to ask the person how they are feeling. Students are encouraged to wait until an upset or angry person calms down before talking to them.

Use of measures of teachers' attitudes are helpful when teachers are trained to use published, validated scales or systems to measure their attitudes toward teaching, their students, etc.

To obtain information about teacher attitudes about their schools' discipline program and school climate, a survey is generally used. *A Sample Staff Discipline Survey* and a *Sample Staff Opinion Survey* (Keating, Pickering, Slack, & White, 1990) may help obtain this information. It uses a Likert scale, which has four categories, from strongly agree, agree, disagree, to strongly disagree. Some of the questions include, "I spend too much time on our present school discipline plan," "I think the principal should be involved in the school discipline plan," and "I think teachers need more support with discipline."

Measures of students' attitudes can be helpful in evaluating the quality of teacher–student interactions as perceived by the students. Student feedback about teacher behavior can be obtained by informal, teacher-made scales or by use of published scales. Valid results accrue when students do not put their names on the scales, because they are more likely to be honest if their responses are anonymous (Jones & Jones, 1990).

Sample questions a teacher may ask include the following (Jones & Jones, 1990): Am I courteous toward you? Do I listen to you when you want to talk? Am I willing to admit I'm wrong? Can you ask me questions? For middle and high school students, teachers are rated on a five-point scale ranging from a home run to a strikeout. For elementary students, teachers are rated on a three-point scale that has a frog jumping up, a frog sitting down, and a frog sitting down with a sad face.

To obtain information about student attitudes, feelings, and perceptions of the school discipline program and school climate, a survey specifically worded for students can be used. These have been described previously and may be distributed to students, teachers, or parents. A typical student opinion survey (Keating et al., 1990) also uses a Likert scale that has four categories, from strongly agree, agree, disagree, to strongly disagree. The areas measured include school climate, achievement, instructional excellence, curriculum content, leadership, and parent involvement.

Modifying the Ecology of the Classroom and the School

Table 9.5, on page 290, presents the variables identified in the area of curriculum, classroom ecology, and systems.

Classroom ecology refers to teacher control and modification of the classroom environment to facilitate good behavior and prevent misbehavior. These approaches are based in great part on the teacher efficacy literature discussed previously.

Structuring classroom activities requires (1) structuring activities or curriculum to maximize engaged time by all students, (2) assuring that lessons are within the ability and interest levels of all students, (3) using a balance of direct or indirect teaching methods, and (4) using examples and evaluation to assure mastery at each student's ability level to minimize boredom if the work is too easy or frustration if it is too difficult.

When planning and teaching classroom rules and procedures, you must decide the rules governing acceptable and unacceptable behavior (Evertson & Harris, 1993). Rules and procedures should be taught systematically by providing explanation, rehearsal, and feedback. Good procedures make students responsible for completing their work but depend on an accountability system that regularly and clearly informs students about what to do, how to do it, and when and where to submit their work. This includes consistent and timely grading and feedback to the students.

Provision of appropriate learning activities for all students in the class involves (1) appropriate time allotments, (2) recognition of constraints, (3) consideration of individ-

TABLE 9.5   Features of Programs That Instruct Teachers on Techniques in Classroom and School Ecology

Variable	1995 Data (N = 80)		1982 Data (N = 27)		% Change	
	f	%	f	%		
Classroom ecology						
Structuring classroom activities/curricula	67	84	14	52	+	32
Structuring classroom physical facilities	42	53	11	41	+	11
Use of teacher efficacy for questioning, lecturing, homework, etc.	18	23	9	33	–	10
Use of teacher-determined rules, conduct codes, etc.	48	60	6	22	+	38
Cooperative learning/discipline*	49	61				
School ecology*						
Use of code of conduct/ teacher rights/student rights	14	18				
School safety procedures	3	4				
Systematic reporting of misbehavior	6	8				
Conducting needs assessment	6	8				
Conflict mediation	23	29				
Peer counseling	11	14				
Training in violence prevention	10	13				
Training in physical restraint	3	4				

Note. *These are new processes that were not used in the 1982 study.

ual student's attention spans and learning patterns within the context of the overall curriculum, (4) wise use of work centers and stations, and (5) an appropriate variety of instructional formats, including whole group, small group, and individual instruction.

Structuring classroom physical facilities is an important procedure to minimize misbehavior that we have already discussed. It includes appropriate arrangement of the room, equipment, and basic supplies to promote effective classroom instruction. Evertson and Harris (1993) suggest three guidelines including (1) good visibility so that all students can easily see all the instructional presentations and displays and can be easily seen by the teacher; (2) good accessibility in high-traffic areas and access to frequently used teaching materials and student supplies; and (3) student placement free from distracters such as doors, open windows, high-traffic areas, computer stations, etc.

The teacher efficacy literature is reflected in programs that improve discipline by clarifying the use of strategies such as questioning, lecturing, and assigning and using homework to promote student achievement (Levin & Nolan, 1991). These procedures maximize student time on task, thereby minimizing time spent waiting for activities to get started, making changes between activities, and passive time with nothing to do. Effective techniques include (1) providing clear oral and written directions to complete an activity, (2) providing clear expectations and assuring that students have the skills and materials to complete assignments, and (3) monitoring seatwork.

Teacher-determined rules, conduct codes, and guidelines maximize student understanding of expectations and consequences for rule breaking. They should be stated in a positive manner and clearly posted.

There are "rules for the use of rules" (Goldstein, 1988). Rules should be made at the start of the school year and should be fair, reasonable, and enforced equitably. You must first define and communicate them in clear, specific, behavioral terms. For instance, use, "Raise your hand before asking a question," rather than, "Be considerate of others." The rules should state what to do rather than what not to do. For example, use, "Students should use words and compromise to resolve disagreements," rather than, "Do not fight." Rules should be as few as possible, simple, easy to memorize, and developmentally appropriate.

Even though the teacher has the final discretion about rules, student compliance is more likely if students have had a role in their development, modification, and implementation.

Cooperative learning/cooperative discipline is a teaching philosophy as well as a series of different but related teaching methods (Goldstein, 1988). It is rooted in John Dewey's belief that in a democracy, schools should provide students with sufficient opportunities to learn cooperation and participation in decision making. Based on these concepts and Adlerian theory, Albert (1989) developed Cooperative Discipline. This program, which we discussed previously, trains teachers to identify the goals of misbehavior and how to intervene.

Students misbehave to achieve attention, power, revenge, or avoidance of failure. Albert's Action Plan has five steps, including (1) pinpointing and describing the student's behavior, (2) identifying the goal of the misbehavior, (3) choosing an intervention technique for the moment of misbehavior, (4) selecting encouragement techniques to build self-esteem, and (5) involving the parents as partners in the action plan.

School ecology is included in all programs that emphasize that classroom discipline is ultimately influenced by the total school environment. Teachers must work with other school staff, parents, students, or community members to develop schoolwide rules, regulations, and programs to maintain discipline. Ecological improvement at the school level may include (1) conducting school discipline needs assessments, (2) development of codes of conduct that spell out teacher/student rights, and (3) training of teachers in legal and ethical considerations in school discipline.

Legal aspects of school discipline (Froyen, 1993) include (1) due process considerations, (2) corporal punishment, (3) negligence, (3) suspension, (4) detention, (5) assault and battery, (6) grade reduction as an academic sanction, (7) defamation and rights to privacy, and (8) injuries that occur in, around, and in transit to and from school. These are complicated issues.

The Family Educational Rights and Privacy Act gives parents the right to challenge grades and other information in the student's records. The courts have allowed school authorities the right to use academic sanctions for poor academic performance. But there is less agreement in allowing school authorities to reduce a student's grade as a punishment for absences or misbehavior. Grades should be objective, measurable indicators of students' mastery of material and not instruments of punishment.

Legal challenges may be successful when teachers lower grades because of poor attendance, nonacademic reasons, or those that reflect malicious or arbitrary responses to student misbehavior. However, you may give separate grades for academic and behavioral progress. If grade reduction is used throughout the school or in your classroom, these rules should be published in the school's student handbook as well as in the teacher's course syllabus as a legal protection for teachers.

Ethical considerations discussed by Long, Frye, and Long (1985) include (1) goals and methodology involved in behavior modification; (2) issues of student rights, including due process and equal protection; and (3) parental rights. Teachers can use Long, Frye, and Long's *Legal Issues Checklist* to make sure that they have made every effort to accommodate students' legal rights. You can insure equal protection and students' rights by (1) treating all students the same way, (2) making sure that all groups of students are included in all activities, and (3) only excluding students from activities if there is adequate, documented justification and the students have been afforded due process before exclusion.

School safety procedures are basic for establishing good school discipline (Goldstein, Glick, Reiner, Zimmerman, & Coultry, 1987). Development and enforcement of policies are shared by school board members and district and building administrators. Safety plans should be written and provide for staff training and supervision. Crisis teams use prevention and intervention measures to deal with such problems as suicide threats and violent incidents. There should be systematic reporting of misbehavior.

Jones & Jones (1990) suggest that the major components of good discipline codes include:

1. A focus on a positive school climate and positive consequences for appropriate behavior
2. Initial emphasis on the teacher's responsibility for adjusting the student's instruction and implementing behavioral interventions
3. Appropriate, ongoing training for students and staff
4. Rules that are clear and concise, and systematically communicated to students, parents, and staff
5. Clear consequences for violations of school rules
6. Consistent responses to similar misbehaviors when students are referred by school staff
7. Systematic procedures for involving parents in prevention and remediation of misbehavior
8. Periodic evaluation of success in meeting desired behavioral outcomes

Teachers need to know about the school discipline policy (McQueen, 1992). They need to adhere to the reporting requirements and follow school policy with regard to disciplinary measures. If you are strongly opposed to the underlying philosophy of your school's discipline policies, you may want to consider working in a district with more compatible views.

Needs assessments have been discussed. Any comprehensive change in a school's discipline program should begin with needs assessment (Keating, et al., 1990).

Conflict mediation is becoming increasingly popular to prevent student aggression. In recent years the focus has shifted to training students in peer mediation techniques (Aetna, 1992). Peers are taught active listening, understanding body language, discovering common ground between the participants, uncovering the hidden agendas, using I-statements, and asking open ended questions as described in Chapter 8. Then, instead of referring the feuding students through the school discipline procedures, the students are given the option of having their dispute settled by a peer mediator.

Peer counseling uses students who are natural leaders to counsel their classmates (Nelson, 1987). Training involves teaching skills in (1) making friends; (2) finding out what happened to cause the problem by asking what, who, when, where, and how questions; (3) asking what the consequences of the inappropriate behaviors are; (4) working with the referred student to develop a plan to do better; and (5) getting a commitment from the student to implement the plan. Peer counselors work under an adult supervisor. Students in need of counseling are referred by teachers who fill out a referral slip. The peer counselor conducts the counseling and then writes the solution to the problem on the slip, sends one copy back to the teacher, and keeps the other copy.

Training in violence prevention is reflected in many programs that use prevention as a primary approach to school discipline (Valentine, 1987). These plans usually include teachers, staff, administrators, parents, students, and the community. Teachers are trained to develop appropriate, effective interventions for dealing with student discipline issues with parent support. If these efforts fail, then the school psychologists and counselors are requested to provide additional interventions. If these efforts are unsuccessful, the school administration intervenes. If all interventions fail, then community and legal interventions are requested.

Physical restraint techniques are rarely taught as part of most discipline training programs. As mentioned previously, these methods require intensive training and should be used only when absolutely necessary.

Training in Reward, Punishment, and Ignoring

Table 9.6, on page 294, presents the variables identified in the programs that teach teachers how to use various types of rewards and punishment.

Almost all discipline training programs address the issues of reward and punishment. Although language and conceptualization differ, everyone agrees that students develop best when they feel good about themselves and benefit from both internal and external systems of reward and motivation.

A teacher can indicate high regard and faith in students by affirming their positive traits, having high, realistic expectations, and tailoring activities to the students' abilities (Albert, 1989). High regard is demonstrated by positive comments, such as "You can handle it" and "I know you can do it." Verbal or written affirmation statements recognize students' positive personality traits such as ambition or cheerfulness. Affirming statements encourage students to believe in their known positive traits, as well as encourage them to become aware of hidden traits. Low expectations indicate low confidence in students and may result in poor performance.

Encouragement and praise are not considered the same by some theorists (Nelson et al., 1993). It is easy for a teacher to praise students when they are making good progress in class, but it is difficult to do when a student is not doing well. Although encouragement recognizes effort and improvement, praise recognizes only complete, perfect productions. Encouragement incorporates a respectful and appreciative attitude toward students, while praise is seen as patronizing and manipulative. Therefore, some advocate the use of encouragement rather than praise. Encouragement tells students that they are good enough just the way they are, and separates what they do from who they are. Encouragement teaches students that mistakes are not something to be ashamed of, but are opportunities to grow, learn, and enhance self-esteem.

Praise is a positive social reinforcer promoted by most behavioral programs to maintain or increases appropriate behavior (Savage, 1991). Social reinforcers occur during any social

TABLE 9.6   **Features of Programs That Instruct Teachers in the Use of Reward, Punishment, and Ignoring**

Variable	1995 Data (N = 80)		1982 Data (N = 27)		% Change	
	f	*%*	*f*	*%*		
Reward						
Express high regard for students	35	44	15	56	−	22
Use of encouragement	52	65	14	52	+	13
Use of praise	66	83	13	48	+	35
Use of material reinforcers	50	63	7	26	+	37
Punishment						
Time out	46	58	6	22	+	36
Loss of privilege	34	43	4	15	+	28
In-school suspension	11	14	2	8	+	6
Out-of-school suspension	17	21	1	4	+	17
Detention*	18	23				
Expulsion	7	9	1	4	+	5
Ignoring of misbehavior	51	64	10	39	+	25

Note. *This is a new process that was not used in the 1982 study.

interaction and include positive statements, words of approval, smiles, and laughter when students are humorous.

Material *rewards* include money, tokens, stickers, food, earned time in desired activities, and other tangible rewards (Buckley & Walker, 1978). Material rewards are given with the expectation that the students will maintain or increase their good behaviors.

Punishment is a procedure for reducing misbehavior. It includes giving students a consequence for misbehavior such as doing an activity they do not like to do or taking away a favored activity. Punishment includes time out from positive situations (Alberto & Troutman, 1990).

Loss of privilege is widely used in homes as a mainstay of punishment. In schools it may include staying in during recess, or denial of other favored activities. It is not as widely used in schools because so many school activities are required by the curriculum or by law.

Response cost is a method to reduce inappropriate behavior by removing reinforcers (Alberto & Troutman, 1990). It has been found to be most effective within a token, checklist, or point system. For instance, a student can start with ten points each day. Each time a misbehavior occurs, one point is removed from the pool.

In-school suspension varies widely in its application. The essential elements are that the student (1) is removed from a reinforcing setting, (2) is sent to a nonreinforcing setting, and (3) understands the contingencies that govern the student's passage from one environment to another. This type of punishment should only be used for severe behavior problems (Froyen, 1993). Although the student is in school, the student generally remains in one room all day and has to complete all classwork under conditions that are more demanding and stringent than those in the regular classroom. They are not usually able to go to the lunchroom or any class they may enjoy. It removes the student from the mainstream of student life and the sources of satisfaction or reinforcement the school offers. In these situations, the student must rely on his own resources to make the changes in attitudes and behaviors. A written contract between the student and the teacher should be developed before the student returns from the in-school suspension.

Out-of-school suspension is one of the least effective and desirable punishments, because it is often desired by the student. Federal laws limit the maximum period, for all but extreme misbehaviors, to ten school days (Hartwig & Ruesc, 1994). The use of out-of-school suspension has serious implications and should be carefully considered before it is applied.

Systematic exclusion from school can be effective only if the teacher has the cooperation of the parents and principal (Canter & Canter, 1992). In these situations, the teacher, parents, and principal need to write the details of the plan before the exclusion to be sure that everyone is clear about the conditions and requirements of the exclusion. If the student then displays the severe behavioral problem, the student is excluded from school for the rest of the day. Parents are expected to pick the student up from school, and to have the student stay in his or her room at home for the rest of the day completing the assigned work. This may be effective because it demonstrates to the student that the teacher and parents are working together. Of course, some students enjoy being home in their rooms doing work. An alternative to exclusion is for the parent to spend the day in school with the student.

Detention is when the student is expected to come into school early, stay after school, or return to school on the weekend. This is probably the only truly punishing situation for most students, but it is least used because of the demands for teacher or staff supervision of the students.

Expulsion, which is recommended in few discipline training programs, has serious legal consequences (Froyen, 1993). The student must be given due process, parents and student must receive written notice of the charges, and a hearing date must be scheduled to give the student time to prepare a defense, which is usually within two weeks of the offense. At the hearing, the student has a right to be represented by legal counsel, face his accusers, cross-examine witnesses, and present a defense. The student has a right to an impartial tribunal whose decision must be based solely on the facts presented at the hearing. Beginning in the early 1990s, states have begun to pass laws that require automatic, one-year expulsions for some offenses. Most frequent is the possession of a gun or other weapon in school.

Ignoring of misbehavior is a technique that weakens inappropriate behavior by removing the reinforcers that have been maintaining it. It is a basic technique in both behavioral and humanistic approaches and is widely used in the programs examined. Too many teachers pay too much attention to student misbehaviors. Many students find this attention reinforcing, so they continue with their inappropriate behaviors in order to obtain the teacher's attention (Alberto & Troutman, 1990). This can be true even if the teacher criticizes, corrects, or threatens the student, although these are not appropriate teacher behaviors. Of course you can not ignore potentially violent or dangerous misbehaviors, but there are many irritating behaviors that can be disregarded.

If your attention has consistently followed a student's out-of-seat behavior, and you withhold attention each time the student is out-of-seat, such behavior will be weakened over time if your attention is the reinforcer. At first, you may see an increase in the undesirable behavior. You must maintain consistency during this period. If you cannot tolerate a temporary increase in misbehaver, ignoring is not a good choice.

Training in Democratic Classroom Procedures

Table 9.7 presents the variables identified in the programs that teach teachers how to use democratic classroom procedures.

Classroom problem-solving techniques are designed to teach teachers and students to be more effective and efficient problem solvers. The most popular cognitive–behavioral curricula focus on teaching students how to (1) identify and define a problem, (2) collect relevant information, (3) brainstorm potential solutions, (4) implement and evaluate the results of a chosen solution, (5) give self-reinforcement, and (6) obtain corrective feedback regarding the efficacy of the chosen solution (Elias & Clabby, 1989). The methods of instruction include modeling, social skills training, role playing, cognitive techniques, and behavioral practice. Students can learn anger control through relaxation training and cognitive techniques. Teacher procedures in groups can be used to defuse potentially explosive situations. Family meetings and group discussion also may be used to teach problem-solving techniques.

Student–teacher rule setting occurs when classroom rules are developed jointly by the teacher and students. Research has demonstrated that classroom rules are most effective if teachers and students develop them together. Emphasis should be on establishing a "just society" rather than simply adhering to a "law and order" approach.

The benefits are (1) a higher motivation on the part of children to implement or comply with the rules; (2) decisions of higher quality; (3) closer, warmer relationships between children and adults; (4) higher self-esteem, self-confidence, and sense of control over fate on the part of children; and (5) more personal responsibility and self-discipline (Gordon, 1991).

Student–teacher contracts result from written agreements between students and the teacher. Contingency contracting is a widely used reinforcement program (Long et al., 1985). The teacher and the students indicate the appropriate behaviors that are expected and the consequences for inappropriate behaviors. These contracts can take a variety of forms. Some contracts are based on a point system in which the students earn points for appropriate behaviors that can be exchanged for agreed-on reinforcers such as material rewards, free time, etc.

TABLE 9.7   Features of Programs That Instruct Teachers in Democratic Classroom Procedures

Variable	1995 Data (N = 80)		1982 Data (N = 27)		% Change	
	f	*%*	*f*	*%*		
Classroom problem solving	37	46	16	59	–	13
Student–teacher rule setting	39	49	11	41	+	8
Student–teacher contracts	51	64	7	26	+	38
Class meetings	26	33	6	22	+	11
Use of curricula and/or classroom procedures that promote democratic process*	31	39				

Note. *This is a new process that was not used in the 1982 study.

Class meetings can reflect concepts of participatory democracy. Students can learn the use of parliamentary procedures to resolve problems, learn cooperation, and develop mutual respect.

Developing skills in the effective use of class meetings takes some time and training (Nelson et al., 1993). To use this process, the teacher is taught to replace authoritarian, directive, controlling behaviors with more cooperative behaviors, such as giving fewer lectures and asking the students more questions to find out their opinions and thoughts. The students are encouraged to express their own opinions and are given choices instead of edicts.

Class meetings should be scheduled at least once a week to encourage true communication between teachers and students. Class meetings have eight building blocks, which include (1) forming a circle, (2) practicing compliments and appreciation, (3) creating an agenda, (4) developing communication skills, (5) learning about separate realities, (6) solving problems through role playing and brainstorming, (7) recognizing the four reasons people do what they do, and (8) applying logical consequences and other nonpunitive solutions. An example of the guidelines for developing better communication skills includes suggesting that the teacher have all the students talk at the same time, and then ask the students how many of them felt heard by each other (Nelson et al., 1993).

Curricula or classroom procedures that promote democratic processes improve student behaviors (Long et al., 1985). Although many teachers report that students lack interest, the students may only be disinterested in what the teacher has in mind. To increase student interest and motivation, teachers should always give students some alternatives. Students at all levels can be given choices among at least two different things. Student interest can be heightened by the way the material is presented and relating the topic to the students' occupational goals. The teachers can also use the students' interests to involve them in the curricula.

Training Teachers to Express Emotions Effectively

Table 9.8, presents the variables identified in the programs that teach teachers how to appropriately express their feelings. These programs offer techniques that provide constructive outlets for teachers' emotions while providing feedback to students regarding their behavior.

TABLE 9.8 Features of Programs That Instruct Teachers on the Effective Expression of Emotions

Variable	1995 Data (N = 80)		1982 Data (N = 27)		% Change	
	f	%	f	%		
Displeasure	15	19	12	44	–	25
Anger	28	35	9	33	+	2
Disgust	6	8	7	26	–	18

Displeasure should be expressed immediately and should not include any putdowns or other type of emotional maltreatment. Without overreacting, teachers can use subtle eye contact, soft reprimands, and proximity as means of communicating expectations.

Teacher expressions of annoyance may reinforce students' needs for attention (Nelson et al., 1993). This happens when teachers respond by coaxing noncompliant students. Instead, it is better to tell students that they will obtain the teacher's attention at a later time and redirect them to desired behaviors.

Anger is the most critical of negative emotions felt by teachers regarding students' inappropriate behaviors. Rather than expressing inappropriate anger in the classroom, teachers should attempt to recognize the cause of the anger and direct it appropriately.

Some advocate that when teachers are confronted with an angry student, they need to remain calm and distance themselves from the student's anger. The paradoxical response should be used, which means that the more upset the student becomes, the calmer the teacher has to become (Canter & Canter, 1992).

Anger control training (Goldstein et al., 1987) helps teachers as well as students. Self-instructional training has four major components. First, the teacher has to prepare for the confrontation by making self-statements such as, "This is going to upset me, but I know I can handle it" and "I can work out a plan to handle this."

To cope with anger arousal, self-statements include, "Getting upset will not help," "It's not worth it to get angry," and so forth. After the provocation, teacher reflection includes self-statements such as, "It could have been a lot worse," and "It wasn't as hard as I thought."

Disgust is a natural reaction in some situations, but it should be minimal in classrooms. Feelings of disgust are often accompanied by feelings of guilt (i.e., How can a teacher loathe a student?). However, keeping in mind that it is the student's behavior that is inappropriate allows teachers to provide feedback regarding both the student's behavior and their own feelings regarding the behavior.

When teachers feel disgusted, they may react by retaliating and getting even with the student, which usually intensifies the student's response (Nelson et al., 1993). A more appropriate response would be for the teacher to deal with the hurt feelings by sharing them with the student and by using reflective listening techniques that show the teacher cares.

Training Teachers in Therapeutic Techniques

Table 9.9 presents information regarding various therapeutic techniques that can be used in the classroom. The variables identified in the programs teach teachers how to use these therapeutic techniques.

Affective education techniques are based on curricula that focus on teaching students how to identify and appropriately express their feelings (Dupont et al., 1974).

To teach students to understand and communicate feelings, you can read aloud vignettes about classroom situations and ask the students how the various people in the vignettes feel. Most tend to assume that one feeling is the "right" answer; yet this is not the case. They must learn to respect each person's feelings about a situation.

Students may need to develop cooperative social skills, experience the difficulties in trying to work together, and understand their own expectations and feelings when participating in a group. One way to accomplish these goals is to pick five students whose last names are alphabetically first on the class roster. Ask them to pick three students whose last

TABLE 9.9   Features of Programs That Instruct Teachers in the Use of Therapeutic Techniques

Variable	1995 Data (N = 80)		1982 Data (N = 27)		% Change	
	f	*%*	*f*	*%*		
Affective education	36	45	15	56	−	11
Role playing	41	51	13	48	+	3
Psychodrama	3	4	4	15	−	11
Cognitive techniques (replacing irrational thoughts)*	32	40				
Social skill training (with actual practice)*	28	35				
Self-esteem enhancement*	38	48				
Moral or character development*	18	23				

Note. *These are new processes that were not used in the 1982 study.

names are alphabetically last. The rest of the class is told that these five students are a special new group, and will now select the rest of the members of this group. The rest of the class are asked to write their birth dates and last names on a piece of paper, and then stand up in front of the class in groups of five to be interviewed to see if they will be selected into the special group.

At the end of the process, only eight students will be left in front of the class. The rest of the class is then asked why they think they did not qualify for the group, and how they feel about not being selected. The class is then brought into a semicircle discussion group, and if they can not guess the group membership requirements, they are told. Through this process, the students learn the feelings involved in group acceptance and rejection.

Role playing, which fits theoretically in almost all teacher variance approaches, can be conducted in two ways (Dupont et al., 1974). Students can express their own thoughts and feelings and what they would do in a variety of situations. This method encourages awareness of the students' perceptions, expectations, feelings, and actions.

In role taking, students act out another person's role. For instance, a student may take the role of a teacher handling a typical classroom discipline problem. This enables the student to understand how the teacher may think and feel when dealing with students.

To develop role playing skills, students can be given a script entitled *The New Student* (Dupont et al., 1974). Each student is asked to play a role. In the discussion period after the role play, the students are asked how they interpreted the character's statements, and how these feelings influenced the students' interpretation of the situation.

Children in kindergarten through the primary grades can learn role playing through "make pretend" play (Shure, 1992). To do this, the teachers have to pretend to be tying their shoes, brushing their teach, and so on, and ask their students to guess what they are doing as an introduction to role playing. Then teachers can assign two students to roles such as pretending to be turning a jump rope, one student jumping, and another pushing the student who is jumping. The rest of the class is asked to guess what is going on in the role play, and what is the problem in the role play. Then the students are asked why the student was pushing, what other things could be done instead of pushing, and so forth.

Psychodrama, which was developed by J. L. Moreno as a group psychotherapy technique, did not appear in the 1995 review. However, even though the psychodynamic theory and techniques of this approach are not recognized in most contemporary programs, many role playing concepts and techniques actually stem from psychodrama.

Cognitive techniques are based on the belief that students learn irrational thoughts that lead to inappropriate behaviors. Teachers help students identify their irrational beliefs and replace them with more rational thoughts.

Systematic desensitization is a cognitive behavioral technique that has been most widely used in the treatment of children's fears and phobias (Elliot & Gresham, 1991). Systematic desensitization is a three-step process that teachers can be trained to use in the classroom. The first step requires that the teacher train the students in relaxation techniques, which include tensing and then relaxing various parts of the body in a sequence. Students practice the relaxation steps for 30 minutes daily.

The second step involves developing an anxiety hierarchy in which the students rate anxiety-provoking incidents on a scale of least to most anxiety producing. In the last step, the students relax while visualizing the events from their anxiety hierarchy. They go from the least to the most anxiety-provoking situation. When the images become too anxiety-provoking, students signal by raising their fingers. Then the teacher instructs students to relax and asks them to imagine a scene from a lower level of their hierarchy. These sessions continue until students are able to imagine their most anxiety-provoking incident without experiencing undue anxiety. Students are expected to generalize these skills in the actual situations, using the relaxation techniques to cope with their anxiety.

Social skills training with actual practice appears in programs that provide teachers with lessons or a curricula. In comparison with cognitive training, these programs focus on the development of actual skills in real-life situations. The goal is to help students internalize the skills learned by providing activities and practice of the skills that relate to their own lives and experiences (Elliott & Gresham, 1991). For instance, if a student is practicing to refuse unreasonable requests from others, the generalization skills include: assign homework in which the student has to discuss refusal skills with his or her parents and ask the parents for two or three situations in which the parents have to use refusal skills; discuss how peer pressure influences their decisions; and encourage self-monitoring, in which the student reports his or her use of this skill for one week.

Many students report using the skills they learned through the social skills training in other situations, such as in the classroom (62 percent), with their parents (60 percent), and outside school with friends (59 percent) (Elias & Clabby, 1989). Examples of students' reports include the following:

"One day I forgot my homework at home. I told my teacher calmly, after counting to ten, and using the social problem-solving steps." "My best friend was feeling bad. She walked around the playground sadly, so I asked her what was wrong and she told me and I just made her happy and we played."

Self-esteem is related to the quality of positive or negative views about oneself (Jones & Jones, 1990). The major components of training programs include developing positive feelings of significance as a person, developing competence, and acquiring power.

The *Building Blocks of Self Esteem* (Jones & Jones, 1990) program helps students feel capable, even when they make mistakes. This involves building confidence by focusing on improvement, remembering past successes, and recognizing achievement by teacher-administered material or social rewards. Helping students "connect" with others is accomplished through the five As: acceptance, attention, appreciation, affirmation, and affection. Students learn to accept others' personal styles, greet and listen to them, offer verbal or written appreciation and affirmation, and show affection and kindness when things go bad. Helping students contribute to others is accomplished by encouraging and requesting students to help others with tasks and ideas. This can be put into practice by participation in programs such as peer tutoring, peer counseling, and peer mediation (Albert, 1989).

Moral (character) development programs train teachers to help their students develop values that may be incorporated into any learning program (Ellsworth & Monahan, 1987). This approach was discussed in Chapter 1.

Developmental Discipline (Ellsworth & Monahan, 1987) is a program that uses Kohlberg's stages of moral development to help students understand and develop good character traits and ethical behavior. At Level I (kindergarten through third grade), students generally have needs to satisfy the teacher. These needs can be harnessed by use of clear plans for approved thinking and actions. On Level II (grades 4–6), students' needs for socialization and self-control must be channeled into good character. The teacher must provide the students with opportunities for working in a fair, equitable manner in groups. At Level III (grades 7 through high school), students are developing their self-identity within the context of various subgroup, institutional, and societal values. For instance, within the context of the school, students need to feel that schoolwide rules are fair, consistently enforced, and provide for mitigating circumstances. The student handbook or school discipline policy can promote good moral development if it reflects the values of a just society.

Home Involvement

Table 9.10 presents information on home involvement, which was a minimal part of teacher training in 1982.

Teaching parents specific techniques related to classroom or school discipline enables parents and teachers to develop the most effective techniques for each student. These programs also promote consistency of discipline procedures in the two major settings of children's lives. For instance, Albert (1989) maintains that parents must be informed about the use of her cooperative discipline program before any problems occur. Once parental cooperation is assured, parents will feel free to participate in the school action plan by

TABLE 9.10   Features of Programs That Instruct Teachers in Techniques to Foster Home/School Cooperation

Variable	1995 Data (N = 80)		1982 Data (N = 27)		% Change
	f	*%*	*f*	*%*	
Teaching parents specific techniques related to classroom or school discipline*	30	38			
Use of regular teacher–parent procedures such as a homework checklist*	26	33			

Note. *These are new processes that were not used in the 1982 study.

implementing a complimentary home action plan. Parents are asked to cooperate with the plan either silently or actively.

In a silent partnership, parents agree to receive periodic reports about their child's progress. In an active partnership, parents agree to develop a home action plan. If the parents agree with the latter, the student is invited to a conference during which misbehaviors are identified, intervention strategies are jointly developed, and consequences at school and at home are set. A follow-up conference is arranged to discuss progress and to make any changes needed.

Elias and Clabby (1989) also promote parent involvement in their school-based programs. Training workshops teach parents to develop their own problem-solving skills, which they teach their children. To use the problem-solving steps, you should (1) look for signs of different feelings, (2) tell yourself what the problem is, (3) decide on your goal, (4) stop and think of as many solutions as you can, (5) for each solution, think of all the things that might happen next, (6) choose your best solution, (7) plan how to carry out your solution and make a final check, (8) try the solution, and (9) rethink it if it is not working well.

Use of regular teacher–parent procedures is important to the success of any school-based program involving the home. This requires regularly scheduled teacher–parent conferences to exchange information about both negative and positive situations. In addition, teachers may initiate the use of a homework checklist. The teacher helps students write out all of their assignments for the next day on a small pad or notebook. Parents monitor their children's daily homework assignment and indicate successful completion each day by signing the homework pad, which is then checked by the teacher. If students do not comply, parents and teachers "team up" to improve the process.

Home notes are a variation of homework checklists (Jackson, Jackson, & Monroe, 1983). At the end of each classroom lesson, students are given feedback about their progress. A home note is completed by the teacher for each student. The home notes are printed sheets of paper that summarize the social skill lesson objectives, behaviors the student was taught, and the quality of the work on the top half of the paper. The bottom half of the page asks the parents to observe the child at home and watch for and support the individually noted new skills and behaviors the child was taught. This is expected to help the child to try out the new behaviors at home and obtain the support and encouragement of the parents in their skill development. Then the home note is returned by the child to the teacher, who continues to encourage and support the child's progress.

Summary, Research, and Critique

This last of three chapters on the ESA offers an eclectic overview of major, contemporary discipline training programs. Not included in this review are the 45 processes that are unique to particular programs and so little used that we did not feel it necessary to report them within this context. Although it is probably true that some readers will view this process approach as the ultimate bag of discipline tricks, we hope that these techniques will be adapted within each person's theoretical frame work.

Fifty-six (70 percent) of the programs reviewed in the 1995 study were identified generally as behavioral/cognitive–behavioral, eleven (14 percent) psychodynamic-interpersonal, seventeen (21 percent) ecological/systems, twenty-five (31 percent) humanistic, one biophysical, and fourteen (18 percent) eclectic. The total is more than 100 percent because some of the programs had strong elements of more than one approach.

We have speculated about why so few programs, except behavioral ones, are eclectic. Our data indicate that academic researchers, most often behaviorists, who base their programs on their own studies, usually remain faithful to their theoretical orientations. Many of the most popular programs, especially those developed by entrepreneurs rather than behavioral scientists, may have begun with a specific theoretical orientation. However, as the programs and workshops become increasingly popular and profitable, many authors tend to revise their books and materials by adding new procedures that are contributed by workshop participants, updated reviews of the literature on discipline, and pop psychology. Furthermore, contemporary "buzz words" change in the political climate of the country, and contemporary educational panaceas are introduced into popular programs. As product developers need to expand their offerings, they add new elements to their workshops and, despite their original theoretical orientations, their programs lose the original focus.

The ESA has the advantage of incorporating the best elements of all of the training programs available. Because it is based very much on either systematic observation or empirical studies, it is appealing in terms of its emphasis on actual classroom behavior. However, there are problems with many of the model programs discussed.

None of the models that seek to integrate or synthesize the teacher efficacy literature or combine elements of many approaches can be singled out as the best or most effective. Only specific teacher traits such as enthusiasm, clarity, and businesslike manner have strong empirical support. The borrowing of techniques of models and strategies from each other makes them difficult for all teachers to implement in the same way and difficult to research. Regardless, most if not all of the programs under the heading of ESA that we reviewed embody important concepts and ideas about classroom management.

We hope, by this point, that you will be able to recognize the roots of "new" discipline techniques. Although the ESA tends to use what works best from an ecological perspective, the teacher variance approach also can be used to tease out why a procedure did not work by understanding the underlying theory. This idea leads us to the final chapter, which focuses on the TVA as it applies to some special discipline problems.

Key Terms

action
authoritarian
body language
broken record
classroom ecology
democratic
educational/diagnostic feedback
group alerting
I-messages
ignoring
momentum

open-ended class meeting
overlapping
prevention
problem-solving meeting
punishments
reality therapy
resolution
rewards
smoothness
with-it-ness

Application Activities

1. Develop a lesson plan using Hunter's eight steps of effective instruction.

2. Ask a teacher or your instructor about their class climate. Ask them if you can administer the Hyman A–D scale to a class to assess the class climate. Discuss the results with the teacher or the class.

3. Assess Kounin, Canter, Duke, and Curwin and Mendler's discipline theories using the ecological/systems process approach by categorizing their components. How are they similar? How are they different?

4. Arrange the class into three groups, assign a leader, and practice Glasser's three class meeting approaches. Discuss the advantages and disadvantages.

5. Assign the class into eight groups, each taking one category of the ecological/systems process approach, and assess your instructor according to the variables over a period of a month. How would you characterize your instructor's style?

Books and Manuals Analyzed for Process Analysis

Aetna Life and Casualty Company. (1992). *Resolving conflicts through mediation.* Hartford, CN: Author.

Albert, L. (1989). *Cooperative discipline.* Circle Pines, MN: American Guidance Service.

Alberto, P., & Troutman, A. (1990). *Applied behavioral analysis for teachers* (3rd ed.). Columbus, OH: Merrill.

Alschuler, A. (1980). *School discipline: a socially literate solution.* New York: McGraw Hill.

Axelrod, S. (1983). *Behavior modification for the classroom teacher.* New York: McGraw Hill.

Bash, M., & Camp, B. (1985). *Think aloud.* Champaign, IL: Research Press.

Bauer, A., & Sapona, R. (1991). *Managing classrooms to facilitate learning.* Needham Heights, MA: Allyn & Bacon.

Buckley, N., & Walker, H. (1978). *Modifying classroom behavior.* Champaign, IL: Research Press.

Cangelosi, J. (1993). *Systematic teaching strategies.* White Plains, NY: Longman.

Canter, L. (1992). *Assertive discipline* (rev. ed.). Santa Monica, CA: Lee Canter & Associates.

Cartledge, G., & Milburn, J. (1986). *Teaching social skills to children* (2nd ed.). Needham Heights, MA: Allyn & Bacon.

Charles, C. (1992). *Building classroom management.* (4th ed.). White Plains, NY: Longman.

Clarizio, H. (1980). *Toward positive classroom discipline.* New York: John Wiley.

Curwin, R., & Mendler, A. (1988). *Discipline with dignity.* Alexandria, VA: Association for Supervision and Curriculum Development.

Deutsch-Smith, D., & Rivera, D. (1993). *Effective discipline.* Austin, TX: PRO-ED.

Dinkmeyer, D., McKay, G., & Dinkmeyer, D. Jr. (1980). *Systematic training for effective teaching (STET).* Circle Pines, MN: American Guidance Service.

Duke, D. (1982). *Helping teachers manage classrooms.* Alexandria, VA: Association for Supervision and Curriculum.

Dupont, H., Gardner, O., & Brody, D. (1974). *Toward effective development (TAD).* Circle Pines, MN: American Guidance Service.

Elias, M., & Clabby, J. (1989). *Social decision making skills.* Rockville, MD: Aspen.

Elliot, S., & Gresham, F. (1991). *Social skills intervention guide.* Circle Pines, MN: American Guidance Service.

Ellsworth, J. (1993, Fall). *Developmental management system: Teacher development manual.*

Northern Arizona University: Kurriculum Publishing.

Ellsworth, J., & Monahan, A. (1987). *A humanistic approach to teaching and learning through developmental discipline.* New York: Irvington.

Emmer, E., Evertson, C., Sanford, B., & Worsham, Murray E. (1994). *Classroom management for secondary teachers* (3rd ed.). Englewood Cliffs, NJ: Prentice Hall.

Ernst, K. (1972). *Games students play.* Berkeley, CA: Celestial Arts.

Evertson, C., Emmer, E., Clements, B., Sanford, J., & Worsham, M. (1989). *Classroom management for elementary teachers.* Englewood Cliffs, NJ: Prentice Hall.

Evertson, C., & Harris, A. (1993). *Classroom organization and management program (COMP).* Nashville, TN: Peabody College/Vanderbilt University.

Froyen, L. (1993). *Classroom management* (2nd ed.). New York: Macmillan.

Ginott, H. (1971). *Teacher and child.* New York: Macmillan.

Glasser, W. (1969). *Schools without failure.* New York: Harper & Row.

Glasser, W. (1984). *Control theory in the classroom.* New York: Harper & Row.

Glasser, W. (1992). *The quality school* (2nd ed.). New York: Harper Perennial.

Goldstein, A. (1988). *The prepare curriculum.* Champaign, IL: Research Press.

Goldstein, A., Glick, B., Reiner, S., Zimmerman, D., & Coultry, T. (1987). *Aggression replacement training.* Champaign, IL: Research Press.

Goldstein, A., Sprafkin, R., Gershaw, N., & Klein, P. (1980). *Skillstreaming the adolescent.* Champaign, IL: Research Press.

Good Shepherd Neighborhood House Mediation Program. (1993). *Student mediators training manual.* Philadelphia, PA: Author.

Gordon, T. (1991). *Discipline that works: Promoting self-discipline in children.* New York: Plume-Penguin Group.

Hargis, D. (1992). *The power of anger control: An anger management program for students and adults.* Lenexa, KS: People in Control.

Hunter, M. (1990). *Discipline that develops self discipline.* El Segundo, CA: TIPS.

Idol, L., & West, J. (1993). *Effective instruction of difficult to teach students.* Austin, TX: PRO-ED.

Jackson, N., Jackson, D., & Monroe, C. (1983). *Getting along with others.* Champaign, IL: Research Press.

Johnson, D., & Johnson, R. (1991). *Learning together and alone.* Needham Heights, MA: Allyn & Bacon.

Jones, F. (1987). *Positive classroom discipline.* New York: McGraw Hill.

Jones, V., & Jones, L. (1990). *Comprehensive classroom management.* Needham Heights, MA: Allyn & Bacon.

Kaplan, J., & Drainville, B. (1991). *Beyond behavior modification.* Austin, TX: PRO-ED.

Kauffman, J., Mostert, M., Nuttycombe, D., Trent, S. C., & Hallahan, D. (1993). *Managing classroom behavior: A reflective case-based approach.* Needham Heights, MA: Allyn & Bacon.

Keating, B., Pickering, M., Slack, B., & White, J. (1990). *A Guide to positive discipline.* Needham Heights, MA: Allyn & Bacon.

Kindsvatter, R., & Wilen, W. (1992). *Dynamics of effective teaching.* White Plains, NY: Longman.

Kohl, H. (1976). *The open classroom.* New York: Schocken Books.

Kounin, J. (1970). *Discipline and group management in the classroom.* New York: Holt, Rinehart, & Winston.

Larivee, B. (1992). *Strategies for Effective Classroom Discipline.* Austin, TX: PRO-ED.

Levin, J., & Nolan, J. (1991). *Principles of classroom management.* Austin, TX: PRO-ED.

Long, J., Frye, V., & Long, E. (1985). *Making it till friday.* Princeton, NJ: Princeton Book Company.

Madsen, C. Jr., & Madsen, C. (1981). *Teaching/discipline: a positive approach for educational development.* Needham Heights, MA: Allyn & Bacon.

Mannix, D. (1986). *I can behave.* Austin, TX: PRO-ED.

McGinnis, E., & Goldstein, A. (1990). *Skill-streaming in early childhood.* Champaign, IL: Research Press.

McGinnis, E., Goldstein, A., Sprafkin, R. P., & Gershaw, N. (1984). *Skillstreaming the elementary school child.* Champaign, IL: Research Press.

McQueen, T. (1992). *Essentials of classroom management.* New York: Harper Collins.

Nelson, J., Lott, L., & Glenn, H. (1993). *Positive discipline in the classroom.* Provo, UT: Sunrise, Inc.

Nelson, J. (1987). *Positive discipline.* New York: Ballantine.

Page, P., & Cieloha, D. (1990). *Getting along: A social skills program.* Circle Pines, MN: American Guidance Service.

Paine, S., Radicchi, J., Rosellini, L., Deutschman, L., & Darch, C. (1983). *Structuring your classroom for academic success.* Champaign, IL: Research Press.

Painter, G., & Corsini, R. (1990). *Effective discipline in the home and school.* Muncie, IN: Accelerated Development, Inc.

Rath, L., Harmin, M., & Simon, S. B. (1978). *Values & teaching* (2nd ed.). Columbus, OH: Charles Merrill.

Redl, F., & Wattenberg, W. (1951). *Mental hygiene in teaching.* New York: Harcourt, Brace & Jovanovich.

Sabatino, D., Sabatino, A., & Mann, L. (1983). *Discipline and behavioral management.* Rockville, MD: Aspen.

Sadalla, G., Holmberg, M., & Haligan, J. (1990). *Conflict resolution: An elementary school curriculum.* San Francisco, CA: The Community Board.

Savage, T. (1991). *Discipline for self control.* Needham Heights, MA: Allyn & Bacon.

Schrumpt, F., Crawford, D., & Usadel H. (1991). *Peer mediation.* Champaign, IL: Research Press.

Schumaker, J., Hazek, J., & Pederson C. (1988). *Social skills for daily living.* Circle Pines, MN: American Guidance Service.

Shure, M. (1992). *I can problem solve* (ICPS). Champaign, IL: Research Press.

Stephens, T. (1992). *Social skills in the classroom.* Odessa, FL: PAR.

Swift, M., & Spivack, G. (1975). *Alternate teaching strategies.* Champaign, IL: Research Press.

Tauber, R. T. (1990). *Classroom management: From A-Z.* Fort Worth, TX: Holt, Rinehart, & Winston.

Valentine, M. (1987). *How to deal with discipline problems in the schools.* Iowa: Kendall-Hunt.

Vernon, A. (1989). *Thinking, feeling, behaving.* Champaign, IL: Research Press.

Waksman, S., Messmer, C., & Waksman, D. (1988). *The Waksman social skills curriculum* (3rd ed.). Austin, TX: PRO-ED.

Walker, H., McConnell, S., Holmes, D., Todis, B., Walker, J., & Golden, N. (1988). *The Walker social skills curriculum: The ACCEPTS program.* Austin, TX: PRO-ED.

Walker, H., Todis, B., Holmes, B., & Horton, G. (1988). *The Walker social skills curriculum: The ACCESS program.* Austin, TX: PRO-ED.

Walker, J., & Shea, T. M. (1991). *Behavior modification.* St. Louis: C. V. Mosby.

Wolery, M., Bailey, D., & Sugai, G. (1988). *Effective teaching: Principles and procedures of applied behavioral analysis with exceptional students.* Needham Heights, MA: Allyn & Bacon.

Wolfgang, C., & Glickman, C. (1986). *Solving discipline problems* (2nd ed.). Needham Heights, MA: Allyn & Bacon.

Wood, M., Combs, C., Gun, A., & Weller, D. (1986). *Developmental therapy in the classroom.* Austin, TX: PRO-ED.

Wood, M., & Long, N. (1991). *Life space intervention.* Austin, TX: PRO-ED.

Workman, E. (1982). *Teaching behavioral self control to students.* Austin, TX: PRO-ED.

$$C \; h \; a \; p \; t \; e \; r \quad \textbf{\textit{10}}$$

Special Issues: Victims and Victimizers

Chapter Objectives

After reading this chapter, you should know:

1. The history and research on school violence
2. How to apply the teacher variance approaches to deal with school violence
3. How to define and identify sexual harassment in the schools
4. How to apply the teacher variance approaches to deal with sexual harassment
5. Kinds of and effects of substance abuse
6. How to apply the teacher variance approaches to deal with substance abuse
7. The definition, research, and effects of psychological maltreatment in the schools
8. How to apply the teacher variance approaches to deal with psychological maltreatment in the schools
9. The history and research on corporal punishment in the schools
10. The relationship between corporal punishment and violence in the schools
11. How to apply the teacher variance approaches to deal with corporal punishment in the schools

Through the case of Chris, and the many examples offered throughout this book, we have discussed typical discipline problems. We now address less frequent, high-impact offenses that can terrorize, intimidate, and destabilize schools. Educators and school staff fear rape, extortion, gang warfare, substance abuse, attacks on teachers and students, and weapons offenses, despite their low incidence in most schools. Serious offenses may occur in any school, but data indicate that reported crimes and levels of student and teacher fear are most frequent in impoverished communities with high crime rates.

The media often sensationalizes student victimization of peers and teachers, exaggerating the popular conception of student crime and school disruption. Conversely, public policymakers and school authorities often mask victimization of students by teachers and other school personnel. Acquiescence, trivialization, and cover-ups of student maltreatments can create a climate that increases student anger, aggression, violence, and criminal behaviors. These issues are rarely discussed in the most frequently used survey textbooks on school discipline (Blum, 1994). Yet, educators should be familiar with all of these issues.

In this chapter, we present data about the two faces of school victimization. In the first section, teacher variance is applied to the problems of school violence, sexual harassment, and substance abuse. The final section discusses psychological maltreatment and corporal punishment of students by educators. In these situations, disciplinary excesses of teachers result in victimization of students and create more, rather than fewer, problems.

The Problem of School Violence

Historians say that disorder and violence have been intrinsic to European, English, and American schools for centuries. For example, schoolchildren in seventeenth century France were often armed, feared by their schoolmates and ordinary citizens alike (Aries, 1962). It was not uncommon for French students to engage in duels, brawls, mutinies, and beatings of teachers. In English public schools, between 1775 and 1836, mutinies, strikes, and violence were frequent. These uprisings were sometimes so severe that schoolmasters sought intervention by the military (Newman, 1980). American schools also have had a history of violence, including attacks on teachers by both students and parents (Finkelstein, 1989).

Contemporary studies indicate that American society has the highest rate of interpersonal violence of all Western democracies (American Psychological Association, 1993). Behavior involving sex, drugs, gambling, and violence was common among children throughout the centuries; what has steadily increased is our concern over the behavior (Moles, 1990).

How Bad Is the Problem?

The landmark research on school violence was the Safe School Study, which represented one of the earliest attempts to study school violence systematically. Despite grave concerns about the problem, data (National Institute of Education, 1978) indicated a relatively low increase and then a tapering off in the late 1970s. For instance, percentages of teachers who were victims of violence in 1956 were 1.6 percent; in 1972, 2.2 percent; in 1974, 3.0 percent; and in 1976, 2.9 percent.

Media hype has historically depicted schools as extremely dangerous places. Rubel (1977) tracked the number of articles about school violence which appeared in the *New York Times* between 1960 and 1975. Ganci and Kleiman (1996) conducted a similar analysis for the period between 1990–1995. The results of these two studies are shown in Figure 10.1.

Rubel included all types of articles in his analysis. In order to improve on that methodology, Ganci and Kleiman separated articles into two categories. As can be seen, the number of articles reporting actual incidence in the schools is relatively low. The majority of articles report opinions and discuss policy issues regarding school violence.

School crime and violence are a problem, but data do not indicate dramatic increases in recent years. Although any school violence is too much, crimes such as student victim-

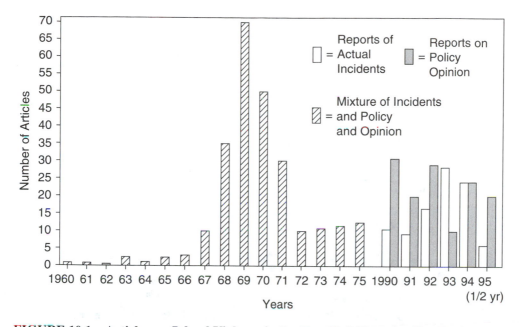

FIGURE 10.1 **Articles on School Violence in the *New York Times* for Two Periods**

ization have remained relatively stable from 1980 to 1994. Figure 10.2, on page 310, displays information to illustrate this.

Despite public perceptions, in 1991, nearly seven of ten high school teachers thought they had substantial or complete control over students in their classrooms. Only 1 percent believed they had no control. These percentages have remained stable from 1988 (National Center for Education Statistics, 1992). Depending on their school district, 0 to 2 percent of teachers felt unsafe in their schools during the school day, but 15 percent of urban teachers did not feel secure in their buildings after school hours. Furthermore, in a 1991 study of teacher victimization, from 12 percent to 28 percent reported verbal abuse within the four weeks preceding the study, 4 percent to 15 percent reported threats of injury, and fewer than 1 to 3 percent were physically attacked within the 12 months preceding the study. Teachers in urban schools represent higher percentages and were therefore much more likely to have been victimized (National Center for Education Statistics, 1992). As with all crime reports, accuracy is a problem. The data presented here indicate modest fluctuations of school violence over the last several decades. Large fluctuations in reports may be artifacts of reporting procedures, reflections of larger social problems, or actual increases in certain more violent activities, such as shootings.

In 1994, data compiled by the U.S. Department of Education indicated that within a twelve-month period, 46 percent of teachers reported that student misbehavior interfered substantially with their teaching. In 1993, 23 percent of eighth-graders were involved in serious student fights; 19 percent of teachers were verbally abused; 12 percent of teachers feared for their safety; 8 percent of teachers were threatened with bodily harm; 2 percent of teachers were physically attacked.

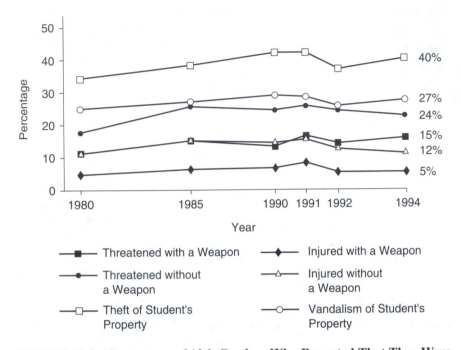

FIGURE 10.2   Percentage of 12th Graders Who Reported That They Were Victimized at School during the Previous Year, 1980 to 1992 and 1994

This information is presented in the 1992 and 1995 National Education Goals Report.
Source: University of Michigan, 1993, 1995.

Schools as Safe Havens

In response to public rhetoric about school crime, we conducted a systematic examination of the data on the relative dangers in schools and found that schools are one of the safest institutions for children and youth (Hyman, Olbrich, & Shanock, 1994).

The Criminal Victimization in the United States Reports (U.S. Department of Justice, 1991, 1992, 1993, 1994) indicate that rape, robbery, and assault are more likely to occur in the home than in school. Table 10.1 presents data that compares national crime rates in different settings, including the school.

As may be seen, homes are actually one of the most dangerous places for children. In 1992, 91 percent of the approximately 2.9 million abused or neglected children were victimized by family members (U.S. Department of Health and Human Services, 1994). Family members accounted for 91 percent of the abuses. This resulted in 1,068 deaths in forty-four reporting states (The National Committee for the Prevention of Child Abuse estimates 1,260 deaths nationwide). Even in the most violent cities, children are safer in schools. In 1991, the aggravated assault rate in Chicago, a highly violent city, was 1,502/100,000, whereas in 1992, the public school rate was 325/100,000 (Chicago Public Schools, The Bureau of Safety and Security, 1994).

TABLE 10.1   Percent Distribution of Crime Incidents, by Type of Crime and Place of Occurrence

Type of Crime	Number of Incidents	At/In Home	Near Home	Street Near Home	In School Building	On School Property
1992	5,964,090	12.0%	7.3%	4.3%	6.2%	5.9%
Rape	131,530	16.3	7.9	4.5	7.1	0.9
Robbery						
Armed offender	600,790	7.5	6.2	5.6	0.6	1.0
Unarmed offender	369,410	16.7	5.8	8.1	6.8	2.4
Assault						
Armed offender	1,499,410	9.1	8.7	6.2	2.0	5.7
Unarmed offender	2,729,100	15.3	7.4	2.5	10.3	8.4
1991	5,836,160	10.9	7.1	3.7	5.4	5.6
Rape	171,420	26.8	3.2	2.1	2.1	1.0
Robbery						
Armed offender	584,660	8.3	6.6	5.3	0.0	1.7
Unarmed offender	329,370	12.7	4.1	4.9	4.2	4.2
Assault						
Armed offender	1,265,580	11.4	8.4	4.4	2.1	4.3
Unarmed offender	2,854,730	11.3	7.0	2.7	9.3	7.9
1990	5,251,000	13.1	7.1	4.0	5.3	4.5
Rape	124,480	35.0	10.3	2.0	0.0	0.0
Robbery						
Armed offender	514,480	7.9	3.6	6.2	0.9	0.9
Unarmed offender	394,540	13.0	2.4	1.3	7.1	2.0
Assault						
Armed offender	1,177,100	11.5	8.3	4.7	1.8	3.6
Unarmed offender	2,566,320	14.8	7.6	3.1	8.3	6.3

Source: Criminal Victimization in the United States, 1993, 1992, 1991.

School Homicides

According to the Center to Prevent Handgun Violence, seventy students were shot to death in 1990. Even one death is too many, but when compared with homicides in other settings, schools are still relatively safe.

In 1986 to 1990, at least seventy-one persons were killed with guns at school (U.S. Department of Education, 1993). To compare school and home violence rates, we selected some states with very high crime rates. These data are reported in Tables 10.2 on page 312 and 10.3 on page 313.

Between the academic years of 1992 and 1993, the Los Angeles Public Schools reported three homicides. One of those deaths was accidental (Los Angeles Unified Public Schools—Department of Security, 1994). The Los Angeles homicide rate for 1991 was 29.30/100,000 persons (California Department of Justice, Division of Law Enforcement, 1993), and for the schools in 1992, it was 0.12/100,000.

TABLE 10.2   Violent Crime Rates in Florida Counties and Public Schools

Region or School District	No. of Incidents	Rate per 100,000
Homicide Rate per 100,000 Persons and Number of Homicides Occurring in Selected Florida Counties and Public Schools, 1993		
Florida*	1,187	8.70
Florida Public Schools†	18	00.91
Dade County‡	339	17.38
Dade County Public Schools§	3	1.02
Hillsborough County‖	74	8.35
Hillsborough County Public Schools¶	0	0.00
Robbery Rate per 100,000 Persons and Number of Robberies Occurring in Florida Counties and Public Schools, 1993		
Florida*	47,742	350.80
Florida Public Schools†	424	21.39
Dade County‡	17,705	907.90
Dade County Public Schools§	339	115.30
Hillsborough County‖	4,173	470.90
Hillsborough County Public Schools¶	7	5.51
Aggravated Assault per 100,000 Persons and Number of Aggravated Assaults Occurring in Florida Counties and Public Schools, 1993		
Florida*	99,108	728.30
Florida Public Schools†	11,060	558.39
Dade County‡	21,819	1118.00
Dade County Public Schools§	1,947	662.10
Hillsborough County‖	9,337	1042.00
Hillsborough County Public Schools¶	9	7.08
Rape per 100,000 Persons and Number of Rapes Occurring in Florida Counties and Public Schools, 1993		
Florida*	13,752	101.10
Florida Public Schools†	23	7.82
Dade County‡	1,659	85.02
Dade County Public Schools§	23	7.82
Hillsborough County‖	1,149	100.60
Hillsborough County Public Schools¶	0	0.00

*Florida Department of Law Enforcement, 1994.
†Florida Department of Law Enforcement, 1994.
‡Dade County Police Department, 1994.
§Dade County Public Schools—Office of School Police, 1994.
‖Hillsborough County Law Enforcement, 1994.
¶Hillsborough County Public Schools—Department of Security, 1994.

School Responses to Violence

Most violence prevention approaches include such methods as metal detectors, increased police presence in schools, uniformed or nonuniformed guards, student and staff I.D. cards, and forbidding beepers on school grounds. Punishment alternatives such as boot camps, wil-

TABLE 10.3   Homicide Rate per 100,000 Persons in Selected Large Cities and Public Schools, 1993*

Region or School District	Year	Rate
Texas*	1991	15.30
Dallas†	1991	48.60
Dallas ISD‡	1993	00.71
Houston§	1991	36.50
Houston ISD‖	1993	00.48
Chicago¶	1991	29.30
Chicago Public Schools#	1992	00.24
Los Angeles**	1991	29.30
Los Angeles Public Schools††	1992	00.12
Aggravated Assaults per 100,000 Persons		
Texas*	1991	485.00
Dallas†	1991	1308.00
Dallas ISD‡	1993	16.00
Houston§	1991	657.00
Houston ISD‖	1993	38.00
Chicago¶	1991	1502.00
Chicago Public Schools#	1992	325.00*
Los Angeles**	1991	1324.00
Los Angeles Public Schools††	1992	47.00

Homicide rates for states and cities are from published sources. School rates were determined by number of homicides for each school as a ratio of each 100,000 students in the school.

*Texas Police Department, 1992.
†American Almanac, 1993.
‡Dallas Independent School District, Department of Safety, 1994.
§American Almanac, 1993.
‖Houston Independent School District, 1994.
¶Illinois State Police, 1992.
#Chicago Public Schools—Bureau of Safety and Security, 1992.
**California Department of Justice, 1992.
††Los Angeles Unified School District, 1993.

derness camps, mandatory drug offender penalties, and adjudicating delinquents as if they were adults have been instituted. However, although these and similar measures may be necessary parts of a total system, they do not address the underlying issues, which involve attitudes of students and staff, social contracts, and school discipline policies. Social scientists frequently, and often impotently, point out the lack of evidence for the success of most of these approaches. Despite this, programs shown not to reduce recidivism, such as boot camps, continue to be funded (American Psychological Association, 1993).

Studies of teachers and administrators suggest that discipline and school violence are important issues, but other matters such as lack of financial resources for school-based programs, inadequate parenting of students, the culture of poverty, and student substance abuse are of equal or greater concern to school staff (Elam, 1989; Elam & Rose, 1995; Hyman, 1990a; Hyman & D'Allesandro, 1984a; Moles, 1990). Yet, most polls fail to recognize the complex relationship between all of the above-mentioned problems. Nor do most educators consider a theory-driven approach such as teacher variance, which we apply here.

Behavioral/Cognitive–Behavioral Approach to School Violence

Behavioral theory treats violence as a learned response. Violent youth invariably learn their aggressive behaviors from their parents or other role models. Furthermore, when violence works to obtain desired ends, it becomes reinforcing for the aggressor (Goldstein, 1989; McCord, 1991; Patterson, 1982). Aggressors learn early in life that they can get what they want by their behavior and consequently never learn alternate ways of solving problems. They usually have an impoverished repertoire of responses to frustration and little knowledge or skills to handle their stress appropriately.

Any institutional response to violence must arrange the physical and psychological environment so that violence is not rewarded. For instance, if suspension is the major punishment for fighting, and if suspension is desired by the students, it is reinforcing rather than punishing. If gang activity and the streets offer more reinforcement than school, the school must mobilize to become more rewarding and relevant to the students' lives. Schools in severely depressed, violent areas, which offer so-called wraparound services, may provide the best opportunity for a reinforcing environment. They can offer meals, medical services, counseling, social and work opportunities, sports activities such as night basketball leagues, and other activities important to adolescents.

The most difficult aspect of extinguishing aggression may involve training parents not to model or reward aggression. Most parents of aggressive children were themselves treated aggressively by their parents. They often do not know alternative ways to discipline children and youth.

Recognizing the importance of early modeling, behaviorists and cognitive–behaviorists promote early prevention and intervention through curriculum approaches, which teach problem-solving skills and clearly work to extinguish aggression.

To control violence, all contingencies must be controlled. This requires a clearly articulated program that is maintained by all school staff. If contingencies cannot be controlled in the regular class and school, students should be placed in special settings that include a system of levels based on conduct. Students must earn the privileges that accrue from appropriate behavior at each level until they can function adequately without all reinforcements being strictly controlled by school staff.

Behaviorists and cognitive–behaviorists recognize that successful programs will provide students with adequate opportunities to replace antisocial behavior with prosocial behavior and that the goal is that social reinforcement, self-praise, and praise by authorities will shape good behavior.

Psychodynamic/Interpersonal Approach to School Violence

The psychodynamic approach views school violence as resulting from students' failure to develop proper ego and superegos. Superegos that are underdeveloped or harsh and punitive may cause conduct problems. Psychological evaluations of violent youth invariably indicate that something went wrong during the early stages of development.

Interpersonal violence results from a total distortion of a child's development of morality and indicates a failure to reach higher levels of morality. This distortion is caused by caregivers whose relations with children have been typified by use of denial or withdrawal of love, emotional rejection, severe punishment, inconsistent rule enforcement, or lack of limits of inappropriate behavior.

The violent student views others as objects to be manipulated or as people whose basic motives are malevolent. Others are incapable of providing for normal need fulfillment and therefore are not worthy of consideration for reciprocal caring. Authoritarian teachers and administrators and useless rules and regulations are perceived as further sources of frustration. In essence, the violent student is often a product of an uncaring, demeaning, and emotionally and physically deprived environment. Therefore, the solution is to provide an environment that can help to undo the harm that was done.

Normal schooling is replete with sanctions, opportunities for rejection, and constant pressure for conformity, academic productivity, and impulse control. This environment cannot even begin to heal students who are prone to violence. Therefore, schools need to provide therapeutic alternative schools, therapeutic summer camps, individual and group therapy, and esteem-building activities to stem violence. School staff must provide for informal and formal learning. However, they must tie the learning to the needs of the student and not be bound by academic curricula.

Treatment requires uncovering the root causes of the problem and attempting to help individuals to work through the problems that accrued at specific developmental stages. Schools need to develop therapeutic alliances with mental health professionals while students are working through their problems. This can be accomplished by activities that promote self-esteem and fair, nonpunitive approaches to discipline.

Humanistic Approach to School Violence

Humanistic alternative schools begin with the assumption that the most important goal is to provide unconditional positive regard for each student. Each teacher assumes, and conveys to the students, the belief that every person has an innate desire to be good, to do good, and to be perceived as good. Misbehavior is treated as a reflection of underlying feelings of frustration and unhappiness caused by rigid rules and regulations and uncaring bureaucracies. When the student's behavior impinges on the rights of others, the student is helped to understand why he or she committed the act. This process may be conducted individually or as part of ongoing group meetings.

The alternative school may provide daily small group meetings to help students to explore their feelings and to solve individual and school problems. Depending on the expertise of the group leaders, these groups offer various levels of therapy. The therapy is often based on gestalt approaches that encourage members to express their innermost feelings and provide for exercises and experiences that teach members to trust each other and the group leader. Once the basic needs for trust and safety are satisfied, the school can provide for the other needs in the hierarchy that leads toward self-actualization. This will result in cultivation of the student's innate desire to develop empathy and caring for others and cessation of violent, antisocial behavior.

Biophysical Approach to School Violence

Growing evidence indicates a substantial biological basis for violence, especially in extremely aggressive career criminals. Recent research implicates malfunctioning in the frontal lobes of the brain. Brain malfunctioning, sometimes due to heredity, may also cause high levels of depression, anxiety, and psychoses that cause violence. Students with head trauma and those with attention deficit hyperactivity disorder are also prone to loss of control and acting out behavior.

The biophysical approach suggests that problems of violence be treated on an individual basis. Psychological, neurological, and psychiatric diagnoses should be considered in all cases in which children demonstrate an early lack of impulse control, aggressive response styles to frustration, and early learning problems.

Short-term hospitalization may be required in some cases to determine appropriate types and levels of medication. Furthermore, all school districts should provide for classification of students whose aggressive behavior may be driven by brain dysfunction and other biophsyical problems. Some of these students may require highly restrictive and structured special school placements.

Ecological/Systems Approach to School Violence

The ecological/systems approach to school violence is based on the assumption that the problem is systemic. A true understanding begins with an analysis of community attitudes, resources, and behaviors toward youth violence. The school is a reflection of the surrounding community, and therefore violence prevention is dependent on mobilizing community agencies to promote cooperation in all areas that may impact on school violence. This approach is illustrated in Chapter 8, where we present a problem-solving matrix for dealing with school violence. Levels of intervention and diagnosis categories are discussed there in detail.

Sexual Activity and Sexual Harassment in Schools

Sexual Activity

Since colonial times, American schools have been concerned with controlling students' sexual behavior. Despite this concern, we have one of the highest teenage pregnancy rates in the industrialized world. Our rates are twice as high as those of England, Wales, France, and Canada; three times as high as those in Sweden; and seven times as high as those in the

Netherlands (Kaplan, 1992). Until relatively recently, pregnant students were subject to severe disciplinary sanctions, which included suspension or expulsion from school. Yet, attempts by school boards to provide preventive efforts such as sex education and condoms to prevent pregnancy and sexually transmitted diseases frequently provoke politically and religiously based resistance. Opponents of these programs claim that sex education encourages sexual activity and that teaching abstinence is the only approach that is morally acceptable in a school setting.

School-based prevention measures are based on the assumption, supported by historical evidence and contemporary research, that it is virtually impossible to stop students from engaging in sexual activities. Most school authorities, medical experts, and mental health practitioners, without encouraging premarital sex, attempt to promote safe sex practices to help students avoid diseases and unwanted pregnancies. However, these approaches, based on research and successful public policy experiences in other countries, sometimes result in loss of school board seats and firing of staff. For instance, in 1993, plans for preventive curricula and distribution of condoms were among the major causes for the dismissal of the New York City school superintendent.

In a speech in 1994, former Surgeon General Dr. Jocelyn Elders indicated that masturbation is a natural human activity, implying it is a better alternative to sexual intercourse and it does not lead to disease and unwanted pregnancy. Elders's opponents distorted her words, claiming she advocated teaching masturbation in school. This, of course, sparked considerable public controversy, resulting in her dismissal.

We are overly concerned with the punishment of unauthorized sexual activities, even when those activities include talking about sex, looking at pictures depicting nudity, or writing about sex. For instance, at least once in their careers, almost every teacher catches a student passing a sexually explicit note, picture, or limerick to a classmate. Although we are quick to mete out punishment for such behavior, we are less willing to seek out and understand the sexual concerns and questions reflected in these acts. The reluctance to deal with teenage sexuality was illustrated by a successful effort led by Senator Jesse Helms of North Carolina to quash a proposal for a major national study of teenage sexual activity. The results were meant to provide a clear picture of adolescent sexual activity and offer guidelines that would provide us with policies to prevent the spread of sexually transmitted diseases.

Sexual Harassment

Sexual harassment is a disciplinary problem because it creates a hostile learning environment in which victims may become fearful, anxious, withdrawn, angry, or suffer severe loss of self-esteem. Their lack of faith in school authorities' ability to protect them may result in lower academic performance, retaliation, withdrawal from school, or acceptance of their role as sexual victims. Considering the extent of the problem, it is poorly addressed. As one fifteen-year-old girl reported, "Teachers and other students can do it and students don't want to say anything. If I complain to my classmates, they will think that I'm full of myself. There's no point."

The inability to address issues of teenage sexuality explains why sexual harassment in the schools was not acknowledged as a problem until recently. Previously, such unwanted activities as flirting, sexually suggestive comments, and touching were seen as an inevitable consequence of having males and females attend school or work together. Many believed that men should not be held responsible for their behavior when they were in close proximity to women. Therefore, sexual harassment, especially in schools, was considered a trivial matter, explained away by the belief that "boys will be boys." This type of thinking excused the need to examine the issue of sexual harassment.

A victim of sexual harassment was, and often still is, more likely to be blamed than to be treated as an unwilling participant. Sexual harassment has generally been viewed as an isolated, interpersonal problem. In the early 1990s, after the famous Senate hearings during which Anita Hill accused Justice Clarence Thomas of sexual harassment, the problem has been identified as widespread. Yet, our difficulty in dealing with the issue has historical roots within the schools.

What is sexual harassment, and how widespread is it in our schools? We define sexual harassment in the educational environment as any unwanted sexual attention from administrators, teachers, peers, or school staff. The range of behaviors includes leering, pinching, grabbing, suggestive verbal comments, pressure for sexual activity, spreading sexual rumors, making sexual or sexist jokes, pulling at another student's clothing, cornering or brushing up against a student in a sexual way, insulting comments referring to students' sexual orientation, date rape, sexual graffiti about a student, or engaging in any other actions of a sexual manner that might create a hostile learning environment.

Sexual harassment is widespread in schools. In 1993, the American Association of University Women (AAUW) conducted a study of sexual harassment in public schools. More than 75 percent of the girls and 66 percent of the boys said they had been the target of unwanted sexual comments, jokes, gestures, or looks. Sixty-six percent of the girls and 42 percent of the boys reported having been touched, grabbed, or pinched. Student-to-student harassment was the most common, accounting for 80 percent of the harassment, whereas teachers, custodians, and coaches were responsible for 20 percent. The results of the study are summarized in Figure 10.3.

Other studies have found equally alarming evidence of adult-to-student sexual harassment. For example, a study by Strauss (1988) indicated that 30 percent of victims reported having been harassed by teachers. Another study reflected that American schoolchildren consider sexual aggression to be an expected part of school life (AAUW, 1993). In this study of 1,700 sixth-graders, 65 percent of the boys and 47 percent of the girls agreed with statements indicating that it was acceptable for a man to force a woman to have sex after they had been dating for six months. This attitude may account for the fact that, in a recent ten-year period, rape arrests for boys younger than fourteen years almost doubled.

Myra and David Sadker (1994) claim that a hostile school setting discourages girls from fully participating in their own education. They learn to devalue themselves and their academic potential. Furthermore, boys often receive mixed messages about sexual harassment. In too many schools, athletes receive subtle and sometimes overt approval from fathers, male coaches, and peers that "sowing their wild oats" is a perfectly normal, macho behavior. This is often seen as approval for behaviors ranging from unwanted touching to date rapes and "gang bangs" (Gelman & Rogers, 1993).

School administrators may be inconsistent in dealing with sexual harassment between students and even between faculty and students. From our personal observations, we would

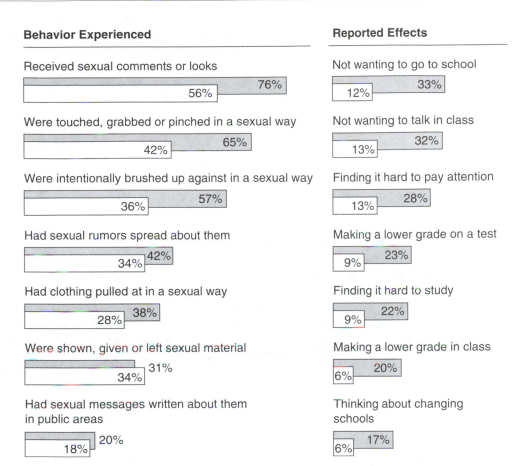

Behavior Experienced

Received sexual comments or looks
76%
56%

Were touched, grabbed or pinched in a sexual way
65%
42%

Were intentionally brushed up against in a sexual way
57%
36%

Had sexual rumors spread about them
42%
34%

Had clothing pulled at in a sexual way
38%
28%

Were shown, given or left sexual material
31%
34%

Had sexual messages written about them in public areas
20%
18%

Reported Effects

Not wanting to go to school
33%
12%

Not wanting to talk in class
32%
13%

Finding it hard to pay attention
28%
13%

Making a lower grade on a test
23%
9%

Finding it hard to study
22%
9%

Making a lower grade in class
20%
6%

Thinking about changing schools
17%
6%

FIGURE 10.3   **Two-Thirds of All Students in Grades 8 through 11 Have Experienced Unwelcome Sexual Behavior in School**

Source: American Association of University Women, 1993

guess that there are few high schools, within any given five- to ten-year period, where at least one faculty member has not had sexual relations with a student. Most often, even though the affair is known by others, it is either unreported to authorities or the authorities quietly end it without any publicity or punishment for the educator.

Behavioral/Cognitive–Behavioral Approach to Sexual Harassment

Inappropriate sexual behavior is learned and reinforced by both social factors and physiological responses. There is ample evidence that the nature of early sexual exposure and experiences can establish lifelong patterns of sexual behavior. If these early experiences are related to deviancy or are misinterpreted because the child is unable, because of his or her developmental stage, to process the experience appropriately, aberrant sexual orientation may occur. Classical conditioning occurs when early sexual stimulation and arousal (physiological responses) are paired with social stimuli. This latter could include molestation; inappropriate sexually arousing words, pictures, and thoughts; and observations of deviant sexual activities. The pairing of sexual activity with violence, male domination over women, and other situations in which sex is an expression of power can set the stage for sexual harassment behaviors in school.

A behavioral/cognitive–behavioral approach would try to extinguish the behavior through a combination of education and punishment. If the school creates a climate in which peer approval of sexual harassment is significantly reduced, the likelihood for reinforcement lessens. Also, girls could learn more assertive behaviors and try various types of deterrence and refusal skills.

Punishment can be based on repression of the behavior by helping the boys to think about how their mothers, sisters, or girlfriends would react to molestation. This can cause a reduction in physiological arousal if negative thoughts or rejection from loved ones are associated with this type of sexual behavior.

Uncontrolled sexual impulses invariably relate to unresolved issues in early parent–child relations. Sexual repression used by parents and society can cause deviant sexual orientations. The behavioral–cognitive approach stresses the recognition and acceptance of sexual drives and the need to provide students with healthy, appropriate expressions of their needs. Students who act improperly must develop internal dialogues to attack sexual thoughts and feelings that might cause them to act inappropriately.

Psychodynamic/Interpersonal Approach to Sexual Harassment

The psychodynamic/interpersonal approach to sexual harassment recognizes that sexual drives are instinctive and cannot be continually repressed without the development of neurosis. However, mature and appropriate expression of sexuality cannot occur without the development of adequate ego and superego controls. The PI approach stresses the importance of early education so that from their first explorations of their own bodies children learn that sexual expression is natural and healthy. They also learn that these drives must be controlled and expressed in socially approved ways. These messages are reinforced by the implementation of developmentally appropriate sex education courses from kindergarten through high school.

A major way to divert unhealthy sexual expressions is to provide many opportunities for productive rechanneling or sublimation of sexual drives into activities such as sports, music, academic studies, community service, and other socially approved endeavors. Those who sexually harass others may suffer from feelings of sexual impotence, regressed sexuality, or a neurotic need for power. Sexual harassment may be socially acceptable and encouraged by peer groups; therefore, intervention may require education and short-term therapy groups. However, repeat offenders are probably expressing neurotic needs and should be treated in psychotherapy.

Schools need to provide for the development of sublimating activities for all students. However, students must learn to feel successful to sublimate.

Humanistic Approach to Sexual Harassment

Sexual behavior between consenting persons is a natural expression of our needs and is never viewed as sinful by the humanist. All individuals should be entitled to consensual sexual activities as long as no one is harmed. Sex is appropriate for any two partners who seek the pleasure and closeness of the activity. This perception of sexual activity has resulted in periodic attacks on humanists by the religious and political right. Sex education programs promoted by humanists have been misinterpreted as encouraging students to engage in premature and self-destructive sexual activities. However, this is not the case.

Humanists' goals regarding sex education are to provide students with factual information about the physical and emotional aspects of sex. However, the actual decision to engage in sex is up to the individual student. Students are encouraged to discuss their feelings, their readiness for sex, and the bases of their decisions to engage in physical intimacy with another person. Within the humanist framework, sex is immoral if it involves coercion, manipulation, or if it hurts the partner.

The solution to student sexual harassment, date rapes, and sexism is to help every student to understand what harm these activities do to victims. If the school promotes an atmosphere of caring and concern for others, these problems will not occur. But strict rules, repression, condemnation, and a variety of sanctions regarding sexual thoughts, discussion, and activities will only serve to increase student desires.

Biophysical Approach to Sexual Harassment

The biophysical approach to sexual harassment focuses on medical or psychiatric causes of harassment, especially when the behavior results from poor impulse control. There is special concern when the behavior goes beyond the "norms" of the harasser's peer group. For instance, although some groups of boys might believe that it is OK to make obscene comments or gestures to girls passing in the school hallway, most will cease if the behavior is appropriately sanctioned. Students who may have serious problems are likely to continue the misbehavior. They may become obsessive or loud or begin to confront angrily or grab passing girls. Increases in intensity or frequency of this sexually harassing behavior could indicate serious emotional or neurological problems. Examples of such problems include obsessive–compulsive disorder, lowering of normal levels of inhibition because of alcohol or drug use, closed-head brain trauma, or delusional thinking.

Rather than focusing on punishment of students who seem unable to desist from harassing behavior, it is important to provide a complete medical/psychological/neurological/psychiatric evaluation. This behavior may be the harbinger of more serious sexually related, illegal activities.

Ecological/Systems Approach to Sexual Harassment

The ecological/systems approach to sexual harassment is based on the assumption that this behavior is maintained and encouraged by systemic approval or indifference. As with other problems, the ESA tends to focus on prevention. Prevention is most effective when it places sexual harassment within its social context. The cause is neither the failure of the particular school nor the inabilities of specific individuals to handle interpersonal problems. Rather, it is the failure of the community and culture to spell out the extent, nature, meaning, and implications of sexual harassment.

Prevention of sexual harassment within the ESA should include clear guidelines and educational programs that sensitize students and faculty to causes and consequences of sexual harassment regarding both the victims and victimizers. Curricula should be developmentally appropriate and offer lots of concrete examples.

School staff should develop systemwide plans for employee and student training and guidelines to help students who have been sexually harassed. Staff and students need to understand their rights and responsibilities and should become aware of appropriate responses to harassment. Such a plan will enable students to identify their legal and administrative options for responding to sexual harassment.

Staff and student training may be accomplished through formal curricula, videotapes, and role playing. The goal is to provide prevention of, early identification of, and clear guidelines for the elimination of sexual harassment at institutional and individual levels.

Students should be trained to respond effectively to sexual harassment. Responses may include:

1. Talking to a friend, counselor, or relative about the situation to place the facts in perspective and develop solutions
2. Learning not to laugh at the harassing behavior
3. Learning skills to confront the harasser with a firm NO at the first sign of sexual harassment and letting the harasser know that this behavior will not be tolerated
4. Avoiding being alone with harassers
5. Talking with other students to see if they have been harassed and, if so, petitioning school authorities to deal with the problem
6. Obtaining eyewitnesses to verify experiences of harassment
7. Keeping a written record documenting all incidents, with dates, times, places, and persons who have seen the activity, and recording physical and emotional reactions
8. Filing complaints

Substance Abuse

Cigarettes

Table 10.4 provides an indication of the problems associated with six frequently used substances that cause dependency. Nicotine, one of the most addictive of all drugs, is readily available to any student who wants it.

Cigarettes rank as major addictors. Research indicates that 45 percent of cocaine addicts, 38 percent of heroin addicts, and 50 percent of alcoholics rank cigarettes to have addictive qualities as strong as their major drug (Hilts, 1994). Because of wide availability of cigarettes and our knowledge of its powerful physiological and psychological addictive qualities, many school discipline policies toward smoking create a dilemma for those who understand the problem. Should smoking be treated as a medical/psychological issue or should smokers be treated as rule breakers?

TABLE 10.4   How Experts Rate Problem Substances

Substance	Withdrawal	Reinforcement	Tolerance	Dependence	Intoxication
Henningfield Ratings					
Nicotine	3	4	2	1	5
Heroin	2	2	1	2	2
Cocaine	4	1	4	3	3
Alcohol	1	3	3	4	1
Caffeine	5	6	5	5	6
Marijuana	6	5	6	6	4
Benowitz Ratings					
Nicotine	3*	4	4	1	6
Heroin	2	2	2	2	2
Cocaine	3*	1	1	3	3
Alcohol	1	3	4	4	1
Caffeine	4	5	3	5	5
Marijuana	5	6	5	6	4

Source: Hilts, P. J. (1994, August 2). Is nicotine addictive? It depends on whose criteria you use. *New York Times,* p. C3.

NOTE. Dr. Jack E. Henningfield of the National Institute on Drug Abuse and Dr. Neal L. Benowitz of the University of California at San Francisco ranked six substances based on five problem areas. 1 = Most serious; 6 = least serious.

Definitions: *Withdrawal:* Presence and severity of characteristic withdrawal symptoms; *Reinforcement:* A measure of the substance's ability, in human and animal tests, to get users to take it again and again, and in preference to other substances; *Tolerance:* How much of the substance is needed to satisfy cravings for it, and the level of stable need that is eventually reached; *Dependence:* How difficult it is for the user to quit, the relapse rate, the percentage of people who eventually become dependent, the ratings users give their own need for the substance and the degree to which the substance will be used in the face of evidence that it causes harm; *Intoxication:* Though not usually counted as a measure of addiction in itself, the level of intoxication is associated with addiction and increases the personal and social damage a substance may do.

*Equal ratings.

In 1994, as this book was being written, the government decided that nicotine, the major addictive element in cigarettes, is a drug. By 1996, it became increasingly apparent that the CEOs of the major tobacco companies have long known about the addictive quality of nicotine. Ongoing governmental and private investigations strongly suggest that some companies manipulated the amount of nicotine and targeted advertising in certain cigarettes in order to "hook" adolescents.

Because addictive drugs are normally controlled and not available for over-the-counter sales, the moral, legal, economic, and practical implications of the above will not be known until long after this book is published. However, schools will have to deal with the consequences of government actions in terms of the potential escalation of drug enforcement policies in hallways, lavatories, and school grounds.

Most, if not all, schools do not permit indoor smoking by students. Some allow students to smoke outdoors in designated areas. Classically, schools have created discipline problems by allowing teachers to smoke in designated areas while forbidding this privilege to students. Student smokers often demand their own smoking area, despite the reality that it is illegal for minors to smoke. They may claim, correctly, that their parents allow them to smoke at home. Some use the rationale that they are legal adults (age 18), and some use their perception of the hypocrisy of the situation as an invitation to try to beat the system. It is clear that determined efforts to eliminate student smoking require great disciplinary resources, especially when one considers the problems of restricting smoking among the public.

Despite the fact that cigarettes are responsible for the deaths of more than 420,000 persons yearly, educators often find that their attempts to prevent smoking among students are frustrated by many factors. Policymakers must function within a society troubled by personal addiction to cigarettes, government addiction to the taxes generated by tobacco sales, and worker addiction to the salaries provided by tobacco companies. For instance, in 1992, Phillip Morris paid $4.5 billion in direct taxes and billions more in other types of taxes, making it the largest taxpayer in the country. It employed 92,000 people in America (161,000 people worldwide) and is one of the major supporters of American farming (Rosenblatt, 1994). Nicotine is the only drug that gives addicts a high when they are down and calms them when they are agitated. Without knowing it, many smokers may become agitated as a result of withdrawal, and therefore, they stave off the symptoms of withdrawal by constantly smoking. It also appears to aid in weight control, helps relieve boredom, and is often part of social interactions. Nicotine is so addictive that two completely smoked cigarettes will convince 85 percent of experimental teens to become regular smokers (Perry, Klepp, & Sillers, 1987).

Why children and youth first smoke may not account for their continued smoking. Students who initially smoke cigarettes or marijuana because of peer pressure will most likely smoke in high school. Early smokers of large numbers of cigarettes will probably continue to smoke heavily in middle school and beyond (Ary & Biglan, 1988). Habitual smoking was found to develop slowly. Peer smoking was a big influence and predicted continuation of smoking after initiation.

Studies show that some students smoke to alleviate the stress of adjusting to high school (Penny & Robinson, 1986). Students who smoke are less able to cope with change and tend to have lower self-esteem, a more external locus of control, and a higher level of trait anxiety (Penny & Robinson, 1986). Not surprisingly, most frequent smokers have smoking parents (Kanbayashi, Kono, Ikeda, & Nishikawa, 1986).

The Tobacco Product Education and Health Protection Act of 1990 was enacted to amend the Public Service Act to establish a center for tobacco products, to inform the public concerning the hazards of tobacco use, to disclose and restrict additives to such products, and to require labeling of such products to provide information concerning such products to the public. Despite warning labels on cigarette packages, children have been enticed to smoke through the modeling of smoking behavior, advertisements that glorify smoking, and easy availability of cigarettes. This will likely change drastically by the turn of the century.

State laws generally require posting of warning labels on cash registers and store windows, stating that it is illegal to sell cigarettes or chewing tobacco to anyone younger than eighteen years. A study by Barovich, Sussman, Dent, Burton, and Flay (1991) attempted to determine the availability of tobacco products for junior high and high school students at stores located nearest the schools. They interviewed store personnel, recorded types and locations of tobacco products, promotional items, and legal age warning signs within stores, and observed purchasing behavior (Barovich et al., 1991). Results showed that store personnel used tobacco at twice the rate of the general public (national average is 28 percent), and they often used tobacco while working. They therefore might be less conscientious about restricting sales to minors. Promotional advertisements were present at most stores, whereas warning age signs were present at few of the stores (Barovich et al., 1991). Smokeless tobacco look-alike products were observed at many of the stores (i.e., Big League Chew bubble gum).

Approximately 50 percent of the personnel in the Barovich et al. (1991) study said they would sell tobacco products to a minor, and many said they observed minors using tobacco near the stores. Several apparently illegal purchases of tobacco were observed (Barovich et al., 1991). This study shows the importance of targeting local stores for community action measures to prevent the purchase of tobacco products by minors.

Although no one has developed a definitive program to prevent or stop smoking, researchers at the Oregon Research Institute (1994) have studied the problem extensively. They developed and evaluated a diversion program that includes police citations for students caught smoking in school. Students are then given the alternatives of fines and suspension or attendance at the diversion program. They report that only about 4 percent of students who attend the program received a second citation over a three-month period. The results are too tentative to predict long-range success, but the program includes many elements that might help. They use education about the law, medical, social, and emotional implications of use, and rewards for cessation. However, with this or any successful program, it is crucial to convince adolescents, who often view themselves as invulnerable, that they themselves need to stop smoking, not to please others, but because they should for their own health.

Alcohol and Other Drugs

According to a 1988 survey by the U.S. Public Health Service (Melear, 1991), high school seniors' self-reports of at least one use of a drug indicated that 92 percent tried alcohol; 66 percent, cigarettes; 47 percent, marijuana; 20 percent, stimulants other than cocaine; 17 percent, inhalants; 12 percent, cocaine; 9 percent, tranquilizers, narcotics, or hallucinogens; 8 percent, sedatives; and 5 percent, crack cocaine. In 1989, 70 percent of public school students and 52 percent of private school students aged twelve to nineteen years reported that drugs were available at their school (U.S. Dept. of Education, 1993).

There are few, if any, schools, including public, private, and religious schools, where students cannot obtain drugs. Drug use, especially marijuana, provides the major activity and the group identity for many moderate to heavy users. It often provides for group cohesion and bonding among students who are alienated from the mainstream, disaffected and plagued by poor academic and behavioral records. In my private practice, a very high percentage of oppositional, defiant, and angry adolescents with learning disabilities or attention deficit disorders are moderate to heavy users of drugs. They groom, dress, and talk the language of the drug culture.

Some studies have investigated the relationship between drugs and dropouts. Potential high school dropouts, as compared with peers, tend to (1) use a larger variety of drugs, (2) have better access to drugs, (3) have fewer people or environmental forces controlling their drug use, (4) engage in more frequent use, and (5) have a physical, psychological, and social network that enables drug use and mediates against adverse consequences (Eggert & Herting, 1993). These studies indicate the necessity of targeting high-risk students, their peers, families, and communities, and developing preventive programs.

Research has well established the role of peer influence on adolescent drug use. This includes teaching peers proper techniques for use and how to experience the pleasurable effects of drugs. Most studies have focused on marijuana or other common illicit, less expensive drugs. Peer cluster theory posits that nearly all drug use occurs within the peer context (Dinges & Oetting, 1993). An extremely important area of interest, therefore, concerns the particular kinds of drugs that friends use.

Peer groups greatly determine the kinds of drugs that adolescents use. They tend to socialize around the use of specific drugs, and the effects of those drugs will determine the nature of their social activities. They are less likely to have friends who use other drugs or no drugs. It is very important for educators to be aware of the various drug subcultures in their schools. Groups tend to distinguish themselves by dress, attitudes, and the types of concerts members attend. The implications of these findings suggest that early, peer-based strategies should focus on teaching students refusal techniques for use when friends push drugs on them.

The problems associated with alcohol use are similar to those of other drugs, except that alcohol is more easily obtained. However, educators should be familiar with the differences between social drinking, binge drinking, and alcoholism. Some students, because of the need for excitement and experimentation, will try almost anything to get high. We have worked with adolescents who have sniffed and snorted powdered Ritalin, the fumes from cigarette lighters, glue, paint thinner, and nitrogen oxide. One student tried to get high on lemon extract because he believed it has a high alcohol content. He ended up with no high and a very sore stomach. In coming decades, with the current structure of society and schools, it is clear that there are many exotic, and perhaps not so exotic, substances waiting in the wings for their reign of popularity. The question is whether schools should put their resources into prevention, punishment, or rehabilitation. Or should the problem be completely shifted to other agencies?

Behavioral/Cognitive–Behavioral Approach to Substance Abuse

Drugs, including nicotine, are powerful physiological and social reinforcers. Although behaviorists and cognitive–behaviorists recognize the physiological component of addiction, they focus on the social reinforcers associated with the addiction. For instance, initial smoking experiences of adolescents are invariably accompanied by peer reinforcement. Cigarette use is also reinforced by the media and smoking by adult role models.

The physical aspects of addiction can be controlled with substitute, nonaddicting drugs, different methods of delivery of the drug, such as nicotine patches, or the use of aversives paired with smoking. But the behavioral/cognitive–behavioral approach requires provision of powerful reinforcers and competing activities to extinguish the addictive behavior. Because social reinforcement by peers is so important, this may mean limiting contact with addicted peers and teaching refusal skills.

Two conditions must exist before behavioral approaches can be successful with addictive behavior. First, as with violence, the treatment must allow for reasonable and sometimes total control of the contingencies. Second, the treatment depends on finding more powerful reinforcers. These may be based on the desire of the addict to have a normal or better life, which is a reality that many addicts do not believe is possible. Money, accomplishment in school or work, and feelings of self-worth also may be powerful reinforcers. Without these two conditions, behavioral treatments will surely fail.

Psychodynamic/Interpersonal Approach to Substance Abuse

Problems of substance abuse must be understood and treated, as would other antisocial, self-destructive behaviors, in terms of early causes. Substance abuse suggests either a narcissistic orientation toward pleasure or a need to escape the anxiety aroused by the pressures of life. In the latter case, the primary problem is one of low self-esteem, complete lack of confidence, and perceived incompetence to deal with reality. Individual treatment focuses on the same approaches as used with other anti-social problems. However, because the addict is a master in the uses of inappropriate defenses such as denial, rationalization, and avoidance, long-term intensive treatment is usually necessary.

Schools should focus early on prevention in terms of addiction. Actual school treatment must focus on helping the student to make small but solid steps toward becoming competent. Without feelings of competence and insight into the nature of one's addictions, there is little hope in solving the problem. Adolescent addicts, because of the many normal developmental tasks they must accomplish, develop strong rationalizations for their activities. These are invariably supported by self-selected peer groups. Therefore, it is important to attack the values promoted in the peer group by providing psychodynamically oriented group therapy.

Humanistic Approach to Substance Abuse

Student substance abuse may present a particular problem for the humanist. Humanists assume that individuals should be free to explore their own beliefs, experiences, feelings, and existential realities. As long as they do not harm others, their choice to experiment with mind-altering drugs should not be fettered. Conversely, it is against our innate needs to use substances that would cause us mental or physical harm. We normally should not need to use drugs or alcohol to seek joy and pleasure because these feelings are available to those whose needs are met. The joy of actualization and accomplishing goals is the sign of a healthy person.

Despite a relatively open attitude toward the use of drugs, humanists would never subscribe to overuse or dependence. These activities are unnatural and harmful to the body and mind. Furthermore, humanist educators recognize that children and youth may not be mature or emotionally ready to deal with drugs that alter the mind and emotions. Although it may be acceptable for adolescents to experiment with alcohol and drugs, those whose emotional and developmental needs have not been met will be particularly susceptible to abuse and addiction.

Early education about the harmful effects of drugs is important from a humanistic perspective. However, this education should be based on facts. There should be no attempt to scare children with false information that they may later learn is untrue. For instance, they should learn that many cultures use hallucinogens, marijuana, alcohol, and other drugs as part of religion and healing. Once given accurate information about the use and abuse of these substances, they can make their own decisions about personal use.

Healthy, actualized people do not need to rely on drugs and alcohol for happiness and joy. However, as long as they do not hurt themselves and others, society should not restrict their freedom to use alcohol and drugs for social, religious, medical, or recreational reasons. Adolescent abuse is a sign of self-hatred and is usually indicative of unmet needs for competence and mastery. Therefore, treatment of substance abuse is similar to that used with violent offenders. Abuse will not stop until the student begins to feel competent and good about himself or herself. This can best be accomplished in an alternative school setting, where the abuse is seen as a symptom incidental to the real underlying problem.

Biophysical Approach to Substance Abuse

The biophysical approach is based on the assumption that substance abuse is caused by both physical addiction and psychological dependence. Many addicts actually self-treat their anxiety and depression with everything from caffeine and nicotine to cocaine. Therefore, it is important to determine the causes of their addictive behavior. This involves a complete psychological, medical, and drug use evaluation. It may be coordinated by your school psychologist or school drug and alcohol counselor. It can be done at a clinic that specializes in drug problems. In some cases, especially where there is imminent danger to the student, short-term hospitalization may be necessary. This will allow for intensive observation, evaluation, and detoxification, a period in which the patient is drug free. Patients are discharged with a treatment plan, and often they have signed a contract with their families, outlining the behaviors that will help them remain substance free.

In some cases, patients may be provided nonaddictive substitutes such as methadone, antidepressants, and antianxiety medications that will help to relieve the symptoms related to the addiction. Also, nicotine patches or inhalants may succeed with patients who really desire to give up smoking.

Students with known addictions should be involved in a treatment plan that requires periodic, random urine, breath, or blood tests to monitor continued use. Treatment should include regular psychotherapy, drug and alcohol counseling, and regular attendance at some group such as Alcoholics Anonymous or Narcotic Anonymous. Families need to be involved, and attempts to redirect the patient from the drug and alcohol culture are important. Research shows that success is very much dependent on a multifaceted approach, with good medical evaluation and monitoring.

Ecological/Systems Approach to Substance Abuse

Because of the medical nature of addictions, the ecological/systems approach to substance abuse fits within the multifaceted approach described. Although it must be recognized that cigarettes, drugs, and alcohol are illegal in schools, a law enforcement approach should not dominate the thinking in any plan. Rather, these problems should be viewed as being basically social, psychological, and medical. Therefore, prevention, treatment and rehabilitation should be the focus of any school plan.

From an ESA perspective, prevention must begin at the earliest stages. Drug education should be included in all grades. It should be presented in an informed manner and not as a scare tactic that includes unproven assertions. However, prevention is also dependent on early screening and identification of children with learning problems, ADHD, abusive parents, and other early predictors of later substance abuse. Early identification requires early treatment, before the problem becomes serious. This can begin as early as the primary grades, where the seeds of low self-esteem are sown. Middle school efforts should focus on training in refusal skills and efforts to provide esteem-enhancing activities for all vulnerable students.

Schools need to constantly involve parents and the community in the battle to deglamorize drug and alcohol use. This is difficult at the high school level, where there are often groups of students who are identified as the druggies. They often provoke school authorities by creating personas that reek of the drug culture. The may wear only black clothes and tee shirts advertising rock groups that glamorize drugs. They may wear multiple earrings, shave their heads, or have very long hair. They also may pierce their noses, tongues, or other body parts. All of this angers faculty and creates a hostile climate that often prevents the development of treatment programs. Schools need to recognize these behaviors as signs of alienation, hopelessness, and failure to make it in the mainstream school culture.

Alternative schools offer an important equivalent educational program for students who are enmeshed in the drug culture. Their behavior may be so provocative to staff and peers that they are often constantly in trouble. The result, frequent suspensions, cut classes, and truancy, is that they are diverted from resources that they need to help them. It is better to provide special settings where their problems can be addressed in a productive manner. There are many models for alternative schools, but it is important that your district's alternative school or program be sensitive to the unique needs, resources, and limitations of your community.

Psychological Maltreatment

Psychological maltreatment of students by educators is an issue that has received relatively little attention in schools and is not generally associated with misbehavior. In general, it takes many forms, including mental cruelty, sexual exploitation, allowing children to live in dangerous or unstable environments, encouraging or permitting children to use destructive drugs, providing negative and destructive role models, exposing children to systematic bias and prejudice, emotional neglect, and subjecting children to institutional practices that are clearly demonstrated to inhibit maintenance of basic human needs (Hart & Brassard, 1987). The latter occurs when children in schools do not receive appropriate human contact and attention because they are unattractive or because teachers are overburdened or burned out (Hart, 1987).

Studies conducted at the National Center for The Study of Corporal Punishment and Alternatives (NCSCPA) indicate that at least 50 percent to 60 percent of all schoolchildren suffer from at least one occurrence of maltreatment by an educator that leads to stress symptoms (Lambert, 1990; Lambert, Witkowski, Hyman, Alderman & Tucker, 1988; Vargas-Moll, 1992; Zelikoff, 1990). Approximately 1 percent to 2 percent develop symptoms of sufficient duration, intensity, and frequency that they develop a clinical syndrome called posttraumatic stress disorder (PTSD) as a consequence.

Although 1 to 2 percent might not seem to be a large percentage of a school-age population, in a system like New York City, this would be about 10,000 children so traumatized by educators that they may suffer lifelong emotional problems. A good percentage of these develop angry and aggressive responses and are a pool of students whose misbehavior is created by the school. Yet, emotional abuse and its relation to misbehavior in schools receives little pedagogical, psychological, or legal attention and is rarely mentioned in textbooks on school discipline (Pokalo & Hyman, 1993; Sarno, 1992).

Verbal assaults, ridicule, and excessive criticism in classrooms often represent attempts by teachers to discipline or correct student misbehavior. These types of disciplinary excesses are often excused on the grounds that they are meant to correct and not to harm students, and that they are normal and accepted methods of motivating children (Hyman & D'Allessandro, 1984b). For instance, sarcasm, name calling, and ridicule may be done in a joking manner by a teacher or coach who is completely unaware of the damaging impact these acts might have on individual students. However, when faced with the reality, the educator may rationalize, insisting that the remark was not meant to harm the child. Or the teacher might defend the act on the basis that most students "can take it." Besides being unaware of limits, abusers are often ignorant about appropriate disciplinary procedures (Blum, 1994; Hyman & Lally, 1982; Pokalo, 1986).

Definitions of Emotional Maltreatment

Educators, legislatures, judges, child protective workers, clinicians, and researchers have all attempted to define emotional abuse from their own perspectives (Brassard & Hart, 1989; Hyman & Weiler, 1994). There is some debate over the semantics of the terms "abuse" and "maltreatment." Abuse usually implies a crime of commission, whereas maltreatment may imply both commission and omission. However, the terms are used interchangeably here, where we deal with the issue from the perspective of schools and classrooms.

There are some legal definitions of emotional maltreatment by teachers. Case law indicates that emotional distress, another term for emotional maltreatment, is a basis for civil litigation (Hyman, 1985, 1987, 1990a; Hyman & Weiler, 1994; Hyman, Zelikoff & Clarke, 1988; Pokalo & Hyman, 1993; Sarno, 1992). In most state education regulations, psychological maltreatment is either absent or not well defined. In states with statutes that forbid it, few cases of abuse are processed, and even fewer are won by plaintiff students and their parents in tort litigation (Connecticut, 1993; Hart, Brassard, & Germain, 1987; Pokalo & Hyman, 1993; Sarno, 1992).

Connecticut has attempted to prevent emotional maltreatment in schools by including it as a forbidden activity in their code of professional standards for teachers (Code of Professional Responsibility for Teachers, 1992). However, even here, translating a few sentences into legally binding operational definitions has not been accomplished. Transforming vague language into effective legislative mandates requires consideration of three factors. The regulation/law must (1) define the act, (2) address the results (symptoms) in relation to the act, and (3) consider whether intention should limit culpability.

We have extensive data on the acts that constitute psychological maltreatment in schools, and these can be relatively easily translated into legislative language. Furthermore, we have clearly documented the range of student symptoms that result from maltreatment. The approach that we have used depends to a great extent on symptomology. Some may question a symptom-based approach to studying psychological maltreatment. They may believe that direct observation is the most appropriate way to study the extent and effects of the problem. However, educators are unlikely to engage in questionable classroom practices while under observation.

We have found few schools willing to invite researchers to investigate the nature and extent of emotional damage their practices may cause children. In clinical evaluations involving litigation, we have found denial ranging from claims of ignorance of a teacher's abusive behavior to outright perjury. In these cases, observations by administrators, testimony by students and parents who support the abusing teacher, and character references are often biased and of little help in determining the impact of teachers on individual students (Pokalo & Hyman, 1993).

In cases in which school authorities have documented symptoms and required abusive teachers to change their techniques, the schools have been successful in disciplining offending teachers (Pokalo & Hyman, 1993). So, whether school boards have been plaintiffs or defendants, documentation of symptoms has been a successful method for amelioration and is amenable to translation into legislation.

The question of intention involves legal and psychological consideration. If a teacher claims that he or she did not mean to embarrass a student, is the teacher relieved of responsibility? There are numerous cases in which the teacher claimed not to have any malicious intent, but the results were nevertheless devastating (Pokalo & Hyman, 1993). However, we think that proper training of teachers can sensitize most to the nature of psychological maltreatment.

Research on Psychological Maltreatment

Psychological maltreatment consists of (1) discipline and control techniques that are based on fear and intimidation; (2) low quantity of human interaction in which teachers communicate a lack of interest, caring, and affection for students; (3) limited opportunities for students to develop adequate skills and feelings of self-worth; (4) encouragement to be dependent and subservient, especially in areas in which students are capable of making independent judgments; and (5) denial of opportunities for healthy risk taking such as exploring ideas that are not conventional and approved by the teacher (Brassard, Hart & Germane, 1987; Hyman, 1990a). Teachers may maltreat students by being overdemanding or perfectionistic with children who are vulnerable as a result of parental pressure or self-demands.

Although psychological maltreatment is believed to occur more often than other forms of abuse, it is difficult to determine rate of occurrence in specific regions or schools, because schools are not anxious to investigate their own malfeasance. Our research on both physical

TABLE 10.5   Comparison of Educator-Induced Stressors from Three Studies

Symptoms*	Retrospective/Adults		Junior High School		Hispanic	
	N	%	N	%	N	%
Verbal assault	163	53.3	47	17	18	22
Ridicule	160	52.3	92	34	2	2
Isolation and rejection	124	40.5	22	8	2	2
Physical abuse	72	23.5	36	13	48	59
Punitive sanctions	54	17.6	57	21	4	5
Peer humiliation	57	15.4	5	2	7	9
Sexual corruption	6	2	6	2	—	—

*Percentages in the first sample do not equal 100 because subjects could list more than one stressor.

and psychological abuse by educators suggests that maltreatment in general includes (1) verbal assault, (2) ridicule, (3) isolation and rejection, (4) punitive sanctions, (5) peer humiliation, (6) sexual corruption, and (7) physical assault (Hyman, 1990a; Hyman, Zelikoff & Clarke, 1988). Table 10.5 shows school stressors identified by three samples that filled out our research instrument, which is called the *My Worst School Experience Scale* (MWSES) (Hyman, 1990a; Hyman, Zelikoff & Clarke, 1988; Lambert, 1990; Vargas-Moll, 1992).

The three samples include teachers and other adults (Zelikoff, 1990), high school students from a middle class school (Lambert, 1990), and inner-city Hispanic elementary schoolchildren (Vargas-Moll, 1992) seen in Table 10.5.

Effects of Psychological Maltreatment

Studies of psychological maltreatment by caretakers indicate that preschool and school-age maltreated children perform at lower levels than control children on measures of (1) ability, (2) academic achievement, and (3) social competency (Brassard & Hart, 1989). Maltreated children also display more behavior problems, including aggression, and poor interpersonal competencies as rated by teachers (Sakowski, 1993). In addition, their feelings of inadequacy and resentment may lead to violence.

We have identified one hundred specific psychological reactions to both physical and psychological maltreatment, which are measured by MWSES (Hyman, 1990a; Hyman, Zelikoff & Clarke, 1988; Lambert, 1990; Lambert et al., 1988; Vargas-Moll, 1991; Vargas-Moll & Hyman, 1992; Zelikoff, 1990). The types of stress symptoms that occur as a result of all school abuses are presented in Table 10.6. Although these data include the results of both physical and psychological abuse, in most cases psychological maltreatment may be considered a major component of the stressor.

As shown in Table 10.6, personality changes, avoidance (often of school, schoolwork, and the teachers who cause the problems), school problems, and aggression are all common results of psychological maltreatment.

As with corporal punishment, the frequency of emotional maltreatment in schools is too often a function of socio-economic status of the school population (Hyman, 1990a).

TABLE 10.6   Comparison of Symptoms Resulting from Educator-Induced Stressors from Three Studies*

Symptom Category	Retrospective/ Adults Sample		Junior High School Sample		Hispanic Sample	
	n	*%*	*n*	*%*	*n*	*%*
Personality changes	178	82	185	55	—	—
Avoidance	172	79	194	58	62	76
Reexperience trauma	166	77	164	49	38	46
School problems	159	73	232	69	25	29
Hypervigilance	126	58	90	27	63	77
Aggression	115	53	214	64	31	38
Memory problems	65	30	45	13	—	—
Somatic complaints	66	30	68	20	27	33
Withdrawal	57	26	65	19	39	48
Dependency	42	19	55	16	27	3
Habit disorder	28	13	34	10	4	4
Sleep distress	24	11	13	4	—	—
Confusion	—	—	—	—	32	39
Low self-esteem	—	—	—	—	28	34
Anxiety	—	—	—	—	20	24
Manipulation	—	—	—	—	16	20
Guilt	—	—	—	—	15	18

*Percentages are more than 100 percent since students can report multiple symptoms.

Evidence suggests that poor children are at greater risk than are other children. However, high-SES students are not immune from psychological abuse in schools (Hyman & Pokalo, 1993).

One study, using the MWSE scale on a total high school population, identified three clusters of stress symptoms: (1) reexperiencing the trauma, (2) school-related problems, and (3) increased arousal (Lambert, 1990; Lambert et al., 1988). Other research with the scale indicates seven symptom factors, which are (1) depression /avoidance, (2) oppositional/defiant, (3) avoidant/hypervigilant, (4) somatic complaints, (5) reexperiencing and intrusive thoughts, (6) depression/hopelessness/suicidal ideation, and (7) disturbing dreams and memories (Berna, 1993; Berna & Hyman, 1993).

In addition to the maltreatment described in most of our research, students are now being abusively strip searched. In 1985, in the case of New Jersey v. T. L. O., the Supreme Court lowered the standard for permission of school districts to search students. As a result of this ruling, some school districts have been encouraged to increase the use of strip searches. Our clinical investigations of the victims of strip searches indicate that asking students to remove their clothes as part of disciplinary procedures can result in serious emotional damage. Interviews with parents and adolescents in a recent case (Tipper et al. v. New Castle, Pennsylvania, Area School District et al., 1993) indicated that many of the students who were stripped developed a loss of faith in the previously admired administrator who conducted this search, loss of interest in academics, depression, and anger. In some students, tardiness and truancy increased and fantasies of revenge were harbored.

In summary, we believe that there is ample evidence that psychological maltreatment in schools can be prevented. Clinical and anecdotal evidence suggest that a significant reduction could result in increases in learning, more satisfaction with school, and a possible decrease in school violence. We have presented sufficient data to support legislative efforts. However, there are political and social reasons why this type of punitiveness may not be soon addressed in any significant manner.

Corporal Punishment

Since 1974, two decades of research, advocacy, and policy efforts to abolish the use of corporal punishment in American education show pervasive and troubling attitudes of approval for the infliction of pain on children (Greven, 1980, 1991; Hyman, 1990a; Hyman & Pokalo, 1993; Straus, 1994). In 1974, only New Jersey and Massachusetts forbade paddling schoolchildren. In the rest of the country, estimates suggested at least three million paddling incidents per school year (Glackman et al., 1978; Hyman, 1990a). By 1995, twenty-seven states had outright prohibitions, and eleven states, by local rules, banned corporal punishment of more than half of the children in their public schools. In addition, in a turnabout considered incredible by many former students, most Catholic schools now forbid the use of the infliction of pain. By 1995, the yearly paddlings were probably about ¾ million. Among these, an unknown but possibly large number occurred in fundamentalist Christian schools and academies.

I have written extensively about this problem (Hyman, 1990a) and originally had not intended to discuss it in this book. But, in recent years, some legislatures in states that had banned corporal punishment have made attempts to reinstate the practice. Furthermore, abolishment efforts have been frustrated by conservative politicians and educators in the southern and southwestern states; this despite the overwhelming research showing that this is an ineffective, unnecessary, counterproductive and potentially harmful practice.

Corporal punishment is generally defined as the purposeful infliction of pain or confinement as a penalty for an offense (Hyman & Wise, 1979). In most schools it involves the use of a wooden paddle. Studies of instruments used, types of offenses, intentions of paddlers, and consequences to children and their families indicate that a simple definition offers, at best, a convenient starting point for understanding it from legal, demographic, educational, and psychological perspectives.

For instance, the usual legal definition cited above was used by a defendant teacher in litigation against the Washington, D.C., School Board. The plaintiff student had been blowing spit bubbles in the air, and the teacher claimed that this " disgusting, unsanitary act" had caused her to "instinctively" strike out. Her smack on his mouth caused bleeding, pain, and emotional trauma (Robinson v. District of Columbia, 1987). Her defense was based, in part, on the school board regulations that defined corporal punishment as an "intentional" act. She stated that she had not intended to hit the child; therefore, her instinctive act had not violated the school board sanctions. Rather than face the plaintiffs in court, the defendants settled the case through attorneys and removed the term "intentional" from the definition.

Teacher resistance to banning corporal punishment is often based on the argument that its use, or at least the threat that it can be used, is needed to stem student violence. However, all laws and regulations regarding corporal punishment in schools protect educators' rights to use force to quell disturbances, and to protect themselves, others' property, or students from self-injury. An educator is not liable for the incidental infliction of pain as a result of the legitimate use of any of the aforementioned. In any event, most hitting occurs in the lower grades (Hyman & Wise, 1979; Russell, 1988, 1989). Teachers and administrators rarely paddle big, strong, potentially violent students who could retaliate.

Because disciplinary procedures that directly inflict pain are varied, corporal punishment should be broadly defined to include unreasonable confinement in a restricted space (Hyman, 1989b), forcing children to assume fixed postures for unreasonable periods, excessive exercise and drills, forced ingestion of noxious substances, and exposure to painful environments or psychological maltreatment that causes emotional pain. The data clearly demonstrate that the potential duration, intensity, and frequency of psychological symptoms resulting from traumatic physical or psychological assaults by educators are the same (Hyman, 1990a).

Research Findings Used to Encourage Policy Changes against Corporal Punishment in Schools

The movement to totally eliminate the use of corporal punishment in our society has been supported by emerging studies of family violence that suggest a link between spanking and child abuse (Haeuser, 1991; Hyman & Gasiewski, 1992; Straus, 1994; Straus & Gimpel, 1992). Current research indicates correlations between spanking and such demographic factors as social class, religion, geography, and race (Frazier, 1993; Hyman, 1989a; Kelly, Power, & Wimbush, 1992; McDowell & Friedman, 1979; Pokalo, 1986; Portes, Dunham, & Williams, 1986; Russell, 1988, 1989; Wiehe, 1989).

Because of obvious ethical and legal limitations on experimental studies of corporal punishment in schools, the research base has been varied. Our arguments against corporal punishment in schools have been based on sources such as the Bible (Barnhart, 1972; Greven, 1980, 1991), literature (Gibson, 1978), medicine (Krugman & Krugman, 1984; Pynoos & Eth, 1985; Radbill, 1974) history (Gibson, 1978; Manning, 1979; Miller, 1980), government studies (Glackman et al., 1978; Russell, 1988, 1989), newspaper articles (Clarke, Erdlen, & Hyman, 1984; Clarke, Liberman-Lascoe, & Hyman, 1982; Hyman, Clarke and Erdlen, 1987), special education (Hyman & Bogacki, 1984), personal anecdotes (Hyman, 1990), cross-cultural studies (Babcock, 1977; Haeuser, 1991, 1992; Levinson, 1989), experimental studies (Bandura, 1973; Bandura & Huston, 1961; Bandura & Walters, 1973; Bongiovanni, 1979), and sociology (Straus, 1989, 1991, 1992). The following is a summary of some of the findings:

- Contrary to popular belief, studies of corporal punishment in schools indicate that it is not used as a "last resort." It is too often the first punishment for nonviolent and minor misbehaviors (Hyman, Clarke & Erdlen, 1987). Also, most incidents of physical abuse of children begin as corporal punishment and then escalate (Hyman, 1990a; Kadushin & Martin, 1981).
- Corporal punishment occurs more frequently in the primary and intermediate levels (Hyman & Wise, 1979).
- Boys are hit much more frequently than girls (Glackman, et al 1978).

- Minority and poor white children receive beatings four to five times more frequently than middle- and upper-class white children (Farley, 1983; Jones, 1993; Richardson & Evans, 1992).
- Most of the corporal punishment in America occurs in states in the South and Southwest—Florida, Texas, Arkansas, and Alabama have consistently been among the leaders in the frequency of hitting schoolchildren (Farley, 1983; Rose, 1984; Russell, 1988).
- The least use of corporal punishment occurs in schools in the Northeast (Farley, 1983; Rose, 1984; Russell, 1988).
- There is evidence that corporal punishment may be one of the causes of school vandalism (Hyman & Wise, 1979).
- In descending order of support for corporal punishment are school board members, school administrators, teachers, parents, and students (Reardon & Reynolds, 1979).
- Very violent children are almost always frequent recipients of severe corporal punishment at home (Eron, Walder & Lefkowitz, 1971; Hyman & Gasiewski, 1992; Straus, 1989, 1994).
- Because hitting at home does not help them, it is just as useless and counterproductive in school. The old saw that "violence breeds violence" is supported by this finding (McCord, 1988a, 1988b, 1991).
- Corporal punishment is forbidden in the schools of continental Europe, England, Japan, Israel, the former Communist nations, Ireland, parts of Australia, Canada, and at the high school level in New Zealand, Puerto Rico, twenty-seven states, many suburban upper-middle-class schools, and most of the largest cities of America (Hyman & Wise, 1979; Hyman, 1990a).
- Teachers who frequently paddle may be authoritarian, dogmatic, relatively inexperienced, impulsive, and neurotic as compared with their peers (Rust & Kinnard, 1983).
- Teachers who do not paddle are most often those who were rarely if ever spanked or paddled as children. This modeling effect has been repeatedly demonstrated. The more teachers were hit as children, the more they tend to hit their students (Lennox, 1982).
- Witnessing and experiencing corporal punishment, a form of aggression, results in modeling of aggression (Bandura, 1973; Bandura & Huston, 1961; Bandura & Walters, 1963; Bongiovanni, 1979; Gil, 1970; Skinner, 1979). Studies of parents (Eron, Walder & Lefkowitz, 1971; Graziano & Namaste, 1990; Hyman, 1989a; Mishkin, 1987) and psychologists (Sofer, 1983) indicate that the best predictor of support for the use of corporal punishment is the amount of corporal punishment received as a child. Modeling is so powerful that childhood experiences of some psychologists distort their interpretations of theories that they use to support the use of corporal punishment. In a national study, psychologists most likely to support the use of corporal punishment frequently used Skinnerian theory to support their beliefs (Sofer, 1983). Yet B. F. Skinner was absolutely against the use of corporal punishment (Skinner, 1979).
- People who indicate that they are Fundamentalists, Evangelicals, Literalists, or Baptists tend to respond more punitively in disciplinary situations than those who identify with other major religions and orientations. Demographic studies of corporal punishment in schools support these findings (Barnhart, 1972; Greven, 1980, 1991; Pokalo, 1986; Wiehe, 1989).

- Schools with high rates of corporal punishment also have high rates of suspensions and are generally more punitive in all discipline responses than schools with low rates of corporal punishment (Farley, 1983). The connection between high rates of misbehavior and high rates of punishment are confirmed by the Safe Schools Study (National Institute of Education, 1978), which indicated that punitive climates actually exacerbate the problem. Among the traits of safe schools were student perceptions of fairness in the administration of discipline and the beliefs that they could influence what happened in their lives and that teachers taught what the students wanted to learn. Although principals in safe schools were considered strict, they were not considered mean or authoritarian, which are traits associated with punitive schools and teachers (Rust & Kinnard, 1983).
- Corporal punishment of various frequencies, durations, and intensities can result in posttraumatic stress disorder (Hyman, 1990a; Hyman, Zelikoff, & Clarke, 1988; Pynoos & Eth, 1985).
- Excessive use of corporal punishment is frequently associated with conduct disorders and comorbid with PTSD (Hyman & Gasiewski, 1992; McCord, 1988a, 1988b; Pokalo, 1992).
- Studies demonstrate that eliminating corporal punishment does not increase misbehavior (Farley, 1983).

Relation between Corporal Punishment and Student Violence

To examine the possible relationship between corporal punishment and the prevalence of other types of violence, Straus used an innovative approach. He weighted states in four categories based on an analysis by Friedman and Hyman (Hyman & Wise, 1979): the higher the weight, the greater the legal authorization for the use of corporal punishment. He thereby created a Corporal Punishment Permission Index. Using the index, he analyzed states on two dimensions. He correlated it with the within-school assault rate and the homicide rate by children in each state. His analysis was used to study what he calls "cultural spillover theory." This theory suggests that legitimized violence in one sphere of society spills over into other spheres. The data gathered by Straus demonstrate that states with high rates of homicide committed by children tend to have high rates of corporal punishment in schools. Also, where corporal punishment of students is high, there are high rates of inter-student violence.

Conclusion

In a country where shootings are the greatest single cause of death among teenage boys, we must be doing something wrong. Certainly, homes, churches, government and politicians are not doing their jobs. Once again, the schools are called on to deal with problems they did not create. You may agree with the view that a teacher's main job is to teach children the academic curriculum, and if they can not conform, or they interrupt the learning of others, that is their problem. From a discipline perspective, this translates to the notion that children should be good because that is the way things should be. If they can not conform, kick them out. Or you may believe that if schools do not teach values and discipline, if they do not realistically and rationally deal with problems such as substance abuse, sexual harassment, or violence, society will be the worse for not having done what needed to be done.

Key Terms

corporal punishment of students
Criminal Victimization in the United States Reports
cultural spillover theory
drug culture
New Jersey v. *T.L.O.*
nicotine
peer humiliation
Posttraumatic Stress Disorder (PTSD)
psychological maltreatment
punitive sanctions
refusal techniques
ridicule, isolation, and rejection
Safe School Study
school crime

school violence
sexual corruption
sexual harassment
smoking diversion program
strip searches
student victimization
substance abuse
teenage sexuality
Tobacco Education and Health Protection Act of 1990
urine, breath, and blood tests
verbal abuse
verbal assault
violence prevention

Application Activities

1. Tabulate the results of the Teacher Variance Survey and Survey of Attitudes toward Children in your class by sex, age, and future profession. Are there trends in your class? Are there differences between the scores and the students' attitudes and behavior?

2. How were you disciplined at home as a child? In school as a child? How do you think it has affected your attitude toward children and discipline?

3. Research the National Education Association, American Psychological Association, National Association of School Psychologists, and other professional organizations' resolutions regarding corporal punishment and discipline.

4. Obtain a copy of the United Nations Convention on the Rights of the Child. What countries have ratified them to date?

5. Get the latest copy of the Phi Delta Kappa/Gallup Poll's Public Attitudes Towards the Public Schools and their Teacher's Attitudes Towards the Public Schools. What are the national trends regarding discipline in the schools?

Suggested Readings

American Psychological Association. (1993). *Violence and youth: Psychology's response.* Volume 1: Summary report of the American Psychological Association Commission on Violence and Youth.

Brassard, M., Hart, S., & Germain, B. (1987). *Psychological maltreatment of children and youth.* Elmsford, NY: Pergamon Press.

Greven, P. (1991). *Spare the child: The religious roots of punishment and the psychological impact of physical abuse.* New York: Knopf.

Hyman, I. (1990). *Reading, writing and the hickory stick: The appalling story of physical and psychological abuse of American school children.* Lexington, MA: Lexington Books.

Moles, O. (Ed.). (1990). *Student discipline strategies.* Albany, NY: State University of New York Press.

Sadker, M., & Sadker, D. (1994). *Failing at fairness: How America's schools cheat girls.* New York: Macmillan Publishing Co.

United Nations Convention on the Rights of the Child: Unofficial summary of articles. (1991). *American Psychologist, 46*(1), 50–52.

References

Adelman, H. S. (1994). Learning disabilities: On interpreting research translations. In N. C. Jordan & J. Goldsmith Phillips (Eds.), *Learning disabilities: New directions for assessment and interventions.* Boston: Allyn & Bacon.

Adorno, T. W. (1950). *The authoritarian personality.* New York: Harper & Brothers.

Aetna Life and Casualty Company. (1992). *Resolving conflicts through mediation.* Hartford, CT: Author.

Albert, L. (1989). *Cooperative discipline.* Circle Pines, MN: American Guidance Service.

Alberto, P. & Troutman, A. (1990). *Applied behavior analysis for teachers* (3rd ed.). Columbus, OH: Merrill Publishing Co.

Altemeyer, B. (1988). *Enemies of freedom: Understanding right-wing authoritarianism.* San Francisco: Josey-Bass.

American Association of University Women. (1993). *Hostile hallways.* A national survey conducted by Louis Harris & Associates.

American Psychiatric Association (1994). *Diagnostic and statistical manual of mental disorders-fourth edition.* Washington, DC: American Psychiatric Association.

American Psychological Association. (1993). *Violence and youth: Psychology's response.* Volume 1: Summary report of the American Psychological Association Commission on Violence and Youth.

Amidon, E. J., Flanders, N. A., & Casper, I. G. (1985). *The role of the teacher in the classroom.* St. Paul, MN: Paul S. Amidon & Associates.

Anderson, H. H., & Brewer, J. E. (1946). Studies of teachers classroom personalities, II: Effects of teachers' dominative and integrative contacts on childrens' classroom behavior. *Psychological Monographs,* No. 8.

Anderson, L. M., Evertson, C. M., & Brophy, J. E. (1979). An experimental study of effective teaching in first grade reading groups. *Elementary School Journal, 79*(193), 222.

Angier, N. (1994, January 23). Elementary, Dr. Watson, the neurotransmitters did it. *New York Times Week in Review,* 1, 3.

Anthony, E., & Kohler, B. (Eds.). (1987). *The invulnerable child.* New York: The Guilford Press.

Aries, P. (1962). *Centuries of childhood: A social history of family life* (Translated by Robert Baldick). New York: Alfred A. Knopf.

Ary, D. & Biglan, A. (1988). Longitudinal changes in adolescent cigarette smoking behavior: Onset and cessation. *Journal of Behavioral Medicine, 11*(4), 361–382.

Ashton-Warner, S. (1963). *Teacher.* New York: Simon & Schuster.

Aspy, D. (1977). *Newport News, Virginia School District CT.E.T. Evaluation.* Washington, DC: The National Consortium for Humanizing Education.

Atwell, B. M. (1982). A study of teaching Reality Therapy to adolescents for self-management (Doctoral dissertation The University of North Carolina at Greensboro). *Dissertation Abstracts International, 43,* 669.

Axelrod, S. (1983a). *The effects of punishment on human behavior.* New York: Academic Press.

Axelrod, S. (1983b). *Behavior modification for the classroom teacher* (2nd ed.). New York: McGraw-Hill.

Axelrod, S. (1993). Integrating behavioral technology into public schools. *School Psychology Quarterly, 8*(3), 1–9.

Babcock, A. (1977). A cross cultural examination of corporal punishment: An initial theoretical conceptualization. In J. Wise (Ed.), *Proceedings: Conference on corporal punishment in schools.* Washington, DC: National Institute of Education (N.I.E. pp. 77–99).

Bandura, A. (1973). *Aggression: A social learning analysis.* Englewood Cliffs, NJ: Prentice Hall.

Bandura, A. (1977). *Social learning theory.* Englewood Cliffs, NJ: Prentice Hall.

Bandura, A. & Huston, A. (1961). Identification as a process of incidental learning. *Journal of Abnormal and Experimental Psychology, 63,* 311–318.

Bandura, A., & Walters, R. (1963). *Social learning and personality development.* New York: Holt, Rhinehart & Winston.

Barbetta, P. (1990a). GOALS: A group-oriented adapted level system for children with behavior disorders. *Academic Therapy, 25,* 645–656.

Barbetta, P. (1990b). Red light-green light: A classwide management system for students with behavior disorders in primary grades. *Preventing School Failure, 34,* 14–19.

Barker, R. G. (1968). *Ecological psychology.* Stanford, CA: Stanford University Press.

Barker, R. G., & Wright, H. F. (1949). Psychological ecology and the problem of psychosocial development. *Child Development, 20,* 131–143.

Barker, R. G., & Wright, H. F. (1955). *The midwest and its children: The psychological ecology of an American town.* New York: Harper & Row.

Barkely, R. A. (1990). *Attention deficit hyperactivity disorder: A handbook for diagnosis and treatment.* New York: Guildford.

Barnhart, J. (1972). *The Billy Graham religion.* Philadelphia: The Pilgrim Press.

Baron, R. A., & Ramsberger, V. M. (1978). Ambient temperature and the occurrence of violence: The long hot summer revisited. *Journal of Personality and Social Psychology, 36,* 351–360.

Barovich, M., Sussman, S., Dent, C., Burton D., & Flay (1991). Availability of tobacco products at stores located near public schools. *International Journal of the Addictions, 26*(8), 837–850.

Barrow, J. (1982). Coping skills training: A brief therapy approach for students with evaluative anxiety. *Journal of American College Health, 30*(6), 269–274.

Bechstrand, P. E. (1973). TA as a means of teaching writing in high school. *Transactional Analysis Journal, 3*(3), 9–31.

Becker, J., Velasco, M., Harmony, T., Marosi, E., & Landazuri, M. (1987). Electroencephalographic characteristics of children with learning disabilities. *Clinical Electroencephalography, 18,* 93–101.

Begley, S. (1993, June 28). The puzzle of genius. *Newsweek,* 46–53.

Behrman, R. E. (Ed.). (1992). *Nelson textbook of pediatrics* (14th ed.). Philadelphia: W. B. Saunders Company.

Bellack, A., & Hersen, M. (1985). *The dictionary of behavior therapy techniques.* New York: Pergammon Press.

Benedict, R. (1974). *Patterns of culture.* Boston: Houghton Mifflin.

Bennett, C. (1995). *Comprehensive multicultural education: Theory and practice* (3rd ed.). Des Moines, IA: Longwood Division of Allyn & Bacon.

Benson, A. J., & Benson, J. M. (1993). Peer mediation: Conflict resolution in schools. *Journal of School Psychology, 31,* 427–430.

Berkowitz, G., Hyman, I., & Lally, D. (1984). *The development of a school wide computerized, uniform discipline reporting system.* Paper presented at the Annual Convention of the National Association of School Psychologists, Philadelphia, PA.

Berna, J. (1993). *The worst experiences of adolescents from divorced and separated parents and the stress responses to those experiences.* Unpublished doctoral dissertation, Temple University, Philadelphia, PA.

Berna, J., & Hyman, I. (1993, April 17). *Stress responses of children from divorced and separated families.* Paper presented at the 25th Annual Convention of the National Association of School Psychologists, Washington, DC.

Berne, E. (1969). *Games people play.* New York: Grove Press.

Biddle, B. J., & Thomas, E. J. (Eds.). (1966). *Role theory: Concepts and research.* New York: John Wiley & Sons.

Blackham, G., & Silberman, A. (1975). *Modification of child and adolescent behavior.* Belmont, CA: Wadsworth Publishing.

Bloom, A. (1988). *The closing of the American mind.* New York: Touchstone Books.

Blum, M. (1994). *The pre-service teacher's educational training in classroom discipline: A national survey of teacher education programs.* Unpublished doctoral dissertation, Temple University, Philadelphia.

Blume, D. M. (1977). Effects of active listening training on verbal responses of University of Florida preservice childhood education teachers (Doctoral dissertation, The University of Florida). *Dissertation Abstracts International, 39,* 232A.

Bogacki, D. (1980). *Issues in physical restraint: A procedural and legal perspective.* Philadelphia: National Center for the Study of Corporal Punishment and Alternatives.

Bogacki, D. (1981). *Attitudes toward corporal punishment: Authoritarian personality and pupil control ideology of school personnel.* Unpublished doctoral dissertation, Temple University, Philadelphia, PA.

Bongiovanni, A. (1979). An analysis of research on punishment and its relation to the use of corporal punishment in the schools. In I. Hyman and J. Wise (Eds.), *Corporal punishment in American education.* Philadelphia: Temple University Press.

Borg, W. R., & Ascione, F. R. (1979). Changing on-task, off-task, and disruptive pupil behavior in elementary mainstreaming classrooms. *Journal of Educational Research, 72,* 243–252.

Borg, W. R., & Ascione, F. R. (1982). Classroom management in elementary mainstreaming classrooms. *Journal of Educational Psychology, 74,* 85–95.

Brassard, M., & Hart, S. (1989). *Development and validation of operationally defined measures of emotional maltreatment.* Research workshop presented at the Eighth National Conference on Child Abuse and Neglect, Salt Lake City.

Brassard, M., Hart, S., & Germain, B. (1987). *Psychological maltreatment of children and youth.* Elmsford, NY: Pergamon Press.

Brody, M. (1974). *The effects of rational-emotive affective education on anxiety, self-esteem, and frustration tolerance.* Unpublished doctoral dissertation, Temple University, Philadelphia, PA.

Brooks-Klein, V. (1995). *Validation of the Teacher Variance Inventory-R and its relationship to the Survey of Attitudes toward Children.* Unpublished doctoral dissertation, Temple University, Philadelphia, PA.

Brophy, J. E. (1983). Classroom organization and management. *Elementary School Journal, 83,* 254–285.

Brophy, J. E. (1986). Educating teachers about managing classrooms and students. *Teacher & Teacher Education, 4,* 1–18.

Brophy, J., & Evertson, C. (1976). *Learning from teaching: A developmental perspective.* Boston: Allyn & Bacon.

Brophy, J. E., & Good, T. L. (1986). Teacher behavior and student achievement. In M. C. Wittrock (Ed.), *Handbook of research on teaching* (3rd ed., pp. 328–375). New York: Macmillan Publishing Co.

Brophy, J., & Evertson, C. (1976). *Learning from teaching: A developmental perspective.* Boston: Allyn & Bacon.

Brown, D., Pryzwanksy, W., & Schulte, A. (1991). *Psychological consultation.* Boston: Allyn & Bacon.

Brown, R. & Borden, K. (1989). Neuropsychological effects of stimulant medication on children's learning and behavior. In C. Reynolds & E. Fletcher-Janzen (Eds.), *Handbook of clinical child neuropsychology.* New York: Plenum Press, p. 7

Brown, R., Dingle, A., & Landau, S. (1993). Overview of psychopharmacology in children and adolescents. *School Psychology Quarterly, 9,* 4–25.

Browning, B. D. (1978). Effects of Reality Therapy on teacher attitudes, student attitudes, student achievement and student behavior (Doctoral dissertation, North Texas State University). *Dissertation Abstracts International, 39,* 4010A.

Buckley, N., & Walker, H. (1978). *Think aloud.* Champaign, IL: Research Press.

Budd, K., Leibowitz, J., Riner, L., Mindell, C., & Goldfarb, A. (1981). Home-based treatment of severe disruptive behaviors: A reinforcement package for preschool and kindergarten children. *Behavior Modification, 5,* 273–298.

Burton, A. (1976). *What makes behavior change possible.* New York: Brunner/Mazel.

Bybee, R., & Gee, E. (1982). *Violence, values and justice in schools.* Boston: Allyn & Bacon.

Cady, M. C. (1983). The effects of classroom teachers receiving instruction in reality therapy and Adlerian techniques on the attitudes of teachers toward authority in the classroom. (Doctoral dissertation,

University of Maryland). *Dissertation Abstracts International, 45,* 1679A.

California Department of Justice, Division of Law Enforcement. (1993). *Profile 1992.* Sacramento: Author.

Canter, L. (1989). Let the educator beware: A response to Curwin and Mendler. *Educational Leadership, 47,* 71–73.

Canter, L., & Canter, M. (1976). *Assertive discipline: A take charge approach for today's educator.* Los Angeles: Canter and Associates, Inc.

Canter, L., & Canter, M. (1992). *Assertive discipline* (rev. ed.). Santa Monica, CA: Lee Canter & Associates.

Caplan, G. & Caplan, R. B. (1993). *Mental health consultation and collaboration.* San Francisco: Jossey-Bass.

Carlson, C., & Brunner, M. (1993). Effects of methylphenidate on the academic performance of children with attention-deficit hyperactivity disorder and learning disabilities. *School Psychology Review, 22*(2), 185–198.

Carr, E., Newsom, C., & Binkoff, J. (1980). Escape as a factor in the aggressive behavior of two retarded children. *Journal of Applied Behavior Analysis, 13,* 101–117.

Ceci, S., & Bruck, M. (1995). *Jeopardy in the courtroom.* Washington, DC: American Psychological Association.

Chance, E. W. (1985). *An overview of major discipline programs in the public schools since 1960.* Unpublished doctoral dissertation, University of Oklahoma, Norman, OK.

Chanow, K. J. (1980). Teacher Effectiveness Training: An assessment of the changes in self-reported attitudes and student observed attitudes of junior high school teachers (Doctoral dissertation, St. John's University). *Dissertation Abstracts International, 41,* 3421-A.

Charles, C. M. (1985). *Building classroom discipline: From models to practice* (2nd ed.). New York: Longman.

Charles, C. M. (1989). *Building classroom discipline: From models to practice* (3rd ed.). New York: Longman.

Chicago Public Schools, The Bureau of Safety and Security. (1994). *Annual report.* Chicago: Author.

Children's Defense Fund. (1991). *Child poverty in America.* Washington, DC: Author.

Christie, D., Hiss, M., & Lozanoff, B. (1984). Modification of inattentive classroom behavior: Hyperactive children's use of self-recording with teacher guidance. *Behavior Modification, 8,* 391–406.

Clarke, J., Erdlen, R. J., & Hyman, I. (1984). *Analysis of recent corporal punishment cases reported in national newspapers.* Paper presented at the Annual Meeting of the National Association of School Psychologists.

Clarke, J., Liberman-Lascoe, R., & Hyman, I. (1982). Corporal punishment in school as reported in nationwide newspapers. In R. Hansen (Ed.), *Child and youth services.* New York: Haworth Press.

Code of Professional Responsibility for Teachers. (1992). Hartford, CT: Connecticut Advisory Panel For Teacher Professional Standards: Connecticut State Department of Education.

Cohen, D. L. (1994, October). Study charts dramatic rise in suburban child poverty. *Education Week,* p. 5.

Connecticut Advisory Council For Teacher Professional Standards. (1993). *Code of professional responsibility for teachers.* Hartford, CT: State of Connecticut Department of Education.

Conoley, J., & Conoley, C. (1992). *School consultation: Practice and training* (2nd Ed.). New York: Macmillan.

Cooper, F. P. (1977). *A study of the effects of instruction in TA on selected teacher behaviors.* Unpublished doctoral dissertation, University of Arkansas, Fayetteville, AK.

Cordasco, F. (1963). *A brief history of education.* Paterson, NJ: Littlefield, Adams & Co.

Covault, T. J. (1973). The application of values clarification teaching strategies with fifth grade students to investigate their influence on students' self-concept and related classroom coping and interacting behaviors (Doctoral dissertation, Ohio State University). *Dissertation Abstracts International, 34,* 2199A.

Crespi, T. D. (1990). Restraint and seclusion with institutionalized adolescents. *Adolesence, 25,* 825–829.

Curwin, R. L., & Mendler, A. N. (1988). *Discipline with dignity.* Alexandria, VA: Association for Supervision and Curriculum Development.

Dahbany, A. (1996). "A process analysis of school discipline programs." Unpublished doctoral dissertation, Temple University, Philadelphia, PA.

Dahbany, A., & Hyman, I. (1995). *A process analysis of contemporary discipline training programs for teachers.* Unpublished manuscript, Temple University, Philadelphia, PA.

Dallas ISD—Department of Safety and Security (1994). *Categories of major offenses as reported to the DIS-D.* Dallas, TX: Author.

Davidson, R. F. (1953). *Philosophies men live by.* New York: The Dryden Press.

Decker, T. N., & Howe, S. W. (1981). Auditory tract assymmetry in brain stem electrical responses during binaural stimulation. *Journal of the Acoustical Society of America, 69,* 1084–1090.

Dennehy, M. N. (1981). *An assessment of Teacher Effectiveness Training on improving the teacher–student relationship, maintaining classroom discipline, and increasing teacher and student capacity for problem-solving.* Unpublished doctoral dissertation, Temple University, Philadelphia, PA.

De Santis, J. F. (1975). *The effects of Transactional Analysis on self-concept, locus of control, and behavior in suspended high school students.* Unpublished doctoral dissertation, Georgia State University, Atlanta, GA.

Dewey, J. (1961). *Philosophy of education.* Paterson, NJ: Littlefield, Adams & Co.

Diamanti, A. (1992, December 24). The teen years don't have to be dreaded. *Philadelphia Inquirer,* pp. F2, F3.

Dillard, J. W. (1974). An investigation of the effects of Teacher Effectiveness Training on the types of verbal responses and attitude change of pre-service teachers. (Doctoral dissertation, George Peabody College for Teachers). *Dissertation Abstracts International, 35,* 4282A.

Dinkmeyer, D., McKay, G. D., & Dinkmeyer, D., Jr. (1980). *Systematic training for effective teaching.* Circle Pines, MN: American Guidance Service.

Dinges, M. & Oetting, E. (1993). Similarity in drug use patterns between adolescents and their friends. *Adolescence, 28,* 253–266.

Donovan, J., Sousa, D., & Walberg, H. (1987). The impact of staff development on implementation and student achievement. *Journal of Educational Research, 80,* 348–351.

Dougherty, K. (1991). *Preliminary item development for the cross-national survey of attitudes toward school misbehavior and corrective methods in schools.* Unpublished doctoral dissertation, Temple University, Philadelphia, PA.

Doyle, W. (1990). *Classroom management techniques.* In O. C. Moles (Ed.), *Student discipline strategies:*

Research and practice (pp. 113–129). Albany, NY: State University of New York Press.

Dreikurs, R. (1968). *Psychology in the classroom: A manual for teachers.* New York: Harper and Row.

Dreikurs, R. (1971). *Maintaining sanity in the classroom: Illustrated teaching techniques.* New York: Harper and Row.

Dreikurs, R., & Cassel, P. (1972). *Discipline without tears.* New York: Hawthorn.

Dreyer, S. (1992). *The best of bookfinder.* Circle Pines, MN: American Guidance Service.

Duke, D. (1978). Can the curriculum contribute to resolving the educator's discipline dilemma? *Action in Teacher Education, 1,* 17–35.

Duke, D. (1980). *Managing student behavior problems.* New York: Teachers College Press.

Duke, D. (Ed.). (1982). *Helping teachers manage classrooms.* Alexandria, VA: Association for Supervision and Curriculum Development.

Duke, D. L., & Jones, V. F. (1984). Two decades of discipline: Assessing the development of an educational specialization. *Journal of Research and Development in Education, 17,* 25–35.

Dupont, H., Gardiner, O. & Brody, D. (1974). *Toward effective development (TAD).* Circle Pines, MN: American Guidance Service.

Durkheim, E. (1951). *Suicide.* New York: Free Press.

Durkheim, E. (1956). *Education and Sociology.* New York: Free Press.

Eggert, L. L., & Herting, J. (1993). Drug involvement among potential dropouts and "typical" youth. *Journal of Drug Education, 23,* 31–55.

Elam, S. (1989a, June). The second annual Gallup/Phi Delta Kappa poll of teacher's attitudes toward the public schools. *Phi Delta Kappa, 70*(10), 785–798.

Elam, S. M. (Ed.). (1989b). *The Gallup/Phi Delta Kappa Polls of attitudes toward the public schools: A twenty year compilation of educational history.* Bloomington, IN: Phi Delta Kappan.

Elam, S. M., & Rose, L. C. (1995, September). The 27th annual Phi Delta Kappa/Gallup poll of the public's attitudes toward the public schools. *Phi Delta Kappa, 77*(1), 41–59.

Elias, M., & Clabby, J. (1984). Integrating social and affective education into public school curriculum and instruction. In C. Mahar, R. Illback, and J. Zins (Eds.), *Organizational psychology in the schools: A handbook for professionals.* Springfield, IL: C. C. Thomas.

Elias, M., & Clabby, J. (1988). Teaching social decision making. *Educational Leadership, 45*(6), 52–55.

Elias, M., & Clabby, J. (1989). *Social decision making skills.* Rockville, MD: Aspen Publishers.

Elliot, S., & Gresham, F. (1991). *Social skills intervention Guide.* Circle Pines, MN: American Guidance Service.

Ellis, A. (1979). Rational emotive therapy. In A. Ellis & J. Whiteley (Eds.), *Theoretical and empirical foundations of rational emotive therapy.* Monterey, CA: Brooks-Cole.

Ellsworth, J. (1993, Fall). *Developmental management system: Teacher development manual.* Northern Arizona University: Kurriculum Publishing.

Ellsworth, J. T., & Monahan, K. A. (1987). *A humanistic approach to teaching/learning through developmental discipline.* New York: Irvington.

Emmer, E. T., & Aussiker, A. (1990). School and classroom discipline programs: How well do they work? In O. C. Moles (Ed.), *Student discipline strategies: Research and practice* (pp. 129–167). New York: State University of New York Press.

Emmer, E., & Evertson, C. (1981). Synthesis of research on classroom management. *Educational Leadership, 38,* 342–347.

Emmer, E. T., Evertson, C. M., & Anderson, L. M. (1980). Effective classroom management at the beginning of the school year. *The Elementary School Journal, 80,* 221–231.

Emmer, E. T., Evertson, C. M., Sanford, J. P., Clements, B. S., & Worsham, M. E. (1989). *Classroom management for secondary teachers* (2nd ed.). Englewood Cliffs, NJ: Prentice Hall.

Engleman, S. (1969). *Preventing failure in the primary grades.* New York: Simon and Schuster.

Eno, M. (1985). Children with school problems: A family therapy perspective. *Adjunctive techniques in family therapy.* New York: Grune & Stratton.

Erikson, E. H. (1964). *Childhood and society.* New York: W. W. Norton & Co.

Erikson, E. H. (1968). *Identity, youth and crisis.* New York: W. W. Norton & Co., 1968.

Erikson, E. H. (1982). *The life cycle completed: A review.* New York: Norton.

Ernst, K. (1973). *Games students play, and what to do about them.* Mellbrae, CA: Celestial Arts.

Eron, L., Walder, L., & Lefkowitz, M. (1971). *Learning aggression in children.* Boston: Little, Brown, & Co.

Evertson, C. M. (1985). Training teachers in classroom management: An experimental study in secondary school classrooms. *Journal of Educational Research, 79,* 51–58.

Evertson, C. M. (1988). *Improving elementary classroom management: A school-based training program for beginning the year.* Tennessee: Peabody College, Vanderbilt University (ERIC Document Reproduction Service No. ED 302 528).

Evertson, C. M. (1989). Improving elementary classroom management: A school-based training program for beginning the year. *Journal of Educational Research, 83,* 82–90.

Evertson, C. M., & Emmer, E. (1982a). Effective management at the beginning of the school year in junior high classrooms. *Journal of Educational Psychology, 74,* 485–498.

Evertson, C. M., & Emmer, E. (1982b). Preventive classroom management. In D. Duke (Ed.), *Helping teachers manage classrooms.* Alexandria, VA: ASCD.

Evertson, C. M., Emmer, E. T., Clements, B. S., Sanford, J. P., & Worsham, M. E. (1989). *Classroom management for elementary teachers* (2nd ed.). Englewood Cliffs, NJ: Prentice Hall.

Evertson, C., & Harris, A. (1993). *Classroom Organization and Management Program (COMP).* Nashville, TN: Peabody College/Vanderbilt University.

Farley, A. (1983). *National survey of the use and nonuse of corporal punishment as a disciplinary technique within the United States public schools.* Unpublished doctoral dissertation, Temple University, Philadelphia, PA.

Featherstone, J. (1971). *Schools where children learn.* New York: Liveright.

Fine, M. (1994). A systems-ecological perspective on home–school intervention. In M. Fine and C. Carlson (Eds.), *The handbook of family-school intervention: A systems perspective.* Boston: Allyn & Bacon.

Finkelstein, B. (1989). *Governing the young: Teacher behavior in popular primary schools in 19th century United States.* New York: The Falmer Press.

Fisher, D. (1989). *Albion's seed.* New York: Oxford University Press.

Fisher, L. (1986). Systems based consultation with schools. In L. C. Wynne, S. H. McDaniel, & T. T. Weber. (Eds.), *Systems consultation: A new perspective for family therapy* (pp. 342–356). New York: Guilford.

Flanders, N. (1960). *Interaction analysis in the class-room: A manual for observers,* Minneapolis, MN: University of Minnesota, College of Education.

Fletcher, J., Shaywitz, S., Shankwieler, D., Katz, L., Liberman, I., Stuebing, K., Francis, D., Fowler, A., & Shaywitz, B. (1994). Cognitive profiles of reading disability: Comparisons of discrepancy and low achievement definitions. *Journal of Educational Psychology, 84*(1), 6–23.

Ford, R. (1984). *Discipline strategies for teachers of problem students.* Washington, DC: National Institute of Education. (ERIC Document Reproduction Service No. ED 253 529).

Fowler, S. (1982). Peer-monitoring and self-monitoring: Alternatives to traditional teacher management. *Exceptional Children, 52,* 573–581.

Foxx, R. (1982). *Decreasing behaviors of severely retarded and autistic persons.* Champaign, IL: Research Press.

Frazier, D. (1993, September). *Examination of the demographic influences on the belief and use of corporal punishment in the African American community.* Unpublished paper, Temple University, Philadelphia, PA.

Freer, M., & Dawson, J. (1987). The pudding's the proof. *Educational Leadership, 45,* 67–68.

Freud, A. (1965). *Normality and pathology in childhood.* New York: International Universities Press.

Freud, S. (1933). *New introductory lectures on psychoanalysis.* New York: Norton.

Froyen, L. (1993). *Classroom Management* (2nd ed.). New York: Macmillan.

Fuller, P. W. (1977). Computer estimated alpha attentuation during problem-solving in children with learning disabilities. *Electroencephalography and Clinical Neurophysiology, 42,* 149–166.

Fuster, J. M. (1989). *The prefrontal cortex* (2nd ed.). New York: Raven.

Gadow, K. D. (1992). Pediatric psychopharmacology: A review of recent research. *Journal of Child Psychology and Psychiatry, 25,* 204–207.

Galbo, J. J. (1984, Winter). Adolescents' perceptions of significant adults: A review of the literature. *Adolescence, 19*(95), 549–556.

Galbo, J. J. (1987). An exploration of the effects of the relationships of adolescents and adults on learning in secondary schools. *High School Journal, 71*(2), 97–102.

Galbo, J. J. (1989, Fall). The teacher as significant adult: A review of the literature. *Adolescence, 24*(95), 549–556.

Gamble, C. W., & Watkins, C. E. (1983). Combining the child discipline approaches of Alfred Adler and William Glasser: A case study. *Individual Psychology, 39,* 156–164.

Gang, M. J. (1974). Empirical validation of a Reality Therapy intervention program in an elementary school classroom (Doctoral dissertation, The University of Tennessee). *Dissertation Abstracts International, 35,* 4216A.

Garbarino, J., Guttman, E., & Seeley, J. (1986). *The psychologically battered child.* San Francisco: Jossey-Bass.

Garinger, G. H. (1936). *The administration of discipline in the high school.* New York: Teachers College Press.

Gelman, D., & Rogers, P. (1993, April 12). Mixed messages. *Newsweek, 121*(15), 28–29.

Geoghin, (1986, March). Teaching emotionally handicapped adolescents. *Exceptional Children, 33*(1), 77–86.

Gibboney, R. (1987a). A critique of Madeline Hunter's teaching model from Dewey's pespective. *Educational Leadership, 44,* 46–50.

Gibboney, R. (1987b). The vagaries of turtle research: Gibboney replies. *Educational Leadership, 44,* 54.

Gibson, I. (1978). *The English vice.* London: Duckworth.

Gil, D. (1970). *Violence against children.* Boston: Harvard University Press.

Ginott, H. (1969). *Between parent and child.* New York: Avon.

Ginott, H. (1971). *Between parent and teen ager.* New York: Avon.

Gittins, N., & Walsh, J. (1990). *Sexual harassment in the schools: Preventing and defending against claims.* Alexandria, VA: National School Boards Association.

Glackman, T., Berv, V., Martin, R., McDowell, E., Spino, R., & Hyman, I. (1978). Corporal punishment in the schools as it relates to race, sex, grade level, and suspensions. *Inequality in Education: Center for Law and Education, 23,* 61–65.

Glasser, W. (1969). *Schools without failure.* New York: Harper & Row.

Glasser, W. (1978). Disorders in our schools: Causes and remedies. *Phi Delta Kappan, 59,* 331–333.

Glasser, W. (1985). Discipline has never been the problem and isn't the problem now. *Theory Into Practice, 24,* 241–246.

Glasser, W. (1986). *Control theory in the classroom.* New York: Harper & Row.

Glasser, W. (1992). *The quality school* (2nd ed.). New York: Harper Perennial.

Glickman, C., & Wolfgang, C. (1978). Conflict in the classroom: An eclectic model of teacher-child interaction. *Elementary School Guidance and Counseling, 12,* 82–87.

Goffin, S. G. (1989, Winter). How well do we respect children in our care? *Childhood Education, 66*(2), 68–74.

Goldberg, S., & Markovitch, S. (1989). Temperament in developmentally disabled children. In G. Kohnstamm, J. Bates, & M. Rothbart. *Temperament in childhood.* New York: John Wiley & Sons.

Goldstein, A. (1988). *The prepare curriculum.* Champaign, IL: Research Press.

Goldstein, A. (1989). Refusal skills: Learning to be positively negative. *Journal of Drug Education, 19*(3), 271–283.

Goldstein, A., Glick, B., Reiner, S., Zimmerman, D., & Coultry, T. (1987). *Aggression replacement training.* Champaign, IL: Research Press.

Goldstein, A., Sprafkin, R., Gershaw, N., & Klein, P. (1980). *Skill streaming the adolescent.* Champaign, IL: Research Press.

Good, T. L., & Brophy, J. E. (1994). *Looking in classrooms* (6th ed.). New York: Harper Collins College Publishers.

Good, T., & Grouws, D. (1977). Teaching effects: A process product study in fourth grade mathematics classrooms. *Journal of Teacher Education, 28,* 49–54.

Goodlad, J. I. (1984). *A place called school: Prospects for the future.* New York: McGraw-Hill.

Gordon, T. (1974). *TET: Teacher effectiveness training.* New York: David McKay Company, Inc.

Gordon, T. (1991). *Discipline that works: Promoting self-discipline in children.* New York: Plum-Penguin Group.

Graziano, A., & Nameste, K. (1990). Parental use of physical force in child discipline: A survey of 679 college students. *Journal of Interpersonal Violence, 5,* 449–463.

Greenwood, C., Carta, J., & Hall, R. (1988). The use of peer tutoring strategies in classroom management and educational instruction. *School Psychology Review, 17,* 258–275.

Greven, P. (1980). *The Protestant temperament.* New York: Alfred Knopf, Inc.

Greven, P. (1991). *Spare the child: The religious roots of punishment and the psychological impact of physical abuse.* New York: Knopf.

Gross, R., & Gross, B. (Eds.). (1969). *Radical school reform.* New York: Simon & Schuster.

Gump, P. V., & Kounin, J. S. (1961). Milieu influences in children's concepts of misconduct. *Child Development, 32,* 711–720.

Guziak, S. J. (1975). The use of values clarification strategies with fifth grade students to investigate the influence on self-concept and values. (Doctoral dissertation, Ohio State University). *Dissertation Abstracts International, 36,* 1389A.

Haeuser, A. (1991). *Reaffirming physical punishment in childrearing as one root of physical abuse.* Paper presented at the Ninth National Conference on Child Abuse and Neglect, Denver, CO.

Haeuser, A. (1992). Swedish parents don't spank. *Mothering, 63,* 42–49.

Hall, C. (1979). *A primer of Freudian psychology.* New York: New American Library (a Mentor Book).

Hall, C. S., & Lindzey, G. (1970). *Theories of personality.* New York: John Wiley & Sons, Inc.

Hamlet, C. C., Axelrod, S., & Kuerschner, S. (1984). Eye contact as an antecedent to compliant behavior. *Journal of Applied Behavior Analysis, 17,* 553–557.

Harbin, S. L. (1975). *The effects of a teacher workshop in Transactional Analysis on teacher flexibility in thinking, locus of control, flexibility in use of ego states and on teacher-pupil interactions.* Unpublished doctoral dissertation, Georgia State University, Atlanta, GA.

Hardetsy, L. (1978). *Pupil control ideology as it relates to middle school concepts.* Paper presented at the Annual Meeting of the American Educational Research Association, Toronto, Canada.

Harris, A. H. (1991). Proactive classroom management: Several ounces of prevention. *Contemporary Education, 62,* 156–160.

Harris, T. (1969). I'm ok—You're ok. New York: Harper Row.

Hart, S. (1987). Psychological maltreatment in schooling. *School Psychology Review, 16*(2), 169–180.

Hart, S., & Brassard, M. (1987). A major threat to children's mental health: Psychological maltreatment. *American Psychologist, 42*(2), 160–165.

Hart, S., Brassard, M., & Germain, B. (Eds.). (1987). *Proceedings of the international conference on psychological abuse of children and youth.* Indianapolis, IN: Center for the Study of the Psychological Rights of the Child, University of Indiana–Indianapolis.

Hartwig, E., & Ruesc, G. (1994). *Discipline in the school.* Horsham, PA: L.R.P. Publications.

Hedges, L. V., Laine, R. D., & Greenwald, R. (1994, April). Does money matter? A meta-analysis of studies of the effects of differential school inputs on student outcomes. *Educational Researcher, 23(3),* 5–14.

Henson, K. (1977, October). A new concept of discipline. *The Clearing House, 51,* 89.

Herrnstein, R., & Murray, C. (1994). *The bell curve: Intelligence and class structure in American life.* New York: The Free Press.

Hike, E. V. (1990). *Cooperative learning.* Bloomington, IN: Phi Delta Kappa Educational Foundation.

Hilgard, E., & Bauer, G. (1981). *Theories of learning* (5th ed.). Englewood Cliffs, NJ: Prentice Hall.

Hilts, P. J. (1994, August 2). Is nicotine addictive? It depends on whose criteria you use. *New York Times,* p. C3.

Hinshaw, S. P. (1992). Externalizing behavior problems and academic underachievement in childhood and adolescence: Causal relationships and underlying mechanisms. *Psychological Bulletin, 111,* 127–155.

Hodes, R. L. (1989). The biofeedback treatment of neurological and neuropsychological disorders of childhood and adolescence. In C. R. Reynolds and E. Fletcher-Janzen (Eds.), *Handbook of clinical child neuropsychology.* New York: Plenum Press.

Hodgkinson, H. (1991). School reform vs. reality. *Phi Delta Kappan, 73*(1), 9–16.

Holt, J. C. (1969). *How children learn.* New York: Delacorte Press.

Holt, J. C. (1982). *How children fail* (Rev. Ed.). New York: Delacorte Press.

Homme, L. (1970). *How to use contingency contracting in the classroom.* Champaign, IL: Research Press.

Houston Independent School District (1994). *Campus based police related incidents: Summary report.* Houston, TX.

Houton-Slowick, C. (1982). The effects of reality therapy processes on locus of control and dimensions of self-concept in the school setting of Mexican–American seventh and ninth grade students. (Doctoral dissertation, University of Houston). *Dissertation Abstracts International, 43,* 2238A.

Hunter, M. (1990). *Discipline that develops self discipline.* El Segundo, CA: TIPS.

Hyman, I. (1964). *Some effects of teaching style on pupil behavior.* Unpublished doctoral dissertation, Rutgers—The State University, New Brunswick, NJ.

Hyman, I. (1984, August 24). *School psychology and school discipline: Reaganspeak in 1984.* Paper presented at the Annual Convention of the American Psychological Association, Toronto, Canada.

Hyman, I. A. (1985a, August). *Psychological abuse in the schools: A school psychologist's perspective.* Paper presented at the meeting of the American Psychological Association, Los Angeles.

Hyman, I. (1985b, September/October). Corporal punishment: Is it a simple answer to your discipline problems? Part I. *Educational Oasis, I*(2), 6–7 (First of two-part series).

Hyman, I. (1987a). Corporal punishment: Does it have a place in the schools? *Children, I*(3), 70–74.

Hyman, I. (1987b, Winter). Corporal punishment: Who needs it? *School and Community,* Magazine of the Missouri State Teachers, 12–14.

Hyman, I. (1988). Getting your goat: The story of an underachieving student. *Educational Oasis, 3*(4), 7–9.

Hyman, I. (1989a). *Using advocacy research to change public policy: The case of corporal punishment in the schools.* Paper presented at eighty-seventh Annual Convention of the American Psychological Association, New Orleans.

Hyman, I. (1989b). Time out: How to use it without getting sued. *Educational Oasis, 4*(5), 11–13.

Hyman, I. (1989c, September/October). Rebel with a cause: The art of the gifted underachiever. *Challenge: Reaching and teaching the gifted child, 8*(1), 13–18.

Hyman, I. (1990a). *Reading, writing and the hickory stick: The appalling story of physical and psychological abuse of American school children.* Lexington, MA: Lexington Books.

Hyman, I. (1990b). Class cutting: An ecological approach. In R. Gupta & P. Coxhead (Eds.), *Intervention with children* (pp. 107–129). London: Routlage.

Hyman, I. (1991, May/Summer). Characteristics of "good" teachers, Part III. *Educational Oasis, 6*(5), 20–21.

Hyman, I. (1995). Corporal punishment, psychological maltreatment, violence and punitiveness in America: Research, advocacy and public policy. *Journal of Applied and Preventive Psychology, 4,* 113–130.

Hyman, I., Bilus, F., Dennehy, M. N., Feldman, G., Flanagan, D., Maital, S., & McDowell, E. (1979). Discipline in American education: An overview and analysis. *Journal of Education, 161*(2), 51–70.

Hyman, I., & Bogacki, D. (1984). Legal and ethical issues in the discipline of emotionally disturbed children. In M. Fine (Ed.), *Systematic intervention with disturbed children.* New York: S. P. Medical and Scientific Books.

Hyman, I., Bogacki, D., Dennehy, N., Feldman, G., Lovoratano, J., Maital, S., McDowell, E., Pfeffer, J., & Spino, P. (1979). *An analysis of studies on the effectiveness of training and staffing to help manage student conflict and alienation* (Contract No. NIE-P-78–0063). Washington, DC: National Institute of Education.

Hyman, I., Clarke, J., & Erdlen, R. (1987). An analysis of physical abuse in American schools. *Aggressive Behavior, 13,* 1–7.

Hyman, I. & Dahbany, A. (1994). *Process Analysis of School Discipline Programs.* Unpublished research report, National Center for the Study of Corporal Punishment and Alternatives. Philadelphia, PA: Temple University.

Hyman, I., Dahbany, A., Weiler, E., Shanock, A., & Britton, G. (1994, October 28). *Policy and practice in school discipline: Past, present and future.* Paper presented at The National Education Goals Panel/National Alliance of Pupil Services Organizations Conference on Safe Schools, Safe Students, Washington, DC.

Hyman, I., & D'Allesandro, J. (1984a). Good old fashioned discipline: The politics of punitiveness. *Phi Delta Kappan, 66,* (No. 1), 39–45.

Hyman, I., & D'Allesandro, J. (1984b, January 24). *School discipline in America: Violence to and by teachers.* Testimony before the Subcommittee on Elementary, Secondary and Vocational Education of the Committee on Education and Labor, United States House of Representatives.

Hyman, I., Flanagan, D., & Smith, K. (1982). Discipline in the schools. In C. Reynolds & T. Gutkin (Eds.), *A handbook for the practice of school psychology* (pp. 454–580). New York: John Wiley and Sons.

Hyman, I., & Gasiewski, E. (1992). *Corporal punishment, psychological maltreatment and conduct disorders: A continuing American dilemma.* Paper presented at the 24th Annual Convention of the National Association of School Psychologists, Nashville, TN.

Hyman, I., & Grossman, A. (1993, November 4). *Corporal punishment, poverty and child abuse: Issues, research and policy implications.* Paper presented at the Second Annual Head Start Research Conference, Washington, DC.

Hyman, I., & Kaplinski, K. (1995). Will the real school psychologist please stand up: Is the past a prologue for the future of school psychology? *School Psychology Review, 22*(4), 564–583.

Hyman, I., & Lally, D. (1982). The effectiveness of staff development programs to improve school discipline. *Urban Review, 14*(3), 181–196.

Hyman, I., & Lamberth, R. (1987). Discipline climate of educational oasis readers. *Educational Oasis, 3*(2), 10.

Hyman, I., Olbrich, J., & Shanock, A. (1994). *A perspective on violence: Reasons, trends and solutions.* Address presented at the 1994 Convention of the National Association of School Psychologists, Seattle, WA.

Hyman, I. A., & Pokalo, M. (1993). *Spanking, paddling and child abuse: The problem of punitiveness in America.* Paper presented at the Eighth Biennial National Symposium on Child Victimization, coordinated by Children's National Medical Center, Washington, DC.

Hyman, I., & Weiler, E. (1994). Emotional maltreatment in schools: Definition, incidence and legal implications. *Illinois Law School Quarterly, 14,* 125–135.

Hyman, I. A., & Wise, J. (1979). *Corporal punishment in American education.* Philadelphia: Temple University Press.

Hyman, I., Wojtowicz, A., Lee, K., Storlazzi, J., Foley, K., Haffner, M., & Rosenfeld, J. (1996, August). *School based methyphenidate placebo protocols: Methodological and practical issues.* Paper presented at the 104th Annual Convention of the American Psychological Association, Toronto, Canada.

Hyman, I., Zelikoff, W., & Clarke, J. (1987, August 31). *The effects of severe disciplinary practices in the schools.* Paper presented at the Annual Convention of the American Psychological Association, New York City.

Hyman, I., Zelikoff, W., & Clarke, J. (1988). Psychological and physical abuse in the schools: A paradigm for understanding PTSD in children. *Journal of Traumatic Stress, I,* (2), 243–267.

Jackson, N., Jackson, D., & Monroe, C. (1983). *Getting Along with Others.* Champaign, IL: Research Press.

Jenson, A. (1980). *Bias in mental testing.* New York: The Free Press.

Jernigan, T. L., Hesselink, J., & Tallal, P. (1987). Cerebral morphology on magnetic resonance imaging in developmental dysphasia. *Society for Neuroscience Abstracts, 13*(1), 1–651.

John, E. R., Prichep, L., Ahn, H., Easton, P., Friedman, J., & Kaye, H. (1983). Neurometric evaluation of cognitive dysfunctions and neurological disorders in children. *Progress in Neurobiology, 21,* 239–290.

Johnson, D., & Johnson, R. (1991). *Learning together and alone.* Boston: Allyn & Bacon.

Johnson, D., & Johnson, R. (1987). *Learning together: Cooperative, competitive, and individualistic learning.* Englewood Cliffs, NJ: Prentice-Hall.

Jones, A., Gasiewski, E., & Hyman, I. (1990). *Factors related to the development of punitive discipline styles in educators.* Paper presented at the Tenth Annual Conference on the Future of Psychology in the Schools, Temple University, Philadelphia, PA.

Jones, F. H. (1987). *Positive classroom discipline.* New York: McGraw-Hill.

Jones, F. H., & Jones, L. S. (1990). *Comprehensive classroom management.* Boston: Allyn & Bacon.

Jones, L. (1993, March) Why are we beating our children? *Ebony.*

Jones, V. (1982). Training teachers to be effective classroom managers. In D. Duke (Ed.), *Helping teachers manage classrooms.* Alexandria, VA: ASCD.

Jones, V. F., & Jones, L. S. (1990). *Comprehensive classroom management: Motivating and managing students* (2nd ed.). Boston: Allyn & Bacon.

Kadushin, A., & Martin, J. (1981). *Child abuse: An interactional event.* New York: Columbia University Press.

Kanbayashi, Y., Kono, Y., Ikeda, Y., & Nishikawa, Y. (1986). A study of mental health of junior high school students. *Journal of Mental Health, 14*(2), 1–15.

Kaplan, J. (1992). *Attitudes on childhood and adolescent sexuality: A cross-cultural comparison.* Unpublished manuscript, School Psychology Program, Temple University, Philadelphia, PA.

Kaplan, J. (1994). *Psychologists attitudes toward corporal punishment.* Unpublished doctoral dissertation, Temple University, Philadelphia, PA.

Kaplan, J. (1995). *Psychologists' attitudes toward corporal punishment.* Unpublished doctoral dissertation, Temple University, Philadelphia, PA.

Kazdin, A. (1984). *Behavior modification in applied settings* (3rd ed.). Homewood, IL: Dorsey Press.

Kearney, D. (1988). Assertive discipline or assertive relationships. *Educational and Child Psychology, 5,* 48–60.

Keating, B., Pickering, M., Slack, B., & White, J. (1990). *A Guide to Positive Discipline.* Boston: Allyn & Bacon.

Keller, B., & Hyman, I. A. (1973, November 16). *A student response inventory for measuring open education at the high school level.* Paper presented at the Anuual Convention of the New Jersey Education Association, Atlantic City, NJ.

Kelly, M., Power, T., & Wimbush, D. (1992). Determinants of disciplinary practices in low income black mothers. *Child development, 63*(3), 573–582.

Kendall, P., & Braswell, L. (1982). Assessment for cognitive-behavioral interventions in the schools. *School Psychology Review, 11*(1), 21–31.

Keogh, B., & Burstein, N. (1988). Relationship of temperament to preschoolers interactions with peers and teachers. *Exceptional Children, 54,* 69–74.

Kibler, V. E., Rush, B. L., & Sweeney, T. J. (1985). The relationship between Adlerian course participation and stability of attitude change. *Individual Psychology, 41,* 354–362.

Kindsvatter, R., & McLaughlin, M. (1985). Discipline mystique and discipline practice. *Clearing House, 55,* 403–407.

Kindsvatter, R., Wilen, W., & Ishler, M. (1992). *Dynamics of effective teaching* (2nd ed.). White Plains, NY: Longmen.

Kinitzer, J. (1984). Mental health services to children and adolescents: A national view of public policies. *American Psycholgist, 38,* 905–911.

Kirp, D. (1973). Schools as sorters. *University of Pennsylvania Law Review, 121,* 705.

Kirp, D. (1982). *Just schools: The idea of racial equality in American education.* Berkeley: University of California Press.

Kirp, D., & Yudoff, M. (1974). *Educational policy and the law.* Berkeley, CA: McCutchen Press.

Kochman, T. (1981). *Black and white styles of conflict.* Chicago: University of Chicago Press.

Kohl, H. R. (1969). *The open classroom.* New York: Vintage Books.

Kohl, H. R. (1979). *The open classroom.* New York: Shocken Books.

Kohlberg, L. A. (1980). *The meaning and measurement of moral development.* Worcester, MA: Clark University Press.

Kohn, A. (1986). *No contest: The case against competition.* New York: Houghton Mifflin.

Kohn, A. (1990). *The brighter side of human nature: Altruism and empathy in everyday life.* New York: Basic Books.

Kohn, A. (1991). Caring kids, the role of the schools. *Phi Delta Kappa, 72*(7), 496–506.

Kolata, G. (1993, September 30). Women pay price for being obese. *New York Times,* 18.

Kolko, D. J. (1992). Characterisitics of child victims of physical violence: Research findings and clinical implications. *Journal of Interpersonal Violence, 1*(19), 27–36.

Kotzen, A. (1994). *Establishing validity and reliability of the survey of attitudes toward children.* Unpublished doctoral dissertation, Temple University, Philadelphia, PA.

Kounin, J. S. (1970). *Discipline and group management in classrooms.* New York: Holt, Rinehart & Winston.

Krauss, C. (July 23, 1995). Mystery of New York, the suddenly safer city. *New York Times—Week in Review,* pp. 1 & 4.

Kruesi, M. J. P., Rapoport, J. L., Hamburger, S., Hibbs, E., Potter, W. Z., Lenane, M., & Brown, G. L. (1990). Cerebrospinal fluid metabolites, aggression, and impulsivity in disruptive behavior disorders of children and adolescents. *Archives of General Psychiatry, 47,* 419–426.

Kreutter, K. (1982). *Student and teacher attitudes toward disciplinary practices in a junior high school setting.* Unpublished doctoral dissertation, Temple University, Philadelphia, PA.

Krugman, R. D., & Krugman, M. K. (1984, March). Emotional abuse in the classroom. *American Journal of Diseases of Children, 138,* 284–286.

Kuriloff, P. (1973). The psychoecological counselor. *Personnel and Guidance Journal, 51*(5), 321–327.

Lally, D. (1982). *Administrator's perceptions of the effectiveness of discipline codes in New Jersey high schools.* Unpublished doctoral dissertation, Temple University, Philadelphia, PA.

Lambert, C. (1990). *Factoral structure and reliability of a scale measuring stress responses as a result of maltreatment in schools.* Unpublished doctoral dissertation, Temple University, Philadelphia, PA.

Lambert, C., Witkowski, B., Hyman, I., Alderman, L., & Tucker, E. (1988). *Psychological and physical abuse in the schools: A survey of students.* Paper presented at the Annual Meeting of the National Association of School Psychologists, Chicago.

Laseter, J. C. (1981). An investigation into the effect of Teacher Effectiveness Training upon student achievement in reading and mathematics (Doctoral dissertation, Georgia State University). *Dissertation Abstracts International, 42,* 937A.

Leffler, A. (1988). *The invisible scars: Verbal abuse and psychological unavailability and relationship to self-esteem.* Paper presented at the 96th Annual Convention of the American Psychological Association, Atlanta, GA.

Leming, J. S. (1981). Curricular effectiveness in moral/values education: A review or research. *Journal of Moral Education, 10,* 147–164.

Lennox, N. G. (1982). *Teacher use of corporal punishment as a function of modeling behavior.* Unpublished doctoral dissertation, Temple University, Philadelphia, PA.

Levin, J., & Nolan, J. (1991). *Principles of classroom management.* Austin, TX: PRO-ED.

Levinson, D. (1989). *Family violence in cross-cultural perspective.* Newbury Park, CA: Sage Publications.

Lewin, K. (1951). Psychological ecology. In D. Cartwright (Ed.). *Filed theory in social science: Selected theoretical papers by Kurt Lewin.* (pp. 170–187). New York: Harper & Row.

Lewin, G., Lippitt, R., & White, R. (1939). Patterns of aggressive behavior in experimentally created social climates. *Journal of Social Psychology, 10,* 271–279.

Liebert, R. M., & Sprafkin, J. (1988). *The early widow: Effects of television on children and youth* (3rd ed.). Elmsford, NY: Pergamon Press.

Litovsky, V. G., & Dusic, J. B. (1985). Perceptions of child rearing and self-concept development during the early adolescent years. *Journal of Youth and Adolescence, 14*(5), 373–387.

Long, J., Frye, V., & Long, E. (1985). *Making it till friday.* Princeton, NJ: Princeton Book Company.

Los Angeles Unified Public Schools—Department of Security. (1994). *Annual Report.* Los Angeles: Author.

Lunenburg, F. (1984). Pupil control ideology and behavior as predictors of the quality of school life. *Journal of Research and Development in School Life, 22*(4), 36–44.

Lynch, K. W. (1975). A study of the effect of inservice training on teachers in the use of some principles of reality therapy upon student achievement of basic mathematical competencies. *Dissertation Abstracts International, 36,* 7978A (University Microfilm No. 76-13, 340).

Maccoby, E., & Zellner, M. (1970). *Experiments in primary education: Aspects of follow-through.* New York: Harcourt, Brace & Javanovich.

Madsden, C. H., & Madsden, C. K. (1991). *Teaching discipline: Behavioral principles toward a positive approach* (2nd ed.). Boston: Allyn & Bacon.

Mandeville, G., & Rivers, J. (1991). The South Carolina PET study: Teacher's perceptions and student achievement. *The Elementary School Journal, 91,* 37–47.

Mandlebaum, L., Russel, S., Krousa, J., & Gonter, M. (1983). Assertive discipline: An effective classroom management program. *Behavior Disorders, 8,* 258–264.

Manning, J. (1979). Discipline in the good old days. In I. A. Hyman & J. Wise. (1979). *Corporal punishment in American education.* Philadelphia: Temple University Press.

Manuel, F. E., & Manuel, F. P. (1979). *Utopian thought in the western world.* Cambridge, MA: The Belknap Press of Harvard University.

Marandola, P., & Imber, S. C. (1979). Glasser's classroom meetings: A humanistic approach to behavior change with preadolescent inner-city learning-disabled children. *Journal of Learning Disabilities, 12,* 383–387.

Marchon-Tully, S. (1987). *Teacher's attitudes toward child variance: Development of the child variance instrument and its relationship to psychological control ideology.* Unpublished doctoral dissertation, Temple University, Philadelphia, PA.

Marotz, B. (1983). *Alternatives to behavioral classroom management.* Paper presented at the Annual International Convention of the Council for Exceptional Children (61st, Detroit, MI, April 4–8, 1983). (ERIC Document Reproduction Service No. ED 229 987).

Martens, B., & Meller, P. (1989). Influence of child and classroom characteristics on acceptability of intervention. *Journal of School Psychology, 27,* 237–245.

Martens, B. K., & Meller, P. J. (1990). The application of behavioral principles to educational settings. In T. B. Gutkin and C. R. Reynolds (Eds.), *The handbook of school psychology* (pp. 612–634). New York: Wiley & Sons.

Martin, R. (1988). Child temperament and educational outcomes. In A. D. Pelligrini (Ed.), *Psychological bases for early education.* New York: John Wiley & Sons.

Martin, R. (1989). Activity level, distractibility and persistence: Critical characteristics in early schooling. In G. Kohnstamm, J. Bates, & M. Rothbart (Eds.), *The handbook of temperament in childhood.* New York: John Wiley & Sons.

Martin, R. P., Nagle, R., & Paget, K. (1983). Relationships between temperament and classroom behavior, teacher attitudes, and academic achievement. *Journal of Psychoeducational Assessment, 1,* 377–386.

Maslow, A. H. (1962). *Toward a psychology of being.* Princeton, NJ: Van Nostrand Co.

Masters, J. R., & Laverty, G. E. (1977). The relationship between changes in attitude and changes in behavior in the schools without failure program. *Journal of Research and Development in Education, 10,* 36–49.

Matthews, D. B. (1972). The effects of Reality Therapy on reported self-concept, social-adjustment, reading achievement, and discipline of fourth graders and fifth graders in two elementary schools (Doctoral dissertation, University of South Carolina). *Dissertation Abstracts International, 33,* 4842A.

McCord, J. (1988a). Parental behavior in the cycles of aggression. *Psychiatry, 51*(1), 14–23.

McCord, J. (1988b). Parental aggressiveness and physical punishment in long term perspective. In G. Hoatling, D. Finkelhor, J. Kilpatrick, & M. Straus (Eds.), *Family abuse and its consequences.* Newbury Park, CA: Sage Publications.

McCord, J. (1991). Questioning the value of punishment. *Social Problems, 38,* 167–179.

McCormack, S. (1985). Students' off task behavior and assertive discipline (Doctoral dissertation, University of Oregon). *Dissertation Abstracts International, 46,* 1880A.

McCormick, B. G. (1973). *Evaluation strategies for reducing violence and vandalism: Project Revive.* Los Angeles, CA.

McCrosky, J., & Richmond, V. (1983). Power in the classoom: Teacher and student perceptions. *Communication Education, 32,* 175–183.

McDaniel, T. (1989). The discipline debate: A road through the thicket. *Educational Leadership, 47,* 81–82.

McDowell, E., & Friedman, R. (1979). An analysis of editorial opinions regarding corporal punishment: Some dynamics of regional differences. In I. A. Hyman & J. Wise (Eds.), *Corporal punishment in American education* (pp. 329–334). Philadelphia: Temple University Press.

McGinnis, E., & Goldstein, A. (1990). *Skillstreaming in early childhood.* Champaign, IL: Research Press.

McGinnis, E., Goldstein, A., Sprafkin, R. P., & Gershaw, N. (1984). *Skillstreaming the elementary school child.* Champaign, IL: Research Press.

McQueen, T. (1992). *Essentials of classroom management.* New York: Harper Collins.

Meichenbaum, D. (1977). *Cognitive–behavior modification.* New York: Plenum Press.

Melear, L. (1991). *Educator's guide to drug prevention.* Atlanta: Melear Multi-Media Inc.

Merrett, F., & Houghton, S. (1989). Does it work with the older ones? A review of behavioral studies carried out in British secondary schools since 1981. *Educational Psychology, 9,* 287–310.

Meyers, J., Parsons, R., & Martin, R. (1979). *Mental health consultation in the schools.* San Francisco: Jossey-Bass.

Mezzacappa, D. (1992, March 1). In a class by itself. *Philadelphia Inquirer,* Sunday Magazine Section, pp. 19–20, 21–24.

Miller, A. (1980). *For your own good.* New York: Farer, Straus & Giraux.

Miller, D., Walker, M. C., & Friedman, D. (1989). Use of holding techniques to control the the violent behavior of seriously disturbed adolescents. *Hospital and Community Psychiatry, 40,* 520–524.

Mishkin, A. (1987). *Corporal punishment: Why some parents use less severe discipline practices than they experienced as children.* Unpublished doctoral dissertation, Temple University, Philadelphia, PA.

Moles, O. (Ed.). (1990). *Student discipline strategies.* Albany, NY: State University of New York Press.

Morse, W., & Smith J. (1980). *Understanding child variance.* Reston, VA: The Council for Exceptional Children.

Multhauf, A., Willower, D., & Licata, J. (1978, September). Teacher pupil control ideology and behavior and classroom robustness. *Elementary School Journal, 79,* 40–46.

National Center for Education Statistics (1992, April). *Public school district survey on safe, disciplined and drug-free schools.* Washington, DC: U.S. Department of Education—Office of Educational Research and Improvement.

National Commission on Children. (1991). *Beyond rhetoric: A new American agenda for children and families.* Washington, DC: U.S. Government Printing Office.

National Committee for the Prevention of Child Abuse. (1991a). Public attitudes and behaviors with respect to child abuse prevention, 1987–1991. Chicago: Author.

National Committee for the Prevention of Child Abuse. (1991b). Current trends in child abuse reporting and fatalities: The results of the 1990 annual fifty states survey. Chicago: Author.

National Education Goals Panel. (1994). *National education goals report, 1994.* Washington, DC: Author.

National Institute of Education. (1977). *Safe school study* (Vols. 1-3). Washington DC: U.S. Department of Health, Education and Welfare.

National Institute of Education. (1978). *Violent schools—safe schools: The safe school study report to the congress.* Washington, DC: Superintendent of Documents.

National School Resource Network. (1980). *Resource handbook on discipline codes.* Cambridge, MA: Oelgeschlager, Gun & Hahn, Pubishers.

Neill, A. S. (1960). *Summerhill.* New York: Hart Publishing Co.

Neill, A. S. (1966). *Freedom Not License.* New York: Hart Publishing Co.

Nelson, J. (1987). *Positive Discipline.* New York: Ballantine.

Nelson, J., Lott, L., & Glenn, H. (1993). *Positive discipline in the classroom.* Provo, UT: Sunrise, Inc.

New England Journal of Medicine, February 3, 1994, *330*(5), 301–307.

Newlon, B. J., & Arciniega, M. (1983). *Adlerian classroom management: An inservice model.* Paper presented at the Annual Convention of the American Psychological Association (91st, Anaheim, CA, August, 1983). (ERIC Document Reproduction Service No. ED 237 483).

Newman, J. (1980). From past to future: School violence in a broad view. *Contemporary Education, 52*(1), 8.

Niblett, J. O. (1979). Measuring the effects of a training sequence in transactional analysis, self-awareness, and values clarification on educators (Doctoral dissertation, Georgia State University). *Dissertation Abstracts International, 40,* 3029A.

Nummela, R. M. (1978). The relationship of Teacher Effectiveness Training to pupil self-concept, locus of control, and attitude (Doctoral dissertation, The University of Florida). *Dissertation Abstracts International, 39,* 6035A.

Obrzut, J. E., Morris, G. L., Wilson, S. L., Lord, J. M., & Caraveo, L. E. (1987). Brainstem evoked response in the assessment of learning disabilities. *International Journal of Neuroscience, 32,* 11–823.

Odom, S. L., Hoyson, M., Jameison, B., & Strain, P. A. (1985). Increasing handicapped preschooler's peer social interactions: Cross-setting and component analysis. *Journal of Applied Behavior Analysis, 18,* 3–16.

O'Hagan, R., & Edmunds, G. (1982). Pupil attitudes toward teachers' strategies for controlling disruptive behavior. *British Journal of Educational Psychology, 52,* 331–340.

O'Leary, K. D. (1977). *Classroom management.* New York: Pergamon Press.

O'Leary, K., Kaufman, K., Kass, R., & Drabman, R. (1970). The effects of loud and soft reprimands on the behavior of disruptive students. *Exceptional Children, 37,* 145–155.

Oregon Research Institute (1994). *Diversion program for minors in possesion of tobacco.* Unpublished Technical Report, Oregon Research Institute, Eugene, OR.

Overman, W. (1979). Effective communication: The key to student management. *NASSP Bulletin, 63,* 34–39.

Papas, B. (1993, March/April). Managing aggression: New stategies for the hospital setting. *Headlines,* pp. 2–6. Boston: J. R. Publishing.

Patterson, G. (1982). A social learning approach to family intervention: III. *Coercive Family Process.* Eugene, OR: Castalia.

Patterson, G., Capaldi, D., & Bank, L. (1990). An early starter model for predicting delinquency. In D. Pepler & K. Rubin (Eds.), *The development and treatment of childhood aggression* (pp. 139–168). Hillsdale, NJ: Lawrence Erlbaum.

Peek, J. H. (1975). *The effect of Transactional Analysis upon the self-concept of adjudicated delinquents.* Unpublished doctoral dissertation, Georgia State University, Atlanta, GA.

Pehlam, W. (1993). Pharmacotherapy for children with attention-deficit hyperactivity disorder. *School Psychology Review, 22,* 199–227.

Pehlam, W., Carlson, C., Sams, S., Vallano, G., Dixon, M., & Hoza, B. (in press). Separate and combined effects of methylphenidate and behavior modifications on the classroom behavior and academic performance of ADHD boys: Group effects and individual differences. *Journal of Consulting and Clinical Psychology.*

Pellow, R., & Jengeleski, J. (1991). A survey of current research studies on drug education programs in America. *Journal of Drug Education, 21*(3), 203–210.

Penny, G., & Robinson, J. (1986). Psychological resources and cigarette smoking in adolescents. *British Journal of Psychology, 77*(3), 857–862.

Percy, R. L. (1990). The effects of teacher effectiveness training on the attitudes and behaviors of classroom teachers. *Educational Research Quarterly, 14,* 15–20.

Perlmutter, B. F. (1994, August 12). *Teaching distractible students: Modifications in seating arrangements and classroom strategies.* Paper presented at The Annual Convention of the American Psychological Association, Los Angeles, CA.

Perry, C., Klepp, K., & Sillers, C. (1989). Community wide stategies for cardiovascular health: The Minnesota Heart Health Youth Program. *Health Education Research, 4*(1), 87–101.

Pfifner, L., & O'Leary, S. (1987). The efficacy of all-positive management as a function of the prior use of negative consequences. *Journal of Applied Behavior Analysis, 20,* 265–271.

Philips, P., & Nasr, S. J. (1983). Seclusion and restraint and the prediction of violence. *American Journal of Psychiatry, 140,* 229–232.

Piaget, J. (1932). *The moral development of children.* London: Routledge & Kegan Paul.

Plas, J. M. (1994). The development of systems thinking: A historical perspective. In M. Fine & C. Carlson

(Eds.), *The handbook of family–school intervention: A systems perspective.* Boston: Allyn & Bacon.

Plowden, J. P. (1967). *Children and their primary schools.* Report of the Central Advisory Council for Education, England. London: Her Majesty's Stationary Office.

Pokalo, M. (l986). *Caregivers' attitudes toward the severity of punishment for forty-four misbehaviors in mental retardation institutions.* Unpublished doctoral dissertation, Temple University, Philadelphia, PA.

Pokalo, M. (1992). *The relationship between severe discipline, conduct disorders and PTSD.* Paper presented at the 24th Convention of the National Association of School Psychologists, Nashville, TN.

Pokalo, M., & Hyman, I. (1993). *Case studies in community sanctioned abuse of school children.* Paper presented at the 25th Annual Convention of the National Association of School Psychologists, Washington, DC.

Portes, P., Dunham, R., & Williams, S. (1986). Assessing child rearing styles in ecological settings: Its relation to culture, social class, early age intervention and scholastic achievement. *Adolescence, 21*(83), 723–735.

Prescott, D. A. (1957). *The child in the educative process.* New York: McGraw-Hill.

Proshansky, H. M., Ittleson, W. H., & Rivlin, L. G. (1970). *Environmental psychology: Man and his physical setting.* New York: Holt, Rinehart & Winston.

Purvis, J. (1976). *Critical behavioral incidents checklist.* Unpublished manuscript, University of Southern Mississippi, Hattiesburg, Mississippi.

Pynoos, R., & Eth, S. (1985). Developmental perspectives on psychic trauma. In C. R. Figley (Ed.), *Trauma and its wake* (pp. 36–52). New York: Brunner/Mazel.

Quay, H. C., & Werry, J. S. (Eds.). (1986). *Psychopathological disorders of childhood.* New York: John Wiley & Sons.

Radbill, S. (1974). A history of child abuse and infanticide. In R. Helford and C. Kempe (Eds.), *The Battered Child.* Chicago: University of Chicago Press.

Raths, L. E., Harmin, M., & Simon, S. B. (1966). *Values and teaching.* Columbus: Charles E. Merrill Publishing.

Raths, L. E., Harmin, M., & Simon, S. B. (1978). *Values and teaching* (2nd ed.). Columbus: Charles E. Merrill Publishing.

Reardon, F., & Reynolds, R. (1979). A survey of attitudes toward corporal punishment in Pennsylvania schools. In I. Hyman & J. Wise (Eds.), *Corporal punishment in American education.* Philadelphia: Temple University Press.

Redl, F., & Wattenberg, W. W. (1951). *Mental hygiene in teaching.* New York: Harcourt, Brace, and World.

Reimers, T. M., Wacker, D. P., & Koeppl, G. (1987). Acceptability of behavioral interventions: A review of the literature. *School Psychology Review, 16,* 212–227.

Render, G. F., Padilla, J. N., & Krank, H. M. (1989a). What research really shows about assertive discipline. *Educational Leadership, 47,* 72–75.

Render, G. F., Padilla, J. M., & Krank, H. M. (1989b). Assertive discipline: A critical review and analysis. *Teachers College Record, 90,* 607–630.

Rhodes, W. C., Tracy, M. L., & Head, S. (Eds.). (1977). *A study of child variance* (Vols. 1–3). Ann Arbor, MI: University of Michigan Press.

Rich, J. M. (1979). Glasser and Kohl: How effective are their strategies? *Nassp Bulletin, 63,* 19–26.

Rich, J. M. (1985). *Innovative school discipline.* Springfield, IL: Charles C. Thomas.

Richardson, R., & Evans, E. (1992). *African American males: An endangered species and the most paddled.* Paper presented at the Seventh Annual Conference of the Louisiana Association that is Multicultural, Baton Rouge, LA.

Riley, V. (1992). *Corporal punishment: The attitudes and perceptions of students in the public elementary grades.* Unpublished doctoral dissertation, Temple University, Philadelphia, PA.

Roberts, M. (1988). Enforcing chair timeouts with room timeouts. *Behavior Modification, 12*(3), 353–370.

Robinson, A. W., & Hyman, I. A. (1984). *A meta-analysis of human relations teacher training programs.* Paper presented at the Annual Convention of the National Association of School Psychologists.

Robinson et al. vs. *District of Columbia, et al.* (1987). Civil Action No. 2484–87, Superior Court of the District of Columbia.

Rogers, C. (1969). *Freedom to learn.* Columbus: Charles E. Merrill Publishing.

Rogers, C. R. (1987). Rogers, Kohut, and Erickson: A personal perspective on some similarities and differences. In J. K. Zeig (Ed.), *The evolution of psychotherapy* (pp. 179–187). New York: Brunner/Mazel.

Rogers, C. R., & Skinner, B. F. (1976). *A dialogue on education and the control of human behavior* (Cassette Recording). New York: Jeffrey Norton Publishers.

Rose, T. (1984). Current uses of corporal punishment in American public schools. *Journal of Educational Psychology, 76*(3), 427–441.

Rosen, H., & DiGiacomo, J. (1976). The role of physical restraint in the treatment of psychiatric illness. *Journal of Clinical Psychiatry, 39,* 228–232.

Rosenblatt, R. (1994, March 20). How do they live with themselves? *New York Times Magazine,* pp. 34–76.

Rosenblatt, R. (1995, August 30) Teaching Johnny to be good. *New York Times Magazine,* 36–41, 50–74.

Rosenfield, S. (1987). *Instructional consultation.* Hillsdale, NJ: Lawrence Erlbaum Associates.

Rosenshine, B., & Furst, N. (1973). The use of direct observation to study teaching. In R. M. Travers (Ed.), *Second handbook of research on teaching.* New York: Longman.

Rosenthal, R., & Jacobson, L. (1968). *Pygmalion in the classroom: Teacher expectation and pupils' intellectual development.* New York: Holt, Rinehart, & Winston.

Rothenberger, A. (1990). The role of frontal lobes in child psychiatric disorders. In A. Rothenberger (Ed.), *Brain and behavior in child psychiatry.* New York: Springer-Verlag.

Rubel, R. (1977). *The unruly school.* Lexington, MA: Lexington Books.

Runes, D. D. (1955). *Dictionary of philosophy.* Ames, IA: Littlefield, Adams & Co.

Russell, W. (1988). *Analysis of OCR data from 1978–1986.* Unpublished paper, Philadelphia: NCSC-PAS, Temple University.

Russell, W. (1989). *The OCR data on corporal punishment: What does it really mean?* Paper presented at the Third National Conference on Abolishing Corporal Punishment in the Schools, Sponsored by the National Committee for the Prevention of Child Abuse, Chicago, IL. (Obtainable from NCSCPAS).

Rust, J., & Kinnard, K. (1983). Personality characteristics of the users of corporal punishment. *Journal of School Psychology, 21*(2), 91–95.

Rutter, M., Maughan, B., Mortimore, P., & Ouston, J. (1979). *Fifteen thousand hours: Secondary schools and their effects on children.* London: Open Books.

Sadker, M., & Sadker, D. (1994). *Failing at fairness: How Americas' schools cheat girls.* New York: Charles Scribners & Sons.

Sakowski, L. (1993). *A study of pre and post-trauma adjustment in corporally punished students.* Unpublished doctoral dissertation, Temple University, Philadelphia, PA.

Sanford, J. P., & Evertson, C. M. (1981). Classroom management in a low SES junior high: Three case studies. *Journal of Teacher Education, 32,* 34–38.

Sarno, G. G. (1992). Emotional distress by school teacher or administrator. *18 Am Jur Proof of Fact 3rd, 103.*

Satterfield, J. H., Schell, A. M., Backs, R. W., & Hidaka, K. C. (1984). A cross-sectional and longitudinal study of age effects of electrophysiological measures in hyperactive and normal children. *Biological Psychiatry, 19,* 973–990.

Savage, T. (1991). *Discipline for self control.* Boston: Allyn & Bacon.

Scarr-Salapatek, S. (1971). Race, social class and IQ. *Science, 174*(4016), 1285–1295.

Schatzberg, A., & Cole, J. (1986). *Manual of clinical psychoparmacology.* Washington, DC: American Psychiatric Press.

Schrumpf, F., Crawford, D., & Usadel, H. C. (1991). *Peer mediation: Conflict resolution in schools.* Champaign, IL: Research Press.

Selz, M., & Wilson, S. (1989). Neuropsychological bases of common learning and behavior problems in children. In C. R. Reynolds & E. Fletcher-Janzen (Eds.), *Handbook of clinical child neuropsychology.* New York: Plenum Press.

Short, R. J., & Shapiro, S. K. (1993). Conduct disorders: A framework for understanding and intervention in schools and communities. *School Psychology Review, 22*(3), 362–376.

Shure, M. (1992). *I can problem solve.* Champaign, IL: Research Press.

Silberman, C. (1971). *Crisis in the classroom.* New York: Vintage Books.

Silberman, C. (1973). *The open classroom reader.* New York: Vintage Books.

Simon, S. B., Howe, L. W., & Kirschenbaum, H. (1972). *Values clarification: A handbook of practical strategies for teaching students.* New York: Hart Publishing Co.

Skinner, B. F. (1953). *Science and human behavior.* New York: Macmillan.

Skinner, B. F. (1968). *The technology of teaching.* New York: Appleton-Century-Crofts.

Skinner, B. F. (1971). *Beyond freedom and dignity.* New York: Knopf.

Skinner, B. F. (1979). Corporal punishment. In I. Hyman & J. Wise (Eds.), *Corporal punishment in American education*. Philadelphia: Temple University Press.

Skinner, B. F. (1982). *Skinner for the classroom: Selected papers*. Champaign, IL: Research Press.

Skinner, L. (1995). *Peer mediation manual*. Unpublished manuscript, Temple University, Philadelphia, PA.

Skinner, M., & Hales, M. (1992). Classroom teachers' "explanations" of student behavior: One possible barrier to the acceptance and use of applied behavior analysis procedures in the schools. *Journal of Educational and Psychological Consultation, 3,* 219–232.

Slavin, R. (1986). The Napa evaluation of Madeline Hunter's ITIP: Lessons learned. *The Elementary School Journal, 87,* 165–171.

Slavin, R. E. (1987). Cooperative learning: Where behavioral and humanistic approaches to classroom motivation meet. *The Elementary School Journal, 88,* 30–37.

Smith, S. J. (1983). The effects of assertive discipline training on student teachers' self-perceptions and classroom management skills. (Doctoral dissertation, University of South Carolina). *Dissertation Abstracts International, 44,* 2690A.

Sofer, B. (l983). *Psychologists' attitudes toward corporal punishment*. Unpublished doctoral dissertation, Temple University, Philadelphia, PA.

Spivack, G., Platt, J., & Shure, M. (1976). *The problem solving approach to adjustment*. San Francisco: Jossey-Bass.

Stagliano, P., & Hyman, I. (1983). Analysis of state departments of education activities regarding violence and vandalism in the public schools. *Phi Delta Kappan, 65*(1), 67–68.

Stankovich, K., & Seigel, L. (1994). Phenotypic performance profile of children with reading disabilities: A regression-based test of the phonological-core variable-difference model. *Journal of Educational Psychology, 86*(1), 24–53.

Stewart, J. S. (1975). Clarifying values clarification: A critique. *Phi Delta Kappan, 56,* 684–688.

Straus, M. (1989). *Corporal punishment and crime: A theoretical model and some empirical data*. Unpublished paper presented at the Department of Criminal Justice, Indiana University. Publication of the Family Violence Research Program of the Family Research Laboratory, University of New Hampshire, Durham.

Straus, M. (1989). Discipline and deviance: Physical punishment of children and violence and other crime in adulthood. *Social Problems, 38*(2), 101–123.

Straus, M. A. (1992). *Corporal punishment of children and depression and suicide in adulthood*. Paper presented at The Society for Life History Research, Philadelphia, PA.

Straus, M. A. (1994). *Beating the devil out of them: Corporal punishment in American families*. New York: Lexington Books.

Straus, M., & Gimpel, H. (1992). *Corporal punishment by parents and economic achievement: A theoretical model and some preliminary data*. Paper presented at the 1992 meeting of the American Sociological Association. Durham, NH: Family Research Laboratory, University of New Hampshire.

Strauss, S. (1988). Sexual harassment in the school: Legal implications for principals. *NASSP Bulletin*. Reston, VA: National Association of Secondary School Principles.

Strauss-Fremuth, C. (1991). Teacher's attitudes toward punishment severity for specific behavioral transgressions. Unpublished doctoral dissertation, Temple University, Philadelphia, PA.

Swett, C., Michaels, A. S., & Cole, J. O. (1989). Effects of a state law on rates of restraints on a child and adolescent unit. *Bulletin of the American Academy of Psychiatry and the Law, 17,* 15–19.

Tallal, P., and Curtis, S. (1990). Neurological basis of developmental language disorders. In A. Rothnberger (Ed.), *Brain and behavior in child psychiatry*. New York: Springer-Verlag.

Tallal, P., Sainburg, R. L., & Jernigan, T. (1991). The neuropatholgy of developmental dysphasia: Behavioral, morphological, and physiological evidence for temporal processing disorder. *Reading and Writing, 3,* 363–378.

Tannen, D. (1990). *You just don't understand: Women and men in conversation*. New York: Ballantine Books.

Tauber, R. T. (1990). *Classroom management: From A to Z*. Fort Worth: Holt, Rinehart, and Winston.

Templer, D., Spencer, D., & Hartlage, L. (1993). *Biosocial psychopathology epidemiological perspectives*. New York: Springer.

Texas Department of Public Safety (1993). *State crime report for twelve months—1992 data*. Austin, TX: Author.

Thomas, A., & Chess, S. (1977). *Temperament and development.* New York: Brunner/Mazel.

Thomas, A., Chess, S., & Birch, H. (1968). *Temperament and behavior disorders in children.* New York: New York University Press.

Thompson, J. L. (1975). The effects of the I-message component of Teacher Effectiveness Training (Doctoral dissertation, George Peabody College). *Dissertation Abstracts International, 36,* 2139A.

Tipper, et al., v. The New Castle Area School District, et al.; Civil Action No. 93-0501. In the United States District Court for the Western District of Pennsylvania, 1993.

Torello, M. W., & Duffy, F. H. (1985). Using brain electrical activity mapping to diagnose learning disabilities. *Theory into Practice, 24,* 95–99.

Tramontana, M. G., & Hooper, S. R. (1989). Neuropsychopathology of child psychopathology. In C. R. Reynolds & E. Fletcher-Janzen (Eds.), *The handbook of clinical child neuropsychology.* New York: Plenum Press.

Travers, P. D. (Summer, 1980). An historic view of school discipline. *Educational Horizons, 58*(4), 184.

Tully-Marschon, S. (1987). Teacher's attitudes toward child variance: Development of the child variance inventory (CVI) and its relationship to pupil control ideology. Unpublished doctoral dissertation, Temple University, Philadelphia, PA.

U.S. Department of Education. (1993). *Reaching the goals—Goal 6: Safe, disciplined and drug-free schools.* Washington, DC: Office of Educational Research and Improvement.

U.S. Department of Health and Human Services. (1994). *Child maltreatment 1992: Reports from the states to the National Center on Child Abuse and Neglect.* Washington, DC: U.S. Printing Office.

U.S. Department of Justice. (1991). *Teenage victims: A national crime survey report.* Washington, DC: U.S. Government Printing Office.

U.S. Department of Justice. (1992). *Criminal victimization in the United States, 1990.* Washington, DC: U.S. Government Printing Office.

U.S. Department of Justice. (1993). *Criminal victimization in the United States, 1991.* Washington, DC: U.S. Government Printing Office.

U.S. Department of Justice. (1994). *Criminal victimization in the United States, 1992.* Washington, DC: U.S. Government Printing Office.

U.S. Department of State (1993). *Country reports on human rights practices for 1993.* U.S. Government Printing Office, ISBN-0-16-043627-3.

Valentine, M. R. (1987). *How to deal with discipline problems in the schools: A practical guide for educators.* Iowa: Kendall/Hunt Publishing Company.

Van Houten, R., Mackenzie-Keating, S., Sameoto, D., & Coleavecchia, B. (1982). An analysis of some variables influencing the effectiveness of reprimands. *Journal of Applied Behavior Analysis, 15,* 65–83.

Van Slyck, M., & Stern, M. (1991). Conflict resolution in educational settings: Assessing the impact of peer mediation programs. In K. G. Duffy, J. W. Grosch, & P. V. Olczak (Eds.), *Community mediation: A handbook for practitioners and researchers* (pp. 257–274). New York: Guilford.

Vargas-Moll, I. (1992). *A descriptive study of school induced stressors among Hispanic students.* Unpublished dissertation, Temple University, Philadelphia, PA.

Vargas-Moll, I., & Hyman, I. (1992, March 6). *Psychological and physical maltreatment of inner city Hispanic school children.* Paper presented at the Eleventh Annual Conference on the Future of Psychology in the Schools, Sponsored by the School Psychology Program, Temple University, Philadelphia, PA.

Veaco, L., & Brandon, C. (1986, Fall). The preferred teacher: A content analysis of young adolescents' writing. *Journal of Early Education, 6*(3), 221–229.

Veaco, E. S., & Smith, R. S. (1982). *Vulnerable but invincible: A longitudinal study of resilient children and youth.* New York: Adams, Bannister and Cox.

Walberg, H. J. (1986). Synthesis of research on teaching. In M. C. Wittrock (Ed.), *Handbook of research on teaching* (3rd ed., pp. 214–229). New York: Macmillan Publishing Co.

Walker, L. (Ed.). (1988). *Handbook of sexual abuse of children.* New York: Springer.

Walker, J., & Shea, T. (1976). *Behavior modification: Practical approach for educators.* St. Louis: C. V. Mosby.

Webber, J., & Coleman, M. (1988). Using rational-emotive therapy to prevent classroom problems. *Teaching Exceptional Children, 21,* 32–35.

Welch, F. C., & Dolly, J. (1980). A systematic evaluation of Glasser's techniques. *Psychology in the Schools, 17,* 385–389.

Welsh, C. (1994). Executive function and the assessment of attention deficit hyperactivity disorder. In N. C. Jordan & J. Goldsmith-Phillips (Eds.), *Learning disabilities: New directions for assessment and intervention.* Boston: Allyn & Bacon.

West, K. (1994). *An investigation of client characteristics contributing to the frequency of physical restraint in child residential treatment.* Unpublished doctoral dissertation, Temple University, Philadelphia, PA.

Wiehe, E. (1989). *Religious influence of parental attitudes toward the use of corporal punishment.* Unpublished manuscript, Department of Social Work, University of Kentucky, Lexington, KY.

Willower, D. J., Eidell, T., & Hoy, W. (1967). *The school and pupil control ideology.* The Pennsylvania State University Studies, 24, University Park, PA.

Wilson, C., Robertson, S., Herlong, L., & Haynes, S. (1979). Vicarious effects of time-out in the modification of aggression in the classroom. *Behavior Modification, 3,* 97–111.

Witt, J., & Elliot, S. (1982). The response cost lottery: A time efficient and effective classroom intervention. *Journal of School Psychology, 20,* 155–161.

Wolery, M., Baily, D. B., & Sugai, G. M. (1988). *Effective teaching: Principles and practices of applied behavior analysis with exceptional children.* Boston: Allyn & Bacon.

Wolfgang, C. H., & Glickman, C. D. (1980). *Solving discipline problems: Strategies for classroom teachers.* Boston: Allyn and Bacon.

Wolfgang, C. H., & Glickman, C. D. (1986). *Solving discipline problems: Strategies for classroom teachers* (2nd ed.). Boston: Allyn & Bacon.

Wood, M., Combs, C., Gun, A., & Weller, D. (1986). *Developmental therapy in the classroom.* Austin, TX: PRO-ED.

Wood, M., & Long, N. (1991). *Life space intervention.* Austin, TX: PRO-ED.

Zelikoff, W. (1990). *A retrospective study of school related stressors of educators.* Unpublished doctoral dissertation, Temple University, Philadelphia, PA.

Survey of Attitudes Toward Children—Scoring Key

Part A

Enter the number you circled in responding to the following questions:

Question	Response # Circled	Question	Response # Circled
1	_____	19	_____
4	_____	21	_____
6	_____	22	_____
9	_____	23	_____
11	_____	24	_____
12	_____	27	_____
16	_____	Part A Total: (add all scores)	_____

Part B

For the following questions, you must change the response you circled to obtain a new score. This is for scoring purposes only. Use the following key for changing your original scores to a changed (new) score for each of the questions numbered below.

If you circled 1, record a 5 as the new score.

If you circled 2, record a 4 as the new score.

If you circled 3, record a 3 as the new score.

If you circled 4, record a 2 as the new score.

If you circled 5, record a 1 as the new score.

Question #	New Score	Question #	New Score
2	_____	14	
3	_____	15	_____
5	_____	17	_____
7	_____	18	_____
8	_____	20	_____
10	_____	25	_____
13		26	_____
		Part B Total: (add all scores)	_____

Add A + B = TOTAL SCORE: _____

Raw Scores and Percentiles for the Survey of Attitudes Toward Children (SATC)

Score Percentile	Score Percentile	Score Percentile	Score Percentile	Score Percentile
36 = 2	51 = 22	59 = 42	70 = 62	84 = 82
39 = 4	52 = 24	60 = 44	70 = 64	85 = 84
41 = 6	54 = 26	61 = 46	72 = 66	85 = 86
43 = 8	54 = 28	62 = 48	73 = 68	87 = 88
43 = 10	54 = 30	63 = 50	74 = 70	88 = 90
45 = 12	55 = 32	64 = 52	77 = 72	90 = 92
46 = 14	56 = 34	65 = 54	78 = 74	91 = 94
48 = 16	57 = 36	66 = 56	80 = 76	93 = 96
49 = 18	57 = 38	67 = 58	80 = 78	98 = 98
50 = 20	58 = 40	69 = 60	82 = 80	

Appendix 3

Teacher Variance Inventory Scoring Key

Rate your assessment as to the level of importance for each available response (1–5). Then select one of the five responses (A–E) as the **single best answer** by circling the letter before that response in each scenario.

Section 1

	Not Important		Important		Very Important
Question #1					
A Psychodynamic	1	2	3	4	5
B Behavioral	1	2	3	4	5
C Ecological	1	2	3	4	5
D Biophysical	1	2	3	4	5
E Humanistic	1	2	3	4	5
Question #2					
A Biophysical	1	2	3	4	5
B Behavioral	1	2	3	4	5
C Ecological	1	2	3	4	5
D Psychodynamic	1	2	3	4	5
E Humanistic	1	2	3	4	5

		Not Important		Important		Very Important
Question #3						
A	Biophysical	1	2	3	4	5
B	Ecological	1	2	3	4	5
C	Psychodynamic	1	2	3	4	5
D	Humanistic	1	2	3	4	5
E	Behavioral	1	2	3	4	5
Question #4						
A	Ecological	1	2	3	4	5
B	Humanistic	1	2	3	4	5
C	Biophysical	1	2	3	4	5
D	Behavioral	1	2	3	4	5
E	Psychodynamic	1	2	3	4	5
Question #5						
A	Ecological	1	2	3	4	5
B	Humanistic	1	2	3	4	5
C	Psychodynamic	1	2	3	4	5
D	Biophysical	1	2	3	4	5
E	Behavioral	1	2	3	4	5

Section 2

Rate your assessment as to the level of effectiveness (1–5) for each scenario. Then select one of the five responses (A–E) as the **single best answer** by circling one letter in each scenario.

		Not Effective		Effective		Very Effective
Question #6						
A	Behavioral	1	2	3	4	5
B	Biophysical	1	2	3	4	5
C	Psychodynamic	1	2	3	4	5
D	Ecological	1	2	3	4	5
E	Humanistic	1	2	3	4	5

		Not Effective		Effective		Very Effective
Question #7						
A	Humanistic	1	2	3	4	5
B	Ecological	1	2	3	4	5
C	Biophysical	1	2	3	4	5
D	Behavioral	1	2	3	4	5
E	Psychodynamic	1	2	3	4	5
Question #8						
A	Psychodynamic	1	2	3	4	5
B	Behavioral	1	2	3	4	5
C	Ecological	1	2	3	4	5
D	Biophysical	1	2	3	4	5
E	Humanistic	1	2	3	4	5
Question #9						
A	Biophysical	1	2	3	4	5
B	Psychodynamic	1	2	3	4	5
C	Behavioral	1	2	3	4	5
D	Humanistic	1	2	3	4	5
E	Ecological					
Question #10						
A	Humanistic	1	2	3	4	5
B	Psychodynamic	1	2	3	4	5
C	Ecological	1	2	3	4	5
D	Biophysical	1	2	3	4	5
E	Behavioral	1	2	3	4	5

Determine Your Best Score and Relative Strength Scores

You will notice that each letter (A, B, etc.) is followed by the full or partial name of one the five TVI orientations. To determine your "best choice" for each scenario, go back and add up the number of times you circled the letter corresponding to each orientation to indicate your first or best guess as to the importance of the approach (Section 1) or the effectiveness of the approach (Section 2).

Total Times Selected

Behavioral/Cognitive–Behavioral _____

Psychodynamic/Interpersonal _____

Ecological/Systems   _____

Humanistic   _____

Biophysical   _____

Now, to determine the weight of each of your responses, go back and add up all the numbers circled on the five-point scale corresponding to the importance or effectiveness of the approach for each orientation. After summing the scores of from 1 to 5 for each orientation, fill in the sums below.

Score For Each Orientation

Behavioral/Cognitive–Behavioral   _____

Psychodynamic/Interpersonal   _____

Ecological/Systems   _____

Humanistic   _____

Biophysical   _____

Index